THE SOVIET ECONOMY IN TURMOIL, 1929–1930

THE SOVIET ECONOMY IN TURMOIL, 1929–1930

R. W. DAVIES

Professor of Soviet Economic Studies
University of Birmingham

Harvard University Press
Cambridge, Massachusetts
1989

Printed in China

10 9 8 7 6 5 4 3 2 1

Library of Congress Cataloging in Publication Data
Davies, R. W. (Robert William), 1925–
The Soviet economy in turmoil, 1929–1930/R. W. Davies.
p.   cm.—(The Industrialisation of Soviet Russia: 3)
Bibliography: p.
Includes index.
ISBN 0–674–82655–8
1. Soviet Union—Economic policy—1928–1932.   I. Title.
II. Series: Davies, R. W. (Robert William), 1925–.
Industrialisation of Soviet Russia: 3.
HC335.4.D38   1989
338.947—dc19
88–21318
CIP

In memory of my mother
GLADYS HILDA DAVIES
1899–1984

CONTENTS

Contents ix

LIST OF TABLES

xi

PREFACE

The present volume deals with developments in the Soviet industrial economy in the year and a half between the summer of 1929 and the end of 1930. This was a crucial period in Soviet history. By the summer of 1929, the centralisation of political power within the Communist Party, and the personal domination of Stalin, were already far advanced. The Politburo majority, with the support of many party members, had by this time firmly resolved to embark on the rapid transformation of the Soviet Union into an advanced industrial power. Stalin insisted in November 1928 that the Soviet Union must 'catch up and surpass' the capitalist countries, where technology was 'simply rushing ahead'; otherwise, he claimed, 'they will destroy us'. By the summer of 1929 the first serious efforts to increase investment in industry in the previous three years had already imposed considerable strain throughout the economy; the New Economic Policy, with its attempt to combine plan and market, was in disarray. From the summer of 1929 the pressures of industrialisation greatly increased. In the calendar year 1930 investment in industry was twice as high in real terms as in the economic year 1928/29, and more than three times greater than the highest pre-revolutionary level. This dramatic acceleration was accompanied by an immense upheaval in every aspect of Soviet life.

In the first two volumes of this series, *The Socialist Offensive, 1929–1930*, and *The Soviet Collective Farm, 1929–1930*, I examined the effects of this upheaval on agriculture. The Soviet authorities, confronted with the deepening agricultural crisis, sought to break down the established peasant economy, and replace it by kolkhozy (collective farms) subordinate to the will of the state and to the interests of socialist industrialisation. In the first great wave of collectivisation in the winter of 1929–30 more than half the peasantry were cajoled and bullied into joining kolkhozy. But the disorder and peasant resistance which the campaign evoked led to a hasty retreat, and by the summer of

1930 less than a quarter of Soviet peasant households remained in the kolkhozy. This retreat was purely temporary. By the autumn of 1930 the collectivisation drive was again resumed, at first more cautiously, and then in 1931 with great ruthlessness. The experience of the winter of 1929–30 nevertheless persuaded the authorities of the need for some circumspection. They relinquished the concept of kolkhozy as huge agricultural economies in which almost all economic activities were socialised. The collective-farm compromise, in which the personal economy and the socialised economy coexisted in uneasy harmony, proved to be a permanent feature of the Soviet economic system.

The new social and economic structure of agriculture was erected on very shaky foundations. Disruption prevailed over construction; and only the luck of exceptionally favourable weather in 1930 temporarily mitigated the consequences.

In the industrial economy, the state was confronted with a less formidable task. It was already in charge, and in 1929–30 it sought to adapt the existing structure to the accelerated pace of industrial transformation. Difficulties and tribulations were not avoided; but in the capital goods industries at least there was rapid growth in 1929–30. This was a significant stage in the burgeoning of the Soviet system of administrative planning.

*   *   *

In the present volume the two introductory chapters, complementary to Chapter 1 of Volume 1, summarise the state of the industrial economy in the mid-1920s, and briefly trace the formation and triumph of the policy of rapid industrialisation in the economic years 1927/28 and 1928/29. The October Revolution in 1917 brought about vast social and economic changes: large-scale industry, the banks and wholesale trade were transferred to state ownership; the private industrialist and the big private merchant vanished. The state economy was now managed by the party; in the 1920s many former workers became managers of state enterprises. By 1926/27 a rudimentary system of central planning succeeded in achieving a level of industrial investment exceeding that of 1913.

But in 1926/27 the level of industrial production, and the technical structure of industry, still closely resembled that of

1913. This meant that the relative backwardness of Soviet industry, measured against its counterparts in the major capitalist countries, was even greater than under the tsars. And the decline in agricultural marketings discussed in vol. 1 hampered the consumer industries, and retail trade, and crippled the export programme.

From the mid-1920s, the Soviet authorities embarked on their unprecedented endeavour to create a great industrial power by means of comprehensive state planning. An inexorably increasing share of resources was directed towards industrialisation. These policies, which did not avoid errors and inconsistencies, resulted between 1927 and 1929 in the breakdown of the New Economic Policy and were accompanied by a 'socialist offensive' in trade and industry which destroyed or absorbed most of the private sector (see Chapter 2).

The further expansion of industrialisation in 1929–30 – the main theme of this book – was accompanied and supported by a vast upheaval in every aspect of Soviet life. The urban labour-force expanded rapidly in 1929–30; this was what Moshe Lewin has called 'a quicksand society'. In an endeavour to enlarge the active support for the party leadership and its policies, large numbers of workers were recruited into the party. Simultaneously, many 'bourgeois specialists' and state officials were dismissed or arrested, and many party members were expelled (see Chapter 3). These upheavals in urban society were accompanied by the destruction of the relatively flexible intellectual framework of NEP. In every profession militant marxists sought to predominate. Before the end of 1930, however, they in turn began to yield to the advance of a tough-minded dogmatism imposed or endorsed from above (see Chapter 4). But a firm intellectual framework was not yet established. The simultaneous growth of dogmatism and confusion is exemplified by the inconclusive debates among marxist economists. They sought to establish a doctrine on the transition to socialism, and the nature of the socialist economy, which would encompass and justify Soviet experience. But many years elapsed before an agreed doctrine emerged (see Chapter 5).

The central chapters of this volume (Chapter 6–11) provide a narrative of the development of economic policy and of the economy itself between the summer of 1929 and the end of

1930. The changes in the annual, five-year and long-term plans are described in some detail; I seek to show how exaggerated plans came to be adopted, and to be enthusiastically supported by many party members (Chapter 6). The following chapter describes the rapid expansion of the industrial economy in the first seven months of 1929/30, the inflation which accompanied it, and the impact of this expansion on the major sectors of the economy (Chapter 7). This precipitate advance contrasts sharply with the simultaneous temporary retreat from the comprehensive collectivisation of agriculture (see Vol. 1), which dominated the proceedings of the XVI party congress in June–July 1930; this was the first congress at which no voices of political opposition were heard (Chapter 8). But the industrial triumphs of the first half of 1929/30 were followed by a severe if brief economic crisis. I discuss this crisis in some detail and seek to place it in the context of the advances and failures of the economic year 1929/30 as a whole (Chapters 9 and 10).

This was a further moment of choice. An unorganised minority, of which Syrtsov was the most articulate representative, sought to bring greater realism into economic policy. But Stalin and the majority of the Politburo resolved to maintain the pace of industrialisation, and to enforce it by better organisation and further repression. During the special quarter, October–December 1930, the crisis was overcome and industrial expansion resumed. The 1931 plan was the most ambitious – and one of the least realistic – of all the annual plans adopted during the course of industrialisation (see Chapter 11).

The urgency with which industrialisation was regarded by the party leadership, and by many Soviet citizens, was certainly partly due to the military dangers which hung over the USSR. While immediate military requirements often took second place to long-term industrial goals at this time, the needs of defence were a central preoccupation of the Soviet authorities and of Soviet plans (see Chapter 12).

*   *   *

While this volume was being completed, the Soviet Union embarked on a vast reconsideration of the Stalin period in general, and the turning-point of 1929–30 in particular. In the decade from 1956 to 1966, the de-Stalinisation policy launched by Khrushchev enabled much greater frankness by Soviet writers and historians, though their analysis was generally placed within the simplistic official view that all errors and disasters were due to the 'cult of personality' and to Stalin personally. In the 1970s, some useful historical publications about the 1930s continued to appear, but a much narrower range of information was published, and fresh analysis almost completely ceased. But since the beginning of 1987 publications by authors of creative literature, by journalists and economists, and to a lesser extent by historians, have been much franker and more thoughtful than in the days of Khrushchev. Senior party figures have encouraged this revaluation. In April 1987, A. N. Yakovlev, now a Politburo member, posed a series of problems to the historians: Why was the New Economic Policy departed from at the end of the 1920s? How was it that 'administrative-bureaucratic methods of management' were strengthened? Were there alternatives and, if so, why did they remain unrealised? (*Vestnik Akademii Nauk*, 6, 1987, 61, 68–70). In November 1987, Gorbachev's report on the occasion of the 70th anniversary of the October revolution characterised the system established in the early 1930s as an 'administrative-command system of party-state management of the country'. According to the report, while these arrangements 'in general gave results' in industry, such a strict system was unsuitable for agriculture and had a harmful effect on society generally. (P, November 3, 1987).

In the debates which began in 1987 widely different approaches to the upheavals of 1929–30 have been voiced in the Soviet press, from the blunt assertion that the market relation with the peasants should have continued, to the almost equally blunt claim that collectivisation, dekulakisation and central planning were essential to industrialisation, and were marred by relatively minor errors (see my article in *The Socialist Register 1988* (London, 1988)).

My volumes on *The Industrialisation of Soviet Russia* form part of the similar discussion that has been raging among western historians for some years, and I hope that they may also be seen by Soviet scholars as a contribution to their own debate. Some years ago I was a keen advocate of the view that the fateful changes at the end of the 1920s were substantially the necessary consequence of rapid industrialisation. I now regard this conclusion as naive. But it seems to me to be equally naive to argue, along lines very familiar nowadays in the Soviet Union as well as in the West, that the great shifts in policy and system at the end of the 1920s were almost entirely due to the ideologically motivated decisions of a centralised political dictatorship, or can even be attributed simply to Stalin's efforts to maximise his personal power. I am still convinced that rapid industrialisation was incompatible with the market economy of NEP; the industrial objectives of the leadership required the replacement of NEP by some kind of administrative planning system. As I see it, the ideology and political practice of the Bolshevik party, the heritage from the pre-revolutionary past, and the personality of Stalin, together with the imperatives of industrialisation in a hostile and dangerous world environment, all played their part in imparting to the Soviet economic and political system of the 1930s its particular characteristics, its paradoxical combination of enthusiasm and achievement with vicious repression and waste. Moreover, the economic policies and system adopted at the end of the 1920s proved temporary and even experimental in the sense that they immediately began to be modified under the impact of the practical experience of the industrialisation drive. The way in which the complex interrelationships between the internal and external environment, ideology, political structure and practical experience developed in 1929–30 are further considered in the Conclusions below (Chapter 13).

* * *

In the Preface to Volume 1, I expressed regret that it had proved impossible to work in Soviet archives. Like a number of other western historians, I have now been able to use archives relating to this period; I worked on material in the Central State Archives of the National Economy (TsGANKh) in the spring of 1981 and on two occasions in 1984. The archives of the Politburo and other party agencies and of the Council of People's Commissars and its commissions, and the *opisi* (catalogues) for all archives of the Soviet period, have not yet been available to western scholars. But the files I received from the archival funds of Vesenkha and Narkomtorg/Narkomsnab and their agencies proved most informative. I am grateful for the assistance of Professor F. M. Vaganov and his colleagues in the State Archives Administration, especially Mrs L. E. Selivanova, and to Dr Tsaplin and his colleagues in TsGANKh. I also worked in the rich sources of the Lenin Library, the Public History Library, and the Library of INION in Moscow, and of the Saltykov-Shchedrin Library in Leningrad, and again had profitable discussions with Yu. A. Polyakov, V. P. Danilov, V. Z. Drobizhev, I. N. Olegina, and other Soviet historians.

The Hoover Institution records of American Engineers in Russia, the US State Department archives and the Trotsky archives in the Houghton Library at Harvard University also proved valuable, and I am grateful to all those concerned for their assistance. In April 1982 I was able to undertake a programme of interviews in Jerusalem and Tel-Aviv with 25 former Soviet citizens who worked in the Soviet economy in the early 1930s, mainly in a managerial or technical capacity. The programme was arranged and the interviews were organised by Mr K. Miroshnik, to whom I am most grateful for his indefatigability, wide knowledge and objectivity.

Soviet archival documents, American engineers and former Soviet citizens presented sharply different viewpoints on the Soviet economic system; and these various sources dealt with some important issues which were virtually excluded from Soviet newspapers and periodicals of the early 1930s. But I was gratified to find that in most respects their account of events and institutions fitted well with the picture of Soviet economic life which I had obtained from a critical scrutiny of the published Soviet records.

In this volume I have been able to draw to a greater extent than in previous volumes on the work of western and Soviet scholars. While few studies have examined agriculture in the 1930s in any depth, many valuable books and articles have appeared on various aspects of the industrial economy. Western authors to whose writings I am particularly indebted include Bailes, Barber, Berliner, Gardner Clark, Cooper, Dobb, Dohan, Filtzer, Fitzpatrick, Granick, Holzman, Hunter, Jasny, Kirstein, Kuromiya, N. Lampert, R. A. Lewis, Nove, Rees, S. Schwarz, Shimotomai Shiokawa, Siegelbaum, Westwood and Zaleski. The pioneering and detailed statistical studies of Bergson and his colleagues, and of Hodgman, Moorsteen, Powell and Nutter have also been constantly at hand while writing this book.

I have greatly benefitted from comments and advice at various stages in the work from colleagues, who painstakingly read chapters, answered queries and supplied information. I should particularly mention Julian Cooper, who read an early draft and made valuable suggestions and comments, and Vladimir Andrle, John Barber, Peter Gatrell, Mark Harrison, Jonathan Haslam, David Holloway, Nicholas Lampert, Moshe Lewin, Catherine Merridale, Alec Nove, Mario Nuti, Arfon Rees, Michal Reiman, John Russell, Nobuo Shimotomai, Nabuaki Shiokawa and, last but not least, Stephen Wheatcroft, who departed to Melbourne in 1985 and has been sorely missed. I am most grateful to him, and Hiroaki Kuromiya and Nabuaki Shiokawa, for providing me with copies of scarce Soviet documents.

Most of my material was again supplied by the Baykov Library of the Centre for Russian and East European Studies at Birmingham University, and I am most grateful to our former librarian, Jennifer Brine, and her worthy successor Jackie Johnson, for their help. Hugh Jenkins once again efficiently undertook the burdensome task of preparing the index. Jean Fyfe again coped speedily and meticulously with typing my various drafts, together with Betty Bennett and Nancy Moore. My wife Frances was an unfailing and indispensable source of support and encouragement.

My work on this subject was greatly facilitated by successive grants from the British Economic and Social Research Council for the research projects on Soviet economic development based at Birmingham. These funds made it possible for me to devote the academic year 1984/85 full-time to these studies, and enabled the employment of Dr Wheatcroft and the project secretary Mrs Bennett. They also facilitated the regular meetings of the 'SIPS' seminars (Soviet Industrialisation Project Seminars) at Birmingham, and the conferences of the International Work-Group on Soviet Inter-War Economic History, which were a constant source of intellectual inspiration.

June 1988   R. W. DAVIES

CHAPTER ONE

THE INDUSTRIAL ECONOMY IN THE MID-1920s

(A) THE SOCIAL TRANSFORMATION

The revolution and civil war eliminated, perhaps for ever, private landowners and all substantial private capitalism. The new social and political structure which emerged during the 1920s was profoundly influenced by this transformation. The revolution flattened the top and extended the sides of the steep pre-revolutionary social pyramid. In the countryside, private peasant farming continued, but much greater equality prevailed than before the revolution (see vol. 1, pp. 23–4). In trade and in small-scale industry, some private businessmen prospered, but only 76,000 persons were recorded as employing any kind of hired labour in the whole non-agricultural sector even in 1926/27, the year in which private businesses were most numerous; and of this total only 30,000 were classified as 'middle and large capitalists'.[1] In Moscow, the number of factory owners declined from 1,791 in 1912 to 145 in 1926, and the number of owners of small-scale industry who were employers of labour from 20,600 to 2,800.[2] The recorded earnings of the top 30,000 private entrepreneurs were substantially greater than average earnings, amounting to 7,352 rubles a year as compared with 729 rubles for the non-agricultural population as a whole.[3] These data based on tax returns are doubtless underestimates. But the average incomes of private entrepreneurs were certainly lower, and their opportunities for accumulating wealth far more limited, than before the revolution.

[1] *Tyazhest' oblozheniya* (1929), 74–81; these data are discussed in Lewin (1985), 213–6, and in Wheatcroft (1984).
[2] BP (Prague), lxx (June–July 1929), 25–6.
[3] *Tyazhest' oblozheniya* (1929), 74–81.

If the old tsarist estates and new capitalist classes had almost completely evaporated, the new ruling élite – consisting largely of senior party and state officials and economic managers – as yet existed only in embryonic form; it was far more modest in its way of life than the leading noble and entrepreneurial families of tsarist Russia. This was most clearly shown by the decline in the number of domestic servants from over $1^1/_2$ millions in 1897 to 339,000 in 1926/27.[4] Even in Moscow, in spite of the large increase in the number of senior government officials and professional people consequent upon the shift of the capital from Petrograd in 1918, the number of domestic servants declined by 57 per cent between 1912 and 1926.[5]

No reliable comparison between the number of leading officials and specialists in the mid-1920s and in 1913 has been possible; accurate data for 1913 are lacking. But such figures as are available indicate a net increase in the number of trained specialists. While some members of the professional classes emigrated in the first few years after the revolution, many more were trained. In 1914/15, there were already 124,700 undergraduate students in tsarist Russia, nearly equal to the total stock of graduates. The number of students increased during the civil war, and, although it declined in the early 1920s, remained substantially greater than before the revolution.[6] Some 90,800 students graduated in the four years 1924–7.[7] The official claim that the total number of graduates increased from 136,000 in 1913 to 233,000 in 1928 is therefore not implausible.[8]

Taking senior administrators, managers and specialists

---

[4] For 1897, see *Obshchii svod* (St. Petersburg, 1905), ii, 264–5; for 1926/27 see *Tyazhest' oblozheniya* (1929), 74–81. In the 1926 census, the number of personal servants was recorded as 319,000 in the towns; a further 133,000 were employed in the countryside, and 13,000 as a secondary occupation (*Vsesoyuznaya perepis'*, xxxiv (1930), 160–1).

[5] While the number of domestic servants in Moscow fell from 97,600 to 42,200 between 1912 and 1926, the number of persons in non-industrial employment and the free professions increased from 55,650 to 131,600 (BP (Prague), lxx (June–July 1929), 25–6).

[6] See *Nar. kh.* (1932), 507.

[7] *Izmeneniya* (1979), 166.

[8] Sketchy data for individual professions also point to an increase in the number of specialists between the eve of the first world war and the mid-1920s (thousands):

together, the administrative and professional élite in the Soviet Union in the mid-1920s was a tiny minority of the population. According to the returns of the 1926 census, it amounted to only about half-a-million persons out of a total working population of 86,220,000. This included 311,854 in 'leading posts' (senior administrators, and managers of enterprises and their deputies) and 167,065 persons in specialist posts classified as 'higher technical' and 'higher'.[9] With the promotion of former workers and others, many of those employed in both 'leading' and specialist posts were 'practicals' without higher education. A survey of 3,554 administrators and technical staff in higher posts at certain major factories and industrial building

	Eve of first world war	1926 census[c]
Doctors	31·4[a]	51·4[d]
Dentists	5·8[a]	10·0
Teachers in higher education	6·7[b]	13·2

[a] See Leikina-Svirskaya (1981), 50–1; in addition there were 5·4 thousand pharmacists.

[b] *Izmeneniya* (1976), 269.

[c] *Vsesoyuznaya perepis'*, xxxiv (1930), 144–80.

[d] *Bulletin* of the Society for the Social History of Medicine, 34 (1984), 19–24 (Wheatcroft), shows that 25·5 thousand of this total were trained before 1917; as there were only about 30,000 doctors in 1917, only a small number of doctors could have emigrated after 1917.

According to the data in Leikina-Svirskaya (1981), there were in excess of 190,000 secondary and elementary school-teachers in 1914, as compared with 326,000 in 1926 (see note 9 below). This implies a considerable improvement in the teacher–pupil ratio, which seems unlikely.

[9] Estimated from *Vsesoyuznaya perepis'*, xxxiv (1930), 144–80. These figures exclude military officers and specialists, literature, journalism and the arts, libraries and museums, as 'higher' occupations in these fields are not listed separately; on the same grounds I have excluded 326,265 teachers from the total. The total includes 'free professions' as well as those in employment. The principal sub-groups are as follows:

Leading personnel:

Administrators, etc.	197806
Managers	114048
Total	311854

(*continued*)

sites in 1929 revealed that 916, or 25·8 per cent of the total, were practicals.[10]

While a high proportion of specialists in the middle and late 1920s had received their training before the revolution, in the state administration personnel already employed before the revolution were in a small minority. A comprehensive survey of 10,832 persons employed in TsIK (the Central Executive Committee of Soviets) and in the all-Union People's Commissariats in October 1929 claimed that only 1,178 of them, 10·9 per cent of the total, were in state service before the revolution.[11] These figures do not, however, adequately indicate the importance as distinct from the total numbers of pre-revolutionary personnel. A 1929 survey of industrial staff in higher posts disclosed that of 1,819 with higher specialised education, 872 had qualified before the revolution; 124 of these were former factory owners or directors, and their influence on economic decisions must have been considerable.[12]

The social transformation of the administration was also limited in three other respects. First, the workers' revolution had not yet brought about workers predominance in high office. The survey in October 1929 of TsIK and the commissariats showed that most of those who replaced the pre-revolutionary staff were from the middle classes: only 11·9 per cent were former workers, and a further 4·5 per cent children of former

---

Technical and other listed higher posts:

Engineers and architects	30235
In higher education	13236
Agronomists	16832
Land surveyors, etc.	12906
Veterinary	5013
Doctors	51430
Dentists	9969
Legal professions	18206
Other	9238
Total	167065

Of the total technical and other higher posts, 10,237 are in 'free professions' working independently, the rest are wage earners.

[10] EO, 12, 1929, 102–22 (Kheinman); a further 10·6 per cent only had secondary specialised education.

[11] The survey is reported in SO, 2, 1930, 82–92 (Latsygina).

[12] EO, 1, 1930, 161–5.

workers. The percentage was somewhat greater in the very highest administrative posts, but reached 39 per cent only for the lowest groups in the hierarchy, janitors, cleaners and other services ('junior ancillary personnel' or MOP). With the exception of the ancillaries, all grades were dominated by former white-collar workers, and their children.[13]

Secondly, there were very few women in administrative or specialist posts. Only 23,700, or 7·6 per cent, of the 311,900 'leading' posts recorded in the December 1926 census were occupied by women, and among the higher ranks the proportion was much lower still. In industry, the proportion of women in administrative and specialist posts was also very low; only 597 of the 37,898 leading posts (1·6 per cent) and 392 of the 16,517 higher technical posts (2·4 per cent) were occupied by women.[14]

Thirdly, while a substantial proportion of leading posts were held by party members, many of them were 'practicals'; party membership among graduates was insignificant. The 1929 survey of administrative and technical staff in industry showed that only 5·2 per cent of those with higher education were party members:[15] in the mid-1920s the proportion would have been even lower. But as many as 10·7 per cent were classified as 'alien to us in their political complexion'.[16] In 1927/28, qualified engineers working in industry included a mere 39 party members, and only 12 of these worked in the mining industry.[17]

In the first decade after the revolution, the expansion in 'secondary specialised' education – which encompassed technicians, midwives and others of similar skills – was even more rapid than the expansion of higher education. According to the official statistics, the number of pupils in secondary specialised technical colleges (tekhnikumy) of various kinds, and in the *rabfaki*, the 'workers' faculties' providing an adult road to higher education, increased from 48,000 in 1914/15 to

[13] SO, 2, 1930, 82–92 (Latsygina). It should be noted, however, that on the same date 72 per cent of foremen in factories were ex-workers or workers' children (see Kuromiya (forthcoming), ch. 7).

[14] *Vsesoyuznaya perepis'*, xxxiv (1930), 144–80. Women played an important part in medicine and education: 40 per cent of doctors, 80 per cent of dentists and 61 per cent of school teachers were women.

[15] EO, 12, 1929, 120–1 (Kheinman).

[16] EO, 1, 1930, 167–8 (Kheinman).

[17] Carr and Davies (1969), 580, n. 5.

as many as 236,000 in 1928.[18] In consequence, the total number of persons with secondary education also rose rapidly, from 54,000 in 1913 to 288,000 in 1928.[19] The percentage of party members was much higher at this level of qualification than among graduates. In the 25 factories and sites surveyed in 1929, 17·5 per cent of the 1,487 persons with secondary specialised education were party members or candidates, and a further 3·8 per cent belonged to the Komsomol. Not surprisingly, the higher percentage of party members and candidates, 29·2 per cent, was found among the 4,062 practicals without any specialised education.[20]

At the bottom of the educational ladder, 48·9 per cent of the population were recorded as illiterate in the 1926 census.[21] This was a considerable improvement on the situation at the time of the 1897 census, when 76 per cent were illiterate. But the number of children attending school rose rapidly in the last decades of the tsarist period, and a Soviet historian has estimated that the proportion of illiterates had declined to 61–2 per cent on the eve of the war.[22] The rise in the number of children attending school continued after 1917, with a brief break in the early 1920s.[23] In the 1920s young workers entering industrial and other occupations were therefore more literate than the older generation: in 1929 13·9 per cent of all workers in census industry were illiterate, but the percentage varied from 30·9 per cent for those aged 40 and over to only 5·2 per cent for those under 23. But the educational level of factory workers, though rising, was not high; in 1929 the average worker had attended school for 3·5 years, the average worker under 23 years of age for 4·3 years. The proportion of illiterates

[18] *Sots. str.* (1934), 408–9; *St. spr. 1928* (1929), 879; of these the number in *rabfaki* amounted to 49,000; see also Fitzpatrick (1979), 62. An alternative series for all lower trade education (profobrazovanie) shows an increase from 267,000 in 1914/15 to 594,000 in 1926/27 (*Nar. kh.* (1932), 507).

[19] *Narodnoe obrazovanie* (1971), 233.

[20] EO, 12, 1929, 120–1 (Kheinman).

[21] Illiterates for the purpose of this figure were those not recorded as 'able to read', aged nine and over (Lorimer (1946), 198–9).

[22] Rashin (1956), 311; this is for the population aged eight and over.

[23] The total number of schoolchildren in attendance increased from 7,802,000 in 1914/15 (including children at church schools) to 10,727,000 in 1926/27; the number in forms 5–10 (roughly 12–17 year olds) increased from 565,000 to 1,205,000 (*Sots. str.* (1934), 399).

was higher among women and among workers in those industries which involved a great deal of unskilled manual labour. Thus the percentage of illiterates was higher in the textile industries, employing a high proportion of women, and in the coal industry, than in metalworking and engineering.[24]

During the early and mid-1920s, with the rapid recovery of industry, railway transport and other non-agricultural sectors of the economy, numbers employed expanded rapidly; in industry and on the railways, the number employed in 1926/27 was substantially higher than in 1913 (see p. 28 below). Many, perhaps most, of those recruited to industry in 1922–5 had worked there before the revolution: a 1929 survey recorded that 50·7 per cent of all workers began work in industry before 1917.[25] This was in considerable part a second-generation working class, a working class which had lost close connections with the countryside in the form of land holding.[26] But, according to one survey, as many as 54 per cent of workers starting work in industry in 1926–7 were previously engaged in agriculture, most as peasants, some as agricultural labourers.[27] In the building industry, as before the revolution, workers were mainly seasonal, and were closely tied to the land.[28]

The industrial workers were the heroes of the October revolution, and its major beneficiaries. It is true that their

---

[24] *Trud* (1930), 30–1; this is the report of a survey of 382,000 workers in the metal, textile and mining industries (20 per cent coverage) carried out by the trade unions in April–May 1929 (*ibid.* xii).

[25] Barber (1978), 2–5.

[26] According to the 1929 survey, 52·2 per cent of industrial workers came from working-class families, while 20·6 per cent held land; in the case of the coal industry, where ties with the land were closer, the respective percentages were 34·4 and 24·6 per cent (*Trud* (1930), 28–9; Barber (1978), 8–14). Comparable data for the other major section of the working class, the railway workers, have not been traced.

[27] *Profsoyuznaya perepis'*, *1932–1933*, i (1934), 94–5; for this survey of trade union workers remaining in industry in 1932–3 see p. 127 n. 149 below.

[28] A 1929 survey of building workers showed the following (in percentages):

	Permanent workers	Otkhodniki
In industry before 1918	37·1	35·9
Working-class parents	37·6	9·2
Own agriculture in countryside	19·9	90·0

(*Trud* (1932), 83, 85; *Izmeneniya* (1961), 152, 180, 194 (Gol'tsman)).

political strength greatly diminished between 1917 and the mid-1920s. Many politically-active party and Komsomol members were promoted out of the ranks of the working class to official positions; and ever since 1917 the party authorities had circumscribed and destroyed any political opposition which sought to base itself on the working-class interest. The workers had effectively lost their hard-won right to strike; the penalties against strikers were already more severe than before the revolution. By the mid-1920s the Soviet working class had virtually ceased to engage in the stormy political activities, or exercise the political initiative, which distinguished it in 1917. But in other respects the revolution had brought a vast enhancement in the status of the industrial workers, in their rights and privileges, and in their material position relative to the peasants, the professional classes and the minor officials. At the place of work, it brought new organisations and new practices. Nearly all industrial and railway workers, and even most permanent building workers, belonged to trade unions. According to the party census, on January 1, 1927, nearly one industrial worker in ten, and at least one transport worker in thirteen, were party members or candidates, as compared with one qualified industrial engineer in 100, and one peasant in 650.[29] The proportion of party members varied widely between different industries, ranging from 13·5 per cent in the oil industry to 6·2 per cent in the textile industry; surprisingly, it

---

[29] The number of party members and candidates on January 1, 1927, was as follows (thousands):

Workers in industry	215·6
Workers in transport	94·3
Other workers	33·2
Non-manual employees	438·8
Peasants	116·2
Other	163·8
Total	1061·9

(*Itogi* (n.d. [?1928], 22–3; these figures exclude the Red Army and Navy). The total number of workers in census industry on January 1, 1927, amounted to 2,365,800 (*Trud* (1930), 7); the total number of persons employed in transport in 1926/27 (average) amounted to 1,257,000 (*Trud* (1930),7) (this figure includes non-manual employees, so the party membership among workers will be higher than one in thirteen); the total number of peasants working in individual households recorded in the 1926 census was 73,456,000 (*Vsesoyuznaya perepis'*, xxxiv (1930), 2–3). For party membership among engineers, see p. 5 above.

tended to be smaller in the larger factories.[30] But virtually every worker must have been personally acquainted with a party member.

The trade unions and the party cells drew factory personnel closely into the political and administrative system, acting both as agents of higher authority and, to a diminishing extent, as representatives of the workers. During the industrial difficulties of 1926, they played an important role in imposing the 'regime of economy' on the workers, and some role in its subsequent relaxation.[31] But they also guarded workers against the depredations of managers, and protected them from arbitrary dismissal. As compared with pre-revolutionary times, the authority over the worker of the factory engineer and the foreman, if not of the factory manager, had considerably diminished.[32]

The enhanced status of the worker brought important material changes, including greater equality of income not only between masses and rulers but also within the industrial working class itself. The differentiation in earnings between higher-paid and lower-paid workers declined substantially between 1914 and 1928.[33] This was the result of deliberate policy. Strenuous efforts to narrow differentials between skills during the civil war gave way in the early 1920s to some increase in differentiation, but at the end of 1926 a new drive was launched for wage equalisation (vyravnivanie) between skilled and unskilled.[34]

War and revolution also brought wide job opportunities and less economic inequality to women workers. As in other

[30] See Carr (1971), 108–9; this was only partly explained by the fact that most of the cotton textile industry, where female labour predominated, was organised into large units.

[31] For the regime of economy, see Carr and Davies (1969), 333–8.

[32] On the role of the factory engineer, see Carr (1958), 378–9, and Carr and Davies (1969), 578–80; on the foreman, see *Predpriyatie*, 12, 1926, 13–14 (Gastev), 22 (Kotel'nikov).

[33] See Bergson (Cambridge, Mass., 1944), 69; the quartile ratio, which is a measurement of equality, increased substantially in seven out of eight industries studied.

[34] For the changes in policy, see Carr (1958), 376–7, Carr and Davies (1969), 529–37, and Bergson (1944), 69, 180–9. For conflicting evidence on the success of the 1926–9 drive for equalisation, see Carr and Davies (1969), 533, especially note 3, and Bergson (1944), 188.

belligerent countries, the war considerably widened the range of jobs accessible to women, and in 1914–18 female employment increased rapidly as a percentage of all workers in census industry. After declining in the first two years of NEP, it then increased steadily between 1923/24 and 1926/27, but did not recover to its wartime peak.[35] Simultaneously the wage gap tended to narrow between industries dominated by men, such as metalworking and mining, and industries in which the percentage of women was substantial, such as textiles and food.[36] The narrowing of the gap was partly due to the introduction of equal pay for equal work, accomplished in the Soviet Union earlier than in any other country.[37] A careful study

[35] For twelve industries for which data are available for the whole period, covering 76 per cent of industrial workers, the percentages were as follows:

1913	30·7	1922/23	34·7
1915	36·0	1923/24	32·8
1917	39·7	1924/25	34·2
1918	41·2	1925/26	34·3
1921/22	38·0	1926/27	35·0

For all census industry, the percentage increased from 25·2 in 1913 to 29·5 per cent in 1926/27. (*Ocherki* (1957), 244–5, 206.)

[36] According to Soviet estimates, real wages changed as follows:

	Women as % of number of workers[a]		Real wages[b] (1913 = 100)
	1913	1926/27	1926/27
Metalworking	4·8	10·2	85·0
Mining	8·0	14·5	75·0
Woodworking	8·2	16·4	108·2
Printing	9·1	22·1	106·8
Food	21·3	26·8	158·1
Paper	36·7	29·3	126·0
Chemicals	31·3	31·2	127·3
Textiles	56·1	60·2	120·0
All industry	25·2	29·5	99·6

[a] *Ocherki* (1957), 206–57 (Mints).

[b] EO, 10, 1927, 144–7 (Kheinman).

[37] This did not, however, result in equal earnings for men and women, as female labour was concentrated in the less remunerative jobs. According to surveys of the central bureau of labour statistics, the average daily earnings by adult women increased from 63·4 per cent of adult male earnings in March 1926 to 67·2 per cent in March 1928; the equivalent percentage for June 1914 was only 51·1 (*Statistika truda*, 9–10, 1928, 2–48 – Rashin).

of Soviet data by an American economist shows a substantial but irregular rise in the daily wages of women relative to those of men between 1914 and 1928; in the eight industries studied the increase varied between 1·8 and 23·3 percentage points.[38] But the relative improvement in women's wages was also partly and perhaps mainly due to the fact that it was easier in conditions of NEP to raise prices and pay higher wages in the consumer industries, where most women worked.[39]

But perhaps the most important reform in working conditions for everyone employed by the state was the introduction of the eight-hour day, the call for which was emblazoned on the banners of every European socialist party.[40] The normal length of the working day declined by over 20 per cent from 9·9 hours in 1913 to 7·8 hours in 1928.[41] On the occasion of the tenth anniversary of the revolution in 1927 further legislation authorised the gradual introduction of the seven-hour day.[42]

The pleasures of increased leisure resulting from the reduced working day were moderated by the possibility of being condemned to an enforced life of complete leisure through unemployment. Unemployment statistics in the Soviet Union, as in capitalist countries, were very unreliable. Estimates for the beginning of 1927 ranged from 1·0 to 2·3 millions. But even on the narrow definition used in the population census of December 1926, unemployment amounted to some 9 per cent of the employed population; and numbers increased continuously

[38] Bergson (1944), 73–6.

[39] A Soviet economist wryly commented: 'We are maintaining a definite policy of eliminating the pre-revolutionary gaps in the payment of male and female labour. But generally the shift in the former relationship of wage payments between the producer goods and consumer goods industries is the result of disruption of the planned control of wages, a disruption due to market conditions' (EO, 9, 1929, 147 – Kheinman).

[40] See Carr (1952), 104.

[41] *Trud* (1936), 98, 371; according to this source, ' "the normal length of the working day" refers to the number of hours of work which are fixed for the given worker by existing legislation or the conditions of the labour contract'. These figures are for adult workers. According to *Trud* (1930), 37, the actual average length of the working day amounted to 7·45 hours in 1926/27 and 1927/28 (including 0·1 hours overtime) and 7·37 (including 0·13 hours overtime) in 1928/29; this figure presumably includes adolescents, who worked a shorter day.

[42] See Carr and Davies (1969), 495–500.

throughout the 1920s.[43] No reliable estimate of unemployment before the revolution is available; the estimate of a Soviet economist, an average of 400–500,000 in 1900–13,[44] is certainly less than half the number of unemployed in the Soviet Union in 1928 by the same definition.

In contrast to Western Europe and the United States, unemployment in the USSR was not the result of economic depression. The number of employed persons increased from 6·7 to 10·4 millions between 1924/25 and 1929, sufficient to absorb more than the natural increase in the able-bodied urban population.[45] But the growth in employment was outweighed by the continuous pressure of the migration of adult labour from country to town; according to Soviet estimates, annual net migration increased from one-third of a million to nearly one million people a year during 1923–6.[46] The reasons for the huge increase in rural–urban migration compared with the pre-revolutionary period have not yet been satisfactorily elucidated. But the growth of job opportunities, and the high prestige of the town and of urban labour, must have played a major part.

The intensity of unemployment varied considerably between different industries and professions. In metalworking, chemicals and mining, the percentage of unemployment was low, especially among certain types of skilled workers. In other industries, labour legislation and the trade unions protected established workers from arbitrary dismissal. But for large numbers of urban workers unemployment was an ever-present menace. A survey by the information department of the party central committee admitted that because of unemployment workers were constantly afraid of losing their jobs.[47] A large and increasing number of workers held purely temporary jobs. This doubtless provided a means of enforcing discipline and was in

---

[43] All these definitions of unemployment covered only those seeking work and not obtaining it; they did not include those in work but in some sense 'under-employed'. For these statistics, see Lane, ed. (1986), 19–35 (Davies), 36–49 (Wheatcroft and Davies); the 'employed population' excludes all self-employed, including peasants not working for hire.

[44] BSE, v (1930), col. 214; the sketchy data on pre-revolutionary unemployment are examined in Davies, ed. (1988) (Shapiro).

[45] *Nar. kh.* (1932), 410–11 (total excluding agricultural workers).

[46] See Carr and Davies (1969), 454.

[47] Cited from the archives in Suvorov (1968), 80.

any case a major source of uncertainty and frustration for the workers concerned.[48] The complete lack of job opportunities for many young people, including children of workers as well as migrants from the towns, was frankly acknowledged by the party to be a major source of disturbance and hooliganism.[49]

Unemployment was also a constant reproach to the authorities, an urgent reminder that the New Economic Policy was grounded in the capitalist economics of the market. It provided one of the most telling Left Opposition criticisms of official policies. The Opposition platform of September 1927 claimed that 'the number of unemployed is growing faster than the total number of employed workers', and plausibly attributed this gross defect to the slow growth of industrialisation.[50] But the Opposition, like the party leadership, was committed to the stability of the currency and to the market relation with the mass of the peasantry. The drive for economy and rationalisation, by increasing productivity, necessarily reduced employment possibilities, and sometimes resulted in an increase in unemployment. 'Individual groups of workers', Kuibyshev reluctantly admitted in April 1927, 'may suffer from rationalisation, thanks to reduction [of employment] in a given enterprise'.[51] Until the very end of the 1920s it seemed to all concerned that the early stages of Soviet industrialisation might alleviate, but could not eliminate, mass unemployment.

(B) CONTINUITY AND CHANGE IN THE INDUSTRIAL ECONOMY

In the early 1920s Soviet politicians and economists, like their counterparts elsewhere in war-devastated Europe, anticipated that full economic recovery would require many years. In Gosplan, one of the most optimistic projections prepared in 1923 forecast that the production of census industry would reach a mere 70 per cent of the pre-war level by 1926/27; and a plan for the iron and steel industry prepared in the same year

---

[48] See Filtzer (1986), 26–7.
[49] Resolution of XV party conference, November 1926, in *KPSS v rez.*, ii (1954), 324–5.
[50] *The Platform of the Joint Opposition (1927)* (London, 1973), 17.
[51] See Carr and Davies (1969), 464.

estimated that rolled steel production would amount to a mere 27 per cent of 1913 in 1926/27.[52] A year later, a transport plan prepared in Gosplan calculated that the pre-war level of freight traffic would not be reached until 1936, and a commission of Sovnarkom, even though it was working under the influence of the always optimistic People's Commissariat for Workers' and Peasants' Inspection (Rabkrin), predicted that the pre-war level of freight traffic would not be reached until 1929.[53] Even in 1925, Gosplan estimated that the demand for pig iron ten years later in 1935 would amount to a mere 4·8 million tons, slightly higher than in 1913.[54]

But the pace of economic recovery swept aside these gloomy prognoses. By 1925, agricultural production already exceeded the 1909–13 average level; by 1926, it approximately equalled the level of 1913, an exceptionally good harvest year.[55] Industry, transport and internal trade had also approximately regained the pre-war level.[56] The main lagging sector in 1926/27 was the building industry, classified separately from 'industry' as 'construction' in Soviet statistics. According to the estimates of Gosplan, which were usually optimistic, in 1926/27 the value of construction amounted only to 610 million rubles against 730 millions in 1913.[57]

---

[52] PKh, 3, 1924, 90; *Byulleten' Gosplana*, 5, 1923, 55ff. In fact rolled steel production reached 75 per cent of the 1913 level in 1926/27.

[53] See Rees (1982), 208; the 1913 level on railways and inland waterways was in fact already reached by 1926/27 (see *Nar. kh.* (1932), pp. xlii–xliii). These and other early draft plans are discussed in Strumilin (1958(1)), 273–307 (originally published in PKh, 12, 1930, 241–62), and in Zaleski (Chapel Hill, 1971), 40–7.

[54] EZh, May 27, 1925 (F. Portenkov); production in 1935 was 12.5 million tons.

[55] See estimates by Wheatcroft in Davies, ed. (1988); in 1926 gross agricultural production reached 112 per cent of the 1909–13 and 102 per cent of the 1913 level; the equivalent percentages for net production were 109 and 98.

[56] For industry, see p. 16 below. For transport, see Davies, ed. (1988) (Westwood). For trade, Gosplan estimated net income at 1,350 million rubles in 1913 and 2,734 million rubles in 1926/27, both estimates in current prices (the 1913 estimate is in EO, 9, 1929, 117 (Gukhman), the 1926/27 estimate in *KTs . . . na 1928/29* (1929), 436); on the basis of the price index, these amounts are roughly equal in real terms, but in view of the decline in the number of trading units and trading personnel between 1913 and 1926/27 (see pp. 31–2 below), some scepticism is in order.

[57] EO, 9, 1929, 117; *KTs . . . na 1928/29* (1929); these figures are in 1913

These data for the major sectors of the economy indicate that total national income as measured by sector of origin is likely to have been approximately the same in 1926/27 as in 1913, for a population which had increased by 5$\frac{1}{2}$ per cent, from 139·3 to 147·0 million persons.[58]

The economy of the mid-1920s was restored with little substantial change in the stock of basic capital. While much capital repair took place in the early 1920s, there was very little net capital investment. Even in 1926/27 net capital investment in the economy as a whole had not fully regained the 1913 level. Net capital investment (including the value of new equipment and net additions to livestock as well as construction) amounted to roughly 1,700 million rubles in 1926/27, as compared with 1,890 million rubles in 1913.[59]

In spite of the continuities between the pre-revolutionary and post-revolutionary economies, the social transformation following the Bolshevik revolution, together with the establishment of a one-party state dedicated to industrialisation and the construction of a socialist society, had brought about profound changes in the economic structure and the economic mechanism. The pages which follow trace the impact of the consequences of war, revolution and civil war, and of the first phase of planned industrialisation, on the structure of industry, on labour productivity, and on internal and foreign trade; a final sub-

---

prices. Falkus estimates construction in 1913 at 878 million rubles (*Economica*, 35 (1968)). For the number of building workers, which also declined, see the hazardous suggestions based on Gukhman's estimate for 1913 and on the population census for 1926 in Davies, ed. (1988) (Perrie and Davies).

[58] In his careful study *Russian National Income, 1885–1913* (1982), 112–13, Gregory estimates that even in 1928 national income measured by end-use was still some 5–10 per cent below the 1913 level; taking the average 1909–13 harvest instead of the 1913 harvest, the equivalent figure would be 2–7 per cent below the '1913' level. For the view that Gregory somewhat underestimates the extent of recovery, see EHR, 2nd series, xxxix (1986), 267–70 (Wheatcroft, Davies and Cooper). For population figures, see *Arkheograficheskii ezhegodnik: 1968* (1970), 243, 248 (Danilov).

[59] For the 1913 figure, see Gregory (1982), 56–7 (multiplied by 0·815 to adjust Russian Empire territory roughly to Soviet territory); for the 1926/27 figure, see EHR, 2nd series, xxxix (1986), 268–9. These figures are in 1913 prices.

section places these changes in comparative international perspective.

(i) The changing shape of industry

The production of census or large-scale industry, which had declined to less than 20 per cent of the 1913 level in 1921, expanded extremely rapidly in the first half of the 1920s, increasing by as much as 60 per cent in the single year 1924/25. By 1926/27 it already exceeded the 1913 level.[60] Production had not yet, however, recovered to the 1916 level, when it was some 17 per cent higher than in 1913.[61] Small-scale industry also recovered substantially. According to a Soviet estimate made in the 1920s, production amounted to 2,040 million rubles in 1913, 2,040 millions in 1926/27 and 1,940 millions in 1927/28, measured in 1913 prices.[62] On the other hand, the number engaged in small-scale industry, in terms of full-time equivalents, is estimated to have declined from 2,263,000 in 1913 to 1,878,000 in 1926/27.[63] This is uncertain territory. But it seems probable that by 1926/27 the production of large-scale and small-scale industry taken together had approximately regained the 1913 level.[64]

In the mid-1920s the industrial economy consisted in large part of the pre-revolutionary factories, mines, railways, shops and offices, reassembled, patched up and put to work. New

[60] 'Census' or 'large-scale' industry normally included industrial units with the qualification (tsenz) of employing 16 workers or more in units using mechanical power, or 30 workers or more in other units; there were many exceptions. All other industry was classified as 'small-scale'. For these definitions see Grossman (Princeton, 1960), 34–5, *Fabrichno-zavodskaya promyshlennost'* . . . *za 1924/25, 1925/26, 1926/27 gg.* (1929), 30. For a discussion of the main Soviet and Western estimates of industrial production, see Davies (1978).

[61] *Ibid.* 66.

[62] EO, 9, 1929 (Gukhman); in terms of current prices, Kaufman (Washington, D.C., 1962), 79–83, estimates gross production of 2,167 millions in 1913 and 4,364 millions in 1926/27 (logging and fishing have been excluded from his totals).

[63] Estimated from Kaufman (Washington, D.C., 1962), 64–74 (excluding logging and fishing); Kaufman's calculations are based on estimates by TsSU of the number of weeks worked per year, which is inexplicably supposed to have declined substantially between 1913 and the mid-1920s.

[64] No allowance is made here for deterioration in the quality of production, which is believed to have been significant.

industrial investment on any significant scale did not take place until the 1925 building season. The fixed capital of factories newly constructed or fundamentally reorganised between 1917 and 1926 amounted to less than 10 per cent of all fixed industrial capital.[65] But important changes took place in the purposes for which industrial capital was utilised.

Largely as a result of state priority for investment in industry, the producer goods (capital goods) industries as a whole regained the pre-war level of production before the consumer goods industries. According to official Soviet statistics for the whole of industry, in 1927 the production of producer goods or Group 'A' industries was as much as 27·5 per cent greater than in 1913; the equivalent figure for the consumer goods or Group 'B' industries was only 2·2 per cent.[66]

There were important exceptions to this general pattern. The production of iron and steel failed to recover to the pre-war level. These industries had suffered great destruction and neglect during the civil war: production declined by 1920 to a mere 3·6 per cent of 1913.[67] No substantial investment was undertaken between 1914 and 1924. In spite of substantial expenditure on repair and restitution in the mid-1920s, in 1926/27 the production of rolled steel amounted to only 75 per cent, and of pig-iron to only 70 per cent, of 1913. Railways and ship-building, two voracious consumers, received smaller supplies of metal than before the revolution, and this alleviated the position of the engineering industries. Engineering and metalworking were disproportionately concentrated in Poland and the Baltic areas before the revolution, and their separation from the Soviet Union reduced the relative demand for iron and steel.[68] Even so, metal shortages were endemic.[69]

The production of non-ferrous and precious metals also collapsed during the civil war, and also failed to recover to the

[65] See PI, 14, 1930, 48; *KTs . . . na 1929/30* (1930), 446.

[66] See 1938 industrial census cited in Buzlaeva (1969), 111, 113; the census itself has not been available. The extent of the exaggeration in these figures is discussed in Davies (1978), 25–9.

[67] *Dinamika*, i, iii (1930), 176–7, 190.

[68] The lost areas produced 39 per cent of all metalworking and 22 per cent of all engineering production in 1913, but only 12 per cent of iron and steel (PI, 17–18, 1930, 72).

[69] For surveys of the state of the industry in the mid-1920s, see *Pervye shagi* (1959), 120–42, and Den, ed. (1926), 245–318.

pre-war level by the mid-1920s. To compensate for the deficiency of copper, imports were substantially increased.[70] The decline in gold production struck a heavy blow at Soviet exports.[71] In the summer of 1927, the gold industry attracted Stalin's attention, and he appointed the prominent and successful oil engineer Serebrovsky as its manager.[72] But many years and much human sacrifice would be required before gold exports earned much foreign currency for the USSR

In other major capital goods industries, the position was much more favourable. Fuel and power output was substantially greater than in 1913. The production of electricity more than doubled between 1913 and 1926/27, from small beginnings; and, with the steady development since the early 1920s of an impressive programme for the construction of power stations, including Dneprostroi, rapid future expansion was assured.[73] In 1926/27 the production of both coal and oil was over 10 per cent greater than in 1913. The oil industry was substantially modernised. The cost of extracting oil fell by over 40 per cent between 1923/24 and 1926/27, and in consequence the industry, dubbed 'the golden egg' by Kuibyshev, was able to supply substantial levies to the state budget and substantial quantities of oil for export.[74] By 1926/27 oil exports had increased to 2,086,000 tons as compared with 952,000 tons in 1913; the increase was primarily in the form of benzine, refining of which increased substantially.[75]

The chemical industry underwent a vast expansion for

[70] See *KTs . . . na 1928/29* (1928), 410; *Vneshnyaya torgovlya* (1960), 214–15. The import of copper increased from 6,200 tons in 1913 to 18,200 tons in 1926/27; cable and wire imports increased from 500 to 1,100 tons.

[71] The Russian Empire supplied 50 per cent of the world's gold before 1914; in 1926 production had recovered to only 28 per cent of the 1913 level (*Sed'moi s"ezd* (1927), 544); according to TPG, September 21, 1927, the number of prospectors declined from 60,000 before the war to 15,000 in 1927.

[72] Serebrovskii (1936), 15–16; Stalin reportedly displayed an enthusiastic familiarity with the Californian gold rush and the writings of Bret Harte, as well as of the Russian writer Maimin-Sibiryak. For the efforts to restore and modernise the industry in 1927–9, see Carr and Davies (1969), 715.

[73] For a survey of investment in the electricity industry printed from the archives, see *Pervye shagi* (1959), 75–84.

[74] See *Promyshlennost'* (1928), 9–10, 153–8; for Kuibyshev's praise see *SSSR: 4 s"ezd sovetov* (1927), 326–7.

[75] *Vneshnyaya torgovlya* (1960), 45, 94; for a comparison of oil-refining in 1913 and 1926/27, see EO, 10, 1927, 107; *Predpriyatie*, 3, 1927, 84.

military purposes during the first world war; this greatly facilitated its recovery. By 1926/27 basic chemical production was substantially larger than in 1913, though still much less than the 1916 peak.[76]

The outstanding achievement of Soviet industry in the mid-1920s was the increase of the quantity and range of civilian engineering production. Gross production increased from approximately 300 million rubles in 1913 to 477 million rubles in 1926/27 (both measured in 1913 prices).[77] In the years of recovery Soviet industry began to produce oil-mining equipment, turbines and other types of engineering products which had been almost entirely imported before the war.[78] The electrical industry, which before the revolution mainly produced fairly simple components, expanded particularly rapidly, manufacturing dynamos, transformers and telephone and cable equipment, as well as electric light bulbs and accumulators. The mid-1920s saw the flourishing, from small beginnings before the revolution, of the Elektrosila and Svetlana factories in Leningrad, and the launching of Elektrozavod and the Dinamo works in Moscow; these all still play a major part in the Soviet electrical industry.[79]

Technical developments in the engineering industries were by no means confined to equipment for use in the producer goods industries. The New Economic Policy anticipated that the expansion of producer goods would be supported by improved conditions for the consumer, and above all for the peasant. The production of textile machinery hitherto imported from Britain was initiated at the 'Karl Marx' factory, Leningrad.[80] In the agricultural engineering industry, which was almost entirely concerned with manufacturing horse-drawn machinery and implements for the individual peasant household, by 1926/27 production was far larger than in 1913.[81] The first

---

[76] See the circumstantial account in Lel'chuk (1964), 71–87.

[77] For the 1913 figure, which may be an overestimate, see Davies, ed. (1988) (Gatrell and Davies); the 1926/27 figure is from *St. spr. 1928* (1929), 317–18.

[78] See the survey in *Promyshlennost' 1927/28*, ([i]) (1930), 176–83.

[79] See Carr and Davies (1969), 406; for the Svetlana factory, see TPG, November 12, 1927. The young Bulganin, future Soviet prime minister, was director of Elektrozavod, which was formally established at the beginning of 1928 (see TPG, December 2, 1928).

[80] See *Predpriyatie*, 5, 1926, 93; this was previously the 'Novyi Lessner' factory.

[81] See Carr and Davies (1969), 951.

Soviet tractors were produced in small numbers at several different factories in 1925.[82] The rival claims of agriculture and industry on Soviet machine building were neatly balanced in the STO decision in the spring of 1927 to construct a tractor factory at Stalingrad, and a heavy-engineering factory at Sverdlovsk.

The mass production of tractors, lorries and other major lines of production novel for Soviet industry seemed to require the construction of new factories (though this was sometimes disputed). But for the moment nearly all engineering development took place at established factories. The capacity of both civilian and military engineering works had been substantially enlarged during the feverish wartime expansion of armaments production, but by 1926/27 Soviet armaments production had barely regained the 1913 level.[83] Much of the war-time and some of the pre-war armaments capacity was reconverted to civilian use in the mid-1920s, the most famous case being the production of tractors in the old cannon shop of the Putilov works in Leningrad. But further unused capacity remained in both military and civilian engineering factories, and most of the facilities of the great military shipyards lay idle.[84] Including the defence industries, the number of workers employed in the engineering industry regained the 1913 level in 1925/26, but did not regain the 1916 level until the end of 1930.[85]

The crucial problem for the Group B industries was the shortage of agricultural raw materials, essential for the production of food, drink and tobacco, and textiles and clothing; together these comprised over 90 per cent of all consumer

---

[82] *Ibid.* 448.

[83] The statistics are imprecise. Armaments production in 1913 probably exceeded 200 million rubles (see EHR, xxxv (1982), 104–7 (Gatrell)). Total 'technical supply' in the defence item of the budget amounted (measured in 1913 prices) to roughly 140 million rubles in 1925/26 and 225 million rubles in 1927/28 (including imports) (I have assumed that prices increased by the same percentage for armaments as for the metal and chemical industries as a whole). For these data, see Davies (1978), 28–9, 37.

[84] On the Nikolaevsk shipyards, see *SSSR: 4 s'ezd sovetov* (1927), 387.

[85] For 1913 and 1925/26, see *Ocherki* (1957), pp. 252–3 (Mints), for 1930, see *Nar. kh.* (1932), 426 (these figures, for 'machine-building' and 'electrical' industries, roughly correspond to Mints' figures for 'metalworking', and doubtless include the armaments' industries).

goods' production in the case of census industry, and over 65 per cent in the case of small-scale industries.[86]

The shortages were due to insufficient marketing rather than to a decline in the total production of these materials by agriculture. According to a Vesenkha study of agricultural raw materials, total production in 1926/27 was only slightly lower than in 1913. But the proportion retained by agriculture increased from 42·7 to 62·8 per cent, and in consequence the amount available for industry, and for export, declined by 37·5 per cent. Exports, which were substantial before the revolution, were drastically reduced. Even so, total supplies available to industry declined by at least 9 per cent between 1913 and 1926/27.[87]

As a result of this decline in supplies, the production of food, drink and tobacco in 1926/27 was lower than in 1913 in both census and small-scale industry. Production statistics partly reflect this decline, but are confused and unreliable. Employment figures, however, are more conclusive. In census industry, the number employed in food, drink and tobacco fell by 17·4 per cent, from 342,700 to 283,100;[88] this decline, in conjunction with the reduction in the length of the working day, indicates that the fall in production may have been substantial. The total number employed in food, drink and tobacco in small-scale industry declined from 616,000 to 587,000; as the working season was apparently shorter in the 1920s, small-scale production is also unlikely to have regained the 1913 level.[89]

In the production of textile yarn and fabrics, the other major group of consumer industries, the statistics in physical terms

[86] Estimated from data for 1927 in *Sots. str.* (1935), 14–15, and for 1926/27 in Kaufman (Washington, D.C., 1962), 75–81.

[87] *Materialy* (1927), 464–76; the study did not include grain, where extra-rural marketings declined by almost 50 per cent, or meat and dairy products, where some decline also took place (see vol. 1, pp. 17–18); the estimate for the year 1926/27, made early in 1927, is preliminary. Similarly Narkomfin estimated, using Gosplan data, that between 1913 and 1926/27 extra-rural sales declined from 20·3 to 14·7 per cent of the output of grain, from 73·1 to 53·1 per cent of the output of industrial crops, and 30·9 to 25·0 per cent of livestock products (for this study see vol. 1, p. 17n).

[88] *Ocherki* (1957), 255 (Mints).

[89] Kaufman (Washington, D.C., 1962), 65, excluding fishing; Kaufman estimates that the full-time equivalents were 347,000 in 1913 and 259,000 in 1926/27 (pp. 70–1).

indicate that in 1926/27 production had approximately recovered to the 1913 level; the official statistics in value terms, which show a substantial increase in production, are evidently exaggerated.[90]

During the first world war and the mid-1920s, the textile industry began to enter a new stage. The factory production of lengths of cotton fabrics and woollen cloth had driven out, or partly driven out, homespun garments in the nineteenth century; but the lengths were made up into garments at home or by artisans. After 1914, the garments themselves began to be produced in factories on a substantial scale for military purposes.[91] The age of mass armies pushed Russia towards the mass production of consumer goods. By 1926/27, production of garments and knitwear by large-scale industry, from small beginnings, was recorded as eight times as large as in 1913. But these two industries still employed only 41,700 workers, mainly in factories controlled by the local soviets.[92] Small-scale industry continued side by side with the new factories; the data for 1913 are uncertain, but according to one estimate artisan production of clothing, hats and knitwear actually increased between 1913 and 1926/27.[93] By 1928, over 55 per cent of woollen cloth was made into garments by census or small-scale industry, but the equivalent figure for cotton textiles was still only 11 per cent.[94] Thus men's suits were normally made by a tailor; shirts and frocks were usually made at home. Leather footwear began to tread the same path: the proportion made by factory industry increased from 12 per cent in 1913 to 19 per cent in 1926/27. This shift was accompanied by a smaller increase in the production of small-scale industry.[95] But in other industries, including metal goods, the increase in factory production was accompanied by a sharp decline in artisan production.

[90] See Davies (1978), 42–3; the number of workers in the census textile industry, including the clothing industry, increased from 712,300 in 1913 to 716,000 (or 751,100) in 1926/27 (*Ocherki* (1957), 246–9 (Mints)).

[91] Compare the production data for 'clothing and toilet goods', in 1913 and 1915, in *Dinamika*, i, iii (1930), 176–9.

[92] *St. spr. 1928* (1929), 347–8.

[93] *Na putyakh* (1929), 15–16.

[94] See data in *Materials* (1985), 365–70. Comparable data for 1913 and 1926/27 have not been available.

[95] The increase in production of the leather footwear industry was reported as follows (million rubles at 1913 prices):

In view of the small amount of new investment in the first eight years after the 1917 revolution, no substantial change took place in the regional location of industry. On the eve of the revolution, census industry was overwhelmingly concentrated into four main economic regions.[96] First, the ancient home of Russian industry was the Central Industrial region, the successor to medieval Muscovy. This was a relatively densely populated economic region, where by 1913 20 million people, one-seventh of the population of the Russian Empire, lived on 2 per cent of its territory, an area the size of France.[97] Here cotton textiles, the first truly modern industry in Russia, had been added to traditional handicrafts in the course of the nineteenth century. One million industrial workers, 37 per cent of the total for the Empire, were employed in the Central Industrial region in 1915.[98] Although the rise of modern engineering industry in the region accompanied the coming of the railways, it was primarily a centre for consumer goods: textiles alone provided over 60 per cent of total industrial output. One-third of the industrial production of the region was manufactured in Moscow itself and its suburbs, but important segments of industry were located over a wide area: Ivanovo–Voznesensk was the centre for cotton textiles, giant engineering works were established at Nizhnii Novgorod (Sormovo) and Kolomna.[99] And in the Central Industrial region outside Moscow a high proportion of

	1913	1926/27
Census industry[a]	30	61
Small-scale industry[b]	233	267
Total	263	328

[a] *Trudy TsSU*, xxxvi, i (1926), 70; *St. spr. 1928* (1929), 316–23.

[b] *Na putyakh* (1929), 15.

[96] The account below excludes the Baltic states, Poland, and the other parts of the Russian Empire which did not form part of the USSR pre-1939 territory. This important industrial area produced 17·1 per cent of all production of census industry, and employed 17·8 per cent of industrial workers in 1913 (555,500 out of 3,114,900). (*Dinamika*, i, iii (1930), 176–7.)

[97] *Pyatiletnii plan* (1930), iii, 42.

[98] For the data relating to 1915 in the following paragraphs, referring to a total of 2,730,000 workers (pre-1939 USSR frontiers) producing a gross output of 6,411 million rubles in current prices, see *Dinamika*, i, iii (1930), 178–89; a regional breakdown for 1913 is not available, and the breakdown for 1912 excludes most workers in the armaments industries.

[99] *Pyatiletnii plan* (1930), iii, 43–4, 50.

the factories, and of the labour force, were located not in the towns, but in villages or in industrial settlements which had grown out of villages.[100]

While industry in the Central Industrial region developed from the fifteenth century onwards, largely with private capital and in response to the growth of the market, our second region, the Ural economic region, provides a major example of industry founded and nurtured by the state. Here Peter the Great forced the rapid growth of the charcoal-based iron industry at the beginning of the eighteenth century, using serf labour. By 1915 the region employed 263,000 industrial workers. As many as 224,000 of these worked in mining and metalworking; industries based on agricultural raw materials were weakly developed. The Urals still employed 49 per cent of all workers in the iron and steel industry, though its ancient mines and ironworks provided only 19 per cent of the output.

From the 1880s, the mining and metal industries of our third region, the Ukraine, like those of the Urals, were developed with state assistance and encouragement. Foreign capital and technology poured into the Ukraine, and by 1915 the Ukraine together with the contiguous industry of the North Caucasus, was responsible for 85 per cent of all coal, 64 per cent of iron and steel, and about 19 per cent of engineering and metal products. The Ukraine, occupying approximately the same area as the Central Industrial region, had a population of 30 millions and was thus even more densely populated. But in contrast to the Central Industrial region, the soil and climate of the Ukraine enabled its agriculture to flourish, and it developed sugar-refining and other food industries based on agricultural raw materials. In 1915, 272,000 of its 499,000 industrial workers were employed in mining and metals, and a further 148,000 in the food industry. The Ukraine and the North Caucasus imported their textiles and other industrial consumer goods from the Central Industrial region, exporting coal, metal and food products to other parts of the Russian Empire and providing most of the grain for export.

Our fourth economic region, the North West, also developed largely as a result of state initiative. The town of St. Petersburg, like the iron industry of the Urals, was constructed by serfs at

---

[100] See Crisp (1976), 44–8; Rashin (1958), 206–11.

the behest of Peter the Great; and the great engineering industries of the region developed partly in response to the state-induced boom of the 1890s. The engineering industry of the region was overwhelmingly concentrated in St. Petersburg and its suburbs, which contained the most modern and sophisticated factories and the most skilled workers in the Russian Empire; it was the main centre for electrical engineering, armaments and naval shipbuilding. Of the 358,000 industrial workers employed in the region in 1915, 181,000 worked in metalworking and engineering, and a further 42,000 in the chemical industry; the region manufactured 36 per cent of all Russian engineering products.[101] A wide range of industrial consumer goods was also produced.

These four economic regions, with only 42 per cent of the population of the Russian Empire, employed 83 per cent of all workers in census industry in 1915. Some important industries were located elsewhere: oil in Baku, manganese in Georgia, gold and platinum in Siberia. And other regions contributed agricultural raw materials, and labour, to the four industrial regions. Cotton, when not imported, was supplied from Turkestan; and the over-populated Central Black-Earth region, the old centre of agriculture, was a constant source of seasonal and permanent labour for both the Central Industrial region

---

[101] The high share of armaments in the production of the region is indicated by a comparison between 1912 (excluding armaments) and 1915 (including armaments):

	1912		*1915*	
	Gross output (mln. rubles)	*Workers (thousands)*	*Gross output (mln. rubles)*	*Workers (thousands)*
a *Chemicals*				
North-West	101·1	15·8	171·3	41·5
Total Russian Empire	333·6	50·8	592·5	108·7
b *Metalworking and engineering*				
North-West	93·2	38·5	480·0	180·8
Total Russian Empire	335·6	108·7	1330·9	536·7

The number of industrial establishments in the North-Western region was reported at 48 for chemicals and 130 for metalworking and engineering in 1912 (excluding armaments); the equivalent figures for 1915 (including armaments) were 85 and 336. (From *Dinamika*, i, iii (1930), 24–7; 178–89.)

and the Ukraine.[102] But most industrial locations outside the four main economic regions were oases linked to the four regions, and exercised little influence on the economy of their own region.[103] The emigration of labour from the over-populated agricultural regions alleviated their economic situation, but did not substantially improve it.

Over vast areas of the Russian Empire no modern industry existed. In the whole of Siberia in 1915, with a population of over 11 million, only 106,000 workers were employed in mines and factories; and of these 71,000 laboured in the coal, gold and platinum mines. Only 3,334 Siberian workers were employed in the metalworking and engineering industries, including armaments. In Central Asia and Kazakhstan virtually no factory industry existed.

Moreover, this survey in terms of very large regions underestimates the extent to which census industry was concentrated into a small part of the territory of the Russian Empire. Within the major industrial regions, whole provinces had little modern industry. Five of the fifty provinces of European Russia contained 49 per cent of the industrial labour force in 1913.[104]

In the mid-1920s, pulling up the underdeveloped areas of the USSR remained a task for the future. The proportion of workers in census industry situated in the four main economic regions very slightly increased, from 82 per cent in 1912 and 1915 to 84 per cent in 1926/27. The Central Industrial region, where consumer goods predominated, occupied the same proportion of total production as in 1912. On the other hand, the North-Western region, the heart of the armaments' industry, declined slightly in significance, and in the mid-1920s much war-time capacity was still not in use. The Ukraine, the North Caucasus and the Urals suffered most from destruction and decline during the civil war; but they recovered at sharply different rates. By 1925/26 the number of workers employed in the Ukraine was absolutely higher than in 1913 or 1915, and had increased from 18·9 per cent to 23 per cent of the total number of workers. In the North Caucasus, on the other hand, the number of workers

---

[102] *Kontrol'nye tsifry . . . na 1927/28* (1927), 428.
[103] See *ibid.* 438–9.
[104] Rashin (1958), 193.

was lower than in both 1912 and 1915. The relative importance of the Ural economic region also declined sharply.[105]

According to Gosplan, the proportion of investment allocated to the North-Western and the Central Industrial regions since the revolution was relatively small. In the North-Western region there was capacity in hand; the Central Industrial region mainly produced consumer goods and also lacked raw materials rather than capacity. Instead, such investment as had taken place since the revolution had been directed primarily to the Ukraine and the Urals, regions where capital repairs were most urgently required.[106] The success of the relatively modern Ukraine, in contrast to the relative failure of the Urals, with its ancient industries, provided strong support for the Ukrainian view that it could achieve the quickest and highest return on investment.[107]

The different rates of recovery resulted in widely varying rates of unemployment. In the Ukraine, where the number employed had substantially increased since 1915, the unemployment rate was relatively low. In the North-Western region, where employment was much lower than in 1915, and in the Central Industrial region, which continuously attracted labour from the neighbouring over-populated agricultural areas, the unemployment rate was considerably higher than average. The unemployment rate was also high in some regions with little industry, such as Siberia, where the population was growing rapidly owing to resettlement, and in the Central Black-Earth region, the classic region of agricultural over-population.[108] At the end of 1926/27 Gosplan was thoroughly pessimistic about the prospects for the full employment of the population of these areas:

[105] The data for 1925/26 in the above paragraph are from *Dinamika*, i, iii (1930), 210–49.

[106] *KTs . . . na 1927/28* (1928), 414, 430–1; Gosplan also explained the lack of investment in Leningrad by 'restraint on new construction in this frontier region'. The crude indicator of the level of capital investment used by Gosplan was investment in state industry in 1926/27 as a percentage of gross industrial output in that year: USSR – 17·1; Ukraine – 20·2; Urals – 21·9; Leningrad – 10·1; Central Industrial region – 8·9.

[107] See the report by Grin'ko, then chairman of the Ukrainian Gosplan, to the first Gosplan congress, in PKh, 6, 1926, 179–80.

[108] The unemployment rate as a percentage of all hired labour in non-agricultural activities in 1926/27 was: Leningrad – 32·6; Central Black-Earth region – 31; Siberia – 30; Central Industrial region – 24·1; Ukraine – 21·2; Urals – 21 (*KTs . . . na 1927/28* (1928), 416–34).

The rate of development is still insufficient to absorb the surpluses of unutilised labour which the areas with over-populated agriculture are supplying. In some areas the unemployment situation is deteriorating owing to spontaneous processes of migration which are not under sufficient state control.[109]

(ii) Productivity and the length of the working day

The principle that social improvement temporarily hinders economic development was amply illustrated in NEP Russia. Social reformers have often argued that long hours are exhausting, so that more will be produced in a shorter working day. But Soviet experience in the 1920s was not encouraging. The introduction of the eight-hour day after the revolution reduced working hours by some 20 per cent (see p. 11 above). This reform, and its retention in the difficult years after the revolution, certainly helped to persuade workers that the new regime identified itself with their interests, and encouraged a minority to work enthusiastically. But hourly labour productivity rose above the 1913 level only after painful efforts to reorganise work or to increase the capital equipment available per worker. Perhaps this was hardly a fair test of the optimistic hypothesis. The greater part of the capital equipment at the disposal of the worker was by the mid-1920s a dozen years older than in 1913, and had often suffered years of neglect.

On the railways, where post-revolutionary investment in improved rolling stock was very small, and the state of the track left much to be desired, traffic was restored to the pre-war level by 1925/26 only because the number of personnel increased to as much as 39 per cent above the 1913 level.[110]

In industry, in contrast to the railways, the pre-war level of production was achieved by a combination of increased employment and increased hourly productivity. The number of workers in census industry rose by about 5 per cent between 1913 and 1926/27, indicating that the total number of hours

---

[109] *KTs . . . na 1927/28* (1928), 441; the preface is dated September 30, 1927.
[110] For data see Strumilin (1958) (2)), 670–1, and *Ocherki*, iii (1960), 126 (Mints).

worked decreased by some 15 per cent. According to official figures, gross production increased in the same period by 5–12 per cent.[111] These figures almost certainly overestimate the increase in production. But, even allowing for overestimation, hourly labour productivity probably increased by something like 10–15 per cent between 1913 and 1926/27.[112]

This substantial improvement was partly obtained by concentrating production into a smaller number of mines and factories, by standardising output, and to a lesser extent by introducing modern machinery.[113] The success of these measures distinguished industry from the railways, where reorganisation was technically more difficult, and capital repair and investment were less generously financed.

Both in industry and on the railways increases in labour productivity also involved economic and administrative pressure on the workers. From the end of 1924 onwards, the authorities, supported half-heartedly and intermittently by the trade unions, insistently demanded that labour productivity should increase more rapidly than the average wage, and sought to bring this about by systematically increasing output norms (i.e. cutting the rate for the job). The campaign was more successful in industry than on the railways, but even in industry wages outpaced productivity in two of the four years 1924/25–1927/28.[114]

[111] See Davies (1978), 58, 60.

[112] For number of workers, see *Ocherki* (1957), 192–3 (Mints); for the production index and its defects see Davies (1978), 13–31.

[113] For the concentration of manufacturing industry, see *Ocherki* (1957), 228–9, which shows that between 1914 and 1927 the percentage of workers in census industry in factories employing over 500 workers increased from 56·5 to 72·1, while the percentage in factories with 50 workers or less declined from 10·2 to 3·4. This continued the trend of 1907–1914 (see Davies, ed. (1988) (Gatrell and Davies)). For examples of standardisation, see Carr and Davies (1969), 343. For an authoritative account of specialisation and standardisation in the cotton textile industry, see *Predpriyatie*, 10, 1927, 10–15 (Nol'de). For the introduction of machinery into the oil industry, see *Pervye shagi* (1959), 161–90; in oil mining and extraction, production increased from 390 million rubles in 1913 to 663 millions in 1926/27 (in 1913 prices), but the number of workers declined from 49,700 to 43,600 (*Ocherki* (1957), 208, 226 (Mints); *Trudy TsSU*, xxvi, i (1926), 69–73; *St. spr. 1928* (1929), 316–23).

[114] On the productivity: wage drive, see Carr (1958), 389–92; Carr and Davies (1969), 487–511.

(iii) Internal trade

After the collapse of all organised trade during the civil war, the New Economic Policy encouraged the revival of private trade. In May 1924, the XIII party congress warned against 'any measures in the sphere of private trade which would lead to a curtailment of, or interference with, the general process of exchange of goods'.[115] But large-scale private trade was always regarded as incompatible with Soviet principles. Where pre-revolutionary private wholesale enterprises remained in existence, they were almost invariably in state or cooperative ownership or control. Even in 1923/24 private wholesale trade accounted for only 18 per cent of total wholesale turnover,[116] and by 1926/27 the proportion had declined to a mere 4·6 per cent.[117] The wholesale trade of state industry was increasingly conducted by national or regional syndicates modelled on the pre-revolutionary private syndicates not only in the capital goods industries but also in cotton textiles and other consumer goods industries in which they did not exist at all before the revolution.[118]

Retail private trade, mainly carried on by individual traders, sometimes assisted by members of their families, was allowed to develop much more freely in the early stages of NEP: in 1922/23 it amounted to 75·3 per cent of all retail trade. According to the concept prevalent until 1927, private retail trade would continue insofar as the socialist sector was not strong enough to take over its activities. In the mid-1920s, this policy was occasionally departed from in practice when the police descended on a market and arrested groups of 'Nepmen' (private traders) for infringement of regulations.[119] But such cases were exceptional. With the rapid recovery of the economy, private retail trade flourished and expanded, doubling in volume between 1922/23

---

[115] See Carr (1958), 245.
[116] Dikhtyar (1961), 212.
[117] Dikhtyar (1961), 303.
[118] See Carr and Davies (1969), 636–50.
[119] In April 1926, for example, 400 traders in the central Moscow market were arrested by the OGPU for allegedly purchasing goods for re-sale, in one of a series of raids carried out by the OGPU at the request of Moscow soviet (TPG, April 16, 1926).

and 1926. But state and cooperative trade, more strongly and much more consistently supported by the authorities, expanded even more rapidly. By 1926 the share of private trade in retail turnover had declined to 40·7 per cent.[120]

The restriction of private trade in circumstances where the state was unable to build up a modern trading system in its place prevented the recovery of the retail trading network to its pre-war size. The total number of trading units (excluding trade from carts and by pedlars, which cannot be accurately estimated) amounted to 930,700 in 1912, but had reached only 645,300 by April–September 1926. Of these, 468,500 were privately owned.[121] But very few private traders risked the employment of an assistant. Only 22,896 traders by main occupation were recorded in the 1926 population census as 'employers',[122] and according to labour statistics the total number of persons employed in private trade in 1926/27 amounted to only 63,900.[123] Even allowing for the under-reporting which no doubt occurred it is certain that private trading units were smaller as well as less numerous than before the revolution. State and cooperative trade was organised in somewhat larger units. But the total number of persons

---

[120] Dikhtyar (1961), 239. These figures all exclude direct sales by peasants and others in bazaar trade.

[121] See Strumilin (1958(2)), 675–95; *Materialy po istorii SSSR*, vii (1959), 124–8. The following table compares the estimates for licensed trading units in 1912–13 and 1926, based on tax data (thousand units):

	1912–13	*1926*[a]
Wholesale, etc.	8[a]	18
Shops (magaziny)	149[a]	62
Small trading units (lavki)	486[a]	259
Stalls and kiosks (lar'ki)	289[a]	306
Carts and pedlars	310[b]	160
Total	1242[b]	804

[a] Official estimate for 1912.
[b] Strumilin's estimate for 1913.
[c] Whole column, including carts and pedlars, is based on official tax returns, so may be underestimated, particularly in the case of persons selling from carts, and pedlars, who found it easier to evade registration.

[122] *Vsesoyuznaya perepis'*, xxxiv (1930), 118–19.
[123] *Trud* (1930), 3.

employed in state and cooperative trade amounted to only 451,300, for a total of 178,908 trading units, a mere 2·5 persons per unit.[124] Taking the private and socialised sectors together, the total number of wage and salary earners employed in trade was no larger than before the revolution, and the number working in trade on their own account was substantially smaller.[125] Nevertheless, according to Soviet estimates the amount of retail trade in real terms in 1926 had reached 94–98 per cent of the 1913 level.[126] Whether the increase in turnover per person engaged in trade is regarded as an increase in efficiency depends on the definition of efficiency; it certainly resulted in more frequent queues.

(iv) Foreign trade and foreign technology

Foreign economic relations were profoundly affected by the consequences of the revolution. In February 1918 the Soviet authorities cast off the capitalist and feudal past by abrogating the national debt. While this act of defiance fuelled the lasting hostility and suspicion of foreign governments and foreign capitalists, its consequences for the balance of payments were favourable. The balance of payments was also improved by the drastic decline in tourist expenditure abroad (this has remained a feature of the Soviet scene). Net payments abroad on interest, dividends and tourism, amounting to 693 million rubles in 1913, had fallen virtually to zero throughout the 1920s.[127] This meant that the substantial surplus of exports of commodities over imports, which was a necessary feature of the pre-

---

[124] For the numbers employed, see *Trud* (1930), 3; for the number of units, see Strumilin (1958 (2)), 694–5.

[125] Strumilin estimated the total number of persons engaged in trade in 1913 as 1,185,000 owners plus 487,000 employees, 1,672,000 persons altogether (Strumilin (1958) (2), 678). The equivalent figures for 1926/27 were 628,644 private owners plus 515,200 employed in all sectors of trade, 1,143,844 altogether; this no doubt underestimated the numbers of pedlars and persons selling from carts. (For the numbers employed, see *Trud* (1930), 3; for the number of private owners, see Strumilin (1958) (2), 694–5.)

[126] Dikhtyar (1961), 238, 240.

[127] For the 1913 figure, see Gregory (1982), 97–8; the figure above is the sum of his cols. 2–6. The positive effect on the invisible items was partly counteracted by a relatively small increase in payments for carriage of Soviet goods in foreign ships, consequent upon the decline of Russian merchant shipping.

revolutionary balance of trade, no longer had to be maintained.[128]

But the revolution and civil war also had extremely damaging consequences for Soviet economic relations with foreign countries. Foreign capital was a major source of investment before 1914, and the main vehicle for transferring advanced technology to Russian industry. In the 1920s the financial inducements offered to foreign companies to invest in the Soviet Union were by no means negligible; the urgent Soviet need for new investment and new technology led the authorities to sporadic but ambitious attempts to attract foreign capital. But the political hostility to the Soviet Union was intense, and was supported by indignation at the abrogation of the national debt. The Soviet Communists for their part were extremely reluctant to become in the least dependent on foreign capitalism. The policy of offering 'concessions' to invest in Soviet industry to foreign businessmen therefore had little practical outcome: only the Harriman manganese concession in Georgia was of substantial industrial importance.[129]

Foreign trade, which virtually ceased during the Civil War, recovered very slowly, and throughout the 1920s was far below the pre-war level. The decline in agricultural marketings resulted in a drastic reduction of every kind of agricultural export. Even by 1926/27 total exports reached a mere 36·7 per cent of the 1913 level.[130] The only major export item which increased substantially was petroleum (see p. 18 above). This huge decline in export earnings meant that the Soviet government was constantly faced with the need to restrict imports; in 1926/27 they amounted to 36·2 per cent of 1913.[131]

[128] The positive balance of trade in 1926/27 was exceptional (see Table in Carr and Davies (1969), 971).

[129] Concessions were responsible for less than 0·5 per cent of the production of census industry in 1926/27; in addition, mixed trading companies handled 5·9 per cent of total foreign trade turnover in 1926/27 (*Materialy po istorii*, vii (1959), 48–61; Carr and Davies (1961), 950, 971). Of some historical interest are the British Lena Goldfields concession, which renewed a pre-revolutionary activity, and the pencil company of the American Armand Hammer, now a famous oil magnate.

[130] See data in pre-war prices in *St. spr. 1928* (1929), 717–18; in a careful estimate in terms of 1926/27 prices, Dohan gives the percentage as 32·9 (*Slavic Review*, xxxv (1976), 606–7).

[131] Dohan's equivalent percentage in 1926/27 prices is 38·4. He shows that the terms of trade were somewhat more favourable to the USSR in the 1920s than

The chains wrought by the shortage of foreign currency hindered every step towards industrialisation. In 1925/26, the failure of the export plan and the consequent reduction in imports was a major cause of the industrial crisis, and led to the permanent withdrawal of the ruble from the foreign exchange market.[132]

The shortage of foreign currency was alleviated by a fairly strict application of import controls. Imports in all the commodity groups of the official foreign trade classification declined substantially in absolute terms, but imports of foodstuffs and consumer goods were reduced far more drastically: these constituted 44 per cent of all imports in 1913, but only 20 per cent in 1926/27. In absolute terms, the import of foodstuffs was reduced to 20 per cent and of consumer goods to a mere 11 per cent of 1913.[133] The import of items such as coffee, tea, wines and spirits, and clothing, declined to almost negligible quantities.[134]

Two sub-groups of imports were singled out for special favour. First, in the case of industrial crops, where exports before the revolution were substantial, the urgent requirements of Soviet industry compelled the authorities not only to reduce the amount of exports drastically but also to continue imports at a fairly high level. Net imports of wool, 38,000 tons in 1913, still amounted to 28,000 tons in 1926/27; and net imports of leather actually actually increased from 14,000 to 53,000 tons. The decline in the marketing of the products of farming thus imposed a severe burden on the balance of trade.

The second sub-group which received special priority in the import plan was machinery. Here the shortage of foreign currency was alleviated not merely by affording priority to these imports, but also by a determined effort to secure earmarked foreign credits. The most important achievement in this respect was the German credit of 300 million marks (140 million rubles) awarded in 1926 and spent on German capital

---

in 1913: the export price index in 1926/27 was 139, the import price index 128 (1913=100, 1927/28 price weights) (*loc. cit.* 606–7, 614–15).

[132] See Carr (1958), 445, 484–7.

[133] Estimated from data in *St. spr. 1928* (1929), 716–22, deducting an estimated value for raw cotton from 'spinning materials and products'.

[134] Compare the physical data for 1913 and 1926/27 in *Vneshnyaya torgovlya* (1960).

equipment in the course of the next two years.[135] In 1926/27 the import of machinery for use in production, together with electrical engineering products, already amounted in real terms to approximately 58 per cent of 1913. In 1927/28 these imports again increased more rapidly than imports as a whole, and reached 83 per cent of 1913. Together with the substantial increase in Soviet production, this enabled total supplies of production engineering and electrical engineering goods to exceed the 1913 level by some 15 per cent in 1926/27, and by some 60 per cent in 1927/28.[136] Foreign trade planning thus made an essential contribution to the high level of industrial investment, perhaps the most important accomplishment of Soviet planning in the mid-1920s.

The import of foreign capital equipment was coupled with the first stages of a determined effort to acquire technical knowledge and experience from abroad. This effort took four main forms, which have not since changed fundamentally. First, foreign technological developments were attentively studied in the USSR, partly through the scrutiny of foreign technical literature, partly through the practice, already established by this time, of dismantling imported equipment and attempting to copy it.[137] Secondly, Soviet citizens were sent on missions abroad to study foreign technology and to improve skills. They ranged from senior officials of Vesenkha to inexperienced young specialists. The success of the missions varied; the most serious drawback was that most of those sent lacked knowledge of the language.[138] But such missions abroad were widely reported in the Soviet economic and technical press; and much information was conveyed about American and German technology, usually in enthusiastic terms.[139]

[135] See Carr and Davies (1969), 712; the German credit was roughly equal to the value of one year's import of machinery.

[136] Estimated from data for imports in *Vneshnyaya torgovlya* (1960) and for production as estimated in Davies, ed. (1988) (Gatrell and Davies).

[137] Thus in 1924 the first turbine motor to be received from the United Kingdom after the revolution was dismantled by Soviet engineers, who were impressed by the advance in western technology thus revealed (P, May 27, 1930). I do not know how significant industrial espionage was at this time.

[138] *Predpriyatie*, 4, 1928, 83.

[139] A. M. Ginzburg, a senior Vesenkha economic official with critical views, was despatched to the United States in 1927; on his return he published a series of well-informed reports on different American industries in the industrial

Thirdly, foreign specialists and workers were employed in Soviet industry, providing advice and training Soviet workers and engineers. The movement of specialists in both directions was small, though increasing rapidly. The number of Soviet citizens sent abroad on technical missions increased from 131 in 1925/26 to 260 in 1926/27. Only 135 foreign engineers and technicians were working in the whole of Soviet industry in the autumn of 1926;[140] the number increased to 197 in the autumn of 1927.[141] Fourthly, and undoubtedly potentially the most important channel for the transfer of technical knowledge, technical assistance contracts were signed with foreign companies, and – sometimes in association with these contracts, and sometimes separately – foreign patents and drawings were purchased. By the end of 1928 40 such contracts were in operation, mainly with American and German companies. In March 1927, Sovnarkom approved a five-year technical assistance contract between Lenmashtrest and Metro-Vickers, U.K., Ltd., awarded after an international competition. The collaboration involved the manufacture of steam turbines under licence in Leningrad, the sale of equipment and patents and the transfer of information to Lenmashtrest, and work by Soviet and British engineers in each other's factories.[142] This contract was typical of the arrangements made during the next few years in all the capital goods industries and in other sectors of the economy. The technical assistance contracts were the most expensive of the four main forms of technical assistance. Taken together, however, all forms of technical assistance in 1926/27 or

---

newspaper (see, for example, TPG, January 5, 1928). At a more practical level, a Soviet engineer visited the Ford works in Detroit in 1926 and studied their repair shops, returning well-equipped with appliances; he wrote a practical manual based on his experience (A. V. Ostavnov, *Avtomobili Forda: modeli A i AA* (1931), especially pp. 3–4). Such examples could be multiplied.

[140] TPG, November 13, 1926; 70 of these were engineers, 65 were foremen.

[141] TPG, November 24, 1927; Kolomenskii, (1930), 11, 17. In addition to the engineers and technicians, 62 foreign workers were employed in Soviet industry in November 1927.

[142] See P, March 15, 1927; *British–Russian Gazette*, iii (1927), 378; *Machinery*, vol. 94 (1959), 165–6, 777–8. The later fate of the collaboration will be discussed in vol. 4.

1927/28 cost only a small percentage of the amount spent on the import of capital equipment.[143]

(v) The comparative perspective

In spite of the progress between 1914 and 1927, the Soviet economy continued to lag far behind the great industrial powers. Straddling Europe and Asia, the Soviet Union, like the Russian Empire, presented a dual face to the world: the most backward of the great European powers, the most industrially advanced of the great peasant countries. The immensity of the gap to be bridged, in terms of both production and technology, was described frankly and more or less accurately in numerous contemporary Soviet publications and pronouncements. In terms of employment, 69 per cent of the independent Soviet population worked in agriculture in 1926, as compared with less than 19 per cent in the United States and Germany.[144] And industry continued to be dominated by the production of consumer goods to a greater extent than the major industrial countries.[145] The first five-year plan, trenchantly complaining about the 'burdensome inheritance' from tsarism, pointed out that the return to the pre-war level 'reproduced the main disproportions' of the tsarist industry; the high share of the textile and food industries in total production was combined with 'very weak development of machine building and electrical engineering, a relatively small percentage of iron and steel and the almost complete absence of the chemical industry'.[146]

The comparative statistics for output per head of population, which were frequently cited, showed that in the Soviet Union the production of consumer goods was lower, and of capital goods much lower, than in any of the other great powers. Even

[143] It may be estimated from data in Kolomenskii (1930), 11–57, that the total cost of all four forms of technical assistance was some 3 million rubles or so in 1926/27 (it increased to 13 million rubles in 1928/29).

[144] *Na novom etape* (1930), ii, 465; these figures exclude members of the family assisting the householder.

[145] The percentage of workers in census industry employed in mining, metals and engineering remained at 37·2 in 1926/27, the same as in 1913, while the equivalent percentage in Germany increased from 41·3 to 46·5 between 1913 and 1925 (*Na novom etape* (1930), ii, 594–5; the figures for 1913 are from *Dinamika*, i, iii (1930), 176–7, and Umanskii, ed. (1928), 89–91).

[146] *Pyatiletnii plan* (1930), ii, i, 98–9.

the amount of paper consumed per head of population in 1926/27, in this land abundant in forests and hungry for knowledge, had reached only 14 per cent of the German and a mere 6 per cent of the United States' consumption.[147] Soviet national income as a whole was estimated to have been no higher in 1927 than the national income of the United States half a century earlier in 1880, even though the population of the USSR was substantially larger.[148]

The gap between the Soviet Union and the industrialised countries was dramatically indicated by the minute quantities of mechanical energy and mechanical motive-power used in the Soviet economy. The total consumption of energy per head of population, including human and animal muscle-power as well as the mechanical energy provided by coal and other fuels, reached only 41 per cent of the equivalent figure in the case of Germany and a mere 13 per cent in the case of the United States. The difference was almost entirely due to the small amount of mechanical energy available in the Soviet Union, which obtained two-thirds of its energy inputs from human beings and animals, lagging behind such semi-industrialised countries as Italy and Japan, and ahead only of the Asiatic countries.[149] 'The Soviet producer', Gosplan commented when

[147] *Materialy* (1927), 29.

[148] *Problemy rekonstruktsii* (1929), 338 (Eventov). This volume contains the proceedings of the V Congress of Gosplan in March 1929; L. Ya. Eventov's informative report sums up the Soviet view at that time of the comparative economic level of the Soviet economy.

[149] The following instructive comparisons, measured in horse-power hours per head of population per year, were presented in *KTs ... na 1927/28* (1927), 444–5, with a further breakdown for each type of fuel:

	Living energy (human and animal)	*Mechanical energy (coal, peat, oil, firewood and water power)*	*Total*
United States	207·3	1818·9	2026·3
Great Britain	57·4	999·5	1052·9
Germany	93·2	571·2	664·4
Italy	84·8	206·2	291·0
Japan	59·3	190·5	249·8
USSR	181·8	88·4	270·2
India	155·3	17·9	173·2
China	52·7	11·0	63·7

it presented these estimates in the summer of 1927, 'is worse equipped for the struggle with nature as a result of this burdensome inheritance than the producers of other countries'.[150]

Soviet dependence on human and animal power, while in large part a function of the technical backwardness of agriculture, extended to the whole of the economy with the exception of the most modern segment of factory industry. A circumstantial comparison between bricklaying in Germany and the Soviet Union by a German bricklayer working in the USSR plausibly argued that the much lower Soviet productivity resulted partly from the lower skill of the Soviet bricklayer, who did all the fetching and carrying himself rather than being supported by unskilled labour, and partly on the quality of the tools used.[151] The quality of Soviet small tools was a very frequent matter of complaint, and affected workers in every sector of the economy.[152]

In factory industry itself, the gap was not so forbidding. The total mechanical power available in Soviet industry, owing to its relatively small size, was naturally much smaller than in the industrial countries, amounting to 3·3 million horse-power as compared with 15·8 millions in the United Kingdom and 52·5 millions in the United States.[153] But such industries as iron and steel and cotton textiles, and important sections of the engineering industry, used relatively modern equipment and modern production methods, as they had in 1913. Horse-power

---

An alternative measure (*Pyatiletnii plan* (1930), ii, ii, 407) showed that the motive power available from animals and machines in the Soviet Union in 1927/8 amounted to only 33·5 million horse-power (some 20 million of which came from animals) as compared with 662·6 millions in the United States. A large part of the difference was explained by the almost complete absence of lorries and motor cars in the Soviet Union; but even if these were deducted the United States figure still reached 155·3 million horse-power.

[150] *KTs . . . na 1927/28* (1927), 446.

[151] TPG, May 10, 1928 (Konshtadt); the author claimed that German bricklayers were able to lay the bricks at once, without knocking and pushing them, and did not have to use a level after every three or four bricks; German trowels, made of good steel, were five or six times as large as Soviet trowels, so the German worker could use one trowel of mortar for three bricks while the Soviet worker used three trowels for one brick.

[152] See for example *Istoriya Moskovskogo Instrumental'nogo Zavoda* (1934), 114–15.

[153] *Fabrichno-zavodskaya promyshlennost'*, i (1928), 9–22 (Veits); the Soviet figure refers to October 1, 1926.

available per worker in factory industry was estimated at 1·4 in the Soviet Union as against 2·0 in the United Kingdom, 2·1 in Germany and 4·3 in the United States.[154] But Soviet workers were less skilled than workers in the major industrial countries, and Soviet industry was poorly provided with technical staff. In every industry what might be called the 'technical-staff gap' was at least as substantial as the technological gap.[155]

As a result of the smaller amount of mechanical power available per worker, and the lower level of skills, labour productivity (output per person employed) even in census industry was lower in the Soviet Union than in the advanced industrial countries. A Soviet estimate indicated that the average industrial worker in 1926/27 produced only one-half as much as a British worker and a mere one-seventh as much as a United States' worker.[156] The variation between industries was considerable. Output measured in tons per worker in 1928/29 was 24·9 per cent of the United States' level in the sugar industry, 17·2 per cent in the iron industry, 28·6 per cent in cotton textiles and as much as 84·0 per cent in the case of crude oil.[157]

In France, Germany and the Soviet Union industrial production approximately recovered to the pre-war level by 1926/27. The Soviet achievement was impressive. The decline in production, and the damage and destruction of industrial plant, had been far greater than in the other belligerent countries. But production in the United States and in the smaller industrial countries which had suffered no war damage far exceeded the

---

[154] *Problemy rekonstruktsii* (1930), 336 (Eventov).

[155] The number of engineering and technical workers as a percentage of total personnel was given as follows:

Coal	USSR 1·45; Germany 4·25; US 25
Chemicals	USSR 5·7; Germany 31·3
Electrical industry	USSR 6·0; US 19

(*Predpriyatie*, 8, 1928, 13; 10, 1928, 12).

[156] *Na novom etape* (1930), ii. 642–5; this gives the ratio for 1928/29, when Soviet productivity was approximately 28 per cent higher than in 1926/27, at 1:5·5 in the case of the United States and 1:1·55 in the case of Britain (the United States figures are for 1927, the British for 1924); all figures are for net output measured in pre-war prices and adjusted for the over-valuation of the ruble.

[157] *Na novom etape* (1930), ii, 643–4; the percentages for 1926/27 would have been lower, as Soviet productivity was lower in that year.

pre-war level. In consequence, the Soviet share in world industrial output declined.[158] The comparative Soviet position varied greatly between different industries. In some established Soviet industries, including coal and textiles, production had not fallen much further behind the rest of the world. But in other established industries, such as iron and oil, the lag had considerably increased.[159] Production of tractors, lorries and motor cars in the US, and to a lesser extent in Western Europe, had vastly increased since the end of the war; and major technical advances were achieved in several other industries. The Soviet Union, largely cut off from world technology between 1917 and 1923, and unable to undertake substantial new investment, had made little progress.[160] Gosplan pointed out in relation to what it termed 'new' industries that the USSR 'the electric power and oil industries, in spite of high rates of growth, are still lagging considerably behind international progress in terms both of their level and the absolute increase in their output, while in other industries (e.g. chemicals, motor vehicles) the position is definitely unfavourable'.[161] A young power engineer drew attention even more dramatically to the nature of the technological race with capitalist industry:

> We must naturally take as our models the achievements of the west and America, we must catch up and overtake them. But there is no kind of static situation over there in the creation of these models. We can observe the uniquely stormy dynamics of the process over there.[162]

---

[158] According to Gosplan, the index of the industrial production of the major powers in 1926/27 was approximately as follows (1913 = 100): USSR 104 (census industry); Germany 105; France 113; United States 152 (manufacturing), 156 (mining); Britain 89 (estimated from data in *KTs . . . na 1928/29* (1929), 383).

[159] The Soviet percentage share in world production in 1926 was estimated by Vesenkha as follows (with the tsarist share in 1913 in brackets): coal 2·1 (2·4), cotton (consumption) 7·1 (8·7), sugar 4·3 (6·7), iron 3·0 (5·6), oil 5·3 (16·7) (*Vypolnenie* (1931), 38).

[160] See the discussion of high technology engineering industries in Davies, ed. (1988) (Cooper and Lewis).

[161] *KTs . . . na 1928/29* (1929), 378; this passage was written in the summer of 1928.

[162] *Predpriyatie*, 10, 1927, 72 (Flakserman); the author pointed out that the Shatura power station was planned with the latest design of turbo-generator,

While the production gap between Soviet and western industry in 1926/27 was as wide as in 1913, and the technological gap yawned even wider, the rate of growth of Soviet industry in the mid-1920s was already higher and more consistent than in the capitalist countries. The Gosplan control figures for 1926/27 noted with some satisfaction that the plan to increase industrial production by 13 per cent 'has no parallel in the development of the US'.[163] A year later, after this plan had been exceeded, Gosplan remarked, in the control figures for 1927/28, that *'periodical crises'* were 'inevitable companions of capitalist development', and contrasted the 'sharp breaks and zig-zags' in the growth-curves of capitalist countries with the 'unbroken advance' which had already characterised Soviet economic growth for several years.[164] This achievement was undeniable. But could this rapid rate of growth be maintained within the framework of NEP once recovery was complete?

(c) INSTRUMENTS OF PLANNED INDUSTRIALISATION

During the years of economic recovery the Soviet authorities maintained – and, where it was absent, established – an imperfect but on the whole effective machinery for planning the economy – or at any rate for its central management. The tsarist government had controlled or influenced the economy partly through the state budget, and partly by protecting Russian industry with the aid of customs tariffs.[165] These instruments were also wielded effectively by the Soviet state; but they were supplemented in the now much larger state-owned sector of the economy by controls over finance, prices and wages. The scissors' crisis of 1923 (see vol. 1, pp. 28–9) impelled the party to authorise the use of a combination of

---

with a capacity of 16,000 kW, and its present extension would have generators with a capacity of 44,000 kW each; but meanwhile a 70,000 kW turbo-generator had been installed in Germany, and one with a capacity of 200,000 kW was planned (for Shatura, see *Promyshlennost'* . . . *1926/27* (1928), 281).

[163] *KTs . . . na 1926/27* (1926), 166 (approved by the presidium of Gosplan on August 16, 1926).

[164] *KTs . . . na 1927/28* (1928), 442, 449–51 (dated September 30, 1927).

[165] For further discussion, see Davies, ed. (1988) (Gatrell and Davies).

fiscal, credit and price policies to restore the delicate balance between industry and the peasantry. During the next four years, until the balance was finally upset at the end of 1927, the central aim of Soviet economic policy was to manipulate the scissors between agricultural and industrial prices so as to place an upper bound on the exploitation of the peasants by the state while at the same time directing resources into state industry.

In manipulating the financial controls, the Soviet government, following the successful currency reform of 1924, for a couple of years sought almost as vigorously as any capitalist government to maintain the stability of the currency, or even to enhance its value. This required a balanced budget. To this end the principal pre-revolutionary revenues were restored (see Table 22(a)). The most notable impost was the revenue from the state vodka monopoly, which had disappeared during the first world war when the tsarist government introduced prohibition. State vodka sales did not return to the pre-war level. But the restoration of the notorious 'tax on drunkenness' as the most important single source of revenue was a dramatic instance of the victory of economic expediency over social principle.[166] Excises were also imposed on textiles and other industrial consumer goods, which did not bear tax before the revolution. Other new sources of revenue included a personal income tax, directed at recovering some of the profits of private traders and other 'Nepmen', and an agricultural tax (a direct tax on peasant incomes). The system of mass loans from the population also began to be introduced in the mid-1920s. But the most striking change in the post-revolutionary budget was the large increase in various kinds of taxes and other imposts levied on the income and profits of state industrial and trading enterprises.

The relations between the state budget and state industry were confused and complicated. From 1922 onwards, the principal state industries acquired monopolistic or oligopolistic powers through the formation of national or regional syndicates (cartels) (see p. 30 above). During the scissors' crisis of 1923, the central state authorities introduced price controls so as to close the scissors by reducing the prices charged by the syndicates. Price controls were quite effective in relation to

[166] For the reintroduction and subsequent history of the vodka monopoly, see Carr (1954), 35, n. 2, Carr (1958), 465–8, Carr and Davies (1969), 759–62.

producer goods. But pressure from the continuous increase in the purchasing power of the population on the retail market for consumer goods tended to push up their prices in spite of the controls. In any case, unlike consumer goods, most producer goods were sold to other state enterprises, and ultimately paid for by the state budget, and this provided a powerful argument for keeping their prices particularly low. Both prices and profits therefore tended to be much higher for consumer goods than for producer goods. The cotton textile industry was the most prominent example of a consumer goods industry which financed its own investment, and also provided a substantial proportion of its profits to the state budget and the banks for general use. In contrast, investment in the producer goods industries, including electric power, was provided almost entirely by the state budget and the various state banks.

As well as providing a mechanism for transferring profits from high-profit to low-profit sectors, the state budget also exercised other major economic functions. As compared with 1913, budget expenditure on defence had been drastically reduced, and the large pre-revolutionary expenditure on interest and repayment of state loans vanished from the budget with the abrogation of the national debt.[167] In place of these items, expenditure on the national economy greatly increased (see Table 22(b)). Industry was the principal recipient of the additional allocations. According to a Vesenkha report, net allocations from budget and banks to Vesenkha-planned industry, after deducting taxes and other payments made to the budget and the banks by industry, amounted to 193 million rubles in 1925/26 and 309 million rubles in 1926/27.[168]

While the crucial means of implementing state policies in the mid-1920s was the provision of finance, financial measures were increasingly supplemented by physical controls. The quite detailed import controls were the most effective of all the physical controls wielded by the authorities during NEP. And throughout NEP the Red Army and Navy, the railways and other organisations financed from the state budget directly

[167] The official figures (see Table 22(b)) also show an enormous reduction in administrative expenditure; this remarkable decline requires sceptical investigation.

[168] *Promyshlennost'* . . . *1926/27* (1928), 72; this includes electrification and 'other' (presumably defence) industries.

negotiated their industrial requirements with Vesenkha through the Committee of State Orders.[169] Arrangements for the central allocation of iron and steel, and fuel, supplemented by elaborate detailed negotiations between syndicates, trusts and factories, were also firmly in place by 1926.[170] But the procedures and practice of physical planning were still crude and unsystematic.

The stage which Soviet planning had reached by the mid-1920s may be illustrated by the important case of capital investment. Capital investment in industry was mainly financed by central government. But once the financial provisions had been settled, the implementation of capital investment plans was in large part undertaken without central government intervention. Orders for capital equipment were normally placed direct between trust and trust; no effective syndicate for engineering products was in operation. A committee on engineering, responsible for distributing orders to engineering factories, was not established until the spring of 1927 (see p. 52 below), and the struggle to establish effective methods of planning capital equipment continued into the 1930s. The construction of buildings, as distinct from the provision of capital equipment, was nominally controlled by a Building Commission of the Council of Labour and Defence, and in industry by the Vesenkha Building Committee and Permanent Conference on Building, supported by the very active central committee of the building workers' trade union.[171] All these committees had different chairmen; they did not act in concert; and their influence was small. The majesty of the apparatus of control reflected the impotence of the authorities. The building industry in fact remained at the primitive technical level prevalent before the revolution. It was 'most backward and disorganised', the chairman of its trade union declared;[172] on another occasion he complained, with pardonable hyperbole, that *'our methods of work are still the same as they were in the Stone Age'*.[173] Building materials were produced in numerous small

---

[169] See Carr (1958), 344; Carr and Davies (1969), 829–30.
[170] *Ibid.* 830–1, which also describes the arrangements introduced in other industries in 1926–8.
[171] See TPG, July 23, 1927.
[172] *TsIK 3/IV* (1928), 167–72.
[173] EZh, February 23, 1927 (report of Vesenkha plenum).

factories, usually controlled by the local soviets.[174] Building labour was still largely seasonal, recruited afresh on the market in every building season. The establishment of the State Institute for Projects of Metal Works (Gipromez) in February 1926 was a significant initial step towards central management of the future shape of industry.[175] But much remained to be done.

(D) FIRST STEPS TO INDUSTRIALISATION, 1924–7

Long before the economy had recovered to its pre-war level, the rapid industrial expansion which began in the autumn of 1924 inspired Vesenkha and Gosplan to turn their attention to the future course of economic development, and their debates took specific form in the spring of 1925 when both organisations undertook to prepare their first drafts of the five-year plan, which were completed in the spring of 1926.[176] In the course of 1925 and 1926, the party in a series of resolutions declared its commitment to the cause of planned industrialisation and sketched out its principal features. In April 1925, the XIV party conference resolved that 'the construction of new metal industry factories must be seen as a priority task'.[177] In his report on the conference in the following month, Stalin made a remarkable declaration of intent:

At present we have about 4 million industrial proletarians. This is of course a small number, but nevertheless it is a start towards building socialism and completing the build-up of the defence of our country to the consternation of the enemies of the proletariat. But we cannot and must not stop at this point. We need 15–20 million industrial proletarians,

[174] 'The building materials industry', Kuibyshev complained, 'is unfortunately not under an All-Union organisation which could freely plan the industry as it plans metal, coal, or oil' (TPG, March 4, 1928, report of Vesenkha plenum).

[175] See Carr and Davies (1969), 357–9; this account exaggerates the extent to which detailed planning of investment was undertaken by the central authorities before 1930.

[176] See Carr and Davies (1969), 844–54; for a first-hand account of the enthusiastic atmosphere in Vesenkha in the spring of 1925, see Valentinov (Stanford, 1971), 157–61.

[177] *KPSS v rez.*, ii (1954), 162.

the electrification of the main regions of our country, cooperative agriculture and a highly developed metal industry. Then we shall not be afraid of any dangers. Then we shall conquer on an international scale.[178]

Stalin's figure of '4 million industrial proletarians' evidently referred to those employed in industry, building and transport, amounting to 3·85 millions in 1924/25; even ten years later in 1935 the number employed in these branches of the economy had reached only 12·5 millions.[179] No specific dates were attached to Stalin's proposal, but the scale of industrialisation which it envisaged was for its time exceptionally ambitious. The XIV party congress, held seven months later in December 1925, resolved in a famous decision to 'carry on economic construction from the point of view that the USSR should turn from a country importing machines and equipment to a country producing means of equipment, so that the USSR in circumstances of capitalist encirclement should in no way turn into an economic adjunct to capitalist world economy'.[180] And in November 1926 the XV party conference called for 'an expansion of fixed capital to bring about the gradual reconstruction of the whole economy on a high technical base' and, reviving a famous phrase of Lenin's, announced that 'it is essential to strive within a relatively minimum historical period to catch up and then to surpass the level of industrial development of the advanced capitalist countries'.[181]

By the autumn of 1926 several major features of Soviet industrialisation policy were firmly in place. First, in spite of the relative backwardness of the Soviet economy and the abundant supply of unskilled labour, industrialisation must be based on advanced technology. This injunction had been a familiar theme of Soviet planning literature ever since 1920,

---

[178] *Soch.*, vii (1947), 132 (first published in P, May 13, 1925).

[179] *Trud* (1936), 10–11.

[180] *KPSS v rez.*, ii (1954), 195. According to Kuz'min (1969), 28–9, citing the archives, the draft resolution prepared by Bukharin merely proposed to 'carry on economic construction from the point of view that the USSR should in no way turn into a simple attachment to the capitalist world economy'; it was amended by other Politburo members, including Stalin.

[181] *KPSS v rez.*, ii (1954), 295; in a report to Comintern at this time, Stalin brusquely rejected Trotsky's perspective of fifty or a hundred years for this process (see Tucker (1973), 398).

when the Goelro plan, supported enthusiastically by Lenin, envisaged in specific terms a new technological revolution based on electrification. Krzhizhanovsky, head of Gosplan throughout most of the 1920s, firmly rejected as early as 1920 the view that Russia could utilise huge untapped reserves of labour without machinery, arguing that modern machines were so productive that even the pre-war machinery stock of the Russian Empire could, if worked in two shifts, undertake the work of 200 million manual labourers.[182] Thus the limitations imposed by the backward agrarian environment and the existing level in industry could be swept aside by the transforming power of modern technology. Krzhizhanovsky later added that with this policy the Soviet Union would be following the example of young capitalist nations in borrowing 'the last word in capitalist practice', without going through preliminary stages of mechanisation.[183] Advocacy of advanced technology was often coupled with the view that it should primarily be embodied in new enterprises built from scratch rather than introduced piecemeal into existing factories. Aleksandrov, the designer of the Dnepr hydro-electric project, argued strongly that such new enterprises would provide a nucleus and a training ground for the advanced economy of the future.[184] The construction of new and up-to-date factories was advocated by Dzerzhinsky and Kuibyshev and, more cautiously, by Stalin.[185]

Another major feature of Soviet industrialisation policy sanctioned by the party in the course of 1925 and 1926 was the affirmation that, in spite of the high costs involved, a wide range of new industries must be established, so that the Soviet economy would become more or less self-sufficient. It was no accident that the XIV party congress, which endorsed 'socialism in one country', also endorsed 'economic self-sufficiency'. If the construction of a socialist society was to be completed in the Soviet Union even without a successful proletarian revolution in a more advanced country, then the country must in the process become independent of the capitalist world. The proposition seemed self-evident to the party leaders, who

[182] Krzhizhanovskii (1957), 72.
[183] PKh, 2, 1926, 15; see also Collette (n.d. [1964]), 130.
[184] TPG, November 18, 1926; this proposition was endorsed by Colonel Hugh Cooper, American adviser to Dneprostroi (*Dneprostroi*, 1, 1927, 84–5).
[185] See Carr and Davies (1969), 433, and Khromov (1977), 220.

brushed aside arguments from Sokol'nikov that it would be cheaper to invest in agriculture and from Bazarov that it would be cheaper to invest in industries where mass production was possible.[186]

These ambitious prescriptions were not intended to be absolute or exclusive. Even the most enthusiastic supporters of new technology acknowledged that the reconstruction of existing factories and even the further development of artisan industries must play a significant part in the industrialisation programme. The goal of self-sufficiency was combined with a recognition that, while the new industries were being established, imports of sophisticated machinery would be increased. The pressure for increased output, and the shortage of capital investment funds, together forced the greater use of existing factories, and drove the protagonists of radical technical change towards cheap and expedient solutions; the tension between long-term technological goals and short-term expediency became a permanent feature of Soviet industrial practice.[187] And throughout 1925 and 1926 the party retained its absolute commitment to the maintenance of equilibrium on the peasant market. This placed a firm upper limit on its support for industry. The XIV party conference in April 1925, while proclaiming the importance of the construction of new factories, also marked the high point of concessions to the peasantry.[188] The XIV party congress in December 1925, which insisted on the development of a self-sufficient engineering industry, was held at a time when the state had cut back credits to industry in order to reduce the inflationary pressures induced by the building boom of the summer of 1925 (see vol. 1, p. 30). In the winter of 1925–6 these cuts caused serious financial difficulties throughout industry, and many recently-recruited workers were dismissed.[189] The XV party conference in October–November 1926, while proclaiming the need to catch up and overtake the industry of capitalist countries, at the same time firmly took its stand against obtaining resources for industrialisation through

---

[186] See Carr and Davies (1969), 402–3.

[187] See Feinstein, ed. (1967), 297–305 (Davies).

[188] See Carr (1958), 240–82.

[189] See *Predpriyatie*, 4, 1926, 85–7 (on Leningrad engineering factories); TPG, May 25 and July 29, 1926 (on the southern iron and steel trust Yugostal' and engineering trust Yuzhmashstroi).

taxation and price policies which would bring a halt to the growth of agriculture.[190]

In spite of these constraints, the economic year 1926/27 saw a major advance in planned industrialisation. The production of census industry increased by over 20 per cent, and exceeded the 1913 level. And net industrial investment was higher in 1926/27 than in 1913, amounting to at least 420 million rubles against about 350 millions in 1913 (both measured in 1913 prices).[191] Investment in Soviet industry, almost entirely based on internal sources of finance, exceeded pre-revolutionary industrial investment by both internal and foreign capital.

This was a first fruit of state planning. It was achieved in spite of the fact that capital investment in the economy as a whole had not yet recovered to the pre-war level (see p. 15 above). In contrast to the increase in industrial investment, net investment in both urban and rural housing had sharply declined,[192] and net investment in transport and communications was probably also lower in 1926/27 than in 1913.[193] Net agricultural investment, however, reached approximately 30 per cent above the 1913 level in 1926/27, primarily owing to the

---

[190] *KPSS v rez.*, ii (1954), 297.
[191] See EHR, 2nd series, xxxix (1986), 269 (Wheatcroft, Davies and Cooper).
[192] See EHR, 2nd series, xxxix (1986), 269, n. 20 (Wheatcroft, Davies and Cooper).
[193] It amounted to 162 million rubles in 1913 (measured in 1913 prices) and 319 millions in 1926/27 (measured in 1926/27 prices), and it is certain that the investment costs index for this sector more than doubled in this period. (For the 1913 figure, see Vainshtein (1960), 417; for the 1926/27 figure see *KTs . . . 1929/30* (1930), 446–65.) The principal inputs into investment in the railways, the predominant sector in 'transport and communications', declined as follows:

	1913	1926/27
Rails (thousand tons)	589[a]	331[a]
Steam locomotives (units)	477[b,d]	364[c]
Goods wagons (units)	9700[b,c]	7950[b]
Passenger wagons (units)	1065[b]	726[b]

[a] SMe, 5–6, 1932, 313.
[b] See Nutter (1962), 430, 432–3.
[c] See Hunter (1957), 377, 411.
[d] According to *Promyshlennost'* (1936), 27, production was 664 in 1913. However, Soviet sources claim that the output of steam locomotives in 'conventional units' amounted to only 265 in 1913, as against 478 in 1928,

increased investment in livestock.[194] The first major successes in industrialisation were thus accompanied by something like an equal priority in investment for the agricultural sector.

Throughout most of the economic year 1926/27 the party leaders, and many of their non-party advisers, believed that the plan would be carried out without serious difficulty. The favourable harvest of 1926 was followed by a period of steady growth of industry and trade. In the winter of 1926–7 goods shortages were conspicuously less acute than in previous years. In April–September 1927, a determined rationalisation drive succeeded in bringing about some reduction in industrial costs. Confident in the success of their policies, the party central committee in February 1927 launched a campaign to reduce retail prices by as much as 10 per cent (see pp. 62–3 below); and in May and June 1927 the State Bank permitted a substantial expansion of credit to industry. When a joint session of Sovnarkom and STO in July 1927 reviewed the fulfilment of the 1926/27 control figures, the written report from Gosplan claimed that 'equilibrium on the market and relatively smooth development of national-economic life have in the main been obtained'. At the session Rykov claimed that the results for the year had been 'more favourable and closer to the control figures and annual plans than in previous years', and drew attention to the 'squeezing out of the goods famine' and the 'improvement of currency circulation'.[195] Even the cautious ex-Menshevik specialist Groman, who objected both to low grain prices and to the inadequate supply of consumer goods to the peasants, with unwonted optimism acknowledged 'a gradual drawing together of the output of consumer goods and the purchasing fund' in the course of 1926/27.[196]

But the favourable developments of 1926/27 proved far more costly and vexatious in their consequences than the party

---

when production in physical terms amounted to 458 (*Promyshlennost'* (1957), 220).

  [c] According to *Promyshlennost'* (1936), 27, the production of goods wagons in two-axle units amounted to 14,832 in 1913 and 10,868 in 1927/28, when the number of wagons produced was 7,780.

[194] See Davies, ed. (1988) (Gatrell and Davies).

[195] *Itogi* (1927), [i,] 19, ii, 17; the session met on July 5 and 12.

[196] *Itogi* (1927), [i,] 6; see also his report to Gosplan of June 29, 1927, in PKh, 7, 1927, 124ff.

leaders anticipated. The fate of NEP hung by a thread. All the prerequisite for a renewed goods famine and for the grain collection crisis of the autumn of 1927 were already established by the summer (see vol. 1, pp. 39–41), while an influential group of party leaders and economic officials, including Kuibyshev and Mikoyan, showed an increasing disposition to support courses of action which disrupted the market relation with the peasants (see vol. 1, pp. 35–8). A crucial factor in these developments was the increased pressure on the party leaders to accelerate the rate of industrialisation. In the course of 1926/27 the industrialisation programme took more concrete form. A committee on engineering chaired by Kuibyshev sought to increase the range and quantity of machinery produced in the Soviet Union, and to persuade industrial customers to agree to purchase the new products.[197] In November 1926, the Politburo authorised the construction of the Dnepr power station and the Turksib railway.[198] In May 1927 it approved the construction of the Rostov agricultural engineering factory, and preparatory work on several new iron and steel works, the heavy engineering works at Sverdlovsk and the Stalingrad tractor factory.[199] In August 1927, a study prepared by Serebrovsky, then a senior Vesenkha official, listed 391 new industrial enterprises which Vesenkha had already been authorised to construct at a total cost of 824 million rubles: a further group of factories about which there were 'disagreements with Gosplan' brought the total of the major enterprises in the major industries alone to at least 1,000 million rubles.[200] In the course of these decisions the central authorities approved a substantial increase in the capital investment plan of Vesenkha for 1926/27, while simultaneously both Vesenkha and Gosplan proposed more ambitious versions of the five-year plan.

While these preparations for more rapid industrialisation were being undertaken, the international situation sharply

---

[197] See Carr and Davies (1969), 409–11.

[198] Carr and Davies (1969), 904–7; *Industrializatsiya, 1926–1928* (1969), 511.

[199] *Industrializatsiya, 1926–1928* (1969), 513.

[200] Serebrovskii (1927), 90–189; these figures do not include power stations (the further cost of the first stage of Dneprostroi alone was estimated at 140 million rubles, excluding the cost of constructing factories which would utilise its electricity).

deteriorated, forcing greater attention to the needs of the defence industries and encouraging the conviction that it was essential to force the pace of industrialisation. Throughout the spring and summer of 1927 Trotsky and the United Opposition insistently argued that the fate of the revolution was imperilled by the slow pace of industrialisation, and the appeasement of kulaks and Nepmen. The continued rise in urban unemployment was a further complicating factor which angered the opposition and alarmed the party leaders.[201] At the session of Sovnarkom discussing the control figures in July 1927 Ordzhonikidze passionately if inconclusively declared:

> How else can the productive forces in our country develop than by the expansion of our industry, by industrialisation? There is no other way out. What will you do with the unemployed who came from the villages, and with the workers' children who have grown up and cannot work? What will you do with them? Our works and factories do not any longer need labour. New factories must be built, but where shall we get the resources to build them?[202]

The issue came to a head during the debate on the control figures for 1927/28 in July and August, when strong voices from within Vesenkha clamoured for an increase in the capital investment plan; Serebrovsky's report on capital projects bluntly declared that 'the amount spent on new construction this year has been insufficient, is inadequate to the needs of the country.'[203] The Politburo gave way, and on August 25, 1927, increased the 1927/28 state budget allocation to industry.[204]

The Vesenkha plan for 1927/28 did not involve an abrupt increase in the pace and scale of industrialisation. The capital investment plan for Vesenkha approved by Sovnarkom in September amounted to 1,176 million rubles as compared with the Narkomfin target of 1,000–1,050 million rubles and the Gosplan figure of 1,086 million rubles. The plan approved by

---

[201] See Lane, ed. (1986), 25–7 (Davies).
[202] *Itogi* (1927), ii, 8.
[203] Serebrovskii (1927), 102; for the debate on the 1927/28 control figures, see Carr and Davies (1969), 296–302.
[204] *Industrializatsiya, 1926–1928* (1969), 514; the allocation was increased from 400 million rubles (*Itogi*, [i,] 15) to '450–500 million rubles'.

Sovnarkom was just over 10 per cent greater than actual investment in 1926/27, and only slightly higher than the figure proposed in the draft Vesenkha five-year plan in the spring of 1927.[205] But the battle over less than 100 million rubles was fought with passion and determination on both sides. Those who resisted the claims of industry correctly believed that further encroachments on the budget would endanger equilibrium. 'They have all come down on us', the deputy head of Vesenkha reported in July, 'arguing that our claim for finance and the amount of capital investment cannot be met in the present situation'.[206] In the same month Groman insisted that budgetary revenue was 'tense to the last drop' owing to the requirements of industry.[207] But the protagonists of industry equally passionately believed that the capitalist countries could not be overtaken if industrial investment did not substantially increase. In its draft five-year plan prepared in the spring of 1927, the most optimistic draft so far, Vesenkha stressed that even at the end of five years of rapid industrial development the Soviet Union would still be only slightly more industrialised than the pre-war Austro-Hungarian empire.[208]

[205] See Carr and Davies (1969), 296n.

[206] Kuibysheva *et al.* (1966); letter of Rukhimovich to Kuibyshev, who was on holiday, about the 'stubborn struggle' in the preliminary discussions of the control figures.

[207] *Itogi* (1927), [i,] 6; M. Bogolepov, head of the financial section of Gosplan, concurred.

[208] *Materialy* (1927), 16–18. The indicator of industrialisation used was the ratio of industrial production to the sum of industrial and agricultural production combined. This was 47·8 per cent in Russia in 1913, 44·8 per cent in the Soviet Union in 1926/27, and was planned at 53·5 per cent in 1931/32; the equivalent figure for both the United States in 1880 and Germany in 1905 was approximately 70 per cent. The revised draft prepared in the autumn of 1927 increased the industrial production plan for 1931/32 from 20,407 to 21,782 million rubles (in 1926/27 prices) (*Kontrol'nye tsifry pyatiletnego plana* (1927), 21); but this only improved the above ratio slightly.

CHAPTER TWO

THE TRIUMPH OF RAPID INDUSTRIALISATION, OCTOBER 1927–SEPTEMBER 1929

(A) THE EXPANSION OF INDUSTRY

In the economic years 1927/28 and 1928/29 capital investment in Vesenkha-planned industry increased by nearly 50 per cent, far exceeding even the most optimistic proposals in the draft five-year plans current in the spring and autumn of 1927. The 1927/28 investment target which had been agreed after such travail (see p. 53 above) was soon superseded. Investment in 1927/28 eventually amounted to 1,325 million rubles, 150 million rubles in excess of the plan. In 1928/29 it rose to 1,629 million rubles. Total investment in industry, including the electric power industry and industry not planned by Vesenkha, increased almost as rapidly. By 1928/29 it amounted to 2,300 million rubles, at least 70 per cent higher than investment in 1913 (see Table 2 below and p. 191 above).

All major industries benefited from this rapid expansion. In iron and steel and building materials, which lagged behind the rest of the producer goods industries in the mid-1920s, investment more than doubled in the course of these two years; and it almost doubled in the chemical industry. Most investment was used to improve and extend existing factories, but the share allocated to the construction of new factories steadily increased, rising from 17·6 per cent of all investment in industry in 1926/27 to 34·7 per cent in 1928/29.[1] About one-third of the workers added to the industrial labour-force between 1926 and 1929 was employed at 'new' and 'newly organised' factories completed during this period. Some of these were quite substantial; major completions included three new paper and

[1] See Barun (1930), 265–7.

cellulose factories, a large oil-cracking plant and an oil pipe-
line.[2] Between 1927 and 1929 the number and staff of capital
projects institutes greatly expanded; and foreign engineers and
designers were employed in increasing numbers.[3] But by the
summer of 1929 little progress had yet been made with the
construction of the very large technologically advanced projects
which had been approved in principle in the course of 1926/27
(see pp. 93–4 below).

The lag in investment in the railways, which had failed to
recover to the 1913 level by the mid-1920s (see p. 50, n. 193
above) was partly overcome in 1927/28 and 1928/29. In these two
years investment in all forms of transport by 58 per cent, while
expenditure on the construction of new railways increased by as
much as 350 per cent.[4] In 1928/29 investment in the railways
was nevertheless probably still no higher than in 1913. The
production of locomotives and goods wagons was slightly higher
than in 1913,[5] but the railways received only 335,000 tons of
rails as compared with 589,000 tons in 1913.[6]

In contrast to the rapid expansion of investment in industry
and transport, investment in agriculture as a whole declined in
absolute as well as relative terms. This decline was a result of
the livestock crisis: the total quantity of machinery and
implements, including tractors, supplied to agriculture increased
by 28 per cent between 1926/27 and 1928/29.[7]

Investment in housing was far below the pre-war level in the
mid-1920s (see p. 50 above), and the share of housing in total
investment was squeezed still further in 1927/28 and 1928/29.
According to Soviet estimates, expenditure on urban construction

[2] For details of factories completed in this period, see *Vypolnenie* (1931), 56–
9, and Minaev, ed. (1930), 94, 96–7, 106, 114.

[3] By the summer of 1929 520 foreign engineers and technicians were employed
in the USSR, and in 1928/29 900 Soviet specialists travelled abroad (see
Kolomenskii (1930), 17, Kas'yanenko (1972), 190); the cost of foreign technical
assistance contracts rose from 1·8 million rubles in 1926/27 to 10 millions in
1928/29 (Kolomenskii (1930), 54).

[4] Investment in new railways increased from 38 million rubles in 1926/27 to
169 million in 1928/29 (*Zheleznodorozhnyi transport* (1970), 62, 74–5).

[5] The production of locomotives increased from 664 in 1913 to 713 in 1928/29:
and the production of goods wagons (in 2-axle units) from 14,832 to 15,940
(*Promyshlennost'* (1936), 27); for alternative figures for 1913, see p. 50, note 193
above.

[6] SMe, 5–6, 1932, 313; Hunter (1957), 411.

[7] *KTs . . . na 1929/30* (1930), 447–9; the 1928/29 figures are preliminary.

and repair increased by 20 per cent, but rural construction and repair declined by 14 per cent. As a result, total investment in housing failed to increase in absolute terms, and declined as a proportion of total investment from 25 to 19 per cent.[8]

Investment in housing contrasted sharply with investment in education, health and municipal services, which was also much lower in 1926/27 than in 1913, but more than doubled in the course of the two years.

These two years saw a marked shift in total investment in favour of the socialist sector of the economy. While investment in the socialist sector increased by over 70 per cent, investment in the private sector declined by 9 per cent. This decline was primarily due to the very substantial decline in investment in livestock (see vol. 1, pp. 44–6). In industry, private investment, which amounted to a mere 4 per cent of all industrial investment in 1926/27, had declined slightly by 1928/29 in absolute terms, amounting to only 2·4 per cent of all industrial investment.[9]

Industrial production, like industrial investment, expanded extremely rapidly in 1927–9. According to the official series in 1926/27 prices, the production of census industry increased by 17 per cent in 1927/28 and 15 per cent in 1928/29, or by 35 per cent over the two years, while the production of small-scale industry increased by 3·5 per cent.[10] The official figures

---

[8] Total investment in socialised and private housing was estimated as follows (million rubles at current prices):

	1926/27[a]	1927/28[a]	1928/29
Urban: socialised	420	446	491[b]
: private	191	238	243[b]
Rural	1015	989	877[c]
Total	1626	(1673)	(1611)

[a] See Table 3; for 1927/28, above table shows revised data from note a to Table 3.
[b] *Materials* (1985), 276.
[c] Derived from data in *Materials* (1985), 416, taking 25 per cent of 1928 and 75 per cent of 1929.

Private housing consisted virtually entirely of individual dwellings constructed for personal use.

[9] *KTs . . . na 1929/30* (1930), 454; the figure for 1928/29 is preliminary.

[10] PI, 11–12, 1930, Appendix table; figures for calendar years published later show a higher rate of growth (see Table 7(a)).

exaggerate the real increase: they do not allow for the further decline in quality in census industry, or for the extent to which the increase in the production of small-scale industry was due to the exceptional thoroughness of the 1929 census. But even allowing for these factors the increase was substantial. In contrast, agricultural production, with the exception of industrial crops, stagnated or declined (see vol. 1, Tables 1 and 2).

Production increased in all major branches of census industry. 1928/29 was the first year in which production of rolled steel was greater than in 1913. Steel was increasingly directed towards the engineering and other metal industries in these years, while the amount allocated to individual consumption and to the municipal economy and non-industrial construction declined in absolute as well as relative terms.[11] The shift in distribution enabled engineering production to expand by 74 per cent in the course of two years (see Table 7(a)).

The production of consumer goods by census industry increased almost as rapidly as the production of capital goods. Two principal factors were at work. First, the supply of agricultural raw materials increased. In both 1927 and 1928 the harvest was good for almost all industrial crops, including textile raw materials, sugar beet, oil seeds and tobacco, and the proportion sold to state agencies increased owing to the high state collection prices. At the same time, imports of agricultural raw materials were reduced only slightly in 1927/28 and 1928/29 as compared with 1926/27.[12] In consequence, output increased substantially in the case of cotton and woollen yarn, and cotton, woollen and silk fabrics. That section of the food, drink and tobacco industries which was dependent on sugar, tobacco and oil seeds also expanded rapidly. The second factor leading to the high rate of increase in consumer goods production in census industry was the increase in factory production of goods previously produced domestically or by artisans. This continued the switch to factory production which was already a marked feature of the first world war and the first years of NEP (see p. 22 above). The production of sewn goods, knitwear and leather footwear, measured in 1926/27 prices, which had

---

[11] *Metall*, 7, 1929, 57–74 (Borisov and Feigel'son).
[12] See the figures for imports of cotton, wool and leather in *Vneshnyaya torgovlya* (1960).

increased from 96 to 383 million rubles between 1913 and 1926/27, reached over 1,200 million rubles in 1928/29, and amounted in that year to over 11 per cent of all consumer goods production. The same tendency also occurred to a small extent in part of the food industry: the factory production of confectionery, for example, increased from 94 million rubles in 1926/27 to 235 millions in 1928/29, as compared with 158 million rubles in 1913.[13]

The production of vodka, which grew more rapidly than the rest of the food and drink industry in the mid-1920s, continued to increase in 1927/28. But the vigorous campaign against alcohol pursued by some party members on moral–political grounds was reinforced by the more pragmatic motive that drunkenness was one of the factors undermining industrial labour discipline. In 1928/29 this led to a temporary reduction in state vodka production. In that year 53 million decalitres of vodka were produced by the state as compared with 40 millions in 1926/27 and the huge figure of 119 millions in 1913.[14]

Small-scale industry in 1927–9 was subject to conflicting influences. The rapid rise of factory production, coupled with the shortage of raw materials controlled by state industry, tended to squeeze out the artisan. Some small-scale state and cooperative enterprises expanded in size and were reclassified as part of census industry. The effort to curb and then eliminate private capitalism reduced private supplies to the artisans and frequently deprived them of the private intermediaries who had previously sold their products. All these factors tended to reduce small-scale industrial production. On the other hand, state policy throughout this period attempted to encourage the individual artisan, and strongly supported the artisan cooperatives;[15] even in 1928/29 state supplies of many kinds of raw

[13] For these data see (for 1913) *Promyshlennost'* (1936), 4–22; (for 1926/27 *Fabrichno-zavodskaya promyshlennost'* . . . *za 1924/25, 1925/26 i 1926/27* (1929), 4–7; (for 1928/29) Kaufman (Washington, D.C., 1962), 75–81, based on SO, 12, 1929, 88–93. The data for 1928/29 are in current prices, which were slightly lower than 1926/27 prices.

[14] See Nutter (1962), 454; the output in 1927/28 was 56 million decalitres. For drunkenness see Carr and Davies (1969), 761; for increased revenue from vodka see p. 71 below. Evidence about the amount of home-distilled vodka produced is confused and contradictory.

[15] See Carr and Davies (1969), 394–400.

materials to the artisans substantially increased.[16] At the same
time the shortage of all kinds of consumer goods meant that
there was a ready market for artisan products. The resulting
pattern of decline and expansion was extremely complicated.
Between the two censuses of 1926/27 and 1928/29, small-scale
production of leather goods, especially footwear, of pottery and
utensils for domestic use, and of furniture and other carpentry
products declined substantially. On the other hand, production
of toys and similar craft products increased. In the food
industry, bread-baking declined but the production of butter
and cheese increased; in the textile industry, in face of the
increase in factory production, the production of sewn goods by
artisans declined, but the production of knitwear continued to
increase.[17] For small-scale industry as a whole, some Soviet
estimates show an increase in production between 1926/27 and
1928/29; others show a slight decline.[18] But whichever estimate is
more accurate, the outstanding feature of the artisan industries
in this period was their resilience in face of the strong
competition of powerful state industries.

(B) THE BREAKDOWN OF THE NEW ECONOMIC POLICY

The grain crisis in the winter of 1927–8 persuaded a large
segment of official opinion that the pace of industrialisation

[16] See data in *Vypolnenie* (1931), 204; according to this source, only the supplies
of tobacco and *makhorka* declined substantially.
[17] See data for gross turnover in current prices in *Nar. kh.* (1932), 88–91;
prices increased in this period, so the figures for 1928/29 are exaggerated in
comparison with those for 1926/27.
[18] The following are some of the alternative estimates (million rubles); all
series apparently include flour-milling, but, unlike the data in Kaufman
(Washington, D.C., 1982), exclude logging and fisheries:

	1926/27	1927/28	1928	1929	
(1)[a]	2040	1940	–	–	(1913 prices)
(2)[b]	4603	4962	–	–	(1926/27 prices)
(3)[c]	–	–	1812	1662	(1928 prices)
(4)[d]	4500 (1927)		4600	4700	(1926/27 prices)

[a] EO, 9, 1929, 114 (Gukhman); gross production.
[b] *KTs . . . na 1929/30* (1930), 429, 423; gross production.
[c] See Table 1; net production.
[d] Buzlaeva (1969), 111, citing 1938 industrial census; gross production.

adopted in the summer of 1927 must be reduced, or at the very least must not be further accelerated. Non-party economists in Narkomzem and Narkomfin called for an immediate restoration of market equilibrium. Within the party itself, first Rykov and then Bukharin early in 1928 sought to relegate the compulsory measures of the grain collection campaign to the category of a temporary emergency departure from established principles. When the industrialisation drive was intensified in the course of 1928/29 the Right opposition, headed by Bukharin, Rykov and Tomsky, continued to seek a return to the more cautious pace of 1927 or even 1926. At the end of 1928 former advocates of rapid industrialisation such as Krzhizhanovsky and Strumilin in Gosplan, together with the non-party specialists in Vesenkha, also resisted the more ambitious industrial programme.

The opponents of the new policies were a formidable social force. Rykov was head of the Soviet government and Tomsky of the trade unions, and Bukharin was by far the most prominent of the party intellectuals. Most of the non-party advisers who had served the Soviet government throughout the 1920s shared their approach. Their criticism was passionate, persistent and authoritative. But, in an atmosphere of increasing repression and mounting enthusiasm, it was also muted and divided. The arrest in March 1928 of the prominent engineers working in the Shakhty coal mines launched a campaign to discredit and silence all 'bourgeois specialists' who failed to support the new policies.[19] Uglanov was dismissed from the secretaryship of the Moscow party in October 1928, and this was followed by the enforced resignation of Tomsky from the presidency of the trade unions in December, accompanied by a vigorous press campaign against the Right wing in the party. Though Bukharin, Rykov and Tomsky were not yet mentioned by name, the campaign was clearly directed against them. In April 1929 the XVI party conference, in an unpublished resolution, condemned 'the departure of the Bukharin group from the general line of the party in the direction of a Right deviation', while in its published resolutions it announced that the first 'general purge' of the party since 1921 would be carried out in 1929–30 by the central and local party control commissions, and also authorised Rabkrin to 'organise *a purge of the Soviet*

---

[19] See Carr and Davies (1969), 584–98.

apparatus'. The purge of the *apparat* would free the governmental machine from 'degenerate elements who distort Soviet laws, fuse with the kulak and the Nepman and prevent the struggle with bureaucracy'.[20] These resolutions marked an important shift in the relation of forces in Soviet administration. They consolidated the advance of the 'CCC/Rabkrin' (the party central control commission and the People's Commissariat for Workers' and Peasants' Inspection), the only joint party and governmental organisation, to the centre of the political stage. With the appointment a few months later of Peters as the head of the Rabkrin central purge commission, the position of the OGPU was also strengthened: Peters had long been prominent as a member of both Rabkrin and the OGPU.[21] The triumph of rapid industrialisation, the outcome of a bitter political struggle, was associated with the development of an increasingly repressive political structure.

By the autumn of 1927 Stalin and the party leaders associated with him were firmly convinced that it was essential to accelerate the pace of industrialisation; and they did not retreat from this policy when they were confronted by the grain crisis at the end of 1927. They did not at first envisage that the course on which they had embarked would lead to the complete abandonment of NEP; greater emphasis on industrialisation was accompanied by strenuous attempts – sometimes initiated by the party leaders around Stalin, sometimes merely endorsed by them – to devise measures which would reconcile the interests of industrialisation with the interests of the peasantry. But the successive measures adopted between 1927 and 1929 proved entirely inadequate in face of increasingly intractable economic difficulties, and gave way to harsh compulsion.

The wishful thinking in these endeavours and expedients is strikingly illustrated by the campaign launched in February

---

[20] *KPSS v rez.*, ii (1954), 605–14, 594–7.

[21] For Peters' appointment, see Rees (1987), 172, 278 n. 16. Peters (1886–1938), a farm labourer's son, was a Latvian who after 1905 was imprisoned and tortured; he fled to London in 1909, where he worked as a tailor's presser and was arrested in 1910 on a charge of organising the 'Houndsditch murders' (his cousin, who was his double, was killed in the siege of Sidney Street in 1911); he was acquitted, and returned to Russia in 1917, where he was a prominent member of the Cheka–OGPU from its foundation (see Leggett (1981), 266–8).

1927 to reduce the prices of industrial consumer goods. One of its main objectives was to compensate the peasants for the reduced grain prices introduced at the time of the 1926 harvest.[22] It was undertaken at a propitious time, when industrial consumer goods were in relatively abundant supply. But in 1927 the rise in the purchasing power of the population resulting from the increase in capital investment and other state expenditure far exceeded the supply of consumer goods in real terms. In consequence, the price reductions exacerbated the goods shortages.[23]

Another policy designed to assist relations with the peasantry was the higher priority afforded by Vesenkha to the production of consumer goods in 1928, and the decision to switch consumer goods to the countryside. This achieved some positive results.[24] But the rate of growth of consumer demand was so considerable by this time that the impact of the increased supply of consumer goods on the goods shortages in the countryside was slight.

A policy of stabilising the currency by restricting and reducing the amount in circulation was also pursued with some vigour in the first few months of 1928. But with the start of the new building season it gave way to renewed currency expansion.[25]

Another expedient, designed to resolve the crisis by providing a major new source of urban food supply, was the decision in July 1928 to establish giant grain sovkhozy. But the difficulties of establishing agricultural enterprises on industrial lines were greatly underestimated; and in any case the new sovkhozy were not established soon enough to have any effect on the supply of grain in 1928 and 1929.[26]

Yet another expedient – the renewed offer in September 1928 of industrial concessions to foreign capitalists – was quite unable, in prevailing internal and international conditions, to

---

[22] See the explicit Politburo decision on this point, dated September 16, 1926, reported in *Industrializatsiya, 1926–1928* (1969), 510; this was followed by a further Politburo decision of December 23, 1926, which assessed the reductions which had been achieved as insufficient (*ibid.* 511), and provided the immediate background to the decisions of February 1927 (see Carr and Davies (1969), 684–6).

[23] See Carr and Davies (1969), 683–91.

[24] *Ibid.* 307–11, 635, 647.

[25] *Ibid.* 776.

[26] *Ibid.* 184–91.

provide a substantial supplement to internal sources of investment.[27]

Of all the campaigns to resolve the crisis which were pursued with such ineffective vigour in 1927 and 1928 the most successful sought to save resources by increasing productivity and reducing costs in the state sector, and particularly in industry. This was not so much a new campaign as the successful outcome of an old one. The campaign for a 'regime of economy' in the spring and summer of 1926 had failed to reduce industrial costs. But the 'rationalisation' campaign, launched in March 1927, was followed in the autumn of that year by a drive to increase the rate of growth of labour productivity above the rate of growth of wages, enforced by widespread increases in output norms.[28] The campaign was successful. Productivity, measured in terms of output per work-day, increased by 13·5 per cent in 1927/28 and 16·2 per cent in 1928/29.[29] In both years over 60 per cent of the total increase in industrial production was due to the increase in productivity; this was predominantly 'intensive growth' dependent on productivity rather than 'extensive growth' dependent on the increased recruitment of industrial labour. And in both 1927/28 and 1928/29 productivity increased more than wages; together with other economies, this enabled the costs of comparable industrial production to be reduced by 6 per cent in 1927/28 and 4–4·5 per cent in 1928/29 as compared with a mere 1·8 per cent in 1926/27.[30] These savings enabled industry to make a substantial contribution to the costs of

[27] *Ibid.* 718. According to a German translation (found in the German Foreign Ministry archive) of alleged Politburo papers, Stalin called for a modification of the foreign trade monopoly in December 1926, and this proposal was revived by Chicherin with the support of Stalin a year later, and by Kuibyshev at a Politburo meeting in the following month; a document allegedly written by Stalin claimed that 'no reasonable party member any longer doubts that the heritage of the late Ilyich [Lenin], the socialist construction of our state, would not be practicable without the help of foreign capital' (see Reiman (Bloomington, Indiana, 1987), 128–33, 135–8). Published statements between December 1926 and the summer of 1928 give no indication that such proposals were being floated, and in any case they were without practical outcome.

[28] See Carr and Davies (1969), 333–50, 504–19.

[29] EO, 12, 1929, 16–17; this ignores the decline in quality.

[30] *Ibid.* 954; the whole of the reduction in costs in 1926/27 took place in the second half of the year.

capital investment.[31] The principle that the growth of nominal wages should be lower than the growth in productivity has been applied with varying success in the Soviet Union ever since.

The drive to improve labour productivity and reduce costs carried with it two major consequences. First, it involved the imposition of greater labour discipline. Periodic increases in work norms, always unpopular with the workers, were from 1928 onwards one of the major instruments which brought about first a levelling and then a decline in real wages; this reversed the substantial improvement in urban living standards which had accompanied economic recovery. The five-year plan approved in the spring of 1929 frankly admitted that the proposed increase in the pace of development required 'a complete overhaul (ozdorovlenie) of the production atmosphere – i.e. the creation of real proletarian discipline'.[32] The need to enlist the trade unions as an obedient agent of this policy lay behind the struggle with Tomsky and his supporters. The subordinate and instrumental role of the Soviet trade unions continued throughout Stalin's lifetime and the decades beyond.

The second major consequence of the productivity and economy drive was a further increase in unemployment. The net increase in non-agricultural employment declined from 1,430,000 in 1925/26, when the economy was still rapidly recovering to the pre-war level, to 701,000 in 1926/27, 515,000 in 1927/28 and 628,000 in 1928/29. This reflected the productivity increases in industry and the effects of the economy drive in state administration.[33] The retardation in the growth of the non-agricultural labour force did not stem the relentless migration into the towns from the countryside; the number of permanent annual migrants increased from 895,000 in 1926 to 1,329,000 in

[31] The savings from costs reductions in 1928/29 alone were estimated at 550 million rubles (*Vypolnenie* (1931), 140); as compared with 1926/27, savings may have amounted to over 1,000 million rubles.

[32] *Pyatiletnii plan* (1930), ii, i, 73; on February 21, 1929, an unpublished Politburo letter to all party organisations called in strong terms for improved labour discipline (*KPSS v rez.*, iv (1970), 169–75).

[33] These figures are for 'hired labour', excluding agriculture, forestry and fisheries, and are derived from *Trud* (1936), 10–11, and *Trud* (1930), 3; see also Table 14(a) below.

1929.[34] Simultaneously the natural increase in the adult population of the towns was substantial. In consequence, the number of unemployed grew both in 1927/28 and in the first few months of 1928/29.[35] The economy drive in state administration in 1927/28 resulted in a substantial increase in clerical unemployment;[36] in 1928/29 the dismissal of 'surplus workers' on economy grounds also resulted in a large increase in the number of unemployed textile workers.[37] From the spring of 1929 onwards, with the more rapid expansion in employment, the growth of unemployment at last began to slow down.[38] In the summer of 1929 several categories of skilled workers and specialists were already in short supply. But the total number of skilled and semi-skilled industrial workers registered as unemployed continued to increase until the end of the economic year. Even in the spring of 1929 it was almost universally believed that unemployment would continue for many years; the rate of industrialisation required for its elimination seemed entirely out of reach. In the meantime the problem of rural underemployment in the Central Black-Earth and other over-populated regions was also growing more acute: in spite of the migration to the towns, the net increase in the rural population was still substantial.[39]

The improvement achieved in industrial efficiency in the course of 1927/28 and 1928/29 was undoubtedly impressive. Coupled with higher prices for industrial consumer goods and more rational prices for state purchases from the agricultural

[34] *KTs . . . na 1927/28* (1928), 214–15; *Trud* (1936), 7; the 1926 figure refers to the Russian, Ukrainian and Belorussian republics, but migration into the towns in the other republics was small.

[35] See Lane, ed. (1986), 27 (Davies); the upward trend cannot be measured accurately, owing to changes in methods of registration, but it certainly occurred.

[36] SO, 6, 1929, 53 (Pollyak).

[37] *Vypolnenie* (1930), 24; SO, 12, 1929, 25 (Kalistratov).

[38] According to one account, the improvement in peasant non-agricultural earnings, together with the poor food situation in the towns, 'reduced the pressure of the countryside on the urban labour market' in 1928/29 (SO, 12, 1929, 14 – Kalistratov); but this was not confirmed by the migration statistics. The same source claimed that the rate of growth in the adult population declined both in the towns and the countryside between April 1927–March 1928 and April 1928–March 1929 (*ibid.* 14).

[39] It was estimated at two million a year in *KTs . . . na 1927/28* (1928), 214, but this estimate assumes an exaggerated growth in total population.

producer, it might have maintained market equilibrium with a level of investment somewhat higher than that actually achieved in the building season of 1927. But investment continued to increase extremely rapidly between 1927 and 1929 (see pp. 55–7 above). The average number of construction workers employed in the economy as a whole exceeded the 1927 level by 13 per cent in the summer of 1928 and by as much as 39 per cent in the summer of 1929.[40] The repercussions of this expansion reverberated throughout the economy. Meanwhile, increasingly ambitious industrialisation plans were approved by the authorities. The struggle for increased resources was fierce and continuous. In the debate about the annual investment plan in the autumn of 1928 the leading officials in Vesenkha insisted so determinedly on higher investment allocations that Krzhizhanovsky, who had hitherto always defended the interests of industry, commented that they had 'lost their feeling for reality'.[41] The longer-term investment targets in the successive draft five-year plans, and the specific projects associated with them, were even more ambitious. In the optimum variant of the five-year plan approved in the spring of 1929 capital investment in industry was planned at 3,465 million rubles for the last year of the plan, 1932/33; this was over double the investment proposed for 1932/33 in the draft prepared by Vesenkha eighteen months previously in the autumn of 1927.[42]

The successive revisions of the five-year plan brought the task of overtaking the advanced capitalist countries within measurable distance for the first time. The five volumes of the five-year plan painted an impressive picture of the fundamental changes in the physiognomy of industry which would be brought about within five years. Technologically, the present 'backward universal enterprises with their weak technology' would be replaced by 'giant enterprises with advanced technology, constructed on the rational foundations of specialist mass production'. New developments such as precision engineering,

[40] Average of monthly figures for June 1–October 1 in each year (see *Trud* (1930), 21); these figures, unlike those for 1928–30 in Table 17 below, do not include white-collar employees.

[41] See Carr and Davies (1969), 322.

[42] See Carr and Davies (1969), 982; these figures are in current prices; the proposed fall in investment costs would increase investment in real terms to an even greater extent.

radio and the introduction of higher grades of oil would transform the internal structure of every industry, while in industry as a whole capital and energy available per worker would increase substantially. Organisationally, giant combines would 'unify the production of a number of industries' while territorially whole 'districts and regions, like the Urals, Dneprostroi, Donbass and Leningrad, will be transformed into colossal industrial combines'. Large-scale socialist economy would begin to drive out small-scale private economy.[43] Extrapolating from the optimum variant of the five-year plan, Sabsovich, at this time a leading planner in Vesenkha, estimated in the spring of 1929 that American industrial production, 20–25 times Soviet production in 1927/28, would amount to only twice Soviet production ten years later in 1937/38, and would be substantially less than Soviet production by the end of the third five-year plan in 1942/43.[44] This amalgam of fantasy and reality, in which fantasy predominated, drew attention from the vexing troubles of peasant Russia towards the glorious socialist future. It infuriated sceptical bourgeois specialists, but seized the imagination of many party members, including Stalin himself, and no party member entirely escaped from its lure.

In all these programmes the increased targets were presented as fully compatible with financial equilibrium; they would be achieved, it was claimed, primarily by increased efficiency in the use of the resources of industry itself. The optimum variant of the five-year plan proposed that labour productivity in industry should rise by as much as 110 per cent within five years, so that in spite of an increase in nominal wages of 47 per cent, the costs of industrial production would decline by 35 per cent; this would enable industry not only to provide finance for investment but also to reduce prices by 23 per cent.[45] Such schemes acquired verisimilitude on the basis of two assumptions which were apparently plausible but in practice proved quite unfeasible. First, the cost and productivity achievements of 1927/28 and 1928/29 could be improved upon and continued indefinitely into the future. Secondly, new factories built to the best German and American standards would be able to achieve and improve upon the performance achieved in those countries,

[43] *Pyatiletnii plan* (1930), ii, i, 90–1.
[44] B, 13–14, July 31, 1929, 119–22.
[45] See Carr and Davies (1969), 983.

in spite of the inexperience of Soviet engineers and the lack of Soviet skilled workers.

Vesenkha, which at first itself managed the drive for improved industrial efficiency, came under increasing pressure from Rabkrin to adopt more ambitious plans. From October 1928 onwards Rabkrin scrutinised industrial programmes in detail and insistently demanded their improvement.[46] Sometimes Rabkrin proposals succeeded in revealing latent possibilities. Thus the 1928/29 tractor plan for the Putilov works, insisted upon by Rabkrin in face of managerial resistance, was overfulfilled.[47] But this was exceptional. The most protracted and intense controversy concerned the reconstruction programme of the vast Ukrainian iron and steel trust Yugostal'. Vesenkha insisted that substantial new investment was required, with the scrapping of much of the existing plant, while Rabkrin claimed that much of this investment was not necessary, as the productivity of the existing Ukrainian plant could be further improved by as much as 35 per cent. The issue was debated inconclusively at the XVI party conference in April 1929. The manager of Yugostal', the former Hungarian revolutionary Birman, bitterly criticised Rabkrin and defended Svitsyn, the 'bourgeois specialist' who prepared the Vesenkha project, and had been arrested in the previous year.[48] This debate was the prototype of the future discussions between Rabkrin and the economic commissariats. Rabkrin, though a keen advocate of the construction of large plants employing the latest technology, also strongly argued that investment costs could be substantially reduced by the even fuller employment of all existing capacity. In an economy with abundant supplies of labour, this was a sensible policy; but Rabkrin, by manipulations of already unrealistic coefficients, consistently underestimated the costs and difficulties involved, and overestimated the possibilities.

By this time all possibility of reconciling the investment programme with market equilibrium had long since been overtaken by events. In the two years 1927/28 and 1928/29 state budgetary expenditure increased by as much as 60 per cent, far

---

[46] See Rees (1987), 155–6.
[47] See Kuromiya (forthcoming), ch. 7, and Gan (1931), 58; output was 3,050 tractors against the plan of 2,500.
[48] For the debate on Yugostal' see Rees (1987), 174–8, SS, xxxvii (1985), 158–60 (Fitzpatrick), and pp. 189–90 below.

outpacing the increase in the national income. Over 50 per cent of the increase was allocated to the national economy, primarily to industry and to the socialist sector of agriculture.[49] The railways were the only major sector of the economy which found the resources to cover their own expansion. Rail charges were increased in 1926 and 1927, while the cost per ton-kilometre of freight declined owing to the rapid expansion of traffic. The net allocation of the budget to transport and posts was reduced from 177 million rubles in 1926/27 to 86 millions in 1928/29, even though investment increased from 729 to 1,156 million rubles (see Tables 2 and 22(b)). The reduction in costs of production enabled industry to pay higher contributions to the budget and at the same time to increase the amount of its own resources directly allocated to investment. But the total increase in industrial investment in 1927–9 was so great that the budget contribution to investment also increased,[50] as did its net total contribution to state industry.[51]

[49] See Table 22(b). The increase in expenditure by 2,020 million rubles included 1,029 million rubles on the national economy, 625 million rubles of which were devoted to industry (including electric power) and 293 to agriculture. In addition, expenditure on defence increased by 278 million rubles and expenditure on social and cultural services by 165 million rubles.

[50] According to a Soviet estimate, the annual net increase in fixed capital in industry was financed as follows (million rubles):

	October 1, 1926–October 1, 1927	October 1, 1927–October 1, 1928	October 1, 1928–October 1, 1929
Internal resources	37[a]	156[a]	280
State and local budget	279	397	550
Long-term banks	123	429	391
Short-term credit	47	− 22	− 25
Foreign credit	n.a.	n.a.	− 31
Total	486	960	1165

[a] Includes foreign credit, which increased by 86 million rubles between October 1, 1925 and October 1, 1928.

Estimated from Barun (1930), 298; for an alternative table showing gross investment in fixed and working capital, see Carr and Davies (1969), 744. The long-term banks were primarily provided with finance by allocations from the state budget, but they also received some resources from the profits of Group B industries (see Barun (1930), 310–12); on October 1, 1928, the net contribution of Group B industries to the industrial bank amounted to 138 million rubles, the net borrowings of Group A industries to 119 million rubles (*ibid*. 314).

[51] According to one source, it increased from 39 million rubles in 1926/27 to

Increased budgetary expenditure was covered by taxation. The rates of tax on private industry and trade, and on the personal incomes of Nepmen, were increased, and the taxes were imposed more ruthlessly, but the yield was small owing to the small absolute size of the private sector outside agriculture.[52] Excises remained the main source of revenue, and in the course of 1927–9 the duties charged on vodka and other alcoholic drinks, the principal source of excise revenue, were substantially increased.[53]

The authorities continued to be committed to their increasingly implausible attempt to maintain the stability of the ruble. They resisted all attempts to increase industrial prices, and repudiated proposals to impose additional increases in excise duties and railway charges in 1928/29,[54] on the grounds that rises in retail prices would lead to further wage increases and an inflationary spiral. But the failure to increase official prices did not prevent inflation. While the state budget remained formally in surplus in 1927/28 and 1928/29, bank credits issued outside the budget resulted in a rapid rise in currency issues. Contrary to all plans, total currency in circulation increased by 21 per cent in 1927/28 and as much as 34 per cent in 1928/29 (see Table 23). As the retail prices of industrial goods in socialised trade increased by only 2 per cent between October 1, 1927, and October 1, 1929, while the purchasing power of the population increased rapidly, the shortage of goods grew far more severe. The annual report of Vesenkha for 1927/28 explained that after a 'relative weakening of tension in demand' in the first few months of 1928, from the second half of June 'the market again began to experience tension, continuously increasing'.[55] Shortages grew more severe

---

340 million rubles in 1928/29 (preliminary figure), excluding the armaments inudstries (*Vypolnenie* (1931), 146–7); for a much higher figure for 1926/27, see Table 22(b); see also PKh, 3, 1932, 150. The variations in the estimates were due partly to the difficulty of deciding which taxes were 'paid by' industry, and partly to the difficulty of measuring the amount of investment actually disbursed in a particular year.

[52] See Carr and Davies (1969), 748–52, especially p. 752, n.3.

[53] *Ibid.* 760–3.

[54] *Ibid.* 759–60.

[55] *Promyshlennost'* ... *1927/28*, [i] (1930), 156–7; the pressure of demand resulted in a substantial decline in stocks as a proportion of turnover both in 1927/28 and in 1928/29 (*ibid.*, [i] (1930), 157; *Vypolnenie* (1931), 47).

throughout 1928/29. In consequence prices of industrial goods on the private market increased: according to the official index, the increase between October 1, 1927, and October 1, 1929 amounted to 28 per cent, and this increase does not adequately reflect illegal transactions at even higher prices.

While controls over industrial prices were partially effective, the retail prices of agricultural products rose steeply, contrary to all the plans of the authorities. In socialised trade, the increase between October 1, 1927, and October 1, 1929 amounted to 16·2 per cent, reflecting the increase in official prices paid to the peasants for grain and other products.[56] But the acute scarcity of food in the state and cooperative shops led to the introduction of bread rationing in Leningrad and Moscow in the winter of 1928/29. Rationing was extended to other towns and other foods in the spring and summer of 1929.[57] On the private market (including the peasant 'bazaars') prices increased by 33 per cent in the course of 1927/28 and a further 64 per cent in 1928/29, 117 per cent altogether. On October 1, 1929, the average price of an agricultural product on the private market reached 232 per cent of the retail price in socialised trade.[58]

The food shortages and the consequent price rises resulted in a considerable improvement in the terms of trade for agricultural goods. The blades of the scissors between industrial and agricultural prices, open to the disadvantage of agriculture ever since 1922, closed rapidly. The ratio of the retail prices of industrial products to the planned collection prices of agricultural products declined from 1·39 in September 1927 to 1·26 in September 1929.[59] If prices on the private market are taken into account, the shift in favour of agriculture was much more dramatic. In these terms the blades of the scissors closed in the spring of 1928, and then opened in the opposite direction.[60]

As a result of this marked shift in the terms of the trade in

[56] Mendel'son, ed. (1930), 98–106, 156–7.

[57] See Carr and Davies (1969), 700–4.

[58] For retail prices on October 1, 1927, and October 1, 1929, see Mendel'son, ed. (1930), 98–106, 156–7.

[59] Mendel'son, ed. (1930), 111 (1913 ratio = 100); for an alternative estimate, which shows a slightly greater decline, see *Vypolnenie* (1931), 82–3.

[60] The ratio of the average retail prices of industrial goods in all trade to the average retail prices of agricultural products in all trade changed as follows (ratio in 1913 = 100):

favour of agriculture, coupled with the increased earnings of the agricultural population from non-agricultural activities, peasant incomes increased much more rapidly than urban incomes in 1927/28 and 1928/29, in spite of the increase in urban employment (see vol. 1, p. 48). Retail trade in the countryside increased by 26 per cent in 1927/28 and 1928/29, in the towns by only 19 per cent. This continued the trend prevalent ever since the scissors crisis of 1923: rural retail trade amounted to only 18·3 per cent of all retail trade in 1923/24, and increased to 31·0 per cent in 1928/29.[61] This estimate does not include peasant purchases in the towns, or omit purchases in the countryside by teachers, officials and others who were not peasants; but this correction would hardly modify this steady increase in the proportion of retail sales commanded by the peasants. According to a Soviet calculation, in 1928/29 'in real terms the growth in the purchase of industrial goods by the non-agricultural population amounted to 3·5 per cent and of agricultural products to about 1 per cent, or 2·2 per cent in all, while the size of the non-agricultural population increased by more than 2 per cent; the growth in the acquisition of industrial goods by the agricultural population in real terms amounted to approximately 12·4 per cent'.[62] Although the state succeeded in imposing a higher rate of industrialisation on a reluctant peasantry, the peasants, simply

---

October 1, 1926	1·18
April 1, 1927	1·12
October 1, 1927	1·07
April 1, 1928	1·04
July 1, 1928	0·97
July 1, 1929	0·85
October 1, 1929	0·88

(estimated from Mendel'son, ed. (1930), 98–106, 156–7).

According to Vainshtein (1972), 93–4, 'the blades of the "scissors" closed in 1927/28 . . . the turning point in the price equilibrium was May 1, 1928'. In the urban cost of living index, in spite of rationing, the relative prices of agricultural goods also increased sharply (SO, 12, 1929, 21).

[61] *Tovarooborot* (1932), 18; these figures, measured in current prices, exclude bazaar trade but include all 'stationary private trade by intermediaries'; the figure for rural trade in 1928/29 in the source cited should read 5,151·2 million rubles.

[62] *Vypolnenie* (1930), 50; the figures for industrial goods evidently refer to large-scale industry.

by the increase in the prices the free market would bear, imposed improved terms of trade on a resentful state.

If the rise in agricultural prices was the main symptom of disequilibrium on the internal market in 1927–9, in foreign trade the lack of agricultural products for export remained the crucial source of difficulty. Agricultural exports, already far lower than before the revolution, declined by as much as 21·2 per cent between 1926/27 and 1928/29, owing to the drastic decline in grain exports.[63] This reduction was outweighed by an even more substantial increase in industrial exports, including timber, oil and cotton textiles: the total volume of Soviet exports increased by 12·7 per cent. But imports increased even more rapidly. In 1927/28 the German loan (see pp. 34–5 above) financed a substantial increase in the import of industrial equipment. The policies of support for the consumer adopted after the grain crisis of the winter of 1927–8, although half-hearted, also resulted in a sharp increase in the import of food, including grain. As a result, 1927/28 ended with a substantial deficit in the balance of trade, which necessitated a major depletion of the gold reserves.[64] In 1928/29, gold exports were drastically reduced, and no substantial further foreign loans were forthcoming. In consequence, in spite of an increase in exports, the authorities were compelled to reduce imports in 1928/29 by 11·6 per cent in order to obtain a positive balance of foreign trade. Food imports were curtailed; the Politburo, in spite of the bread shortage, rejected proposals by Rykov and others to import grain (see vol. 1, p. 57). But industry also suffered directly. Imports of industrial raw materials and even of capital equipment were reduced. A foreign trade survey referring to the first nine months of 1928/29 comfortingly explained that 'in spite of the reduction in the import of equipment for the needs of industry and transport by 17·2 per cent, the production needs of industry . . . were adequately satisfied, because equipment to the value of 250 million rubles was imported during 1927/28, and a considerable part of this equipment was not installed in 1927/28,

---

[63] For foreign trade in 1926/27–1928/29, see Davies, ed. (1984), 127 (Dohan) and BP (Prague), lxxiv (December 1929), 8–18.
[64] According to Dohan in Davies, ed. (1984), 127, the gold reserves declined from 347 to 187 million rubles between December 31, 1927, and December 31, 1928.

and was not yet in use when it was transferred to 1928/29'.[65] But this was a purely temporary solution: the investment programme assumed that equipment imports would greatly increase in the next few years.

The desperate efforts of the authorities to solve the agricultural crisis imposed a further burden on the foreign trade balance: while imports of all other kinds of machinery were reduced in 1928/29, imports of tractors and other agricultural machinery for the new sovkhozy and kolkhozy were afforded high priority, and increased rapidly. In the meantime a new difficulty began to make itself felt. Owing to the decline in agricultural prices relative to industrial prices on the world market, the terms of trade turned significantly against Soviet exports. The problems posed by the dominant position of agriculture in the economy loomed over the Politburo at every turn.

(c) THE SOCIALIST OFFENSIVE

In the course of 1927, the policy of tolerating small private traders and industrialists was abruptly replaced by a campaign to curb the private sector and even eliminate it altogether. The assumption that private trade would continue until socialised trade could replace it was swept aside. The economic context of this change in policy was the taut situation on the retail market. In the spring and summer of 1927 demand on the retail market rose steeply, and the consequent shortages were exacerbated both by the reduction of the retail prices of industrial goods (see pp. 62–3 above) and by the hoarding which took place during the war scare following the abrogation by Britain of diplomatic relations with the Soviet Union. In view of the growing gap between demand and supply the private traders were able to sell goods at prices substantially higher than those in state and cooperative shops. 'From this logically flowed the necessity', wrote Vainshtein, Kondratiev's deputy in the Conjuncture Institute of Narkomfin, and one of the most forthright critics of the new policy, 'of controlling private trade, of limiting its volume, of extending socialist trade with the object of replacing private trade, and, in that part of private trade which still

---

[65] *Byulleten' Kon"yunkturnogo Instituta*, 7, June 1929, 16–17.

remained, of controlling the prices of those goods for which prices in socialised trade were fixed or controlled'.[66]

In the spring and summer of 1927 private traders were subjected to a general assault by the state trading and financial agencies, and by the police. They were compelled to reduce their prices, deprived of supplies from the state sector, and in many cases simply removed from the market altogether by a combination of high taxes and enforced administrative action.[67] In July 1927 Mikoyan bluntly admitted at Sovnarkom that sharp price rises had been avoided in the spring only by 'state pressure' in the course of which 'hundreds of people were handed over to the courts'.[68] The campaign resulted in a decline in the official price index for industrial goods in private as well as socialist trade.[69] But this was certainly misleading: there were frequent reports that private trade in practice took place at higher unofficial prices, and that 'official' private trade was supplemented by private transactions at prices which were sometimes double the official level.[70] To counter these developments the authorities took further action against the private traders; and this process continued throughout the worsening goods shortages of 1928 and 1929.

According to Mikoyan, 100,000 private shops or stalls were closed in the course of 1926/27.[71] This was about one quarter of the total; by the end of 1928 more than half of all private shops and stalls had closed; and by the end of 1929 only 47,150 units were officially registered as compared with over 400,000 in 1926/27.[72] In consequence, private retail trade turnover in current prices declined from the peak of 5,064 million rubles in 1926/27, 36·9 per cent of all retail trade turnover, to 2,680 millions in 1928/29, only 16·1 per cent of all turnover (see Table 12). The decline both in the number of private trading units

---

[66] *Byulleten' Kon''yunkturnogo Instituta*, 11–12, 1927, 14.

[67] For examples, see TPG, August 9, 24, September 15, 1927.

[68] *Itogi* (1927), ii, 17.

[69] See Mendel'son, ed. (1930), 102, 105, 108. The old official index for retail prices in private trade declined by 2·2 per cent between October–December 1926 and July–September 1927, and the new index by 6·0 per cent; the equivalent percentage in the socialised sector was 8·7 per cent.

[70] See, for example, SO, 10, 1927, 9 (Pervushin).

[71] See Carr and Davies (1969), 672–3.

[72] The available data was not strictly comparable: see Table 11.

and in private turnover was more rapid in the countryside than in the towns.

The expropriation by the state of the shops and stalls of private traders was not adequately compensated by an increase in the socialised network. The larger private enterprises were transferred to the state or cooperative trading agencies, but most smaller shops and stalls were simply closed. The total number of trading units declined in the towns from about 311,000 in 1926/27 to 215,000 in 1928/29, and in the countryside from 240,000 to 160,000.[73] The decline was particularly harmful to trade in the countryside, for it meant that many rural settlements now lacked any kind of permanent shop or even stall; peasants had to make all their purchases of industrial goods in a neighbouring settlement or in the towns. By the end of 1928, the number of trading units in the USSR was less than 40 per cent of the number in tsarist Russia in 1912.[74] The reduction in the number of trading units may have brought certain economies of scale, but it certainly involved a considerable deterioration in the facilities available to the consumer.

The fundamental shift in approach to the private sector took place two years before the shift in agricultural policy from restricting to eliminating the kulaks, and from voluntary to enforced collectivisation. In retrospect the analogy is obvious between the policy pursued in 1927–9 of eliminating private trade before the socialised sector was able to replace it and the policy pursued in 1929–31 of collectivising agriculture before state industry was able to supply tractors and other machinery in place of peasant horses and implements. At its inception in the summer of 1927, while vigorously opposed by the non-party experts in Narkomfin, the drive against private trade met with little open resistance within the party. In April 1929 Rykov and Bukharin proposed to 'normalise' the market and remove 'pressure in the sphere of trade'.[75] But this was by then an idle dream: it could have been achieved only by drastic measures to

[73] See Table 11; these figures somewhat exaggerate the number of units (see General Note to Table).

[74] See Davies, ed. (1988) (Gatrell and Davies); this figure includes wholesale and some other trading units not included on January 1, 1929; my estimate of the decline in the number of units allows for this.

[75] See Carr and Davies (1969), 633.

restore equilibrium between supply and consumer demand, which no-one contemplated.

State policy towards private industry was more complex and ambiguous. The production of private census industry, even at its peak in 1925/26, amounted to only 3·6 per cent of total production; and the official attitude was more tolerant towards private industry, which was seen as at least having the merit of producing useful goods, than towards private trade, which was regarded as parasitic.[76] Nevertheless, the decline of private census industry began as early as the first half of the economic year 1926/27, and the reduction in production in 1927 and 1928 was precipitate.[77] Between 1925/26 and 1928/29 the production of the private sector declined by as much as 86·5 per cent, and in the latter year it was responsible for a mere 0·3 per cent of the total production of census industry.[78]

Private capital was also influential in small-scale artisan industry, but the extent of its influence is extremely difficult to assess.[79] Larin, who waged a fierce campaign against private capital throughout the 1920s, received the support in 1927 of an authoritative commission, which proclaimed that about 10 per cent of all industrial production was controlled by private capitalists. The commission claimed that this sector, far larger than the officially-recorded capitalist sector, consisted largely of individual artisans, domestic workers and members of bogus artels and cooperatives, who were exploited by private traders who supplied them with raw materials or sold their products.[80] These illegal or 'masked' enterprises were said to continue the evils of '*pre-Soviet times*', working without control over hours or

[76] See Carr and Davies (1969), 386–9, 950; B, 11–12, June 30, 1927, 87 (Larin).

[77] *Materialy*, vii (1959), 63–4; this report from the archives provides (pp. 61–79) an informative account of the decline of private industry in 1926/27 and 1927/28.

[78] See Carr and Davies (1969), 950.

[79] 'All the methods available at present for measuring this "illegal" private capital are so doubtful', Narkomfin told STO in its sceptical report on private capital in 1926/27 prepared in the spring of 1929, 'that it is impossible to pose the question of determining its size' (*Materialy*, vii (1959), 61).

[80] B, 11–12, June 30, 1927 78–89 (Larin); the commission included Ordzhoni-kidze, Mikoyan, Frumkin, Kviring and Strumilin as well as Larin.

working conditions.[81] In December 1927, Larin's campaign was strongly supported by Stalin at the XV party congress.[82]

Between 1927 and 1929 artisans in many industries were removed from the influence of private capital as a result of the drive against private trade. Sometimes the loss of supplies or market outlets compelled artisans to cease work altogether.[83] In spite of these pressures the number of persons engaged in small-scale industry increased between 1926/27 and 1928/29.[84] By 1928/29, however, only 140,000 individual artisans were recorded in the census of small-scale industry as selling their output to the capitalist sector (i.e. mainly to private traders); while this figure was no doubt under-reported, there is no doubt that the influence of private capital on small-scale industry had greatly diminished. Simultaneously the number of artisans in the official producer cooperatives had increased to 869,000 as compared with 178,000 in 1926/27, and a further 420,000 individual artisans sold their output to the socialist sector. Sixty per cent of all artisans remained independent of both the socialist sector and the rapidly declining capitalist sector, and sold their output direct to individual consumers.[85] But the cooperative and state sector was far more productive: although it included only 25 per cent of all participants in small-scale industry, it was responsible for 52 per cent of gross turnover.[86]

---

[81] *Ibid.* 82.

[82] See Carr and Davies (1969), 397.

[83] See, for example, the report on the artisan metal industry in TPG, January 29, 1928.

[84] *Nar. kh.* (1932), 88–91; for the production of small-scale industry, see p. 60 n. 18 above.

[85] Those engaged in small-scale industry in 1928/9 were divided by social sector as follows (thousands):

Capitalist sector		37
Individual artisans		3011
Selling to: capitalist sector	140	
individual consumers	2445	
socialist sector	420	
State industry and public organisations		164
Artisan and other cooperatives		869
Total		4081

(*Melkaya promyshlennost'*, i (1933), 22–3; these figures exclude the flour, groats and vegetable oil industries).

[86] *Loc. cit.*

By 1928/29 the socialist offensive had already made considerable inroads into small-scale industry.

(D) THE INDUSTRIAL ECONOMY, SUMMER 1929

As the economic year 1928/29 drew to a close, contrasting achievements and failures provided ample evidence to justify both optimists and sceptics. Capital investment in industry in 1928/29 failed to reach the very high level planned in the autumn of 1928.[87] It nevertheless increased extremely rapidly during the 1929 season, after a slow start. On April 1, 1929, the total number employed in building was only 17·5 per cent greater than on the same date of the previous year, but by October 1, 1929, the equivalent percentage had reached 29·1 (see Table 17). Capital investment in industry and electrification, measured in real terms, increased by at least 20 per cent in 1928/29, and as a result the stock of fixed capital in industry increased more rapidly than in previous years.[88]

The increase of industrial production in the summer of 1929 also provided cause for satisfaction. The established seasonal pattern was that production rose rapidly in October–December

[87] First reports indicated that the plan had been achieved in monetary terms. The annual report of Sovnarkom predicted that the plan would prove to be 'slightly overfulfilled' (*Industrializatsiya, 1929–1932* (1970), 122; see also Kaganovich in P, November 26, 1929). But investment in Vesenkha-planned industry was eventually reported as 1,627 million rubles as compared with the original plan of 1,650 millions and the final plan of 1,707 millions (*Ob"yasnitel'naya zapiska, 1928–1929* (1930), 78–9), while investment in electrification in Vesenkha amounted to only 218 as against the plan of 311 millions (*Ezhemesyachnyi statisticheskii byulleten'*, 3(78), December 1928, 116–17). The lag was greater in the case of investment in new factories than in the repair and extension of existing factories (*Byulleten' Kon"yunkturnogo Instituta*, 8, July 1929, 3, referring to the period October 1928–July 1929). In real terms underfulfilment was even greater, as construction costs declined by only about 5 per cent in 1928/29 as against the plan of 15 per cent (*Vypolnenie*, June and January–June 1932, 8), and the total price index for fixed capital, including the value of capital equipment as well as the cost of construction, declined by only 1·3 per cent (Minaev, ed. (1930), 60–1). This footnote corrects Carr and Davies (1969), 332.

[88] The series for capital stock vary considerably according to the extent to which stock data allow for depreciation, but they all show an accelerating curve. The following alternative series for fixed capital stock in industry are calculated from Barun (1930), 34, who explains his methods of estimation on

and more slowly in January–March: it then levelled off in the second half of the economic year owing to summer holidays and the return of coal miners and other workers to the countryside for haymaking and the harvest. This pattern was followed in 1925/26, 1926/27 and 1927/28.[89] But in 1928/29 production continued to rise in each quarter of the year, and reached its maximum in July–September 1929, exceeding production in July–September 1928 by as much as 31·2 per cent. This seems to have been due primarily to the sustained production drive which was maintained throughout the summer; the staggering of summer holidays also played its part.[90]

In the second half of 1928/29 a substantial reduction in industrial costs was also achieved. In the first half of the year, October 1928–March 1929, wages increased more rapidly than planned, and costs were only 1.9 per cent below the average level in 1927/28, as compared with the plan of 7 per cent. But, beginning with April 1929, a determined effort to control wages and economise in inputs resulted in a much greater decline in costs, so that costs over the whole year declined by 4.2 per cent.[91] Moreover, Vesenkha claimed that the reduction would have amounted to 5·6 per cent if taxes and the prices of inputs

---

pp. 21–38 (annual percentage increases as compared with the same date of previous year, measured in 1928/29 prices):

	October 1, 1926	October 1, 1927	October 1, 1928	October 1, 1929
At full restoration cost	9·0	11·7	14·4	16·2
At cost with depreciation deducted, as shown in annual balance	10·1	13·3	16·3	18·8
At cost with technical depreciation deducted	11·9	15·0	17·9	20·1
At cost with commercial depreciation deducted	14·3	18·6	22·1	24·3

For other series, see *Na novom etape* (1930), i, 504–5; Minaev, ed. (1930), 69, 71.

[89] In 1927/28, production increased very rapidly in January–March; this increase was a major factor in the fulfilment of the annual plan.

[90] See Table 7(b), and *Byulleten' Kon''yunkturnogo Instituta*, 8, July 1929, 4–5, and SO, 1, 1930, 33.

[91] According to Strumilin, costs declined by as much as 9 per cent in April–September 1929 (TPG, September 24, 1929).

had not increased; on a comparable basis the reduction in costs was somewhat greater than in the previous year.[92]

In 1928/29, as in the previous three years, the increase of industrial production was more rapid than the increase in the stock of industrial fixed capital.[93] Almost all Soviet economists, of whatever school of thought, assumed that virtually the whole of the pre-revolutionary capital stock in industry had already been brought back into use by 1927; a careful estimate concluded that only 7·4 per cent of fixed capital was not 'operational' on October 1, 1927.[94] Hence the rapid increase in production in the later 1920s was usually attributed to improvements in the efficiency with which capital was utilised. An optimistic assessment of future capital–output ratios lay at the heart of Fel'dman's extremely optimistic growth model (see pp. 227–30 below). This rash reasoning did not sufficiently take into account the extent to which capital equipment classified as 'operational' was not in fact fully in operation. The engineering and chemical industries, in particular, had recovered to their 1913 but not yet to their 1916 level. The rapid increase in production in 1927–9 and the accompanying decline in the capital–output ratio was thus partly a result of the last stages of the recovery process.[95] Moreover, the experience of both peace-

---

[92] According to Vesenkha, rises in the prices of inputs increased costs by 0·5 per cent, while increased taxes accounted for 0.9 per cent, whereas in 1927/28 these 'conjunctural factors' had reduced costs by 1·1 per cent; the 'organisational and technical production achievements' of industry had therefore reduced costs by 5·1 per cent in 1927/28 and 5·6 per cent in 1928/29 (*Vypolnenie* (1931), 81–90); it should be borne in mind, however, that costs data were particularly capable of manipulation.

[93] See pp. 80–1 note 88 above. The estimate with 'commercial depreciation' deducted shows an increase in stock in 1928/29 which slightly exceeds the rate of increase in gross industrial production recorded in the official statistics; but in view of the continued use of older capital the application of a commercial rate of depreciation to fixed capital is hardly realistic.

[94] EO, 10, 1929, 134 (Gorelik).

[95] In their obituary of Fel'dman on the occasion of the tenth anniversary of his death A. L. Vainshtein and G. I. Khanin wrote that 'if we consider the restoration period as a process of achieving the full utilisation of the production potential of pre-revolutionary Russia, it was completed not in 1926 but far later, and remnants of the period remained in 1926–1930' (*Ekonomika i matematicheskie metody*, 2, 1968, 298–9). For estimates of the increase in the fixed capital stock of industry between January 1, 1914, and January 1, 1918, ranging from 17·7 to 29·7 per cent, see Strumilin (1958 (2)), 554.

time and war-time booms in all industrial countries has shown that substantial increases in production can be obtained by a more comprehensive use of existing capacity. The expansion of industrial production at the end of the 1920s, and the accompanying rise in labour productivity and fall in costs, depended to a much greater extent on these special conditions than was generally realised.

Several major new developments in the spring and summer of 1929 also encouraged the authorities in their belief that rapid expansion of industry could continue. These months saw the launching on a mass scale of the campaign for 'socialist emulation' between groups of workers and whole factories and the emergence of 'shock-workers (udarniki)'; the increased production achieved by these means was widely publicised. Stalin's only substantial public utterance between April and November 1929 appeared as a preface to a pamphlet on socialist emulation, in which he extolled the new movement as *'the communist method of constructing socialism'*, and condemned bureaucrats who sought to curb popular initiative.[96] By June the campaign implausibly claimed two million participants.[97] But according to a Gosplan survey the initial movement for socialist emulation was 'insufficiently specific', and 'somewhat declined' in June and July 1929 after the first burst of enthusiasm.[98]

The seven-hour day, initiated at the end of 1927, also began to play a substantial part in industry by the summer of 1929. By October 1, 1929, as many as 577,300 workers, 20 per cent of the total, had been transferred. This might have been expected to hinder the expansion of production. But a Vesenkha investigation claimed that the decline in productivity per day had proved temporary; after a period of three–six months, productivity in a seven-hour day already exceeded that previously achieved in an eight-hour day.[99] Whether this success

[96] The preface, dated May 11, 1929, also appeared in P, May 22, 1929. In a letter dated July 9, which was not published at the time, Stalin admitted that the pamphlet contained 'crude mistakes', but defended its publication as an attempt to enable an unknown but talented young author to contribute to the cause (Stalin, *Soch.*, xii (1949), 112–15). The pamphlet was E. Mikulina, *Sorevnovanie mass* (1929).

[97] See Carr and Davies (1969), 515–19.

[98] *Sotsialisticheskoe sorevnovanie* (1930), 32.

[99] SO, 1, 1930, 33–4.

was achieved because of or in spite of the seven-hour day was not satisfactorily established. The main economic purpose of the seven-hour day was to make possible the more intensive use of machinery by increasing the number of shifts. But the success achieved in this respect was very small: the 'shift coefficient' increased by a mere 2·2 per cent in 1928/29.[100]

The economic advantages of the seven-hour day were thus not yet demonstrated. During the summer of 1929 it was overshadowed as a means of increasing production from existing capacity by a novel development which appeared to possess all its advantages without its disadvantages. This was the *nepreryvka*, the continuous working week. Under this system there was no longer a fixed day of rest: factories and offices worked every day of the week, and workers had four or five days on and one day off. In May 1929, Larin argued at the V congress of soviets that the universal introduction of the *nepreryvka* would increase the number of working days in the year from 300 to about 360; in consequence, production could be increased by one-fifth without any additional equipment.[101]

During June and July 1929, the *nepreryvka* was widely discussed at meetings and in the press. By and large it was welcomed in Vesenkha, though some officials doubted whether machinery would be repaired properly if it was in use on every day of the week.[102] On July 18, 1929, the presidium of Vesenkha approved 'in principle' a scheme presented by Kraval', who was in charge of labour in Vesenkha; shortly afterwards Larin's close associate Sabsovich was appointed as plenipotentiary in

[100] The shift coefficient, which showed the ratio of the total number of days worked to the number worked on the shift with the maximum number of workers, increased from 1·491 in 1927/28 to 1·521 in 1928/29 (*Trud* (1930), 20).

[101] *SSSR: 5 s''ezd sovetov* (1929), No. 5, 26–7; EZh, May 29, 1929. The scheme was apparently originated by a Vesenkha engineer, a certain Shauer, who proposed at the beginning of 1927 that it should be combined with a two-shift rather than a three-shift system, thus avoiding the low productivity characteristic of night shifts (for the origins of the scheme, see the discussion in EZh, June 4, 5, 6, July 5, 1929). According to Larin, a certain Rapoport proposed it in Vesenkha in 1927, but the proposal was buried. It was also discussed in the Ukrainian trade unions, and was raised by Larin in the Communist Academy, sometime before May 1929. Larin dismissed the claim from a department of Vesenkha, ORSU, that engineer Aronovich was the originator, suggesting that ORSU stood for '*otdel rasprostraneniya smeshnikh uprekov* (department for the dissemination of ridiculous reproaches)'.

[102] See reports in EZh, May 31, June 1, 2, 9, 16, 1929.

charge of introducing the *nepreryvka*.[103] Gosplan also supported its immediate introduction, envisaging rather cautiously that in 1929/30 industrial production might be increased by between 3 and 6 per cent as a result.[104] The *nepreryvka* was strongly opposed, however, at a large conference of business managers and trade union officials convened by Narkomtrud on July 22. On the following day a note to Sovnarkom from Uglanov, People's Commissar for Labour, and one of his officials claimed that during the next few years the obstacles to introducing the *nepreryvka* would be 'almost insuperable', and listed seven difficulties: (1)–(5) shortages of fuel, raw materials, power, finance and labour; (6) out-of-date equipment; (7) disruption of the worker's life and of cultural services.[105] In the middle of August 1929, Sovnarkom heard a report on the *nepreryvka* prepared by Gosplan arguing that it should be posed as a 'great national-economic political task'. Shortages of fuel and materials could partly be overcome by using them more efficiently; and the *nepreryvka* could help to overcome shortages if it was first introduced into industries producing scarce materials. In the debate at Sovnarkom, Larin claimed that the *nepreryvka* should be introduced even in industries in which materials were scarce, concentrating available materials on the best machines. Uglanov retreated from his position of outright hostility, but warned against undue haste, which would result in declining productivity and rising costs due to the use of inadequately trained labour and to the increasing break-downs of equipment.[106] On August 26, 1929, Sovnarkom decreed that the *nepreryvka* should be introduced in 1929/30, and, 'where possible', even in 1928/29.[107]

---

[103] *Protokol . . . VSNKh, 1928/29*, No. 27, prilozhenie, art. 704; No. 29, prilozhenie dated August 1.

[104] EZh, July 11, P, August 3, 4, 1929.

[105] P, August 3, 1929; the note itself has not been available; this source is an account of the note by Markus, a hostile witness, who described it as 'planning for the bottleneck' and 'the normal Right-wing phrases against the rate of socialist industrialisation'. Uglanov, a former associate of Bukharin, was deposed from the secretaryship of the Moscow organisation and replaced Shmidt as People's Commissar for Labour in November 1928 (see Carr and Davies (1969), 88–92, 555–6). The official who also signed the note was Avdeev, presumably the former Zinovievist (see Carr (1971), 43, 48).

[106] P, August 17, 1929.

[107] SZ, 1929, art. 502; on August 22, the Politburo approved the decree in draft (*Industrializatsiya, 1929–1932* (1970), 585).

On the same day a government commission to introduce the *nepreryvka* was established under the chairmanship of Rudzutak.[108] The scheme seemed to carry social as well as economic advantages. It would reduce the pressure on workers' clubs and other leisure facilities, enabling them to be used in daytime throughout the week. Above all it struck a blow against religion by treating Sunday as a normal working day.

The *nepreryvka* was introduced in individual factories from May 1929 onwards.[109] By the end of the economic year 280,000 industrial workers had transferred to the new arrangements. While some of these were employed in industries where continuous production was already normal practice for technical reasons, such as iron and steel, the *nepreryvka* was already reported to be 'one of the factors assisting the smoothing-out of the seasonal curve' in the summer of 1929.[110]

All these developments – socialist emulation, the seven-hour day and the *nepreryvka* – were in their infancy in the summer of 1929. But their limitations and disadvantages had not yet become obvious; and their potential for increasing production from existing factories without further investment seemed to their protagonists to be very considerable.

But the mounting claims of the industrialisation drive relentlessly increased inflationary pressure in every sector of the economy in 1927–9, and in the spring and summer of 1929 the tense situation was exacerbated by the sharp increase in capital investment, which brought with it rising demand throughout industry. In consequence stocks of fuel, raw materials and other inputs held by industry declined relative to output;[111] and the worsening shortages led to a further extension of the system of physical allocation. With the further rapid expansion of personal purchasing power, shortages also grew far more acute on the retail market. Everyday life began to take on the familiar characteristics of war-time austerity. A Soviet account vividly

---

[108] BFKhZ, 35, 1929; the commission, attached to STO, was eventually disbanded, after completion of its work, on September 21, 1930 (BFKhZ, 28, 1930).

[109] See EZh, May 29, 1929.

[110] SO, 1, 1930, 33 (M. Tsigel'nitskii), VTr, 4, 1930, 3; the figure refers to Vesenkha-planned industry.

[111] *Byulleten' Kon"yunkturnogo Instituta*, 8, July 1929, 7.

describes the change which had already taken place in Moscow by the early summer:

> Only a year or two previously the streets were full of the strident signboards of private traders, pseudo-cooperatives and cooperatives, and the shop-windows lured the purchaser. Now the private trader was not to be seen. The Nepmen did not vanish off the face of the earth, but disguised themselves in protective clothing . . .
>
> The shop-windows grew bare, many shops were locked up. In the windows of the food shops old friends reappeared – jam, 'Hercules' flour, washing blue, 'Health' coffee. The chain of dairies which used to belong to Chichkin and Blandov still existed, but were empty. Here and there the streets looked as they did in the severe years of war communism. The cooperative shops were untidy, dirty and littered. The private dining rooms and cafes were closed. The cooperative dining rooms were filthy and pitiable . . .
>
> The reduction in the number of horse-cabs was startlingly obvious. Ration books were introduced for fodder, but obviously this did not help much. There were no automobiles in the Moscow streets yet, or very few of them. At night people went about only on foot. Moving a load became a serious problem . . .
>
> Moscow lacked fuel. Housing with central heating was badly off, and apartments with their own stoves were even worse off. There were vast queues at the wood stores . . .
>
> Shops selling clothes and footwear were empty . . . Any newly-arrived batch went in half-an-hour. As in 1919 and 1920, people appeared dressed in leather from head to foot. Expensive fur coats vanished from the streets, and the provocative tasteless finery by which Nepmen could be so easily spotted. The streets got grayer.[112]

During the summer, the situation further deteriorated. In Moscow, official trading agencies at first lacked sufficient stocks of meat to enable rationing to be introduced, so during the summer queues formed at two or three in the morning. When

---

[112] *God devyaynadtsatyi. Almanakh devyatyi* (1936), 329–30 (Bogushevskii and Khavin).

rationing of meat, fish and milk was introduced in the autumn, there was only sufficient milk to provide a ration for children.[113] In smaller towns shortages were even more acute, while in the countryside the cooperatives were empty and most private shops were closed.[114]

The worsening shortages meant that, even in the case of producer goods, consumers more and more frequently had to accept what they were offered. In this context the unremitting drive to increase production and reduce costs inexorably led to a decline in the quality of industrial output. In its annual report for 1928/29, Sovnarkom recorded 'many complaints from consumers, trading and cooperative organisations, government departments and production enterprises' about the 'serious deterioration in quality'.[115] Vesenkha recorded equally bluntly 'a general worsening of the quality of output', which reduced the period of useful service; 'in a number of cases the reduction of costs in 1928/29 was achieved by the purely mechanical reduction of the expenditure needed to produce goods of normal quality'.[116] Every stage in the production process and every type of product was affected, from raw material to finished goods, from pig-iron and building materials to clothing, china, sugar and matches.[117] In July–September 1929 a survey of cotton textiles classified 50 per cent as 'spoiled'.[118] The industrial newspaper frankly admitted that '*in expanding production we simultaneously worsen its quality to such an extent that the utility of production as a whole to the consumer does not increase, but declines*'.[119]

Such deficiencies were more or less frankly admitted, but their provenance was increasingly attributed to the failings of the executors of the plans rather than to the strain imposed by the plans themselves. The presidium of Vesenkha attributed poor quality to 'factors of a primarily subjective character,

[113] *Pervaya Moskovskaya konferentsiya* (1929), ii, 25–6 (Bauman).

[114] *God devyatnadtsatyi. Almanakh devyatyi* (1936), 329.

[115] *God raboty pravitel'stva 1928/29* (1930), 155.

[116] SP, 1929/30, No. 1 (resolution of presidium dated October 5, 1929).

[117] For typical accounts, see SO, 1, 1930, 36; PI, 5, 1930, 35–6; *Byulleten' Kon"yunkturnogo Instituta*, 8, July 1929, 18; other references are given in BP (Prague), lxxi (August–September 1929), 10–12.

[118] PI, 5, 1930, 35–6 (Grintser).

[119] TPG, September 20, 1929 (Shukhgal'ter); see also the report of the presidium of Vesenkha and the subsequent editorial, *ibid.* September 22, 24, 1929.

depending on industry itself'. Vesenkha strengthened quality inspection agencies at factories and launched an extensive propaganda campaign to persuade or shame industrial personnel into taking quality more seriously; it also proposed that criminal penalties should be imposed on administrators or workers guilty of an 'intentionally careless attitude to quality'.[120]

Enthusiasm for industrialisation, and a sense that the economic transformation of the Soviet Union was imminent, dominated the local and national party conferences and soviet congresses when they discussed and approved the five-year plan in the spring of 1929. At the V Gosplan congress in March 1929, Krzhizhanovsky succinctly summarised the prevailing attitude of the supporters of rapid industrialisation:

> We may conclude the following. We have clear evidence that we are structurally on the right lines; but quantitatively there is tremendous backwardness. Conclusion – a huge programme of construction.[121]

The rapid expansion of industrial production and investment in the succeeding six months confirmed the Soviet leaders and their immediate advisers in their view that a 'huge programme of construction' was entirely feasible. A significant turning point came in August, when the Politburo supported Rabkrin in its acrimonious dispute with Vesenkha about Yugostal' (see pp. 189–90 below), and issued a directive that industrial capital investment should be increased in 1929/30 by over 80 per cent (see p. 180 below).

These alluring perspectives seized the imagination not only of party officials and leading party members, but also of a significant minority of industrial workers. A hostile American witness emphasised the crucial importance of 'the explosive energy in the minority and the flaming faith in an all-socialist future': 'young communists who had reached maturity in the

[120] SP, 1929/30, No. 1 (resolution of October 5, 1929); the resolution also proposed that prices paid to factories for higher grades of output should be increased.

[121] *Problemy rekonstruktsii* (1929), 337.

last eight years . . . thrilled at the new opportunity for deeds of daring' while 'the politically more conscious sector of the industrial proletariat gratefully rationalized its burdens as temporary war measures'.[122] A student who was at the Leningrad shipbuilding institute between 1928 and 1932 vividly recalled the prevailing atmosphere:

> At that time everyone was an ardent patriot. During all our student days those plans occupied our minds, we were exhilarated by them. If a new blast-furnace started up somewhere, that was a great occasion for us. We were tuned in to the successes in constructing the new factories and improving the old ones, we were very patriotic about it.[123]

How far this mood extended among rank-and-file workers has not been reliably established. Kaganovich bluntly admitted that 'certain groups of workers' were dissatisfied, and had 'influenced the psychology of some leading party members';[124] one of the delegates to the regional Moscow party conference in September 1929 complained that as a result of the worsening conditions of life 'a mood of depression' had replaced the élan of 1925/26, when the workers lived better.[125] At the same conference Bauman, on behalf of the Moscow committee, acknowledged 'a certain nervy state, a certain tension', but praised the emergence of 'new militant activists' among the workers, and claimed that the working class could now see the prospects for the future more clearly, and 'accept temporary adversities in order to win tomorrow'.[126] Other commentators noted, no doubt correctly, both greater enthusiasm among some workers and 'certain vacillations' among others.[127] A recent study plausibly argues that the core group which maintained the shock-brigade movement consisted neither of the older established workers nor of the new unskilled workers from the

---

[122] Lyons (1938), 197–8; for similar accounts see the émigré Menshevik journal, SV (Paris), 18 (207), September 27, 1929, 16, and M. Fischer (New York and London, 1944), 41.
[123] Interview No. 12 (April 1982).
[124] P, November 1, 1929.
[125] *Pervaya Moskovskaya* (1929), ii, 194–5.
[126] *Pervaya Moskovskaya* (1929), ii, 195–6.
[127] EO, 9, 1929, pp. iii, v–vi (editorial).

countryside, but of young skilled workers, 'probably of urban origin'.[128]

In the summer of 1929, the party leaders sought to consolidate their authority by a mixture of repression, persuasion and appeals for loyalty at a time of crisis. Bourgeois specialists who were hostile, or were believed to be hostile, to the new policies were more savagely repressed than at any previous period of Soviet history. Arrests and executions of 'counter-revolutionaries' were briefly but frequently reported throughout the summer (see vol. 1, p. 117). In September Molotov reported to the Moscow regional party conference that 'Whiteguard groups of wreckers, linked to the foreign bourgeoisie and the White emigration, have been found in the Donets coal trust, in Narkomput' and in the gold and platinum industry, and also in the shipbuilding trust, in war industry, and in Gosplan, and in Narkomtorg, and in the headquarters of Vesenkha itself'. Molotov bluntly condemned leading officials who 'firmly impose their bourgeois line on particular agencies ... masked with external loyalty and even with some learning', and he called upon them to choose '*Either – or!* – there is not and there cannot be any third road'.[129]

Simultaneously, supporters of the Right wing in the party were systematically removed from their posts (see vol. 1, pp. 117–19). In August 1929 Bukharin was publicly condemned for the first time. A statement by the Comintern listed errors which included 'attempts to reduce the rapidity of the rate of industrialisation carried out by the party', and 'spreading pessimism, depression and lack of belief in the strength of the working class'.[130] Opponents and critics rallied to the party leadership not only as a result of intimidatory measures but also because of their support for the cause of industrialisation, and their belief in the need for loyalty to the party at a time of crisis (see vol. 1, p. 118). An American observer noted that in 1929 'many heartsore old Bolsheviks ... suddenly woke to a new zest in revolution'.[131] Perhaps the most dramatic example

---

[128] SR, 44 (1985), 295 (Kuromiya).

[129] *Pervaya Moskovskaya* (1929), i, 161–4.

[130] The resolution, approved by the X Plenum of IKKI which met from July 3–19 (*Kommunisticheskii Internatsional* (1933), 911–13), was published in *Pravda*, August 21, 1929.

[131] Lyons (1938), 198.

of this return from recusancy was the statement of August 1929
signed by 500 members of the Left Opposition which, while
strongly criticising the bureaucracy, declared that the fate of
the October revolution could depend on the success of the five-
year plan, and, reversing the previous policies of the United
Opposition, agreed in principle to renounce fractional activity,
condemned 'Trade-Union tendencies' among the workers, and
warned against attempts to use workers' dissatisfaction for
counter-revolutionary purposes. Reflecting the atmosphere of
the time, Trotsky, from his place of exile in Turkey, somewhat
reluctantly added his signature.[132] The Right wing in the party
was less easily persuaded to fall into line. For the moment
Bukharin and Tomsky remained silent, though Rykov, who
retained his post as chairman of Sovnarkom, publicly supported
party policies unreservedly.[133]

The VI Gosplan congress, which assembled on September
22, 1929, fully reflected the mood of enthusiasm. In his opening
address, Krzhizhanovsky applauded the 'new red energy of our
labour', as a result of which socialist emulation and the
nepreryvka had become powerful factors for future growth, and
announced that 'WE ARE ON THE THRESHOLD OF A
REAL ENERGY OCTOBER'.[134] Strumilin, who a year earlier
had strongly resisted the industrial investment plan for 1928/29,
admitted in his report to the congress that the view that the
1928/29 plans were 'extremely strained' must now be revised;
the achievements of industry and transport were a 'lesson' to
the planners, which must be taken into account in the future:[135]

> Contrary to the widespread opinion of our sceptics and
> Right-wing cynics [Strumlin declared], our industrialisation
> programme is not only not exaggerated; on the contrary, it is

[132] For this document see vol. 1, p. 119.

[133] See for example his report to the Moscow regional soviet congress in P,
September 28, 1929.

[134] TPG, September 24, 1929. This 'congress of planning agencies of the
USSR' was held from September 22–27; the main reports were published
separately, with revisions, as Krzhizhanovskii *et al.*, *Osnovnye problemy kontrol'nykh
tsifr narodnogo khozyaistva SSSR na 1929/30 god* (1930). For the congress
discussions on the 1929/30 control figures, see pp. 182–3 below.

[135] TPG, September 24, 1929; this passage does not appear in Krzhizhanovskii
et al. (1930).

even too cautious and should be subject to an upwards correction.[136]

With the ambitious industrialisation programme on which the Soviet Union had now embarked, it already seemed entirely feasible to catch up and overtake the advanced countries in the course of two or three five-year plans. Kviring, reporting on capital construction to the Gosplan congress, presented a calculation which purported to show that, while 'rich America is far ahead of us in investment in services, distribution and housing', in industry alone 'the scale of our construction is somewhere not very far behind the scale of construction in the USA.'[137] This greatly exaggerated the achievements of Soviet industrial construction.[138] In fact the construction programme of the five-year plan was only just getting under way in the summer of 1929. While considerable progress had been made with Dneprostroi, the Stalingrad tractor factory, the Rostov agricultural engineering factory and the Turksib railway, the other major projects had scarcely been started. By the close of the 1929 building season some auxiliary buildings had been erected at the engineering factory Uralmash in Sverdlovsk, but work on the main buildings had not yet begun.[139] On the site of the Berezniki chemical factory the old salt sheds were still being dismantled. At Magnitogorsk strings stretched across the ground showed where the foundations would be. The first workers and the first building materials did not arrive at the site of the

[136] Krzhizhanovskii *et al.* (1930), 19.

[137] Krzhizhanovskii *et al.* (1930), 86–7. Kviring claimed that total 'pure construction' in the USA amounted to some 21 milliard rubles in real terms, including over 8 milliards in housing and 1·8 milliard rubles in industry; in 1929/30 Soviet 'pure construction' would amount to only 6 milliard rubles, 29 per cent of the United States' level, but 1·6 milliard rubles of this would be allocated to industry, only 1 milliard to housing. 'Pure construction' is building work, and excludes the value of equipment installed, etc.

[138] According to a plausible estimate by the American engineer Zara Witkin, total 'pure construction' in the Soviet Union in 1928 amounted not to 29 per cent as Kviring claimed (note 137), but to between 4 and 9 per cent of the average amount of construction in the United States in 1925–9 (see Davies, ed. (1984), 149–50); on this estimate, Soviet industrial construction planned for 1929/30 amounted to between 12 and 28 per cent of industrial construction in the United States.

[139] *Ural'skii zavod* (Sverdlovsk, 1933), 11.

Nizhnii-Novgorod automobile factory until October 1929.[140] And the basic projects for all these sites were still being negotiated and revised.

The hopes of 1929, for industry as well as for agriculture, were based on optimistic calculations which always gave the more favourable assessment the benefit of the doubt, on the grounds that the human will, in the context of socialist relations of production, could overcome all obstacles. These assumptions were about to be tested.

---

[140] *God devyatnadtsatyi. Almanakh devyatyi* (1936), 347.

CHAPTER THREE

THE SOCIAL CONTEXT, 1929–30

(A) THE SOCIALIST OFFENSIVE RENEWED

In his famous article 'The Year of the Great Break-Through', published on the twelfth anniversary of the Bolshevik revolution (November 7, 1929), Stalin succinctly summarised the prevailing mood in leading party circles.[1] According to Stalin, a 'decisive *offensive* by socialism' had occurred in the course of the economic year 1928/29, and had resulted in three major achievements. First, a '*decisive break-through*' in the productivity of labour had been achieved. This was a result of the 'unleashing of the creative initiative and creative élan of the masses', and was supported by the struggle against bureaucracy by means of self-criticism, the struggle against poor labour discipline by means of socialist emulation, and the struggle against production routine via the introduction of the *nepreryvka*. Secondly, in 1928/29 '*the problem of accumulation* for capital construction in heavy industry was solved in principle, an *accelerated rate* of growth of production of means of production was adopted, and the prerequisites were established for transforming our country into a country *based on metal*'. According to Stalin, while other countries had required colossal foreign loans, the USSR was solving the problem of accumulation with its own resources. Now only the problem of cadres had to be solved in order to ensure the development of heavy industry. Thirdly, in 1928/29 the socialist reconstruction of agriculture had been initiated. Stalin concluded with the famous peroration:

> We are going full steam ahead to socialism along the road of industrialisation, leaving behind our traditional 'Russian' backwardness.

[1] Stalin, *Soch.*, xii (1949), 118–35, dated November 3, 1929. For agricultural aspects of this article see vol. 1, pp. 155–6.

We are becoming a country of metal, a country of the automobile, a country of the tractor.

A few weeks after the plenum, in a private letter to Maxim Gorky, Stalin assessed much more frankly the strains and stresses of the socialist offensive:

Not everyone has the nerves, strength, character and understanding to appreciate the scenario of a tremendous break-up of the old and a feverish construction of the new, as a scenario of what is *necessary* and therefore *desirable*. This scenario does not in the least resemble the heavenly idyll of a 'general well-being' which provides the possibility of 'taking it easy' and 'relaxing pleasurably'. Naturally with such a 'baffling turmoil' we are bound to have those who are exhausted, distraught, worn-out, despondent and lagging behind – and those who go over to the enemy camp. These are the inevitable 'costs' of revolution.[2]

Perhaps the outstanding feature of Soviet economic policy between the summer of 1929 and the end of 1930 was its overwhelming emphasis on the human will as a factor which might hinder or ensure the achievement of the plan. Failures were attributed to the activity of enemies or the insufficient activity of those in authority; success was sought through acts of labour heroism and improved leadership and organisation. Economic and financial incentives were down-graded, to some extent in theory and to a greater extent in practice. At the XVI party congress Stalin insisted that the essence of the Bolshevik offensive was primarily the mobilisation of the masses against capitalist elements and against bureaucracy, together with the development of the creative initiative and hard work of the masses.[3]

The socialist offensive was seen to involve both the collectivisation of agriculture and a thorough reconstruction of urban society. The remnants of capitalism must be eliminated in industry and trade. The old specialists in leading positions must be replaced by new specialists enthusiastic for the socialist

[2] Stalin, *Soch.*, xii (1949), 174; this letter, dated January 17, 1930, was first published in 1949; for another passage see SR, 44 (1985), 294 (Kuromiya).
[3] *Soch.*, xii (1949), 311.

cause; the untapped energies of the working class must be released, and a new generation of workers brought into the industrial economy.

Simultaneously with the drive against the kulaks in the countryside, the authorities accordingly intensified the campaign against the private trader and the remaining petty capitalists in industry. The plenum of the party central committee in November 1929 called for the 'decisive strengthening of the *socialist sector*', and drew attention to the 'sharpening of the class struggle and the stubborn resistance by capitalist elements to socialism on the offensive'.[4]

As in the previous three years, the private sector in trade and industry was assaulted by a combination of high taxes and administrative harassment. At the beginning of the economic year, personal income tax on small businessmen was increased to a marginal rate of 54 per cent, plus a surcharge by local soviets.[5] The rates of industrial tax (promnalog) paid by private enterprises on their turnover were also sharply increased,[6] and new regulations provided for prompter payment from the private sector.[7] The incidence of tax continued to differentiate sharply between petty and larger-scale capitalism. In 1930 the nominal rate of all forms of direct tax on incomes up to 200 rubles a month amounted to only 14·1 per cent, but the rate on incomes above 3,000 rubles was now in excess of 100 per cent.[8]

Tax evasion was widespread. Direct tax was a comparatively recent innovation, so the experience of the tax authorities was limited. In the conditions of worsening goods' shortage and rising free-market prices which prevailed after 1927, the possibilities of tax evasion greatly increased, particularly for the large number of petty traders without fixed premises. Most tax was paid by the minority reported as earning higher incomes:

[4] *KPSS v rez.*, ii (1954), 626, 631.

[5] SZ, 1929, art. 639, dated October 28; this rate was now applied to those employing three persons or less; the rate of 54 per cent had already been imposed on other businessmen in December 1927 (SZ, 1928, art. 2, dated December 14, 1927).

[6] The maximum rate was increased to 29·6 per cent of turnover as compared with the previous 17·15 per cent (Davies (1958), 111, and SZ, 1930, art. 53, dated January 13).

[7] SZ, 1929, art. 662, dated November 11.

[8] See Davies (1958), 112; average monthly earnings of insured persons in the state sector in 1928/29 amounted to only 70 rubles (see Table 20).

those with incomes above 3,000 rubles a year (which was more than treble the average wage in the state sector) received 55·4 per cent of recorded 'non-labour incomes' and paid 82·4 per cent of the income tax on these incomes.[9] Throughout this period the efforts of the authorities to obtain tax from the private sector greatly intensified; high rates of tax were frequently imposed more or less arbitrarily by the tax inspectors and their voluntary assistants. But, with the decline in the private sector, the rising diligence of the tax collectors confronted a diminishing resource. According to Narkomfin experts, private turnover subject to industrial tax declined by 26 per cent in 1928/29. Nevertheless, as a result of the increase in tax rates and the pressure on the private sector, the amount of industrial tax declined by only 15 per cent.[10] But many private businesses were unable to cope with the depredations of the tax officials. By October 1, 1929, arrears owed by the private sector amounted to over 100 million rubles.[11]

In the autumn of 1929, the purge commission investigating Narkomfin sought to increase the tax pressure on the private sector still further. It strongly criticised the tax department for its claim that high taxation was leading to the decline of private trade, and accused tax inspectors of a 'careless attitude' to tax debts. In one notorious case of tax arrears a woman whose husband had been exiled to a concentration camp for speculation was alleged to possess foreign currency amounting to $80,000 and £1,200.[12] During the winter of 1929–30 the workers' brigades which participated in the purge of Narkomfin also went out in search of tax arrears from the private sector, and purported to have recovered 40 million rubles.[13] A simultaneous drive against hoarding was supported by a decree which provided that those who discovered gold and other hidden valuables could retain 25 per cent of the proceeds.[14] This

[9] *Ob''yasnitel'naya zapiska* . . . *za 1928–1929* (1930), 30.
[10] *Ob''yasnitel'naya zapiska* . . . *za 1928–1929* (1930), 26–7.
[11] The amount quoted ranged from 130 million rubles (P, November 10, 1929, report of central control commission) to 108 million rubles (FSKh, 6, 1931, 48, report of Narkomfin collegium).
[12] P, November 11, 1929; *Chistka* (1930), 15. For the purge of Narkomfin, see also pp. 117–118 below.
[13] *Chistka* (1930), 15; over 10 million rubles were recovered in Moscow alone (EZh, March 5, 1930).
[14] SZ, 1930, art. 48, dated January 3.

campaign against the private sector, like the simultaneous dekulakisation campaign in the countryside, was later criticised for its over-zealousness. Between October 1, 1929, and May 1, 1930, the amount of tax collected from the private sector increased considerably; but simultaneously its tax arrears swelled from 100 to 500 million rubles.[15]

The penal taxation imposed on private enterprise at this time was vividly described by the organiser of an independent artel of six members, which manufactured spoons and then sold them direct on the market. For some years the artel avoided paying taxes altogether; and then in 1929 or 1930 it was treated as a private enterprise and forced to close. According to the organiser:

> The inspector for indirect and other taxes appeared ... They began to impose such taxes! Hand it over or be dekulakised. They taxed each and every one of us with huge sums of money. I sold everything that was at home to pay all that, everything I had earned, you know. Yes, those who could not pay, or did not want to pay for some reason, were exiled ... We sold the premises, the building, the presses and everything else and eventually got out of it.[16]

Private trade and industry also suffered other grave disadvantages. According to Gosplan, by the autumn of 1929 'the restriction and in some places the complete cessation of the supply of scarce commodities to private trade, together with the cessation of credit from state organisations and banking establishments, struck it a most powerful blow'.[17] During 1929/30, tighter state controls were introduced over both industrial raw materials and foodstuffs, and state controls were extended to new ranges of goods; in consequence the sources of supply for private trade declined even further. But the greatest disincentive to private trade was undoubtedly harassment and persecution by the soviet authorities, especially the OGPU. Raids were launched against speculators intermittently throughout NEP; but from 1927 they increased in frequency. In 1929/30

---

[15] FSKh, 6, 1931, 48 (report to the collegium of Narkomfin).
[16] Interview No. 10; for his subsequent fate, see p. 103, n. 28 below.
[17] *KTs ... na 1929/30* (1930), 188.

the OGPU arrested not only the private traders themselves but also numerous state and cooperative trade officials and shop assistants, who were accused of selling consumer goods and food to private traders.[18]

These hazards were overshadowed in the autumn of 1929 by a new menace: systematic eviction of Nepmen in large cities from their apartments, followed by exile. In Leningrad the first eviction decree was promulgated at the beginning of 1928; but firm action did not follow until the summer of 1929. By October 1929 Nepmen had been evicted from 300 rooms in Leningrad and some 800 or 900 in Moscow; in Moscow 'commissions to exile the non-working element' were established at a district level.[19] Indignant letters from factory workers about the slowness of the procedure were published in *Pravda*, and convey a flavour of the times:

> Housing departments and administrative agencies [a Leningrad worker complained] *stand too much on ceremony about the exiling of bourgeois elements, to the harm of our vital interests.* In their day, when all this crowd were still in power, they did not stand at all on ceremony with us. My family was thrown on to the street in 1914 without any ceremony.[20]

During the succeeding months substantial numbers of Nepmen were evicted and exiled. A Moscow shopkeeper has vividly described his own fate:

> They sealed up my shop. I didn't know, and when I set off for it from home in the morning, they seized me on the way, and that was it. There was no questioning, nothing . . . I was put in Taganka jail, room 369, and worked in a cardboard workshop in the jail . . . I was there from December [1929] to February. Three months . . . I was in the workshop, and some one came in and said you've got six years . . . They said it was exile to West Siberia for six years under article 59³. Nothing else was said. Later, when I enquired what

[18] See, for example, P, October 25, 1929, describing arrests by the OGPU in the Yaroslavl' and Pokrovsk workers' cooperatives.

[19] P, October 12, 1929.

[20] P, October 12, 1929 (Karl Marx engineering factory).

article this was, they told me that in the Criminal Code of the RSFSR this was for banditism.[21]

The persecution of the private sector resulted in its almost complete elimination as a legal activity. The number of registered private retail trade enterprises declined from 153,000 on January 1, 1929, to a mere 17,700 on January 1, 1931, as compared with over 400,000 in 1925–7 (see Table 11). The volume of private retail trade, measured in current prices, declined from 2,680 million rubles in 1928/29 to 1,240 million rubles in 1929/30; this was a mere 7 per cent of all retail trade.[22] According to TsUNKhU estimates, the 'capitalist groups' of the population, excluding petty traders, declined from 167,000 persons in 1928, including family members, to 83,000 in 1930; their consumption per head also declined drastically.[23] As a result of the strenuous exertions of the tax collectors, the amount collected in tax from the private sector, including the petty traders, was only slightly lower in 1929/30 than in the previous year, though it fell short of the budget estimate.[24] The bulk of tax from the private sector, as in previous years, was obtained from the larger private trading and industrial enterprises: in 1929/30 only 13 million of a total industrial tax paid by the private sector amounting to 144

[21] Interview No. 2; he worked as a clerk in a remote timber office for five years, and was then amnestied; from 1936 he worked as chief book-keeper in the Kiev tram department.

[22] See Table 12; in real terms this represented a decline of about two-thirds.

[23] See *Materials* (1985), 219, 207.

[24] The following table shows the approximate amounts of direct tax on the private sector (million rubles):

	1928/29[a]		1929/30[b]	
	Estimate in budget	Actual	Estimate in budget	Actual
Industrial tax	198	170	176	144
Tax on excess profits	23	19	18	19
Income tax ('non-working incomes')	n.a.	72	107	83
Total	n.a.	261	301	246

[a] *Ob''yasnitel'naya zapiska . . . za 1928–1929* (1930), 25–32.

[b] *Otchet . . . za 1929–1930* (1931), ob. zapiska, 19–22.

million rubles was obtained from the group classified as 'personal activities'.[25]

The fate of those driven out of the private sector was recorded, albeit imperfectly and incompletely, in a survey conducted by Narkomfin in 1929/30 of 34,242 owners and co-owners of enterprises which ceased to operate in 1928/29.[26] The largest single group of those whose future occupation is known, 16 per cent of the total, became artisans of various kinds; only 5·4 per cent resumed private trade or private industrial activities; and only 3·7 per cent went to work in state and cooperative enterprises. But as many as 30 per cent of the total left their okrug altogether or could not be traced.[27] It may be presumed

[25] *Otchet . . . za 1929–1930* (1931), ob. zapiska, 20.

[26] FP, 7–8, 1930, 91–6; the survey covered 12 large towns and 17 okrugs, and included 31,538 of the approximately 136,000 private enterprises closed in 1928/29 (the last figure is estimated from Table 11 below).

[27] The following table has been compiled from FP, 7–8, 1930, 91–6, and from data in the archives reported in *Izmeneniya* (1979), 128–9 (Morozov):

Subsequent activity	No. of persons	% of total
Independent artisans	4169	12·2
Official industrial cooperatives	(925)	2·7
Independent industrial cooperatives	(274)	0·8
Izvozchiki (cab-men)	(103)	0·3
Resumed private trade or industry	1840	5·4
Employed in private enterprises	240	0·7
Employed by state or cooperative enterprises	1267	3·7
Casual labour	753	2·2
Agriculture	(2460)	7·2
Maintained by relatives	2914	8·5
Living off capital, renting rooms, etc.	3203	9·4
Imprisoned or exiled	1721	4·9[a]
Left okrug	8370	24·5
Not traced	(1300)	3·9
Illegal activity	(1160)	3·4
No definite occupation	(850)	2·5
Not clear [sic]	(1000)	2·9
Other	(1700)	4·9
Total	(34250)	100·0

The figures in brackets were estimated from the percentages by the present author.

[a] This category is listed as 'other' in the source, but this is the only item in the sub-table which could refer to prison and exile, which are said to be included in the total.

that many of these went to work in state industry, disguising their previous activity.[28]

The drive against the Nepmen reached its peak in January and February 1930, simultaneously with the eviction and exile of the kulaks in the countryside. In January 1930, a joint plenum of the Moscow party committee and control commission, inspired by the enthusiastic Moscow party secretary Bauman, resolved to extend the official formula about the kulaks to the Nepmen:

> The plenum of the Moscow committee and control commission points out that the whole party, and the Moscow regional organisation, are facing, as a most important political task proposed by the central committee, the elimination of the kulaks *and the new bourgeoisie as a whole* as a class in the Soviet state.[29]

This formulation was indignantly repudiated by the central party authorities. In his reply to Sverdlov University students on February 9, 1930, Stalin criticised 'certain of our organisations' which had made the mistake of 'trying to "supplement" the slogan of the elimination of the kulaks as a class with the slogan of the elimination of the urban bourgeoisie'. These organisations had forgotten the distinction between Nepmen, who did not have any serious influence on economic life because they had already been deprived of a production base, and the kulaks, whose production basis gave them a huge economic influence.[30] A few days later, on the instructions of the party central committee, the bureau of the Moscow party committee adopted a much more cautious formula, which was then approved by the Moscow committee as a whole:

> The plenum of the Moscow committee and control commission points out that the whole party, and the Moscow regional organisation, are facing, as a most important political task

---

[28] The spoon-manufacturer whose cooperative was closed down went to work in an engineering factory, where he eventually became a shock-worker (Interview No. 10).

[29] EZh, February 14, 1930 (my italics). For Bauman's similar role in collectivisation, see vol. 1, pp. 215, 262–3.

[30] *Soch.*, xii (1949), 186.

proposed by the central committee, the elimination of the kulaks as a class in the Soviet state, on the basis of comprehensive collectivisation and in conformity with the real participation of the mass of poor and middle peasants in kolkhoz construction.

It is also to continue the further squeezing out of the capitalist elements of the town on the basis of . . . systematic and even fuller taking-over of the market by state and cooperative trade.[31]

At the XVI party congress in July 1930 Bauman conceded that the original formula was a mistake in principle, and reiterated Stalin's statement of February 9. Bauman added that the practical effect of the original formula was harmful, as it had resulted in pressure on the petty trader and the artisan.[32]

The distinction between the Nepman and the independent individual producer or petty trader proved as difficult to maintain as the distinction between kulak and middle peasant. The general principle that artisan production should be encouraged was never abandoned. But throughout the 1920s the principle had been inhibited by the fear that the existence of individual producers, if not carefully regulated, would encourage the growth of capitalism. In the winter of 1929–30, with the growing scarcity of consumer goods and raw materials, the fear became paramount. The 1929/30 control figures, drafted in the autumn of 1929, reflected the prevailing atmosphere, noting that in 'connection with the narrowing of the legal sources of supply, artisan industry (private and bogus cooperatives) plays a growing role in supplying the private sector'; 'the private sector supplies scarce goods obtained via bagmen and various commission agents, buyers up and people who stand in queues'.[33] The vast majority of the private trading units which closed down in 1929 and 1930 were family enterprises or individuals working on their own. During the collectivisation drive of the winter of 1929–30, individual

[31] EZh, February 14, 1930; the resolution was adopted by the plenum 'by correspondence'. For the role of the central committee, see *XVI s"ezd* (1931), 214 (Bauman).

[32] *XVI s"ezd* (1931), 214. Bauman was dismissed from the post of Moscow party secretary in April (see vol. 1, pp. 279–80).

[33] *KTs . . . na 1929/30* (1930), 188–9.

artisans were frequently treated in practice as petty capitalists. At the time of the purge of Narkomfin in November 1929, a report to the party central control commission complained that artisans had paid insufficient tax;[34] in order to secure payment, their property, including their tools, was frequently removed.[35] At the height of the collectivisation drive, an article in the economic journal claimed that 'an increase in tendencies hostile to the Soviet system' could be observed among artisans and artisan cooperatives, and called for 'the elimination of the kulak as a class in the sphere of small-scale industry'. The article also reported with enthusiasm that state and cooperative trading organisations had ceased to supply credits and raw materials to individual artisans; this was described as 'a powerful and decisive blow against private-entrepreneurial economic initiative'.[36] Cases of the 'dekulakisation' of artisans were not infrequent.[37]

Strong pressure was exerted on individual artisans to join the cooperatives, and on independent cooperatives to join the official cooperative network. A resolution of the party central committee on February 16, 1930, called for the overfulfilment of the plan to recruit the artisans into cooperatives; the cooperatives should switch from supply and marketing activities to cooperation in production, and 'independent artels should be fully included in the system, cleansing them thoroughly from kulak–Nepman elements'.[38] The artisan cooperatives suffered the pressures of rapid industrialisation and collectivisation. Accounts written after the publication of Stalin's article 'Dizzy with Success' on March 2, 1930, complained that in the first weeks of 1930 many officials believed that previous party decisions in favour of the artisans were no longer effective; some local officials even thought that artisans should be eliminated altogether.[39] The presidium of Vesenkha decreed that large numbers of artisans working in the metal industry should be

[34] P, November 10, 1929 (Peters).

[35] P, April 2, 1930.

[36] EO, 2, 1930, 74–5 (Shiryaev).

[37] See, for example, *Istoriya industrializatsii* (Gor'kii, 1968), 121 (report of June 1930).

[38] SPR, vii, i (1930), 240; for an example of an independent cooperative which was dissolved as a result of penal taxation, see p. 99 above.

[39] P, May 6, 1930 (Lobov); I, September 6, 1930 (Shapiro).

transferred to the state-owned engineering factories; and, following an agreement between Narkomtrud and Vesenkha, members of artisan cooperatives were sent in teams (brigades) to major building sites.[40] Many artisan cooperatives in the towns did not receive ration cards for their members, who promptly left.[41]

In the countryside, particularly in the RSKs, artisan cooperatives as well as individual artisans were compulsorily assimilated into the kolkhozy. According to the chairman of the union of artisan cooperatives (Vsekopromsoyuz) 'numerous swoops were made against the industrial cooperatives', and their buildings and capital were sometimes seized. In a typical case, the kolkhoz chairman and the party secretary told the cooperative in their village that its members would be treated as counter-revolutionaries if they did not transfer it to the kolkhoz.[42] The results were sometimes disastrous. One report noted a general tendency to abolish the artisan cooperatives without replacing them by an alternative, as a result of which 'whole sectors of production have been denuded'.[43] Thus in Vyatka okrug 'all the artisans, who were incidentally all middle peasants, were "dekulakised" and sent away to timber cutting and logging'; as a result production ceased of cigarette cases and small wooden boxes, which were partly made for export.[44]

With the retreat from collectivisation in the spring of 1930, the status of the artisans was restored. According to one account, 'the liquidationist wave' against the artisan cooperatives began to recede with the publication of the central committee resolution of February 16.[45] But this resolution was in reality more in harmony with the spirit of uninhibited collectivisation than in conflict with it. While it called for an increase in artisan production, it also proposed very restrictively that artisan

---

[40] ZI, May 25, 1930 (editorial); PI, 5–6, 1931, 80; Buzlaeva (1969), 114. The dates of the decree and the agreement are not stated.

[41] Thus in Leningrad only 18,000 cards were issued as against the 48,000 planned (P, May 12, 1930 – report of session of STO Committee on Artisan Cooperatives).

[42] *XVI s"ezd* (1931), 629 (Beika).

[43] ZI, March 28, 1930; the process was described as 'de-artisanisation (raskustarivanie)', by analogy with 'dekulakisation (raskulachivanie)'.

[44] *Loc. cit.*; for similar examples from the Urals, Tula and Nizhnii-Novgorod see NPF, 11, 1930, 24 (Kh. Gurevich) and P, May 12, 1930.

[45] P, July 8, 1930, disk. listok 29 (E. Ivanov and A. Baulin).

cooperatives should concentrate primarily on semi-finished products for reworking by state industry, and should use locally-produced raw materials which were not in short supply; and it even suggested that the artisan cooperatives should draw on membership fees to a greater extent for their finance. After Stalin's article of March 2 and the subsequent central committee resolutions (see vol. 1, pp. 269–83), more serious efforts were made to revive the fortunes of the artisans. On April 21, an all-Union committee was established for the industrial cooperatives and the artisan industry.[46] The new committee, which was attached to STO, had a higher status than its predecessors, which were subordinate to Vesenkha or to the republican governments. On April 28, Vesenkha ruled that the transfer of artisan enterprises to state industry must cease.[47] On June 2, a Sovnarkom decree stressed the 'tremendous significance' of artisan industry and the industrial cooperatives, and criticised 'underestimation by some local authorities'. The decree sought to preserve the independence of the artisan cooperatives in rural areas, insisting that they should form part of the kolkhoz only when they were reworking agricultural raw materials or serving the needs of the kolkhoz; where artisan production predominated, the normal kolkhoz should be replaced by an industrial kolkhoz (promkolkhoz) which formed part of the artisan cooperative system.[48]

These measures did not fundamentally improve the position of the artisans. Spokesmen for the artisan cooperatives continued to complain that in the towns they were treated as part of the private capitalist sector, and not supplied with food rations, while in the countryside many kolkhozy and kolkhozsoyuzy underestimated the importance of artisan production.[49] Vesenkha frequently took over artisan cooperatives rather than working with them,[50] and continued to recruit metalworking artisans for the state engineering industry.[51] Sometime in 1930

---

[46] SZ, 1930, art. 281 (decree of STO); similar committees were to be established in the republics.

[47] SP VSNKh, 1929/30, art. 1313.

[48] SZ, 1930, art. 338.

[49] P, July 8, 1930, disk. listok 29 (Ivanov and Baulin).

[50] ZI, April 23, 1930 (report of sitting of Sovnarkom of the RSFSR).

[51] A Vesenkha report claimed that at least 155,000 out of 470,000 metalworkers could be retrained for the engineering industry (ZI, May 29, 1930); later Vesenkha clashed with Vsekopromsoyuz on this issue (ZI, July 30, 1930).

Narkomtrud and Vesenkha reached an agreement on 'directing cooperative artisan workers in brigades to the large new construction sites (Kuznetskstroi, Magnitostroi)'.[52] But, as in previous years, artisan production proved surprisingly resilient. According to official figures the net production of small-scale industry declined only slightly in 1930, and the total number of persons engaged in small-scale industry slightly increased (see p. 383 n. 31 below and Table 16). The importance of the cooperatives greatly increased in the course of 1929/30; the number of members of the Vsekopromsovet system increased from 1,183,000 on October 1, 1929, to 1,566,000 on October 1, 1930,[53] and the number of artisans who belonged to all kinds of cooperatives in the summer of 1930 amounted to some two million persons out of an estimated total of five million.[54]

Considerable efforts were made to reorganise the cooperatives into common workshops in the course of 1929/30. On October 1, 1930, the number of artisans in common workshops amounted to 774,000, as compared with 465,000 on October 1, 1929.[55] A substantial number of these were in workshops sufficiently large to be classified with census rather than small-scale industry.[56] According to one report, as much as three-quarters of all the production of industrial cooperatives came from the common workshops.[57] But, while the output per worker per year in the cooperative sector was much higher than in the individual sector, the productivity gap between cooperative and individual artisans narrowed with the entry of large numbers of artisans into the cooperatives. In 1928/29 21 per cent of artisans belonged to cooperatives and produced 44 per cent of gross turnover. But although 40 per cent of artisans belonged to cooperatives on October 1, 1930, the socialised sector, including small-scale

---

[52] PI, 5–6, 1931, 80.

[53] *Promyslovaya kooperatsiya* (1934), 9.

[54] *XVI s"ezd* (1931), 629 (Beika); I, September 6, 1930 (Shapiro).

[55] PI, 5–6, 1931, 73. These figures refer to the Vsekopromsovet system; about one million persons in all worked in common artisan workshops (*XVI s"ezd* (1931), 629 (Beika)).

[56] The average number of cooperative artisans employed in census industry in 1930 amounted to 292,000 as compared with 180,000 in 1929 (NPF, 23–4, 1930, 47–8); according to Beika, the total in census industry in the summer of 1930 had already reached 500,000 (*XVI s"ezd* (1931), 629).

[57] *XVI s"ezd* (1931), 629.

state enterprises, was responsible for only 61·2 per cent of the net output of small-scale industry in 1930.[58]

The socialist offensive was also directed against the only form of private foreign investment permitted in the Soviet Union, the concessions (which would nowadays be known as joint ventures). Concessions had never been an important instrument for the acquisition of foreign technology, and the fleeting attempt to encourage them in 1928 was undermined in advance by the abrogation of the Harriman manganese concession.[59] In December 1929, the OGPU raided the headquarters and local offices of the British-owned Lena Goldfields Co., the other concession of some industrial significance.[60] On April 18 Soviet employees of Lena Goldfields were put on trial for political spying and a 'diversionary act', and were sentenced to between 1 and 10 years.[61] After this, the company withdrew its employees and repudiated further responsibility; long wrangles about the financial settlement continued for many years.[62]

The action against Lena Goldfields formed part of a more general policy. In December 1929, Rykov, who launched the new decree in favour of concessions in 1928 (see pp. 63–4 above), brusquely announced at TsIK that 'the conditions for concessionaires are: work with your own money, don't rob us, and don't engage in counter-revolution'.[63] Counsels were evidently divided. In the economic newspaper a senior official concerned with industry in Rabkrin published a series of articles critical of the past behaviour of concessionaires but strongly insisting that concessions which invested substantially and were satisfied with reasonable profits 'have every chance to develop in the conditions of our infinite market with its huge demand'.[64] But in the same month a Politburo commission decided that the further existence of concessions contradicted

[58] *Materials* (1985), 156.

[59] See Carr, iii, i (1976), 90–1.

[60] For rival British and Soviet accounts of grievances see Woodward and Butler, eds., vii (1958), 58–9; Sutton (1971), 23–7, and *Dokumenty vneshnei politiki*, xiii (1967), 86–8, 250–2; I, June 3, 1930 (Gurevich, dated May 13).

[61] ZI, May 10, 1930; in the alleged 'diversionary act', carried out on August 31, 1929, a former prison warder and policeman who served under the White general Kolchak set the factory on fire.

[62] Woodward and Butler, eds., vii (1958), 58–9.

[63] *TsIK 2/V*, No. 1, 7.

[64] EZh, February 16, 23, 25, 1930 (Gurevich).

the tasks of socialist industrialisation.[65] On February 26 Litvinov told the German ambassador Dirksen that the concessions sector had 'become a negative factor slowing down and retarding the fulfilment of our five-year plan', though some concessions would continue temporarily.[66] By this time, one of the most famous concessions, the Moscow Industrial Co. of Armand Hammer, had asked to be bought out, on the grounds that it was unable to obtain from abroad the resources needed for further expansion.[67] The industrial newspaper published an interview with Hammer in which he agreed that the USSR had been 'completely reliable (loyal'nyi)' and criticised the foreign press for its attitude of 'financial boycott as a part of a general attack'.[68] This did not prevent *Pravda* from describing him as a 'cunning entrepreneur' who had offered large bonuses to buy the support of his workers and had won over the factory committee to his side.[69] Some concessions lingered on: 59 were operative in October 1929, and 24 still continued in March 1932.[70] But after the Lena Goldfields and Hammer incidents, concessions finally lost any remaining significance as a means of acquiring foreign technology.

(B) THE SPECIALISTS

In the last months of 1929, the drive against disloyal specialists and the efforts to train a new generation of loyal Soviet specialists were accelerated.[71] The November plenum of the party central committee, following a report by Kaganovich, condemned the 'social and political instability, neutrality and

[65] *Leninskii plan* (1969), 186.
[66] *Dokumenty vneshnei politiki*, xiii (1967), 112.
[67] ZI, February 28, March 14, 1930; Hammer applied to be bought out in December 1929 and agreement was reached on February 18.
[68] ZI, February 28, 1930.
[69] P, March 15, 1930; an earlier criticism of Hammer appeared in P, May 16, 1928.
[70] *Leninskii plan* (1969), 187. On February 28, 1930, shortly after the general decision hostile to concessions, *Ekonomicheskaya zhizn'* announced, perhaps as a sop to Dirksen, that a concession for the manufacture of 'Chlorodont' toothpaste had been agreed with Leo Werke, Dresden.
[71] For the earlier stages in the drive against the specialists, see pp. 61 and 91 above.

even hostility' of a section of the specialists, and declared that the training of new cadres, in spite of the 1928 reforms, 'completely failed to match up to the rate of industrialisation and socialist reconstruction of agriculture'. The resolution also stressed the urgency of promoting young graduates and former workers to 'positions of command'.[72]

The dangers to the regime presented by disloyal specialists formed a central theme of Kaganovich's report to the plenum.[73] He announced the discovery of 'a number of major cases of wrecking in our major industries'. In the metal group of industries Khrennikov and Zhdanov, responsible for technical leadership within Vesenkha, had both been exposed as wreckers, together with the key figures concerned with the metal industry in Gipromez and in the industrial section of Gosplan.[74] Kaganovich presented similar alarming revelations about other industries. He alleged that most of the wreckers were former factory owners and shareholders, and accused them of attempting to create 'continuous crises' in industry with the aim of restoring capitalism.[75] According to Kaganovich, the management of higher education was also unsatisfactory. The election of Rectors (Vice-Chancellors) and Deans of Faculties by the academic staff meant that 'people alien to us' predominated; election should accordingly be replaced by appointment.[76]

The charges of spying and sabotage, and of conspiracy to overthrow the Soviet regime, were accepted at face value by many party members and ordinary citizens; some foreign engineers working in the USSR were also persuaded that sabotage was widespread.[77] But at first such charges were

---

[72] *KPSS v rez.*, ii (1954), 632–42; for thorough accounts of the problem of the specialists in this period, see Fitzpatrick (1979), chs. 6, 9, and Lampert (1979), chs. 3–4.

[73] A 'shortened and reworked stenogram' of the report was published in B, 23–4, December 31, 1929, 50–71.

[74] *Ibid.* 50–1; the principal figures in Gosplan were Taube and Gartvan (see Carr and Davies (1969), 803).

[75] B, 23–4, December 31, 1929, 51–2; Khrennikov, Zhdanov, Taube and Gartvan were all managers and shareholders of iron and steel works before the revolution; however, Kaganovich later stated (p. 62) that only 29 per cent of those arrested in industry were former capitalists and landowners.

[76] *Ibid.* 56–7.

[77] Gnedin, who attended the Shakhty trial on behalf of Narkomindel, noted

regarded with great scepticism by many Soviet officials with a close knowledge of economic affairs, including party members.[78] There is of course no doubt that the more serious charges, and many of the lesser ones, were entirely fabricated.[79] They afforded a convenient means of personifying the lack of effort and lack of faith which the party leaders believed was the only major obstacle to the success of the industrialisation plans. Disorder and disruption in industry and other sectors of the economy were frequently attributed to deliberate sabotage by the specialists.[80]

But this is not the whole story. Behind the crudeness and brutality of the attacks on the bourgeois specialists lay a serious political issue. While some specialists had decided to cooperate fully with the Bolshevik regime in the 1920s, others remained hostile or at best neutral. A Soviet émigré who knew some of the mining engineers in Shakhty has described their luxurious parties and their bitter criticisms of the Soviet leaders.[81] The turn to rapid industrialisation and forced collectivisation was resisted by many specialists who had previously worked conscientiously with the authorities. Non-party officials in Gosplan, Vesenkha and the other economic commissariats, as well as many party officials, regarded the policies adopted after

---

in his reminiscences published in exile that, 'like most of us', he believed in the guilt of the accused (Gnedin (Amsterdam, 1977), 268–70). Rukeyser, an American engineer, claimed that the existence of 'a great deal of premeditated sabotage' seemed obvious to most US specialists with whom he discussed the matter (Rukeyser (1932), 233). See also pp. 409–10 below.

[78] See Lampert (1979), 44. Chicherin, People's Commissar for Foreign Affairs, asked Gnedin 'Why do you think they confessed? . . . Did they beat them? They beat them, beat them!' (Gnedin (Amsterdam, 1977), 271). The Menshevik journal in exile in a report from Moscow firmly attributed the confessions to persistent questioning and lack of sleep under a bright light which broke the nerves (SV (Paris), 24 (214), December 21, 1929, 14–16). See also pp. 340–1 below.

[79] See Lampert (1979), 43–4.

[80] See the quotations from Kaganovich and Kuibyshev in Lampert (1979), 94.

[81] Borodin (London [1955]), 62–5, 75–6; Baganov, the most prominent of them, called Stalin a 'great Khan', and expressed the wish that the leaders would tear each others' throats. On the political attitudes of the specialists, see Carr and Davies (1969), 580–1, and the more subtle discussion in Lampert (1979), 46–8.

1927 as foolish and dangerous, and, when they could, advised against them.[82]

For their part, the Soviet leaders resolutely determined to create a loyal and enthusiastic cadre of specialists and managers. As one Soviet writer put it, an engineer should be 'a representative of the Soviet state in the production-technical process'.[83] This was not simply a matter of securing their support for official policies. Russian engineers were regarded as suffering from a 'caste spirit', and as being too isolated, in outlook, training and work, from the practical problems of production. The leading Russian engineer Grum-Grzhimailo claimed that engineers merely directed others rather than doing the hard work themselves: during his whole life he had met only a few iron and steel engineers 'who work personally with a pencil; chemical experiments are equally rare'.[84] Russian engineers were frequently accused of being *beloruchki* – people who don't get their hands dirty. Littlepage, an American engineer who worked in the Soviet gold industry between 1928 and 1937, reported that at the beginning of his stay 'Russian engineering traditions tended to keep engineers and officials in good clothes and in their offices, well out of the dirty mine-shafts'. According to Littlepage, Serebrovsky, head of the Soviet gold industry, was astonished when he met a general mine superintendent in Alaska who wore digging clothes and sat down in them to eat with the miners.[85] The view that Russian engineers of the older generation were too theoretical in their approach and lacked practical experience was almost universally held by American engineers working in the Soviet Union.[86]

---

[82] Their point of view was well put by an émigré economist: 'They were undeniably hostile to the existing system, which was purely political in its tendencies. They could not possibly connive at such cruel measures as the raising of monstrous levies, the enforced collectivity, the 'Dekulakization' and others. They endeavoured to put a brake on these activities, relying for support on the Right Wing's disaffection. But in the communist state every dissenting opinion is branded as sabotage and hunted down' (Brutzkus (London, 1935), 233–4).

[83] *Front nauki i tekhniki*, 7–8, 1931, 7, *cit.* Lampert (1979), 47.

[84] *Predpriyatie*, 7, 1926, 38–9.

[85] Littlepage and Bess (London, 1939), 48–9.

[86] See Hoover, AER, Box 2, J. S. Ferguson ms, p. 6 (Kuznetskstroi), J. H. Gillis ms, p. 5 (non-ferrous metals), L. M. Banks ms, p. 5 (Ridder combine); Box 3, F. R. Harris ms, p. 6 (waterways and shipbuilding).

Some Americans saw Russian engineers as 'permeated with the European custom and tradition'.[87] An engineer who worked in Gipromez from 1929–33 plausibly argued that the experience of the older engineers was 'almost entirely confined to German or Continental practice', which was quite different from the American tradition of production in large quantities with simple and rugged equipment, which he saw as the way forward for the Soviet Union.[88] The new training programmes for Soviet specialists set out to overcome these deficiencies. The plenum of the party central committee in November 1929 called for a substantial increase in production practice, on a 'sandwich' basis, and, following the transfer of technical institutes to the control of Vesenkha, for improved 'organic links' between industry and higher education.[89]

At the TsIK session in December 1929, Krzhizhanovsky, widely respected among non-party specialists, firmly declared that 'there can be no apoliticism in our country' and condemned the 'marsh' as amounting to wrecking. He announced a threatening new slogan, adapted from Christ's declaration that 'He that is not with me is against me' (Lk. 11.23; but see Lk. 9.50):

> *Who is not with us is against us.*[90]

In 1930, the ferocity of the campaign against bourgeois specialists greatly increased. An unsigned feature article in the industrial newspaper condemned 'neutrality' on the part of many engineers, declaring that the old formula:

> '*Rely on the Soviet engineer, make an agreement with those that are neutral, declare war on the wreckers*'

should now give way to

> '*Rely on the Soviet engineer, declare war on neutralism, destroy the wreckers*'.[91]

[87] Hoover, AER, Box 3, Harris ms, p. 6.
[88] Hoover, AER, Box 3, W. S. Orr ms, pp. xi–xii.
[89] *KPSS v rez.*, ii (1954), 635–6; see also Fitzpatrick (1979), 192–3.
[90] *TsIK 2/V*, No. 1, 6. The slogan was repeated as the main heading to a speech by Kuibyshev to Leningrad engineers, published in ZI, February 2, 1930 (speech of January 28).
[91] ZI, February 16, 1930.

This new formula reflected a very substantial shift in attitude. In the 1920s, the mass of the specialists were treated as analogous to the middle peasantry: Bolshevik policy had shifted from 'neutralising' them in the first phases of the October revolution to a policy of winning them over to a stable alliance from 1919 onwards. But the new formula of 1930 treated the mass of the specialists hardly more favourably than the bourgeoisie. The bourgeoisie, in the Bolshevik concept, was 'neutralised' during the 1905 revolution, but treated as a hostile class from 1917 onwards.[92]

Rykov, who had strongly resisted the campaign against the bourgeois specialists at the time of the Shakhty trial, now came out in favour of the harsher approach. He accused the 'largest group' of old engineers and technicians of a mere formal loyalty to the Soviet regime. Insisting that 'neutrality in relation to us is neutrality or semi-sympathy in relation to our enemies', he bluntly insisted that the old specialists must transform themselves or be 'crushed by the wheel of history'. He claimed that their attitudes had facilitated large-scale acts of wrecking, and the core of his speech was an extensive presentation of OGPU evidence about wrecking. He praised the OGPU officials for their diligence, and firmly rejected the 'numerous complaints' he had received about the arrests of specialists:

We gave the OGPU the opposite advice – arrest everyone who is caught wrecking. I am completely unable to understand how honest people can be worried about themselves when a thief or murderer is arrested.

He blithely assured the assembled engineers that evidence was always cross-checked in detail so that the investigating agencies could act with confidence.[93] In retrospect, these passages are redolent with irony: seven years later it was the turn of Rykov to be destroyed by the wheel of history after his public trial on similar charges.

The sword of the OGPU hacked into every profession and every branch of the economy. In the Academy of Sciences,

---

[92] On these shifts in policy, see Stalin, *Soch.*, ix (1948), 205–20, 269–81 (letters of April and May 1927).

[93] ZI, February 20, 1930 (speech of February 16).

prominent historians were accused of preparing a coup d'état; the new monarchist government, headed by Platonov and Tarlé, would rely on the network of regional studies' groups for their local government. The germ of truth in these remarkable revelations seems to be that some of those arrested had remained monarchists by conviction throughout the vicissitudes of revolution and recovery, and did not disguise their views.[94] In the Ukraine, a 'Union for the Liberation of the Ukraine' was accused of attempting to establish an independent Ukrainian bourgeois state; 45 members of the alleged Union were put on trial in March 1930. According to the official account, the Ukrainian Academy of Sciences acted as the general staff of the organisation and its research institutes acted as auxiliaries.[95] In industry, the extensive arrests announced by Molotov in September 1929 (see p. 91 above) were followed by secret trials and further arrests. In October 1929, five former generals working in war industry were found guilty of spying and wrecking, and sentenced to death; their associates were imprisoned in concentration camps.[96] In February 1930, Krzhizhanovsky in two lengthy articles in *Pravda* reported extensive spying and wrecking in both capital and consumer goods industries, as well as in military industry and transport;[97] in June, Kirov claimed that 'there is no industry in Leningrad in which our GPU agencies did not find wrecking'.[98]

The number of specialists arrested during 1929 and 1930 is not precisely known. According to a Soviet account, 'no more than 2–3,000 were wreckers' out of some 30,000 old engineers;[99] according to the émigré Menshevik journal, over 7,000 out of

[94] Extensive accounts of these cases appear in *Pamyat'* (Paris), iii (1980), 474–84 ('A. Rostov'), iv (1981), 58–109 (Antsiperov); see also Barber (1981), 40–1, and Graham (1967), 121–30. The accused were arrested in January 1930 and sentenced to between three and ten years' imprisonment on February 10, 1931; Platonov died in exile in November 1931, but Tarlé later became prominent as a patriotic historian of the resistance to Napoleon. (Graham misdates the arrests as occurring in November 1930–February 1931 rather than at the beginning of 1930.)

[95] P, November 22, 1929 (statement by Ukrainian GPU): SGRP, 5–6, 1930, 272–3; *Dokumenty vneshnei politiki*, xiii (1967), 147, 788. For the alleged monarchist organisation in the North Caucasus, see P, October 25, 1929.

[96] P, October 20, 1929.

[97] P, February 12, 13, 1930.

[98] Kirov (1930), 13. See, however, p. 340 below.

[99] Trifonov (1960), 160–1.

35,000 engineers had been arrested by the spring of 1931.[100]
Some industries were particularly badly hit: thus half of all
engineering and technical workers in the Donbass were arrested
by 1931.[101] The effects of the campaign spread far beyond the
individuals who were arrested. While the proportion of
specialists occupying higher posts who were arrested was
particularly high, many cases were also reported of the arrest of
factory engineers. Members of research institutes and of local
studies' groups were arrested as well as senior scientific
administrators.[102] Every professional person must have been
acquainted with colleagues who were arrested.

The activities of the OGPU were accompanied by a systematic
purge of state, governmental and other public organisations.
The purge announced at the XVI party conference in April
1929 (see pp. 61–2 above), was directed towards the removal
from office of bureaucratic and degenerate officials, and those who
'solidarised' with Nepmen or kulaks, as well as those who were
outright saboteurs and wreckers. The purge was carried out by
Rabkrin, with the support of activists both from the institutions
being examined and from outside.[103] Those deemed to be
inadequate for their office were divided into four categories:
Category I, the worst offenders, were permanently barred from
working in the Soviet service; milder offenders were merely
demoted.

The purge campaign started slowly. It got seriously under
way in the autumn of 1929 in the financial and agricultural
agencies; here hostility to the policies of the socialist offensive
was most pervasive. It was extended to Vesenkha and
Narkomtrud in March 1930. A later Rabkrin report complained
that, owing to the reluctance of the staff, including party
members, to participate in the purge process, '*big pushes from
outside*' were needed.[104] Together with the staff of Rabkrin,
teams of factory activists investigated the views and activities of
governmental personnel; Elektrozavod was appointed 'patron
(shef)' of Narkomfin, and the AMO vehicle factory of Vesenkha.
In all 35,000 workers and 25,000 peasants participated in

[100] SV (Paris), 6–7 (244–5), April 3, 1931, 19.
[101] Bailes (1978), 150, citing a Soviet source.
[102] See sources cited on p. 116, n. 94 above.
[103] *KPSS v rez.*, ii (1954), 594–5; see also Carr (1971), 310.
[104] *Chistka* (1930), 8–9.

running the purge; according to the Rabkrin report, 'only the workers' brigades *were capable of and succeeded* in "loosening the tongues" of the officials'.[105] Following the purge of Narkomfin, a preliminary report from Rabkrin strongly criticised the whole work of its planning and tax departments, complaining that they had favoured the private sector; 11 per cent of the central staff were dismissed.[106] Similar purges were undertaken in every locality.[107] In every unit, individual reports (kharakteristiki) were prepared on senior personnel; the purge commissions also received and adjudicated on denunciations and complaints from the staff.[108] By June 1930, 454,000 of the two million members of administrative staffs had been investigated; 51,000 were dismissed.[109] By mid-1931 the number investigated had risen to 1·6 million, of whom some 11 per cent were dismissed.[110] The percentage dismissed varied from 8·6 per cent in the central staff of Vesenkha to 14·6 per cent in Narkomfin and as many as 20·2 per cent in Narkomput'.[111]

The campaign to force the specialists to support official policies without reservation was pursued in every government department. During the 1920s a strong tradition had been established among Soviet party and non-party intellectuals, including economists and planners, that they should refrain from political invective in their discussions, in the interests of freedom of debate. At a discussion in the Communist Academy in January 1926, a speaker who attacked his opponents on

---

[105] *Ibid.* 9.

[106] P, November 10, 1929 (report by Peters to V Plenum of central control commission).

[107] See, for example, the report on the Dnepropetrovsk okrug in P, December 4, 1929.

[108] In the research institute for vehicle- and aircraft engines, NAMI, only two out of thirty senior staff were party members; only three of the thirty were declared to be 'more or less alien', five were classified as belonging to the 'marsh', 22 as satisfactory. Members of staff were denounced for supporting the Whites during the Civil War, for having owned a pre-revolutionary car-hire firm, and for being related to a high official in the tsarist Ministry of War; a party member was accused of extreme rudeness by a member of the Komsomol. (See TsGANKh, 7620/1/20.)

[109] *XVI s"ezd* (1931), 316 (Ordzhonikidze); 11,000 of those dismissed were placed in Category I.

[110] *Za tempy, kachestvo i proverku*, 6–7, 1931, 13. I am grateful to Dr. E. A. Rees for this reference.

[111] *Chistka* (1930), 22.

political grounds met with vocal disapproval.[112] Even in 1928 and 1929 non-party specialists displayed considerable frankness in expressing their opinions in governmental agencies. But this tradition was rapidly eroded. At the beginning of 1929 Strumilin made his revealing comment that specialists 'are already admitting in the corridors that they prefer to stand up for high rates of expansion rather than to sit in jail for low ones'.[113] In his speech at the TsIK session in December 1929, Krzhizhanovsky frankly declared that, at a time when the fate of the whole world depended on Soviet economic success, all economic activity must also be seen as political activity. 'Every economic manager must understand that he is also a politician'; groups of specialists could not act as 'a kind of special little wedge in this great construction', taking the attitude that 'they are doing their job but don't interfere in politics'.[114]

At the end of 1929 a particularly vigorous campaign of denunciation was launched against the principal non-party officials in Gosplan. Even at this late date Gosplan was intellectually dominated by the ex-Mensheviks who had occupied senior positions on its staff since the early 1920s, including Groman and Bazarov. A few prominent party members acted as a powerful counter-weight: Krzhizhanovsky as chairman, Strumilin as a deputy chairman, and more junior figures such as Vaisberg. But even in April 1929 400 of the 500 staff were not party members.[115] In 1925–7 Gosplan led the campaign for an increase in the rate of industrialisation; but in 1928 and 1929 first the key non-party officials and then even Strumilin, an enthusiastic advocate of purposive planning, resisted the higher five-year plan targets proposed by Vesenkha.[116] In the course of 1929, a number of junior and some senior Gosplan officials were arrested on charges of wrecking. Simultaneously the views of the key non-party Gosplan officials were strongly attacked. The denunciation of Groman for his pessimistic but accurate forecast of the 1929

---

[112] VKA, xv (1926), 187–91; the offending speaker was Motylev; Pashukanis was reproved for a similar offence by Preobrazhensky, amid applause (pp. 167–72, 232).

[113] See Carr and Davies (1969), 886.

[114] *TsIK 2/V*, No. 1, 6.

[115] Carr and Davies (1969), 803.

[116] Carr and Davies (1969), 874–86.

harvest (see vol. 1, pp. 64–7, 176–7) was followed by two lengthy and widely reported meetings of Gosplan specialists at which non-party officials were denounced by their party colleagues. At the first meeting, on December 15, a report from Vaisberg denounced Groman's 'geneticism' as *'objectively justifying the necessity of returning to pre-war class relations'.*[117] The basis for this specious charge was evidently Groman's view that if industrial production increased, its prices would fall, so that the ratio of marketed agricultural to marketed industrial production, measured in current prices, would remain at the pre-war figure of 63:37.[118] Vaisberg also accused Bazarov, another well-known non-party specialist in Gosplan, of denying that it was possible to catch up the capitalist countries, and of wanting to make the USSR dependent on international capital. Here Vaisberg was distorting Bazarov's view that investment should be concentrated on industries such as textiles in which mass production would give high returns.[119] The views of Groman and Bazarov were certainly incompatible with the Bolshevik goal of rapidly overtaking the advanced countries; they advocated a slower pace of industrialisation, more limited in scope. But Vaisberg's interpretation of them was a political smear. Strumilin, no doubt uneasy at the crudeness of Vaisberg's charges, more honestly admitted that *'it is not a matter of the fine points of the theoretical dispute'* but of *'the scepticism of these people which brought tremendous harm to planning work'*; Groman and his colleagues were waging an *'ideological struggle within Gosplan, which must be brought to an end'*. At a second meeting, on December 24, the pressure on the recalcitrant non-party officials increased. Grin'ko announced that 'a long list of wreckers' had been exposed in Gosplan, while Krylenko, prosecutor at the Shakhty trial and at the future Industrial Party trial, demanded that the struggle against wrecking should not be left to the OGPU but actively supported by the general public.[120]

[117] EZh, December 18, 1929.

[118] For Groman's classic 1925 article, see Carr (1958), 495–6; it assumed no major change in fixed capital. In P, September 20, 1929, Groman defended his 'law', merely conceding that the ratio had now shifted to 65:35 (EZh, November 13, 1929; this seems to have been his last published article). For Vaisberg's previous role, see Carr and Davies (1969), 792, 796, 884.

[119] For Bazarov's view, see Carr and Davies (1969), 403.

[120] EZh, December 26, 1929. These anti-specialist measures were separate from the Rabkrin purge of Gosplan, which was undertaken as late as January

Persistent harassment and prosecution silenced the critical voices of the bourgeois specialists. But mere silence was also treated as a hostile act, so many specialists were induced to publicly renounce their previous views. Vainshtein, in a letter to Mikoyan dated December 18, 1929, declared that he had 'to a considerable extent' abandoned the position he adopted in 1927, and had 'at present no really substantial disagreements with the policy of industrialisation being carried out by the party'; he would devote himself to implementing the general line.[121] Kafengauz, prominent statistician in Vesenkha, declared in the industrial newspapers that he fully supported the policy of industrialisation as expressed in the latest drafts of the five-year plan.[122] But such declarations were not enough. In response to his letter, Vainshtein was urged to denounce 'Kondratievshchina' as the 'ideology of the restoration of capitalism'.[123] In spite of their avowals, both Vainshtein and Kafengauz were arrested.[124]

These developments broke the resistance of the bourgeois specialists. But their long-term effect was more insidious. The bounds of freedom of discussion were considerably narrowed both within government and in the press. Criticism of official policies, even on minor matters, became more hazardous. For the old specialists, caution and acquiescence were much safer than the exercise of initiative.[125] The consequence for economic discussions, distinguished in the 1920s by their wide scope and their frankness, was disastrous. In the spring of 1930 the range

---

1931 with the support of the Komsomol (NPF, 17–18, 1930, 64, 66–7 – Priduvalov).

[121] VT, 1, 1930, 126–7; Vainshtein had been transferred from the Conjuncture Institute of Narkomfin to the Institute of the Monopoly of Foreign Trade, which formed part of Mikoyan's commissariat. Such statements cannot of course be taken at face value. When I met Vainshtein in 1963, he was vehemently critical of the whole line of policy pursued from 1928 onwards – 'the whole intelligentsia of Moscow and Leningrad was against it', he assured me.

[122] ZI, April 4, 1930; an article *ibid.* March 27, 1930, criticised his anti-Bolshevik newspaper articles published in 1918.

[123] VT, 1, 1930, 127 (note by editors of the journal).

[124] Vainshtein spent the years between 1930 and 1955 in custody or in exile, with a short interval in the mid-1930s; for part of this time he worked as a minor planning official in Siberia.

[125] See Lampert (1979), 96–7.

of economic publications was very greatly reduced. The daily economic newspaper, *Ekonomicheskaya zhizn'*, ceased to be a general economic newspaper on the ostensible grounds that this function was performed by the agricultural and industrial newspapers, and responsibility for it was transferred from STO of the USSR and the Economic Council of the RSFSR to the three commissariats of trade, transport and finance.[126] Shortly afterwards, one of the major monthly economic journals, *Ekonomicheskoe obozrenie*, and the two main statistical journals, *Vestnik statistiki* and *Statisticheskoe obozrenie*, merged with the Gosplan journal.[127] Henceforth the amount of published statistical material was greatly reduced, and the treatment of general economic issues tended to be much more superficial. Discussion was truncated. Thus in a striking but characteristic example an editorial on the XVI party congress in the Gosplan journal was denounced in the following issue by its editorial board on the grounds that 'instead of evaluating the Rights as an agency of the kulaks in the party, their position is merely characterised as "cowardly doubts" and "theoretical shortsightedness"'. The principal editor was forthwith dismissed.[128]

Even in 1930, cautious attempts were still made to limit the effects of the anti-specialist campaign. In February, the industrial newspaper criticised the slandering of honest specialists, citing the rival economic newspaper for an example of this error.[129] In June, the procurator of the People's Commissariat of Justice of the RSFSR, after examining recent cases of the prosecution of specialists and managers, commented that '*criminal prosecution is often started without sufficient justification against personnel who are valuable and necessary to production*'; he was supported by Krylenko.[130]

Despondency and fear among the old specialists contrasted

[126] See EZh, February 22, 1930; Vaisberg replaced Svetlov as editor. The new arrangements came into effect on March 1.

[127] See EO, 3, 1930, 2, and PKh, 5, 1930, 3.

[128] PKh, 6, 1930, 5–11, and 7–8, 1930, 4; Kovalevskii (principal editor) was replaced by Shakhnovskaya; Gatovskii, Kviring and Maimin were added to the editorial board (compare the title pages of nos. 6 and 7–8, 1930).

[129] ZI, February 16, 1930.

[130] ZI, June 11, 14, 1930; this did not of course include cases handled by the OGPU, which were sacrosanct.

sharply with the mood of elation and enthusiasm among many of the supporters of the programme of rapid industrialisation. During 1929 and 1930, with the demotion or arrest of many of the old specialists, the rate of promotion of young Soviet-trained specialists or 'practicals' increased. At the higher level, perhaps the most famous appointment in 1930 was that of Zavenyagin, who became head of Gipromez two days after graduating from the Moscow Mining Academy.[131] But this was only the start of what later became a major social transformation. Even the accelerated completion of courses in higher education establishments under Vesenkha made available only 3,166 new graduates in October 1929–March 1930 as compared with 1,282 in 1928/29.[132] This supply of inexperienced graduates was insufficient to replace the old specialists who had been removed, and could not begin to meet the increased requirements of the five-year plan, particularly in the new industries.

In these circumstances the November 1929 plenum of the party central committee stressed even more strongly than previously that 'the maximum utilisation of foreign technical assistance and foreign specialists must be expanded on an even wider scale'.[133] The number of foreign personnel employed increased from 884 in November 1928 to an estimated 2,950 in 1929/30.[134] Foreign engineers were employed on almost every major project of civilian industry and in almost every new factory; in major new factories, such as the Stalingrad tractor works, foreign foremen and skilled workers helped to train the Soviet workers.

Soviet engineers and officials were expected to learn more advanced European and American technology from their foreign colleagues, and were warned that resources must not be wasted

[131] Abramov (2nd edn, 1978), 260–1; *Novyi mir*, 1, 1967, 18 (Emel'yanov). Zavenyagin (1901–56) later occupied a series of posts in heavy industry, including director of the Magnitogorsk works; from 1938 he was head of the non-ferrous metal project at Noril'sk, largely carried out by forced labour (Solzhenitsyn, ii (London, 1976), 262, 517, 673); in 1955 he was appointed a deputy chairman of the Council of Ministers of the USSR.

[132] P, May 11, 1930 (D. Petrovskii).

[133] *KPSS v rez.*, ii (1954), 628.

[134] Kolomenskii (1930), 17; *Memorandum* (Birmingham), 4 (February 1932), 11; the latter figure excludes foreign workers not under contract.

on looking for 'Americas' which had already been discovered.[135] But this willingness to learn technology from the West was combined with a strong conviction that the Soviet political and economic system was superior, and would outpace its capitalist rivals. For their part most foreign engineers shared the prejudices of their class and generation. They were normally hostile to or unsympathetic with socialism in any form, and very impatient with its Soviet version. They were often racially prejudiced. In a typical comment, an American engineer complained in his unpublished memoirs that the head of Magnitostroi was a Jew surrounded by engineers who were Jews 'almost to a man', and was succeeded by another Jew who brought in his own followers.[136] Nevertheless foreign engineers were able to distance themselves from Soviet politics and to offer technical judgments with little fear of persecution. They were also much more free than their Soviet colleagues to object to the tight building schedules which the Soviet authorities endeavoured to impose in every industry. As seen through the eyes of almost all the American engineers, the older Russian engineers displayed some reluctance to learn from them and were fearful of exercising initiative; in contrast, the young engineers, while eager to learn from foreign experience, pressed forward their own ideas into areas where they lacked experience.[137]

With these contrasting outlooks and approaches, the collaboration was often placed under great strain. Soviet relations with the McKee Co., which worked on the design and construction of Magnitostroi, were particularly chequered. Stuck, one of their principal engineers, complained that the main reason for poor progress was 'inexperienced engineers trying to do something about which they knew but little',[138] while Shmidt, the Soviet head of Magnitostroi, bitterly commented about McKee and Co. that 'all we got from them was that our technical thought was stimulated to build large

---

[135] Kolomenskii (1930), 5–6, who even compared existing Soviet industry with an 'old broken primus' which had been repaired but now needed to be replaced. See also Carr and Davies (1969), 413–15.
[136] Hoover, AER, Box 4, R. W. Stuck ms, p. 39.
[137] See the judicious comments in Hoover, AER, Box 3, Orr ms, p. v.
[138] Hoover, AER, Box 4, R. W. Stuck ms, p. 29.

blast furnaces'.[139] At other projects relations were far less tense. In their memoirs of Kuznetskstroi, Frankfurt, the head of the construction, and Bardin, the chief engineer, criticised the leisurely approach of the American engineers, and complained that the Freyn Engineering Corporation sent 'second-grade personnel'; but they nevertheless acknowledged their significant role in Soviet technological development.[140] On two public occasions in 1930, Stalin explicitly acknowledged the important role played by foreign engineers. In June 1930, in a message to the newly-opened Rostov agricultural engineering works he thanked 'all those foreign specialists – engineers and technicians – who have helped in the construction of Sel'mashstroi'; and in a similar message to the Stalingrad tractor factory he thanked 'our teachers in technology, the American specialists and technicians'.[141] (On foreign specialists see also pp. 216–18 below.)

(c) THE WORKERS

Even on the broadest definition, the Soviet working class in 1929–30 was a small segment of the total population. In 1929 the total number of persons employed in 'productive activities', primarily industry, building and transport, amounted to some six millions, and of these perhaps $4^1/_2$ million were manual workers. A further $3^1/_2$ million persons were employed in trade, banking, social and cultural services, administration and other activities officially classed as 'non-productive'; only a small proportion of these were engaged in manual labour.[142] Even on the widest Soviet definition of the 'proletariat', which included all wage labour – manual, clerical, professional and managerial –

---

[139] *Slovo o Magnitke* (1979), 40; for Gugel's criticism of Stuck's high-handedness, see *ibid.* 94. For an even sharper conflict in the asbestos industry, which ended in litigation, see the rival accounts by the American consultant Rukeyser (1932), *passim*, and the head of the trust Paramanov (2nd edn, 1970), 266–73.

[140] Bardin (Novosibirsk, 1936), 126–9; Frankfurt (1935), 131.

[141] Shtikh (1931), 22 (dated June 16); P, June 18, 1930 (dated June 17). These phrases are omitted in the version published in *Soch.*, xii (1949), 233, 234; the extent of Soviet acknowledgement of foreign technological assistance in the early 1930s has varied considerably in successive publications.

[142] See Table 14(a) and (b), and further data in *Nar. kh.* (1932), 410–11, 416–17, 465, 470–1; the number of manual workers employed on the railways, out of a total of about one million, has not been available.

the total hired labour force in 1928/29 amounted to only about ten million persons out of a total active population of over 60 million persons.[143]

The increase in employed labour in the single year 1930 exceeded all expectations. The optimum variant of the five-year plan approved in the spring of 1929 envisaged an increase from 9·7 million persons in 1928/29 to 12·9 millions in 1932/33.[144] In fact, employed labour already reached 12·3 millions as early as 1930; employment in industry and transport already equalled the plan for 1932/33 (see Table 14(a)). The total number of persons employed in census industry increased from 3·61 millions on January 1, 1930, to 4·96 millions on January 1, 1931, an increase of 37·6 per cent in a single year (see Table 15(a)). In 1930 the average increase per quarter in the number of industrial workers equalled the total increase in the whole of 1929 (see Table 15(b)). The expansion of employment in capital construction was even more dramatic, rising by 76·8 per cent.[145]

The increase in non-agricultural employment by over $2^1/_2$ million persons in a single year, as compared with a mere $1^1/_4$ millions in the previous two years, transformed the situation of urban labour. As the natural wastage from the employed labour force was approximately 500,000 per year, the total addition to the labour force in 1930 amounted to three million persons, nearly a quarter of the total.[146] Unemployment, expected to continue throughout the first five-year plan, was almost completely absorbed by the autumn of 1930. The composition of the labour force began to change significantly. Between January 1, 1930, and January 1, 1931, the number of industrial workers aged 22 or less increased from 24·7 to 32·8 per cent of the total, and the number of female workers from 28·4 to 29·9

---

[143] See Table 14. The figure for 'hired labour' (the employed labour force), here and elsewhere in this book, excludes agriculture and forestry unless otherwise stated. The active population is estimated as 63·9 million in December 1926 in Wheatcroft (1982), 13, using the definition of the 1939 census.

[144] *Pyatiletnii plan*, ii, i (1930), 206–7; these figures are annual averages.

[145] See Table 17; the seasonal peak was 2,116,000, and the annual average 1,623,000. The five-year plan anticipated that the number employed in building would amount to 1,662,000 in 1931/32 and 1,883,000 in 1932/33 as compared with 796,000 in 1928/29.

[146] For an estimate of natural wastage, see Vdovin and Drobizhev (1976), 109.

per cent.[147] According to a Soviet estimate, the number of persons in all state employment who had been employed in any capacity for less than one year also increased from 12·7 per cent in 1929 to 23·5 per cent in 1930.[148] There was no increase in 1930 in the percentage of industrial workers recruited from the countryside. As in the later 1920s, about half the new workers in industry came from previous agricultural occupations, while the other half came from school-leavers (the second largest group), housewives, domestic workers and the unemployed.[149] The percentage recruited from agriculture varied widely between industries, from about 30 per cent in cotton textiles and electrical engineering to nearly 90 per cent among permanent workers in the peat industry, but did not increase substantially in any industry in 1930. However, the proportion of new workers who were of peasant social origin (i.e. whose fathers were peasants) rose considerably. And in the building industry the proportion of ex-peasant workers, already high in the mid-1920s, increased particularly sharply.

Simultaneously with the increased recruitment of young and inexperienced workers into industry, the labour force at existing factories was further diluted in several significant ways. The promotion of politically active workers to posts of responsibility had taken place ever since the revolution, but in 1929–30 the proletarianisation of the state administration was pressed forward more rapidly than at any time since the Civil War. Other experienced workers were transferred from established factories to the new factories such as the Stalingrad tractor factory and Rostsel'mash, which were completed in the summer

---

[147] *Sots. str.* (1934), 344–5; these figures are for workers and apprentices in large-scale industry.
[148] Vdovin and Drobizhev (1976), 112–13; no source is given; according to the authors, the percentage further increased to 27·6 per cent 'at the beginning of 1931', but this seems to be an error as their underlying data are in terms of the annual average. These data cover all employment, including about two million persons employed in agriculture (mainly sovkhozy) and forestry, and so are not strictly comparable with our figures for non-agricultural employment.
[149] According to a census of trade union members carried out in 1932–3, of those new recruits still remaining in industry at that time, the percentage coming from agriculture was 54 in 1926–7, 49·6 in 1928–9 and 49·4 in 1930 (estimated from data in *Profsoyuznaya perepis', 1932–1933*, i (1934), 94–155). The survey excluded miners, who were particularly closely linked with agriculture.

of 1930. To the requirements of industry was added the pressing need to transfer active workers to the countryside to support collectivisation and the food collections. Comprehensive figures for these transfers are not available. But from Leningrad alone 13,000 party and non-party activists were transferred to the countryside between March 1929 and May 1930, in addition to a substantial number of temporary workers' brigades.[150]

The unfavourable consequence of the recruitment of new workers and transfers of established workers for the political consciousness of the working class was countered by intensive efforts to provide political education for the remaining workers, and by the recruitment of large numbers of shop-floor workers to the party (see pp. 135–7 below). Simultaneously the dilution of skills was countered by radical measures to train new workers and improve the skills of the remainder. 'The possibilities of the labour market as a source of skilled labour,' Gosplan declared in the control figures for 1929/30, 'are as a rule almost exhausted at present, and we must meet the inevitable shortage of mass cadres by shock and extraordinary measures.'[151] A drive was launched to achieve universal elementary education, and the number attending technical colleges (technicums) and factory apprenticeship schools (FZU) was greatly expanded.[152] The number of apprentices in census industry alone, including both the pupils of FZU and those being trained on the job, increased from 136,000 on January 1, 1930, to 353,000 on January 1, 1931.[153] As in higher education (see p. 114 above), the severely practical was strongly emphasised: in the summer of 1930 most upper forms of secondary schools were closed down in order to make way for technicums. Training schemes for unemployed

---

[150]   Gooderham (1983), i, 22–3.

[151]   *KTs . . . na 1929/30* (1930), 245.

[152]   The expansion was as follows (thousand pupils):

	1928/29	1929/30	1930/31
Elementary and secondary	12075	13504	17770
Technicums	208	236	594
FZU, etc.	273	323	585

(*Nar. kh.* (1932), 507–19; these figures are for the school year beginning September 1). For these developments, see Fitzpatrick (1979), chs. 7–9.

[153]   *Trud* (1932), 17; these figures are included in the total figures for industrial employment above.

workers also expanded rapidly in 1930.[154] In addition to various forms of formal industrial training, many workers continued to be trained solely on the job.[155]

This larger and less experienced labour force was confronted with an economic and social environment which was fundamentally different from that of the 1920s. Since 1924 the authorities had sought to improve efficiency and discipline through a centrally-organised drive for higher productivity and lower costs. But in the mid-1920s the productivity drive was accompanied by a more or less continuous improvement in the standard of living. From 1928 onwards the pressures for improved discipline further increased, but simultaneously urban living standards declined. Although official ideology insisted that real incomes were rising (see pp. 308–9 below), official statistics admitted that consumption per head by the non-agricultural population had declined slightly in 1930.[156] The rationing system protected industrial and other manual workers from the worst effects of the goods shortages, but even the official figures show a slight decline in the food consumption of manual workers.[157]

Simultaneously with the decline in living standards, the rapid expansion of the industrial economy confronted the authorities with an unexpected development. With the diminution of urban unemployment and the continued expansion of the labour force, all kinds of skilled and semi-skilled labour became scarce, and this provided the working class – in spite of the weakness of the trade unions – with an unexpected source of economic strength. Henceforth managers were anxious to retain labour, and unwilling to discharge all but the most incompetent workers. In the second half of the 1920s, with the extension of the maximum period of temporary employment from 2–4 weeks to 2–4 months,

[154] 55,000 unemployed were trained in 1928/29 and 336,000 in 1929/30 (*Industrializatsiya, 1929–1932* (1970), 572–3).

[155] Even on January 1, 1931, at the height of the campaign to base apprenticeship on FZU and other forms of formal training, 95,000 industrial apprentices (26·8 per cent of all industrial apprentices) were being trained on the job ('individual and brigade apprenticeship') as compared with 66,000 (48·2 per cent) on January 1, 1930 (percentages from *Nar. kh.* (1932), 438–41, applied to absolute figures, *ibid.* 424–9).

[156] *Materials* (1985), 204; these figures certainly underestimate the decline.

[157] *Ibid.* 207; these figures make no allowance for the substantial decline in the quality of consumer goods.

the practice was widespread of taking on temporary workers.[158] Temporary workers lacked the privileges of permanent workers: they received no compensation when they were dismissed, and were not paid for stoppages. With labour readily available, this enabled management to select the best workers for their permanent work-force. But in 1930 these possibilities greatly diminished. As a leading labour economist put it, 'with the colossal growth in the labour power needed by the economy, hire for *permanent* work was naturally a greater incentive to attract and retain labour than hire for "temporary work"'. The stronger position of the working class on the labour market was reflected in the decline in the proportion of temporary workers among all newly-recruited workers from 70 per cent at the end of 1929 to 40 per cent at the end of 1930.[159]

Soviet workers, called upon to accept greater sacrifices in the name of socialist industrialisation, were divided and often perhaps uncertain in their response. Should they willingly acquiesce in harder work and poorer living standards for the sake of the socialist future, or seek to preserve their existing practices and privileges? This question confronted every worker, and every working group, not in abstract terms but in daily practice whenever they entered their place of work. A significant minority of rank-and-file workers enthusiastically supported the taxing goals of the plan and actively sought to achieve them. Their efforts to overcome difficulties by heroic exertions, and to acquire new skills, which will be described on many occasions in the pages which follow, were a crucial factor in the huge expansion of Soviet industry in the early 1930s. But these enthusiasts were certainly a minority of the urban work-force. Many workers resisted, and still more resented, the growing pressure to increase output, and their deteriorating living conditions. Bitter hostility both to the increases in output norms and to the shock brigades was frequently reported (see pp. 269 and 260–1 below). At some factories, mines and docks, workers

---

[158] For the change in the law on temporary workers in 1927, see Mordukhovich (1931), 83–5.

[159] Mordukhovich (1931), 87; the decline in temporary workers was facilitated by a decree of Sovnarkom RSFSR dated January 11, 1930, which provided that decisions about what work should count as temporary should be left to the collective agreements in each industry, rather than being subject to provisions in central legislation (*ibid*. 86, 154–7).

went on strike in the spring and summer of 1930 in protest against poor food supplies.[160]

The Soviet leaders, in their public statements and policy decisions in 1929–30, sought to combine a wide-ranging appeal to the socialist consciousness of the working class with a firm insistence on the need for hard work and discipline.

On the one hand, they placed greater stress than at any time since the Civil War on the support, enthusiasm and active collaboration of the working class. Stalin, in his article dated November 3, 1929, stressed the crucial role played by the 'creative initiative and creative élan of the masses' in the great break-through achieved in 1929 (see p. 95 above). Kaganovich, in an address to the Institute of Soviet State and Law on November 4, 1929, claimed that 'socialist emulation is laying the foundations of the dying-away of the compulsory character of labour'. He also envisaged that the proletarianisation of administration would be accompanied by the replacement of paid officials by elected voluntary personnel, combining the administration of the country with productive labour.[161] At the shock-brigade congress, which met in December, Kuibyshev praised the 'unprecedented and increasing activity of the broadest masses of the working class', and claimed that this represented 'an historical break-through in the psychology of the worker'. According to Kuibyshev, the worker 'feels himself to be the representative of his class, the master of his country':

A new human being is being created in production.[162]

And Bukharin, in an article conceding that 'the party was right' in its disputes with him about the correct path for economic development, dramatically stressed the crucial role of the working class in the major developments of the past $1^1/_2$–2 years, which he compared to the energy which would be liberated as the result of a successful atomic fission:

With us the working class is placed in conditions – and it must be even more so every day – where it can uncover,

---

[160] See Filtzer (1986), 82–3.
[161] SGRP, 1, 1930, 39–41.
[162] Kuibyshev (1930), 13–14, 17; part of this report is reprinted in *Pervyi Vsesoyuznyi s"ezd* (1959), 41–55; for this congress see p. 256 below.

foster and develop all the wealth of its internal energies. *And our main wager must be placed here.*[163]

Bukharin's readers would have been aware that he was silently counterposing this 'wager on the working class' to Stolypin's 'wager on the sober and the strong' peasant in 1907, and to Bukharin's own 'wager on the kulak' in the spring of 1925.[164] Kuibyshev returned to the theme at a joint meeting of the staff at Vesenkha with workers of the AMO automobile factory in Moscow, who had assumed 'patronage' over Vesenkha:

> The Soviet state apparatus [Kuibyshev declared] is gradually fusing with the working class. *We are approaching the wiping out of any boundary between them.*[165]

But the party leaders, while strongly emphasising the transformation which was taking place in the relationship between the working class and the state, were also well aware that the working class was by no means unanimous in its enthusiasm and willingness to make sacrifices. This lack of unanimity was attributed primarily to the social heterogeneity of the working class. At the shock-brigades congress Kuibyshev frankly admitted that '*petty-bourgeois psychology* is still strong in certain strata of the working class', and offered a rather pessimistic analysis of the 'lack of uniformity in its composition'. A huge number of workers had begun work since the revolution, and in many industries '*completely new working cadres*' had been recruited in the past three years; in many industries and areas '*children of peasants, people who have left the peasantry are a very considerable percentage*'.[166] Kuibyshev's diagnosis wrongly implied that discontent was found solely among inexperienced or ex-peasant workers, or could be attributed solely to their influence. In fact skilled workers also resented the deterioration in their working conditions. Kuibyshev also underestimated the

[163] P, December 15, 1929; this is the 'revised stenogram' of a speech at a conference of engineers and shock brigades in the Sokolniki district of Moscow.
[164] In April 1925, Bukharin, in announcing proposals to remove restrictions on well-to-do and kulak farms, unconvincingly denied that they constituted a 'wager on the kulak' (see Carr (1958), 260–1).
[165] ZI, January 19, 1930.
[166] Kuibyshev (1930), 19–20.

proportion of the labour force which consisted of long-established workers from proletarian families (see p. 7 above). But behind his diagnosis lay a recognition that the working class of 1929 did not correspond to its heroic image: 'the vanguard of the working class,' he acknowledged, 'must struggle very very strongly against all these attitudes and re-educate all strata of the working class.'[167]

The Soviet authorities also acknowledged, somewhat grudgingly, that the pressures of industrialisation placed additional strains on the working class. The control figures for 1929/30, as approved by Sovnarkom, admitted that in view of the large planned increase in output per worker the planned increase in wages was 'fairly modest'.[168] Syrtsov more frankly acknowledged 'the non-fulfilment of the plan to increase real wages, and in individual cases even a reduction in the level of real wages', though he also claimed that real wages did not reflect the 'whole material situation' of the working class.[169]

Confronted with sceptical specialists, and with a working class heterogeneous in its composition and outlook, the Soviet authorities insisted that if their plans were to succeed the industrial economy must be subordinated to the will of the state by even firmer controls. The expansion of the urban labour force, Krzhizhanovsky insisted, made it necessary to exercise 'the iron firmness of party levers of control'.[170] Stalin later looked back on the first five-year plan as a time when 'the party as it were whipped on the country, accelerating its advance'.[171] Firm central control was regarded as entirely compatible with an enhanced role for 'proletarian democracy' in the economy, providing that the participation of trade unions, production conferences and worker-managers in economic decisions and administration was confined to supporting rather than assessing or modifying the goals set by the Politburo.

---

[167] Kuibyshev (1930), 21.

[168] *KTs . . . na 1929/30* (1930), 15.

[169] Syrtsov, *Nakanune* (1930), 29 (prepared at end of May or beginning of June 1930).

[170] Krzhizhanovskii *et al.* (1930), 10 (opening speech at VI Gosplan congress, October 1929).

[171] *Soch.* xiii (1951), 183; this report, delivered on January 7, 1933, will be discussed in vol. 4.

(D) THE PARTY

The decision to launch a purge of the entire party membership, the first general party purge since 1921, was adopted simultaneously with the decision to purge the state administration (see pp. 61–2, 117–18 above), and was frankly linked with the requirements of the socialist offensive. Announcing the purge, the XVI party conference in April 1929 emphasised the sharpening class struggle which made it essential to 'strengthen resistance to the influence of petty-bourgeois spontaneity' and free the party from 'everything non-communist'. Those to be expelled should include 'alien elements', bureaucrats, anti-semites and supporters of anti-party groups. No party organisation should be exempted from the purge: even the factory cells, although 'the healthiest section of the party', had been penetrated by associates of the kulaks, purveyors of 'petty-bourgeois influences' and 'self-seeking elements which do not actively participate in the improvement of labour discipline'.[172]

The party purge proceeded far more rapidly than the purge of the administration. In the course of the fourteen months between the XVI conference and the XVI congress, the vast majority of party organisations were subjected to the purge; party members and candidates were required to justify their views and conduct at meetings open to non-party workers and peasants, which attracted large audiences.[173] By May 1930, 99,610 members and candidates had been expelled, 7·8 per cent of those who went through the purge.[174] The purges hit the rural party most severely, the industrial cells much more mildly.[175] The rather vague information available about the reasons for expulsion makes it clear that political opposition, indiscipline, links with kulaks or Nepmen, laziness and criminality were all involved.[176]

---

[172] *KPSS v rez.*, ii (1954), 605–12; see also Carr (1971), 143–6.

[173] In the Ukraine alone, at least 3¹/₄ million people attended the purge meetings (P, April 23, 1930).

[174] Andrukhov (1977), 138; this figure is net of those reinstated after appeal; a further 17,835 left voluntarily (P, April 23, 1930). For an alternative figure of 133,000, see Rigby (1968), 178–9. Between the XV and XVI party congresses, a further 34,309 (2·3 per cent of the membership) were expelled on an individual basis (P, June 9, 1930).

[175] See Carr (1971), 146, and the figures for the Ukraine in P, April 23, 1930.

[176] *XVI s"ezd* (1931), 349; P, April 23, 1930; see also Carr (1971), 147.

While the purge eliminated the lazy, the disobedient and those who hankered after NEP, a mass recruitment drive sought to bring untapped proletarian enthusiasm into the party. Long before 1929, the Lenin enrolment of 1924 and the October enrolment of 1927 increased the size of the party, and sought to raise to 50 per cent the proportion of party members who were workers at the bench. Party membership expanded from 446,000 on January 1, 1924, to 1,535,000 on January 1, 1929, and the proportion of party members who were workers by occupation increased from 18·8 per cent in 1924 to 41 per cent in 1929 (see Table 21). In January 1929, central committee directives provided that at least 90 per cent of new recruits to the party in the industrial provinces, 70 per cent in the agricultural provinces, and 60 per cent in the national republics should be workers by occupation.[177] During 1929 party membership increased more slowly. At the beginning of 1930, however, a second 'Lenin enrolment' was announced, and recruitment was very rapid during the first few months of the year. Few barriers were placed in the way of workers who wished to join the party; in 1929, 70 per cent of all applicants for party membership were accepted, as compared with 44 per cent in 1927, and the percentage remained high in 1930.[178] In some large factories, whole workshops proposed to join the party collectively. The practice was strongly encouraged by some party officials and activists. At the 'Serp i Molot' factory, Moscow, election slips for Soviet elections carried the line 'I join the party' at the bottom, which had to be deleted by those workers who did not wish to join.[179] In February 1930, Stalin praised collective recruitment to the party as 'a sign of very great revolutionary upsurge', but nevertheless insisted on retaining 'the trusted method of *individual* approach to everyone who wishes to join the party'.[180] Collective recruitment henceforth greatly diminished, but even in June 1930 73 'communist workshops' remained in Leningrad alone.[181] Party membership, which had increased by 140,000 in 1929, increased by over 500,000 in 1930 and reached 2·2 millions (see Table 21). While over two-thirds

[177] See Schlesinger (Bombay, 1977), 276.
[178] See *Sostav VKP(b)* (1930), 50, and Gooderham (1983), i, 2, ii, 6.
[179] TsGAOR 7952/3/267, 12, cited in Merridale (1987).
[180] *Soch.*, xii (1949), 189.
[181] See Gooderham (1983), ii, 5–6.

of those recruited to the party in 1929 and 1930 were workers by occupation,[182] even larger numbers moved from the factory floor into administration or full-time education. The proportion of the total membership who were workers by occupation reached a peak of 45·5 per cent in April 1930; the goal of 50 per cent was never achieved.

In industry in 1930, party membership expanded somewhat more rapidly than the number of workers employed; party membership expanded particularly rapidly in the larger factories, so that by the beginning of 1931, except in the textile industry, it was the largest factories which had the highest proportion of members.[183] Party saturation increased in almost all industries in 1930, but huge variations remained between industries, so that on January 1, 1931, the percentage for the oil industry was 19·7, the percentage for textiles only 12·2.[184] The variation between different factories was also very great: on April 1, 1930, as many as 47·3 per cent of workers at the Kolomna factory and 26·9 per cent at the Putilov works belonged to the party, as compared with only 10·8 per cent at the Rykov iron and steel works and 10·9 per cent at the Kharkov loco works.[185] The proportion of party members in the building industry remained low: even at Dneprostroi it was only 9·6 per cent, and at the Stalingrad tractor site it was a mere 5·8 per cent.[186] Within each factory, the percentage of

[182] See Gooderham (1983), Table II.
[183] The table below presents somewhat inconsistent data on party saturation in larger industrial enterprises, from two different sources (in percentages of total number of workers):

	April 1, 1929[a]	January 1, 1930[a]	January 1, 1930[b]	April 1, 1931[b]
1000–3000 workers	14·8	13·3	12·4	13·9
3000–5000	13·4	13·6	12·2	14·5
Over 5000	11·4	11·2	13·3[c]	15·4[c]
Over 10000	n.a.	n.a.	13·9	15·8
Average for above:	13·2	12·6	n.a.	n.a.

[a] *Sostav VKP (b)* (1930), 58–9; sample data for 306 enterprises.
[b] PS, 13, 1931, 5.
[c] 5000–10000 workers.
[184] See Sadler (1979), 139.
[185] *Sostav VKP(b)*(1930), 61.
[186] *Sostav VKP(b)*(1930), 61.

party members varied greatly between shops; in many factories party members were transferred between shops to rectify the anomaly.[187]

With the expansion of party membership in industry, the number of factory party organisations substantially increased. In the larger factories party cells were established in each shop, sometimes for each separate shift; and factory party committees were established at several hundred of the largest factories, with a status between that of a cell and that of a district committee, and responsibility for coordinating the work of the shop cells.[188] Elektrozavod, Moscow, with a factory party committee, 18 departmental cells, 40 shop cells and numerous party groups provided an example of a model factory party organisation.[189] In Leningrad alone, the number of factory party committees increased from 7 in January 1929 to 53 in January 1931, the number of shop cells rising from 1,129 to 2,600.[190] In the course of 1930, strenuous efforts were made to establish groups or links down to the level of the brigade, so that the organised influence of the party would be brought to bear at the point of production.[191] The shop and the brigade became the focus of party work in the enterprise.[192] But the attempt to organise a rapidly-growing and largely inexperienced membership involved much experiment and uncertainty. To assist the establishment of party organisations within factories, *orggruppy* (organising groups) were sent in from outside; their members ranged from young communists to senior local party officials.[193] Within the factories, different forms of party organisation proliferated.[194]

Uncertainty in organisation was coupled with uncertainty about the division of functions between the party and the factory management. In April 1930, the party central committee declared that 'at the vast majority of enterprises the CC

[187] This policy was announced by Kaganovich (*XVI s"ezd* (1931), 65). See for example P, October 1, 1930 (Karlik), B, 2, January 31, 1931 (Semenov).

[188] Sadler (1979), 77.

[189] Sadler (1979), 84.

[190] Gooderham (1983), Table V.

[191] P, October 1, 1930 (Karlik).

[192] These tendencies were consolidated in a central committee resolution 'On Party and Mass Work in the Shop and the Brigade', dated March 21, 1931 (SPR, viii (1934), 417–19); see also *Istoriya KPSS*, iv, ii (1971), 123–4.

[193] See Merridale (1987).

[194] See Sadler (1979), 100–4.

directive of September 5, 1929, has not been put into practice',
so that one-man management was not yet effective.[195] In
September, 1930, on the other hand, it complained that senior
managers often failed to understand their obligation to combine
one-man management with 'relying upon' the party, the
Komsomol and the trade union.[196] The broad injunction that
the party must not interfere in operational matters in the
factory, but must give support and advice to the management,
was inherently ambiguous; and the difficulties it entails still
remain a central problem of factory organisation today.

[195] P, April 12, 1930 (resolution of April 10).
[196] P, September 3, 1930.

CHAPTER FOUR

THE INTELLECTUAL
FRAMEWORK, 1929–30

'We are going full steam ahead by means of industrialisation to socialism', Stalin announced in November 1929.[1] The Politburo under Stalin's leadership sought to subordinate every aspect of society, and every citizen, to the tasks of the socialist offensive. In December 1929, Stalin, in an unconventional reply to birthday greetings, drew attention to the heroism and self-sacrifice required in the battles which lay ahead by proclaiming his own readiness 'to devote to the cause of the working class, the proletarian revolution and world communism all my strength, all my abilities, and if necessary all my blood, drop by drop'.[2]

In their struggle to impose the 'socialist offensive' on society, Stalin and his closest allies strongly emphasised the crucial role of the proletarian state in the transition to socialism. In 1926, advocating 'socialism in one country', Stalin stressed the primacy of politics over economics. 'We have victoriously achieved the dictatorship of the proletariat', he assured the executive committee of Comintern in December 1926, 'and have thus created the *political* base (baza) for the advance to socialism'; the possibility now existed to create the *economic* base of socialism.[3] In November 1928, explaining that he was merely 'paraphrasing Lenin's words', he declared that 'We have caught up and *overtaken* the advanced capitalist countries in a political respect by constructing the dictatorship of the proletariat' and now 'We must use the dictatorship of the proletariat ... in order to catch up and *overtake* the advanced capitalist countries *economically* as well'.[4] By this time Stalin had already tacitly

[1] P, November 7, 1929.
[2] P, December 22, 1929, reprinted in *Soch.*, xii (1949), 140.
[3] *Soch.*, ix (1948), 22–4.
[4] *Soch.*, xi (1949), 250–1.

abandoned the notion of the immediate withering away of the state. 'The proletarian state is necessary', he wrote in March 1927, 'to suppress the resistance of exploiters, to organise socialist construction'.[5] At the XVI party congress in June 1930, he frankly insisted that state power must be strengthened:

> We are in favour of the withering away of the state. And we are also in favour of the strengthening of the dictatorship of the proletariat, which is the most powerful and the mightiest power of all state powers which have so far existed. The higher development of state power in order to prepare conditions *for* the withering away of state power – this is the marxist formula.[6]

The case for strengthening the proletarian state in order to transform the backward economy inherited from tsarism was put even more harshly by Kaganovich. Frankly admitting that the Soviet state was not a 'law-governed (pravovoe) state', he bluntly asserted that 'our laws are governed by revolutionary expediency at each given moment':

> The state is a superstructure above the economic basis; but this does not merely not exclude the active reverse influence of the state on the economic basis, but presupposes it.[7]

Praising the role of 'extra-economic measures', Kaganovich proclaimed that the state was driving out the law of value and strengthening planning 'by the whole force of the laws of the proletarian state':

> Do not expect any softening of the proletarian dictatorship in the immediate period. On the contrary, for the next period the slogan of the party is not the softening, but the all-round strengthening of the proletarian dictatorship, the strengthening of it in all spheres.[8]

Spokesmen for the party leadership rejected Bukharin's call in

[5] *Soch.*, ix (1948), 182–3.
[6] *Soch.*, xiii (1951), 369–70.
[7] SGRP, 1, 1930, 9, 25 (report of November 4, 1929).
[8] *Ibid.*, 29, 43.

'Notes of an Economist' for 'a few steps towards the Leninist commune-state', which he had coupled with a strong criticism of 'over-centralisation'. Kaganovich insisted that centralisation and stronger control of the economy were entirely compatible with an increased role for elected voluntary administrators, which were 'links in the unified chain of construction of the commune-state'.[9] The prominent Rabkrin official Gol'tsman even claimed that 'the Soviet state will not be a commune-state only in the future; it is already one at present'.[10] But use of the term 'commune-state' even in the context of further centralisation was soon rejected as inappropriate, on the grounds that it led to an underestimation of the role of the state in repressing hostile classes.[11]

Stalin had long held that this transformation of society led by the state could be accomplished only if the party maintained iron discipline, unity of will, and 'complete and absolute unity of action'; no fractions or groups must be permitted within the party, and it must maintain its ideological integrity by purging itself of opportunist elements: 'the party', Stalin asserted, 'is the General Staff of the proletariat'.[12]

Stalin took an equally uncompromising view of the place of theory in the struggle for socialism. In December 1929, at the conference of agrarian marxists, he insisted that theory must be subordinated to the practical needs of the socialist offensive:

> we have a certain gap between practical successes and the development of theoretical thought. It is necessary, however, for theoretical work not merely to run after practical work, but to move ahead of it, arming our practical workers in the struggle for the victory of socialism.
>
> ... Theory, if it is really theory, must provide practical workers with ability to find the right direction, clarity of perspective, confidence in work, belief in the victory of our cause.[13]

[9] SGRP, 1, 1930, 40–1; for Bukharin's call, see P, September 30, 1928.
[10] P, January 20, 1930.
[11] SGRP, 5–6, 1930, 47 (Berman).
[12] These principles, drawing on various statements of Lenin, were first systematically expounded by Stalin in his lectures of April 1924 on 'The Foundations of Leninism' (*Soch.*, vi (1947), 69–188).
[13] *Soch.*, xii (1949), 142 (speech of December 27); for other aspects of this speech see vol. 1, pp. 197–8, 391–2, vol. 2, p. 87, and pp. 150, 158–9 and 165 below.

These pragmatic criteria were a short step from the belief that the party and its supreme agencies, on the basis of their assessment of society's needs, should be the ultimate arbiter in all intellectual as well as practical issues. As a party official put it a few months later, 'it is clear to everyone that all efforts to think of any theory, of any scholarly discipline, as autonomous, as an independent discipline, objectively signify opposition to the party's general line, opposition to the dictatorship of the proletariat'.[14] But this austere prescription merely provided the framework of intellectual subordination and obedience. The road to socialism was uncharted, and even the major features of the future society were conceived by the party only in broadest outline. Stalin and most of his immediate associates, all former members of the pre-revolutionary underground, were shrewd men toughened in the upheaval of revolution and civil war. They were convinced that the 'bourgeois specialists' – and more generally all the non-marxist intellectuals in every profession – were blocking the triumph of socialism and the progress of marxism at every turn; and sought to destroy their influence by means of the mass purge and the political police. Similar methods of coercion disposed of the Nepmen and the kulaks. This work of destruction was relatively simple to organise. But the construction of the institutions, ideas and ethos of a new socialist society was much more difficult. They did not spring from the heads of the members of the Politburo. Instead the Politburo had to rely on smaller or larger groups of marxists in every walk of life, accepting, rejecting or modifying their ideas and proposals.

In some activities, the role of the Politburo in 1929–30 was quite limited. In relation to the natural sciences, it almost never took the initiative, and rarely acted as adjudicator in disputes. Instead it entrusted Kol'man, a militant party mathematician, with responsibility for science in the apparatus of the central committee. He later claimed that in this capacity 'I was free to act on my own ... There was not a single competent person who could intervene'.[15]

[14] Kol'man, speech of November 29, 1930, cited in Fitzpatrick, ed. (1978), 109 (Joravsky).
[15] See *Canadian Slavonic Papers*, xxi (1979), 231–2 (Rabkin); this is an interview with Kol'man, an émigré from Czechoslovakia, who worked in the agitation and propaganda department (from January 1930 renamed the culture and

In education, the Politburo played a much more active role. In 1928, Stalin took the initiative in seeking to adapt the education system to the needs of industrialisation, supported by Kuibyshev and the departmental interests of Vesenkha. Lunacharsky, People's Commissar for Education since 1918, resisted these decisions, and resigned in the spring of 1929. No other party member of sufficient political standing had substantial experience of education. Instead, after some months' delay, Bubnov was appointed to replace Lunacharsky in September 1929. Bubnov was a former Left Communist, who had been head of the Red Army Political Administration since 1925. He had to rely on critics of Lunacharsky within the education system to determine the shape of the education reforms. According to his own account, he appointed Shulgin and other radical educationists to leading positions in Narkompros not because he agreed with their views but because their 'militant political spirit' conformed with the 'requirements of our epoch'. Bubnov also accepted the demands of the dominant militant group in the Komsomol for a fundamental reform of the secondary school.[16] The decision to restructure the education system was taken by the Politburo; but the shape of the reform was largely determined by militant party educationists.

In the winter of 1929–30, when the socialist offensive against kulaks, Nepmen and recalcitrant bourgeois specialists was at its most vigorous, the Politburo at first almost everywhere encouraged such radical initiatives. The spirit of these months was dramatically embodied in the discussions about the reform of the calendar. In the 1920s, the rival merits of calendar year, economic year (October–September), and agricultural year (July–June) were hotly debated without any outcome. But at the beginning of 1930, two government commissions seriously considered fundamental changes, following the example of the French revolution. A commission chaired by Ryskulov, a deputy chairman of Sovnarkom of the RSFSR, proposed that 1930

---

propaganda department) from August 1929 to March 1931 (Kol'man (New York, 1982), 161). According to Kol'man, the successive heads of the department at this time were ignorant of the natural sciences.

[16] See Fitzpatrick (1979), chs. 6–7, esp. pp. 144–5; for the education reform of 1929–30, see pp. 114, 128–9 above.

should be renamed Year 13, and that each new civil and economic year should begin on November 1.[17] An even more authoritative commission chaired by Rudzutak, a deputy chairman of Sovnarkom of the USSR, and a Politburo member, resolved to introduce a five-day week to conform with the continuous working week. In consequence there would be twelve thirty-day months each containing six weeks; five festival days which did not belong to any particular month would complete the revolutionary year.[18] The new calendar was partly introduced by some local authorities.[19] But caution eventually prevailed. Delegates at a Gosplan conference criticised the reform on the grounds that it would produce a calendar out of line with the rest of the world.[20] The Soviet government, unlike the French Convention, never brought itself to adopt a new calendar of its own.

Every branch of learning and every cultural activity were affected by the rise to predominance of militant marxists which accompanied the drive against the bourgeois specialists. Throughout the USSR enthusiastic teams removed 'harmful literature' from public libraries and destroyed it, with the support or acquiescence of the authorities.[21] In the winter of 1929–30 the anti-religious campaigns of the 'militant Godless' were particularly ferocious (see vol. 1, pp. 118, 246, 273).

In creative literature, at the end of 1929 *Pravda* offered its authoritative support to the proletarian writers' association RAPP.[22] The heroic literature of the collective struggle for victory on the production front was everywhere in favour.[23]

[17] SKhG, January 1, 1930; for Ryskulov's role in collectivisation, see vol. 1, pp. 154, 178–80, 199.

[18] ZI, February 25, 1930; the Rudzutak commission presumably coincided with the commission for the introduction of the continuous working week (see p. 86 above). This scheme was proposed in October 1929 by the director of the Pulkovo observatory at a conference of Glavnauka (P, October 31, 1929).

[19] In Yaroslavl, the local newspaper *Severnyi rabochii* continued to describe 1932 as 'the fifteenth year' on its mast-head during the first few months of that year.

[20] ZI, February 25, 1930; they also argued that it would be difficult to record production in industries which continued to operate during festivals.

[21] P, November 4, 1929; *Pravda* reported sympathetically complaints that 'useful' items like the Granat encyclopedia had been destroyed, but raised no objection to book-destruction on principle.

[22] P, December 4, 1929.

[23] See Fitzpatrick, ed. (1978), 189–206 (K. Clark).

Those who would not conform to this approach were deprived of all possibility of publication. In March 1930, Bulgakov, who refused friendly advice to write a 'communist play', declared in a letter to the Soviet government 'I have been destroyed . . . I am faced with poverty, the street and destruction'; and asked permission to emigrate.[24] Other literary groups were forced to conform: Pereval, a group of fellow-travellers who emphasised the importance of literary skills, was disbanded.[25] This triumph of one form of Bolshevik orthodoxy in literature was accompanied by the administrative imposition of political conformity. Mayakovsky, who joined RAPP two months before his suicide, referred in his last letter not only to his personal troubles but also to his clash with a leading RAPP official about the banning of an agitational slogan in verse which had decorated the auditorium during the performance of his satirical play *Banya* (The Bath-House). 'Tell Ermilov it's too bad he removed the slogan', Mayakovsky wrote. The slogan castigated 'the bureaucratic swarm . . . given aid and comfort by critics like Ermilov'.[26]

After the arrest of many non-marxist historians (see pp. 115–16 above), by the spring of 1930 Pokrovsky was effectively in charge of all historical studies. But this did not end controversy: Pokrovsky's own school contended with rival marxist historians in a series of fierce debates throughout 1930.[27]

In philosophy, the second half of the 1920s was dominated by a long and increasingly bitter dispute between two groups of marxists – the 'mechanists' and the Deborinists. The 'mechanists' held that living organisms must be seen as complex mechanisms, receiving energy and transforming it; Deborin and his followers argued that this was an anti-dialectical approach, which reduced the complex to the simple, and quality to quantity. The 'mechanists' in their turn insisted that Deborin's wish to impose dialectics on the natural sciences from outside was merely a sterile 'revival of the idealistic dialectics of Hegel'.[28] By the end

[24] *Politicheskii dnevnik* (Amsterdam, 1972), 206–13 (dated March 28, 1930).

[25] See Fitzpatrick, ed. (1978), 195, 293 (referring to April 1930).

[26] See Brown (1969), 37–9; the suicide note, dated April 4, 1930, was published in *Literaturnoe nasledstvo*, lxv (1958), 199.

[27] See Barber (1981), chs. 4–8.

[28] See Yakhot (New York, 1981), ch. 5; until his death in 1928 the principal mechanist was the old Bolshevik Skvortsov-Stepanov; Deborin, at first a

of 1929 the Deborinists, who accused their opponents of providing the ideological foundation for the Right deviation, had apparently triumphed.[29]

In the natural sciences, the necessity for a marxist approach was asserted at a series of conferences;[30] and 'the discovery by agronomist Lysenko' that winter seed could be frozen artifically and planted in the spring was applauded in the national press, with the support of Shlikhter and the Narkomzem of the Ukraine.[31]

Militant marxism was particularly assertive in disciplines with a direct influence on the restructuring of society. In legal studies, by the end of the 1920s the bourgeois jurists had been swept aside by marxists headed by Pashukanis, who held that all law was derived from contractual relations based on commodity exchange. With the demise of the latter as a result of the great break-through, legal institutions would wither away, and law would be replaced by regulation and socio-economic norms. By the winter of 1929–30 the doctrines of Pashukanis predominated in legal education, where new syllabuses described the forthcoming replacement of civil law by technical rules, and of criminal law by the 'principle of expediency'.[32] In November 1929, the chief justice of the Supreme Court of the RSFSR announced that the process of the withering away of law had already begun.[33]

In urban and social planning, the campaign for the socialisation of *byt* (everyday life) reached its height in 1929–30. It was led by Sabsovich and Larin, who in the later 1920s had both been vigorous supporters of industrialisation and planning.[34]

Bolshevik, joined the Mensheviks in 1907 and strongly criticised Lenin's major philosophical work *Materialism and Empirio-Criticism*; he rejoined the Bolsheviks in 1917.

[29] See Joravsky (New York, 1961), esp. pp. 50–7, 228–9.

[30] For example, the congress on human behaviour in January 1930 (see SR, xliv (1985), 642 (M. Miller)).

[31] EZh, August 4, 1929; P, October 8, 1929.

[32] See Fitzpatrick, ed. (1978), 169–81 (Sharlet); the earlier controversies are discussed in Carr (1971), 373–6, which exaggerates the extent to which Pashukanis' views were cognate with those of Bukharin.

[33] See *Review of Socialist Law* (Tokyo), 2, 1980, 146 (Oda).

[34] For Sabsovich, see Carr and Davies (1969), 841, 877, 881–2, and pp. 152–3 and 225–8 below; for Larin, see Carr and Davies (1969), 892, pp. 152–3 and 226 below, and vol. 2 of the present work, pp. 41, 85–7.

Sabsovich rejected as incompatible with socialism the out-dated notion that individual families should each live in a separate house or flat. Instead, he called for dwellings in which separate bedrooms were provided, but otherwise all services were in common, and children were separated from their parents and brought up communally. The new socialist cities would be relatively small communities of 40–60,000 people, joined by an integrated electric power supply.[35] The proposal to construct small socialist towns was endorsed by Strumilin, who reported that the Stalingrad combine would be served by a population of 300,000, which would be located in five towns several kilometres apart from each other.[36] Proposals for communal living received the authoritative endorsement of two government commissions and a commission of Rabkrin, which proposed that new blocks of flats should have no individual kitchens, and that living in collectives should be encouraged by higher rations; food combines in each town should supply meals to flats, schools and other institutions.[37]

In almost every arena, however, the victory of militant marxism in its 1930 variant was superficial or temporary. In most natural sciences, little changed beneath the political rhetoric. According to Joravsky, the scientists were ideologically disarmed 'in principle', but 'in practice still enjoyed almost unimpaired autonomy in their subject matter'. At the conferences of 1930, most papers were not affected by the prevailing marxist wind, and in the scientific press learned articles continued to appear in profusion.[38] So this was not a dress rehearsal for the Chinese Cultural Revolution of 1966–7, which brought nearly all non-military research to a halt. But even this superficial politicisation of science led some scientists, including the leading chemist Ipatieff, to emigrate, while others refrained from research which they believed to be politically risky.

In virtually all the humanities and social sciences it is obvious

---

[35] Sabsovich, *Gorod budushchego i organizatsiya sotsialisticheskogo byta* (1929); for these and rival proposals see Fitzpatrick, ed. (1978), 207–40 (S. F. Starr).

[36] PKh, 5, 1930, 98–9.

[37] EZh, February 26, 1930; this was a draft governmental decree prepared jointly by the everyday-life commission of CCC/Rabkrin, the Rudzutak commission on the continuous working week, and a commission to improve labour and everyday-life attached to TsIK.

[38] Joravsky (New York, 1961), 248, 240–1.

to the historian, with the advantage of hindsight, that the new marxist masters were purely temporary appointments; within a few years they were replaced by or submerged in rival trends. But in 1930 party intervention against the militant marxists was usually a mere preliminary almost inaudible rumble of approaching thunder. In education, for example, Shulgin and the Komsomol continued their activities almost unimpaired.

In the field of law, Pashukanis' commodity theory was not yet challenged directly. But laws and legal institutions began to be implicitly treated as a permanent feature of Soviet society. At the XVI party congress Krylenko, obviously with the support of the higher party authorities, criticised as a violation of Soviet law the Moscow party committee resolution of February 7, 1930, on the elimination of the bourgeoisie (see p. 103 above), and reproved judges and procurators who had failed to conform to Soviet law during the collectivisation drive. According to Krylenko, this 'contemptuous attitude to laws as revolutionary norms' must give way to 'revolutionary legality'.[39] This did not imply that law should be in any way independent of the political authorities. Krylenko, both at the congress itself, and in an article in *Pravda* just before the congress, insisted that all Soviet law must be subordinate to the unrestrained right of the Politburo and other 'leading agencies of the proletariat' to change the law.[40] But within these narrow and shifting limits legal norms and a legal system would operate. Stalin's insistence at the XVI congress that the proletarian state must be strengthened before it began to wither away (see p. 140 above) also undermined the Pashukanis approach to law. Henceforth Pashukanis no longer asserted that the withering away of law had already begun: 'the disappearance of law will begin', he explained in November 1930, 'when the dominating [i.e. socialist] sector has swallowed everything up'.[41]

In creative literature, while official party policy continued

[39] *XVI s"ezd* (1931), 351–3.
[40] *Loc. cit.*; P, June 25, 1930.
[41] SGRP, 12, 1930, 47 (speech of November 10). On October 6, 1930, an article in *Izvestiya* accused Pashukanis of 'slurring over Bukharin's errors about the doctrine of the state' (see Carr (1971), 376n.); in his speech reported in SGRP Pashukanis admitted that he had failed to recognise that not only bourgeois but also other forms of property, such as feudal property, had given rise to corresponding systems of law (SGRP, 12, 1930, 33).

strong support for RAPP, behind the scenes Stalin began in 1930 his more or less arbitrary interventions in literary matters which continued throughout the 1930s. In response to Bulgakov's letter (see p. 145 above), Stalin telephoned him on April 18, 1930, and told him to ask for work in the Arts Theatre, remarking 'I think they will agree'.[42] This was the first of a series of minor actions by Stalin on behalf of persecuted writers which helped him to acquire a certain reputation for liberalism among the Soviet intelligentsia. But Stalin was no liberal in relation to creative literature. In January 1930, he condemned Voronsky's call for the publication of literature exposing the horrors of war as 'hardly any different from the approach of bourgeois pacifists'.[43] In December, in a letter to Demyan Bedny, he strongly defended a central committee resolution which criticised Bedny's poems as a slander on the Russian past. Stalin added, no doubt with some exaggeration, that 'the central committee has rebuked dozens of poets and writers when they made mistakes'.[44]

In the Communist Academy, the first signs appeared that the party was not prepared to give unqualified backing to Pokrovsky and his school. In June 1930 Pokrovsky was strongly attacked, not yet for his views, but for his conduct as president of the Academy. These attacks were evidently supported by Kaganovich, and indicated that Pokrovsky's position as the leader of the marxist historians was not inviolable.[45]

These were relatively minor interventions. In a few fields the party acted much more decisively.[46] In philosophy, the

[42] *Voprosy literatury*, 9, 1966, 139.

[43] *Soch.*, xii (1949), 176 (letter to Gorky dated January 17, first published in 1949). Voronsky, a former Trotskyist, was one of the moving spirits in the literary organisation Pereval, which closed shortly afterwards (see p. 145 above).

[44] *Soch.*, xiii (1951), 23–7 (letter dated December 12, first published in 1951).

[45] See Fitzpatrick, ed. (1978), 161–2 (Enteen); Kaganovich in June 1930 was the director of the Institute of Soviet Construction, from which most criticisms of Pokrovsky emanated. In January 1931 Kaganovich, now a secretary of the party central committee, drafted a statement signed by three members of the Communist Academy calling for a thorough examination of Pokrovsky's Institute of History (see Barber (1981), 124). One would suspect that Kaganovich's action had Stalin's approval, but, according to a prominent Soviet historian, Stalin at that time supported Pokrovsky (see *op. cit.* 173, n. 38, citing Sidorov in IS, 3, 1964, 136).

[46] For its role in political economy, see pp. 156–9 below.

temporary victory of Deborin in December 1929 (see pp. 145–6 above) was immediately followed by Stalin's general complaint to the agrarian marxists that 'theoretical thought' was lagging behind practice.[47] Early in 1930 the party bureau in the Institute of Red Professors, headed by the young Deborinite philosophers Mitin and Yudin, called for a new advance on the philosophical front in the light of Stalin's statement.[48] It is not known whether this move was undertaken on their own initiative. But on March 30, Yaroslavsky, a member of the party central committee, who rarely acted independently, criticised the 'dialecticians' (i.e. the Deborinites) and partially defended the 'mechanists'.[49] A few weeks later, on June 7, 1930, a letter was published in *Pravda* from Mitin, Kol'tsevich and Yudin, strongly criticising the Deborinists for 'passivity' towards Trotskyism and inadequate criticism of idealist theories. In a note, the editors of *Pravda* 'solidarised with its main propositions', thus indicating powerful party support.[50] This was the beginning of the end for the Deborin school, which was attacked in further articles by Mitin for underestimating Lenin, overestimating Plekhanov, abstract separation of politics from philosophy, and formalism.[51]

Within a few months, Yudin, Mitin and the 'Bolshevisers' had taken over the management of Soviet philosophy and deprived it of any serious philosophical content. On December 9, 1930, Stalin directly intervened in the controversy at his famous meeting with the bureau of the party cell of the Institute of Red Professors of Philosophy and Natural Science.[52] In the course of the conversation he placed very great emphasis on the importance of Lenin's work on marxism in general and philosophy in particular, claiming that 'Lenin elevated dialectical

[47] The conference of agrarian marxists met immediately after a Communist Academy meeting which supported Deborin, and in the same building.

[48] Yakhot (New York, 1981), 61; no source is given; the author is a former Soviet philosopher, whose information seems generally reliable.

[49] See Yakhot (New York, 1981), 63–4.

[50] P, June 7, 1930; Trotsky supported and contributed to Deborin's journal in its early years (see Yakhot (New York, 1981), 63–4).

[51] P, August 8, 9, 1930; in P, August 24, 1930, the editors condemned Deborin for 'insufficient self-criticism on the philosophical front'.

[52] Mitin's summary of the conversation, evidently authorised by Stalin, appeared in PZM, 1, 1936, 25–6; my quotations from this account are all in indirect speech in the original.

materialism to a new stage'; according to Stalin, materialism had been 'atomistic' before Lenin, while Lenin 'analysed the electron theory of matter from the point of view of marxism'. Stalin urged the philosophers to expose 'a number of false philosophical statements by Plekhanov, who always looked down on Lenin', and by Machists like Valentinov, Bazarov and Bogdanov.[53] 'Go through (pereryt') all their work so as to recall how they criticised Lenin and what their attitude was to *Materialism and Empirio-Criticism*', Stalin advised. But his main fire was reserved for the Deborin group, which he castigated as '*a menshevising idealist revision*' of marxism. 'Deborin masks his own idealism, and even fires off broadsides against open idealism of the Losev type'.[54] Stalin described the Deborin group as 'great masters at presenting their material covered by every kind of "left" sauce, relying on the fact that youth is susceptible to every kind of leftism'. It was 'necessary to dig about in everything that had been written by the Deborin group – everything erroneous on the philosophical sector'.

Stalin's notorious malediction of the Deborin group as a '*menshevising idealist revision*' of marxism adapted a phrase which had already been used in slightly different forms in the economic and philosophical discussions in the course of 1930 (see pp. 159–60 below). It neatly impugned both Deborin's reprehensible political past and his alleged Hegelianism. On January 25, 1931, the party central committee enshrined the phrase in a resolution on the philosophical journal *Pod znamenem marksizma* (Under the Banner of Marxism). The resolution criticised the

[53] Valentinov, Bazarov and A. A. Bogdanov were close to the Bolsheviks in 1905, but differed with Lenin about philosophy and political tactics after 1905. Valentinov (Vol'skii), a Menshevik during the Civil War, from 1922 worked as deputy editor of *Torgovo-promyshlennaya gazeta*, the industrial newspaper, but remained abroad while on a mission in 1929 (see Valentinov (1968) and (1971)). Bazarov also supported the Mensheviks during the Civil War, and became a leading adviser of Gosplan in the 1920s (see Carr and Davies (1969), 788–9); he was one of the accused in the Menshevik trial of March 1931. For Bogdanov, an influential and unorthodox philosopher and economist in the 1920s, see Susiluoto (Helsinki, 1982); a doctor by profession, he died in a blood transfusion experiment in 1928.

[54] A. F. Losev (b. 1892) was a non-marxist philosopher and logician who published learned works on ancient philosophy and aesthetics in the 1920s. His life-work on classical aesthetics, *Istoriya antichnoi estetiki*, began publication in the 1960s; six volumes had appeared by 1986, when it was recommended for a state prize (*Literaturnaya gazeta*, August 13, 1986 (Bychkov)).

'lack of party approach (partiinost') in philosophy and natural science', condemned the Deborin group slightly more cautiously than Stalin as 'going over in a number of questions to the position of menshevising idealism', and called for a fight on two fronts against mechanism, which was still the main danger, as well as idealism. Philosophy should develop 'in close connection with the practice of socialist construction and world revolution', and to this end militant dialectical materialists should unite.[55]

In urban and social planning the party also intervened directly. Larin was a long-established eccentric; during the collectivisation drive, he enthusiastically defended ambitious schemes for agro-towns.[56] With the retreat from collectivisation, all immediate plans for agro-towns were abandoned. Then on May 16, 1930, a resolution of the party central committee criticised schemes for replanning existing towns and constructing new ones 'solely at state expense', with completely socialised catering, housing and upbringing of children. The resolution supported a more modest programme of social services in new towns, including a green belt between the factory and the housing area. It singled out for strong condemnation

the extremely unjustifiable semi-fantastic and therefore extremely harmful attempts of certain comrades (including Yu. Larin and Sabsovich) to leap 'in a single jump' over the obstacles to the socialist reconstruction of everyday life. These obstacles are grounded on the one hand in the economic and cultural backwardness of the country, and on the other hand in the necessity at the present moment of concentrating maximum resources on the most rapid industrialisation of the country. Only this will create real material conditions for a fundamental transformation of everyday life.[57]

One of the principal targets for criticism was Sabsovich's notorious commission to the Stalingrad tractor factory, which recommended Utopian schemes for a new town, including

[55] P, January 26, 1931; it appointed a new editorial board to the journal including Mitin, Kol'man and Yudin as well as Deborin and A. K. Timiryazev (a former 'mechanist').

[56] See vol. 2, p. 41; in December 1929 he clashed with Stalin about the nature of the kolkhoz (see *ibid.*, pp. 85–6).

[57] P, May 17, 1930.

separate upbringing for children. Sabsovich was castigated in *Pravda* as 'the principal phrase-monger', and later appeared in a fictionalised history of the Stalingrad factory as head of the commission which proposed a town costing 4,000 million rubles, one hundred times the cost of the factory.[58]

The authoritative intervention of the party central committee did not immediately halt the discussion between the proponents of rival town-planning schemes. In the debate preceding the XVI party congress Larin claimed that at the Stalingrad factory mass meetings of workers had protested about the construction of ' "family flats" of a petty-bourgeois type', and argued that it was essential to liberate women from the individual kitchen if the new Gosplan proposals to employ four million additional women in production during the five-year plan were to be achieved.[59] There is no doubt that at Stalingrad communal living was popular among many young workers, and central attempts to interfere with it were resented.[60] But in practice, whether their everyday life was organised communally or individually, at Stalingrad as at other new factories, young workers lived in 'Asiatic conditions' in rather primitive barracks, or in tents; bugs prevented sleep, the roofs leaked and water supplies were inadequate.[61] These miserable circumstances provided a convincing basis for replacing the Utopian dreams of Sabsovich and Larin by the harsh realism of Kaganovich.

---

[58] P, June 12, 1930; Il'in (1934), 75, 104–5; the novel barely disguises his name as 'Bashkovich'. For criticisms of Sabsovich's long-term plans for the economy, see pp. 225–8 below.

[59] P, June 24, 1930, disk. listok 19.

[60] Il'in, ed. (1933), 180, 183, 190.

[61] P, July 31, 1930 (Osinskii); Il'in, ed. (1933), 134.

CHAPTER FIVE

ECONOMIC DOCTRINES IN TRANSITION, 1929–30

In the economic debates of the mid–1920s, Bukharin argued that during the transition from NEP to socialism the 'planning principle' would struggle and cooperate with the 'principle of spontaneity' on and through the market, so that the market would be the sole regulator of the economy. But the doctrine was challenged in practice in 1928–9 by the use of coercion to obtain agricultural products from the peasantry, and by the pressures of inflation which disrupted the market. In April 1929 the party central committee rejected proposals from Bukharin and Rykov that the market should be 'normalised' and that 'pressure in the sphere of trade' should be removed, castigating them as 'an interpretation of NEP in a liberal sense', which would lead to 'the renunciation of the control of market relations by the proletarian state'.[1] Preobrazhensky's rival doctrine held that two independent and hostile laws or regulators were in conflict in the Soviet economy, 'the law of socialist accumulation' and 'the law of value'; the fate of socialism depended on the success of the former law in driving out the latter. At the plenum of the party central committee in April 1929, Stalin acknowledged that 'tribute' or surtax must be exacted from the peasants, and argued that there were 'two aspects' to NEP, *the controlling role of the state on the market* and 'freedom of private trade, the *free* play of prices on the market'; the former aspect was 'more important to us' than the latter.[2] This came close to accepting Preobrazhensky's struggle between two regulators. But it was unthinkable that Preobrazhensky's notorious economic doctrine, developed in the service of the Left opposition, should be separated from its tainted political

[1] See Carr and Davies (1969), 633.
[2] *Soch.*, xii (1949), 43–56.

context and taken over by the party leadership. At the end of the 1920s the victors over Bukharin and Preobrazhensky were faced with the necessity of developing their own theory of the transition to a socialist economy.

(A) POLITICAL ECONOMY AND ECONOMIC THEORY

In 1929, economic theory in the USSR was in disarray. In the absence of any agreed principles for the analysis of the transition to socialism, the economic theorists in the Marx–Engels Institute, the Communist Academy and the Institute of Red Professors devoted most of their attention to capitalism. Almost all marxist economists held that 'political economy' was by definition concerned exclusively with the study of the capitalist economy, in which the exploitation of the working class by the capitalist class was concealed behind the exchange of commodities. The economic theory of other social formations, including socialism, must be studied by different analytical tools.[3] Political economy, like law in Pashukanis' theory of commodity law, would come to an end when capitalist economy came to an end.

In 1928–9 the political economy of capitalism was itself the arena for a fierce dispute between two major groups: Rubin and his followers, including at this time Leontiev and Borilin, known by their oppenents as 'idealists', and Bessonov, Kon and others, known by their opponents as 'mechanists'. In his *Ocherki po teorii stoimosti*, which was published in several editions in the 1920s, the fourth and last in 1929, Rubin argued that political economy must be concerned solely with production relations, the social form of capitalist society. The forces of production, or production technology, were merely a 'starting point' for Marx's

[3] Engels had referred (in *Anti-Dühring* (n.d. [?1939], first published in 1878), p. 171) to political economy concerned with 'various human socieites' as 'political economy in this wider sense', and 'still to be brought into being'; and Lenin in May 1920 wrote 'a step back as compared with Engels' and 'not only!' against Bukharin's claim in *Economics of the Transition Period* that political economy is concerned exclusively with commodity production (*Leninskii sbornik*, xl (1929), 349 – Lenin's marginal comments were first published in 1929). But only Skvortsov-Stepanov, A. Bogdanov and Pokrovsky argued for the wider definition of political economy at a famous debate in the Communist Academy in 1925 (see Valovoi and Lapshina (1972), 366–7).

research and must be studied by a separate science.[4] But according to the 'mechanists' Bessonov and Kon, political economy should comprise the study of both the forces of production and production relations, and the interaction between the two. Behind this definitional dispute lay a serious disagreement about the proper focus for research. The 'mechanists' believed that Rubin dealt with production relations abstractly, and paid inadequate attention to their technical and historical context; the Rubinists argued that the mechanists tended to confuse the study of material production with the study of social relations, and hence to exaggerate the role of technology.

In the autumn of 1929 the two schools each prepared polemical collections of articles criticising their rivals, and each wrote angry letters to *Pravda* denouncing the other side.[5] At this point the party authorities took a hand, and on October 10, 1929, *Pravda* published an editorial note, obviously with the support of the central committee apparatus, calling for 'a struggle against both the idealist danger, which often disguises itself in marxist clothes, and against the mechanist survivals of Bogdanovism'; this would require 'the unification of all forces of the scientific thought of the party on the basis of consistently applied marxism–leninism and its revolutionary dialectical method'.

[4] The third edition of Rubin's book (1928) is translated as I. I. Rubin, *Essays on Marx's Theory of Value* (Detroit, 1972), see esp. pp. 1–3. Rubin (1886–(?)1938), was first a member of the Jewish socialist Bund, and then a Menshevik; he became a research worker at the Marx–Engels Institute, directed by Ryazanov, in 1926; he was a defendant at the Menshevik trial in March 1931, where he was compelled to testify falsely against Ryazanov (see his sister's memoir in Medvedev (London, 1971), 132–6).

[5] The books were B. Borilin and A. Leont'ev, eds., *Protiv mekhanisticheskikh tendentsii v politekonomii* (1929), and S. A. Bessonov and A. F. Kon, *Rubinshchina ili marksizm?* (1930). The 'letter of the ten', dated August 1929, criticising a hostile review of the former book by Butaev in P, August 4, 1929, was signed by Berezin, Borilin, Kruglikov, Leont'ev, I. Litvinov, L. Mendel'son, Mekhlis, Ostrovityanov, Eventov and Khmel'nitskaya. The 'letter of the twelve', dated September 1929, was signed by Bessonov, Bumber, Butaev, Kats, A. Kon, Laptev, Mednikov, Rappoport, Saigushkin, Kholmyanskii, Chernomordik and Shumskii. They were both transmitted by *Pravda* to the economic journals, and were published in PZM, 10–11, 1929, 250–8. Skvortsov-Stepanov, a 'mechanist' in philosophy (see p. 145 n. 28 above), would no doubt have supported the 'twelve'.

Events now moved swiftly towards a denouement. The central committee plenum which denounced Bukharin and the Right danger in strong terms met from November 10–17. While it was in progress, on November 16, a general meeting of the economists at the Institute of Red Professors, while criticising 'the idealist trend in political economy', reserved its main fire for the mechanists. It was unable to identify them politically with Bukharin and the Right wing deviation, but it accused them in effect of guilt by potential ideological association:

The meeting considers that the mechanist tendencies which are to be found in the sphere of political economy may in the future come together with the non-marxist non-dialectical mechanist assumptions which are characteristic of Bukharin and his 'school'.[6]

According to one of the participants, at this point, on the initiative of the party bureau in the economics division of the Institute of Red Professors, the economists 'turned to the CC of the party with a request to help them to take a correct position in the questions of the discussion'. This was followed by 'a discussion in the CC with the participation of representatives of the "Rubin" trend and a group of supporters of the struggle on two fronts' – the mechanists were apparently excluded.[7] At the meeting unnamed party officials stressed the political danger both of the mechanists, whose views were 'directly linked' with the standpoint of Right-wing opportunism on topical questions of the building of socialism, and of the idealists, whose views were 'directly linked' with 'Menshevik and Trotskyist conceptions on questions of the building of socialism' and with the views of the Second International. Following this broadside, the economists agreed to write an article criticising both trends; the article, though signed by Milyutin and Borilin, was 'a result of the collective creativity of the economists who participated in

---

[6] PZM, 10–11, 1929, 259; in P, February 17, 1930, an unsigned article castigating both schools in political economy again admitted that the mechanists were 'politically separate' from Bukharin, but argued that they were influenced by his 'mechanist conceptions'.

[7] Pashkov (1970), 82–3. According to Pashkov, early supporters of the 'struggle on two fronts' included Abezgauz, Dukor and Notkin.

the conference in the CC CPSU'.[8] Milyutin, himself once a Menshevik, had been a member of the central committee since 1917, and had held a variety of senior party and government posts, and his signature gave the article a stamp of authority; Borilin, a young economist, until this point had been a follower of Rubin. The article, published in the party journal _Bol'shevik_ and in two other journals at the end of January 1930, attacked the '_emptiness_' and '_scholasticism_' of the whole discussion, and made a strong link between errors in economics and political deviation, condemning Rubin in unprecedently harsh terms for his 'anti-revolutionary general political line'. It concluded by appealing to 'communist economists' to assist the planning agencies and the main economic departments of state such as Vesenkha. An editorial note attached to the article reiterated its major arguments, condemned both deviations as 'equally hostile to marxism', and announced that with the publication of the article 'the discussion must come to an end'.[9]

On December 27, 1929, in the midst of these discussions, Stalin publicly expressed his views about the state of economics in the course of his speech to the agrarian marxists. He attacked a variety of existing theories which 'choke the heads of our practical workers', and drew attention to the kind of urgent investigation which economists should undertake. In particular, he condemned all existing work on the balance of the national economy. The 1923/24 balance published by the Central Statistical Administration in 1926 was 'not a balance, but playing with figures', and the approach of Bazarov and Groman 'will not do'. Instead, 'a scheme for the balance of the national economy of the USSR must be worked out by revolutionary marxists, if they in general want to occupy themselves with elaborating questions of the economy of the transition period'. More generally, 'it would be desirable for our marxist economists to appoint a special group to elaborate problems of the economics

[8] Pashkov (1970), 82–3. The author naively comments that his narrative refutes assertions that the discussion was 'broken off artificially, by administrative interference from above', and claims that 'it was brought to an end by the economists themselves with the assistance of the CC CPSU'. This ignores the obvious fact that the economists' appeal for party intervention was triggered off by the unexpected and unprecedented condemnation of both schools in the authoritative _Pravda_ note of October 10, 1929.

[9] B, 2, January 31, 1930, 48–63; see also PE, 1, 1930, and PKh, 1, 1930.

of the transition period in the new situation'.[10] Six weeks later, in the midst of his travails with the collectivisation of agriculture and the elimination of the kulak, Stalin summed up the discussion on economics in his answers to questions from the students of Sverdlov Communist University:

> It seems to me that in the disputes between the economists there is much that is scholastic and contrived. If the outer shell of the disputes is discarded, the main mistakes of the parties to the dispute are as follows:
>
> (a) neither party has been able to apply properly the method of the struggle on two fronts, both against 'Rubinism' and against 'mechanism';
> (b) both parties have been distracted from the basic questions of the Soviet economy and world imperialism into the sphere of Talmudic abstractions, and have thus wasted two years of work on abstract themes, to the gratification and profit of our enemies, of course.[11]

Stalin's comment of February 9 appeared some days after the publication of the article by Milyutin and Borilin, and thus merely confirmed an official viewpoint which had already been announced in principle several months before. We do not know what part Stalin personally played in the preparation of the *Pravda* note of October 10, 1929, or in the discussions with the economists in the central committee at the end of the year. The three interventions by the party authorities pushed the economists to renounce both the main trends in political economy, encouraged the denunciation of errors in economics as political deviation, or even as counter-revolution, and directed economic theory towards propagandist support for current party policies.

In the first few weeks of 1930 many harsh criticisms of both mechanism and Rubinism appeared in the press.[12] Motylev, a

[10] *Soch.*, xii (1949), 171–2.
[11] *Soch.*, xii (1949), 190, dated February 9, 1930 (originally published in P, February 10, 1930).
[12] See, for example, P, January 6 (Ronin), March 1 (Motylev), 1930. An unsigned article 'On New Rails: the Results of the Economic Discussion' appeared in P, February 17, 1930.

strong advocate of rapid industrialisation, condemned Rubin
for his '*menshevik idealist revision of marxism*'.[13] This was nine
months before Stalin's famous conversation with the philosophers
in which he applied the term '*menshevising idealist revision of marxism*'
to Deborin (see p. 151 above).

In spite of the strong appeals to the economists to turn their
attention to the economics of socialist construction, during 1930
few contributions of substance were made to the marxist theory
either of the socialist economy, or of the transition to socialism.
Throughout 1930, the view that political economy was concerned
only with the capitalist mode of production continued to prevail:
summing up, Lapidus and Ostrovityanov, two well-known
young economists, declared that societies which were 'organised
and directed by the conscious human will', from the peasant
economy in kind to the communist economy, 'do not contain
material which political economy could study'.[14] It is surprising
that the party authorities did not bring themselves to adjudicate
in favour of Engels' political economy 'in the wider sense',
particularly after the publication of Lenin's remarks on
Bukharin. The narrow definition of political economy certainly
diminished the importance of the economic theory of socialism
in the eyes of the theorists: according to *Pravda*, 'some circles'
regarded the theory of the Soviet economy as 'theory of a lower
order'.[15] In the 1930s the party authorities, and Stalin personally,
confined themselves to setting limits to the permissible theories
of the socialist economy and did not rule in favour of
a particular theory. But in the prevailing political atmosphere
the economists were reluctant to advocate theories of their own.
The reply to a long discussion in the Communist Academy in
May 1930 revealingly pointed out that 'people do not want to
speak out in advance of the [party] congress', citing an
economist who refused to write a discussion article for *Bol'shevik*
until after the congress was over.[16]

The discussion was in any case confined within narrow

---

[13] P, March 1, 1930; for Motylev, who pioneered the attack on the 'attenuating
curve' in the drafts of the five-year plan, see Carr and Davies (1969), 841,
876–7.

[14] Lapidus and Ostrovityanov (1930), 11.

[15] P, February 17, 1930 (unsigned article).

[16] VKA, xxxvii–xxxviii (1930), 101 (K. Rozental'); the discussion took place
between April 29 and May 23.

bounds, as economic theorists had to establish a hierarchy of laws, regularities or regulators for the transition period which did not involve either the Right-wing heresy of Bukharin's single market regulator or the Trotskyist heresy of Preobrazhensky's two regulators. The young economist Gatovsky attempted to subsume all previous discussion by the bold proposition that the plan was both the 'regulator' and the 'basic law of motion' of the Soviet economy, and that this had been true throughout NEP. The plan 'asserts its dominance in the struggle with spontaneous tendencies', but even at the time of the scissors' crisis of 1923 the plan had proved to be dominant.[17] Other economists sought other devices to maintain the principle of a single regulator which was neither the market nor the 'law of value'. S. L. Rozental', arguing that in the early stages of NEP 'we counterposed the dictatorship of the proletariat and not the plan to spontaneous movement and the development of the capitalist elements', concluded that at that time the proletarian dictatorship was itself the regulator, and was gradually replaced by the plan.[18] Stetsky made the anodyne suggestion that 'in the transition period the law of extended reproduction lies at the basis of our movement to socialism'; this sidestepped all the problems.[19] Raskin, however, plausibly argued that the law of motion of the transition economy should incorporate the relation between the socialist sector and the other sectors, as well as the main tendency of the socialist sector itself. He therefore suggested that the basic economic law was the 'law of socialisation'.[20] Lapidus and Ostrovityanov, in the 1930 version

[17] See the discussion in the Institute of Economic Research of Gosplan, reported in PKh, 4, 1930, 130–91, esp. 171–3. Gatovsky also advanced these propositions in articles in B, 13–14, July 31, 1929, 80, 85, and in PE, 1, 1930, 80, 82.

[18] PKh, 4, 1930, 150; from 1933 onwards the view was widely held that the dictatorship of the proletariat continued to be the law of motion of the Soviet economy even in the 1930s (see Shirokorad (Leningrad, 1974), 85–90).

[19] B, 3–4, February 28, 1930, 106; the article was signed 'A.S.'; Stetsky was a member of the editorial board of the journal. A. I. Stetskii, a former supporter of Bukharin, later became head of the culture and propaganda department of the central committee and a member of the Orgburo. According to SV (Paris), 23(308), November 25, 1933, 9–10, he was small, with large spectacles, democratically dressed in a ragged jacket and a Russian shirt, and looked like a zemstvo statistician; this account portrays him as an intelligent man who did not allow himself to think for himself.

[20] PE, 4–5, 1930, 49–50.

of their well-known textbook, sought to attach more weight to the role of the law of value without lapsing into the errors of Bukharin or Preobrazhensky, and ambiguously suggested both that the law of value was dying out and being replaced by the planning regulator, and that it was being 'transformed into' the planning regulator; they ineptly likened this to 'the transformation of a caterpillar into a butterfly, which takes place inside the cocoon'.[21]

The party authorities did not attempt to adjudicate on this tedious discussion about questions of principle for many years.[22] As a result, entirely contrary to their intentions, the teaching of socialist economic theory remained vague and confused; not even a systematic textbook existed in this period.[23]

(B) THE TRANSITION FROM NEP TO SOCIALISM

It was common ground for all marxists in the Soviet Union in the 1920s that under the New Economic Policy the economy was moving through a long transition period between capitalism and socialism. Socialism, the first phase of communism, would be reached by the end of this period. In this first phase the social product would still be distributed according to work done, but it would be characterised not only by the elimination of capitalist relations of production and hence of exploitation, but also by the complete replacement of trade, the market and the money economy by direct planning and product-exchange; the state, as an agency for the repression of the exploited classes, would begin to wither away. In the second, higher phase of communism, distribution according to work done would be replaced by distribution according to need; the distinction between town and country and between mental and manual labour would disappear; the state would finally wither away.

[21] Lapidus and Ostrovityanov (1930), 464–5, 472–3; on this view see Illarionov (1984), 86–7. If the law of value was the caterpillar and the planning regulator the butterfly, what was the cocoon?
[22] A Soviet historian of the economic thought of this period remarked with some restraint 'the methodological aspects of the problems of the basic economic law had not yet been elaborated' (Shirokorad (Leningrad 1974), 83).
[23] See Guznyaev (Kazan', 1976), 87.

These were the general principles; and they did not formally contradict the classical concept of socialism advanced by nineteenth-century marxism. But for Marx and Engels socialism was not only a new economic system but also a new form of social relations. Lenin, in his 1914 article on 'Karl Marx' for the Granat encyclopedia, also firmly declared that 'Socialism, leading to elimination of classes, will thereby also lead to the elimination of the state', and in this context cited with approval Engels' dicta that in the new society 'government over persons will be replaced by the administration of things and the management of the process of production', and that society would 'reorganise production on the basis of a free and equal association of the producers'.[24] The notion that under socialism society would be controlled not from above but by the associated producers themselves was not explicitly rejected by the Bolsheviks after the revolution. But by the end of the Civil War it was undermined – or its application was delayed until the indefinite future – by the stress on central planning as the essential means of developing the Soviet Russian economy, and on one-man management in state enterprises. In the 1920s, with the triumph of the doctrine of socialism in one country, the withering away of the state was also delayed to an indefinite future (see pp. 139–40 above). The party leadership vituperatively condemned as unscrupulous demagogy the successive appeals from Left and Right oppositions for greater democracy in the state, the party and the factories.

The upheaval of 1929–30 saw a temporary recrudescence among Stalin's supporters of notions of workers' management and of the greater democratisation of the state (see pp. 141 above and 272–8 below). But throughout the 1930s discussions of the transition to socialism were almost entirely concerned with its economic aspects. Neither the withering away of the state nor the rights of the associated producers again found a place on the Soviet agenda until Khrushchev's political reforms of the early 1960s.

Within this restricted framework, in the course of 1929–33 the Soviet political leaders and their economic advisers, moulded

---

[24] Lenin, *Soch.*, xxi, 57–8; the section on Socialism did not appear in the encyclopedia (*ibid.* 422). Engels's statements are in *Anti-Dühring* (n.d. [? 1939]), 315, and in *The Origin of the Family* (1940, first published 1884), 198.

by their practical experience, evolved a fundamentally new concept of the nature of the socialist economy. After a few months of Utopian optimism, the first major steps were taken in this direction in the course of 1930.

The evolution of thought was prompted by the far-reaching changes in the economy and in economic policy in 1927–9, which posed crucial issues for the economists and the political leaders. What was the relation of these changes with the economics of the transition period? Did they amount to a new phase of NEP, or its abandonment? Were they to lead directly to the first, socialist, phase of communism, or would another stage in the transition period be interposed between NEP and socialism?

For the 'bourgeois economists' and the Right wing in the party, the NEP economy was essentially a market economy in which the state influenced the economic activity of the peasant indirectly through price and taxation policy and not directly through administrative coercion. The new policies of 1928–9 represented to them a reversion to war communism, and the end, or the beginning of the end, of NEP. At first Stalin did not openly disagree with the view that the market was at the heart of NEP. In his speech to the party central committee in July 1928, he insisted that NEP was not just a retreat, but was 'directed towards overcoming capitalist elements and constructing a socialist economy'; he still acknowledged, however, that this was 'by means of utilising the market, via the market, not avoiding the market'.[25] But by the spring of 1929, anxious to guard against the charge that the new policies meant the abandonment of NEP, Stalin perceptibly shifted his position. At the plenum of the central committee in April 1929 he argued that both 'a *certain* freedom for private trade' and '*the controlling role of the state on the market*' were aspects of NEP. This was almost unexceptionable. But he then proceeded to claim that the new system of making contracts with the peasants in advance for the sale of their products and the purchase of industrial commodities did not contradict the requirements of NEP, even though these transactions took place at prices fixed by the state; this 'method of contracts' had established 'new forms of trade turnover'. Though Stalin did not specifically say

[25] *Soch.*, xi (1949), 144–5.

so, the implication was that the whole of the new phase of development since 1927, described by Stalin as 'the period of *reconstruction* of the whole economy on the basis of socialism' formed part of the New Economic Policy.[26] Stalin's view was frequently reiterated by party spokesmen in the course of their veiled attacks on Bukharin in the summer of 1929.[27]

In his address to the conference of agrarian marxists on December 27, 1929, Stalin, whose pronouncements were now acquiring the characteristics of dogma, stressed that 'new practice is giving birth to a new approach to the problems of the economy in the transition period', and sought to expose certain deep-seated 'bourgeois prejudices, which are called theories'. According to Stalin, the theory of 'equilibrium', which was particularly identified with Bukharin, held that the socialist and capitalist sectors of the economy were like two boxes which would 'roll ahead peacefully on separate tracks', two parallel lines which contrary to the rules of geometry would eventually meet to produce socialism. Stalin objected that Soviet power and socialist construction could not be based over a long period on both large-scale industry and the backward petty-commodity economy of the individual peasant; the theory of equilibrium was a Utopian attempt to find a 'non-existent third road' between the capitalist and socialist roads to the unification of agriculture. A second bourgeois theory, the theory of 'spontaneous flow', asserted that the individual peasant would spontaneously follow the socialist town, whereas in fact the socialist town would have to lead the countryside by '*implanting* kolkhozy and sovkhozy'. Stalin concluded with some reflections on NEP, which seemed to imply that its days were numbered. Emphasising that 'NEP is not confined to a retreat, but also means preparation for a new decisive offensive on the capitalist elements in town and country', he indicated that NEP was only acceptable as a link between town and country insofar as it would 'secure the victory of socialism':

If we support NEP it is because it serves the cause of socialism. And when it ceases to serve the cause of socialism, we shall throw it to the devil. Lenin said that NEP had been

[26] *Soch.*, xii (1949), 43–9, 27; for contracts see vol. 1, esp. pp. 62–3, 68–9.
[27] See for example P, August 4, 1929 (Krumin).

introduced seriously and for a long time. But he never said that NEP had been introduced for ever.[28]

The notion that NEP was soon to be discarded appealed to the most vocal industrialisers of the period. On January 19, an article in the industrial newspaper declared that 'the stage we are entering ... is THE BEGINNING OF THE END OF NEP.' Two days later an editorial firmly proclaimed that NEP is '*NOT for ever*': while the struggle for socialism within the USSR was 'far from finished', it had entered a new period 'when victory is *predetermined*, when the competition ("who will defeat whom!") is finished and the question is merely one of completing the victory and realising its fruits'.[29] In a sharp exchange, the economic newspaper accused the industrial newspaper of being 'hoorah-optimistic' and disorienting its readers; the industrial newspaper in turn replied that its critics were 'panic-mongers' who were not used to the new rates of growth.[30]

Bogushevsky, the editor of the industrial newspaper, who was presumably responsible for the editorial of January 21, now embarked on a more wide-ranging reconsideration of NEP. Stressing that the crucial feature of NEP was the existence of commodity turnover, he argued that NEP and the period of transition to socialism were coterminous: the next stage after NEP would be the first phase of communism, in which the state would begin to die away. The present stage was the 'beginning of the end of NEP'. NEP was, however, only formally the means of completing the building of socialism, and was 'negated' in its present last stage. It was already possible to go over to 'direct operational action in all branches of the economy', as

[28] *Soch.*, xii (1949), 141–9, 179; for other aspects of this speech see vol. 1, pp. 197, 391–2, vol. 2, p. 87 and pp. 141, 150, 158–9, 165 above. At the X party conference in May 1921 Lenin cited with approval Osinsky's remark that the tax in kind had been introduced 'seriously and for a long time' (Lenin, *Soch.*, xxxii, 406). Six months later, at the IX Congress of soviets on December 23, 1921, he remarked about the New Economic Policy that 'we shall carry out this policy seriously and for a long time, but, of course, as has already been correctly pointed out, not for ever', and added that NEP was 'a response to our state of poverty and destruction and the great weakness of our large-scale industry' (Lenin, *Soch.*, xxxiii, 135).

[29] ZI, January 19 (Chernykh), 21, 1930.

[30] EZh, January 22, 1930; ZI, January 24, 1930.

the country was now an 'unbroken socialist plateau, intersected only in certain places by fissures of the private-economy sector'. It might therefore be better to call the present stage not NEP but PEPP (poslednii etap perekhodnogo perioda – the last stage of the transition period).[31] Simultaneously with the publication of Bogushevsky's article, a Gosplan report at a conference of planning and statistical agencies also stressed the element of novelty in recent developments. 'Market relations controlled by the state', which had been presented by Stalin in April 1929 as an essential aspect of NEP, were now described as giving way to *'planned and organised product-exchange'*.[32] The approach of the end of NEP was boasted about rather than denied.

At this point in the discussion, Stalin injected a note of mild caution. On February 9, in the course of his reply to the Sverdlov University students (see p. 159 above), he criticised party organisations which were endeavouring to eliminate Nepmen in the towns immediately, and provided a gloss to his earlier remarks about NEP:

> The well-known phrase in my speech at the congress of agrarian marxists should be understood as meaning that we shall 'throw NEP to the devil' when we no longer need to concede a certain freedom for private trade, when this concession gives purely negative results, when we have the possibility of arranging economic links between town and countryside via product-exchange, without trade with its private turnover, with its concession of a certain revival of capitalism.[33]

The logic of Stalin's position was that NEP involved private trade, that the existence of trade in any form presupposed the existence of private trade, and that NEP would come to an end

---

[31] ZI, February 9, 11, 1930; for Bogushevsky see SR, 43 (1984), 204–5 (Davies). He was first appointed editor of ZI early in 1929 (Valentinov (Stanford, Cal., 1971), 253n.), and resumed the editorship on January 11, 1930, after a period in which he had been replaced by Mezhlauk (SP VSNKh, 1929/30, art. 586).

[32] EZh, February 9, 1930 (V. A. Levin).

[33] P, February 10, 1930; the version in *Soch.*, xii, 186–7, published in 1949, replaces 'product-exchange' by 'our trading organisations' and adds 'private' before 'trade'.

only when trade was replaced by product-exchange. This implied that no intermediate period would intervene between NEP and the first or socialist phase of communism, and was on the whole consistent with his argument against the Right wing in April 1929. Some ambiguity, however, still surrounded such new phenomena as the contracts between the state and the peasant. Classified as forming part of the controlling role of the state on the market in April 1929, and therefore as part of NEP, or at least as not inconsistent with it, such developments might have been more consistently treated as elements of the future system of product-exchange which was emerging within NEP.

Stalin's remarks supported Bogushevsky's contention that the transition period and NEP were coterminous, but were clearly at variance with Bogushevsky's optimistic assertion that capitalist elements were already virtually elminated. After the reversal of the collectivisation drive at the beginning of March, numerous attacks appeared on Bogushevsky's rash assertion that 'the competition ("who will defeat whom!") is finished' and on his description of the Soviet economy of February 1930 as an 'unbroken socialist plateau'.[34] He soon conceded his error, explaining that it had been inspired by the beginning of the world crisis in the United States, but admitting that it objectively reflected 'dizzy' attitudes to the rate of collectivisation.[35]

A new chapter in the discussion was opened with the publication in *Bol'shevik* of an article by K. Rozental' entitled 'The New Stage'. While rejecting any notion that NEP would be eliminated immediately, Rozental' argued, with the aid of numerous quotations from Lenin, that the essence of NEP was the use of 'indirect controls (oposredstvuyushchie zven'ya)' to create a large-scale socialist industry, as distinct from *direct* 'socialist construction'. While the transformation of NEP into direct socialist construction was only just beginning, 'a whole number of economic and political measures which we have *already begun* to carry out do not fit into the framework of the "new economic policy"'. In Rozental''s conception, the transition from trade to socialist product-exchange formed part of a

---

[34] For example, P, March 20, 1930 (K. Rozental'): EZh, March 20, 1930 (Gatovskii); B, 7–8, April 30, 1930 (Vaisberg).

[35] B, 7–8, April 30, 1930, 77.

transition from NEP to direct socialist construction, and
product-exchange did not form part of NEP.[36] The notion that
only indirect controls formed part of NEP was vigorously
assailed as Bukharinist by Bogushevsky and others.[37] More
constructively, another contributor proposed to define the new
stage as the last stage of NEP, one in which 'we have gone over
to a policy of direct transition to socialism' without any
intervening stages, and which would be concluded when NEP
Russia had become socialist Russia:

> NEP is a form of movement of the contradiction between the
> socialist economy of the working class and the private-
> property economy of the small-scale peasant. At the same
> time development of its content ensures *the resolution of this
> contradiction and thus its 'removal' as a form of movement of this
> contradiction.*

'Product-exchange' thus formed part of NEP and Bukharin had
been wrong to describe recent developments as a 'reduction of
the volume of NEP'.[38] The issue was, however, not yet closed.
In the pre-congress discussion, an attempt was made to
distinguish the tumultuous changes of 1929–30 as a stage in the
transition period which was neither part of NEP nor not a part
of it: it was rather a 'dialectical synthesis of war communism
and NEP'.[39]
At the XVI party congress Stalin bluntly rejected the notion
that the socialist offensive was incompatible with NEP,

[36] B, 5, March 15, 1930, 60–84. A few days earlier, on March 13, 1930,
Pravda, in an exchange with *Za industrializatsiyu*, endeavoured to cite Lenin in
proof of the view that product-exchange was a possible form of NEP, but on
the following day, March 14, it conceded that Lenin had held that product-
exchange was a possible form of NEP only if the private commodity producer
had freedom to trade and certain concessions were made to capitalism: ZI,
March 15, 1930, was triumphant about *Pravda*'s rare lapse.

[37] B, 7–8, April 30, 1930, 78–88; an indignant refutation by Rozental'
appeared in *ibid.* 95–117; participants in a protracted discussion at the economic
section of the Communist Academy in April–May 1930 were reproved by
Milyutin in his closing remarks for concentrating on the search for a Right-
wing deviation in Rozental''s thought (PE, 4–5, 1930, 219–21).

[38] B, 7–8, April 30, 1930, 121, 126–8; 10, May 31, 1930, 87, 97–8 (Butaev);
Bukharin's phrase appeared in P, February 19, 1930.

[39] EZh, June 25, 1930 (Veisbrod).

condemning it as a stupidity derived either from Trotskyists who believed they could abolish NEP in a flash or from Right wingers who wanted to stop the offensive:

> In going over to the offensive along the whole front, we are not yet abolishing NEP, for private trade and capitalist elements still remain, commodity turnover and the money economy still remain. But we are certainly abolishing the initial stage of NEP, and developing its following stage, the present stage of NEP, which is its last stage.[40]

This firmly incorporated the collectivisation of agriculture, forced industrialisation and centralised administrative planning within the framework of NEP.[41] Stalin remained fully committed to the view that product-exchange and the elimination of the monetary economy were crucial features of socialism. This was still common ground to all participants in the discussion. On February 13, 1930, a decree of TsIK and Sovnarkom on internal trade spoke matter-of-factly about preparations for 'the gradual transition from the general planning of commodity turnover to planned socialist product-exchange'.[42] In a pamphlet on the *genplan* prepared for the XVI party congress, Krumin even argued that the transition period would not be replaced by the first socialist phase of communism until everyone was employed by the state: by then the last kulak would have been eliminated and the last private shop closed, and the whole economy of the

[40] *XVI s"ezd* (1931), 37; in Stalin, *Soch.*, xii, 306–7, published in 1949, the phrase 'commodity turnover and the money economy still remain' is replaced by '"free" commodity turnover still remains'.

[41] In accordance with this dictum, NEP came to an end only when socialism was declared to be 'established in principle' with the virtual completion of collectivisation in 1936. In Soviet discussions about NEP in the early 1960s, several leading historians argued that NEP came to an end in 1929, on the sensible grounds that NEP was based on a market relation with the peasants. The Brezhnev period saw a return to orthodoxy. 'Bourgeois authors', according to Polyakov *et al.* (1982), 228–9, citing *inter alia* the present author, 'date NEP from 1921 to 1928'; 'the objective of this chronological scheme is clearly to distort the true essence of NEP by separating its first years from the period of the decisive offensive against the capitalist elements in town and country, when the socialist nature of NEP disclosed itself most clearly'. However, in *Moskovskie novosti*, November 9, 1986, Ambartsumov denounces 'the renunciation of NEP at the end of the twenties'.

[42] SZ, 1930, art. 181.

kolkhozy socialised; no basis for underground trade would exist.[43] In another collection of articles prepared by Gosplan for the XVI party congress, Gatovsky explained that in a socialist economy, an economy in kind would replace the market, indirect plan control via price and the market would give way to direct planning, and 'moneyless service to the working people' would replace distribution via money. 'Moneyless service' would be achieved by a form of rationing, probably by using a 'labour book' with a fixed upper limit to consumption so that free choice was available. According to Gatovsky's then entirely orthodox view rationing was not just a result of temporary food difficulties:

> Is there not something here of the inevitable process of turning the economy into an economy in kind? We think there is, and to no small degree![44]

The achievement of a fully socialist economy was also assumed to involve the central planning of labour, though the implications of this were seldom discussed.[45]

The hopes of achieving product-exchange and a moneyless economy in the immediate future were gradually abandoned in the course of 1931 and 1932. The postponement of these goals eventually led the party leadership to abandon the daunting assumption that socialism would not be established until they were achieved, in favour of the more restricted notion that socialism simply required the social ownership of the means of production. Stalin took a first step towards the redefinition of socialism at the conference of agrarian marxists in December 1929, when he insisted that the kolkhoz was a form of socialist economy.[46] But throughout 1929 and 1930 it was still universally supposed that the personal ownership of farm animals and implements by collective farmers was private ownership, and

---

[43] Krzhizhanovsky *et al.* (1930), 40–5.

[44] *Na novom etape* (1930), ii, 7–51.

[45] See Mordukhovich (1931), 12, 14–15, who cites with approval the statement in the party programme of 1919 about the distribution of labour between geographical regions and branches of the economy, and declares that it is essential to 'reduce the spontaneous movement of labour to a minimum and then eliminate it', using both 'administrative' measures and income and housing incentives.

[46] For this controversy see vol. 2, pp. 85–7.

that bazaar trade by collective farmers was private trade, and incompatible with socialism. For the moment, then, the original definition of a socialist economy remained.

How long it would take to complete the transition to socialism was strongly disputed. In the spring of 1929, Sabsovich, in putting forward his version of the general plan (*genplan*), assumed that it would take fifteen years to eliminate classes and complete the building of socialism.[47] This was soon to seem unduly modest. In November 1929, an article in the economic newspaper, with the blessing of its editors, called for the preparation of a 'general plan for the construction of socialism' in which both collectivisation and the 'construction of socialism in principle' would be achieved in 7–8 years.[48] Not to be outdone, the industrial newspaper a few weeks later proposed a much more exacting time-table. Zolotarev, a prominent Vesenkha official, contended that all remnants of capitalism could be eliminated within two years, and that the first phase of communism would be completed by 1936/37 during the course of the second five-year plan; the higher phase of communism, when the state began to wither away, would then follow.[49] This article perhaps presented the most optimistic of all the long-term prognoses circulating at that time. It was immediately criticised by the economic newspaper for jumping a phase.[50] A few months later, in the less heady atmosphere of the spring of 1930, Kviring in a pamphlet on the *genplan* for the XVI congress contended that the most that could be achieved in 10–15 years was '*to complete the transition period and to construct in principle the first phase of communism*'; how quickly the first phase would grow into the second could not be predicted.[51] But even Kviring expected that 'simple commodity economy' could be eliminated within 5–7 years, and that during the lower phase of communism the kolkhoz peasant would go over to a wage system and gradually become equal to a worker, possibly within the period of the *genplan*.[52] It eventually proved possible to achieve the first, socialist, phase of communism by 1937 only by making

[47] See Sabsovich (1929), and B, 13–14, July 31, 1929, 119–22.
[48] EZh, November 24, 1929 (Mindlin).
[49] TPG, December 7, 1929.
[50] EZh, December 8, 1929.
[51] Krzhizhanovsky *et al.* (1930), 37–42.
[52] *Ibid.* 45–9.

drastic changes in its definition, so as to incorporate socialised trade, the kolkhoz market and the money economy within the first phase of communism.

(c) MONEY AND SOCIALISM

Throughout 1930 it was taken for granted that the establishment of socialism would involve the abolition of money. The strengthening of planning and the state sector, accompanied by the decline of the free market, was therefore universally presumed to mean that money relations would give way to relations in kind.

The protracted dispute in the 1920s about the nature of exchange relationships within the state sector had already posed the problem of the role of money and prices in the transition period. Preobrazhensky argued that within the state sector, as far as means of production were concerned, price was 'merely the title' to the receipt of resources and to the maintenance of a certain level of accumulation; thus a locomotive, though 'sold' within the state sector, was a product (produkt), not a commodity (tovar). Within the state sector a new content was filling the old form, and the money form of exchange was in many respects empty and could be replaced.[53] His opponents, with varying degrees of vehemence, rejected the notion that the state sector was independent of market forces or could become independent of them. Protagonists of sound finance such as Yurovsky strongly insisted that the situation on the market was the sole criterion of equilibrium between the state and the private sector. Prices and plans must be adjusted to the market situation; even within the state sector the 'law of value', and money relations derived from the market, predominated.[54]

By this time exchange within the state sector itself was almost universally regarded as product-exchange. This interpretation was taken to its logical conclusion by Mekhlis, who argued that because the category of value did not dominate in socialist industry, the worker did not sell his labour power to the state, and did not create surplus value for the state; 'wages' in state

[53] Preobrazhensky (1965), 162–4; he added the qualification that the 'law of value', by which he roughly meant the free play of supply and demand on the market, influenced price via the payment of the worker for his labour power.

[54] Yurovskii (1928), 372–6.

industry were really a new type of production relation, and their present capitalist form would gradually be replaced.[55]

The emergence after 1927 of non-market coercive relations between the state and private sectors added a further complication. In April 1929 Stalin argued that state contracts with the peasantry did not contradict the requirements of NEP (see p. 164 above). But exchange of this kind was generally treated in the literature of 1929–30 as a further form of product-exchange.

The partial supersession of the market by product-exchange implied that the role of money was changing substantially. In the journal of Gosplan in August 1929, G. Kozlov argued that money as an economic category was coincident with the law of value as a regulator of the economy. Within the socialist sector, what appeared to be money was 'mimicry, assisting a calmer development of the new relations':

> Money, as real money, is needed by the plan as long as it is still an independent force as a regulator . . . As the plan becomes a regulator of the economy, money is transformed into accounting units (raschetnye znaki).[56]

Maimin, who was rapidly becoming prominent in Narkomfin, welcomed Kozlov's article as 'the first serious marxist attempt' to pose the problem of the nature of finance in the transition period, and argued that it was essential to establish the stages in which the existing financial system would '*gradually die out and become an economy* in natura (naturalizovan), *and be reconstructed into a planned system of accounting units*'. He also announced that the whole question would be the subject of a special report by Gosplan to the government in June 1930.[57]

The theme was taken up by Krzhizhanovsky in lyrical terms when he presented the 1929/30 control figures to the TsIK

---

[55] B, 3–4, February 28, 1930, 40–4. The maintenance of this position was stubbornly insisted upon in the debates about the economic theory of socialism many decades later. In 1969 I attended a Soviet conference at which a well-known economist indignantly repudiated someone who had incautiously suggested that the Soviet worker created surplus value, remarking that in the past he would have been put up against the wall for the error.

[56] PKh, 8, 1929, 114–38.

[57] EZh, October 12, 1929 (discussion article).

session of December 1929. He admitted that a huge distance had to be covered before the language of money could be dropped, but claimed that it was not the market but the plan and public opinion which were decisive in the new situation. This meant that money would increasingly become 'an accounting unit', and 'a receipt for labour':

> If the present control figures are studied attentively, it will become clear that behind the monetary language the language of products (blagi) in kind, which directly serve the mass of working people, is growing.

Krzhizhanovsky looked forward to a time when the control figures would be replaced by a red book, showing what the worker would accomplish and receive, a blue book showing the energy plan (including solar energy), and a yellow book presenting the plan in money terms. The yellow book would be less important than the other two, and would only be retained at all 'insofar as monetary language is retained'.[58]

In the first few weeks of 1930 a number of articles supported the view that the transition from capitalism to socialism automatically involved the gradual elimination of money as a category. A discussion article in the financial journal referred to the 'degeneration' of money, and held that with the growth of the state sector money in the USSR was becoming 'labour coupons'; the 'irrational money form' was retained solely because of the existence of a non-socialist sector.[59] Z. Atlas, later the most prominent Soviet scholar in the field of money and banking, hailed the credit reform as a 'major step on the road to the preparation of the socialist organisation of product distribution'. In this socialist society, 'there is no money, credit or commodities', and all output is measured in 'labour-rubles', distributed to workers in 'labour bonds', and recorded and supervised by Gosbank:

> Of course the distribution apparatus of socialist society can be called 'cooperation' or 'state trade', and the central recording and supervising agency can be called a bank, and

---

[58] *TsIK* 2/V, No. 2, 11–12.
[59] VF, 2, 1930, 31, 36 (Berkovetskii).

labour bonds can be called 'money', and the movement of the latter can be called 'bank credit', *but all these terms are entirely free from the meaning they possess in unorganised commodity society.*[60]

Encouraged by this enthusiastic atmosphere, a young theoretician was alleged to have calculated at this time that money would no longer be required after April 1, 1931.[61]

Such rashness was not universal. D'yachenko, later a major specialist on money and prices, while envisaging that the major changes taking place within the socialist sector would be 'the beginning of the end of khozraschet', also firmly insisted that money transactions would be required as long as the non-socialist sectors continued. Even within the socialist sector itself the 'labour-hour' would not always represent the amount of socially-necessary labour; and money, though 'distorted' by the rise of planning, must remain the common unit for transaction between sectors.[62] Another economist, while envisaging that 'in the long run the solution of the problem of currency issue in Soviet conditions will rest on payment of wages in kind and on the collectivisation of all economic processes', nevertheless insisted that the purchasing power of money in the meantime must remain stable.[63]

The more cautious approach was soon to prevail. In an interview on the occasion of the sixth anniversary of the currency reform of March 1924, Bryukhanov, the People's Commissar for Finance, complained that many people considered money to be superfluous, and argued that money remained a measure of value, an instrument of circulation, a means of savings and a general means of payment. On the same day an editorial in the economic newspaper criticised the 'dizziness from success' of those who treated Soviet money as mere accounting units:

Such a 'leftist' conception leads to an indifferent attitude to questions of currency circulation, and to its planning and

[60] Atlas (1930), 435–6; the preface is dated April 28, 1930. For his later account of the debate on money in 1930, see Atlas (1969), 264–6.
[61] *XVI s"ezd* (1931), 343 (cited by Bryukhanov).
[62] VF, 1, 1930, 59–63 (report for Institute of Marxism, Leningrad).
[63] EO, 2, 1930, 30 (Blyum).

control. It creates a harmful temptation to follow the line of least resistance, the line of unlimited currency issue, of turning so-called accounting units into a supplementary bottomless source for financing the national economy.

The policy of 'victory by numbers' must be decisively abandoned.[64]

These pragmatic considerations were not, however, accompanied by any change in views about the future role of money. The editorial in the economic newspaper stood by the position that money would no longer exist in 'developed socialist society'.[65] A few weeks later, a discussion article in the financial journal sought to show that money would continue to be a 'useful method for measurement and evaluation' even in the longer term.[66] But such attitudes were rare at this time. The view that the role of money was being steadily restricted in the new phase of Soviet development continued to prevail. Gatovsky argued that what was taking place in the USSR was 'the inevitable process of the turning of the economy into an economy in kind' (see p. 171 above). Noting that transactions within industry were already 'in substance socialist product-exchange', he looked forward to the development of non-monetary accounts in relation to the population, which would eventually lead to the keeping of all records in terms of labour units.[67]

The discussions on money and socialism acquired an air of fantasy not merely because of their Utopianism but also because the authorities would not permit open acknowledgement of the existence of inflation (see p. 311 below), facilitating this proscription by preventing publication of any systematic data about retail prices. Nor was it possible to discuss the multiplicity of prices and their effect on the nature of money. Maimin,

---

[64] EZh, March 11, 1930; a similar line was taken by Butkov in *Finansovye problemy planovogo khozyaistva*, 3, 1930, 6–8; this is the successor journal to *Vestnik finansov*, the last issue of which was No. 2, 1930.

[65] EZh, March 11, 1930.

[66] FP 4, 1930, 37–48 (Dobrogaev); the article was rhetorically entitled 'Does Finance Have a Future?', and was ambiguously welcomed by the editors for 'posing the problem'.

[67] *Na novom etape* (1930), ii, 36–9; see also his article in B, 19–20, October 30, 1930, 81.

endeavouring to come to grips with this problem, argued that a single stable monetary unit no longer existed:

> Today we are concerned not with a single ruble, but with rubles of various kinds. We have a 'workers'' ruble, a 'peasant' ruble, and also a 'Nepman' ruble.[68]

But this attempt to introduce elementary realism into the discussion was repudiated as a 'Trotskyist approach' which took the line *'either accept inflation or abandon the agreed rates of construction'*, and failed to recognise that the Soviet economy was an integrated whole, which must participate in the world economy 'with a single world measure of value (tsennost') in terms of gold'.[69] A few months later Kozlov, repudiating his own earlier view that money had already turned into 'accounting units' as 'a very "leftist" "theory"', rejected both Maimin's 'three-ruble theory', as originating from Preobrazhensky, and the 'Right wing' proposal that the ruble should be based on gold, but did not propose a further theory of his own.[70] The question of the place of money in the emerging socialist economy was not resolved for several years. In the meantime economic analysis gave way to a pragmatic insistence, in conditions of growing inflation, on the importance of currency stability.

[68] EZh, May 9, 1930.

[69] EZh, August 5, October 21, 1930 (both articles by Bronskii); for Maimin's reply, in which he accuses Bronskii of wanting to subordinate the plan to the gold ruble, see EZh, September 23, 1930.

[70] ZI, December 29, 1930 (report of December 25 to Economic Institute of Red Professors and the Institute of Economics of the Communist Academy).

CHAPTER SIX

PLANS FOR A HEROIC AGE, 1929–30

'We are convinced that 1940 will see only one great world power – the USSR!'

L. M. Kaganovich, speech to Moscow regional party conference (P, June 8, 1930).

(A) THE CONTROL FIGURES FOR 1929/30

Two weeks before it was finally approved by the V congress of soviets, the optimum variant of the five-year plan was already being nudged aside by the imperative claims of industry. On May 7, 1929, the presidium of Vesenkha, in its preliminary discussion of the control figures for the economic year October, 1, 1929, to September 30, 1930, approved production targets for several major industries which exceeded the figures for 1929/30 set out in the official five-year plan.[1] Immediately after the congress of soviets, Gosplan made a short-lived attempt to prevent further escalation of the plans, proposing to Vesenkha and the other commissariats that the 1929/30 figures in the five-year plan should be taken as the basis for the control figures.[2] But in the course of July and August the five-year programmes for several individual industries were revised upwards under pressure from Rabkrin (see pp. 187–90 below). In this context a crucial unpublished directive was issued by the central authorities, probably in August, which ruled that capital investment in Vesenkha-planned industry should amount to 3,000 million rubles, 30 per cent above the five-year plan target

[1] *Protokol VSNKh, 1929*, No. 17, art. 418.
[2] *Informatsionnyi byulleten' Gosplana*, 2, June 1929, 12–15 (theses presented to conference on the control figures, May 22 and 27).

for 1929/30. Capital investment in industry in 1928/29 was already about twice as high as in 1913, and was now planned to increase by over 80 per cent in a single year.[3] Kviring, first deputy chairman of Gosplan, later pointed out that the investment proposed for 1929/30 meant that 'almost the whole increase in national income will be utilised for the needs of the economy'.[4] Even the very high figure of 3,000 million rubles concealed the extent of the proposed increase, as it excluded certain investments which formed part of the five-year plan figure; the comparable figure is apparently 3,200–3,300 million rubles (see Table 5).

On August 25, following this directive, Kuibyshev announced the main features of the Vesenkha draft of the control figures. The production of Vesenkha-planned industry would increase by 31·2 per cent, most of this increase being made possible by a rise in labour productivity (output per man-year) of 23·5 per cent. Wages, however, would rise by a modest 8·1 per cent, thus enabling production costs to be reduced by as much as 9·5 per cent. Capital investment in industry was planned at 3,070 million rubles, as much as 2,538 million rubles of this being allocated to Group A industries.[5]

These ambitious plans were justified by the plausible but unrealistic assumption that the rate of progress achieved in the summer of 1929 could continue throughout the following year. In June–July 1929, production in Vesenkha-planned industry was 29·2 per cent and labour productivity 20·4 per cent higher

---

[3] The existence of the directive is referred to in TPG, October 13, 1929, by G. Smirnov; he explained that a Vesenkha proposal to plan on the localities to plan on the basis of a total Vesenkha investment of 2,700 million rubles was based on the directive of 3,000 millions, which was reduced in order to hold back inflated claims. The directive may be roughly dated from Bogushevsky's statement in TPG, October 9, 1929, that the Vesenkha proposal of 2,700 million rubles was made two to three months previously, and by Kviring's statement in EZh, August 9, 1929, which implies that Gosplan was then working with a lower investment plan.

[4] P, October 11, 1929, reporting discussion at session of Sovnarkom and STO on October 6; for this discussion see pp. 183–4 below.

[5] TPG, August 25, 1929; the Vesenkha control figures submitted to Gosplan were published as a separate volume, *Kontrol'nye tsifry promyshlennosti na 1929/30 g.: materialy k dokladu VSNKh SSSR Gosplanu SSSR* (n.d. [1929]). On August 14, the presidium had approved a preliminary plan to increase production by 28 per cent (*Protokol VSNKh, 1929*, No. 29, art. 743).

than in the equivalent months of 1928.[6] The planners argued
that in 1929/30 labour productivity could be expected to
increase more rapidly than in 1928/29, because capital per
worker was planned to increase by as much as 30 per cent;[7] a
leading industrial statistician pointed to the 'decisive significance'
for improved productivity, both of the reconstruction work
carried out in past years and of the completion of new
enterprises.[8] The planned reduction in costs would in turn
result in a substantial increase in industrial profits, and these,
together with some other economies, and a further increase in
the budget allocation, would provide the basis for the proposed
increase in the capital investment plan.[9]

The reasoning was circular: higher productivity enabled higher
investment, higher investment enabled higher productivity. Such
reasoning had increasingly dominated planning ever since
Strumilin's draft five-year plan alarmed the second Gosplan
congress in the spring of 1927.[10] Its fundamental weakness was
that the so-called 'qualitative indicators' for cost and productivity
were adjusted to fit in with and sustain the quantitative
production and investment plans. As Syrtsov delicately put it,
'disputes about whether particular qualitative indicators can be
achieved usually begin only after claims and requirements have
been examined and to some degree approved'.[11] The procedures
for deriving the cost reduction plan were later candidly described
by a Gosplan official:

> How is the cost reduction plan obtained? The potentialities
> of various factories and what can be obtained there should be
> analysed. But this is not what happens. An output of a
> certain magnitude is required, a certain level of costs is
> required, and this requires a certain amount of resources for
> capital construction; in order to obtain the necessary amount
> we distribute it over total output. In this way a particular

[6] *Byulleten' Kon''yunkturnogo Instituta*, 8, July 1929, 16–17; these figures are
measured in pre-war prices, and do not take account of the decline in quality.
Labour productivity was measured in output per work-day.

[7] Krzhizhanovskii *et al.*, *Osnovnye* (1930), 28 (Strumilin).

[8] EO, 10, 1929, 8 (Gukhman).

[9] VF, 9, 1929, 6-7 (Gerchuk).

[10] See Carr and Davies (1969), 854–64.

[11] SKhG, October 15, 1929.

percentage is obtained, which we call the required percentage of cost reduction. To a certain extent all this is pure arithmetic.[12]

Even enthusiastic advocates of these neat calculations admitted that the effort to achieve the 1929/30 plan would put the whole economy under further strain. In the three months following the publication of the Vesenkha draft control figures, Gosplan sought to achieve a rough balance in the control figures for the national economy as a whole, both by cutting down claims and by forcing every sector into greater reliance on its own resources. After various preliminary meetings in Vesenkha and Gosplan, the VI planning congress, which met from September 22 to 27, 1929, was entirely devoted the 1929/30 control figures. On behalf of Gosplan, Strumilin proposed that in order to balance income and expenditure the costs of production in industry should be reduced not by 9·5 but by 11 per cent, while Kviring proposed to reduce the capital investment plan of Vesenkha from 3,069 to 2,922 million rubles and of transport from 1,332 to 1,215 million rubles. The proposed changes were vigorously opposed by Vesenkha; and the representative of Narkomput', pointing out that the freight plan for 1929/30 was larger than the proposal in the five-year plan for 1931/32, insisted that without the additional investment *transport will inexorably become a bottleneck for the stormily-developing national economy*. In his reply to the debate Kviring revealed the difficulty or impossibility of reconciling the plan with financial stability in a cry of despair:

Ronin proved here that it would be absolutely impossible to carry out the Vesenkha plan without obtaining an additional 600 million rubles. But where can they be obtained? What shall we cut? Transport, agriculture, trade, housing? There is nothing which can be cut anywhere.

The congress ended in deadlock on this crucial issue: in his

[12] PKh, 9, 1930, 43 (Vizhnitser, in conversation with shock workers, October 6, 1930); technical indicators such as metal consumption per unit of construction were derived in a similar way.

final speech Krzhizhanovsky noted that 'major financial disagreements were not finally eliminated'.[13]

The debate now moved to a series of joint sessions of Sovnarkom and STO. Kviring continued to defend the Gosplan proposals for industrial investment, while Kuibyshev, although conciliatory in tone, even insisted that the Vesenkha plans for capital investment should be increased still further, and, in a revealing passage, criticised Gosplan for approaching the question 'not from the point of view of the economy but from the point of view of balancing the plan'.[14] The debate, like others at this time, was heroic or militant in tone. At the Sovnarkom session on October 3, Pyatakov, in a dramatic intervention, frankly described the three years 1927/28 to 1929/30 as 'the most difficult, the most serious, the most tense years' and praised the control figures of Gosplan as 'a very bold and it may be said heroic stance'.[15] Krzhizhanovsky addressed the session of October 6 in equally eloquent terms:

The control figures have the object of mobilising 50 per cent of the national income in the current year for financing the economy. Such a goal can be posed only when a war is taking place. In the name of this war, declared by the control

[13] For reports of the congress see TPG, September 24, 26, 27, 28, 1929, and Krzhizhanovskii *et al.*, *Osnovnye* (1930); the figures set out in this volume are not the Gosplan proposals presented at the congress, but the final control figures approved by Sovnarkom.

The discussions of the control figures were supplemented by the preparation of an 'iron-clad minimum' capital investment plan. This was supposed to cover merely the continuation of existing work, plus essential safety measures, etc., and was intended to facilitate the transition from one budget year to the next (see TPG, August 14, 1929). At a meeting of the Gosplan presidium in August, however, Vesenkha presented proposals amounting to 2,117 million rubles, a figure considerably more than the total industrial investment in the current year 1928/29. After a confused discussion, the presidium resolved that the approval of the 'iron-clad minimum' should be delayed until after the approval of the control figures (TPG, August 16, 1929). Nevertheless a minimum plan of 2,144 million rubles for Vesenkha-planned industry was approved by STO on October 3, 1929, and included at least 134 million rubles investment in entirely new projects or extensions (see SP VSNKh, 1929/30, art. 107). This odd episode illustrated the difficulty of maintaining ordered planning at a time when extraordinary pressure was being exerted for the expansion of capital investment.

[14] P, October 11, 1930.

[15] TPG, October 5, 1929; see also vol. 1, pp. 148, 388.

figures, a war with the highest goals, it is necessary to require an improved quality of labour, and tension of the will.

Protected by these rhetorical flourishes, Krzhizhanovsky rejected Kuibyshev's strictures on the inadequacy of the control figures, which he extolled as 'a plan of national economic development' which was a 'monolithic whole'. But, on behalf of Sovnarkom and STO, Rykov came down on the side of Vesenkha. He supported the proposals to increase the investment allocations to industry, and announced a compromise plan to reduce industrial costs by 10 per cent; no greater reduction in costs was possible because it was urgently necessary to improve the quality of production. Sovnarkom and STO resolved to approve the Gosplan proposals 'in principle', a formula indicating that disagreements still remained. A commission was established under Kviring's chairmanship to draw up detailed directives based on the 'exchange of opinions' at the sessions.[16]

These meetings were accompanied by a bitter controversy between Vesenkha and Gosplan in the press. In the industrial newspaper, Gordon, a Vesenkha official, described the Gosplan proposals for capital investment as 'not financial disagreement but a blow at the volume of capital work'. Kviring retaliated by attacking the industrial newspaper at Sovnarkom, and the party cell in Gosplan unanimously condemned the newspaper for its 'completely impermissible' hints that Gosplan was taking a Right-wing position.[17]

At the VI plenum of Vesenkha, held two weeks after the Sovnarkom session, objections to the control figures unexpectedly appeared from another direction. Kuibyshev was confronted by strong protests from representatives of major trusts and factories, who argued that the control figures even in their Vesenkha variant failed to provide sufficient resources to enable the production targets to be met; and they also strenuously objected to the proposed cost reductions as unrealistic. Several representatives of Yugostal' complained that the targets for production and costs in the iron and steel industry did not take into account the poor quality and insufficient quantity of coke

---

[16] P, October 11, 1929, EZh, October 11, 1929.
[17] TPG, October 5 (Gordon), 6 (G. Smirnov), 9 (Bogushevskii), 13 (G. Smirnov); EZh, October 6 (Maimin), 8 (A. M. [Maimin]), 10, 1929.

and ore, or the cuts which had been made in the plans for investment in existing plant; these were so considerable that 'all allocations for rationalisation have been crossed out to the last kopek'. Lomov, the head of Donugol', complained that its production target had crept up from 29 million tons in the five-year plan to 33 million tons, and insisted that in view of the appalling conditions of food supply, and the inadequate provision of finance, this was 'beyond the power of Donugol' enterprises'. Something of the sceptical atmosphere behind the scenes was indicated by his remark 'I am for rates of growth, but for realistic and not paper rates'. Kuibyshev, resisting all these attempts to revise the plan, sternly warned the assembled members of the Vesenkha plenum:

> The task of every industrial official is not to prove the impossibility of the target, or to advance arguments against the possibility of fulfilling it, *but to present to the appropriate higher authorities the conditions under which these targets will be fulfilled.*[18]

On October 20, 1929, the Politburo discussed the control figures in preparation for the central committee plenum due to be held in the following month. It approved draft Sovnarkom directives on the control figures, but rejected theses on the control figures prepared by Rykov, not because of their economic content but because they failed to provide a political characterisation of the Right-wing deviation; Krzhizhanovsky and Kuibyshev were appointed joint rapporteurs to the plenum in Rykov's place.[19] The Sovnarkom directives retained the capital investment plan proposed by Vesenkha almost in its entirety, even adding at the suggestion of Gosplan an additional 100 million rubles for the reconstruction of the building industry; they also accepted the Gosplan proposal that industrial costs should be reduced by 11 per cent.[20] On October 23, Kuibyshev reported these and other changes to the presidium of Vesenkha, frankly admitting that they were 'so substantial that to fulfil the plan of industry necessitates additional tension of the entire

[18] TPG, October 11, 12, 13, 1929.
[19] *Industrializatsiya, 1929–1932* (1970), 586.
[20] *Loc. cit.*; TPG, October 25, 1929.

economic apparatus'.[21] No open objection to these plans was recorded. But at a Komsomol conference held soon after these decisions Kaganovich denounced unnamed persons for proposing a reduction in the industrial investment plan from 3,500 to 2,500 million rubles, and roundly declared that such proposals would prevent new factories from being built, and would result in the triumph of capitalism due to the weakness of the Soviet Union and its out-of-date equipment.[22]

At the central committee plenum which met from November 10 to 17, 1929, the control figures were the first item on the agenda, and the rest of the proceedings, though primarily concerned with agriculture, were coloured by recognition of the magnitude of the burden placed on the whole economy by the vast industrialisation programme. The resolution on the control figures accepted the main provisions already agreed by the Sovnarkom commission.[23] Capital investment in planned industry plus electric power was to amount to some 4,000 million rubles in 1929/30 as compared with the 2,800 millions proposed in the five-year plan. The round figures left room for further argument, but apparently assumed that investment in Vesenkha-planned industry would amount to 3,331 million rubles, and in electric power to 614 million rubles.[24] To make this investment possible, industrial costs were to fall by 11 per cent and building costs in industry by 14 per cent; production by Vesenkha-planned industry would increase by 32 per cent and productivity of labour by 25 per cent. Capital investment in transport and agriculture were also planned to increase more than had been proposed in the five-year plan, though the increase would be smaller than in the case of industry. Total investment would amount to 13,000 million rubles against the 10,200 millions proposed for 1929/30 in the five-year plan and 8,500 millions actually invested in 1928/29. The resolution acknowledged 'the complexity and difficulty of the tasks confronting us', but expressed an astonishing degree of optimism about the urban standard of living and the situation on the market, proposing that the rise in nominal wages by 9 per cent

---

[21] TPG, October 25, 1929; a meeting of the presidium of Gosplan on the decisions of the commission is reported *ibid.* October 24, 1929.

[22] P, November 1, 1929.

[23] *KPSS v rez.*, ii (1954), 620–32.

[24] Krzhizhanovskii *et al.*, *Osnovnye* (1930), 4–5.

should correspond to an increase in real wages of at least 12 per cent; the excess of real above nominal wages was to be achieved by a reduction in the prices of industrial goods.[25] On December 1, 1929, the control figures were endorsed by TsIK without further substantial change.[26] In an impassioned report, Krzhizhanovsky described 1929/30 as the 'spinal year' of the five-year plan; this became the phrase by which it was generally known.[27]

(B) THE TRANSFORMATION OF THE FIVE-YEAR PLAN

(i) The plan as a whole

In the summer of 1929, the targets of the optimum variant of the five-year plan were revised upwards in several major industries. On June 20, following a circumstantial and ambitious report from Rabkrin of the RSFSR, the Politburo recommended that the five-year plan for timber production and export should be increased.[28] A month later, on July 18, a further Politburo decree increased the five-year plan for the domestic production of cotton fibre; if achieved, the new plan would enable the elimination of all cotton imports in the course of the five-year plan.[29] On July 25, the Politburo approved resolutions on the Leningrad engineering and shipbuilding trusts, incorporating Rabkrin proposals.[30] Taken together, these changes already signalled an abandonment of the five-year plan in favour of much more ambitious objectives. Kuibyshev was at this time a fervent advocate of forcing the pace, and in a private letter of

[25] *KPSS v rez.*, ii (1954), 620–32; for the controversy about industrial prices, see pp. 300–1 below.

[26] SZ, 1929, art. 724.

[27] Krzhizhanovsky's report appears as *TsIK 2/V*, No. 2. On April 2, 1930, Sovnarkom authorised an additional expenditure of capital investment by Vesenkha-planned industry of 339 million rubles (see Table 5, note k).

[28] *Industrializatsiya, 1929–1932* (1970), 584; see also Zaleski (Chapel Hill, 1971), 95, note 36; for the Rabkrin report, see Rees (1987), 181–2, 280 n. 84.

[29] *Resheniya*, ii (1967), 85–93; Rabkrin proposed an output of 917,000 tons of cotton fibres in 1932/33 against the five-year plan of 589,000 tons; the central committee on July 18 approved a compromise figure of 785,000 tons.

[30] *Industrializatsiya, 1929–1932* (1970), 584.

July 30 written from a Crimean resport he expressed the dominant mood among the party leaders:

> The CC dealt a shrewd blow about cotton. I like this very much: bold, with breadth of vision, a bolshevik approach. Although this decision strikes at Vesenkha (we did not manage to shake up Glavkhlopkom), I am ready to applaud. I hear similar decisions have been taken for some other industries (non-ferrous metals, tractors, Leningrad, timber, fish, etc.). Greater investments are being undertaken on a considerably larger scale than in my variant of the five-year plan.[31]

Further party and government decisions about major industries followed in quick succession. On August 2, a STO decree on non-ferrous metals called for a 'fundamental revision' of the five-year plan, increasing the plans for 1932/33 from 85,000 to 150,000 tons in the case of copper and from 5,000 to 20,000 tons in the case of aluminium.[32] On August 13, a STO decree explicitly based on a Rabkrin report called for an acceleration of coal-mine construction in the Donbass, with greater use of foreign technical assistance.[33] On August 27, a further decree of STO increased the timber procurement plan for 1932/33 from 125 to 180 million cubic metres, so as to provide additional timber both for the building programme and for export.[34] This decree broadly followed the earlier recommendations of Rabkrin of the RSFSR and Rabkrin of the USSR, which were considered by a special commission of STO chaired by Syrtsov.[35] Two days later, on August 29, a Politburo resolution entitled 'On the Work of the Northern Chemical Trust', but in fact dealing with the chemical industry as a whole, emphasised the importance of the industry both for economic development and as 'a terrible weapon of destruction and annihilation in forthcoming imperialist wars', strongly criticised the backwardness of the Soviet industry, and called for the revision of the five-year plan and the reorganisation of the industry 'on the basis of the plan

[31] Kuibysheva *et al.* (1966), 302–3.
[32] *Direktivy*, ii (1957), 90–7.
[33] SZ, 1929, art. 487.
[34] SZ, 1929, art. 550.
[35] See Rees (1987), 181–2, and Zaleski (Chapel Hill, 1971), 95, note 34.

agreed by Vesenkha and Rabkrin'. A remarkable feature of this resolution was its insistence that by the beginning of the year 1931/32 all the main orders for chemical equipment should be met within the USSR.[36]

By August 1929 Rabkrin had become the major political instrument for the acceleration of industrialisation by overcoming the inertia and prudence of the commissariats and the *glavki*.[37] Special brigades of CCC/Rabkrin were involved in revising the plans and the organisation of almost every industry, undertaking their own independent examination of production possibilities, for individual factories as well as at the national level. The conflict between Rabkrin and the industrial managers and specialists took its most acute form in the continued debate about the Ukrainian iron and steel industry. Rabkrin relentlessly and enthusiastically advocated its proposals for Yugostal', which sought to increase production plans while simultaneously economising in capital investment through the improved and fuller use of existing capacity (see p. 69 above). Rabkrin insisted that ten old blast-furnaces which Vesenkha intended to scrap should be kept in use, and that all existing furnaces should be used much more efficiently. New increased coefficients of utilisation of furnace area, which Rabkrin worked out individually for each major furnace, should replace those in the Vesenkha plan. Such careful details gave an attractive air of realism to quite wild proposals. The proposals acquired additional authority because they were supported by the German engineer Karner, employed by Rabkrin as a senior consultant. Karner was described at the time by Rabkrin as 'one of the best foreign experts on Russian iron and steel, whose work in the USSR has been of great value, demonstrating in practice that foreign experience is extremely useful'.[38] Forty years later an equally senior Soviet engineer bitterly criticised Karner's 'pedantic estimates': 'he was at the factories and saw nothing, basing himself on the attitude that everything that was needed for the work of the blast and open hearth and Bessemer

---

[36] *Direktivy*, ii (1957), 107–20; the trust was located in the Urals. On August 19, Tomsky was appointed head of Glavkhim and a member of the Vesenkha presidium (P, August 20, 1929; SZ, 1929, ii, art. 185).
[37] For the functions of Rabkrin, see pp. 237, 240–1 below.
[38] *Promyshlennost'* (1930), 25 (Gokhman).

furnaces was available'.[39] For its part, Yugostal' also called foreign consultants to its aid.[40] Faced with conflicting advice, Stalin and his colleagues in the Politburo almost invariably supported the cheaper and more ambitious plans emanating from the politically reliable Rabkrin. According to Ordzhonikidze, the Politburo examined the acrimonious dispute between Vesenkha and Rabkrin about Yugostal' 'in great detail', appointing commissions which included almost all the directors of Yugostal' factories, and 'in the main found our stand correct and developed it further'.[41] The victory of Rabkrin on this issue, a significant moment in the further increase in the pace of industrialisation, was confirmed by a central committee resolution of August 8, 1929, condemning the 'wrecking activity' of previous Yugostal' specialists and accepting the higher production coefficients proposed by Rabkrin.[42]

The successful advance of production in the final months of the 1928/29 economic year provided further encouragement to optimism, and strengthened expectations that the original five-year plan would be completed well ahead of time. On August 1, the local newspaper *Luganskaya Pravda*, in a note on workers' proposals for the five-year plan of the Lugansk locomotive factory, wrote 'Not five, but four, and perhaps 3'.[43] A week later, at a joint session of the presidium of Gosplan and the collegium of the Central Statistical Administration devoted to the preliminary results of the first year of the plan, Milyutin suggested that the control figures of Vesenkha indicated that the five-year plan would be fulfilled in four years in a number of industries.[44] On September 1, *Pravda*, praising the increases in the targets of the 1929/30 control figures as compared with the five-year plan, bluntly declared 'We will fulfil the five-year plan in 4'. Sabsovich, welcoming the slogan, claimed that the optimum variant of the plan, 'which some people thought was

[39] *Byli industrial'nye* (1970), 186–7 (Tochinskii); Karner is not named, but is described as 'a major German specialist, invited for consultation about metallurgy'.

[40] TPG, July 24, 1929; SS, xxxvii (1985), 159–60 (Fitzpatrick).

[41] *XVI s"ezd* (1931), 302–3; for the earlier stages in this dispute, see p. 69 above.

[42] *Direktivy*, ii (1957), 97–107; the decree appeared in P, August 13, 1929.

[43] Cited in *Leninskii plan* (1969), 112.

[44] EZh, August 9, 1929.

too tense and could not be achieved, has been decisively overtaken by life'.[45]

This foreshortening of perspective did not meet with universal approval. At the VI planning congress in September, Strumilin warned that 'the lag of agriculture makes talk of turning the five-year plan into a four-year or even a three-year plan premature'.[46] But in October Syrtsov declared that 'the fulfilment of the targets of the five-year plan in no more than four years is a completely realistic and achievable task'.[47] 'The Five-Year Plan in Four Years', or simply '5 in 4', now became a major slogan. A main heading in *Pravda* on the first day of the November plenum of the central committee announced that 'The Proletariat of the USSR Declares its Inviolable Decision to Fulfil the Five-Year Plan in Four Years',[48] and a *Pravda* editorial published in conjunction with the session of TsIK in the following month was simply headed 'The Five-Year Plan in Four Years'.[49] But the slogan did not yet receive the accolade of formal endorsement by the higher authorities. It did not appear among the official slogans for the twelfth anniversary of the revolution,[50] in Stalin's article 'The Great Break-Through', or in the resolutions of the November plenum. Someone somewhere behind the scenes was evidently still cautious about its feasibility.[51]

Throughout the rest of 1929, the five-year plans for the principal Soviet industries continued to spiral upwards. Various justifications were offered for increases in the plans. In industry

[45] VARNITSO, 6–7, September 20, 1929, p. 1.
[46] See Kuz'min (1976), 92; this sentence does not appear in Strumilin's published report in Krzhizhanovskii *et al.*, *Osnovnye* (1930).
[47] SKhG, October 15, 1929. On the following day, October 16, *Pravda* reported that Vareikis, at a peasant conference in the Central Black-Earth region, had supported amid stormy applause the demand of collective farmers in Khodol village that the five-year plan should be completed in four years.
[48] P, November 10, 1929.
[49] P, December 9, 1929.
[50] P, November 2, 1929.
[51] The slogan received slightly oblique but massive official endorsement on February 21, 1930, when the major mass loan for 1930/31 and 1931/32 was entitled 'The Five-Year Plan in Four Years' (SZ, 1930, art. 137 – decree of TsIK and Sovnarkom). At the XVI party congress in June 1930 Stalin declared 'we can fulfil the five-year plan in four years', and 'in a whole number of industries in three or even two-and-half years' (*Soch.*, xii (1949), 270).

after industry, as in the famous case of Yugostal', Rabkrin sought out additional capacity in existing factories, and then called for higher production plans. Higher plans in an industry imposed higher demands on the supply industries, and their plans were also increased.[52] Higher plans resulted in increased claims for imports of metals and machinery not produced in the USSR. In view of the acute shortage of foreign currency, this in turn gave rise to imperative demands that Soviet industry should take on new types of production previously imported.

In the last few months of 1929, further momentum was imparted to the escalation of the plans by the collectivisation drive. Mechanisation of Soviet agriculture along United States' lines, essential for its ultimate success, required a vast expansion in the supply of tractors and other advanced agricultural machinery. During 1929, the Kharkov and Chelyabinsk factories, both scheduled to be completed in 1931/32, were added to the Stalingrad and Putilov factories, which were already included in the five-year plan approved in April 1929.[53] The Chelyabinsk factory was to produce 40,000 giant caterpillar tractors, the first factory of this kind in the Soviet Union and the largest tractor factory in the world.[54] At the Putilov tractor shop, following the overfulfilment of the high target insisted upon by Rabkrin in 1928/29 (see p. 69 above), an even higher plan for 1929/30 was imposed on the management, and incorporated in the five-year plan.[55] In the revised five-year plan for the tractor industry approved by TsIK in December 1929, the production of tractors in 1932/33 was planned to reach 206,500 as compared with 55,000 in the optimum variant of the five-year plan; and the production of combine-harvesters, which were not included at all in the five-year plan, was planned at

---

[52] See Mednikov (1930), 61–2, for a description of this process by a Gosplan official.

[53] See NAF, 1, 1930, 62–3.

[54] *Protokol VSNKh, 1929*, No. 33, art. 856 (session of September 14, 1929); and STO decision of December 7, 1929 (TsGANKh, 7620/1/22, 65–1). For a comparison with factories outside the USSR, see Dodge (1960), 359.

[55] See Kuromiya (forthcoming), ch. 7. In June 1930 the chief engineer was arrested; in October, following the failure of the plan, the director was dismissed. Output in 1929/30 actually amounted to 8,934 against the original plan of 10,000 and the revised plan of 12,000 (Kostyuchenko *et al.* (1966), 317–20, 334–5).

40,000 in 1932/33.[56] Strong demands were also made for a complete revision of the plan for motor vehicles. Osinsky, the most forthright advocate of the automobile, estimated on the basis of data from 18 countries and the 48 United States of America that a country with the national income and road facilities per head of population of the USSR should produce over a million vehicles a year, one-third of which should be lorries; he accepted a Gosplan conference proposal, as a 'bare minimum plan', that 350,000 lorries and buses and 100,000 cars should be produced in 1932/33.[57] But these proposals were too extravagant even for the enthusiastic mood of 1929/30. In February 1930, Vesenkha had adopted a provisional plan to produce 200,000–300,000 vehicles in 1932/33,[58] and at the XVI party congress Stalin announced that the plan for 1932/33 had been fixed at 200,000 automobiles (see p. 334 below).[59]

The revised agricultural machinery and vehicle plans in turn placed greatly increased demands on the iron and steel industry, accounting for over 40 per cent of the increases made between April and December 1929 in the five-year plan for iron and steel.[60] The increased demand for kerosene and petrol was a major factor in the increase of the plans for oil production (see p. 197 below).

The public facade of enthusiasm for higher targets barely concealed considerable scepticism about their feasibility. S. Kosior, referring to the period October 1929–February 1930, reported in relation to the heavy industry of the Ukraine that 'in many factories and mines the management and technical personnel formed the firm opinion that the programmes are exaggerated and cannot be fulfilled; some local party

[56] *TsIK 2/V*, No. 6, prilozhenie, p. 12; the plan for tractors announced at the XVI party congress was 170,000 (see p. 334 below).

[57] P, June 9, 1929; for Osinsky's earlier support for the automobile, see Carr and Davies (1969), 446–7.

[58] P, February 23, 1930 (Gamarnik); see also Zaleski (Chapel Hill, 1971), 116, 119.

[59] At the congress Osinsky, now in charge of the tractor and automobile industry, again appealed for a further increase in the plan (*XVI s"ezd* (1931), 548–50); for his appointment see SP VSNKh, 1929/30, art. 290 (dated November 28, 1929).

[60] Total demand for pig iron increased from 10 to 17·6 million tons; 3·3 million tons of the increase was attributed to the needs of these industries (EZh, January 12, 1931 – Tseitlin).

organisations were also infected with these attitudes'; a 'shake-up (vstryaska)' had been required as a prelude to 'mobilisation along the entire front'. All leading specialists in the Southern Ore Trust, and the party group in the trust, as well as some of the enterprise managers, opposed its revised five-year plan.[61] Even in the open press, the more extravagant plans were cautiously criticised.[62] In the course of the first few weeks of 1930, the party authorities evidently themselves decided that the escalation of plans had gone far enough. The extremely ambitious plans for coal, oil, iron and steel, tractors and combine-harvesters which were current at the beginning of 1930 now remained more or less stable. In the course of the discussion of the 10–15 year 'general plan' at Gosplan in February 1930, even more extravagant plans were strongly criticised by Strumilin and Krzhizhanovsky; and their authors, including Sabsovich and Fel'dman, were henceforth no longer taken seriously (see pp. 226–8 below). The more cautious mood induced by the retreat from collectivisation in March 1930 no doubt helped to consolidate this partial moderation of fantasy. Voices pleading for caution now occasionally made themselves heard in the press, though any direct criticism of the major revisions of the plan was carefully avoided. Thus a Gosplan official warned in relation to the slogan 'the Five-Year Plan in Four Years' that *'dizziness is dangerous here as well'*; some plans would take more than four years and some less.[63] By the spring of 1930 the five-year plan approved a year earlier had been thoroughly disrupted, but no serious attempt was made to compile a new plan to take its place.[64]

[61] P, March 9, 1930.

[62] EZh, January 16, 1930, for example, reported that at a Sovnarkom commission, Lokshin, a senior official in Sabsovich's planning administration in Vesenkha, had defended a plan to produce 200,000 'children's cameras', accusing his critics of 'a light-minded attitude to the problem of educating the family', but it turned out that he had misread 'cheap (deshevye)' as 'children's (detskie)'.

[63] EZh, May 24, 1930 (V. A. Levin; discussion article).

[64] A coordinated five-year plan, a commentator in the industrial newspaper complained, is 'as necessary to us as air', but 'such a plan does not exist, and, most important of all, we evidently give very little thought to it' (Kapustin in TPG, May 28, 1930). On the other hand, some speakers at the planning conference of February 1930 (see pp. 227–8 below), including Gaister from Vesenkha, argued that *'the five-year plan has become a political document and should*

(ii) The fuel industries

Fuel and iron and steel were seen as the crucial industries on which all other developments depended. The petroleum industry had so far been the fastest-growing industry, and the industry in which technological change was most rapid. The plan for crude oil production in 1932/33 was increased from 22 million to 26 million tons in August 1929, and in October it was further increased to the huge figure of 40 million tons; production in 1927/28 was only 12 million tons. Ordzhonikidze later explained to the XVI party congress that the revision to 26 million tons did not meet the needs of the automobile and tractor industry or of the export plan.[65] Only 25 million tons could be obtained from existing oil-fields; as much as 15 or 16 million tons would have to be obtained from new fields, as yet hardly explored.[66]

Equally serious potential shortages faced the coal industry. In March 1930 a fuel conference sponsored by Vesenkha and Gosplan proposed a production programme of 140–150 million tons for 1932/33 as compared with the five-year plan of 75 million tons.[67] This involved producing 71 million tons of coal as early as 1930/31, the third year of the five-year plan:[68] the central slogan of the fuel conference was 'The Fuel Five-Year Plan in Three Years'.[69] In order to achieve these targets, work would have to be undertaken on 27 large new mines before the

---

not be revised'; while the aim should be to fulfil the existing five-year plan as a whole in even less than four years, modifications should appear only in the control figures (I, February 10, 1930). Whether this argument should be taken at its face value or as a veiled attempt to reduce the proposed rates of growth cannot now be established.

[65] *XVI s"ezd* (1931), 306; the plan of 40 million tons was approved by Soyuzneft', the oil corporation, in February 1930 (ZI, February 12, 1930).

[66] ZI, February 7 (prof. A. Sakhanov), March 14 (Lomov), 1930.

[67] ZI, March 9, 1930 (Krzhizhanovskii); see also Zaleski (Chapel Hill, 1971), 119. Vesenkha, however, did not go above a lower target of 120 million tons (P, April 26, 1930) (Shvarts).

[68] P, April 26, 1930 (Shvarts); an attempt by Chubarov to cut this figure to 68 million tons was curtly rejected at the presidium of Vesenkha by Rukhimovich as beyond the competence of industry (ZI, June 3, 1930).

[69] PI, 6, 1930, 66.

autumn of 1931, in addition to the large mines already under construction, and numerous smaller mines would also have to be started immediately at higher capital cost.[70] Experience with the construction of large mines had not been encouraging: only four of the sixteen planned in 1926 had been completed by the beginning of 1930, and these were expected to produce only 1·7 million tons in 1929/30. The new mines, designed by US and German firms, would have to be completed more rapidly than in German practice at its best.[71] Yet preparatory work was lagging considerably: geological assessments had been completed for only three of the proposed 27 new mines, and the new mines to be started in 1930/31 would absorb all the verified annual stocks of coal.[72] The lag was particularly great in the coal areas outside the Donbass; under the new plan these were to produce half of all Soviet coal in 1932/33, as compared with the 24 per cent proposed in the first five-year plan.[73]

As well as enormous increases in total output, the revised plans for fuel also involved major technological changes. The fuel conference of March 1930 concluded that even the huge new targets were inadequate to cope with the rising demand from industry, the production of which was now expected to increase by as much as 40 per cent in 1930/31, 45 per cent in 1931/32, and 50 per cent in 1932/33. It was therefore much concerned to improve the utilisation of fuel and to seek new simple ways of increasing available energy. But many delegates were cautious about proposals advanced at the conference to increase greatly the production and enrichment of low-grade local fuel. Most delegates were also reported to be sceptical about the plans of the Committee for Chemicalisation to treat Donets coal chemically *in situ* rather than transport it over long distances. On these specific technical innovations, the resolution of the conference was non-committal, admitting that it was impossible to avoid long hauls of fuel for the immediate future. But the conference also urged upon Gosplan and Vesenkha '*a fundamental re-examination of attitudes to the development of the energy economy of the country*'. The revised five-year plan for fuel assumed

[70] ZI, January 19, 1930 (Chubarov); PE, 6, 1930, 42–5; P, April 26, 1930 (Shvarts).

[71] ZI, January 19, 1930; P, April 26, 1930.

[72] PE, 6, 1930, 40; P, April 26, 1930; ZI, May 23, 1930 (editorial).

[73] PE, 6, 1930, 38.

that fuel consumption per unit of industrial output would fall by 40 per cent over the five-year period as compared with the figure of 31 per cent in the five-year plan.[74]

Fuel for tractors was particularly difficult to provide. The increased requirements of petrol and kerosene for 1932/33 now amounted to 18 million tons, as much as 14 million tons of this being needed by the automobile and tractor industry, as compared with the production of only 2·4 million tons in 1928/29. Even if the planned 40 million tons of crude oil were obtained in 1932/33, additional plant would be needed to crack 7 million tons of petrol from heavy oil, and many tractors would have to be redesigned to use petrol instead of kerosene. This was a formidable task. The Soviet Union had virtually no experience of the cracking process, but plants to be installed were the equivalent of over one-third of world cracking capacity.[75] In these circumstances the leading expert Ramzin urged at the fuel conference that tractors should be redesigned to use diesel or heavy oil, or gas generated from straw.[76] The Thermotechnical Congress which followed the fuel conference also urged in its resolution that tractors should go over to heavy or solid fuel.[77] But these proposals were hardly a more practical prospect for the immediate future than the fantastic commitment to develop vast unexplored oil fields in two or three years and revolutionise oil refining. The Rabkrin report on the industry prepared in the summer of 1930 struck an unusually despairing note.[78]

(iii) Iron and steel

The urgent need for rapid growth and technical change was particularly apparent in the case of the iron and steel industry.

[74] The conference is reported in PI, 6, 1930, 66–8; ZI, March 9, 11, 12, 14, 15, 16, 1930.
[75] ZI, February 7, 1930 (prof. A. Sakhanov).
[76] ZI, March 11, 1930.
[77] For this congress, see ZI, March 16, 18, 20, 21, 22, 1930; its resolution took a more favourable attitude to local fuel than that manifested at the fuel conference. The proposal to develop a gas-generating tractor had already been raised by Gosplan with Vesenkha in May 1929 without result; proposals to convert tractors to diesel or gas were placed before STO by Gosplan in May 1930 (P, May 14, 1930).
[78] *Promyshlennost'* (1930), 116–31 (Bulushev and Izrailovich).

This industry lagged behind all the other major heavy industries in the 1920s; and in 1928 the optimum variant of the five-year plan, which planned to increase the production of pig-iron from 4·0 million tons in 1928/29 to 10 millions in 1932/33, was adopted in face of very strong opposition.[79] In February 1930, a leading Gosplan official reminded his colleagues that the target of 10 million tons had been pushed through only by '*the iron will of the party and the working class*, intuitively grasping the impending prospects for development of the economy'.[80] But by that time the debates of the previous winter seemed to belong to a distant and peaceful era. As a result of the investigation of Yugostal' by Rabkrin in the summer of 1929 (see pp. 189–90 above), the Politburo concluded in August 1929 that improvements in the efficiency of blast-furnaces would enable the existing factories of the trust to produce not 5·2 but 6–6·5 million tons of pig-iron, and in December the technical council of Gipromez, the State Institute for Designing Metal Works, increased this figure to 6·9 millions.[81] Faced with an explicit decision by the Politburo, the Soviet specialists ceased open resistance to these proposals, and the Yugostal' board at last accepted them.[82] But the foreign specialists, with the exception of Rabkrin's Dr. Karner, remained sceptical. Specialists from the United States and Germany pointed out that high coefficients of utilisation were achieved in their own industry only through the use of less sulphurous coke and through using quartzite rather than iron ore and complained about the method used to justify the planned Soviet coefficients:

> *The coefficients do not arise from the technical possibilities of the project; it is the technical possibilities which are driven forward by the boldly depicted dynamics of the coefficients.*

An American engineer sceptically commented on the existing furnaces that 'rejuvenation of these old fellows won't give satisfactory results'.[83]

The plans for new iron and steel works were also revised

[79] See Carr and Davies (1969), 886–8, 896.
[80] PKh, 3, 1930, 199 (Kovalevskii).
[81] *Byulleten' Gipromeza*, 7–8, 1929, 95 and 1, 1930, 8.
[82] ZI, January 1, 1930 (Briz).
[83] ZI, January 1, 1930 (report by Briz).

upwards in the autumn of 1929. On November 11, Sovnarkom of the RSFSR, after hearing a report from the head of Magnitostroi, resolved that the capacity of the works should be increased from 650,000 to 1,100,000 tons.[84] The Kuznetsk project was also increased by 50 per cent sometime towards the end of 1929, in spite of Bardin's objections.[85] These changes alone increased the possible output of the whole industry in 1932/33 from 10 to over 12 million tons. Meanwhile the demand for iron and steel continued to spiral upwards. On October 27, 1929, Glavchermet recommended to the presidium of Vesenkha that production in 1932/33 should be increased to 12 million tons in view of the likely shortage of metal.[86] In December, the All-Union Metal Syndicate VMS issued a report calculating the demand for pig-iron and rolled steel for each major consuming department, and concluded that the demand for pig-iron in 1932/33 would reach 17·51 million tons.[87] In December 1929, the total production plan for 1932/33 was increased to over 16 million tons; the planned capacities of both new and existing factories were substantially increased.[88] From the beginning of

---

[84] P, November 1, 1929; *Iz Istorii* (Chelyabinsk, 1965), 56; this decision, presumably because of the level at which it was made, was not regarded as final approval (*TsIK 2/V*, No. 6, 36).

[85] Bardin (Novosibirsk, 1936), 7. For the successive plans for new iron and steelworks, see Table 6 below.

[86] Zuikov (1971), 36, citing the archives.

[87] TPG, December 17, 1929; EZh, January 12, 1930; *Metall*, 1, 1930, 15–26. The report, which was described by Glavchermet as 'very provisional', was prepared by Rikman, Spivak and Tseitlin; Rikman was one of the authors of the previous demand estimates (*Metall*, 1, 1929, 37–46).

[88] The following table compares the main sources of pig-iron production proposed in various drafts of the iron and steel plan prepared in 1929 (million tons):

	1927/28 Actual[a]	1932/33 Basic variant[a]	1932/33 Optimum variant[b]	1932/33 VMS[b]
Existing works				
Ukraine	2·4	5·0	5·2	6·5
Ural	0·7	1·4	} 2·2	2·5
Other	0·2	0·3		1·3
Total	3·3	6·7	7·4	10·3
New factories	–	1·3	2·6	6·1
Total	3·3	9·0	10·0	16·4

[a] *Pyatiletnii plan* (1930), i, 39–44.

[b] TPG, December 17, 1929.

1930 a new plan of approximately 17 million tons was accepted as the framework for the development of the industry. In January 1930, Kuibyshev even spoke of 'a dispute about whether the output of pig-iron should be increased to *17* or to *25* million tons'.[89] In the same month the Urals authorities proposed a target for the Urals alone of 7·5 million tons in 1932/33.[90] But I. Kosior, now responsible for new iron and steel factories, endorsed the target of 17·5 million tons in February;[91] and the Ural target was later cut from 7·5 to 4 million tons by a commission headed by Kuibyshev.[92] In May 1930, the iron and steel corporation Stal' prepared a new variant of 15·2 million tons, 5 million tons of which were to be produced in new works, and Vesenkha in a submission to the presidium of Gosplan envisaged a possible expansion to 18 million tons through the construction of further new works.[93] The target of 17 million tons was eventually endorsed by the XVI party congress.[94]

Although the five-year plan for the industry was not further increased after the beginning of 1930, several major changes were made in the planned pattern of production and technology as compared with the five-year plan. The decision not to replace existing plant, but to continue to use it whenever possible, promoted by Rabkrin in the previous summer, became a firm feature of the new plan, for the Urals as well as the Ukraine. But, in the massive amount of new construction which was to be undertaken, the most advanced Western models predominated. In the five-year plan adopted in April 1929 the proposed new iron and steel works were intended to be based on 'a standard model of a very large enterprise with an annual output of 650,000 tons', with provision for eventually producing double

[89] ZI, January 19, 1930.
[90] ZI, January 26, 1930; in a speech on this date at the presidium of Vesenkha, Kuibyshev implied that 17 million tons would be produced as early as 1931/32 (IA, 3, 1958, 74, printed from the archives).
[91] ZI, February 18, 1930.
[92] ZI, June 1, 1930.
[93] ZI, May 11, 1930 (Mezhlauk); EZh, May 10, 1930; PE, 7, 1930, 59.
[94] See *KPSS v rez.*, iii (1954), and pp. 334, 337–8 below. The increases in the iron and steel plans in turn required equivalent increases in the plans for iron ore and coke; the revised plans for these industries were, however, far less precise than those for iron and steel (see *Promyshlennost'* (1930), 67–90, 132–42, and, for iron ore, the Politburo resolution of April 15 on the Southern Ore Trust (*ibid.* 91–4) and Rees (1987), 183–4.

this output on each site, where raw materials and the nature of the site permitted.[95] This was already very large by Soviet standards: the capacity of the largest pre-revolutionary works, the Dzerzhinsky works in the Ukraine, was about 600,000 tons. But by 1929 the capacity of a modern iron and steel works in the United States was typically one million tons, and the capacity of the Gary works in Indiana, designed by the Freyn corporation, was as much as 3–4 million tons.[96]

The first major step towards the construction of iron and steel works of this size in the USSR was taken in the autumn of 1929, when Glavchermet authorised Gipromez to expand the final capacity of the Krivoi Rog project to 2·6 million tons, 1·2 million tons being reached in the first stage.[97] Meanwhile in the Urals a plenum of the regional party committee, which met from October 6–12, 1929, suggested that the capacity of Magnitogorsk should be expanded to 2·5 million tons.[98] By December, the proposal was seriously under discussion in Vesenkha.[99] On January 26, 1930, in an unpublished speech to the presidium of Vesenkha, Kuibyshev stressed the economic advantages of constructing in Magnitogorsk 'a more powerful works, using the ore of various regions for a single powerful giant' rather than the six smaller factories so far planned for the Urals.[100] A few days later he publicly stated that a sketch project for increasing the capacity to 4 million tons, now being completed in Gipromez, was '*evidently expedient and should be adopted*'.[101] On February 15, 1930, the Politburo approved a capacity of 2·5 million tons, with a subsequent extension to 4

---

[95] *Pyatiletnii plan* (1930), i, 42.

[96] For the Gary works see p. 202 below.

[97] *Byulleten' Gipromeza*, 7–8, 1929, 104.

[98] *Istoriya industrializatsii* (Sverdlovsk, 1967), 184; on the history of the Magnitogorsk decision see Kirstein (Baden-Baden (1979), Berlin (1984)), and Davies, ed. (1984), 88–106 (Kirstein).

[99] It was mentioned in a letter from M. G. Gurevich, head of the foreign department of Vesenkha, to McKee, dated December 10, and printed in *Iz istorii* (Chelyabinsk, 1965), 58–61.

[100] IA, 3, 1958, 71–2; losses from the higher cost of administration, housing and transport, however, were also anticipated (PE, 7, 1930, 61). The economies and diseconomies of scale are discussed in Clark (1956), especially 82–4 and chapter 6.

[101] ZI, February 2, 1930 (speech of January 28).

million tons.[102] The plant was explicitly intended to have a capacity as high as that of the Gary works. Ordzhonikidze later reported:

> Cde. Stalin asked about the capacity of factories in America, and the reply was that large factories in America gave $2^{1}/_{2}$ million tons of pig iron a year. Cde. Stalin said that we must build such a factory here, in the first place for 2–$2^{1}/_{2}$ million tons, and then for 4 million tons.[103]

The other new works which were eventually approved remained on a more modest scale; but it was clear that this expansion, if achieved, would result in an average size of iron and steel works in the USSR which was substantially greater than elsewhere in the world.

The new giant factories were planned to be technologically extremely advanced. Gipromez, the chief institute for designing metal works, claimed:

> In designing production units which are enormous in size and complexity, Gipromez is at the same time resolving the extremely complicated task of inculcating into our industry the most novel methods of production on the basis of the achievements of Europe and America, methods which are frequently very little known, or not known at all, not only in our factory practice, but also to the scientific and technical personnel of our country.[104]

---

[102] Unpublished decision cited from the archives by Zuikov (1971), 127; the first public reference to a project of 4 million tons seems to have been in a speech by Kuibyshev (ZI, January 19, 1930).

[103] Ordzhonikidze, *Stat'i i rechi*, ii (1957), 481 (speech of July 1933); the capacity of the Gary works was stated in the press at this time to be between 3 and 4 million tons, and it was made clear that this was the only United States works with a capacity of this order of magnitude (ZI, February 2 (Kuibyshev), 18 (I. Kosior), 1930; PE, 7, 1930, 61). The Ural authorities proposed at this time that a second works with a capacity of 4 million tons should be constructed at Alapaevsk forthwith (ZI, January 26, 1930); this proposal was not taken up in Moscow. A 4-million ton works was planned for Mariupol', in the Ukraine, and a 6-million ton works in the Urals was also under discussion (ZI, February 18 (I. Kosior), January 28 (Mezhlauk), 1930).

[104] *Byulleten' Gipromeza*, 7–8, 1929, 87 (Burov, director of Gipromez); for another view of Gipromez see p. 217 below.

The blast-furnaces were based on the latest American designs. Gipromez claimed the credit for securing their acceptance, with American assistance, against the opposition of 'the technical thought of our country'.[105] A senior Soviet specialist insisted, however, that even before 1914 'Americanism in blast-furnaces' had been 'stably rooted in the minds of the blast-furnace specialists in the South'; for twenty years all blast-furnace construction 'followed the path of imitating the best American models'.[106] The political authorities strongly supported the more advanced technology. Early in 1929 Kuibyshev, interviewing Bardin on the occasion of his appointment as chief engineer of Kuznetskstroi, asked him whether the blast-furnace in the Freyn project could be enlarged.[107] A test case was provided in October 1929 with the completion at the Tomsky works, Makeevka, of an $842m^3$ blast-furnace, then the largest in the USSR. The furnace worked at low capacity in the first three months, owing to the shortage of iron ore and coke. This led some members of Gipromez council to argue that smaller furnaces were more suitable to Soviet conditions; but this view was over-ruled by the technical council of Gipromez, supported by workers' organisations at the plant.[108] In 1930, engineers from the United States' Freyn Corporation working at Gipromez began to design a standard furnace of $920-930m^3$; this was later used in five different works.[109] McKee and Co. designed a $1,200m^3$ furnace for Magnitostroi, which was later also used in the second phase of Kuznetskstroi.[110] These furnaces were as large as the most advanced American models.[111] Some open-hearth furnaces were to be based on German, a larger number on United States' designs: their proposed capacity varied from 150–250 tons a day, somewhat lower than the most advanced in the United States.[112]

[105] *Ibid.* 89–90.
[106] *Byulleten' Gipromeza*, 3, 1930, 41.
[107] Bardin (Novosibirsk, 1936), 18–19.
[108] *Byulleten' Gipromeza*, 3, 1930, 63, 67–8 (Kotel'nikov); two other furnaces of this capacity were later introduced in this works (BSE, lxi (1934), cols. 265–6).
[109] *Byulleten' Gipromeza*, 3, 1930, 41; Lauer (1933), 40–1.
[110] P, June 8, 1930 (Birman), October 26, 1930 (Frankfurt and Brudnyi); Clark (1956), 321–2.
[111] See Clark (1956), 64.
[112] *Byulleten' Gipromeza*, 3, 1930, 50, 60–2; two recent United States furnaces, designed by the Freyn Corporation, had capacities of 300 and 350 tons.

The provision of rolling mills to handle the increased supply of crude steel was a less immediate problem than the construction of blast and open-hearth furnaces, as over a third of available rolling capacity was not yet in use.[113] The most spectacular longer-term decision was that in the major works under construction modern blooming mills should be installed to handle the large ingots produced by the new open-hearth furnaces: as the annual capacity of a large blooming mill was 750,000 tons, this would in itself make necessary a minimum annual supply of about one million tons of both pig-iron and crude steel for each works, even if only one blooming mill were installed.[114] In association with the bloomeries, the most advanced continuous rolling mills could in turn be constructed.[115] Large-scale capital construction, and in particular the development of tractor, vehicle and defence industries, also involved extensive changes in the use of existing rolling-mill capacity, bringing the pattern of output closer to that of the United States. Merchant bars and concrete reinforcements were required for the construction of the new works, while new machine-building and defence industries required sheet steel and above all high-grade steel of all kinds.[116] Soviet experience in the production of high grade or 'quality' steel (kachestvennaya stal') was limited to tooling steel and small quantities of special steels for the electrical industry.[117] The five-year plan prepared by Vesenkha in the spring of 1929, before the major increases in planned tractor and vehicle production later in the year, provided for the construction of the Dneprostal' and Dneprosplav works in the Ukraine for the production of quality steel and alloys; but assumed that some steels for engineering, vehicles, tractors and aircraft would need to be imported for two or three

---

[113] *Byulleten' Gipromeza*, 1, 1930, 12–13; NPF, 13, 1930, 21 (V. Lenin).

[114] PE, 7, 1930, 60–1.

[115] In P, June 8, 1930, Birman reported that this was to be the system at Magnitogorsk.

[116] *Metall*, 10–12, 1930, 106–9, compares the composition of output of rolled steel in tsarist Russia, the USSR and other countries.

[117] Clark (1956), 14–15, 311. Clark discusses the various Soviet definitions of 'high-grade steel' on pp. 309–11; it should be added that the definition was widened in 1932, so that 1927/28 output was 70,000 tons on the old definition, and 90,000 tons on the new definition (BSE, lxi (1934), cols. 258–283).

years.[118] In the course of 1929/30, a plan was prepared for the production of 1·3 million tons of quality steel in 1932/33 as compared with 70 thousand tons in 1927/28.[119]

The production of quality steel could not await the construction of new specialised factories, and was already undertaken in 1929 and 1930 at four long-established works.[120] In the first few months of 1930, the Soviet authorities decided that existing iron and steel works should be extensively and immediately converted to the production of quality steel pending the construction of new factories. In January 1930, in spite of the strong opposition of the management of both factories, Vesenkha confirmed its earlier decision that the Krasnyi Oktyabr' (formerly Dumo) works should supply quality steels to the Stalingrad tractor factory.[121] In May, the party central committee, reversing the decision in the five-year plan a year earlier to replace charcoal furnaces in the Urals by new coke furnaces, resolved that six of the major Ural charcoal-based works 'should be transformed into a main base for supplying the USSR with quality and high-quality steel and quality pig-iron, increasing the production of charcoal-based pig-iron in 1932/33 to 1–1·1 million tons'.[122] This decision fitted in well both with the principle that maximum use should be made of existing capital equipment and with the policy that a substantial amount of iron and steel capacity should be located in the Urals and beyond; charcoal-smelted pig-iron, being free of sulphur, was

[118] *Materialy k pyatiletnemu planu promyshlennosti VSNKh SSSR na 1928/29–1932/33 gg.* (1929), iii, pp. xxxiii–iv, 613; *Metall*, 1, 1929, 49.

[119] PE, 7, 1930, 48; an output of 1·3 million tons (old definition) was in fact first reached in 1935, when output was 1·57 million tons by the new definition (see Clark (1956), 20).

[120] Elektrostal' (Moscow), Putilov (Leningrad), Krasnyi Oktyabr' (Stalingrad) and at Zlatoust in the Urals (see Clark (1956), 311).

[121] See ZI, January 15, 16, March 28, October 24, 1930; P, July 31, 1930.

[122] *Resheniya*, ii (1967), 202–7, resolution of May 15; the proposals to continue charcoal smelting in the Urals were supported by Vesenkha but resisted by the director of Gipromez on the grounds that it would be more expensive than constructing new factories and displayed a 'barbarous attitude' to the use of timber (*Byulleten' Gipromeza*, 1, 1930, 4; *Gipromez*, 4, 1930, 1–2). For background material on the resolution of May 15 and a subsequent STO decree of June 16, see Zuikov (1971), 42–3, 178; ZI, May 11, 1930 (Mezhlauk), and Kirstein (Baden-Baden, 1979), 248–56.

especially suitable for the production of quality steel.[123] At the same time preliminary plans were prepared to construct largé quality-steel works in Zaporozh'e and in Bakal in the Urals; the Bakal works was intended to supply the Chelyabinsk tractor factory.[124]

The decision to establish two of the largest and most advanced iron and steel works in the Urals and in the Kuznetsk basin was not fortuitous. Increasing emphasis was placed at this time on defence aspects of industrial location, notably by Krzhizhanovsky, who at TsIK in December 1929 openly stressed the importance of the Ural industry for defence:

> One cannot close one's eyes to the fact that the Urals is the *spine* of our defence; the cde. Ukrainians must take this clearly into account, and realise that the Ukraine to a considerable extent is a frontier zone. Much of the construction which it is appropriate to put in the Urals it is inappropriate to put in the Ukraine.[125]

A few weeks later, on February 4, 1930, at the presidium of Gosplan, he defended the 'super trunk-line' associated with the Ural–Kuznetsk combine as justified on defence grounds, describing Siberia as 'our fortress in the world struggle':

> *Let the officials of the People's Commissariat for Transport and the professional railwaymen weigh up in the most serious fashion what a great super trunk-line in Siberia will mean for us in relation to defence. This is a problem of the highest order.* I emphasise this so that your civil conscience should always show a special interest in these problems.[126]

Even at the beginning of 1930 the Ural–Kuznetsk combine,

---

[123] Donbass coal is sulphurous and produces unsuitable pig-iron without special treatment: the proposed Ukrainian special steel plants were to use cheap power from Dneproges, while the Moscow and Leningrad works were primarily fed with scrap (Clark (1956), 312).

[124] ZI, January 26, 28, April 3, August 10, 1930; B, 15–16, August 31, 1930, 160; PI, 2, 1930, 58; PKh, 12, 1930, 277.

[125] *TsIK 2/V*, No. 13, 15.

[126] ZI, February 4, 1930; NPF, 5, March 15, 1930, 8; *Sovetskaya Sibir'*, February 16, 1930 (*cit.* Matushkin (Chelyabinsk, 1966), 376–7).

with its expensive 1,500km coal-ore shuttle, was not yet finally approved. The director of Gipromez argued that the coal deposits at Kizelovsk in the Urals should be urgently explored.[127] Ukrainian engineers, including Dimanshtein, the most stubborn opponent of the UKK, no longer publicly objected to the Magnitogorsk and Kuznetsk projects as such, but instead vigorously defended the immediate construction of the new Krivoi Rog works, for which a project of 2·5 million tons had been approved by Gipromez at the end of 1929.[128] At the presidium of Vesenkha, Kuibyshev took the conciliatory line that 'the speed of development of the economy we have now attained is so great that the Urals and the Ukraine can both be put under its roof': if the Urals were to produce 7 million tons in 1931/32, that left 10 million tons for the Ukraine.[129] But the authorities were soon finally committed to overriding priority for the Ural–Kuznetsk scheme. The central committee resolution on the Ural metal industry of May 15, 1930 declared:

> A vitally necessary condition for rapid industrialisation is to create in the East a second coal and iron and steel centre for the USSR by using the extremely rich coal and ore deposits of the Urals and Siberia.

This was the first central committee resolution to refer to 'combining the stocks of Ural iron ores which exceed one milliard tons with Siberian and Kizelovsk coals' and to 'the possibility of easily obtaining high-quality metal by uniting valuable Ural ores with high quality Siberian coke'.[130] Stalin is said to have insisted in the central committee that everything needed for the sites must be provided, and any opposition, direct or hidden, overcome. On June 1, 1930, a Sovnarkom

---

[127] *Gipromez*, 4, 1930, 4–5. The Ural authorities in their 'Plan for a Great Urals' wanted to base their industry on Ural coke, and attempts to develop coke from Kizelovsk coal were strenuously undertaken (ZI, January 21, 28, February 2, 1930), and the notion that Ural iron ore should be sent to Siberia was criticised at the presidium of Vesenkha (ZI, February 15, 1930).

[128] EZh, February 16, 1930 (Dimanshtein).

[129] IA, 3, 1958, p. 74 (speech of January 26, 1930); '1931/32' may be a slip for '1932/33'.

[130] *Resheniya*, ii (1967), 202–7; the reference to coal from Kizelovsk in the Urals was still an escape clause.

decree provided material support for the projects.[131] Not
everyone was convinced of the viability of the scheme: the
industrial newspaper felt it necessary to attack 'panic' from
'opportunistically inclined elements in our *apparat*', manifested
in 'little conversations' that 'such giants are beyond our
powers'.[132] But by the spring of 1930 the Ural–Kuznetsk
combine had moved to the centre of the industrial stage.[133]

The rise of the UKK was accompanied by the down-grading
of the projects for new factories in the South. In spite of a
stirring resolution by the presidium of Vesenkha urging support
for the new Krivoi Rog works,[134] it was allocated only the
miserly sum of 0·5–0·7 million rubles for 1929/30, as compared
with 58 million rubles to Magnitostroi and 35 million rubles to
Kuznetskstroi;[135] it was eliminated from the May 1930 variant
of the five-year plan prepared by Stal'.[136] A similar fate overtook
the second stage of the Kerch works; the first stage was greatly
delayed because Kerch ore proved to require agglomeration,
and Krivoi Rog ore could not be used successfully with the
Kerch plant owing to its low phosphorous content.[137] The
project to establish a large new works in Mariupol' was also
delayed.[138] By the spring and summer of 1930, the role of the
Ukraine in current projects for new works had greatly declined
as compared with 1929 (see Table 6).

(iv) The engineering industries

With the expansion of the five-year plans for fuel and iron and
steel, the engineering industries were in turn faced in 1929–30

[131] Frankfurt (1935), 268; ZI, September 27, 1930; the Sovnarkom decree
does not appear to have been published.

[132] ZI, June, 5, 1930.

[133] Even now Dimanshtein argued that specialised products such as pipes
should not be manufactured in Siberia (see his discussion with Rikman in
Metall, 6–7, 1930, pp. 7–33, and 8–9, 1930, pp. 44–54).

[134] See Carr and Davies (1969), 444.

[135] EZh, February 16, 1930; FP, 6, 1930, 106.

[136] PE, 7, 1930, 58.

[137] *Ibid.* 58; ZI, June 4, 1930 (Birman).

[138] In ZI, February 18, 1930, Kosior said it was to be started in 1930; in ZI,
April 1, 1930, he announced that the government had ceased construction for
the current year. At the XVI party congress, however, Kuibyshev announced
that it would produce 600,000 tons in 1932/33 (*XVI s"ezd* (1931), 483).

with burgeoning claims for an increased supply of modern machinery for the planned new coal mines, oil wells, iron and steel works and related facilities, and all original plans were swept aside.

In the optimum variant of the five-year plan, production in engineering as a whole was already planned to treble or quadruple by 1932/33.[139] This required fundamental reorganisation of an industry of which large sections were notoriously backward by international standards, and had fallen still further behind the advanced countries since 1916. In spite of some rationalisation during the 1920s, even in 1929 all engineering factories, even the largest, produced a variety of products for a variety of industries, often in small quantities. The five-year plan required the standardisation of output, and the specialisation of factories on particular types of output; auxiliary processes such as casting and forging would be transferred to new specialised factories.[140] Major advances were planned for several branches of engineering. In railway engineering, which was well-established in pre-revolutionary Russia, the production of modern rolling stock would require the fundamental reconstruction of existing locomotive and wagon factories, and the construction of a new wagon factory at Nizhnii-Tagil' in the Urals; the industry would not need to rely heavily on imports.[141] In electrical engineering, which was in its infancy before the revolution, but developed rapidly in the 1920s, expansion of the Soviet industry into new and complex lines of production was planned to be so considerable that imports would decline from 35 per cent of total demand in 1927/28 to 5 per cent in 1932/23.[142]

In view of the backwardness of many branches of engineering,

[139] *Pyatiletnii plan* (1930), ii, i, 157.

[140] *Ibid.* ii, i, 157.

[141] *Ibid.* i, 46–7, ii, i, 158.

[142] *Ibid.* ii, i, 105; in the Soviet classification in the 1920s the 'electro-technical industry' was treated as a separate industry, and engineering was divided into 'agricultural engineering', 'shipbuilding', 'transport engineering', and 'general engineering'; the latter category included all other engineering industries, and transport engineering was sometimes placed within it. The armaments' industries were often classified as part of 'engineering' (see p. 454 and Table 7(c) below). For the agricultural engineering industry, and for the tractor and vehicle industries, which were classified separately from engineering, see p. 219 below.

the five-year plan approved in the spring of 1929 frankly admitted that the next five years would merely 'lay a firm foundation' for the future of the industry, which would remain 'to a considerable extent at only the initial stage of development'.[143] The new Uralmashzavod at Sverdlovsk and the new heavy engineering works at Kramatorsk would not be completed until towards the end of the five years, so during 1929–33 most capital equipment for coal mining and iron and steel would be imported.[144] The infant machine-tool industry would manufacture only 'the most *popular* machines'. The complex special machine tools which would be required for the tractor and vehicle industries (and of course for the production of aircraft, though this was not mentioned in the plan) would be produced only in small quantities in order to gain experience for future developments.[145]

During 1929 and 1930, such caution came to be regarded as pusillanimity, or was even attributed to deliberate wrecking. In the machine-tool industry, the capacity of the new factories scheduled in the five-year plan was greatly enlarged, and the completion dates were advanced from 1932/33 to 1930/31 or even to 1930; and several new factories were added to the building schedule.[146] In May 1929 Vesenkha had planned to increase the production of machine tools from 9 million rubles in 1928/29 to 53 million rubles in 1932/33; by July 1930, the target for 1932/33 had been increased to 150 million rubles.[147] In September 1929, the presidium of Vesenkha condemned the 'extreme backwardness' of the industry, and particularly the 'complete absence of production of the main types of machine tool which determine modern methods of metalworking', including semi-automatic and special machine tools. While Vesenkha did not approve any new plan for 1932/33, it called for the 'complete reconstruction' of existing factories within twelve months.[148]

---

[143] *Ibid.* i, 47–9, ii, i, 156.
[144] The plan usually refrained, evidently for reasons of commercial security, from publishing any specific import targets (*ibid.* i, 101); electrical engineering (see p. 209 above) was a rare exception.
[145] *Ibid.* ii, i, 156–7.
[146] See Cooper (1975), ch. 3.
[147] See Cooper (1975), 47, 63; for production in 1928/29, see I, May 10, 1930 (editorial).
[148] TsGANKh, 3429/1/5195, 86–8 (resolution of September 18).

In heavy engineering, the proposed annual production capacity of Uralmashzavod was increased from 18 to 100 million rubles in the course of 1929/30.[149] Uralmash would produce annually the equipment for a complete new iron and steel works the size of the revised project of the Magnitogorsk works with its pig-iron capacity of $2^{1}/_{2}$ million tons, and would also produce heavy mining equipment for non-ferrous metals and coal. Uralmash was largely modelled on the Krupp works in Essen.[150] Its potential military as well as industrial value was obvious. 'We can make everything that Krupp ever made', a Soviet engineer assured an American visitor to the plant, 'for war as well as for peace'.[151] Uralmash was merely the most outstanding item in a vast programme. On October 29, 1930, the new heavy engineering plan approved by the presidium of Vesenkha required the expansion of production from 130 million rubles in 1928/29 to 1,200 millions in 1932/33, as compared with 460 millions proposed in the five-year plan.[152] The revised plan also envisaged that by 1934/35, when production would have increased to 2,800 million rubles, the needs of the iron and steel, coal, oil and chemical industries would be satisfied from internal production with new types of equipment corresponding to the most up-to-date foreign technology. All factories would work every day of the year for three shifts, and even the largest of the 21 new factories which were to be constructed would be completed in the course of two years.[153]

In January 1930, in the midst of the revision of plans for particular branches of engineering, the presidium of Vesenkha called for an immediate revision of the five-year plan for engineering as a whole in view of the increased plans for investment in the coal, oil, iron and steel, chemical and timber industries. The new plan would provide for the full satisfaction of requirements by the Soviet engineering industry within the

---

[149] Unpelev (1960), 6–7; the planned capacity was trebled in November 1929, and increased again in July 1930.

[150] PI, 23–4, 1931, 74–7, 80; *Ural'skii zavod* (Sverdlovsk, 1933), 13.

[151] Chamberlin (1934), 54; his visit apparently took place in 1933.

[152] ZI, October 22, 1930; *Metall*, 10–12, 1930, 185–6; TsGANKh 3429/1/5195, 145–51 (resolution of October 29, 1930).

[153] *Metall*, 10–12, 1930, 172–92; the data in this article, though published at the end of 1930, coincide with the data in the report of the Vesenkha presidium in ZI, October 22, 1930, and in its resolution of October 29.

next few years with machinery of the latest design, produced by the most recent production processes.[154] But, while new plans were compiled for the crucial items of machinery, no national schedule of supply and demand for engineering products was compiled before 1931, even on an annual basis. The plans for engineering approved by Vesenkha remained broad general targets in value terms, based in large part not on an estimate of requirements, but on inexact guesses by planners and administrators about production possibilities.[155] No revised first five-year plan, even in outline form, was ever approved for the industry as a whole.

(v) Major projects under stress

This account of the revision of the five-year plan in some major Soviet industries has illustrated the intimate connection between the changing production targets for each industry at a national level and the specific capital projects for major factories. The expansion of the national targets led to the enlargement of almost all existing projects for individual factories. The uncertainty which surrounded the five-year plan in each industry encouraged organisations and individuals at every level to advance additional proposals for new factories. The campaign against the bourgeois specialists and the Right wing in the party greatly weakened resistance to extravagant schemes. Many senior specialists were arrested or dismissed (see pp. 116–17 above). Those who remained sought to curb the most extravagant excesses, but at every level in the industrial hierarchy resistance to new claims was hesitant and muted. At a plenum of the Ukrainian Vesenkha, Sukhomlin complained that 'many business managers are poisoned with a kind of gigantomania; as soon as a project has been prepared, they immediately demand that the specifications should be increased'.[156] An industrial journalist – himself at the time a vigorous advocate of forcing the pace – has described how at the end of 1929 the industrial newspaper was reporting uncritically every proposal for a new factory, however fantastic.

---

[154] SP VSNKh, 1929/30, art. 555 (dated January 6, 1930).

[155] *Metall*, 2–3, 1931, 4–7 (Spektor); Mednikov (1930), 28–30.

[156] ZI, May 29, 1930; for a similar view by a Gosplan economist, see *Na novom etape* (1930), i, 435 (Kvasha).

It was stopped from doing so only at the insistence of Mezhlauk, who told a meeting of the editorial staff that they were opening doors to 'Manilovs', and insisted that even Sovnarkom of the RSFSR and the presidium of Vesenkha of the USSR were not authorised to change the five-year plan:

> Vesenkha of the USSR, and even Gosplan of the USSR, may only request the CC of the party and the Sovnarkom of the USSR to make changes in the five-year plan. The five-year plan may not be changed by a single comma without a special decision of the supreme authorities of the country.[157]

In practice the central party and government authorities, as we have seen, frequently approved major and wildly optimistic changes in plans and projects.

While more precise revised plans for the major industries were pending, projects underwent substantial revision. At a conference of project organisations in June 1930, a foreign consultant complained of vagueness, delays, and frequent changes in the specifications from the higher authorities:

> The representative of one republic told me, for example, that he wanted to have a metal works in his republic. We asked him how much he wanted to spend on it and he said he didn't know, maybe half a million, maybe two million, whatever we found necessary.[158]

Similarly Soyuzugol' issued instructions for the construction of first 40 and then 70 coal mines in the Donbass, but without any specific information.[159] This situation forced Gipromez and other capital project organisations to prepare outline specifications for major projects themselves, a situation described by one designer as 'thinking for the boss what he should do and where'.[160] The lack of knowledge by Soviet officials and engineers of the

---

[157] Khavin (1968), 149–150; Manilov, a character in Gogol's *Dead Souls*, exemplified dreamy well-meaning passivity; for an illustration of Mezhlauk's own support for exaggerated plans, see pp. 200 above and 218 below.

[158] *Trudy pervoi konferentsii proektiruyushchikh organizatsii* (1931), 14 (Hyde).

[159] *Ibid.* 41 (Kagan, director of the project administration of the mine construction trust Shakhtstroi).

[160] *Ibid.* 61 (Dubov, from Gipromash).

advanced technologies of the new factories, together with their general inexperience, added to the delays and resulted in unsatisfactory projects. In August 1930, several months after construction should have started, the Soviet project for a large ball-bearing factory was scrapped, and a contract to provide a new project was signed with an Italian firm.[161]

With the heroically short construction periods insisted upon by the authorities, delays of a few months resulting from a dispute about alternative projects became major disasters. At the end of 1928, Graftio, the power engineer responsible for the Svir' hydro-electric project, proposed to construct the first plant on the site by the end of 1933, but was instructed by Sovnarkom to complete it a year earlier. In 1929 Swedish engineers redesigned the foundations so as to speed up construction, but then the whole building season of 1930 was lost in a dispute involving American consultants who wanted to revert to the original scheme for the foundations.[162]

A further subject of complaint was that crucial decisions were delayed by the propensity of Russian engineers, officials and politicians to engage in disputes of principle rather than to reach practical conclusions. Mezhlauk condemned 'the Eastern dreaminess with which many managers and trade-union officials await tomorrow's miracles from new technology',[163] while a German engineer exclaimed:

Why do you love reading and discussing so much (and with high-principled theoretical justification for everything)?[164]

---

[161] For the history of the project for this factory, which eventually became the 'Kaganovich' state ball-bearing factory no. 1 (GPZ-1), see EZh, October 26, 1929; ZI, August 28, 1930; PI, 10, 1931, 49–53; Sutton (1971), 145–6.

[162] *Pervaya vsesoyuznaya konferentsiya* (1931), 59–64; *Elektrifikatsiya* (1966), 110–26 (reprinted from the archives); the first plant was actually completed in December 1933 (*ibid.* 123). Sutton describes a dispute between the American consultants (the White Corporation) and the Soviet authorities; the latter allegedly cancelled the consultancy and paid only $20,000 of a $400,000 claim (Sutton 1971), 263–4). But Graftio claimed in reports to Sovnarkom and Energotsentr of Vesenkha that the Americans had not studied the soil properly and had submitted 'not a sketch project but an opinion' (*Elektrifikatsiya* (1966), 114–16).

[163] B, 11–12, June 30, 1930, 15.

[164] PE, 7, 1930, 51.

All these influences worked towards instability. Bardin complained of an 'epic of variantomania' in Gipromez, and even alleged that it 'did not compile any plans, but loved variants'.[165]

Nearly all the available designers and draughtsmen worked at full stretch on the key projects due for completion within the next year or eighteen months; minor and longer-term projects were neglected. In 1929 and 1930, the Dnepr power station was being constructed rapidly and successfully. But the Dnepr combine, the vast complex of factories which would utilise Dnepr power, still lacked projects, even though it was due for completion in the spring of 1932. Even the general plan for the site was not approved until April 1930. 'Project bacchanalia' continued throughout the summer of 1930, but at the end of the summer only the sketch project for the aluminium factory had made any serious progress.[166]

The project-making crisis was at its most intense in the winter of 1929–30, when all plans were under continuous revision. By February 1, 1930, projects had been approved for only 40 per cent of 1,121 major construction jobs, a serious deterioration as compared with September 1929, when 84 per cent of 433 jobs had approved projects;[167] on February 1, 1930, 37 per cent of the annual capital investment plan for industry was not backed by even a sketch project.[168] The position was naturally worse in the producer goods' industries, where most innovation and expansion were taking place.

After the beginning of 1930, the tacit decision of the authorities not to allow further increases in the main production targets for 1932/33 (see p. 194 above) exercised a marked stabilising influence. New projects were prepared and approved at breakneck speed during the spring and summer of 1930. The decision to build a combine-harvester factory in Saratov was approved in principle on January 12, 1930; the sketch project was ready by April 18 and the final project by June 8.[169]

[165] Bardin (Novosibirsk, 1936), 74.
[166] *TsIK 2/V*, No. 6, 11; No. 10, 8; No. 13, 4–5; EZh, April 10, 1930; ZI, April 10, July 13, September 12, 1930.
[167] *Industrializatsiya, 1929–1932* (1970), 119, 135.
[168] Khmelnitskaya (1931), 522–3; according to *Trudy pervoi konferentsii* (1931), 28–9, on April 1, 1930, only 38 per cent of the building programme of Soyuzstroi was backed by final projects and only 26 per cent had working drawings.
[169] P, August 11, 1930 (I. N. Smirnov).

Foreign and particularly American consultants played a vital role in the preparation of the capital projects. The total number of technical-assistance contracts rose from 45 in October 1928 to 70 in October 1929 and 104 in March 1930; of the latter as many as 81 were contracts with United States' or German firms.[170] On a number of major projects foreign designers worked in the USSR, training and supervising Soviet design teams. The relations between the foreign engineers and their Soviet counterparts were often difficult. American engineers frequently complained of the combination of bureaucratic political interference from above with the pseudo-democracy in decision-making which prevailed at the construction site or in the project office. R. W. Stuck, principal engineer from the McKee Co. at Magnitostroi, complained that Soviet engineers, with the support of the political leaders, tried to incorporate German, French and English features, and their own obsolete ideas, into the American project:

> The Russian engineer is not content to accept the best practice as it has been developed but wants to do it differently . . . with the result that some of the most peculiar and impractical ideas appear at the most inappropriate places.
> . . . Imagine what groups of engineers, and it took many more to redesign the plan than the original design did, would do to such a project when the greater number of them had but little actual steel plant construction and operating experience, yet they were given a free hand in redesigning this project and were to correlate what they thought were the best ideas of the world into a project of their own. It resulted in changing everything that could be changed except the location and design of the blast furnaces.[171]

Soviet accounts in turn blame McKee and Co. for the delays in the drawings, and insist that the project prepared by McKee was too expensive.[172] Relations became so strained that at one point Ordzhonikidze issued a confidential Vesenkha order which set out emergency measures for preparing the detailed

[170] Sutton (1971), 10–11; ZI, February 16, 1930 (A. Gurevich).
[171] Hoover, AER, Box 4, Stuck ms, pp. 30–3.
[172] *Byli industrial'nye* (1970), 296, 298; Galiguzov and Churilin (1978), 26.

drawings 'in connection with the refusal of the firm of A. McKee to fulfil the contract on technical assistance'.[173] I am unable to judge how far these conflicts were a necessary part of the learning process by which Soviet engineers gained their independence as designers. Progress was much smoother when the Soviet engineers were shrewder and the foreign engineers more tactful. According to Soviet accounts, in spite of major and minor clashes, the Freyn Corporation, which worked in Gipromez from 1928 until 1933, transformed the scale and quality of its work. Bardin, the leading Soviet iron and steel engineer, described how the Freyn engineers were involved 'in all questions of project-making and reconstruction for our iron and steel industry':

> The arrival of Americans was a great event. Until then Gipromez was lame in all four legs. It was a puny establishment, highly liable to empty talk and unprincipled chatter, incapable of elaborating technical ideas either in writing or in drawing . . . The Americans left behind them a serious trace. Our young people learned a lot from the Americans; they had borrowed from them both technical knowledge and – the main thing – a way of working.[174]

Designs and drawings for many of the new projects were prepared in the United States or Germany and sent to the USSR. Soviet engineers, often accompanied by high-level officials, visited or worked in these countries, and representatives of the consultant firms frequently visited the USSR. Projects prepared by Soviet organisations, with or without foreign help, were almost invariably sent abroad for expert comment.[175]

As a result of all this feverish activity, by July 1, 1930, projects had been prepared and approved for 62 per cent of jobs under construction, as compared with 40 per cent on February 1,[176] though often their quality left much to be desired. But on many major sites projects and working drawings were

---

[173] TsGANKh, 3429/1/5195, 204–5 (dated December 24, 1930).

[174] Bardin (Novosibirsk, 1936), 10, 13; see also Sutton (1971), 61–4.

[175] For contemporary Soviet accounts of different forms of foreign technical assistance see Kolomenskii (1930), *passim*; *Metall*, 3–4, 1930, 24–9 (Dobrovol'skii).

[176] *Industrializatsiya, 1929–1932* (1970), 135.

received only after construction had started. The contract for the project for the revised Magnitogorsk works was not signed with the McKee Co. until March 14, 1930; not surprisingly, the project was not completed by the agreed date of mid-June 1930.[177] In 1929, Bardin brought arguments about Kuznetsk project variants to an end by 'laying the foundations, thus cutting off the path to a retreat'.[178] In 1930, Bardin and Frankfurt, now in charge of the site, continued construction in spite of specific injunctions to 'cease partisan activities' from Novostal' and from I. Kosior, its head. Kosior, after accusing them of 'prejudging the building plan of the whole factory without either a project or foreign assistance', later condoned them with the familiar proverb 'Victors are not judged'.[179] At the site of the Novosibirsk combine-harvester factory, 'projects and drawings were brought by aeroplane and immediately put into use'.[180] The authorities overlooked these gross departures from agreed procedures. At a conference of giant construction projects Mezhlauk criticised 'out-of-date views that it is impossible to build without final projects and even working drawings', and insisted that preliminary work should be started as soon as the general plan reached the site. He claimed that the cost which was sometimes involved due to the need for rebuilding was more than compensated by the gain in time, citing Magnitogorsk as an example.[181]

In spite of these uncertainties, by the summer of 1930 substantial progress had been made with designing a new Soviet industrial structure. The new production targets for the five-year plan proved to be wildly unrealistic. In some industries they were not reached at all in the 1930s. But in other industries, the new plans for 1932/33 would not have been utterly impossible as targets for achievement in 1936 or 1937, and in practice they provided an ambitious framework within which projects for the major plants were drawn up, and a

[177] *Iz istorii* (Chelyabinsk, 1965), 9, 61, 265.
[178] Bardin (Novosibirsk, 1936), 75.
[179] Frankfurt (1935), 24; Bardin (Novosibirsk, 1936), 117.
[180] ZI, October 4, 1930 (Morin, head of construction).
[181] ZI, October 5, 1930; a similar view was put forward by Vinter, head of Dneprostroi, who pointed out that construction and project preparation had taken place simultaneously, with both the Shatura and Dnepr power stations (ZI, October 1, 1930).

building programme developed which continued into the second five-year plan. By the summer of 1930 major new plants in each industry were firmly included in the building programme. Thus in heavy engineering, the construction of the enlarged Uralmashzavod was under way,[182] and the project for the Kramatorsk works had been approved.[183] In agricultural engineering, the great Rostov factory was complete and was in process of being converted to the production of tractor-drawn implements (see p. 249 below). In the tractor industry, the Stalingrad factory was almost complete; the conversion of part of the Putilov works to tractor production was under way; the project for the Kharkov tractor factory was being prepared on the basis of the Stalingrad factory; the draft project for a caterpillar-tractor factory in Chelyabinsk was complete and was the subject of consultancy abroad.[184] These four giant factories were scheduled to produce between them all Soviet tractors in 1932/33, and eventually were the only tractor factories built in the USSR in the 1930s. Two combine-harvester factories, in Saratov and Novosibirsk, were also under construction (see pp. 192–3 above). In the automobile industry, the project for the AMO motor works in Moscow was approved in February 1930, after heated disputes involving Stalin and the Politburo.[185] In April 1930, the project for the Nizhnii-Novgorod works was completed on time by Ford and Austin, and building started on May 1, 1930.[186] In the mining industries, there was much more uncertainty, though it was reported in June 1930 that projects for 23 of the 26 coal mines being reconstructed by Shakhtstroi, and 48 of the 54 new mines, were now complete.[187]

[182] Unpelev (1960), 6–7; *Ural'skii zavod* (Sverdlovsk, 1933), 13.

[183] *TsIK 2/V*, No. 9, 8 (Kattel').

[184] For the Stalingrad factory see pp. 250–1 below; for the other factories, see ZI, January 11, 1930; EZh, February 25, 1930; P, July 31, 1930 (Osinskii); the design and construction of these factories is extensively described in Dodge (1960), *passim*.

[185] *Istoriya Moskovskogo avtozavoda* (1966), 149–154; *Direktor I. A. Likhachev* (1971), 43–4, 49–52. Sutton (1971), 177–8, describes the factory as 'Brandt-built', but according to *Istoriya Moskovskogo avtozavoda* (1966), 154, the Brandt representatives withdrew in April–June 1930 after the approval of the project.

[186] ZI, April 13, 22, 1930.

[187] *Trudy pervoi konferentsii* (1931), 41–2. With working drawings, however, the position was 'catastrophic': none were available, even for the sixteen mines started five years previously (*ibid.* 42–Kagan).

In the iron and steel industry, the main specifications were agreed for the Magnitogorsk and Kuznetsk works, and the revised projects were being prepared.

For almost all the factories under construction, impossibly short construction schedules were insisted upon by the authorities. But most of the factories discussed above were eventually completed in the middle-1930s; together they provided the backbone of Soviet industrialisation. The revised programme for the five-year plan certainly represented the temporary triumph of Utopianism over realism, but out of this triumph a programme of action emerged which was altogether more ambitious, in both production capacity and technology, than the five-year plan adopted in the spring of 1929.

(vi) 'Giants and dwarfs': the scale of production

The large group of giant factories equipped with the latest technology formed the nucleus of the revised five-year plans, gripped the public imagination, and increasingly received priority in the allocation of resources. The popular phrase that industrialisation was like 'sewing a coat onto a button' encapsulated this approach. But in a country where capital was in very short supply it would have been ludicrous not to involve existing factories in the industrial transformation; and in 1929/30 the drive for their reconstruction, led by Rabkrin, did not lose its momentum. On March 23, 1930, a typical resolution of CCC/Rabkrin criticised the failure of Vesenkha to arrange for redundant capital equipment to be used elsewhere in industry. Rabkrin claimed that such equipment often found its way at high prices to artisan cooperatives or private repair shops, or was simply retained by the original factory.[188] The drive to make maximum use of existing factories and equipment was supported by powerful voices in Vesenkha and Gosplan. The issue was put quite frankly in the Vesenkha report to the XVI party congress:

> The task of securing for the economy the necessary *quantity of production* . . . compels us to a certain extent, as an exceptional

---

[188] P, March 25, 1930 (Roizenman); *Na novom etape* (1930), i, 489–501 (Osip'yan).

measure, to bring back enterprises which have been closed down as unprofitable, or to construct small and medium enterprises. In many cases this less intensive development of the productivity of labour, or of the mechanisation of an industry, which we are compelled to follow by way of a retreat, is wholly repaid by the *general acceleration* of the development of the productive power of social labour . . . But we place the *main* emphasis in all construction on large, mechanised enterprises, and on the struggle for qualitative indicators.[189]

In the iron and steel industry, the revised Urals five-year plan provided the most striking example of the combination of old and new works: Magnitogorsk would be developed side by side with the reconstruction of six of the old charcoal-based iron works.[190] In the coal industry, the urgent need to achieve the revised targets of the five-year plan led to the development of small as well as large pits (see pp. 195–6 above). But the advantages of the reconstruction of existing factories were most obvious in the engineering industries, where much capacity was not fully utilised: in 1930 engineering factories worked on average 9·2 hours per' day, as compared with 13 hours in mining and manufacturing as a whole.[191] During the course of 1929/30 vigorous efforts were made to adapt existing engineering capacity to the growing needs of the five-year plan. On October 21, 1929, Vesenkha established a 'Staff (shtab) for the Mobilisation of Free Production Reserves in the Engineering Industry' using the Russian word for the military General Staff. The Vesenkha Mobilisation Staff sent teams of engineers and managers round the country. They concentrated their initial efforts on smaller factories and workshops attached to the republican and local authorities, and to Narkomput', and then turned their attention to the large all-Union factories.[192] Simultaneously a Directorate for New Machinery designed new machines and adapted foreign models for production by small

---

[189] *Vypolnenie* (1931), 34; 'qualitative indicators' in this context refers to the reduction of production costs.
[190] See pp. 205–8 above; and ZI, May 11, 1930 (Mezhlauk).
[191] I, June 25, 1930 (Kvasha).
[192] TPG, December 25, 1929; PI, 3, 1930, 29–31, 40 (Kostich); *Vypolnenie* (1931), 65.

engineering factories. According to a Soviet report, the experience 'tuned up the industry and gave it confidence in its power to reach new technical objectives at an American tempo'.[193] But these developments were not enough. Soviet planners insisted that a vast expansion of output could be obtained with fairly small investments in casting and forging facilities, which were often already working two or three shifts;[194] and the Vesenkha capital investment allocation was increased for this purpose.[195] In a Gosplan report prepared for the XVI party congress in the summer of 1930, an engineering specialist vigorously attacked the 'epidemic of "gigantomania"', in which every enterprise tried to be super-powerful and narrowly specialised; thus a 'gigantic longitudinal milling machine, second or third in the world' had been installed in a special building, but customers for its production had not yet been found.[196] Kuibyshev, in a frequently-cited article 'On Dwarfs and Giants', also attacked giant factories which wanted to produce everything themselves, and called for the extensive use of local factories and artisan metal workshops, which employed almost as many workers as the factory metalworking industry, to manufacture components for the giant factories.[197] The new long-term plan for the heavy engineering industry envisaged that in 1930/31 production would already exceed the level proposed in the optimum variant of the five-year plan, but only 76 million rubles' production out of a total 508 million rubles would be produced in new factories.[198]

(vii) Specialisation by product and component

In both new and reconstructed factories, the revised five-year plans envisaged that the transformation of Soviet industry

[193] *Metall*, 1, 1930, 27–36 (Perel'man).

[194] I, June 25, 1930 (Kvasha); *Na novom etape* (1930), i, 421–9 (Kvasha).

[195] B, 10, May 31, 1930, 17 (Ostrovskii).

[196] *Na novom etape* (1930), i, 436.

[197] ZI, June 19, 1930; see also his article in *ibid.* June 12, 1930. According to Kuibyshev, in 1930 358,000 artisans were engaged in metalworking, but this figure evidently includes blacksmiths and others in the countryside. The total number of workers employed in factory census industry in engineering and metalworking was 628,000 on January 1, 1930 (*Trud* (1930), 7).

[198] *Metall*, 10–12, 1930, 172; in 1934/35, however, the new factories would supply as much as 1,628 out of 2,802 million rubles.

would involve the elimination of universal non-specialised production in favour of a high degree of specialisation by product and by component. The electrical engineering industry, for example, was strongly criticised for being engaged, in spite of its advanced equipment, in 'artisan production on a large scale': the Kharkov electrical factory, with its variety of production, was known as 'Muir and Merrilees', after the pre-revolutionary Moscow department store.[199] A central committee resolution of March 19, 1930, called for a high degree of specialisation between factories.[200] Central planning would make it possible to concentrate on the batch or mass production of a relatively small number of products. The most conspicuous example of this trend was the tractor industry, where, with an annual production of 200,000, only three or four types of tractors were to be produced.

In other industries, the optimum pattern of production remained unclear or controversial. In the machine-tool industry, some specialists, including Al'perovich, head of the industry, advocated the initial concentration of effort on mass production of a few simple universal machines, while others proposed that the Soviet Union should follow the United States' example and concentrate on productive machine tools adapted for special purposes, such as those imported for the Stalingrad tractor factory. The latter group, which included M. M. Kaganovich, the chief engineering specialist in Rabkrin, tried to get the best of two worlds by claiming that highly-specialised machine tools could also be produced on a mass scale.[201] On the basis of the experience of the Stalingrad tractor factory, Sheboldaev also defended the production of specialised machine tools, claiming that 'European technology suffers from the universalism of its machine tools, and in this respect is backward'.[202] While these arguments were proceeding, factories which produced a mixture of machine tools and other engineering products were reorganised so as to specialise on machine tools, and, following the establishment in Berlin of a German–Soviet Technical Bureau

---

[199] PI, 3, 1930, 26, 48 (Khankovskii).

[200] Kholmyanskii (1933), 45.

[201] See Cooper (1975), 51–3, 107–11, 240–1. The arguments of the main protagonists will be found in ZI, August 5, September 12, 1930 (Al'perovich), and in ZI, July 24, 1930 (M. Kaganovich).

[202] B, 11–12, June 30, 1930, 64–5.

to plan the new factories, the construction of the Nizhnii-Novgorod milling-machine factory and the Moscow turret-lathe factory started belatedly in the summer of 1930.[203]

Both the reduction in the number of types of production and the increase in specialisation by product were an extension on a much larger scale of measures already adopted during the rationalisation drive of the mid-1920s (see p. 29 above). The objective now was to divide up the production process much further, so that eventually each type of component would be produced by a separate factory, and the factories producing the final output would for the most part be assembly plants. Casting and forging operations, and the manufacture of tools, usually undertaken in the same factory that produced the final machines, would henceforth be separated out into giant specialised factories. 'Standardisation in our conditions', one expert declared, 'has a possibility of development which exists nowhere in the world, and can give the most grandiose positive results'; he noted the erroneousness of the popular American opinion that Soviet economic success was already due to the widespread use of standardisation.[204] Vesenkha similarly reported to the XVI party congress that 'we still lag greatly behind the practice of West European and American industry in specialisation and collaboration', and announced that giant central foundries (Tsentrolity) were now under construction in Moscow and Leningrad.[205]

Practical exigencies, which forced the allocation of resources to the reconstruction of existing factories as well as to the construction of new ones, also brought about the pragmatic modification of the ideal of numerous specialised artisan workshops and small and medium-sized factories providing tools, castings and components for giant assembly works. The metalworking artisans in the countryside were often diverted by the kolkhozy and sovkhozy to their own needs; and in both town and country artisans were recruited by large engineering factories desperately short of labour. While Kuibyshev was

[203] For the Berlin bureau, which continued until 1931, see Cooper (1975), 336–8, and I, May 19, 1930 (Zhidovetskii); for the new factories, see *Ocherki*, ii (Gor'kii, 1966), 249, VI, 1, 1978, 92–3, and Kholmyanskii (1933), 28–9; the start of the construction of the Kharkov factory was delayed until 1931.
[204] NAF, 5, 1930, 96 (Korostoshevskii).
[205] *Vypolnenie* (1931), 68; for the Tsentrolity, see also I, May 19, July 6, 1930.

calling for the adaptation of artisan industry to the needs of industrialisation, the party journal simultaneously argued that artisans should be recruited by engineering factories.[206] But it was the shortage of supplies endemic in the central planning system which rendered entirely unworkable the grand schemes for specialisation by component. According to an account published many years after the event, at the end of 1929, following an intense discussion about specialisation in the motor industry 'Stalin gave a very important ruling: the first factories must be built complete – mastering production is a difficult matter, it will be easier to assist one factory than dozens'.[207] If this 'ruling' was in fact made at this time, it did not put a stop to the argument. For several years enthusiasts for specialisation by component continued to proclaim their cause.[208] But in practice shortages forced new factories to become 'universal Empires', and deprived many second-priority factories of essential supplies. And, above all, until 1934 the acute shortage of metal drove the authorities to allocate essential supplies to a relatively small number of high-priority consumers.

(C) THE GENERAL PLAN

During 1929/30 attempts continued to prepare a 'general plan (*genplan*)' covering ten or fifteen years.[209] While the new targets for the five-year plan sometimes proved practicable over a longer period and to that extent retained an element of realism, the general plan soared far beyond all possibility of achievement, and the Utopian strain was overwhelmingly paramount.

In the summer of 1929, Sabsovich, who for some months had been the chief public advocate of ambitious long-term targets, was taken increasingly seriously.[210] In the journal of the presidium of Vesenkha, a reviewer applauded his assumptions that industry would grow fifteen-fold by 1943 and a hundred-fold by 1948, arguing that while his 'fantasy' was not mathematically proved, it was 'a "fantasy" *all the roots of which*

---

[206] B, 10, May 31, 1930, 19 (Ostrovskii).
[207] *Direktor I. A. Likhachev* (1971), 251.
[208] See, for example, I, December 30, 1930 (Sorokin).
[209] For the earlier history of the *genplan*, see Carr and Davies (1969), 837–42.
[210] For Sabsovich's earlier proposals see Carr and Davies (1969), 841.

emerge from and grow out of our reality'.[211] In a trenchant article in *Pravda*, Larin, at this time one of the strongest supporters of Sabsovich's proposals, condemned sceptics for their '*petty perspectives (kurinye masshtaby)*' and criticised Krzhizhanovsky's preface to Sabsovich's pamphlet because he 'carefully disassociated himself from the conclusion'.[212] Krzhizhanovsky's reply indicated the extent to which ambitious plans were now the order of the day. He avoided all criticism of Sabsovich, and also insisted that Gosplan had been responsible for the preparation of the pamphlet, and had provided materials about the *genplan*.[213] Later in 1929 Sabsovich revised his prognoses still further upwards, declaring 'I made a colossal underestimation'.[214] He increased the target for pig-iron production in 1937/38 from 81 million tons in the first edition of his pamphlet to 132 million tons in the third edition; nearly four times as large as United States' production in 1927/28, and 7 per cent greater than total world production.[215] This new revision of Sabsovich's ten-year plan was too fantastic even for this age of fantastic plans. The equivalent Glavchermet estimate for 1937/38 was a mere 38 million tons, roughly equal to the United States' level in 1928, as compared with its earlier figure of 26 million tons, while the group in the metal syndicate VMS which was engaged in revising the five-year plan calculated the demand for rolled steel in 1937/38 at 58 million tons, which would require some 65 million tons of pig-iron, still only half the Sabsovich estimate.[216] The VMS group claimed that Sabsovich's proposals would result in all ore being exhausted within ten to fifteen years.[217] The less extravagant proposals from Glavchermet and VMS also met with some cautious scepticism. At the session of TsIK

[211] PI, 7, 1929, 84–9; his pamphlet was also highly praised as a 'good warrior' for the mobilisation and economic re-education of the masses by a reviewer in B, 13–14, July 31, 1929, 119–122; the reviewer approved his proposed industrial growth rates, while resisting his scheme to replace all existing towns, villages and hamlets in fifteen years.

[212] P, August 29, 1929.

[213] P, August 30, 1929.

[214] PKh, 2, 1930, 18.

[215] *Metall*, 1, 1930, 16.

[216] TPG, December 28, 1929; *Metall*, 1, 1930, 15–26; for the target of 50–60 million tons in 1937/38 approved in May 1931, see vol. 4.

[217] *Metall*, 1, 1930, 16; this claim has of course since been proved wrong, but was true in relation to the ore sites discovered by 1930.

in December 1929, one speaker argued that the Soviet Union would not need to reach the United States' level of metal production within ten to fifteen years: it would neither produce as many motor cars nor build skyscrapers, and these two activities between them consumed some 30 per cent of United States metal.[218] In discussions 'in the corridors' at the December session of Gipromez, cynics commented that 'to demonstrate these needs (which with us can be raised to almost any level) still does not tell us anything about how to meet this requirement'.[219]

Meanwhile Kovalevsky, in charge of the preparation of the *genplan* in Gosplan, worked with Fel'dman to prepare a 'working hypothesis' for the plan; this was eventually presented by Krzhizhanovsky to a conference of planning and statistical agencies which met from February 8 to 10, 1930, and then discussed at two protracted sittings of the Institute of Economic Research of Gosplan on February 25 and March 5.[220] The working hypothesis was more intellectually respectable than Sabsovich's pamphlets, being based on Fel'dman's growth model. Marx's schemes of social reproduction, together with a 'coefficient of tension' (ratio of capital investment to annual national output) and a 'coefficient of effectiveness' (ratio of net output to capital stock or national wealth) were used to generate a number of plan variants. Extremely optimistic assumptions about 'effectiveness', together with a high level of 'tension', provided the grounds for an optimism equal to Sabsovich's in his earlier (but not his later) proposals. The variant for 1937/38 favoured by Kovalevsky would achieve production of coal and oil equal to the United States' 1928/29 level, pig-iron output amounting to 78 million tons, which was 80 per cent above the United States' 1929 level, and $2^1/_2$ times the United States'

---

[218] *TsIK 2/V*, No. 8, 25 (Tochinskii), replying to an earlier statement by Andronnikov (*ibid.* No. 8, 12); for Tochinskii's later role in the adoption of more realistic plans, see vol. 4.

[219] TPG, December 28, 1929.

[220] Krzhizhanovsky's long speech to the planning conference, which met from February 8 to 10, was reported in EZh, February 12, 1930, and published in revised form in PKh, 2, 1930, 7–21 and 3, 1930, 5–16. The discussion at the institute, of which Strumilin was director, was reported in EZh, March 9, 1930, and PKh, 3, 1930, 117–209. Fel'dman's methodology for the plan appeared in his article in PKh, 12, 1929.

output of electric power.[221] At the planning conference, Kovalevsky scathingly rejected a variant of the *genplan* which proposed that by 1938 net production per head should reach a mere 50 per cent of the present United States' level, pointing out that this would achieve a level of consumption which was less than 75 per cent of what he described as the '*hunger consumption norm of the German proletariat*'; he contemptuously dismissed a proposed increase of production by a mere 14 per cent a year as far too low.[222]

By this time Sabsovich's activities were meeting with increasing hostility, and had obviously offended higher party circles. A commentator in the industrial newspaper, probably Kuibyshev, commended him to contemporary novelists as 'an ultra-clear representative of those whose heads have been made dizzy in analysing our perspectives, to such an extent that real calculation begins to be replaced by drunken dreams'.[223] At the planning conference Krzhizhanovsky criticised Sabsovich as 'a very bold man' whose whole scheme suffered from 'an incorrect methodology', and 'an absence of technical and economic argumentation'.[224] In his report of February 25 Kovalevsky pointed out that Sabsovich's scheme was 'internally inconsistent',[225] and claimed that it had failed to resolve the problem of deriving the future general level of production with the aid of Marx's reproduction schemas.[226]

Kovalevsky's working hypothesis was also strongly criticised. At a closed session of Gosplan Strumilin argued that an approach based on the acceptable rather than the feasible could result in an iron output four times the volume of the earth.[227] At the planning conference Krzhizhanovsky argued, taking electric

[221] PKh, 3, 1930, 138, 141; the relatively high production of pig-iron in the USSR was due to the low availability of scrap: crude steel production was planned at 45 per cent above the US level.

[222] PKh, 2, 1930, 204–5.

[223] ZI, January 3, 1930; the article was signed 'V.V.', Kuibyshev's initials; it was published two months before Stalin's famous 'Dizzy with Success' speech.

[224] PKh, 2, 1930, 18.

[225] PKh, 3, 1930, 140.

[226] PKh, 3, 1930, 207; Fel'dman, however, described Sabsovich's plan more kindly as a 'rough but justified sketch' (ZI, March 25, 1930). For Sabsovich, see also pp. 152–3 above.

[227] PKh, 3, 1930, 156; this stricture was cited with approval in the discussion at the Institute of Economic Research by A. Kon.

power as an example, that the proposition that industrial output would reach half the United States' level in 1932/33 was 'risky', and that in general 'cde. Kovalevsky underestimates the "scissors" between the main elements of the industrial structure of the USSR and the USA'.[228] Kovalevsky himself frankly admitted in his report to the institute that his calculations, based on 'economic possibilities' rather than 'concrete engineering calculations' usually seemed 'completely improbable' to 'even the boldest and most talented engineer', as well as to officials in new regions for which a particularly rapid expansion was proposed; but he claimed that 'great incredulity and perplexity' on the part of engineers and officials invariably gave way gradually to full acceptance.[229] Some speakers in the discussion at the institute, on the other hand, including the Gosplan official Vaisberg, a long-established advocate of accelerated growth, claimed that the proposed growth rates were too low, and made fun of the assumption in earlier versions of the *genplan* that the number of individual peasant households would continue to grow.[230] Both the more realistic and the super-optimistic agreed in objecting to what were variously described as 'arithmetical combinations', a 'purely statistical' approach and 'an excessive preoccupation with mathematics, replacing planning'.[231] According to the moderate Krzhizhanovsky, Kovalevsky had rushed through technical and economic analysis at a 'mathematical gallop': the working hypothesis of the *genplan* should be 'not the first stage, but a synthesis of syntheses', and questions of technology should have been fully brought in at this stage of the work.[232] Critics from the Left also objected to the mathematical abstraction of the plan, criticising, however, not the absence of technology but inadequate attention to changes in social structure, and the

---

[228] PKh, 2, 1930, 19; 3, 1930, 10–11.

[229] PKh, 3, 1930, 119–20, 208; thus transport officials could 'neither understand nor accept' the proposal that 75 per cent of the railway network would be electrified, but concurred with it after receiving Kovalevsky's 'working hypothesis'.

[230] PKh, 3, 1930, 151 (Savchuk), 146 (Vaisberg); for Vaisberg, see Carr and Davies (1969), 325, 743, 884.

[231] PKh, 3, 1930, 156 (A. Kon), 172 (Koldobskii); EZh, March 9, 1930 (Shakhnovskaya).

[232] PKh, 2, 1930, 19–20.

attempt to establish regularities independent of particular social structures; Vaisberg characterised this approach as Bogdanovism.[233]

With the announcement of more cautious policies towards collectivisation in March, criticisms of lack of realism in drafts of the *genplan* were made more openly. A discussion article in the industrial newspaper criticised Fel'dman's coefficients as lacking any justification, described this as characteristic of the 'arithmoplans' of mathematical economists, and called for a 'real struggle of planning thought for *realistic* rates of growth, as distinct from the paper complacency which finds its expression in writing down (but merely writing down) high growth rates'. It also castigated as 'a Tugan–Baranovsky standpoint' the attitude of production for production's sake which led Kovalevsky to reproduce the 1929/30 situation in his plan for 1942/43, and others to treat restrictions on consumption as a communist virtue.[234] The furore about the work of Kovalevsky and Fel'dman, in which impatient opponents from both Right and Left objected to the schematism of its approach, was a significant moment in the fate of mathematical methods in planning (see also p. 483 n. 44 below). Summarising the discussion in a pamphlet issued for the XVI party congress, Kviring admitted that it would take eighteen months or two years to compile the *genplan*, and described Kovalevsky's working hypothesis as 'only something of an estimate for our rough orientation', which should be followed by a 'specific elaboration of technical reconstruction in the most important branches of the economy'.[235] The resolutions of the XVI congress made no

[233] PKh, 3, 1930, 146–7, citing Fel'dman in PKh, 12, 1929, 95. In ZI, April 4, 1930, Dol'nikov accused Kovalevsky and Fel'dman of Bukharinism, Bogdanovism and Bazarovism, claiming that 'laws of revolutionary Marxist–Leninist dialectics cannot be replaced by any mathematical exercises or schemas'. For Bogdanov, see p. 151 n. 53 above.

[234] ZI, May 29, 30, 1930 (Birbraer; for Birbraer's later role as an unsuccessful advocate of economic reform see SR, 42 (1984), 201–23 (Davies)). The 'numerical constructs' of Sabsovich and Fel'dman were characterised as 'proposals without proof' by Timrot in NP, 4, 1930, 117–18. Tugan-Baranovsky was an economist and 'Legal Marxist' who argued that the capitalist economy could remain in equilibrium however high the ratio of producer goods to consumer goods.

[235] Krzhizhanovskii *et al.*, *Problemy postroeniya general'nogo plana* (1930), 55; on this pamphlet see PE, 2, 1931, 14 (Larin).

reference to the *genplan*, and it was never completed. But long-term production targets of this order of magnitude for the moment continued to prevail in party thinking.

CHAPTER SEVEN

PROGRESS AND TURMOIL IN THE INDUSTRIAL ECONOMY, OCTOBER 1929–MAY 1930

(A) THE IMPACT OF THE WORLD ECONOMIC CRISIS

In the closing months of 1929, the capitalist world plunged into a protracted economic and social crisis. A year earlier, in August 1928, the VI Congress of Comintern announced that the general crisis of the capitalist system was entering its 'third period' of 'tremendous catastrophes', in which the partial stabilisation of the mid-1920s would give way to growing contradictions within and between the major capitalist countries; the danger of war would increase and the class struggle would intensify.[1] In July 1929, on the eve of the world crisis, the X Plenum of the Executive Committee of Comintern condemned Bukharin for underestimating the contradictions within capitalism, and vigorously proclaimed that a new upsurge of proletarian revolution had begun.[2]

Comintern had thus displayed remarkable foresight, at a time when almost no-one outside its ranks expected that the age of capitalist prosperity was about to come to an end. But its political analysis was seriously flawed: it greatly exaggerated the prospects for proletarian revolution, and underestimated the threat of fascism. Nor did Comintern, or its Soviet mentors, anticipate the profundity of the world economic crisis. The first loud rumbles of crisis in August and September 1929 received little attention in the USSR. Following the Wall Street crash on October 29, however, most Soviet economists soon diagnosed the crisis as serious. On November 2, Osinsky concluded that

---

[1] *Kommunisticheskii Internatsional . . . (1919–1932)* (1933), 769–71; see also Carr, iii, i (1976), 203–4.

[2] *Kommunisticheskii Internatsional . . . (1919–1932)* (1933), 911–13, 882–4.

'a stock-exchange crisis of this scale must influence the general economic situation of the US, and it is more than probable that it will profoundly deteriorate'; 'the whole of bourgeois Europe' would also be affected.[3] On December 15, *Pravda* announced that a general economic crisis was developing in the United States, and contrasted this with Soviet progress.[4] This contrast was a recurring theme in the ensuing months and years. At the XVI party congress in June 1930, the first two sections of Stalin's report contrasted 'The Growing Crisis of World Capitalism' with 'The Growing Upsurge of Socialist Construction' in the USSR. Stalin stressed that the crisis was a *world economic crisis*'. It had profoundly affected agrarian as well as industrial countries, bringing poverty and mass unemployment, and 'destroyed illusions about the omnipotence of capitalism in general and North-American capitalism in particular':

The bourgeoisie will seek a way out in a new imperialist war . . . the proletariat, struggling with capitalist exploitation and the war danger, will seek a way out in revolution.[5]

More or less simultaneously with the onset of world crisis, tension increased between the Soviet Union and several of its neighbours. In Afghanistan, the progressive Sheikh Amanullah, friendly to the Soviet Union, was overthrown at the beginning of 1929; later in the year he was succeeded by King Nadir Shah, who was soon suborned by the British.[6] In July 1929, the local Chinese authorities seized the Chinese Eastern Railway and ejected its Soviet managers; the conflict was brought to an end only six months later, after successful Soviet military action.[7] In Europe, the election of the Labour Government in May 1929 and the restoration of Soviet–British diplomatic relations - in November temporarily strengthened the Soviet position. But in the first few months of 1930, Soviet relations

[3] P, November 2, 1929.
[4] P, December 15, 1929 (editorial). Some Soviet economists argued that what was taking place was a depression rather than a crisis; but this was distinctly a minority view (see EZh, January 10, 1930).
[5] Stalin, *Soch.*, xii (1949), 229–54. For a careful analysis of Soviet interpretations of the crisis, see Day (1981), chs. 5–6.
[6] See Carr, iii, iii (1978), 694–7; Haslam (1983), 32–3.
[7] Carr, iii, iii (1978), 898–9, 909; see also pp. 444–6 below.

with both France and Germany sharply deteriorated; and the anti-religious campaign associated with the forced collectivisation of agriculture in the USSR aroused great hostility in the Vatican, and among Christians generally.[8]

Neither the crisis in the capitalist world nor these unfavourable developments in foreign relations led the Soviet authorities to conclude that there was imminent danger of an imperialist invasion of the USSR. In November 1929, Molotov explicitly noted that 'messrs. the imperialists have not so far decided to attack us directly';[9] and in June 1930, Radek, formerly prominent in the Left Opposition, and now temporarily restored to official favour as a commentator on foreign affairs, concluded that for the moment '*it is very difficult for the anti-Soviet front which is forming against us to go over to active measures*'.[10] But the Soviet authorities were nevertheless strongly convinced that the economic crisis would in the longer run increase the danger of military intervention against the USSR. At the XVI party congress, Stalin bluntly asserted that 'the tendency to adventurist actions against the USSR and to intervention is bound to be strengthened as a result of the developing economic crisis'.[11] These fears greatly strengthened the Soviet resolve to achieve the transformation of the USSR into a great industrial power before the respite came to an end. Radek pointed out that '*huge resources are being taken out of the country and invested in industry, and are not yet yielding a result in terms of commodities, while at the same time the peasant economy is in process of transformation*'. The current period was a '*zone of the greatest dangers*', which must be got through quickly.[12]

(B) THE FRAMEWORK OF CENTRAL POWER

When the five-year plan was approved in the spring of 1929, Stalin, with the support of many leading party figures, had

---

[8] For these events see Haslam (1983), 21–37.

[9] See vol. 1, p. 164; see also *ibid*. p. 117.

[10] I, June 26, 1930; the article was published on the first day of the XVI party congress, which gave it particular significance.

[11] *Soch.*, xii (1949), 255.

[12] I, June 26, 1930.

secured a majority in the Politburo; and at the central committee plenums, in spite of heated discussions, contested issues were never taken to a vote.[13] But advocates of more prudent economic policies still occupied important positions in the supreme agencies of the party. In the Politburo of nine members, Stalin, Molotov, Kuibyshev, and perhaps Rudzutak, gave unhesitating support to the continuation of coercive measures against the peasantry and to further increases in the pace of industrialisation. The Right-wing trio Rykov, Bukharin and Tomsky opposed the new policies; Kalinin, and perhaps Voroshilov, supported the new policies with reluctance. The new policies were also supported by Ordzhonikidze, head of the central control commission, and probably received the backing of seven of the eight candidate members of the Politburo. But Stalin's majority was not absolutely assured; at the crucial meeting which condemned the Bukharin group in February 1929, he secured a firm majority by convening the Politburo jointly with the presidium of the central control commission. And in the Orgburo, often thought of as Stalin's plaything, a majority of the thirteen members are said to have sympathised with the Right, as did two of the five members of the secretariat.[14]

By the end of 1929 Stalin and his supporters had consolidated their authority in the party. The plenum of the central committee in April 1929 condemned the Bukharin group and removed Bukharin from the editorship of *Pravda* and from work in Comintern; this resolution was unanimously approved by the

[13] For the Politburo, see Carr (1971), 60–1; for the central committee plenums, see Cohen (1974), 286–329.

[14] On the Orgburo, see Vaganov (1970), 144, and Bukharin to Kamenev, T 1897; however, of the members elected after the XV party congress in December 1927, only Uglanov, Dogadov, A. P. Smirnov and Kubyak are known to have resisted Stalin's policies. The members of the secretariat, who were also members of the Orgburo, were Stalin (general secretary), Molotov, Uglanov, S. Kosior and Kubyak; the other eight members of the Orgburo elected after the XV congress were Moskvin, Bubnov, Artyukhina, Andreev, Dogadov, A. P. Smirnov, Rukhimovich and Sulimov (SPR, vii, i (1930), 265). According to Vaganov (1970), 144, the unpublished report to the April plenum of the central committee (TsPA, 17/2/415, 5) stated that the Rightists 'counted on' a majority of the Orgburo, on support by the leadership of Sovnarkom and AUCCTU, and on *Pravda*, *Leningradskaya Pravda*, *Rabochaya Moskva* and *Trud*.

party conference later in the same month.[15] In November 1929, the central committee plenum removed Bukharin from the Politburo and warned Rykov and Tomsky that 'appropriate organisational measures' would follow 'the slightest attempt on their part to continue the struggle against the line and decisions of the Comintern Executive Committee and the CC'.[16] A public campaign against Bukharin and the Right, launched in August 1929, continued throughout the winter of 1929–30. And on December 21, 1929, Stalin's birthday provided the occasion for an unparalleled display of enthusiasm and loyalty by his supporters and former opponents.[17]

In the principal government agencies, Sovnarkom and STO, the position was much less satisfactory from the point of view of Stalin and his colleagues. In May 1929, Rykov's position had been weakened when he was replaced by Syrtsov, at this time a loyal supporter of Stalin, as chairman of Sovnarkom of the RSFSR.[18] But Rykov continued as chairman of Sovnarkom and STO of the USSR. While no major decision could be taken by these bodies without the authorisation of the Politburo, Rykov as chairman was responsible for reporting on all matters to the Politburo. Shmidt, one of his three deputies, was also an adherent of the Right.[19] Rykov endeavoured to support official policy conscientiously.[20] But he was a man of caution and compromise – a supporter of a socialist coalition in opposition to Lenin in November 1917, never on the Left of the party, strongly committed to NEP, the first of the Right-wing trio to try to call a halt to the extraordinary measures in March 1928.[21]

---

[15] See Carr (1971), 91–2. At the plenum Uglanov was replaced by Bauman as a candidate member of the Politburo and secretary of the central committee (SPR, vii, i (1930), 304).

[16] *KPSS v rez.*, ii (1954), 662–3. At the plenum Gamarnik (head of the political administration of the Red Army) was elected a member of the Orgburo and Shvernik (secretary of the AUCCTU) a candidate member (SPR, vii, ii (1930), 89).

[17] See vol. 1, pp. 118–19, 174–5.

[18] I, May 19, 1929.

[19] SZ, 1929, ii, art. 124 (dated May 29) confirming previous appointments; the other deputies were Rudzutak and Ordzhonikidze.

[20] See, for example, his speeches of September 1929, and February 16, 1930 (pp. 92 and 115 above).

[21] See Carr and Davies (1969), 58–61.

In the course of 1928 and 1929 the assault against Right-wing tendencies in the party and state administration removed many of those who opposed the new policies, and intimidated others. But every agency of state, as well as some local party organisations, resisted the pace of change which the party leaders attempted to impose. In overcoming this resistance, the role of CCC/Rabkrin, headed by Ordzhonikidze, was crucial. It acted as the chief adviser to the Politburo on economic policy and on all aspects of state administration; and the responsibility placed on it in April 1929 for conducting the purges of party and state further enhanced its authority (see pp. 61–2 above). By the summer of 1929, its staff included 300 Soviet specialists as well as a group of foreign consultants, and it was able to comment in detail on every aspect of economic affairs.[22] In the period from the summer of 1929 to the XVI party congress, it continuously did so, arguing passionately that economic plans were underestimated.[23] In these furious discussions Rabkrin increasingly drew on evidence from the OGPU that the pessimism of state agencies was due to the malevolent influence of wreckers. Many prominent party members who at first doubted the evidence of wrecking were eventually persuaded to accept it. In December 1929, Grin'ko, a senior party member who battled vigorously for high rates of industrialisation as president of the Gosplan commission for perspective planning, commented sharply on the experience of planning in previous years:

> We were compelled to listen for hours and days to the consultancies and drafts of these wreckers; when one looks back now on this activity, one realises how they screwed down all our estimates and plans and held them in strong pincers.[24]

A young party member working in Gosplan added that 'the young group of officials within the walls of Gosplan met with

[22] See Rees (1987), 170–1.
[23] See pp. 188–90 above; for Rabkrin's role in relation to agricultural plans in 1927 and 1928, see vol. 1, pp. 38, 66.
[24] EZh, December 26, 1929 (report of December 24); for Grin'ko's role in the preparation of the five-year plan, see *Material* (1930), 27.

clear sabotage, clear unwillingness to collaborate, an unfriendly attitude'.[25]

The party leaders looked forward from this tension and discord, which had been rife in several of the major commissariats, to an efficient and united state administration working unhesitatingly to carry out the party line. Grin'ko conjured up an alluring vision:

> In the process of implementing the five-year plan we physically feel with all the fibres of our being how much we need to organise a social and political mechanism enabling 150 million people to act guided by a single will, a single striving to accomplish what is laid down in the plan.[26]

Under Sovnarkom, within the commissariats, nervousness and demoralisation spread among the leading non-party specialists as the purge and the arrests proceeded (see pp. 116–17 above). Narkomfin had already been weakened by the campaign which had been waged against its principal advisers since the beginning of 1928. It was now the turn of Gosplan. On December 27, six prominent officials were removed from the Gosplan presidium, including Groman and Kalinnikov, head of the industrial section; Osinsky, the eccentric party member who had expressed sympathies with the Right wing in the past eighteen months, was transferred to work in industry.[27] Then on January 23, 1930, the Central Statistical Administration was amalgamated with Gosplan as its 'economic and statistical sector'.[28] The Central Statistical Administration had operated as an independent government department with the status of a commissariat since its establishment in July 1918. Its tradition of independence had vexed the political authorities for some years; and its stubborn realism about the size of the 1929 harvest (see vol. 1, pp. 64–5) undoubtedly precipitated this administrative upheaval, even though Groman, the principal troublemaker, was a Gosplan official working in the Central

[25] EZh, December 26, 1929 (Turetskii).
[26] EZh, December 26, 1929.
[27] SZ, 1930, ii, art. 7; for Osinsky's view, see Carr and Davies (1969), 76–8; Osinsky was appointed head of the new Vehicle and Tractor Corporation of Vesenkha on November 28, 1929 (SP VSNKh, 1929/30, art. 290).
[28] SZ, 1930, art. 97; the new sector was headed by Strumilin.

Statistical Administration as a coordinator of the two agencies. At the same time the incorporation of the statistical agencies within Gosplan offered a drastic solution to the problem of coordinating planning and statistics, which had become increasingly urgent with the rapid extension of operational planning throughout the economy.[29] Krzhizhanovsky, in his report to the presidium of Gosplan a week after the amalgamation was announced, stressed the crucial importance of up-to-date statistics which would influence events and be fully coordinated with the work of Gosplan.[30] A few days later, a circular from Krzhizhanovsky and Milyutin, the former head of the Central Statistical Administration, bringing together the political and technical problems posed to the authorities by statistics, declared that statistical reports must be 'militant and operational', 'embracing all the phases of the great historical struggle, the main content of which is the full and final extinction of the last remnants of capitalist relations in our country'.[31]

But the reform of Gosplan did not restore its former influence on economic policy. Krzhizhanovsky and his close associate Strumilin had led the campaign for purposive planning in 1927, but in the winter of 1928/29 they resisted the increased plans proposed by Vesenkha. Their resistance failed, but they remained in office, and throughout 1929/30 Gosplan seems to have exercised little initiative. Narkomfin remained equally ineffective after the removal of its principal advisers. A Rabkrin official wrote with some justice in November 1929 that 'Narkomfin no longer carries out a substantial independent policy'.[32] The initiative in financial matters passed to Gosbank and its ex-Trotskyist chairman Pyatakov: Gosbank, though formally part of Narkomfin, in practice often acted autonomously. Narkomtrud, on the other hand, remained unreformed: its Rightist commissar, Shmidt, had been replaced by the Rightist Uglanov in November 1928; its collegium remained intact, and Narkomtrud was later denounced for the Rightism which it

[29] For an earlier attempt to adapt statistics to the requirements of planning, see Carr and Davies (1960), 808.
[30] NPF, 2, 1930, 7–8.
[31] EZh, February 8, 1930.
[32] TPG, November 11, 1929 (Artamanov).

displayed in 1929–30.[33] Vesenkha was in a different category: its chairman, Kuibyshev, was a Politburo member and played a major role in the struggle for more rapid industrialisation and in opposing the Right wing in the party. But by the autumn of 1929 even Vesenkha was in a much weaker position than at any time since 1925. Some of its leading advisers had been accused of wrecking and sabotage, and the proposals of Vesenkha in relation to several major industries had already been overturned by the Politburo on the advice of Rabkrin.

Thus Sovnarkom and its commissariats spoke with uncertain and divided voices. The initiative in preparing economic plans and policies increasingly passed to Rabkrin. According to one of its officials, writing in November 1929, 'the logic of its work, the place of the agency in our system is drawing it to *head the work of planning*'. He claimed that Gosplan had not occupied a leading position in preparing the five-year plan, while Vesenkha had prepared the industrial plan for 1929/30, and Gosplan merely 'attached itself' to it (he could have added that Vesenkha itself was frequently compelled to accept proposals prepared in Rabkrin and approved by the Politburo). Gosplan lacked 'the necessary concentration of authority and power', and so, together with the Central Statistical Administration, it should be joined to CCC/Rabkrin to form a People's Commissariat for Planning, Records, and Supervision of Fulfilment, which would be known from its Russian initials as TsKK–PKI (the Russian initials of CCC/Rabkrin were TsKK–RKI).[34] This proposal came to nothing. But Rabkrin continued to perform the functions of principal planning agency and policy adviser to the Politburo until the XVI party congress and after: at the congress it was described as 'more a planning agency driving things forward than a Rabkrin'.[35] It would be an exaggeration to say that in this period the Politburo and Rabkrin took on the functions performed by Sovnarkom throughout the 1920s; but there was a marked shift in this direction. In one crucial sector of the economy, agriculture, when the Narkomzem of the USSR was established in November 1929 Yakovlev, until then deputy chairman of Rabkrin, was appointed the first Commissar,

[33] For Uglanov's appointment, see SZ, 1928, ii, art. 264 (dated November 29); for the condemnation of Narkomtrud, see pp. 342–3, 419–20 below.

[34] TPG, November 11, 1929 (Artamonov).

[35] *XVI s"ezd* (1931), 386 (Kiselev (Ukraine)).

and Rabkrin officials concerned with agriculture, including Kalmanovich, Tsil'ko and Kindeev, was transferred to its staff.[36] The practice of placing commissariats in the hands of Rabkrin personnel became almost normal (see pp. 417 and 418 below).

The transfer of the management of Vesenkha to the senior officials of Rabkrin did not take place until the end of 1930 (see p. 417 below). But on December 5, 1929, a major resolution of the party central committee 'On the Reorganisation of the Administration of Industry' was strongly influenced by proposals from Rabkrin.[37] During the summer of 1929 Vesenkha and Rabkrin prepared alternative proposals on this reorganisation, which were then reconciled in a joint commission of Vesenkha and Rabkrin.[38] The resolution of December 5, 1929, proposed that the confused division of the management of each branch of industry between *glavki* and syndicates should be brought to an end, and supported the Rabkrin contention that the syndicates, administratively stronger in most industries, should form the basis of the new unified agencies for each industry, which were henceforth known as *ob"edineniya* ('corporations' or 'associations'). The resolution of December 5 was based on premisses which had been strongly asserted at the XVI party conference in April 1929. First, administration should combine '*decentralisation* of operational functions with the simultaneous centralisation of planning and leadership on the main questions'. Secondly, Vesenkha should become an agency concerned not only with planning and economic questions but also with 'technical leadership, based on the achievements both of American and European and of Soviet science and technology'. Thirdly, the economic initiative of factories should be strengthened.[39] The resolution accordingly stressed the need to strengthen the rights of the enterprise, and proposed to concentrate the powers to manage and plan enterprises, including their supplies and sales, in the new corporations, thus seeking to 'reduce the sphere of operational interference' of the central staff of Vesenkha, and also of the trusts subordinate to

---

[36] SZ, 1929, ii. arts. 278, 292, dated December 8, 16; see also Rees (1987), 193.

[37] *Direktivy*, ii (1957), 126–33.

[38] For the Rabkrin proposals, see EZh, August 2, 1929; for the Vesenkha proposals, see P, September 13, 1929.

[39] *KPSS v rez.*, ii (1954), 597–8.

the corporations into which factories were normally grouped. The resolution also placed great stress on the need to replace traditional 'line-and-staff' organisation by 'functional' organisation, which was fashionable in the United States and Germany at the time. At the level of the central staff of Vesenkha, functionalism as applied in practice meant that all instructions were mainly issued through the new 'Planning–Technical–Economic Administration (PTEU)' of Vesenkha and its principal sectors, responsible for the functions of planning, labour, finance, scientific research and so on.[40] No administrative units within the central staff of Vesenkha had overall responsibility for a particular industry, or for a special group of corporations.

Following the promulgation of the reform, a senior official of Vesenkha claimed with satisfaction that it would provide the basis for the successful administration of the goal of catching up and overtaking the capitalist countries.[41] But this assessment proved to be over-optimistic. The reform was carried out at a time when industry was under great pressure to increase production and extend its range. It coincided with frequent changes in personnel at every level, resulting from the purge in Vesenkha (see pp. 117–18 above). The resolution of December 5 established the principles of the reorganisation only in broadest outline, and according to an authoritative commentator '*a general plan of reorganisation was lacking, and Vesenkha was unprepared on a whole number of cardinal questions* . . . the reorganisation was carried out *to a considerable extent in a spontaneous and unplanned way*.'[42] The process of reorganisation was spread over the whole of the first six months of 1930, and the composition of the new

[40] For a list of the sectors, see *Industrializatsiya, 1929–1932* (1970), 223 (report of Sovnarkom administrative department dated June 16, 1930). PTEU was headed by Mantsev, former Left Communist, and Cheka and Rabkrin official, who was brought into Vesenkha by Dzerzhinsky (for Mantsev, see Valentinov (Stanford, 1971), 101–3; for his appointment in 1930 see SP VSNKh, 1929/30, art. 1436, dated May 27).

[41] Lakin (1930), 4 (preface by Mantsev). A similar reform of Narkomtorg established sectors 'mainly constructed according to function' and corporations each responsible for a branch of trade (SZ, 1930, art. 181, decree of TsIK and Sovnarkom dated February 13); in June 1930 Narkomtorg also took over the food industry from Vesenkha (see p. 418 below).

[42] ZI, June 21, 1930 (Gintzburg).

corporations was frequently changed in the course of reorganisation. Confusion reigned:

> *The universal inflation of staffs, the growth of administrative expenditure, the revival of parallelism, increased complexity instead of simplification of the scheme of organisation, duplication of work . . . lack of precision in the allocation of functions – all this, unfortunately, happened everywhere, these infantile disorders of the reorganisation which at times acquired the clear character of an epidemic.*[43]

The upheaval certainly had a damaging effect on industrial performance; throughout the transition there were no clear lines of communication between authority and factory. Some coherence was retained only because the new corporations automatically carried on the functions of the old syndicates.[44]

Perhaps the fundamental reason for the confusion was the inappropriateness to Soviet needs of major aspects of the reform. The planning of production under conditions of scarcity required a clear chain of command, in which instructions about changing priorities were issued to factories from a single authority. The unification of syndicate and *glavk* into a single organisation for each industry was certainly appropriate. But in the circumstances of the 1930s it was futile to attempt to confine the activities of the central staff of Vesenkha largely to the planning of technology, which was the main justification for reorganising it on functional lines. Great confusion also resulted from the interposition of trusts between the new corporations and the factories; the trusts were responsible for technological leadership, rationalisation and reconstruction, but lacked supply and sales functions, or control over production plans. Moreover, the high degree of centralisation in the management of supplies which resulted from the reorganisation effectively deprived the factories of flexibility which proved to be essential to the operation of the system. In the course of the next three years, all these provisions were painfully revised.

[43] ZI, June 21, 1930 (Gintzburg); for a similar account, in more measured terms, by the administrative department of Sovnarkom, see *Industrializatsiya, 1929–1932* (1970), 220 (report of June 16, 1930).
[44] See the article by Dukarevich in *Metall*, 8–9, 1930; and *Industrializatsiya, 1929–1932* (1970), 220.

(C) THE ADVANCE OF INDUSTRIALISATION

In the first eight months of 1929/30, the successful expansion of large-scale industry again seemed to refute the sceptics. According to the official statistics, production increased by 28·5 per cent as compared with the equivalent period of 1928/29, the growth of Group A by 39·8 per cent greatly exceeding the growth of Group B by 20·2 per cent.[45] The statistics for industrial production at this time exaggerate the true rate of growth. They fail to take into account the chronic decline in quality which was a feature of the years 1929–31; and the relentless pressure from above for higher production no doubt led to exaggerated returns, particularly as statistical controls must have been weaker as a result of the confusion which prevailed in the statistical agencies in 1930. The official figures nevertheless portray the general trend; at various stages in 1929/30, they disclosed a decline in a number of industries, and in industry as a whole (see figures for November 1929 below, and also p. 346 below).

The official rate of growth was much higher than in the same period of the previous year, and came fairly close to the ambitious increase of 32·1 per cent in 1929/30 proposed in the control figures approved by Sovnarkom. This success was achieved in spite of a relatively poor performance at the beginning of the economic year. In October 1929, production of Vesenkha-planned industry was approximately the same as in the previous month, and in November it declined by over 5 per cent.[46] On December 22, 1929, A. M. Ginzburg, an ex-Menshevik expert who for the moment retained his post in Vesenkha, reported to a special conference summoned by the Vesenkha presidium that industrial production in November 1929 amounted to only 7·2 per cent of the annual plan, a smaller proportion than in any of the four previous years. Moreover, this increase was primarily due to the introduction of the *nepreryvka*: production per working day increased more slowly than in previous years. Ginzburg explained the lag behind the plan primarily in terms of 'the particularly great importance of

---

[45] SO, 6, 1930, 4; these figures are for Vesenkha-planned industry.

[46] See Table 7(c) below; these figures exclude seasonal industries, but are not adjusted for the varying number of working days in each month (the number of working days in November is usually three less than in October).

conjunctural factors', including the reduced supply of raw materials and the increased number of workers with insufficient training. According to another report to the conference, costs of industrial production in October were only 3–3·5 per cent below the average costs in 1928/29, compared with the annual plan of 11 per cent. In his concluding remarks Rukhimovich, a deputy chairman of Vesenkha, reproved Ginzburg for his exaggerated emphasis on conjunctural factors, and insisted that available resources were inadequately utilised.[47] On December 23, the day after the Vesenkha conference, Mendel'son reported to the presidium of Gosplan in a much more optimistic spirit that with the exception of industry 'in the main the country has got on to the rails of the fulfilment of the plan and the development of the whole economy is more or less satisfactory'. Freight carried on the railways had increased, as compared with the normal seasonal decline, and currency issue would probably be less than planned. Mendel'son placed the blame for the poor performance of industry primarily on subjective rather than objective factors.[48]

Following the Vesenkha conference Kuibyshev, in an article in the industrial newspaper simply entitled 'Shame!', uncompromisingly described the results for October and November as 'a clear defeat on the industrial front', contrasting them unfavourably with the achievements in agriculture, transport and finance. Kuibyshev condemned the inadequate performance of the 'servants of the working class' – the managers, administrators, technicians and party members in the factories – as compared to the leading groups of workers themselves, who were showing 'remarkable heroism', and were achieving the 'great miracle' of 'the transformation of the worker from a slave of the machine into the master of production and of the whole state economy'. Kuibyshev forthrightly condemned those who still criticised the high targets of the plans:

The task has been set. Now is not the time for discussion, the time for querying whether the plan can be fulfilled.[49]

[47] TPG, December 24, 1929.
[48] TPG, December 24, 1929.
[49] TPG, December 25, 1929.

In December, production increased by 13·3 per cent, reaching a higher level than in any previous month (see Table 7(c). But Ginzburg reported to a further Vesenkha conference that production still lagged behind the plan both in December and in the first two weeks of January 1930.[50] Drastic measures seemed to be necessary; and on January 25, 1930, a well-published central committee Appeal, addressed to all party, trade union, Komsomol and economic organisations, bluntly declared that the achievements of industry in the October–December quarter, though an improvement on the same period of 1928/29, were 'completely insufficient from the point of view of the fulfilment of the plan'. It attributed the lag to the insufficient mobilisation of the *aktiv* and the failure to introduce one-man management, complained that a 'considerable number of workers' were 'continuing to work in the old way', and approved the initiative of AUCCTU and the Komsomol in calling for a Lenin enrolment of shock brigades.[51]

The Appeal was followed by a vigorous campaign for an immediate increase in industrial production. In the next few months production increased very rapidly.[52] A survey in the statistical journal hailed February as a 'break-through month in the sense of approaching close to the plan targets'.[53] Ginzburg was able to report to the planning department of Vesenkha that, while the earlier lag of production behind the plan had not been fully made up, '*the March upswing brought production towards the fulfilment of planned tasks*'.[54] A further optimistic report

[50] ZI, January 24, 1930.

[51] P, January 25, 1930; the Appeal appeared in an editorial position under the heading 'A Militant, Shock Task'; for the Lenin enrolment see p. 258 below.

[52] The production of large-scale state industry was reported to be in excess of that in the equivalent month of 1929 by the following percentages (1926/27 prices):

	January	February	March	April	May
Group A	35·9	43·9	50·5	39·5	49·5
Group B	21·6	21·4	26·7	10·0	13·2
Total	27·7	30·7	37·0	22·1	29·4

(SO, 3–4, 1930, 106; 5, 1930, 156; 6, 1930, 152). For slightly different figures, see Table 7(c).

[53] SO, 3–4, 1930, 5.

[54] ZI, April 26, 1930.

by Mendel'son to the presidium of Gosplan announced that in the first six months of the economic year, October 1929–March 1930, industrial production in comparable branches of large-scale industry had increased by 30·4 per cent as compared with the 30·8 per cent planned; the harvest outlook was favourable; transport was 'coping with the plan'.[55] Determined pressure on industry had apparently yielded positive results.

Labour productivity in industry, however, rose less than planned, and as a result additional labour was taken on. Partly because of this, and partly because consumption of fuel and materials increased per unit of output, costs fell considerably less than planned.[56] Nevertheless, some optimism seemed appropriate, as the decline in costs was greater than in the same period in each of the previous four years. Moreover, in March 1930 costs declined substantially; this seemed to anticipate a repetition of the experience of 1928/29, when the main decline in costs took place in the second half of the year.[57]

In spite of the improvement in industrial costs, the financial situation in the economy as a whole deteriorated considerably during the first six months of 1929/30. Both urban and rural earnings increased much more than planned. This increase was absorbed partly by the rise in state and cooperative trade, and partly by the revenue of the state budget: in October 1929–March 1930 trade turnover and budgetary revenue both amounted to a higher proportion of the plan for the whole year than in previous years. But much additional unspent purchasing power remained.[58] Currency in circulation increased by over

[55] EZh, May 13, 1930; for transport, see pp. 348–9 below.
[56] The following results for industry were reported for October 1929–March 1930, as compared with the control figures for the year and the results for October 1928–March 1929 (percentage increase (+) or decrease (−)):

	Control figures	Results
Cost of production	− 11	− 5·5[a]
Numbers employed	+ 5·7	+ 8·6
Labour productivity	+ 25	+ 19·1

(SO, 5, 1930, 156; EZh, May 13, 1930).

[a]Vesenkha claimed a fall of 5·8 per cent
(EZh, May 13, 1930; *Vnedrenie* (1931), 91).

[57] P, May 28, 1930 (Miroshnikov).
[58] For figures see EZh, May 30, 1930.

200 million rubles, whereas in previous years it had always been reduced in the first six months of the economic year (see Table 23). This inflationary pressure resulted in a substantial rise in the uncontrolled prices of private trade in the first three months of the economic year (see Table 24(c)). A temporary halt in the rise in the general price level in January and February was the subject of some self-congratulation,[59] but this was evidently a result of the restrictions imposed on peasant trade during the collectivisation drive, and was not maintained during March.[60]

The financial situation continued to deteriorate sharply in April and May 1930. The further expansion of heavy industry and capital construction involved a rapid increase in the number of workers employed,[61] and hence in urban purchasing power; and supplies were wholly inadequate to meet demand. The situation was exacerbated by the poor performance of the consumer goods industries. In May 1930, production of Group B industries was only 13·9 per cent higher than in May 1929 (see Table 7(c)). This was a result of the reduction in the supply of raw materials, particularly of imported cotton. Kalinin later explained that the Soviet government had decided that the import of machinery was 'more important than cotton', even though the cotton shortage meant that most Moscow textile factories had to close down for ten weeks.[62]

In the producer goods industries, however, the successful production drive of January–March 1930 was maintained in the following two months. In May, Group A production was reported to be as much as 51 per cent higher than in May 1929, which was an even more rapid expansion than the average increase for the year proposed in the control figures for 1929/30 (see Table 7(c)). The authorities were also encouraged by an impressive reduction in industrial costs, by 8·9 per cent in April and 8·6 per cent in May 1930 as compared with the same

[59] EZh, March 28, 1930; according to Table 24(c), bazaar prices continued to rise.
[60] For the restrictions on peasant trade, see vol. 2, pp. 160–1.
[61] The numbers employed in large-scale state industry (excluding MOP) rose by 1·1 per cent in April and 0·5 per cent in May (SO, 6, 1930, 150, 152); numbers employed in construction rose from 1·11 millions on April 1 to 1·84 millions on June 1 (see Table 17).
[62] P, July, 23, 1930. For cotton imports see p. 369 below.

months in 1929.[63] But the most remarkable success was the expansion of industrial capital investment. While it lagged behind the plan, it amounted in the period October 1929–May 1930 as a whole to some 1,450 million rubles, double the investment in the same period of 1928/29.[64] On June 1, 1930, nearly twice as many workers were employed in the building industry as on June 1, 1929 (see Table 17).

In the weeks preceding the XVI party congress the completion of three major investment projects dramatically symbolised the initial successes of the industrialisation drive. On April 25, 1930, the northern and southern sections of the Turksib railway were joined at Aina-Bulak eighteen months ahead of the original schedule.[65] A special train took Soviet officials and workers, and foreign diplomats and journalists, from Moscow to the opening celebrations.[66] On June 1, 1930, the largest agricultural engineering works in Europe, Rostsel'mash, construction of which began in 1927, was completed in Rostov on Don. Rostsel'mash, a highly-mechanised combine consisting of five separate factories on the same territory, was scheduled to employ ten thousand workers when working at full capacity. The factory was originally planned to produce horse-drawn equipment, but, following the unexpected pace of the collectivisation drive, Rostsel'mash was converted to the production of tractor-drawn implements in the last few months of its construction.[67] A message from Stalin congratulated 'workers, technical personnel and all the leading cadres' on their 'great victory' in constructing a factory which would eventually produce output worth 115 million rubles, as compared with a production of only 70 million rubles from all 900 pre-war

[63] *Industrializatsiya, 1929–1932* (1970), 238; these figures exclude the food industry; for the decline in costs in October 1929–March 1930, see p. 247 above.

[64] ZI, July 26, 1930 (report to Vesenkha presidium of July 25).

[65] I, April 27, 1930 (Ryskulov).

[66] For a graphic description of the celebrations, witnessed by 'unsophisticated' Kazakhs from hillside and desert who 'grew as excited as children when they saw their own faces in a mirror', see Lyons (1938), 304–312; the train journey is satirised in I. Ilf and E. Petrov, *The Little Golden Calf* (1932).

[67] P, June 15, ZI, June 15, 1930; Glebov-Avilov (Rostov, 1930), 21–4, 42; Yakovlev (1932), 9. The construction was known as Sel'mashstroi, the completed factory was at first also known as Sel'mashstroi, and eventually as Rostsel'mash.

agricultural engineering factories.[68] Full production was planned for 1930/31, two years ahead of the original plan; to speed up the assimilation of the factory, engineers and workers were brought in from the United States and Germany.[69] Immediately after construction was completed, heroic efforts compressed two to three months' work into two weeks so that the first batch of tractor sowers to be made in the USSR could be presented to the party congress.[70]

On June 17, 1930, the Stalingrad tractor factory completed its first tractor. The Stalingrad factory was intended as a concentrated expression of the essence of the Soviet industrialisation drive. The revised project adopted in February 1929 was based on the most advanced United States' technology. This was the first Soviet factory to produce a single standardised product on a conveyor belt, and equalled in capacity the equivalent International Harvester factory in Milwaukee.[71] American firms, urged on by Walter Duranty, the Moscow correspondent of the *New York Times*, prepared the designs in record time.[72] The factory was constructed at feverish pace under the head of construction V. I. Ivanov, a crude, deep-voiced passionate ex-metal-worker and ex-sailor who had become a Chekist and a party official, and the chief building engineer, John Calder, a calm American who had been responsible for building Ford factories in the United States.[73]

[68] P, June 17, 1930.

[69] Glebov-Avilov (1930), 79–81. Soviet sources (e.g. Glebov-Avilov (1930), 46; P, June 15, 1930) frequently claimed that while foreign machinery was installed, no direct foreign help was received in constructing the factory. Stalin's message, however, thanked 'all the foreign specialists' for their assistance.

[70] Shtikh (1931), 20–1; for the 'chain shock brigade' which was organised to accomplish this see pp. 259–60 below. Knickerbocker (1931), 116–18, who visited Rostov in the autumn of 1930, describes the new factory, 'neat, crowded with busy workmen and girls tending hosts of machines', against the background of a 'city of thieves, goats, Caucasian beer, stenches' in which barefoot women fought to get fly-blown meat.

[71] Il'in, ed. (1931), 12–13; Il'in, ed. (1933), 33–4; Dodge (1960), 355; ZI, June 19, 1930 (Ivanov).

[72] For an account of the role of United States' firms in designing the factory, see ZI, July 5, 1930 (Levenson); for Duranty's role see EZh, July 31, 1929 (Mezhlauk).

[73] I, September 9, 1930; for Ivanov, see Dodge (1960), 242–3; Il'in, ed. (1933), 17–26, 35, 39, 77.

The personalities of Ivanov and Calder typify and contrast the 'Russian revolutionary sweep' and 'American business efficiency' of which Stalin spoke in 1924.[74] The completion date was advanced from the end of 1931 first to the autumn of 1930 and then to July 1, 1930. Building continued in severe weather conditions throughout the winter of 1929–30, and was completed in a 'shock forty days'.[75] By June 17, the factory was hardly yet capable of producing a tractor. Only sixty per cent of the machine tools for the first stage had been installed, the conveyor was not working, and much work had to be carried out by hand.[76] Many troubles lay ahead (see pp. 372–5 below). But for the moment enthusiasm prevailed. As soon as the first tractor was completed a telegram arrived from Stalin congratulating workers and management for making it possible to produce 50,000 tractors a year, which would be '50,000 missiles blowing up the old bourgeois world and laying the road to a new socialist system (uklad) in the countryside'.[77] The factory, in a telegram to Rykov as chairman of Sovnarkom, described the first tractor as the 'steel Chekist of the reconstruction of the Soviet countryside', announced that the factory would go over to 'super-American rates of work', and claimed that its experience demonstrated that 'grumblers and those of little faith' were wrong not to believe that the approved rates of growth could be attained.[78]

(D) THE MANAGEMENT OF LABOUR

The increase in industrial production during the first eight months of 1929/30 was achieved partly by the recruitment of additional workers, partly by an increase in output per worker. In Vesenkha-planned industry, as compared with the same

---

[74] Calder summed up his relationship with Ivanov with the remark that the site needed an axe as well as a saw (Il'in, ed. (1933), 39).

[75] B, 11–12, June 30, 1930 (Sheboldaev); SKhG, October 15, 1929; Il'in, ed. (1933), 35–43; ZI, April 10, June 19 (Ivanov), 1930; Dodge (1960), 282. Apparently Ivanov resisted the advance of the date from the autumn of 1930 to July 1, which was approved while he was in the United States (Dodge (1960), 282; Il'in (1934), 103).

[76] ZI, June 19, 1930 (Ivanov); Dodge (1960), 283.

[77] P, June 18, 1930; Il'in, ed. (1933), 49.

[78] SZe, June 20, 1930.

period of the previous year, the average number of workers increased by 12·2 per cent, output per worker per day by 17·4 per cent. By the end of the period, however, most reliance was placed on recruiting extra labour: in May 1930, the number of workers was 18·9 per cent and output per man-day only 12·0 per cent higher than in May 1929.[79]

(i) *The* nepreryvka *and multi-shift working*

A substantial part of the growth of industrial production in this period was obtained by increasing the number of days a month and hours a day that machinery and buildings were in use, primarily by the *nepreryvka* (see pp. 84–6 above). Vesenkha planned to transfer to the *nepreryvka* 85 per cent of workers in Group A industries and 50 per cent in Group B industries in the course of 1929/30; of the 1,300,000 workers to be transferred, 810,000 would be transferred in the six months October 1929–March 1930.[80] These were ambitious plans, but they were soon exceeded. By the beginning of November 1929, a Narkomtrud commission had reported favourably on the results of the first transfers;[81] 906,000 workers, over 40 per cent of the total, were transferred by December 31, 1929, and as many as 1,257,000, 53 per cent of the total, by February 1, 1930.[82] While practice varied in different enterprises, the five-day week, four working days followed by a rest-day, soon became the general rule.[83] These developments were seen as having considerable revolutionary significance. The journal of the Left opposition in emigration hailed continuous production as a 'principle of socialism' which had been incorporated in the ideals of socialism from the English and French Utopians to the Russian Bogdanov.

---

[79] Calculated from data in *Ezhemesyachnyi statisticheskii byulleten'*, July 1930, 4–5, 15–17, 25–7; the underlying data for production, and output per worker per day, are measured in 1926/27 prices; the figures, which show an increase in production of 30·7 per cent, exclude seasonal industries. For a slightly lower figure for the increase in production, see p. 246 n. 52 above.

[80] VTr, 4, 1930, 3–4.

[81] P, November 1, 1929.

[82] VTr, 4, 1930, 4–5. From November 1, 1929, *Pravda* went over to the continuous week, and was henceforth published on every day of the week; other newspapers continued the previous practice of publication on every day except Monday.

[83] *Trud* (1930), 99.

According to the Left opposition journal, the *nepreryvka* must become not 'continuous gray preoccupation with work' but 'a huge act of *cultural revolution*', replacing the Sundays of class society by continuous leisure facilities for the proletariat. The break with the old calendar was 'a kind of Rubicon'.[84] In the USSR, plans went ahead for a new revolutionary calendar (see pp. 143–4 above), but, like many other schemes of this period, they were not put into effect.

The most obtrusive difficulties in implementing the *nepreryvka* appeared in management and administration. The Politburo swiftly adapted its own arrangements. It traditionally met weekly on Thursdays, as it does at the present day, but between October 1929 and November 1931 it normally met on the 5, 10, 15, 20, 25 and 30 of every month.[85] In all organisations it became extremely difficult to ensure that key officials were all present on the same day. In November 1929, Vesenkha instructed managerial staff to take fixed days off and to appoint deputies;[86] but the trouble persisted, and in March 1930 Vesenkha accepted a recommendation of the Rudzutak commission that meetings should be held only on the first, third and fifth days of every five-day week, and that the rest-days of heads of institutions should fall only on the second and fourth days.[87] The complexities involved in scheduling the use of equipment confronted factory managers with a more fundamental problem. With the traditional system, each machine was used by only one worker, or transferred to regular workers on the second and third shifts. But when the machine was used on every day of the week, timetabling so that workers always returned to their own machines was virtually impossible.[88] For the moment the problem was often avoided by introducing the

---

[84] BO (Paris), vi (October 1929), 23–5.

[85] See the dates of Politburo meetings incompletely listed in *Industrializatsiya, 1929–1932* (1970), 579–615.

[86] SP VSNKh, 1929/30, art. 273 (order of November 26).

[87] ZI, March 18, 1930; SP VSNKh, 1929/30, art. 1071 (order of March 23). For a foreign visitor's impressions of the chaos resulting from a varying rest-day, see Bourke-White (1931), 49.

[88] See, out of a vast literature, the discussion of the experience of 1930 in VTr, 2, 1931, 37–41 (Fal'k); another article in the same issue comments in despair that 'to schedule work on a single machine tool for two or three shifts is mathematically impossible without an inevitable loss of working time' (pp. 43–8 – Al'do).

nepreryvka purely formally, so that equipment was rested on one day in five instead of one in seven.[89]

In spite of all deficiencies, the *nepreryvka* was responsible for a rise in production of 8–9 per cent in 1929/30:[90] by the end of the economic year, 72·9 per cent of workers in Vesenkha-planned industry had been formally transferred to it, as compared with the plan of 67·5 per cent.[91] This would prove to be the highest achievement of the *nepreryvka* campaign.

The *nepreryvka* overshadowed and in practice thrust aside the efforts to increase the use of existing capacity through a multi-shift system. It seemed simpler to introduce, and less troublesome for the individual worker. Its rapid spread throughout industry in 1929/30 swallowed up the resources required by a multi-shift system: the *nepreryvka* drew heavily on technical and skilled labour, absorbed all available agricultural raw materials in the consumer goods' industries, and worsened the metal shortage in producer goods' industries.[92]

The attempt to introduce night shifts also encountered many other obstacles. In a variety of factories surveyed by brigades sent out by the industrial newspaper, production was much lower on the night shift. The night shifts were very unpopular. Technical staff above the level of foreman were almost invariably absent, and canteen and medical facilities were inadequate. The shift was poorly planned.[93] A Vesenkha order of March 22, 1930, complained that *'each shift goes off without waiting for the next'*, and insisted that a responsible member of management must be present at every factory day and night.[94] But this had little practical effect.

More fundamental doubts about the viability of the third shift had not been allayed. Some planners argued that it was unwise to use old equipment so intensively, though others, more optimistic about the future availability of machinery, claimed that it would be advantageous to wear out old

---

[89] *Na novom etape* (1930), i, 456–7 (Kvasha, writing in March 1930); see also Dubner's report to the presidium of Vesenkha, ZI, August 1, 1930.

[90] PI, 19–20, 1931, 8.

[91] VTr, 2, 1931, 39.

[92] See *Na novom etape* (1930), i, 453–4 (Kvasha).

[93] ZI, March 19, 25, 1930.

[94] SP VSNKh, 1929/30, art. 1069.

equipment quickly as it would soon be replaced.[95] Many economists and administrators believed that labour productivity on night shifts was inherently low. The project for the Chelyabinsk tractor factory assumed productivity would fall by 25 per cent in the third shift. Even surveys most favourable to the night shift showed a reduction of 6 per cent.[96]

By the summer of 1930, little progress had been made. A Vesenkha order in April 1930 reported that the coefficient was still barely 1·5.[97] While it increased in Leningrad industry from 1·35 in 1928/29 to 1·63 in 1929/30,[98] this was exceptional. A comtemporary report gave a figure of 1·60 for October 1929–August 1930, but the final figure for 1930 was only 1·55, as against 1·50 in 1928 and 1·53 in 1929.[99]

For the time being the authorities continued to press for the introduction of second and third shifts. Projects of new factories, originally designed for two shifts or even a single shift, were adapted to a night shift; the planned capacity of the Stalingrad factory increased from 50,000 to 75,000 tractors a year.[100] The Vesenkha order of April 12, 1930, called for introduction of a multi-shift system in existing factories even where materials were scarce; production should be concentrated in the best-equipped and most profitable factories.[101] Kuibyshev's resolution for the XVI party congress called for 'an all-out extension of efforts to increase the number of shifts'.[102] Others proposed to go even further. In the discussion which preceded the party congress Larin called for the gradual introduction, beginning in 1931/32, of completely continuous production in four shifts of six hours, which would enable output to increase by a further 15 per cent. This proposal was supported by Dubner, an influential figure in Vesenkha at this time.[103] Another Vesenkha specialist rejected the proposal as a 'leftist' distortion, arguing that it would require a huge increase in skilled and technical

[95] *Na novom etape* (1930), i, 481 (Maksimov); ZI, May 25, 1930.
[96] *Na novom etape* (1930), i, 440–9 (Kvasha), 481 (Maksimov).
[97] SP VSNKh, 1929/30, art. 1188 (dated April 12, 1930).
[98] NFI (Leningrad), 17–18, September 25, 1930, 4.
[99] VTr, 3–4, 1931, 51; *Trud* (1936), 96.
[100] B, 11–12, June 30, 1930, 64.
[101] SP VSNKh, 1929/30, art. 1188.
[102] *KPSS v rez.*, iii (1954), 46.
[103] P, June 24, 1930; ZI, July 3, 1930.

personnel.[104] In any case, strong evidence was available that the halt in production for three hours a day, which was the total available with a three-shift seven-hour day, was insufficient for repair work and smooth production.[105] The proposal to introduce round-the-clock operation, reflecting the wild hopes of these months, had no practical outcome.[106]

(ii) Socialist emulation

The campaign for socialist emulation, which sought to enlist the working class in heroic efforts to increase productivity, continued to be at the centre of party attention throughout 1929/30. The first All-Union Congress of Shock Brigades, which met in Moscow from December 5–10, 1929, heard a report from Kuibyshev in which he claimed that 'socialist emulation in the last resort is the most important factor which will determine the fulfilment and overfulfilment of the five-year plan'.[107] The main resolution of the congress praised socialist emulation as the 'main method of attracting the working masses into the management of the national economy', and called for universal participation. 'All those at work must be attracted into shock brigades; shock brigades must turn into shock shops, shock shops into shock model enterprises.' Socialist emulation should

---

[104] ZI, August 3, 1930 (Shauer); this article followed a sitting of the presidium of Vesenkha at which Dubner reported on multi-shift working (ZI, August 1, 1930); Shauer is said to have initiated the *nepreryvka* (see p. 84 n. 101 above).

[105] *Na novom etape* (1930), i, 481.

[106] The difficulties in the way of increasing the number of shifts eventually proved insuperable. The shift coefficient rose from 1·55 in 1930 to 1·72 in 1933 (*Trud* (1936), 96); but in September 1933 a Narkomtyazhprom order proposed that enterprises should reduce the number of third shifts and work the first and second shifts more intensively (ZI, September 28, 1933); from 1933 onwards the shift coefficient declined, falling to 1·61 in 1935 (*Trud* (1936), 96). In 1988 the Soviet authorities are still strenuously endeavouring to increase the shift coefficient.

[107] *Pervyi Vsesoyuznyi s"ezd udarnykh brigad* (1959), 55. This is the abridged report of the congress, published for the first time on the occasion of its thirtieth anniversary. At the time the resolutions of the congress were published in the daily press (*Trud*, December 7, P, December 11, 1929), and Kuibyshev's report and the congress resolution appeared as a separate pamphlet in 60,000 copies (Kuibyshev (1930)). The verbatim report was never published; to judge by the abridged report, this may have been because it was too frank about workers' resistance to the campaign.

be integrated with the plan in 'economic and political contracts' which disaggregated the control figures to enterprise, shop and shift level.[108]

The importance of socialist emulation was stressed by all the party leaders. Kaganovich praised it as one of the major incentives which would replace the whip of capitalist competition:

> It must be understood, comrades: capitalism has its incentives. Competition whips it on, inflows and outflows of capital from one branch to another whip it on. We don't have this. Our incentive is socialist construction, striving forward, proletarian public opinion, socialist emulation, self-criticism.[109]

At the XVI party congress, Stalin summed up the importance of socialist emulation through rose-tinted official spectacles:

> The most remarkable feature of emulation is that it produces a fundamental revolution in the attitude of people to labour, as it turns labour from the shameful and heavy burden which it was thought to be previously, into a matter of *honour*, a matter of *glory*, a matter of *valour* and *heroism*. Nothing like this exists or could exist in capitalist countries.[110]

The congress resolution on Stalin's report praised 'the broad development of socialist emulation and shock work among the workers' for its major contribution to the successes achieved in industry and agriculture.[111]

In the course of 1929 and 1930 the drive for socialist emulation nominally succeeded in involving the majority of industrial workers. Within the larger category 'socialist emulation', a term which covered all types of competition between and within factories, a smaller number of shock workers (udarniki) were organised into 'shock brigades', which were groups of workers engaged in a particular production task, or operating a group of machines. In addition, a smaller number of 'individual shock workers' were not organised into brigades. At the time of the

---

[108] Kuibyshev (1930), 35–46.
[109] P, June 8, 1930.
[110] Stalin, *Soch.*, xii, 315.
[111] *KPSS v rez.*, iii (1954), 18.

congress of shock workers, only a minority of industrial workers, some 10–15 per cent, had declared themselves to be shock workers.[112] At a conference of local party officials convened by the central committee on January 13, 1930, Kaganovich frankly admitted:

> At present the position is that a small group of shock workers is carrying on an heroic struggle, is working stubbornly and tensely, while a considerable part, and perhaps the majority, of workers is working in the old way.[113]

A determined effort was made to improve matters with the publication of an Appeal by the AUCCTU and the Komsomol in January 1930 for a 'Lenin enrolment' of 500,000 new shock workers to commemorate the anniversary of Lenin's death.[114] Within a month, 1,320,000 shock workers were said to have been enrolled in only twenty regions. Much significance cannot be attached to this figure, which included all workers in shops and factories which declared themselves to be 'shock'.[115] This was the time of the comprehensive collectivisation of agriculture, and the recruitment of shock workers was often carried out indiscriminately. S. Kosior complained that in the Ukraine the formal enrolment of large numbers of shock workers had often been of no help, or had even been a hindrance:

> The more shock brigades there are at an enterprise, the more helpless the trade unions and managers are in organising the whole shop or mine along shock lines.[116]

Both for socialist emulation as a whole, and for the shock brigades, objectives were often vague. A 'mass self-check' carried out by the trade unions in April–June 1930 revealed

---

[112] VTr, 4, 1930, 12; a survey of factories employing 921,000 workers carried out on January 1, 1930, reported that 26 per cent were shock workers (Uglanov, ed. (1930), 89).

[113] P, January 21, 1930.

[114] See Rothstein (London, 1948), 120; for the Appeal, dated January 20, 1930, see P, January 21, 1930. The appeal was approved by the Politburo on January 20 (*Industrializatsiya, 1929–1932* (1970), 588–9).

[115] VTr, 4, 1930, 13–14; the author claimed, however, that the realistic figure was far in excess of the 500,000 planned.

[116] P, March 9, 1930.

that many shock workers were registered only on paper, and others had no specific obligations.[117] There is no doubt, however, that the campaign succeeded by the summer of 1930 in involving a substantial number of workers. A Gosplan survey of several hundred enterprises in the spring of 1930 claimed that 72 per cent of their workers were involved in socialist emulation, including 47 per cent as shock workers organised in shock brigades, and 4·7 per cent as individual shock workers.[118] Following the impetus to the shock-brigade movement at the end of 1929 and beginning of 1930, party and Komsomol groups and group organisers began to function as regular organisers of the shock brigades.[119] At the XVI party congress Shvernik confidently asserted that the campaign had played a large part in the substantial increases of labour productivity in the first few months of 1930.[120]

Novel and ingenious forms of emulation emerged in the spring of 1930. The oddly-named 'voluntary tug-boat (obshchestvennyi buksir)' was a group of the best shock workers in the Artem coalmine in the North Caucasus, who were sent, accompanied by an assistant manager, to a lagging mine to pull up its performance. The works committee at the lagging mine was 're-elected', i.e. replaced, the mine manager was also replaced, and the 'tug-boat' took virtual control of the mine until its performance improved.[121] The 'chain (skvoznaya) shock brigade' at the new agricultural engineering works Rostsel'mash received its name because all the relevant factory shops, together with shops making components in other factories, were linked together in an effort to overcome bottlenecks in the production of new Soviet-designed seeders to be attached to Stalingrad tractors. Two shock workers acted as full-time chasers in the

[117] VTr, 10–11, 1930, 41–3. According to a Gosplan survey (see note 118 below), only 39 per cent of shock brigades had specific production targets in March 1930, and results were recorded for only two-thirds of these; this report was based on data returned by the management which doubtless exaggerated the success (*Sotsialisticheskoe sorevnovanie* (1930), 25–8).

[118] *Sotsialisticheskoe sorevnovanie* (1930), 11–12; the survey covered 491 factories, each employing more than 1,000 workers, with a total labour force of 1,051,000 workers, and was carried out between April 20 and May 20 (*ibid.* 11, 13).

[119] *Sotsialisticheskoe sorevnovanie* (1930), 34.

[120] *XVI s"ezd* (1931), 650 (Shvernik).

[121] *Trud,* June 14, 1930 (reprinted in *Sotsialisticheskoe sorevnovanie* (1965), 91–2).

production shops; 'four shock workers who had completed the FZU courses regularly went to the drawing office after work and helped to prepare the drawings'; and others went to the 'Krasnyi Aksai' agricultural implements factory after work and persuaded a group of its workers to process components in their spare time.[122] On June 28 Rostsel'mash duly reported the completion of the seeder to the XVI party congress.[123] At the Putilov works, 'planning operational groups' more generally acted as chasers and took over minor aspects of the administration of the plans.[124] At Elektrozavod, 'rationalisation brigades' recorded and studied production experience in order to improve their work.[125] All these devices were frequently called upon in later years to assist in overcoming disruptions and bottlenecks in production. Meanwhile the long-established production conferences continued. But they were now primarily concerned with the solution of specific production problems rather than the general examination of the work of the factory; and preference was given to conferences of shops and of groups of workers, rather than to the traditional factory-wide conferences.[126]

It is difficult, perhaps impossible, to assess how far genuine enthusiasm spurred on all these campaigns, and how far they were the result of organised social pressure. Some workers reacted to socialist emulation with extreme hostility. Veinberg, in the main report to the shock workers' congress, frankly admitted that 'alien elements' among the workers regarded socialist emulation as 'sweated labour', greeting it with remarks such as 'they used to feed us with paradise, now they feed us with socialism'. According to Veinberg, 'shock workers are threatened, often in their barracks, and relatives quarrel with them'.[127] Other delegates reported that a worker stood by and failed to stop the machine when a shock worker fell into a vat of

[122] *Trud*, June 5, 1930 (reprinted in *Sotsialisticheskoe sorevnovanie* (1965), 88–90).

[123] *XVI s"ezd* (1931), 102–3.

[124] *Industrializatsiya, 1929–1932* (1970), 520.

[125] B, 18, September 30, 1930, 57–8 (Pavlov). For these various forms of emulation, see also *XVI s"ezd*)1931), 652; Rothstein (London, 1948), 122–4.

[126] ZI, June 6, 1930; B, 18, September 30, 1930, 59; *XVI s"ezd* (1931), 654.

[127] *Pervyi Vsesoyuznyi s"ezd* (1959), 69–70; Veinberg was a secretary of AUCCTU.

boiling dye, while on another occasion 'stokers almost threw a shock worker who cut the rate for the job into a furnace'.[128] In January 1930 Kaganovich complained that a 'section' of the workers 'stands on one side, tittering ironically at what they call "shock worker-idiots (chudaki–udarniki)"'.[129]

But much of the enthusiasm of the shock workers was certainly genuine. Kravchenko, who worked in the Petrovsky iron and steel works, Dnepropetrovsk, in 1928–30, and was later utterly disillusioned, described how in 1929–30 he was part of an enthusiastic minority, 'caught up in a fervor of work at times touched with delirium'.[130] Similar reports appeared in the émigré Menshevik journal from clandestine correspondents.[131]

(iii) Production collectives and production communes[132]

The most spontaneous efforts by workers to increase production through their own exertions were the 'production collectives' and 'production communes'. The first prominent communes were established in the summer of 1929 in the metal works at Zlatoust in the Urals. Wages of members of the commune were recorded on a single account and divided equally; productivity and wages increased.[133] The spontaneous origins of the movement were universally acknowledged. A survey of its history in Nizhnii Novgorod, prepared by the regional council of trade unions in June 1930, described it as a movement 'outside the field of vision and leadership of trade unions and economic organisations'.[134]

According to Shvernik, the collectives began '*spontaneously*', without any leadership.[135] The movement spread rapidly during

---

[128] *Ibid.* 100, 166, 158.

[129] P, January 21, 1930 (speech of January 13).

[130] Kravchenko (London, 1947), p. 50.

[131] See SV (Paris), 18 (207), September 27, 1929, 16; 13 (227), July 12, 1930, 12, 14.

[132] See also Filtzer (1986), 102–7, and SR, xlv (1986), 65–84 (Siegelbaum) – this informative article surveys the history of collectives and communes in 1929–31.

[133] B, 3–4, February 28, 1930, 4–5; *Industrializatsiya, 1929–1932* (1970), 506; SR, xlv (1986), 67 (Siegelbaum).

[134] *Istoriya industrializatsii* (Gor'kii, 1968), 112.

[135] ZI, March 12, 1930; this was a report to a conference called by the party central committee and the AUCCTU.

the first few weeks of 1930, usually in conditions, such as continuous flow production, in which collective work was particularly appropriate.[136] By May 1930, the collective and communes included 9·3 per cent of the workers at factories surveyed by Gosplan, some 100,000 of the 500,000 workers who were members of shock brigades; 14,700 of these were in Leningrad.[137]

The common feature of all production collectives and communes was that their work was recorded collectively and their members drew on a common pool of earnings rather than being paid individually. The Gosplan survey of April–May 1930 distinguished six types of production collectives: (1) members were all of the same grade of skills, and divided wages equally, according to the number of hours worked; (2) members were of different grades, but divided all earnings equally; (3) members were of different grades, and divided basic pay according to their grade, and additional pay (prirabotki) equally, irrespective of skill; (4) members were of different grades, and divided all earnings according to their grade; (5) more rarely, the number of 'eaters' in the family was taken into account; (6) different members were paid on different principles ('mixed forms of distribution').[138] Categories (1) and (2) were known in the press as a production commune, Categories (3) and (4) as production collectives, Category (5) as a production-welfare (byt) commune, and Category (6) was treated as intermediate between commune and collective. A study in the Narkomtrud journal noted that 'definite distinctions between the concepts "production collective" and "production commune" are not found in the localities'.[139] Most of the collectives surveyed by Gosplan were in Category (1); among the remainder, membership was more or less equally divided

---

[136] VTr, 4, 1930, 18–19; *Na novom etape* (1930), i, 177.

[137] *Sotsialisticheskoe sorevnovanie* (1930), 43; B, 17, September 15, 1930, 60; IS, 5, 1961, 63.

[138] *Sotsialisticheskoe sorevnovanie* (1930), 57–64.

[139] VTr, 1930, 20–1; *Industrializatsiya, 1929–1932* (1970), 511–2. A report of the Nizhnii–Novgorod regional council of trade unions in June 1930 made a similar distinction between communes and collectives (*Istoriya industrializatsii* (Gor'kii, 1968), 111–12). One case was reported in which basic pay was divided equally, and additional pay according to grade (ZI, March 7, 1930). The Gosplan survey pointed out that Category (1) collectives in fact usually involved substantial equalisation of earnings, as earnings of different workers

between 'equalising communes' (Category (2) and collectives (Categories (3) and (4)).[140]

The movement was undoubtedly partly inspired by the hopes prevalent among politically-active workers of rapid progress to a more advanced society. Veinberg, in the main report to the congress of shock workers, described the communes as 'cells of the future communist society'.[141] In the Putilov works the Statute of one commune referred to *'the possibility of partial achievement of communist ideas even in the period when we are surrounded by capitalists'*.[142] Collectives and communes may also have drawn on the experience of the artels in the building, timber and mining industries formed by workers who came from a particular area to negotiate pay and conditions, though the collectives and communes tended to be formed in industries such as metalworking and textiles where the artel tradition was weak.[143] In the winter of 1929–30, the rapid progress of the collectivisation of agriculture also encouraged the formation of production collectives in industry. An official trade union pamphlet spoke of the establishment of 'factory shops of comprehensive collectivisation'; in one factory members of communes were referred to as 'collective farmers', non-members as 'kulaks'.[144] But the analogy should not be pressed too far. Even at the height of the drive for collectivisation, the authorities sought to impose individual payment according to work done on the kolkhozy (see vol. 2, pp. 134–40), while many production collectives in factories practised an equal division of wages.

While the collectives and communes partly appealed to the aspirations of their members to participate in socialist forms of works, they were firmly grounded in their usefulness for the

---

with the same grade often varied considerably (*Sotsialisticheskoe sorevnovanie* (1930), 58–9).

[140] The survey covered only 512 collectives with 5,294 members. The membership was divided as follows: Category (1) 3,213 (60·7 per cent), (2) 942 (17·8), (3) 252 (4·8), (4) 679 (12·8), (5) 45 (0·9), (6) 163 (3·1) (*Sotsialisticheskoe sorevnovanie* (1930), 90).

[141] *Pervyi Vsesoyuznyi s"ezd* (1959), 71.

[142] *Na novom etape* (1930), i, 178, 180.

[143] See SR, xlv (1986), 73–4 (Siegelbaum).

[144] Cited in *Na novom etape* (1930), i, 179; an editorial in B, 3–4, February 28, 1930, 7, 10, claimed that mass collectivisation and dekulakisation were the main factors leading to the establishment of production collectives and communes.

workers concerned in improving their working conditions, and in maintaining or increasing their earnings by improving productivity. A report prepared by the sector of production and wages of the AUCCTU noted that the advantages of collectives and communes included 'self-supervision and mutual assistance in work, self-discipline, a more fully utilised working day, rationalisation and correct organisation of labour processes, . . . better utilisation of machinery, tooling and machine tools'.[145] The pooling of wages by the collective helped to even out fluctuations in earnings due to the irregularity of supply and the arbitrariness of norm setting.[146] The collective payment of wages was also defended on the grounds that it provided incentives for members to help each other which were absent in ordinary shock brigades, so that *'wages turn from a factor restraining the development of the cooperation of labour into a factor assisting it'*.[147] Initial reports on the practical value of the movement were favourable. They concurred that both collectives and communes attracted the best shock workers, and usually achieved more rapid improvements in productivity, labour discipline and earnings. Some collectives even volunteered to accept increased norms of output.[148] There is also some evidence that managers were able to use the enthusiasm of their members to reduce job rates below the normal level.[149]

The Gosplan survey of April–May 1930 also noted some serious difficulties with all categories of production collective, though it insisted that only a minority were affected. Members often resented having to 'work for others', and competent workers even reduced their productivity so as to avoid putting money into the pockets of the less successful members. The presence of inexperienced or slow members in the collective was resented by the more capable. According to the survey, failure to choose members carefully 'resulted in many unsuccessful experiences and in the collapse of many collectives', while collectives were successful when their members had previously

[145] *Sotsialisticheskoe sorevnovanie* (1965), 58 (cited from the archives).

[146] See SR, xlv (1986), 74–5.

[147] B, 17, September 15, 1930, 59 (A. P. Pavlov).

[148] ZI, March 3, 1930 (conference called by the Red Directors' journal *Predpriyatie*); March 12, 1930 (Shvernik at conference of March 11 called by the party central committee and the AUCCTU); VTr, 4, 1930, 22–4; *Na novom etape* (1930), i, 182–3.

[149] See Filtzer (1986), 105–6, citing *Na novom etape* (1930), i, 183, 188–9.

worked together.[150] All these problems recurred when production collectives were revived fifty years later.[151]

The party and economic authorities responded to the production collectives and communes with an uncertain voice. At the shock-workers' congress, Veinberg praised shock collectives and communes indiscriminately as deserving all possible help, but Kuibyshev, while endorsing communes of workers of more or less equal skills, warned that equal division of wages might discourage workers from improving their qualifications.[152] The resolution of the organisation section of the congress, while acknowledging that communes should be assisted in every way, called for a study of their experience, and meanwhile cautiously confined its endorsement of communes to cases where a conveyer system existed or where skills were the same. The resolution condemned the 'artificial imposition' of communes; and, where skills varied, called for the distribution of earnings according to skill.[153] But at this stage no firm line was taken by the central authorities on any aspect of the movement. In February 1930, it received its highest party accolade. An editorial in the party journal *Bol'shevik* hailed the improvements in labour organisation and utilisation of capital equipment which had been achieved, and called upon party and trade union organisations to devote 'increased attention to all these new forms of the development of independent activity, of the manifestation of the revolutionary energy and class consciousness of the worker'. It particularly praised communes in which wages were divided equally.[154] Reports from individual factories published in the industrial newspaper as late as March 11 claimed good results from the equal division of earnings.[155]

---

[150] *Sotsialisticheskoe sorevnovanie* (1930), 71–4.

[151] See the informative report in EKO, 8, 1985, 151–99 (Maksimova).

[152] *Pervyi Vsesoyuznyi s"ezd* (1959), 71, 159–60.

[153] *Ibid.* 152.

[154] B, 3–4, February 28, 1930, 4–7. A further paragraph praised workers in the Kolomna factory, in which the commune movement was particularly strong, for declaring 'the Kolomna factory and all Kolomna godless', and described the widespread mass movement from below to close churches as 'unique in history'. This paragraph was later stated to have been printed by mistake, and the bulk of it was withdrawn, but no criticism appeared of the rest of the editorial (B, 5, March 15, 1930, 128; P, March 19, 1930).

[155] ZI, March 11, 1930 (reports from factories in Moscow, Kharkov and Kiev).

From March 1930, however, the central authorities took a harsher attitude to communes which distributed wages equally. At a conference on production communes summoned by the party central committee and the AUCCTU, both Shvernik and Veinberg asserted that equalisation of pay had 'negative results'.[156] During the next few months numerous accounts appeared in the press of cases where as a result of equal pay skilled workers had refused to join communes, or communes had rapidly dispersed, or skill and productivity had declined.[157] Equalisation of wages was criticised by the Gosplan survey of socialist emulation carried out in April–May 1930. The survey claimed that 'attempts to create collectives with a strict egalitarian principle of wage distribution, irrespective of the variation in the skill of the participants, must be recognised to be inexpedient at the given stage of development of the productive forces, as they result in reduced incentives to more intensive work by skilled workers and simultaneously weaken the interest of the low-skilled in improving their skills'.[158] The survey found, not surprisingly, that in 'equalising communes' skilled workers' earnings tended to decline while unskilled workers' earnings increased.[159] But its reports from particular communes revealed that 'in three-quarters of collectives of Categories (1) and (2) a good atmosphere of unity predominates'; progressive skilled workers accepted the equalisation of wages with equanimity when it was in the interests of production.[160] Thus its negative conclusions about egalitarian communes were tailored to the prevailing view of the authorities rather than being drawn from the evidence. In the same spirit a report in the Narkomtrud journal, assserting that 'the principle of equalisation of wages often acts as a brake on the involvement of skilled workers', condemned support for equality as 'a manifestation of tail-endist petty-bourgeois attitudes'. A further article by the author of this study was firmly headed 'For the

---

[156] ZI, March 12, 14, 1930.

[157] See for example ZI, April 9, June 11, 1930; see also *Istoriya industrializatsii* (Gor'kii, 1968), 111–12.

[158] *Sotsialisticheskoe sorevnovanie* (1930), 87 (Pollyak, Batsofen, Semenina); the evidence is displayed on pp. 69–75.

[159] *Sotsialisticheskoe sorevnovanie* (1930), 95; see also SR, 45 (1986), 76 (Siegel-baum).

[160] *Sotsialisticheskoe sorevnovanie* (1930), 73.

Shock Collectives, Against Equalisation'.[161] Another account claimed that egalitarian communes resulted from the 'striving for equality' of young workers just starting work, who wanted to be equal with the highly skilled; this was equivalent to jumping over the agricultural artel to the commune.[162] The rapid expansion of collectives and communes in the first few weeks of 1930 was partly attributed to administrative pressure, which was condemned in industry as it had been in agriculture.[163]

The campaign against egalitarian communes was consolidated at the XVI party congress in June 1930. Kaganovich strongly condemned 'equalising tendencies' in communes and attempts to force factory directors into joining them.[164] But production collectives continued to be regarded with favour. At the congress Shvernik, while criticising 'equalising tendencies', strongly praised both collectives of workers of the same grade, and collectives with earnings in common which were distributed according to grade.[165]

The cause of the egalitarian commune was, however, not yet finally lost. In September an article in the party journal still argued that it would be a 'great mistake' to prevent the formation of communes as well as collectives on a voluntary basis.[166]

(iv) Output norms and wages

Together with their strong appeal to political enthusiasm, the socialist emulation campaigns carried with them powerful material incentives. In August 1929 60·3 per cent of workers in industry were paid on a piece-work basis.[167] Shock workers on piece work automatically earned more for producing more, and the joint incomes of production collectives on piece work were directly related to output, however their income was distributed among the members. Legislation in the autumn of 1929 provided

---

[161] VTr, 4, 1930, 25–6, 29, ZI, April 9, 1930; the author was Zaromskii, who was editor of *Voprosy truda*.
[162] ZI, June 11, 1930 (I. Kondrat'ev (Kiev)).
[163] ZI, March 14, June 11, 1930.
[164] *XVI s"ezd* (1931), 62.
[165] *XVI s"ezd* (1931), 652.
[166] B, 17, September 15, 1930, 59–62 (Pavlov); see also PI, 20, 1930 (Deich).
[167] *Trud* (1932), 49.

for the establishment at enterprise, trust and *glavk* of Funds to Assist Socialist Emulation formed from savings due to emulation. These provided both monetary rewards and improved cultural facilities for shops, shifts, brigades and individual workers successful in the various competitions.[168] In November 1929 Vesenkha announced the award of foreign business visits, places in rest homes, technical books and sets of tools to victors in the competition for the Best Site of 1928.[169] In 1930 the best shock workers were sent on a free European cruise.[170]

A powerful incentive to increased productivity was also provided, in a negative form, by increases in output norms (work norms). An increase in the output norm involved a cut in the 'rate for the job', so that the worker had to produce more in order to receive the same wage. Norms were supposed to be technically based on the capabilities of the worker and the equipment, and to increase in response to improvements in the conditions of production. But in practice substantial norm increases were obtained during annual norm-revision campaigns associated with the signing of collective agreements between management and trade unions, a major feature of the wage system since 1927.[171] A general revision of norms was again undertaken in the winter of 1929–30. In the control figures for 1929/30, the gap between productivity and wages was particularly large: output per worker was planned to rise by 25 per cent, and the average wage by only 9 per cent.[172] The control figures insisted that in order to achieve this result 'in 1929/30 the reexamination of output norms must take place immediately after new machinery is introduced or organisation is improved'.[173] In practice this meant that the rates for the job were to be cut both at the beginning of the year and when production conditions improved, whereas previously norms were not changed in the course of the year.

The annual norm-revision campaign got off to a slow start;

---

[168] SZ, 1929, art. 541 (decree of September 11, 1929); SP VSNKh, 1929/30, art. 267 (order of November 25, 1929).

[169] SP VSNKh, 1929/30, art. 302 (order of November 30, 1929).

[170] Rogachevskaya (1977), 125.

[171] See Carr and Davies (1969), especially pp. 504–7, and the informative article by Siegelbaum in SS, xxxvi (1984), 44–68.

[172] *KTs . . . na 1929/30* (1930), 211.

[173] *Ibid.* 239.

Vesenkha acknowledged that in the first three months of 1929/30 little was achieved.[174] Even as late as March 1930 the iron and steel trust Uralmet had not yet completed its norm revision.[175] In the Donbass coal industry, plans to revise 55 per cent of all the norms in the first six months of 1929/30 'remained on paper'.[176] In Leningrad, in the electrical industry corporation VEO, no substantial reexamination of norms occurred.[177] These shortcomings were partly due to the preoccupation of management at the Vesenkha level with the major industrial reorganisation which took place in the winter of 1929–30; the industrial newspaper complained that at the beginning of 1930 the new corporations even transferred some norm setters (rate fixers) to other work.[178] But the main cause of the delay was the resistance by workers and their représentatives to substantial increases in norms. In the engineering industry the Moscow trust Mosmashtrest was able to reach broad agreements about wages and norms with the metalworkers' union and its regional committee, from which the old leadership had been removed following the defeat of Tomsky and his supporters in the trade union. But negotiations between the factory managements and the factory committees were very protracted. The industrial newspaper complained that the committees had 'not yet turned their faces fully to production', and responded to pressure for higher guaranteed wages from the workers:

> Only after pressure on the factory committees from the regional committee of the trade unions and the party organs, the factory committees began to sign agreements on a timetable for reexamining output norms and rates for the job at the beginning of February.[179]

Eventually, agreement was reached at all factories except one, following a regional conference of management and trade unions attended by factory representatives.[180]

[174] ZI, July 18, 1930 (Vesenkha report to STO); *TsIK 2/V*, No. 8, 22 (Tochinskii).
[175] SP VSNKh, 1929/30, art. 1005 (order of March 13).
[176] ZI, February 27, 1930.
[177] ZI, March 28, 1930.
[178] ZI, March 15, 1930.
[179] ZI, February 14, 1930.
[180] ZI, February 16, 1930.

Following these broad agreements in every industry and factory, strenuous negotiations took place to fit the millions of specific output norms into this framework. In the spring of 1930, the Council of Technical Norms called for norms to be based on the performance of instructors and shock workers;[181] and the agreement between Mosmashtrest and the metalworkers' union stipulated that revised norms should be '*based not on the average but on the best worker*, and that the norms should be the maximum technically possible'.[182] But in practice in the vast majority of factories norms continued to be fixed by rule of thumb. Trained rate fixers were scarce; and managers were anxious to avoid fixing high norms which would cause skilled workers to move elsewhere. Following stringent rate-fixing in one Moscow factory, shock brigades dissolved, and workers quit their jobs or deliberately reduced their output.[183] In a factory near Yaroslavl' party members refused to attend meetings on the grounds that workers were dissatisfied with the new norms.[184] In another Moscow factory, 57 workers, including 17 young party members and candidates, signed a collective protest when the management suddenly cut the rates because wages were rising more than productivity.[185]

In spite of the deficiencies in the norm campaign, the relation between wages and productivity achieved in the first eight months of 1929/30 was reasonably satisfactory. While the planned gap was not achieved, monthly output per worker increased by 16·3 per cent, and the average wage by only 7·9 per cent. The statistical journal commented that 'for the first time in any year the planned wage ceilings still have unused reserves'. But this achievement was due not only to the norm campaign but also to the fact that many unskilled workers were taken on at low grades in the wage scale.[186]

---

[181] See SS, xxxvi (1984), 54 (Siegelbaum).
[182] ZI, February 14, 1930.
[183] ZI, March 15, 1930 (Elektrolampa factory).
[184] *Severnyi rabochii*, March 26, 1930.
[185] P, June 22, 1930 (Burevestnik factory); *Pravda* denounced this as a 'Trotskyist declaration', and claimed that a Trotskyist–Menshevik group was behind it.
[186] SO, 6, 1930, 7–8; PKh, 5, 1930, 213–14 (Mendel'son). The delay in wage and norm agreements paradoxically also cut down the average wage by delaying the payment of general increases in wages due in certain grades and industries (the so-called 'automatic addition (mekhanicheskaya pribavka)')

While the authorities attached great importance to the norm revisions, which in effect cut piece rates, they continued to regard the piece-work system itself with the caution and ambiguity characteristic of the previous three years.[187] Under the collective agreements of 1929/30, all 'normal' work previously paid on a time basis was supposed to be transferred to piece rates but nothing was done to put this into effect.[188] The influential Communist statistician M. N. Smit (Mary Fal'kner-Smith) boldly supported the reduction of piece work, arguing that it had 'ceased to play the role of an incentive to the intensification of labour'[189] In the iron and steel industry, highly skilled workers, and 2,000 workers in blast-furnace shops, were experimentally transferred to time payment, and the advocates of the experiment claimed that this resulted in a fall in wage payments per ton of output for the first time in three years.[190] At the XVI party congress, the party leaders in their various reports were sternly silent about the relative merits of time work and piece work, and the written report of Narkomtrud to the congress also ignored the whole question. In this policy vacuum, the role of piece work in industry declined for the first time for many years: the number of working hours paid by piece rates declined from a peak of 60·3 per cent in August 1929 to 58·1 per cent in February and 55·5 per cent in August 1930.[191]

The campaign against piece work, while it undoubtedly derived strength from the long-standing antipathy of Soviet trade unions and workers to a system typifying capitalist exploitation, found its justification mainly in the changing technology of Soviet industry.[192] In the United States, with the development of the conveyor system, the Ford company paid time rates; and in 1930 both the Stalingrad tractor factory and

---

(ZI, July 18, 1930 – Vesenkha report to STO), though in some cases the continuance of the old norms led wages to increase more than productivity (e.g. in Mosmashtrest (ZI, February 14, 1930) and in Uralmet (SP VSNKh, 1929/30, art. 1005, order dated March 13)).

[187] See Carr and Davies (1969), 534–7.
[188] VTr, 3, 1930, 33.
[189] PE, 3, 1930, 13.
[190] VTr, 2, 1931, 15–23.
[191] *Trud* (1932), 49.
[192] See PE, 3, 1930, 13 (Smit); Burdyanskii (1930), 200.

the Moscow automobile factory AMO made wide use of time payments.[193] In both the chemical and the iron and steel industry, the move to time work was justified on the grounds that productivity did not depend on the worker but on the equipment.[194]

Supporters of greater equality increasingly sought technological and economic rather than social arguments for their views on other delicate aspects of wage policy. The efforts to narrow differentiation in earnings according to skill, which continued during 1929/30, were defended on the grounds that this corresponded to the technological changes which were bringing about a decline in the proportion of skilled 'universalist' workers, and an increase in the proportion of workers with a narrow specialisation or an average skill, requiring less time to train.[195] There is little doubt, however, that here, as in the case of time work, belief in socialist equality was an important motive in the campaign. On the other hand, economic priorities clearly motivated the authorities in their efforts to pull up the average wage in the lagging coal and metal industries, though even here the attempt to add the textile industry to the list was clearly unjustified in terms of the economic priorities of the regime.[196] But perhaps the most outstanding feature of wage policy – or the lack of it – in 1929/30 was that the Politburo evidently regarded it as secondary to socialist emulation in the struggle to raise productivity.

(v) Workers' participation

In the last months of 1929 two major resolutions on industrial administration found a place both for greater worker participation and for tighter controls from above. The first was

[193] See VTr, 6, 1930, 23 (Vladimirov); PE, 6, 1931, 22 (Yampol'skii). On this see Shiokawa (May 1986), 8.

[194] *Formirovanie* (1964), 224 (Lel'chuk); VTr, 2, 1931, 20 (Mokhson); *Predpriyatie*, 3–4, 1931, 18–19 (Gliksman). In the chemical industry, the percentage of hours paid on piece rates declined from 62·1 in August 1928 to 45·7 in August 1930, and in iron and steel from 67·2 to 62·8 per cent (*Trud* (1932), 49).

[195] VTr, 6, 1930, 48 (El'yashevich).

[196] Compare the reference in the 1929/30 control figures to 'the reinforced growth of wages in the coal and metal industries' (*KTs . . . na 1929/30* (1930), 236) with the list in VTr, 3, 1930, 33 (Vasil'ev), describing the collective agreements for 1929/30, which also includes textiles, chemicals and cement.

the famous resolution of September 5, 1929, 'On Measures to Regularise the Administration of Production and Establish One-Man Management'.[197] Its main thrust was to secure 'firm order and strong internal discipline' by establishing – or rather reestablishing – 'management by a single person', the factory director; it insisted that the party and trade union organisations at the factory must not interfere in the 'operational–production work of the management'. At the same time the resolution provided for increased participation of the trade unions and the production conferences in the preparation of plans and in transmitting the views and proposals of the masses to the management (see p. 275 below). The second major resolution, on industrial reorganisation, adopted three months later on December 5, 1929 (see pp. 241–2 above), sought to strengthen the position of the enterprise by increasing the role of khozraschet. The Politburo, while prudently insisting on 'concentrating a small number of really highly competent officials in the higher administrative agencies',[198] added to the draft prepared by Vesenkha and Rabkrin 'a directive on the necessity for the broad participation of the working masses and trade union organisations in the management of production'.[199] In this spirit, the resolution of December 5 called for 'active participation of workers in the resolution of all major questions concerning the leadership of the enterprise and the appropriate branches of industry, in the preparation and elaboration of production plans and targets, and also in the supervision of their fulfilment'.[200]

The resolution on one-man management met with some resentment from workers who regarded it as an attempt to subject them to firmer control. In a major iron and steel works, 118 meetings (*sic*) did not succeed in persuading the work-force that one-man management was desirable; in the tube-casting shop many workers opposed one-man management and objected to the adoption of a specific plan for each piece of machinery.[201] In the Central Volga, the regional party committee reported

[197] *Direktivy*, ii (1957), 120–6.
[198] *Leninskii plan* (1969), 167.
[199] *Industrializatsiya, 1929–1932* (1970), 587.
[200] *Direktivy*, ii (1957), 133.
[201] ZI, February 7, 1930 (Tomsky works, Makeevka).

'very widespread lack of understanding' of one-man management by 'many party members, and even more non-party people'.[202]

Within the framework of the drive for tighter work discipline with which the resolution on one-man management was associated, numerous attempts were made to involve workers directly in state and industrial administration. During the purge of People's Commissariats and other state agencies, workers' brigades assumed some of their administrative functions, and workers were promoted to administrative positions in place of the dismissed specialists. In Vesenkha, one hundred workers were promoted to administrative posts on the central staff during the early stages of the purge.[203] After these initial promotions, the shock-brigade congress in December 1929 resolved that 5,000 shock workers should be retrained for promotion;[204] orders by Vesenkha which followed the congress provided that 500 of the promoted workers should be employed on administrative and managerial work in trusts, the rest in factories.[205]

The whole question of the role of the workers in industrial administration was temporarily open to debate. Lenin's Utopian vision of a society in which every cook would learn to govern the state momentarily seemed to be a practical possiblity. One senior Vesenkha official proposed in the industrial newspaper that workers should occupy administrative posts in factories jointly with specialists, each working $3\frac{1}{2}$ or 4 hours a day.[206] Another senior official proposed that factory and agricultural workers should temporarily occupy a proportion of the permanent senior administrative posts in Vesenkha, each being employed for a period of three–six months.[207] The published comments on these proposals were generally sympathetic; and the editors of the newspaper commended their *'timeliness'*, remarking that 'public opinion has long and stubbornly sought

---

[202] *Istoriya industrializatsii Srednego Povolzh'ya* (Kuibyshev, 1974), 146.

[203] TPG, December 19, 1929; by December 1, 1929, only 315 of the 2,317 staff members of Vesenkha were ex-workers, including 103 recently promoted.

[204] *Pervyi Vsesoyuznyi s"ezd* (1959), 155; this is the resolution of the organisation section of the congress, printed from the archives.

[205] SP VSNKh, 1929/30, art. 606 (dated January 14); art. 700 (dated January 27).

[206] ZI, January 12, 1930 (Dubner).

[207] ZI, February 2, 1930 (M. G. Gurevich).

to find forms of administration which would lead most reliably to the elimination of bureaucratism as a result of the proletarianisation of administration (orabochenie apparata)'.[208]

These developments and proposals were intertwined with a reconsideration of the role in economic management of the trade unions, now purged of their former leadership. The central committee resolution of September 5, 1929 (see pp. 272–3 above) envisaged a more active role for the factory committees in discussion and preparation of economic plans. The plenum of the AUCCTU, which met in November 1929, instructed the trade unions, while continuing to defend the interests of their members, to turn their 'face to production'; this would involve them in discussion and supervision of plans at every level of the economic hierarchy. The plenum also proposed that candidates for all administrative posts at all levels from the factory to the commissariat should be discussed by the appropriate trade union organisation, and 'in especially important cases, at trade union congresses'; in the trade union hierarchy itself a proportion of the occupants of elected posts should be transferred to production or to more junior administrative posts and replaced by promoted workers.[209] A Vesenkha circular at this time pointed out somewhat prematurely that the 'trade unions are on the point of participating in the examination of all major questions of economic life'.[210]

In this atmosphere favourable to workers' participation, significant changes occurred in factory practice. In the first few months of 1930, work-team leaders (brigadiry) were frequently elected by their workers, instead of being appointed by the factory director.[211] The most substantial development was the proposal to appointed chairmen of production conferences as full-time assistant directors of their factory, so as to facilitate the practical implementation of the decisions of the conferences and of workers' suggestions. This was approved as an experiment by the party central committee in its resolution of September 5, 1929 (see pp. 272–3 above). On September 30, the Leningrad party regional committee proposed to introduce these arrangements in twelve of its most important factories; and in the following

---

[208] ZI, February 7, 1930.
[209] VTr, 1, 1930, 9–13.
[210] SP VSNKh, 1929/30, circular no. 18/11 (dated December 11, 1929).
[211] See Kuromiya (forthcoming), ch. 7.

months many other factories were included in the experiment by Vesenkha.[212] At the XVI party congress in June 1930, Kaganovich declared that 'this was done as an experiment, and the experiment fully justified itself',[213] and the congress resolved that the practice should be extended.[214] Following the congress, a 'Statute on the Rights and Obligations of Assistant Directors/Production Conference Organisers' entitled them to a full-time staff, and provided for the appointment of the organisers of production conferences of factory shops as assistants to the head of the shop, in the case of shops employing at least 500 workers per shift.[215]

But all these attempts to strengthen 'proletarian democracy' by involving rank-and-file workers in administration proved unsuccessful. The resolution of December 5, 1929, was followed by considerable administrative confusion in industry (see pp. 242–3 above). From the outset managements frequently treated the experiments with almost complete indifference. In all the commissariats the administrative staff sought, with some success, to limit the impact of the purge and the accompanying workers' brigades on their normal activities. At a mass purge meeting of the financial department of Vesenkha, only 117 of the 700 staff turned up, and members of the Vesenkha presidium allocated to the purge commission failed to attend its meetings.[216] It even proved difficult to persuade Vesenkha staff to work after 5 p.m. so that the AMO workers could observe how Vesenkha functioned.[217] The purge had the backing of Rabkrin and the OGPU; and was eventually forced upon the attention of the commissariat. But the activities of the workers' brigades soon diminished, or were absorbed into normal administration. The trade unions were in a worse position. They lacked any powerful support, and the central committee decisions to increase their role in planning had no substantial consequences. Reports by AUCCTU, endeavouring to display the importance of trade

[212] *Industrializatsiya Severo-Zapadnogo Raiona* (Leningrad, 1967), 58–9; SP VSNKh, 1929/30, arts. 245 (dated November 19, 1929), 706 (dated January 28, 1930).

[213] *XVI s"ezd* (1931), 62; see also p. 654 (Shvernik).

[214] *KPSS v rez.*, iii (1954), 66.

[215] SP VSNKh, 1929/30, art. 1828 (dated August 15, 1930).

[216] ZI, February 20, 1930.

[217] ZI, February 7, 1930.

union influence on planning and in production administration, in fact reveal its triviality.[218] Representatives of the trusts demonstrated their scepticism about the role of trade unions in planning by failing to attend sessions of the trade union central committee for their industry.[219] A Vesenkha order which instructed factories in the defence industry to increase participation of workers in production planning was concealed at some factories and ignored at others.[220] At a conference of assistant factory directors/production conference organisers called by the AUCCTU it was reported that the workers thought of the assistant director as 'our chap' or 'the trade-union director', but the assistant directors themselves normally did not feel stable in their posts, and the managerial staff of the factory were reluctant to carry out their instructions.[221] In the 2,500 orders issued by Vesenkha between October 1929 and December 1930 only a few trivial references appear to all the various forms of worker participation in planning and administration.

The reemergence in 1930 of the worker as something like an associate manager of the Soviet economy thus proved temporary and fragile. Within a few years these experiments were almost forgotten, dismissed as infantile Leftism within the USSR and regarded by outside observers as a smokescreen, designed to distract workers from the increasing exploitation and loss of effective power which was their fate in the early 1930s. But the tradition of worker participation and worker management died hard. In 1935–6 it reappeared temporarily at the time of the Stakhanov movement. In the 1980s it has reemerged far more forcefully as a major theme of the party leadership in its efforts to revive and speed on the Soviet economy.[222] In the 1930s, the

---

[218] *Industrializatsiya, 1929–1932* (1970), 514–16, 522–7 (resolution of April 28, 1930, and survey of October 1930, printed from the archives).

[219] See, for example, SP VSNKh, 1929/30, circular no. 18/11 (dated December 11, 1929), referring to the building industry.

[220] SP VSNKh, 1929/30, art. 454 (order dated December 23, 1929, referring to an earlier order).

[221] ZI, March 8, 1930.

[222] At the XXVII party congress, Mr. Gorbachev, stressing the need to extend '*direct democracy*' and the role of the labour collective, argued that all leaders of brigades (work-teams), should be elected, and that the elective principle should be extended 'gradually to certain other categories of leading officials in enterprises – foremen, heads of shifts, sections and shops'; he

most permanent consequence of the central place occupied by the worker in party doctrine was the promotion of large numbers of workers to administrative posts or their transfer to higher education. The promoted workers wholeheartedly shared the values and supported the policies of the party leadership in its Stalinist variant, and by the end of the 1930s the most successful of them had advanced to key posts in the ruling élite.

(vi) Control over labour

Following the resolution on one-man management, serious attempts were made to strengthen the power of managers over workers. The degree of March 6, 1929, already strengthened the right of managers to dismiss violators of labour discipline;[223] and in 1930 managers acquired the power to allocate workers to wage scales without consulting the Rates and Conflicts Commission.[224] Their powers were also undoubtedly strengthened by the extensive purge of 'Right wingers' from the trade unions.[225] In 1929/30, the number of workers dismissed for violation of labour discipline substantially increased (see Table 19).

But these increased managerial powers were effectively countered by the great expansion of job opportunities in the summer of 1929 and the first six months of 1929/30. This led to the virtual elimination of unemployment among many grades of skilled workers and a reduction in the total number of unemployed registered at labour exchanges from 1,741,000 on April 1, 1929, to 1,081,000 on April 1, 1930.[226] With the

---

justified this proposal by reference to 'experience over many years' (P, February 26, 1986); it has since been experimentally extended to factory directors.

[223] See Carr and Davies (1969), 517.

[224] See Kuromiya (forthcoming), ch. 3.

[225] By April 1, 1930, 59·5 per cent of the membership of the AUCCTU had been removed; the equivalent figures for the trade union central committees and the factory committees were 67·5 and 68·1 per cent (Kul'chitskii (Kiev, 1979), 74, citing a report to the XVI party congress).

[226] See Table 18. Job vacancies per 100 persons registered as seeking work increased from 142·1 in 1928/29 to 181·4 in the first five months of 1929/30 (*Trud* (1930), 36). This Narkomtrud report claimed that the unemployment figure for April 1, 1930, owing to the inclusion of unemployed in transit to other jobs and fictitious registrations, was 'many times as high as the real reserve of labour available to the economy' (*ibid.* pp. xix–xx). For the

prospect of easily finding other employment, workers became less tolerant of managerial pressure and less willing to accept poor housing conditions or deteriorating food supplies. Paradoxically, the increase in labour productivity in 1929/30 was accompanied by deteriorating labour discipline and greater instability in labour relations. In 1930, the average number of days of absence per worker without due cause in the main branches of large-scale industry increased from 4·09 to 4·49 days per year, while the average number of days actually worked fell from 264·2 to 252·3, after a continuous improvement in both respects between 1926 and 1929.[227] The increased dismissals for violation of labour discipline were partly due to deliberate violation of instructions by workers seeking to move elsewhere.[228] Many reports complained that managers frequently failed to dismiss undisciplined workers because of the difficulty of replacing them.[229]

The most striking indicator of increasing instability in labour relations was the sharp increase in labour turnover (see Table 19).[230] The increase was entirely due to what was known as 'pure turnover' or 'turnover from subjective causes', which was deemed to have occurred when workers left at their own request or were dismissed for indiscipline.[231] According to many accounts, turnover was particularly associated with the recruitment of new workers as a consequence of the expansion

---

complexities of Soviet unemployment statistics, see Lane, ed. (1986), 36–49 (Davies and Wheatcroft).

[227] *Sots.str.* (1935), 503; for earlier figures see Carr and Davies (1969), 510.

[228] See Filtzer (1986), 55.

[229] VTr, 6, 1930, 26 (Mordukhovich); the author claimed that the failure to dismiss undisciplined workers exercised 'a disruptive influence on their fellow-workers'.

[230] The measurement of turnover was a complex task, and ten different indicators existed in 1930. The usual indicator is misleadingly large because it includes all temporary workers; on the other hand it does not include transfers of workers within an enterprise. All indicators showed a sharp upward trend. (See ZI, February 16, 1930, Mordukhovich (1931), 63, and *Annals* (Tokyo), xxiii (1982), 65 (Shiokawa)).

[231] Returns for Moscow region show a much lower level of turnover from these two causes than in Table 19 below, but even in the Moscow returns the rate of turnover doubled during 1929/30 (VTr, 2, 1931, 75). For 'pure' turnover' and 'turnover from subjective causes', see VTr, 1, 1931, 90, and Mordukhovich (1931), 39.

of industry, and was higher among unskilled, young and new workers, and lower among skilled workers.[232] But skilled and long-established workers in industries or factories where conditions were poor or pay was low also sought to move to other industries, or to better jobs in their own industry. Skilled textile workers moved to unskilled or semi-skilled jobs in the engineering industry, where the pay was higher.[233] Turnover was high among skilled workers in the coal industry, where living conditions were poor and deteriorating.[234] Major construction sites offered high pay to skilled workers to attract them from established enterprises.[235]

Labour turnover conformed with the plans of the authorities insofar as it resulted in the movement of experienced workers from industries with low priority, such as cotton textiles, to high-priority key enterprises in Group A industries and to major construction sites. But the price of the adjustment was high in terms of the deskilling of the low-priority industries and the disorder consequent upon the instability of the labour force throughout industry.

No clear policy for dealing with labour turnover emerged. As early as May 1928, the party central control commission requested Vesenkha, AUCCTU and Narkomtrud to study the causes of turnover, but without result.[236] Narkomtrud on the whole took a relaxed or even complacent attitude to labour turnover, eschewing undue alarm about its increase, attributing it to deep-seated causes, and proposing to deal with it by long-term solutions. A report to the collegium of Narkomtrud on May 30, 1930, by the prominent labour specialist Gindin rejected the view that labour turnover was harmful and abnormal, and criticised proposals to hinder it by preventing

---

[232] See for example VTr, 6, 1930, 76–82 (a study of two Ural iron works); ZI, March 7, 1930 (Tolokontsev, referring to the Leningrad metalworking industry); *Metall*, 10–12, 1930, 15–29 (Ya. Ossovskii; a study of seven Moscow factories showing that in May 1930 turnover was over 9 per cent in the lowest two grades, and only 1·9 and 1·3 per cent in Grades 7 and 8).

[233] VTr, 6, 1930, 23; ZI, June 21, 1930.

[234] See *Annals* (Tokyo), xxiii (1982), 82 (Shiokawa).

[235] See for example the data on loss of skilled labour from Krasnoe Sormovo engineering factory (Nizhnii Novgorod), ZI, June 15, 1930 (Belyi); turnover among skilled workers is further discussed in *Annals* (Tokyo), xxiii (1982), 71–2, 77–8 (Shiokawa).

[236] ZI, February 16, 1930.

voluntary leavers from re-registering at employment exchanges and depriving them of benefits. In the discussion Uglanov also condemned the use of 'fire-fighting measures' to deal with a 'long-term phenomenon'. The resolution of the collegium attributed increased turnover to labour shortages, pay anomalies, inadequate arrangements for promotion and training, and the pull of the larger towns, and proposed that it should be reduced by improvements in training and housing, better incentives to remain on one job for a long period, and the introduction of long-term contracts between factories and workers.[237]

Ultimately such material incentives became an important instrument, together with compulsion and exhortation, for influencing the movement of labour, and were a necessary consequence of the continued right of most Soviet citizens to change their jobs. But in 1929/30 the cautious approach of Narkomtrud seemed anachronistic, and ambitious legislation sought to plan the allocation of labour on a national scale. From September 1929 students in higher and secondary technical education were subject to compulsory placement for the first three years after completing their course.[238] In 1929/30 these new provisions were largely ineffective.[239] This was also the fate of a far-reaching Sovnarkom decree of November 10, 1929, impressively entitled 'On the Planned Provision of Labour to State Industry and Transport in 1929/30'. This called upon Narkomtrud, together with Vesenkha and Narkomput', to elaborate a plan for the supply of labour, broken down into separate quarters of the year, regions, industries and skills.[240] The decree indicated some scepticism about its own effectiveness, however, by providing that an 'increased level of labour turnover' should 'in appropriate cases' be incorporated in the plan. Vesenkha found it very difficult to persuade its trusts and enterprises even to return the forms indicating their anticipated labour surpluses and shortages.[241] Attempts by the central authorities to control the supply of seasonal labour from the

[237] PE, 4–5, 1931, 48–9; VTr, 6, 1930, 27–8.
[238] Sovnarkom decree of May 18, 1929 (SZ, 1929, art. 298); this regulation continues in force at the present day.
[239] See *Industrializatsiya, 1929–1932* (1970), 362–4, 571.
[240] SZ, 1929, art. 676.
[241] SP VSNKh, 1929/30, arts. 333 (order of December 5, 1929), 617 (order of January 15, 1930), 831 (order of February 13, 1930).

countryside were equally ineffective in 1929/30 (see vol. 2, pp. 162–7). Councils to coordinate and control the planning of labour were established in the course of the first few months of 1930, but like the other measures had little practical outcome.[242]

All this legislation served to underline the contrast between the desire of the authorities to control the distribution of labour and the prevailing freedom of workers of all grades to change their jobs without hindrance, which was enhanced by the shortage of labour. Some initial steps were taken in this period to tighten up control over the movement of industrial workers. In February 1930, a long decree of Sovnarkom extended the power of labour exchanges to remove unemployed persons from their register and deprive them of benefit if they refused to accept jobs offered to them.[243] Vesenkha attempted what might be described as 'allocation by exhortation', calling with some success for specified numbers of volunteers to man the Stalingrad tractor factory, the Rostov agricultural engineering works Rostsel'mash, and the Ural engineering works.[244]

With the crisis in labour supply unsolved, more drastic measures began to be contemplated. The introduction of compulsory obligation to work was advocated by 'some circles of labour officials',[245] but such proposals were strongly resisted by the trade union newspaper.[246] A factory in the Urals proposed to recruit prisoners on the grounds that they 'would not run away'.[247] When a delegate to the XVI party congress reported

---

[242] On January 1, 1930, Sovnarkom of the RSFSR announced the establishment of an inter-departmental Council to Control the Movement of Labour attached to Narkomtrud of the RSFSR, with local councils attached to the labour exchanges (the decree is printed in Mordukhovich (1931), 154–7). In April, Sovnarkom of the USSR established an Inter-departmental Council for the Labour Market attached to Narkomtrud of the USSR, also with appropriate local councils (SZ, 1930, art. 295, decree of April 21); this presumably superseded the RSFSR arrangements.

[243] SZ, 1930, art. 147 (dated February 14); further measures adopted in the spring of 1930 are outlined in a Narkomtrud report of May 1930 reprinted from the archives in *Industrializatsiya, 1929–1932* (1970), 365–6.

[244] SP VSNKh, 1929/30, circular 58/37 (dated February 19, 1930), art. 1010 (order of March 14), art. 1095 (order of March 27); workers for the Stalingrad factory were to be selected by special commissions attached to local labour departments.

[245] VTr, 1, 1930, 34.

[246] *Trud*, March 29, 1930, *cit.* Filtzer (1986), 109, 287.

[247] VTr, 6, 1930, 77.

with disapproval that in the timber industry 'many managers
. . . wait to solve export problems by the widespread labour of
prisoners', delegates shouted from the floor 'That's not a bad
thing!'[248] Narkomtrud discussed proposals to recruit demobilised
conscripts to industry through a system of contracts based on a
labour plan.[249]

These developments reflected the anxiety and uncertainty of
officials and managers confronted with labour shortages and an
increasingly mobile labour force. At the XVI party congress
Stalin castigated Narkomtrud and the trade unions for 'great
confusion' in their data about unemployment, and concluded
that 'there is no *reserve* army or *permanent* army of unemployed
for our industry'; but he had little to say about labour turnover
and labour discipline.[250] The resolutions of the congress placed
their main emphasis on socialist emulation and shock work as
means of overcoming difficulties in the factory, and on
'comradely courts composed of the best shock workers' as
means of 'influencing people who violate labour discipline'.[251]
Until the autumn of 1930 the authorities refrained from drastic
coercive measures to impose discipline and limit the freedom of
the worker to choose his job.

(E) INTERNAL TRADE AND RATIONING

(i) Retail trade

In the first eight months of 1929/30, the continued increase in
the non-agricultural population and in their average income
(see pp. 126 above and 305 below) further disrupted
established patterns of retail trade. To meet rising demand, and
to provide additional commodities for export, the state intensified
and extended the official collections of agricultural products
(see vol. 1, pp. 361–71). The Economic Council of the RSFSR
(Ekoso) even demanded that mushrooms and wild berries
should be intensively collected by women and children, while

---

[248] *XVI s"ezd* (1931), 386; no doubt some of those who shouted were among
the many delegates at this congress who were themselves sent to labour camps
a few years later. The role of forced labour will be discussed in vol. 4.

[249] ZI, July 5, 15, 1930.

[250] Stalin, *Soch.* (1949), xii, 292–3.

[251] *KPSS v rez.*, iii (1954), 45, 65–6.

another central agency required the collection of goats' beards for export, and an okrug consumer cooperative instructed its local societies to collect, salt down and store cows' ears.[252] Such attempts at minute control over agricultural production, reminiscent of War Communism, and inspired by a similar desperation among officials confronted by the breakdown of the market, had almost no practical result; the powers and the personnel to enforce them were lacking. But with major food products, including grain, potatoes, meat and fish, the collections covered a much higher proportion of total production than in 1928/29.[253] The extension of the official collections was accompanied by severe restrictions on the private and the peasant trader, the main alternative sources of supply to the non-agricultural population. While restrictions on peasant bazaar trade were partly lifted in March 1930 (see vol. 1, p. 273), the drive against private intermediary trade continued, and in 1929/30 as a whole the amount of food available on private and peasant markets was much lower in absolute terms than in the previous year. According to Soviet data the increase in the official collections substantially exceeded the decline in private and peasant marketings, and so the total amount of food supplied to the non-agricultural population through socialised and private channels increased. But, even according to the official figures, food supplies failed to keep pace with the growth of the non-agricultural population (see pp. 305–7, 355–7 below).

With industrial consumer goods the position was equally unsatisfactory. Group B production in large-scale state industry in the first eight months of 1929/30 was recorded as 20·2 per cent greater than in the same period of the previous year.[254] But this figure considerably exaggerates the availability of industrial

---

[252] SU, 1930, art. 179 (decree of April 5); Syrtsov, *K novomu khozyaistvennomu godu* (1930), 41–2.

[253] For grain and potatoes, see vol. 1, Table 6; the collections took place mainly in the autumn in the first few months after the harvest (see monthly data *ibid.* Table 8 and, for potatoes, *Tekhnicheskie kul'tury* (1936), 58–9 – the latter refers to 1931/32 onwards but the chronological pattern would have been similar in earlier years). Meat collections more than doubled in October 1929– March 1930 as compared with the same period of the previous year, and then declined sharply in April–June 1930 (see vol. 1, Table 10). Fish collections increased in both 1929 and 1930 (*Tovarooborot* (1932), 103).

[254] SO, 6, 1930, 152 (measured in 1926/27 prices).

consumer goods in this period. An unknown but substantial part of artisan production was absorbed by large-scale industry (see pp. 104–9 above), and appears as part of the increased production of large-scale industry. A growing proportion of industrial production was utilised within the state sector in the 'extra-market fund', and was not directly available to the consumer. According to a Gosplan report, in the economic year 1929/30 the total supply of industrial goods to the mass market, including the countryside, increased by only 4–5 per cent.[255] Moreover, production of goods in particularly short supply increased more slowly than Group B production as a whole: in the economic year 1929/30 the production of twelve planned consumer goods increased by only 5 per cent, and their 'market fund' actually declined by 2·9 per cent.[256]

The small increase in supply utterly failed to match the increase in demand. A careful study in the Soviet statistical journal noted that following the 'extremely tense situation' in August–September 1929 the 'disproportion' between demand and supply increased still further in October–December:

> The list of scarce goods has expanded, and now includes confectionery and preserved foods, and tobacco products in certain areas.

[255] PKh, 7–8, 1930, 43 (Guberman); this estimate is apparently in normal socialised retail prices, which did not increase in 1929/30 (*Tovarooborot* (1932), 126–7); the author states that the increase in supply was 9 per cent 'if dual [commercial] prices are taken into account'. These percentages refer to the whole economic year as estimated towards the end of the year; in the first eight months the increase in supply would be somewhat greater, as the performance of the textile industry deteriorated in the summer of 1930 (see pp. 369–70 below).

[256] *Tovarooborot* (1932), 8–9 (in 1926/27 prices). Data for the period October 1929–May 1930 have not been traced. The twelve groups of goods included cotton fabrics, woollen fabrics, threads, knitwear, sewn goods, leather footwear, galoshes, cigarettes, *makhorka*, household soap, toilet soap and kerosene. This classification is in accordance with the planning arrangements in 1932. In 1929/30 the sale of seven scarce groups of consumer goods was planned by Narkomtorg; these included cotton fabrics, woollen fabrics, clothing, leather goods, leather footwear, metals and window glass. A further twelve groups of consumer goods were planned by Tsentrosoyuz: knitwear, oil-cloth, linen fabrics, *platki* (scarves and handkerchiefs), silk, galoshes, basic metal goods, china and earthenware, glassware, matches, household soap and *makhorka*. Between them Narkomtorg-planned and Tsentrosoyuz-planned sales included less than half of the total retail sales of industrial consumer goods. See SO, 6, 1930, 73–9 (Fomin).

With certain goods the position has deteriorated sharply, including metal goods, shoe leather, chinaware, certain knitted goods and sunflower oil.[257]

Industrial consumer goods were in particularly short supply in the towns after the 1929 harvest because Narkomtorg, to encourage the grain collections, greatly increased the proportion of scarce goods distributed to the countryside.[258] In January–March 1930, supplies were abruptly switched back to the towns, and this was said to have resulted in a 'considerable improvement'.[259] But any improvement which may have occurred did not last. With the removal of the ban on bazaar trade in March and April 1930, purchases by the urban population from the peasants sharply increased, and peasant purchasing-power rose. In May 1930, contrary to the normal seasonal trend, stocks in the trade network fell, and the rate of goods turnover increased; this was described by Gosplan as 'a direct reflection of the influence of the growth of consumer demand'. As a result of the shortage of industrial goods in the countryside goods sold by the state at commercial prices were 'completely bought out by the peasants' in some towns; and trade at the peasant market was frequently replaced by barter of agricultural products for textiles, soap and *makhorka*.[260]

---

[257] SO, 6, 1930, 73–4 (Fomin).

[258] 'The flow of goods to the villages is one of the principal causes of scarcity . . . in urban centers', Duranty reported to the US chargé d'affaires, Berlin, on January 29, 1930 (US State Department 861.00/11414). The allocation of seven 'Narkomtorg-planned goods' was as follows (as a percentage of the total):

| | *1928/29* | | | | *1929/30* | |
	Oct.–Dec.	Jan.–Mar.	Apr.–Jun.	Jul.–Sep.	Oct.–Dec.	Jan.–Mar.
Towns	35·7	32·2	53·9	33·0	24·7	74·0
Countryside	64·3	67·8	46·1	67·0	75·3	26·0

(SO, 6, 1930, 75; PKh, 5, 1930, 119; I have corrected minor inaccuracies in the original figures). These figures exclude Central Asia. The proportion of goods planned by the consumer cooperatives which were supplied to the countryside in October–December 1929 also substantially increased (SO, 6, 1930, 79). Even in October–December 1929, supplies per head of population in absolute terms were higher in the towns.

[259] I, April 2, 1930 (Zal'kind).

[260] SO, 6, 1930, 16–7; this is an unsigned Gosplan report.

Retail trade was further disrupted as a result of the huge number of empty spaces left by the closing down of private trade (see p. 101 above). The Narkomtorg journal frankly admitted 'gaps in organisation and instability of supply' resulting from the fact that 'private traders, including small grocers and greengrocers, are precipitately leaving the market, but the cooperatives have not yet mastered their new market'; and castigated the 'incompetence, inexperience, muddle and negligence' of the trading agencies.[261]

Narkomtorg sought to restrain the increased press of customers in socialised trade by extending trading hours, introducing a 'continuous trading week (NTN)' analogous with the 'continuous working week (NRN)' in industry.[262] In September a decree of STO, complaining of 'worsening service for the mass of the population', urged the state and cooperative trading agencies to take over the buildings vacated by private shopkeepers, and to develop mobile sales to replace itinerant private traders.[263] For its part Narkomtorg of the RSFSR urged the socialised sector to sell consumer goods to peasants at the large seasonal fairs which still assembled in a number of towns. 'At many fairs', Narkomtorg complained, 'the socialised sector is completely absent, and this provides a broad scope for private traders to sell secondary goods which are most in demand (haberdashery, toys, confectionery, etc.)'.[264]

In the autumn of 1929, shopping hours were duly extended and a continuous trading week was introduced. But this was inadequate compensation for the collapse of private trade. According to a Soviet report, the buildings relinquished by the private traders were 'suitable only to an extremely small extent'.[265] But in 1929/30 most investment in trade was allocated to what were seen as the more urgent tasks of constructing public catering facilities, food stores and suburban farms, and

[261] VT, 14, November 1929, 19–20 (Ts. Kron). In equally harsh tones, a Rabkrin official, at a conference on the problem of queues, citing a survey carried out on Ordzhonikidze's instructions, claimed that among trade employees 'drunkenness, theft and a coarse attitude to customers are a normal phenomenon' (EZh, October 5, 1929).
[262] ZART, 1929, No. 47, pp. 1–2 (decree of August 8).
[263] SZ, 1929, art. 544 (dated September 11, and signed by Rykov).
[264] ZART, 1929, No. 61, p. 15 (circular dated October 21).
[265] EO, 1, 1930, 89 (Zhitomirskii).

expenditure by the consumer cooperatives on the construction and repair of shops sharply declined.[266] While some new state and cooperative trade outlets were opened in the countryside, in the towns the number of state and cooperative outlets, contrary to all plans, actually declined. With the precipitate reduction of private trade, the total number of trading outlets in the USSR declined by 31·9 per cent in 1929 and a further 9·7 per cent in 1930, and in the towns the decline was as much as 57 per cent over the two years. (See Table 11.) The development of mobile trade by the socialised sector was characterised by a Soviet investigator as 'miserly'.[267] Retail facilities further deteriorated early in 1930 when, at the height of the campaign against peasant markets, seasonal fairs in provincial towns, instead of being infiltrated by the socialised sector, were banned by the authorities.[268] The ban was not removed during the retreat from collectivisation: on March 16, STO announced the abolition of the great fairs at Nizhnii Novgorod and Baku, explaining disingenuously that this was possible owing to the increase in planned trade and in the sale of artisan goods via the cooperatives.[269] Numerous decisions imperatively requiring improvements in the quality of retail trade were adopted by the Soviet authorities in this period. But supplies continued to be scarce and unreliable, and the number of retail outlets remained far too small. Queues and poor service became a chronic feature of Soviet trade.

---

[266] According to one source, capital investment on 'exchange and distribution' increased from 68·1 million rubles in 1928 to 154·2 millions in 1929 and 340·6 millions in 1930 (*Materials* (1985), 414–17); an alternative source gives 85·3, 178·4 and 472·2 (preliminary) (*Nar.kh. plan 1931* (1931), 90). But between 1928/29 and 1929/30 expenditure on the construction and capital repair of shops by the consumer cooperatives declined from 22 to 10 million rubles (*ibid.* 141). All these figures are in current prices; the data for 1929/30 are preliminary.

[267] EO, 1, 1930, 87–8 (Zhitomirskii). This refers to the end of 1929; no improvement took place in 1930.

[268] See for example SU, 1930, art. 168 (decree of March 3), and note 269 below.

[269] SZ, 1930, art. 209. The closing of fairs was evidently a controversial matter behind the scenes: on March 24 a Narkomtorg circular criticised 'the complete elimination of trade at fairs', pointing out that this trade 'at present in a number of places bears the character of large-scale bazaar trade, associated with the seasonal sale of agricultural commodities' (ZRT, 1930, art. 362).

(ii) Rationing

Following the practice of the Civil War, and of European governments during the first world war, the Soviet authorities responded to the crisis of supply by extending and systematising the rationing of scarce commodities to non-agricultural consumers. Rationing was introduced piece-meal in 1928 and 1929, and by the middle of 1929 had spread to a wide range of food products in many towns.[270] From the outset, in each of the towns where rationing was introduced, consumers were divided into categories with different priorities. Industrial workers received higher rations than other employees; dependants of industrial workers and other employees were placed in a lower group, sometimes with preferential treatment for young children.[271] In July 1929, Narkomtorg, noting that 'a considerable range of food products and mass consumption goods' was already rationed, called for 'the continuation of rationing as a measure to limit consumption of these goods by the non-working population and as a means of affording priority to the satisfaction of the needs of industrial workers'. It also ruled that the 'non-working population'–i.e. petty capitalists and the self-employed – must not draw on state supplies, and instead would have to obtain their food on the market or direct from the producer. Where the state exercised a monopoly, the non-working population should be entitled to a ration lower than that received by the working population, and should be required to buy it at higher prices.[272] It could have added that rationing would also isolate retail supplies from the peasantry who otherwise, amply furnished with money earned on the free market, would eagerly seek to buy up food products and consumer goods.

The emergence of a rationing system covering most of the non-agricultural employed population and their families – over thirty million people in 1929/30 – placed an immense burden on the local agencies of Narkomtorg and the consumer cooperatives. They were able to draw on the experience of the elaborate rationing system introduced during the Civil War,

[270] See Carr and Davies (1969), 700–4, and pp. 72, 87–8 above.
[271] See Carr and Davies (1969), 702–3 (referring to Moscow); EZh, October 2, 1929.
[272] ZART, 1929, No. 39, p. 2 (decree of July 4).

and not finally abolished until the end of 1922. This system, with rations differentiated for different categories of the employed population and their families, closely resembled the arrangements introduced in 1928–30.[273] But in 1928–30, as in the Civil War, rationing was introduced piece-meal, without preparation in advance. In July 1929 Narkomtorg admitted in a circular that it possessed 'no serious material' on trading techniques, on the management of demand, or on the 'struggle with queues'.[274] At the same time, evidently concerned about the administrative complexities of the rationing system, and anxious not to become exclusively responsible for all supplies, the commissariat ruled that no further food products and consumer goods should be rationed without permission from its representatives.[275] Even as late as the autumn of 1929, few specific directives about rationing had been issued by the central authorities; the arrangements for rationing, and the size of the rations, varied from town to town and were controlled by the local authorities.[276] In October 1929, for example, decisions to ration meat, herrings and eggs in Moscow, and to provide supplementary rations for children up to the age of twelve instead of the age of eight were apparently taken by the presidium of Moscow soviet and not by Narkomtorg.[277]

In the autumn of 1929, however, contrary to the earlier intentions of Narkomtorg, the scope and powers of the centralised rationing system greatly increased. Ever since the mid-1920s Narkomtorg had already allocated major food products and consumer goods between different regions (see p. 45 n. 170 above). Where Narkomtorg plans monopolised the supply, as in the case of tea and sugar, and of grain in the regions which were net consumers of grain, the general level of rations in each region was in effect already determined by the

---

[273] See Carr (1952), 232, 321; Malle (1985), 418–25.

[274] ZART, 1929, No. 42, pp. 12–13 (dated July 5); this circular called for intensive study of the experience of a few shops in each town.

[275] ZART, 1929, No. 39, p. 2 (decree of July 4).

[276] VT, 14, November 1929, 17–19 (Ts. Kron). It has not been possible to trace the development of rationing precisely. Throughout the rationing period, information about the level of rations appeared only intermittently in the Soviet press and in reports of foreign visitors; the relevant government and Narkomtorg decrees were published only in part or not at all. This topic deserves a more thorough investigation.

[277] EZh, October 2, 1930 (sitting of plenum of soviet, October 1).

size of its Narkomtorg allocation, so local decisions were made within a severe constraint. After the 1929 harvest the increase in the centralised collections of grain and other agricultural products, together with the closing down of many private trade outlets, reduced food purchases by the local authorities and the volume of sales on the market. In November 1929, the Ukrainian Politburo pointed to the reduction of bazaar trade and petty retail private trade as major factors leading to the extremely unsatisfactory food supplies in major industrial centres in the Ukraine.[278] The range of towns and products covered by the centralised supply system inexorably expanded. By the autumn of 1929 food products subject to ration often included bread, groats, meat, butter, vegetable oil, sugar and tea.[279] The main 'Narkomtorg-planned' industrial consumer goods were also rationed, including fabrics, footwear and ready-made clothing.[280] By the end of 1929 a rough hierarchy of towns for rationing purposes had emerged. At first Moscow and Leningrad received top priority. In October 1929, a government commission chaired by Shmidt resolved that workers in the Donbass and Krivoi Rog should be equated with Moscow and Leningrad for food supplies, and the central commission for workers' supply demanded that the same arrangements should apply to industrial goods.[281] In January 1930, Narkomtorg of the RSFSR added eight Ural workers' centres to towns like Ivanovo–Voznesensk and Nizhnii Novgorod which received 'centralised guaranteed' supplies; this was presumably a high-priority group of towns with slightly less priority than Moscow, Leningrad and the Donbass.[282]

Pressure to extend the rationing system came both from the local trading agencies, anxious to secure reliable central supplies for their area, and from the official workers' organisations,

[278] Moshkov (1966), 121–2, citing the archives.

[279] See, for example, the lists in ZART, 1929, No. 64, pp. 23–6 (referring to a government commission of October 8), and in EZh, October 2, 1929.

[280] See, for example, P, November 6, 1929; ZART, 1929, No. 70, pp. 2–11 (decree of November 26).

[281] ZART, 1929, No. 64, pp. 23–6 (resolution of October 12–13; the Shmidt commission, referred to in this resolution, met on October 8); in November 1929, the Ukrainian Politburo still described food supplies in the Donbass and Krivoi Rog as extremely unsatisfactory (Moshkov (1966), 122).

[282] TsGANKh, 5240/4/490, 198–9 (decree of Narkomtorg of March 6, 1930, approving Narkomtorg RSFSR decision of January 31).

anxious to secure the priority for industrial workers in practice which they were afforded in theory. In October 1929, for example, at a plenum of the Moscow soviet, the trading department of Moscow soviet and the representative of the consumer soviets urged the introduction of rationing for milk.[283] Later in the same month the Central Commission for Workers' Supply urged Narkomtorg to introduce rations of pork fat (salo) for underground workers on the grounds that it was 'a basic product for lunch (zavtrak)' in the Donbass.[284] In January 1930 the Commission called for a unified system which placed towns and categories of consumers in particular supply groups, and urged the strict enforcement of the plan for the centralised supply of meat.[285] By this time a Sovnarkom decree dated December 21, 1929, 'On the Supply of Food Grains', had already indicated that the central authorities had decided to replace the localised arrangements of 1929 by a centralised rationing system managed by Narkomtorg. The decree, perhaps intended to mark Stalin's fiftieth birthday, announced that the planned supply of grain for food would be increased in view of the success of the collections; and for the first time instructed Narkomtorg to establish 'specific rations for workers and their families, divided by region, district, and workers' centre'.[286] Following this decree, in the course of 1930 a nation-wide rationing system, with a hierarchy of towns, products and groups of consumers, was brought into being.

Consolidating previous arrangements, on February 18, 1930, STO issued two priority lists (spiski) of towns with a total population of about 20 million people. List 1 contained 44 major towns and other 'supply points', and List 2 included a further 105.[287] In practice the remaining towns and workers' settlements constituted a lower-priority list (List 3), while Narkomtorg afforded particularly high priority to Moscow, Leningrad and the Donbass (which formed part of List 1). It was therefore in effect already operating with four Lists. But

---

[283] EZh, October 2, 1930 (plenum of October 1).
[284] ZART, 1929, No. 64, pp. 23–6 (resolution of October 12–13).
[285] ZART, 1930, art. 158 (resolution of January 23–5).
[286] I, December 22, 1929.
[287] Moshkov (1966), 123. According to ZRT, 1930, art. 456 (Narkomtorg instruction of April 27, 1930) Lists 1 and 2 appeared as a supplement to a STO decree on measures to increase real wages of workers.

Narkomtorg did not adhere at all strictly to the Lists in practice.[288] According to a Gosplan report, in the course of 1929/30 'the number of people on rationed supply varied greatly from month to month, considerably increasing in the case of most towns'.[289] The variations in the Lists used at different times are illustrated by the following examples:

February (meat)[a]:	Towns with population of 12·6 millions receive uninterrupted supplies.	
February (butter)[a]:	Group 1: 25 main workers' centres	
	Group 2: 80 others.	
March 22 (sugar)[b]:	15 'most important industrial centres'	
	population	8·30 millions
	List 1: large towns	7·47
	List 2: towns	8·53
	Small towns	7·31
		31·61
July 1 (vegetables)[c]:	List 1	11·14 millions
	List 2	10·55
		21·69
July 1 (apples and pears)[d]:	List 1	10·37

[a]EZh, February 14, 1930 (I. Pankratov).
[b]TsGANKh 5240/9/491, 157.
[c]TsGANKh 5240/9/494, 166–8 (plan for 1930/31).
[d]TsGANKh 5240/9/494, 183 (plan for 1930/31).

Thus in the Lists for sugar in March, as compared with the Lists for fruit and vegetables in July, towns covering most of the population on List 1 are included in the list of 15 towns; in

[288] The uncertainties with which the system operated were reflected in a Narkomtorg decree of May 16, 1930, signed by Mikoyan which, long after Leningrad was supposed to be treated as equal with Moscow, instructed all concerned to 'equate Leningrad to Moscow in rations supplied for food products and industrial goods' (ZRT, 1930, art. 494).
[289] *Kon''yunktura . . . za sentyabr' i 12 mesyatsev 1929/30* (n.d. [1930]), Obmen i raspredelenie, p. 7.

addition towns with a population amounting to over 4 million people are in List 1 rather than List 2, and a further 1½ million population are in List 2.[290] The anomalies in the arrangements were not straightened out until the end of 1930, when the two Lists were replaced by a Special List (osobyi spisok), covering Moscow, Leningrad, the Donbass and certain defence factories, and Lists 1, 2 and 3. While the size of each of the four Lists changed considerably in the ensuing years, this division into four Lists remained until rationing was abolished in 1935.[291]

In addition to the allocations to towns as such, further allocations were provided for transport workers, distant areas (including Central Asia), the Red Army, industrial consumption and (in relatively minute quantities, and only in the case of industrial food products such as sugar) the rural sector.[292]

Consumers in towns on higher-priority Lists normally received higher rations, and their rations were more firmly guaranteed. In the decree of Narkomtorg of the USSR dated April 2, 1930, the sugar ration for workers was 1,000–1,500 grams a month in the case of the 15 towns, 1,000 grams for List 1, and 700 grams for List 2. The decree ruled that the rations for the 15 towns were mandatory (direktivnye), but 'in relation to all the rest of the rural and urban sectors they are estimates (raschetnye), which are to be specifically determined locally, in accordance with the allocations despatched'.[293] Even in the case of bread, Narkomtorg of the RSFSR ruled that Lists 1 and 2 were to be given priority in supplies, followed by transport workers and their families, and seasonal workers, with the implication that other towns and groups would not receive an adequate allocation.[294] With those industrial consumer goods which were distributed by a fixed individual ration, for towns in List 1 the ration was firmly fixed in advance by Narkomtorg, for towns in List 2 it was determined by the regional trade department on

[290] The decrees set out the 15 most important towns with their population in the case of sugar, and provide a regional breakdown for Lists 1 and 2 in the case of vegetables, but do not show the precise relation between the Lists for the different products.

[291] *Rabochii klass*, ii (1984), 238; subsequent developments will be discussed in vol. 4.

[292] See, for example, the arrangements for sugar supplies in 1929/30 in TsGANKh, 5240/9/491, 155–60 (decree of April 2, 1930, and attached tables).

[293] TsGANKh, 5240/9/491, 155–7.

[294] Moshkov (1966), 124; this ruling was apparently made in April 1930.

the basis of the earmarked allocation (kontingent) for these towns actually received by the region, and for other towns and workers' settlements the regional trade department was merely instructed to determine the ration 'in accordance with the supply of goods (tovarnye fondy)'.[295] When supplies were particularly scarce, the Lists withered away. Thus in June 1930, only 4,380 tons of butter were available: 4,280 tons were specifically allocated to export, Moscow, Leningrad, Baku, the Donbass, holiday resorts and 'special needs', and the rest of the population of the whole USSR was allocated a mere 100 tons.[296] Outside those towns which were on Lists 1 and 2, food supplies were extremely precarious. As a Soviet scholar delicately remarked, 'some groups of working people fell out of the system of planned supply': in the Lower Volga region, for example, until the party committee rectified the situation no grain was available either through central allocations or on the market for workers and employees in rural districts, or for landless peasants previously supplied from the centre.[297]

The range of products covered by rationing was considerably extended, and by June 1930 eggs, vegetables, apples and pears had been added to the basic foods.[298] Vegetables included onions, carrots and beetroots, in addition to potatoes, cabbage and cucumbers. Narkomtorg also consolidated the rationing

[295] ZRT, 1930, art. 456 (Narkomtorg instruction of April 27).
[296] TsGANKh, 5240/9/492, 14 (Narkomtorg decree of May 31, 1930). The population of towns receiving specific allocations amounted to about 7.5 millions out of an urban population of over 30 millions and a total population of 155 millions. The allocations were as follows (tons):

Export	1500
Moscow	1000
Leningrad	800
Baku	80
Donbass	180
Resorts	250
Special needs	470
Local	100
	4380

[297] Moshkov (1966), 123, citing the archives (undated, but apparently referring to the spring of 1930).
[298] VT, 5, 1930, 20 (for eggs); TsGANKh, 5240/9/494, 163, 166–8 (vegetables) and 5240/9/494, 180, 183 (apples and pears); the last two decrees were plans for the 1930 crop.

system for industrial consumer goods. On April 27, 1930, it ruled that 'to prevent the leak of these goods into the free market (vol'nyi rynok)', all consumer goods in short supply would in future be subject to rationing.[299] At this time the view that trade was in process of giving way to product-exchange was widely held by economists, and influential among the political leaders (see pp. 167–71 above). On February 13, 1930, a decree of TsIK and Sovnarkom, in announcing the reorganisation of internal trade, explained that one of its main functions included the 'supply (snabzhenie)' of personal consumption needs and 'the organisation of planned exchange (obmen) between town and country'; and instructed local trading agencies to prepare for 'gradual transition from general planning of commodity turnover (tovarooborot) to planned socialist product-exchange (produktoobmen)'.[300] The word 'trade' was nowhere mentioned in the decree, except in the official titles of Narkomtorg and its agencies, and already seemed an anachronism.

In practice Narkomtorg was cautious about further extending its powers. The decree of April divided industrial goods into three groups. Only goods in Group 1 were allocated to the consumer by fixed individual rations; these included cotton and linen fabrics sold by the metre, thread and household soap. Group 2 goods were controlled by the regional trading agencies, which were themselves to fix quarterly, six-monthly or annual rations, usually in terms of a money limit which was noted in the ration book as it was spent. Group 3 goods, though formally rationed, were to be sold 'in the normal manner', subject to rules for particular goods laid down by Narkomtorg.[301] This did not represent a change in principle from the established system. In November 1929, shops were already supposed to announce a monthly ration for footwear, ready-made clothing and haberdashery; and to enter amounts bought in the documents of individual purchasers.[302] Narkomtorg operated a similar

---

[299] ZRT, 1930, art. 456.
[300] SZ, 1930, art. 181.
[301] ZRT, 1930, art. 456. Group 2 included finished clothing, knitwear, worsted and woollen pieces, leather footwear, felt footwear (valenki) and galoshes. Group 3 included all other goods.
[302] P, November 6, 1929; for the quarterly ration of cotton fabrics in Moscow, see I, January 7, 1930.

'hierarchy of attention' for food products. Bread and other grain products were specifically rationed on an individual basis, and Narkomtorg established very firm central controls over their distribution from centralised supplies to 26 million people in 1930.[303] But the complexities of administration, together with the partial failure of the agricultural collections, rendered a comprehensive centralised rationing system for all food products unworkable.

A further important step towards uniformity was taken in the middle of 1930, with the replacement of ration books issued by the local cooperatives by a unified ration book (zabornaya knizhka) issued by the central cooperative organisation Tsentrosoyuz. Following existing practice, ration books were supposed to be issued only to persons employed by state and cooperative organisations and their dependants.[304] More or less simultaneously, on May 4, 1930, a Narkomtorg decree divided the population into Categories, systematising arrangements operated by the local authorities since the beginning of rationing. The decree divided the working population into two basic Categories: Category I consisted primarily of factory and railway workers, together with engineers and technicians working in production; Category II consisted of all other working people, and dependants of members of both Categories I and II. A further Category was established for children up to twelve years of age, so that children received a ration even if they belonged to a non-working family which was not entitled to a ration. A fourth Category included various kinds of seasonal workers, but their dependants were not normally entitled to a ration.[305] These Categories also underwent many changes in

---

[303] See Malafeev (1964), 138.

[304] Neiman (1935), 176; Hubbard (1938), 33; but see n. 000 below.

[305] TsGANKh, 5240/9/492, 135. Category I included: factory workers; transport and municipal workers in specified occupations; persons formerly in Category I who occupied posts to which they were elected by their place of production; promoted workers during their first year of office work; engineers and technicians working in socialised production; officers of the Red Army, GPU and convoy defence not receiving rations from their units; apprentices and instructors in FZU; and, during the first three months of unemployment, unemployed persons formerly in Category I. The Category for seasonal workers included: workers in the construction and timber industries; peat sovkhozy and fisheries; seasonal haulers and workers on water transport; teachers, doctors, agronomists, etc. working in villages.

practice, without changing the general principles.[306] All the ration scales adopted by Narkomtorg provided higher rations for those in Category I. The ration-scale for Moscow in April 1930 illustrates the sharpness of the differential (grams per month):[307]

	Workers	*Other employed persons [and dependants of workers]*
Bread (per day)	800	400
Meat	4400	2200
Sugar	1500	1200
Tea	25	25
Butter	300	300
Herrings	1200	800

Certain manual workers received a higher bread ration of 1,000–1,200 grams a day. These included underground workers, workers in hot shops, haulage workers and timber workers producing for export.[308] Thus the size of the ration depended

[306] According to EZh, October 28, 1930, new regulations established five Categories:

Category IA:	workers, etc. (as in former Category I), plus ex-political prisoners and members of the Society of Old Bolsheviks
Category IB:	junior ancillary personnel (MOP); certain artisans; transport workers not in IA
Category II:	relatives of IA
Category III:	relatives of IB; other people in employment
Category IV:	children up to twelve years of age
Special category:	seasonal workers.

[307] Hubbard (1938), 35. For a similar ration-scale for Leningrad in September 1930, which also includes macaroni, groats, sunflower oil and household soap, see BP (Prague), lxxxi (August–September 1930), 31–2, citing *Krasnaya gazeta*, August 29, 1930; in each case the ration for workers in Category I is higher. Children in Leningrad were entitled to an additional ration of oats, groats, butter, eggs and cheese.

[308] EZh, February 14, 1930 (Pankratov); TsGANKh, 5240/9/493, 43 (June 19, 1930), 5240/9/490, 53 (March 24, 1930). The practice of issuing somewhat higher rations of certain products to members of consumer cooperatives, which greatly assisted recruitment, continued in 1930 but gradually declined in significance. In September 1930, cooperative members in Leningrad received an extra ration of macaroni, but the same ration as non-members for all other

partly on the Category of the consumer, partly on the List in which his town or factory was included.

Public catering was an important additional source of food in key factories. In 1928, only about 750,000 urban employees received regular meals in public dining rooms; by 1930 the number had increased to some $2^3/_4$ millions.[309] The works' canteen or buffet helped to retain workers in key industries, and was also intended to facilitate the recruitment of housewives into factory work.[310] Poor food and service were normal: the Narkomtorg journal criticised 'repulsive service, the unsanitary state of the dining rooms, the low quality of the dishes and the malfeasances of the employees'.[311] But the food at the canteens was additional to the ration.[312] At a time of goods shortage there

---

products (BP (Prague), lxxi (August–September 1930), 31–2). The membership of consumer cooperatives increased as follows (in millions):

	Jan. 1, 1929	Jan. 1, 1930	Jan. 1, 1931 (prelim.)
Urban	8·98	12·71	18·9
Rural	14·80	23·83	39·2

(*Nar.kh.plan 1931* (1931), 140).

[309] According to *Sovetskaya torgovlya* (1935[?1936]), 129, the turnover of public catering increased as follows (in million rubles at current prices):

	1928	1929	1930
Urban	300	471	1140
Rural	50	79	150
Total	350	550	1290

In 1928 750,000 customers consumed 2·2 million dishes per day (Neiman (1935), 158); as the price per dish remained roughly constant between 1928 and 1930, the number of customers probably increased in proportion to turnover.

[310] The Commission for Workers' Supply, advocating an expansion of public catering, pointed out 'the need to liberate women from the domestic kitchen in order to utilise them in basic production' (ZRT, 1930, art. 559 (dated May 27–9, 1930)); it failed to suggest that men might lend a hand in the domestic kitchen.

[311] VT, 14, November 1929, 24 (Ts. Kron); see also Filtzer (1986), 94.

[312] Mikoyan suggested at the collegium of Narkomtorg that the normal ration might be reduced – perhaps by a quarter – in the case of those using public catering facilities (EZh, August 6, 1930), but this proposal was not adopted.

was no lack of customers; dining rooms were overcrowded and queues were extremely long.

(iii) Retail prices

In spite of worsening queues and shortages, the Soviet authorities continued the policy of reducing retail prices. In the spring of 1929, when demand already far exceeded supply on the retail market, the five-year plan hopefully assumed that equilibrium between supply and demand would be re-established, and proposed that retail prices of consumer goods should decline by 23 per cent in the course of the plan.[313] Following the further deterioration in the summer of 1929, the wisdom of price reduction policies was strongly challenged during the discussions on the control figures for 1929/30. Gosplan initially proposed a substantial reduction in industrial prices, which would result in a decline in the cost-of-living index (the 'budget index') for workers by 4 per cent.[314] On behalf of Gosplan, Strumilin pointed out that 'if we were to leave prices on the existing level in 1929/30, over the past five years we would have only one year of price reduction, i.e. we would fulfil the directives of the party by only 20 per cent'. Gosplan proposed that prices should be reduced on items consumed by workers and the poorest peasantry, and increased for the more expensive goods; the general level of prices would decline.[315] The Narkomfin collegium remained unconvinced, and at a joint session of Sovnarkom and STO Bryukhanov argued on its behalf that 'this price reduction in present circumstances will inevitably lead to a repetition of negative phenomena which occurred in the past economic year', and advocated price increases differentiated by social class.[316] Syrtsov also opposed the reduction of industrial prices in 1929/30, proposing that the resources saved by refraining from price reduction should be allocated to industry.[317] The final control figures approved by Sovnarkom proposed a modest decline in retail prices by 1 per cent in the course of 1929/30. The budget

---

[313] See Carr and Davies (1969), 983.
[314] TPG, September 24, 1929.
[315] TPG, September 27, 1929.
[316] I, October 9, 1929; for Strumilin's refutation, see EZh, October 11, 1929.
[317] SKhG, October 15, 1929.

index for workers would, however, decline by as much as 2·5 per cent; this would be secured by 'a further reduction in the share of private trade, with its extremely high price-level', in workers' budgets.[318] In accordance with the control figures, Narkomtorg proposed that in 1929/30 the share of the private sector in workers' expenditure should decline from 18 to 3 per cent in the case of food, and from 11 to 2 per cent in the case of industrial goods.[319]

The policy of reducing retail prices was doggedly pursued in 1929/30. In February 1930, Vesenkha and Narkomtorg agreed that, following a reduction in wholesale industrial prices by Vesenkha, urban retail prices of cotton textiles should be reduced by 9 per cent, of clothing by 8 per cent and of footwear by 10 per cent.[320] These reductions resulted in a decline of the general level of urban retail cooperative prices by 3·7 per cent between October 1, 1929, and June 1, 1930; the prices of industrial goods excluding food products declined by as much as 5·2 per cent.[321] The prices of food products were also reduced over the same period.[322] At the XVI party congress in June 1930, Stalin admitted that it would take 'at least a year' to eliminate the 'goods famine' in respect of meat, dairy products and vegetables, but still insisted that 'it is necessary to secure the application of *the policy of price reduction*'.[323]

While the stubborn pursuit ever since 1927 of price reductions in spite of severe goods' shortages was a prime example of dogmatism reinforced by obstinacy, the policy paradoxically acquired a certain logic now that many consumer goods were rationed. Reduced prices made it easier for lower-paid workers to take up their rations,[324] and thus helped to bring about what

---

[318] *KTs . . . na 1929/30* (1930), 218–19.

[319] Cited in ZRT, 1930, art. 158.

[320] SP VSNKh, 1929/30, issue No. 17 (presidium protocol no. 7, dated February 18).

[321] *Tovarooborot* (1932), 134–5.

[322] The price of food products as a whole fell by 2·2 per cent, the price of grain products declining by as much as 5·1 per cent (*loc. cit.*).

[323] Stalin, *Soch.* (1949), xii, 329–30. Price reduction was not mentioned in the congress resolutions on Stalin's report and on the five-year plan, but the resolution on the trade unions briefly noted that 'until recently' trade union attention to 'the struggle for price reduction' had been 'most inadequate' (*KPSS v rez.*, iii (1954), 69).

[324] According to a Soviet study, the lowest-paid group of workers (earning

Syrtsov described as 'a certain equalisation in the standard of life of skilled workers and the mass of unskilled workers'.[325] In 1930, this was still official policy.

The retail price reductions were confined to the urban sector.[326] Retail cooperative prices in the rural sector increased slightly between October 1, 1929, and June 1, 1930.[327] State retail prices were also substantially increased for some transactions at what were variously known as 'dual' or 'commercial' prices. These were intended to mop up the monetary surpluses of Nepmen, and of higher-paid specialists and other senior personnel. In July 1929, a special state fund of sugar was established for sale at higher prices to the non-working population, and these arrangements were gradually extended. From December 1929, 'special market funds' of cotton and woollen fabrics and finished clothing were sold at double or treble the retail price.[328] When commercial trade was first introduced, the rations sold at lower or 'normal' prices to workers and their families were increased.[329] But in practice rationed supplies of consumer goods were intermittent, and if they could afford it ordinary workers also resorted to the special shops.[330] The plenum of the Commission for Workers' Supply, meeting on January 23–25, 1930, complained about this situation, and demanded a further increase in rationed supplies at 'normal' prices, and the restriction of the range of goods available at higher prices to those goods which were also available on the ration.[331] In 1930, when ordinary workers and

---

up to 24 rubles a month per member of their household) were unable to take up the whole of their rations of tea and meat, unlike the higher-paid workers, and were far more dependent on their rations for clothing and footwear (VT, 5, 1930, 16–24).

[325] Syrtsov, *K novomu khozyaistvennomu godu* (1930), 19.

[326] The Commission for Workers' Supply proposed at its meeting of January 23–25, 1930, that price reductions should only be made at industrial centres with a substantial worker population, and where new capital construction was taking place, but on January 26 STO ruled that they should be made at all towns, new sites and workers' settlements (ZRT, 1930, art. 158).

[327] *Tovarooborot* (1932), 131.

[328] Neiman (1935), 238; ZART, 1929, No. 70, pp. 2–11.

[329] I, January 7, 1930.

[330] P, February 8, 1930.

[331] ZRT, 1930, art. 158.

their efforts were everywhere exalted, the commercial fund for the moment remained only a small part of retail trade.[332]

(iv) The peasant market

The Soviet authorities intended, by combining stable or reduced prices in socialised trade with a comprehensive rationing system, to insulate the non-agricultural employed population from the private and peasant market. The peasant market, primarily supplying the 'non-working population' in the towns, would begin to wither away. During the collectivisation drive in the winter of 1929/30, many peasant markets were closed. According to a Gosplan estimate, the percentage of workers' expenditure on all goods which took place on the free market declined from 23 in August 1929 to 14 in March 1930. But with the legal reopening of the markets the percentage again increased, rising to 21 per cent in May and 24 per cent in June, higher than in the equivalent months of 1929.[333] This represented a substantial decline in real terms: between July–September 1929 and April–June 1930 peasant bazaar prices for food products increased by 77·4 per cent, and the prices of industrial consumer goods on the private market increased by 40·6 per cent.[334] These figures are compatible with a Soviet estimate that in real terms workers acquired on the private market in October 1929–July 1930 only about half the quantity acquired in the equivalent period of 1928/29.[335] But the peasant market had not withered away, and eventually its stubborn disruptive strength would force the Soviet leaders to incorporate it within their concept of socialism.

The urban population as a whole was dependent on the free market to an even greater extent than the workers. Urban employees other than workers received smaller guaranteed

---

[332] The gap between the 'normal' and the commercial price was paid into the state budget. Budget revenue from this source amounted to 299 million rubles in 1929/30, as compared with the estimate of 180 million rubles (*Otchet . . . 1929–1930* (1931), ob. zapiska, 31); total socialised urban retail trade amounted to 10,680 million rubles (*Tovarooborot* (1932), 18).

[333] *Kon''yunktura . . . za sentyabr' i 12 mesyatsev 1929/30* (n.d. [1930]), Tablitsy.

[334] Estimated from data in VT, 7–8, 1930, 73, 75 (Averbukh). An alternative Soviet index of urban bazaar prices for peasant sales of five foods shows an increase of 76·5 per cent between October 1, 1929, and June 1, 1930 (see Table 24(c)).

[335] B, 19–20, October 31, 1930, 78 (Gatovskii).

supplies from socialised trade (see pp. 297–8 above), and therefore spent a higher proportion of their income on the private market; in May 1930 21 per cent of all workers' expenditure on goods of all kinds took place on the free market, but the equivalent figure for white-collar employees was 39 per cent.[336] Urban citizens who were not employed in the socialised sector, or were not dependants of people in work, had to rely entirely on the private market or on the small state commercial sales.[337] According to a Soviet estimate, purchases of agricultural goods on the private market by the non-agricultural population as a whole amounted to as much as 49 per cent of all their purchases of agricultural goods in 1930.[338] In his critical speech of August 1930, Syrtsov frankly acknowledged 'a growth in the relative weight of the private trader'.[339]

Regional variations in the role of the free market were extremely large. In May 1930, in the USSR as a whole 37 per cent of the expenditure by workers on agricultural products took place on the free market, but the percentage varied from only 8·4 per cent in Moscow and 16·0 per cent in Leningrad to 43 per cent in the Urals, 54 per cent in Kharkov and 60 per cent in Kiev.[340]

(v) Real wages and living standards

In this economy of multiform prices, any assessment of the increase in the general level of retail prices or the cost-of-living

[336] *Kon''yunktura . . . za sentyabr' i 12 mesyatsev 1929/30* (n.d. [1930]), Tablitsy.

[337] According to *Materials* (1985), 199, of a total expenditure on material goods by the non-agricultural population amounting to 14,409 million rubles in 1930, 2,118 million rubles was spent by artisans, craftsmen, small traders and 'capitalist groups', who had to purchase the bulk of their supplies on the private market. For the higher price increase for non-manual employees which resulted from their greater dependence on the private market, see *ibid.* 147.

[338] Kul'chitskii (Kiev, 1979), 124, using data from the archives, states that 3,455 million rubles out of a total of 7,030 million rubles were purchased from the private trader (this obviously includes peasant trade). According to Gatovsky, writing in May or June 1930, the 'free market', including intra-rural turnover as well as urban peasant bazaars and organised private trade, amounted 'in extremely approximate terms' to 50–52 per cent of all retail turnover in 1926/27, 36·7 per cent in 1928/29, and 30 per cent in 1929/30 (*Na novom etape* (1930), ii, 25).

[339] Syrtsov, *K novomu khozyaistvennomu godu* (1930), 16.

[340] *Kon''yunktura . . . za sentyabr' i 12 mesyatsev 1929/30* (n.d. [1930]), Tablitsy.

index crucially depends on the relative weights attached to the socialised and the free market. The increase in the general urban retail price index between October 1, 1929, and June 1, 1930, is in the range 15–35 per cent, depending on the weights used.[341]

This increase in prices is at least as rapid as the increase in money wages. The average monthly wage of all insured persons employed in the non-agricultural sector increased by 10 per cent between July–September 1929 and April–June 1930 (see Table 20). The average monthly wage of industrial workers did not increase at all in the first seven months of 1929/30, owing to the increase in the proportion of workers with low skills.[342] The cost of living rose less sharply for industrial and other manual workers, who were less dependent on the free market, than for white collar employees.[343] But even for manual workers, the cost of living was estimated to be an average of 8·6 per cent higher in the nine months October 1929–June 1930 than in the equivalent period of 1928/29.[344] Nominal wages rose in the same period by only 8·1 per cent, so the price increase entirely swallowed up the wage increase.[345] Moreover, the price index did not take account of the considerable deterioration in the quality and variety of consumer goods which occurred in this period, or of the atrophy of consumer choice. But even these distorted index numbers showed that the real wage had slightly

[341] In all socialised trade the prices of industrial goods increased by 0·9 per cent and of agricultural goods by 1·6 per cent between July–September 1929 and April–June 1930 (VT, 7–8, 1930, 69, 71); I have assumed a general price increase in urban socialised trade of 1 per cent. Peasant bazaar prices for food products increased by 77 per cent and the prices of industrial consumer goods on the private market by 41 per cent in the same period (see p. 303 above). If private and bazaar trade is given a minimum weight of 20 per cent, the general price increase is over 15 per cent; with a weight of 40 per cent the increase is over 35 per cent, using the relative percentages of food and industrial goods implied by the data in *Kon''yunktura . . . za sentyabr' i 12 mesyatsev 1929/30* (n.d. [1930]), Tablitsy.

[342] The average monthly wage was 76r 28k in September 1929 and 75r 07k in April 1930 (SO, 12, 1929, 94; SO, 6, 1930, 152); see also Table 20.

[343] According to *Trud* (1930), 60–1, white-collar employees with families spent 36 per cent of their food expenditure on the private market in February 1930, and manual workers with families only 20 per cent.

[344] VT, 7–8, 1930, 77 (Averbukh); the index, which incorporated the weighted prices of 39 commodities, showed an increase in the prices of agricultural goods by 16·7 per cent, and a decline in the prices of industrial goods by 1·8 per cent.

[345] *Ibid.* 78.

declined in the case of industrial workers, and fallen sharply for other major sections of the non-agricultural population.[346]

For some urban families this decline in real wages was partly offset by the increase in the number of members of the family who went out to work. Married women entered employment; and men and women of pensionable age postponed their retirement.[347] The average number at work per worker's family increased from 1·23 in October–December 1928 to 1·26 in July–September 1929 and 1·33 in April–June 1930.[348] This trend continued throughout the ensuing decades.

Soviet authors have frequently argued that the 'social wage' increased more rapidly than the money wage, so that the real wage as measured by money earnings does not reflect the true increase in the standard of living. But, even on the broadest definition of the social wage, in 1929/30 the decline per worker in various monetary benefits and in free accommodation offset the increase in education and health expenditure, so the social wage slightly declined as a percentage of the money wage.[349]

---

[346] In October 1929–March 1930 the average monthly money wage in non-agricultural employment as a whole was 10·9 per cent higher than the average for 1928/29; the equivalent figure for industrial workers was only 4·0 per cent (*Trud* (1930), pp. xx, 38). This more rapid increase was certainly more than offset, except for 'leading cadres' with good access to rationed supplies, by their greater dependence on the free market. According to *Materials* (1985), 207, in 1930 workers' consumption per head increased by 2·2 per cent, but consumption per head of other employed persons declined by 3·7 per cent.

[347] For the increase in female employment, see pp. 125–6 above; for pensioners, see PKh, 5, 1931, 86 (Pollyak).

[348] PKh, 5, 1931, 66 (Pollyak); the number rose to 1·35 in July–September and 1·43 in October–December.

[349] The following table, derived from a careful Gosplan investigation, shows the social and individual wage bill (million rubles at current prices):

	1927/28	1928/29	1929/30
Education and student grants	167	214	361
Trade union cultural funds	71	82	(117)
Medical help	242	269	362
Free accommodation	45	41	22
Fund to Improve Workers' Welfare (FUBR)	29	32	44
Insurance and other payments	388	462	477
Payment for holidays	167	194	246
Maintenance of FZU apprentices	19	22	39
Total 'social wage bill'	1128	1325	1669

The decline in real wages was not planned by the Soviet authorities: the control figures for 1929/30 blithely proposed that the real wages of employed persons should increase by as much as 11 per cent in 1929/30.[350] But the decline was the necessary outcome of an increase in non-agricultural employment which was not accompanied by an equal expansion in the supply of food and industrial consumer goods. The decline was at first frankly if circumspectly acknowledged in reports prepared by government departments. In January 1930 the central committee of the Ukrainian party admitted that 'real wages had further declined in the previous quarter, as prices in the private sector and in cooperatives had continued to increase'.[351] A Gosplan survey of the first five months of 1929/30 acknowledged that the budget index for workers, as compared with the same period of 1928/29, had risen as rapidly as nominal wages.[352]

In the discussion before the XVI party congress, a certain N. Kholopov rashly stated that real wages had ceased to rise in 1928/29 and 1929/30, and declined in 1930. A reply by a Narkomtrud official appeared in the same number, obviously solicited by the editors; it claimed that real wages had increased by 4 per cent in 1928/29, and a further 2–3 per cent in the first six months of 1929/30, so that they had now reached the same level as that of a Berlin worker, even if the social wage was not

Money wage bill	3164	3661	4640
Social wage as % of money wage	35·7	36·2	36·0

(PKh, 5, 1931, 62–119 (Pollyak; the study was prepared in collaboration with Kheinman)). The slow rise in 'insurance and other payments' was due to the decline in the number of unemployed, the slow rise in the number of pensioners (see p. 306, note 347 above) and the reduction in sickness benefits for certain groups of workers. If education, student grants, unemployment benefit, pensions and maintenance of apprentices are omitted on the grounds that these do not accrue directly to workers in employment, the percentage is 22·2 in 1928/29 and 21·6 in 1929/30.

[350] *KTs . . . na 1929/30* (1930), 237.

[351] Moshkov (1966), 124; this passage, cited from the archives, is in indirect speech.

[352] NPF, 9–10, May 1930, 42 (Guberman).

taken into account.[353] Two days later a young political economist rushed into the fray, castigating Kholopov as a 'Right-wing opportunist'.[354] Kholopov withdrew his heretical statement, nervously commenting that he should not have been treated as a 'class enemy' because of a single mistake.[355] At the XVI party congress Stalin, in a section of his report entitled 'The Improvement of the Material and Cultural Situation of Workers and Peasants', asserted that real wages, including social insurance and the Fund to Improve Workers' Welfare, were now 67 per cent above the pre-war level, and added that 'real wages are undeviatingly increasing from year to year'.[356] The resolution on the report took the same line.[357]

In spite of these categorical statements, for a few months honesty continued to struggle with political expediency in statements about real wages. Syrtsov, in speeches immediately preceding the congress, cautiously noted the 'non-fulfilment of the plan to increase real wages, and in individual cases even the reduction of the level of real wages', but added that an assessment of the 'material situation' of the working class should also take into account such developments as the decline in unemployment and the increase in the number of workers per family.[358] After the congress, while remarking that he did not intend to join in the 'very numerous disputes about the methodology of estimating real wages', he bluntly declared that 'the feelings of the main strata of the working class are far less erroneous than many index numbers, and indicate an extremely unfavourable situation in this matter, which is getting worse'.[359] In the Gosplan journal, one report hesitantly claimed that 'the real wages of industrial workers have shown a certain tendency to growth' in the first six months of 1929/30, but also admitted that their average consumption of proteins declined by 1·4 per cent as compared with 1928/29, while their consumption of

---

[353] P, June 18, 1930, disk. listok 14 (Kholopov; Tsybul'skii). This assessment about the comparative level of Russian and German wages was extremely inaccurate.

[354] P, June 20, 1930, disk. listok 16 (Markus).

[355] P, June 29, 1930, disk. listok 24.

[356] Stalin, *Soch.*, xii (1949), 290, 296–7.

[357] *KPSS v rez.*, iii (1954), 13.

[358] Syrtsov, *Nakanune* (1930), 29, based on reports of May 26 and June 5.

[359] Syrtsov, *K novomu khozyaistvennomu godu* (1930), 19.

carbohydrates and the calorie content of food remained stable.[360] But a later report, while also claiming that nominal wages had increased slightly more rapidly more rapidly than prices in the first six months, added that in April and May 'the relation between nominal wages and the budget index did not change for the better'.[361] A few months later a survey of the whole economic year insisted, with some civil courage, that 'the increase in nominal wages went to cover the growth of the budget index and enabled only a stable level of wages in comparison with last year'.[362] An article in the Narkomtorg journal published at this time took the same line (see p. 305, note 344 above). And all sources remained silent about the real wages of other non-agricultural employees apart from workers.

Such attempts to present a more or less frank estimate of real wages in the press did not continue beyond the summer of 1930. By this time price indexes and the cost-of-living index from workers' budgets had ceased to be published.[363] Scattered information about retail prices appeared from time to time; but the general retail price index for the early 1930s was not published in the Soviet press until historians obtained access to the archives in the 1960s.[364] Data continued to be circumspectly collected, with some disruption in 1930–1 resulting from the arrest or dismissal of many leading statisticians.[365] The continued decline in real wages must have been obvious to both officials and workers. Many workers accepted the decline in their standard of living as a sacrifice required for the future of their country, and of socialism. But they were firmly assured that, contrary to appearances, their standard of living was continuously increasing. They were required to build their vision of the future on self-deception about the present.

[360] PKh, 5, 1930, 115, 119 (Mendel'son).

[361] PKh, 6, 1930, 88–9 (Averbukh).

[362] PKh, 7–8, 1930, 41–2 (Guberman); the author added that the 'basic cadres of workers' were in a more favourable position.

[363] The general retail price index for February 1930 appeared in the statistical journal SO, 3–4, 1930, 107; and separate price indexes for socialised and private retail trade, without a general index, for March, April and May 1930, appeared in SO, 5, 1930, 158, and in the last number of the journal, SO, 6, 1930, 151, 153.

[364] Notably Malafeev (1964).

[365] See *Materials* (1985), 147 (prices), 192–218 (consumption); this is a Gosplan study issued in 1932 for official use only.

(F) FINANCIAL CONTROLS

(i) Finance and planning

Frumkin, the party member who most zealously defended the cause of financial equilibrium in the bitter debates of 1928–9, was dismissed from the post of deputy People's Commissar for Finance on September 11, 1929.[366] By this time the Narkomfin view that economic growth must not exceed the limits imposed by sound finance had been thoroughly defeated; finance was subordinate to the plan. In November, a financial official writing in the economic newspaper noted that the budget was already in practice 'an institution serving the national-economic plan', and firmly rejected Frumkin's approach:

> It has not been the so-called 'budget possibilities' which have limited the growth of the budget in 1929/30; it is the Balances of the various national-economic plans which have determined the general contours of the budget as derivatives.[367]

A few months later, in its report to the XVI party congress, Vesenkha boasted that 'the financial system of industry even in its external form is more and more sharply distinguished from capitalist forms' and 'more and more closely tied in with the material economy':

> In the general structure of our planned economy finance is beginning to become more and more an apparatus of record and supervision, taking an active part in the organisation of the material processes of production and circulation.[368]

Such sentiments were now established party doctrine. Yet the authorities were also committed to currency stability, and even to steady improvement of the value of the ruble (see p. 300 above). The official attitude to finance was fundamentally ambiguous: both the primacy of the plan and the stability of the currency were regarded as essential. Advocates of the

[366] SZ, 1929, ii, art. 203; for Frumkin, see Carr and Davies (1969), esp. 74–5, 320, 323.
[367] EZh, November 30, 1929 (Lyando).
[368] *Vypolnenie* (1931), 149–50.

replacement of money by an accounting unit were careful to acknowledge that the purchasing power of the ruble should rise as long as it continued to exist,[369] while the economic newspaper, in defending the importance of a stable currency, nevertheless conceded that '*it is not socialist construction which exists for the ruble but on the contrary the ruble which exists for socialist construction*', and condemned those who 'tend to see an inflationary danger in every ruble issued'.[370] Similarly D'yachenko, while insisting on a stable currency, conceded that money should not be 'fetishised', and that currency issues should be used as a 'supplementary lever' in planning.[371]

While a careful balance was maintained in statements of principle, in practice the plan was usually given precedence. A typical confrontation of the two conflicting aspects of Soviet financial policy took place when the preliminary work on the financial plan for 1930/31 was reviewed at an extended session of the collegium of Narkomfin. Anticipating a gap of at least 1,000 million rubles between revenue and expenditure, the senior Narkomfin official responsible for taxation posed an insoluble dilemma: the difficulties in planning for adequate revenue from taxation were 'insurmountable', yet to increase currency in circulation more than the growth of output was 'completely excluded'. In reply to the discussion the spokesman for Narkomfin announced that expenditure would go ahead as planned in spite of inadequate revenue: 'finance must not be a limit to the development of the national economy'.[372]

All concerned continued to deny, at least in public, that inflation could result from these policies. While admitting the 'growth of tension in our currency circulation', D'yachenko insisted that all talk of '*forthcoming* or existing *inflation*' was '*absolutely unjustified*': currency issue could be described as 'absolutely abnormal and crossing the boundaries of inflation' only if it was proved that the planned rate of industrialisation was unrealistic.[373] But in any normal sense of the word what occurred at this time was inflation: currency issues greatly

---

[369] See for example Maimin in EZh, October 12, 1929.
[370] EZh, March 11, 1930 (editorial on occasion of sixth anniversary of currency reform).
[371] FP, 5, 1930, 53–4; for D'yachenko see p. 176 above.
[372] EZh, May 29, 1930 (Teumin, a member of the Narkomfin collegium).
[373] EZh, July 2, 1930.

exceeded the plan, and the pressure of demand led to rapid increases in prices whenever they were not controlled by the state (see pp. 247–8 and 303 above).

(ii) Cost reduction under strain

In industry the drive for improved efficiency in financial terms and the drive for increased production were continuously in conflict. The difficulties and tensions were strongly visible in the outcome of the campaign for cost reduction in industry. The decision to reduce costs by 11 per cent in 1929/30 was a crucial element in the financial plan (see p. 185 above). Successes and failures in meeting this target were frequently discussed at sessions of Gosplan and Vesenkha; and the campaign was conducted with vigour. The drive to increase labour productivity more rapidly than wages, a key element in the cost reduction plan, was zealously pursued (see pp. 268–70 above). Other means of reducing costs were not neglected. At the end of 1929, a 'voluntary society to struggle against losses' was established. The economic newspaper, in the course of an energetic campaign, reproduced by way of example the company newspaper issued by the Oakland Motor Car Co. of the USA, which announced that thousands of volunteers had joined in the War against Waste.[374] In January 1930, Elektrozavod, the electrical engineering factory in Moscow, declared a ten-day campaign against losses. The campaign issued its own newspaper, and party cells were mobilised in support; economies were claimed amounting to at least 300,000 rubles. Similar campaigns were launched by other factories.[375] The first USSR conference on the internal resources of industry met in February 1930, and established a commission headed by Shtern, who was in charge of financial policy in Vesenkha. A 'large group' from Vesenkha and its trusts and factories worked with the commission, supported by the press, to seek out unnecessary stocks and improve supplies.[376]

---

[374] EZh, December 20, 1929. This was one of a Special Battle Series of the American newspaper, dated May 13, 1929; it reported that a Captain Mitchell with a platoon of machine-gunners had opened the final week of the campaign with 'GUNS ABLAZE: Gunfire Symbolises Intensive Drive'.

[375] See Kul'chitskii (Kiev, 1979), 95–6.

[376] For the conference, see ZI, February 21, 22, 25, 1930; for the commission,

The outcome of the cost reduction campaign was paradoxical. The ambitious plan was not achieved, but according to official figures the reduction in costs amounted to as much as 5·5–5·8 per cent in October 1929–March 1930 (see p. 247 n. 56 above), a more substantial reduction than in the same period of 1928/29. Productivity increased more rapidly than wages (see pp. 268–70 above), and, as in previous years, fixed costs declined sharply, almost automatically, as a result of the increase in production from established capacity at existing factories.[377] But in several important respects the campaign was a failure. In spite of the efforts of the Shtern commission, stocks in industry increased between October 1, 1929, and April 1, 1930.[378] And, contrary to the cost reduction plan, the amount of fuel and raw materials consumed per unit of output also increased.[379] This was an important indication that the production drive – and the confusion and shortages it entailed – was increasingly predominating over financial and economic efficiency. The imperative claims of the production drive also resulted in a further steep decline in the quality of production. At a session of STO, a Vesenkha representative tactlessly admitted that 'quantity prevails over quality'.[380] The widespread contempt for the quality of production was reflected in the fate of a conference of managers, workers, trade unions and trading organisations summoned to discuss the quality of output on April 11, 1930,

---

see *Komissiya po mobilizatsii*, svodka No. 6, June 1930, p. 2; the commission continued to issue reports until February 1931. Shtern killed himself on April 22, 1930, and his work was taken over by Khavin, one of his deputies in the department of financial policy of Vesenkha. Shtern suffered from severe heart disease which caused breathing difficulties and tension, and his suicide was attributed to his illness in the Soviet press (*Komissiya po mobilizatsii*, svodka No. 6, June 1930, pp. 1–3); but he was an ex-Menshevik close to the other ex-Mensheviks in Vesenkha (see Valentinov (Stanford, 1971), 136–7, 140–1), and would almost certainly have been one of the accused in the Menshevik trial of March 1931.

[377] PI, 2, 1931, 18.

[378] *Komissiya po mobilizatsii*, svodka No. 7, August 1930, p. 7, svodka No. 8, October 1930, p. 18. This general increase in stocks concealed a precipitate decline in the stocks of fuel and other scarce inputs to dangerously low levels (see *Industrializatsiya, 1929–1932* (1970), 233, and, for October–December 1929, the decree of Vesenkha presidium dated March 8, 1930 – TsGANKh, 3429/1/5193, 65).

[379] PKh, 7–8, 1930, 30 (Guberman), referring to 1929/30 as a whole.

[380] EZh, April 8, 1930.

which had to be cancelled when only fifty people had turned up an hour after it was scheduled to begin.[381] In a vain endeavour to stop the slide to lower quality, Kuibyshev, in an article devoted to this topic in the industrial newspaper, emphasised that the 'shocking quality of our output threatens to reduce a considerable part of our achievements to zero'.[382] As cost reduction was measured in terms of the costs of 'comparable' products, the widespread deterioration in the quality of a 'comparable' product meant that a recorded reduction in the cost of producing it was often spurious. Kuibyshev pointed out that it was 'completely useless' to reduce the cost of a tractor if the tractor subsequently broke down in the field.[383]

(iii) Khozraschet under threat

While the outcome of the cost reduction campaign indicated that industrial enterprises were still under some effective pressure to improve their financial performance, the fate of khozraschet (economic accounting) in industry unambiguously demonstrated that the drive to increase the quantity of output predominated in practice over financial efficiency. The decree on industrial reoganisation of December 5, 1929, strongly emphasised the importance of khozraschet. It claimed that earlier decisions to transfer all industrial enterprises to khozraschet had proved 'entirely justified', and stipulated that in future the difference between planned and actual costs, if requirements for quality of production were met, should be 'a basic indicator of the success of the work of the enterprise'. The decree provided that every enterprise should have a monthly balance, and that shops and other units within the enterprise should keep a careful record of expenditure and results.[384] Detailed legislation soon followed.[385]

---

[381] ZI, April 12, 1930.

[382] ZI, June 14, 1930.

[383] ZI, June 14, 1930; see also the striking comments in Syrtsov, *Nakanune* (1930), 19–20.

[384] *Direktivy*, ii (1957), 126–33.

[385] Model Statute on the Shop in an Industrial Enterprise, approved by Rabkrin and Vesenkha December 23, 1929 (SP VSNKh, 1929/30, art. 662, dated January 20, 1930); joint letter of Vesenkha and AUCCTU (SP VSNKh, 1929/30, art. 997, dated March 11, 1930). The decree of December 5 and the

The legislation on khozraschet was almost entirely ignored in practice. The role of khozraschet continued to decline throughout industry. In June 1930, the Chief Inspectorate of Vesenkha reported that none of the factories it investigated in a recent survey had carried out the directives on transferring shops to khozraschet; often the shops had not even heard of the Model Statute.[386] A Vesenkha report to Sovnarkom also acknowledged that 'the introduction of khozraschet in shops is taking place extremely slowly', but claimed that in most industries factories as a whole had been transferred to khozraschet.[387] But the transfer, when it occurred, was almost never accompanied by greater attention to khozraschet in practice. In retrospect, Molotov claimed that the provisions about khozraschet in the decree of December 1929 had not been applied and that during 1930 attention to khozraschet had fallen off.[388] Birman, the outspoken industrial administrator, characterised the post-1929 period as 'the new non-khozraschet period'.[389] The declining significance attached to khozraschet in 1930 was reflected in public attitudes. At a conference convened by *Pravda*, a representative of the chemical industry tactlessly pointed out that it was absurd to hope to introduce khozraschet in factory shops at a time when the 'principle of khozraschet' was 'dying out' in industrial corporations as a whole, and was 'to a considerable extent a sign of a Right-wing deviation'.[390] Nor were the theorists firmly tied to the principle of khozraschet in the first few months of 1930. In spite of the decree of December 5, 1929, D'yachenko argued that changes were imminent within the state sector which amounted to the 'beginning of the end of "khozraschet"'. This reflected the widespread view that with the growth of comprehensive physical planning no real

---

Model Statute did not specifically use the term 'khozraschet' in relation to the shop, but the joint letter did (see Venediktov, ii (1961), 638).

[386] ZI, June 3, 1930.

[387] *Industrializatsiya, 1929–1932* (1970), 219 (a report to a STO session held on June 16, cited from the archives).

[388] Speech at the first industrial conference, reported in I, February 12, 1931; this conference will be discussed in vol. 4.

[389] PI, 8, 1931, 5.

[390] P, April 16, 1930.

distinction could be made between establishments financed from the state budget and enterprises financed by khozraschet.[391]

(iv) The decline of financial controls

In the winter of 1929–30 significant institutional changes reflected the almost contemptuous attitude of the authorities to financial constraints and controls. In the 1920s the arbitration system, through which organisations and enterprises claimed fines and other penalties from each other for failure to carry out agreed obligations, was an important instrument for maintaining good order in economic relations by financial controls. In addition to the general system of State Arbitration attached to STO, an extensive network of arbitration commissions was established within the People's Commissariats; their function was to adjudicate between organisations when both were subordinate to the same commissariat. A Sovnarkom decree dated December 13, 1929, abruptly abolished all these commissions, and those of the cooperatives; such disputes were henceforth handled through the legal system only by appeal to State Arbitration.[392] Most of the output of enterprises subordinate to Vesenkha was sold to other enterprises within Vesenkha; the effect of the decree was therefore to reduce greatly the influence of contracts as a means of financial discipline for this vast number of transactions.

Long-established instruments for the control of budgetary expenditure were also swept aside. In the spring of 1929 the authority of Gosfinkontrol', the Chief Administration for Financial Supervision, which formed part of Narkomfin, was weakened by limiting its powers to organisations financed entirely from the budget. External audit of the financial activities of organisations on khozraschet was henceforth the sole

---

[391] VF, 1, 1930, 59; see also Maimin, in EZh, October 12, 1929. In EZh, June 25, 1930, Veisbrod even argued that khozraschet within the industrial enterprise was counterposed to the planning principle.

[392] SZ, 1930, art. 60. Like several other important decrees at this time, its transmission and publication were delayed. Vesenkha received it on January 24, 1930, and ordered the abolition of its arbitration commissions with effect from March 15 (SP VSNKh, 1929/30, art. 710, dated January 28).

responsiblity of Rabkrin.[393] In 1929/30, as a result of this measure only a quarter of budgetary expenditure in the case of industry and 22 per cent in the case of agriculture were liable to inspection by Gosfinkontrol'; over 90 per cent of its central staff was engaged in inspecting the accounts of transport, posts and defence.[394] But this reform did not go far enough to satisfy Rabkrin, which argued, with the support of the trade union organisations in Narkomfin, that it should absorb Gosfinkontrol'.[395] Advocates of the Rabkrin proposals insisted that formal checks on budgetary discipline must give way to a broader 'supervision from the point of view of the national economy'; Gosfinkontrol' was accused of being a dilatory and bureaucratic organisation which had to turn to Rabkrin to put its proposals into effect. Narkomfin, however, urged upon Sovnarkom the alternative course of restoring the powers of Gosfinkontrol' over khozraschet organisations.[396] As was normal in 1929/30, the views of Rabkrin prevailed. With effect from February 15, 1930, Gosfinkontrol', the equivalent republican administrations and all their local agencies were abolished.[397] Henceforth the preparation of reports on expenditure by Narkomfin was confined to putting together accounts received from individual government departments and from the union republics; all inspection of documents was entirely the responsibility of the department concerned, under the supervision of Rabkrin, and assisted by voluntary teams of workers.[398] On April 22, 1930, a further Sovnarkom decree greatly reduced the amount of detail required in departmental returns of budgetary expenditure; this reinforced the decision in April 1928 to transfer responsibility for re-allocating expenditure between

---

[393] See *Uproshchenie finansovoi sistemy* (1930), 44–8. Gosfinkontrol' was separated from Rabkrin in October 1923 and closely corresponded to the pre-revolutionary Ministry of State Control; its powers were already limited in practice following a decree of November 1926 (see Carr and Davies (1969), 724).

[394] *Uproshchenie finansovoi sistemy* (1930), 44–8; EZh, November 30, 1929 (Lyando); the latter source reports that Gosfinkontrol' inspected only 20–25 per cent of all budgetary expenditure.

[395] Decision of March 12–17, 1929, reported in EZh, November 30, 1929.

[396] EZh, November 30, 1929 (Lyando); see also EZh, July 2, 1929.

[397] SZ, 1930, art. 99 (dated February 1).

[398] *TsIK 3/V*, No. 5, 2–4 (Chutskaev).

sub-divisions of the state budget from Narkomfin to the commissariat concerned and its major divisions.[399]

(v) The unified financial plan

On May 23, 1930, the decision of TsIK and Sovnarkom to establish a 'unified financial plan' marked the culmination of the efforts to subsume the traditional state budget within a wider financial plan designed to assist economic expansion.[400] The Gosplans of the USSR, the RSFSR and the Ukraine had for several years urged upon the authorities the necessity of compiling what was variously known as a 'financial plan', a 'plan of the financial balance', a 'comprehensive (svodnyi) financial plan' and a 'unified (edinyi) financial plan'.[401] At the beginning of 1929, Narkomfin published what it described as 'a first attempt at constructing a unified financial plan', relating to the economic year 1928/29;[402] and in September 1929 Narkomfin submitted summary tables of a unified financial plan for 1929/30 to Gosplan and Sovnarkom.[403]

The decision of May 23, 1930, resolved three contentious issues about the nature and function of the unified financial plan. First, should the plan incorporate in money terms all transfers of resources in the economy, including all movement of goods and money? Secondly, should it be merely an instrument to assist the planners, or should it have 'operational-directive' functions? Thirdly, should it be the responsibility of Gosplan or of Narkomfin? On the first issue, the Ukrainian

[399] SZ, 1930, art. 278; for the measures of April 1928 see Carr and Davies (1969), 721–3.

[400] SZ, 1930, art. 315; on May 24, a Sovnarkom decree announced arrangements for the immediate preparation of the unified financial plan for 1930/31 (SZ, 1930, art. 370).

[401] For the history of the unified financial plan, see Davies (1958), 152–3, Carr and Davies (1969), 730–2, and Lyando (1963), 65–6; according to Kul'chitskii (Kiev, 1979), 21, Lyando participated in the first attempts at 'synthetic financial planning' at the end of the 1920s; he was apparently a member of Rabkrin transferred to Narkomfin.

[402] VF, 2, 1929, 66–103.

[403] See Lyando (1963), 65–6; this was presumably a response to the instruction of TsIK and Sovnarkom of April 24, 1929, that the 1929/30 draft state budget should be accompanied by a 'comprehensive (svodnyi) plan for financing the national economy' (SZ, 1929, art. 245).

Gosplan strongly contended that the plan should be comprehensive, covering financial flows between units and sectors of the economy as well as financial relations controlled by the state, but Narkomfin rejected this ambitious proposal as premature.[404] The lack of adequate statistical material, and the complexities involved in preparing what amounted to a complete *tableau économique*, dictated the decision of Sovnarkom to uphold the Narkomfin view. The unified financial plan was restricted to the state and local budgets, the financial plans of the various sectors of the economy, social and state insurance and the credit plans.[405] On the second issue, the most enthusiastic advocates of the unified financial plan contended that it should be approved by Sovnarkom as a document with the same legal force as the state budget.[406] Sovnarkom, however, resolved that the unified financial plan should not replace 'the separate operational plans (the state budget, the financial plans of industry, credit plans, etc.)' but would 'facilitate their mutual reconciliation and secure the most suitable direction of resources, and economy in their use'. It was to be integrated with the annual control figures for the national economy, and submitted to Sovnarkom and TsIK for approval, and Sovnarkom would consider reports on its implementation.[407] It was thus an operational rather than a research plan, but without the administrative–executive functions of the state budget.

The third issue was hotly contested. In view of the past hostility of Narkomfin to economic planning, Gosplan officials argued that Narkomfin should retain merely a treasury function, and the responsibilities of its planning departments should be reduced still further.[408] M. Bogolepov, head of the budget and financial section of Gosplan, contended that the authority of the control figures would be reduced if Narkomfin took all financial planning into its own hands.[409] But Narkomfin was now

---

[404] VF, 2, 1929, 67; the view that for successful financial planning all transactions in the economy must be incorporated in the unified financial plan is persuasively argued by one of the authors of the Ukrainian schema in VF, 5, 1929, 48–62.

[405] See Lyando (1963), 66.

[406] VF, 5, 1929, 62.

[407] SZ, 1930, art. 315.

[408] Lyando (1963), 67–8.

[409] NPF, 7, April 15, 1930, 48–50.

Bolshevised and thoroughly reconstituted. In the discussion about the unified financial plan, a senior official of Narkomfin argued that it should be transformed from a government department 'almost exclusively concerned with the budgetary system' into a 'single financial centre controlling directly or indirectly the whole financial economy of the socialised sector'; it should prepare the unified financial plan as a working hypothesis preliminary to the final assembly of the national-economic plan as a whole.[410] In the atmosphere of increased concern for financial stability which prevailed in the spring of 1930, these proposals were accepted: Narkomfin was entrusted with the responsibility of preparing the unified financial plan and submitting it simultaneously to Sovnarkom and Gosplan.[411] At an extended session of the collegium of Narkomfin which met a few days after the publication of the decree on the unified financial plan, the spokesman for Narkomfin hailed May 23 as a 'jubilee date in the history of the development of Soviet finance and in the history of Narkomfin'.[412] Narkomfin was rehabilitated; but in practice the diminution of the status of the state budget further weakened financial control.

(vi) The credit reform

The credit reform of January 1930 was the most far-reaching and remarkable of all the changes in the financial system associated with the industrialisation drive. Throughout the 1920s the State Bank, Gosbank, was the most conservative of all Narkomfin institutions. According to a contemporary account, Gosbank at first took no initiative in the reform, but 'the position changed fundamentally with the advent of cde. *Pyatakov'* as chairman of the bank early in 1929.[413] Pyatakov, former 'super-industrialist' and member of the united opposition, was fully committed to forced industrialisation; the bank under his leadership made 'a sharp turn to the planning principle in credit', and took the initiative in pressing for the reform.[414] In

[410] I, April 16, 1930 (I. Ivanov, discussion article).
[411] SZ, 1930, art. 315.
[412] EZh, May 28, 1930 (Teumin).
[413] PI, 6, 1930, 17 (Kornitskii); for Pyatakov's appointment see Carr and Davies (1969), 738–9.
[414] PI, 6, 1930, 17; EZh, February 19, 1930 (Nagler).

June 1929 the position of Gosbank was strengthened by a new Statute, the first since 1921, which made it independent of Narkomfin.[415] During the summer of 1929 draft proposals for credit reform were submitted to a government commission on the rationalisation of trade chaired by Shmidt.

The most contentious question was the future role of commercial credit created by the issue of promissory notes (vekseli) from purchasers to suppliers. Throughout NEP this was a basic form of payment for goods, used by the suppliers for their own subsequent payments or discounted in the bank. This created a flow of credit which was not directly under the control of Gosbank, and was held to be a serious limitation on central financial planning. The replacement of promissory notes by Gosbank credits was proposed in a project for credit reform prepared by A. V. Veisbrod, a Rabkrin official, and was supported by Gosbank in its own project submitted to the Shmidt commission.[416] While the currency reform of 1924 had been almost universally accepted, the Gosbank project met with 'strong opposition from a number of major financial officials and business managers'.[417] Narkomfin argued that the proposals were premature. Vesenkha officials resisted the reform on the grounds that the right of industrial organisations to issue commercial credit to each other was essential to the maintenance of khozraschet, and also claimed that the abolition of commercial credit would increase the pressure on the state budget.[418] The

[415] EZh, July 24, 1929. The People's Commissar for Finance nevertheless remained chairman of the Council of the bank which replaced the Committee for Bank Affairs, and was responsible for deciding the upper limit of banknote issue on the basis of directives from STO; for the Committee for Bank Affairs, see Carr and Davies (1969), 729. Party influence in the bank was further strengthened by the appointment of A. M. Kaktyn' and M. M. Karklin as deputy chairmen on December 28, 1929 (P, December 30, 1929; SZ, 1929, ii, art. 306).

[416] VF, 6, 1929, 3 (Katsenelenbaum); at the XVI party congress in June 1930 Ordzhonikidze described the reform as 'elaborated by us [Rabkrin] jointly with cde. Pyatakov' (Ordzhonikidze, *Stat'i rechi*, ii (1957), 216).

[417] EZh, May 18, 1930 (Lupandin); PI, 6, 1930, 17 (Kornitskii); Kaktyn' claimed that the 'reactionary bourgeois professors' in the Shmidt commission had also all opposed the reform (EZh, June 28, 1930).

[418] TPG, June 14, 1929 (Birbraer); EZh, July 11 (Barun), 23 (Blyum), 1929. According to BP (Prague), lxxviii (April 1930), 18, behind the public silence of the industrial newspaper throughout nearly all the discussion, in private Vesenkha strongly opposed the reform.

reform was eventually approved in principle by TsIK and Sovnarkom on November 30, 1929.[419] The decision having been made, both Vesenkha and the cooperatives now insisted at a banking conference that it must be carried through rapidly as a single act, and not delayed to the end of 1929/30.[420]

On January 30, 1930, a short decree of TsIK and Sovnarkom set out the main principles of the credit reform, which was to come into operation on April 1. Its objective was to place all short-term credit firmly in the hands of the central authorities. Commercial credit via promissory notes would be eliminated, and short-term credit would in future be available only from Gosbank. The newly-established corporations, each responsible for a branch of industry, would each be allocated in the credit plan an agreed 'general limit' or maximum sum of credit for each quarter. This limit would be distributed in the plan among the enterprises of the corporation, but the latter could vary this allocation in the interests of increased production. On the basis of the credit plan Gosbank would issue credit to enterprises via its branches.[421]

The importance attached by the authorities to the successful implementation of the reform was indicated by the appointment by Pyatakov as a member of STO on February 12, 1930.[422] Pyatakov celebrated his appointment by writing an article in *Pravda* in which he announced in glowing terms that the reform would 'to a considerable extent turn the credit system into an accounting system'. The bank would henceforth operate the principle that the supply of resources would be determined by 'the plan and the real process of material production and distribution'. It would not be 'to any extent an agency administering our economy or economic enterprises'; its work with enterprises would be 'largely automatic'. Pyatakov attempted, however, to show that the reform was compatible with the maintenance of financial control. If an enterprise

---

[419] EZh, June 28, 1930.

[420] EZh, May 29, 1930 (Nagler); the conference was held in January–February 1930.

[421] SZ, 1930, art. 98; the proposals had been approved by the Politburo on January 20 (*Industrializatsiya, 1929–1932* (1970), 588).

[422] SZ, 1930, art. 72. Pyatakov already attended meetings of Sovnarkom and STO: the previous October at a Sovnarkom session he emphatically declared his support for the industrialisation drive (see p. 183 above and vol. 1, p. 148).

exceeded its credit limit, the bank would automatically signal this to the corporation, indicating whether the weakness was in costs, production or stocks; the enterprise would obtain additional credit only if it could prove to the corporation that a mistake had been made in the plan. Pyatakov also stressed that the bank would transfer payments from purchasers to suppliers only after the purchaser had formally accepted the goods, and the purchaser would be obliged to check that the goods had been supplied at the required quality, at the right time and in the right quantity. But the main thrust of Pyatakov's convictions emerged clearly in his peroration:

> The credit cloud is dispersed. The magic of banks gives way to simple economic accounting and calculation. The shell of credit falls off and the clear features of the process of production and circulation in physical terms are emerging.
>
> We are entering the stage of the socialist transformation of credit institutions.[423]

Presiding over a reform in which he had taken a personal initiative, and which he saw as a crucial moment in the transition to a socialist planned economy, Pyatakov must have felt that his achievement fully justified the ignominy of his political capitulation.

Kaktyn', one of Pyatakov's deputies in Gosbank, also presented the reform as contributing both to the advance of physical planning and to financial efficiency. The increase in 'cashless accounting' would 'strengthen the tendency for money gradually to die out as a means of payment and accumulation', turning money increasingly into 'accounting units', which in turn increasingly resembled 'labour units'. But the growth of cashless accounts would also result in a decline in the amount of currency in circulation; the elimination of promissory notes would prevent concealment of financial deficits; the clear enterprise Balances which would be available would assist khozraschet.[424]

In some articles published in connection with the reform the main stress was placed on the contribution of the reform to

---

[423] P, February 14, 1930.
[424] EZh, February 15, 1930.

achieving a moneyless economy, in others on the improvement in financial discipline. A writer in the former category even argued that banking functions were disappearing from the Soviet economy. Bank operations between two parties were dying out altogether because of the decline in private economic relations, and the banks were losing their direct responsibility to provide finance for industry and trade; the time had come to transform Gosbank into 'a grandiose recording and accounting centre for the socialist economy of our Soviet Union'.[425] On the other hand an official of the Ukrainian Gosbank was equally anxious to show that the reform would not provide a basis for the unlimited issue of money. He reported that his bank had already successfully replaced promissory notes by bank credits in its dealings with the Ukrainian coal industry: when obligations were not fulfilled the bank imposed sanctions and in exceptional cases declared a moratorium on payments.[426] An editorial in the industrial newspaper similarly stressed that an enterprise which exceeded its credit limit would inevitably find itself in difficulties because Gosbank would take 'energetic measures' to prevent currency issue and credit in excess of the plans.[427] According to one economist, the reform was 'a change in the forms of pressure on the economic agencies exercised by the credit system', and would result in more severe controls.[428]

If the image of the reform presented in the press was ambiguous, in its application it soon proved to be an instrument for large increases in currency and credit. Several major features of the reform undermined any hope that it would maintain financial disicpline. First, the influence of the purchaser over the supplier diminished rather than increased as a result of the reform. The bank claimed that the intended system by which payments would depend on acceptance by the purchaser was unworkable. Instead payments were automatically debited against the purchaser's account when the standard invoice was presented by the supplier.[429] The bank even refused to handle

---

[425] V. Korobkov, in EZh, January 14, 1930; he cited in favour of this view his own article on 'labour units' published in the same newspaper on February 9, 1919, at the time of War Communism.

[426] EZh, February 21, 1930 (Pevzner).

[427] ZI, February 26, 1930.

[428] EO, 2, 1930, 28, 30 (Blyum).

[429] A standard invoice (schet-faktura) prepared by the Institute of Management Technique of Rabkrin jointly with Gosbank was published in P, May

claims from purchasers against suppliers when goods were inadequate in quantity or quality, claiming that this was the responsibility of the arbitration commissions.[430] Confronted by indignant objections, Kaktyn' told a special meeting of the board of Gosbank with business managers that 'the bank is not a notary or a trading expert'.[431] A leading bank official told a similar meeting that the reform presupposed that 'invoices are accurate and clients are conscientious'; he conceded, however, that it might be possible for the bank to charge claims from purchasers against the suppliers' accounts pending the settlement of the dispute by arbitration.[432]

The second obvious weakness of the reform was that it became very difficult for Gosbank to discover whether or to what extent one of its clients was in debt. Before the reform, the current and loan accounts of the enterprise were separate; on the loan account loans were made and promissory notes discounted for specific purposes. Now each enterprise held a single account (kontokorrent) with the bank on which all debits and credits were recorded; the account did not show separate sources of income or types of outlays. When an enterprise exceeded its credit limit, it was impossible for the bank to know whether this was due to temporary factors, or to excessive costs; it was confronted with demands for additional credit which it was unable to adjudicate upon.[433]

Thirdly, credit was issued, within the credit limit, in accordance with the plan (pod plan), whether the plan had been carried out or not: an enterprise with lower production and higher costs than planned could nevertheless receive the full planned credit.[434]

To these inherent weaknesses in the reform were added enormous confusion and disorder due to inadequate preparation

---

18, 1930; it simply listed the quantity, weight and price of items despatched, and did not have to indicate the plan or the order from the purchaser authorising the supply.

[430] EZh, April 10, 1930.

[431] EZh, April 22, 1930; for typical demands for the introduction of 'preliminary acceptance' see EZh, May 21, 1930.

[432] EZh, May 20, 1930.

[433] FP, 7–8, 1930, 16–18 (Kaktyn'), 19–27 (K. L. [Lupandin], reporting a survey carried out by Rabkrin in July–August 1930).

[434] EZh, May 18, 1930; FP, 7–8, 1930, 22.

and hasty execution. The administrative muddle was in sharp contrast to the systematic care with which the currency reform of 1924 was put into effect.[435] In both conception and execution, the credit reform had obvious features in common with the collectivisation drive which was at its height when the reform was introduced. The volume of business handled by Gosbank suddenly greatly increased, without any corresponding increase in staff.[436] No serious preparation had been made for dealing with the vast accretion of interlocking debts between clients. An editorial in the government newspaper complained of the 'complete absence of a plan': three months after the promulgation of the reform, government departments had not yet presented credit plans which could be used by Gosbank as a basis for compiling the general credit plan and the unified financial plan.[437] Credit limits for the April–June quarter had not been fixed by the bank even by the end of May.[438] Bank officials claimed, and a Rabkrin survey confirmed, that clients used the absence of credit limits to get as much as possible from the bank, and in the absence of clear arrangements for debt settlement simply 'flung' all their debt documents at the bank.[439]

In the first three months following the announcement of the reform, administrative disorder, coupled with a certain caution on the part of Gosbank about the amount of credit it should make available, led to a vast increase in unsettled claims for payments, which reached a peak in the middle of May 1930. Some enterprises found themselves in financial difficulties and were unable to pay wages.[440] But even in these months new credit issues were substantial; and from the middle of May 1930, when the reform began to work better in a technical sense,[441] credit swelled to an unprecedented level. In June, a

---

[435] EZh, May 18, 1930 (Lupandin). Pilot schemes covering various aspects of the reform had, however, been carried out with the Oil Syndicate and Donugol' in the previous two years (VF, 1, 1930, 10–13).

[436] EZh, April 12 (Blyum, a Gosbank official), June 28 (Kaktyn'), August 15 (Zangvill'), 1930.

[437] I, April 20, 1930; the Vesenkha proposals for the April–June quarter were submitted on April 16 (EZh, April 22, 1930 (Kaktyn')).

[438] EZh, May 29, 1930 (Kaktyn').

[439] EZh, April 22 (official of Moscow office of bank), August 15 (Rabkrin survey), 1930.

[440] EZh, April 22, June 28, 1930.

[441] EZh, July 30, 1930 (Kaktyn').

report to a sitting of the board of Gosbank, with Pyatakov in the chair, frankly admitted that financial discipline had declined because the bank was unable to control credit issues.[442] The prevailing atmosphere was vividly portrayed in the Soviet press. The attitude of industrial officials and managers to the reform was 'cool, not to say negligent and contemptuous'.[443] They continuously pressed the bank for additional financial resources, and the bank, just because it was now oriented to the needs of production, felt itself responsible for ensuring an uninterrupted flow of financial resources to industry, and was therefore unwilling to impose strict credit limits.[444]

Only the higher political authorities could bring this situation to an end by firm intervention to control the flow of credit. In June, a government directive imposed specific restrictions on the growth of the debt of industry to the bank for the July–September quarter.[445] But the directives were not enforced, and for the moment the political authorities displayed a remarkable complacency. Stalin reported the reform to the XVI party congress in an uncritical spirit. According to Stalin, the concentration of all short-term credit in Gosbank and the establishment of cashless accounting within the socialist sector had two major consequences, both of which he presented as entirely positive:

> The first is that Gosbank is being transformed into a general state *apparat* for recording the production and distribution of products; the second, that large masses of money are being freed from circulation. There can be no doubt that these measures will lead (they are already leading) to the establishment of good order in the whole credit system and to the strengthening of our ruble (chervonets).[446]

A few weeks later, on August 11, 1930, after Sovnarkom had heard reports from Rabkrin and Gosbank on the results of the reform, it issued a decree which, while admitting 'great difficulties and faults', and that financial and credit discipline

---

[442] EZh, June 24, 1930.
[443] I, April 20, 1930 (editorial).
[444] I, July 30, 1930 (Miroshnikov).
[445] EZh, June 24, 1930.
[446] Stalin, *Soch.*, xii, 330–1.

had been 'considerably weakened', nevertheless claimed that 'the reform was timely and its basic principles were correct', and praised its 'great importance for strengthening the planning principle and the principles of khozraschet'. The decree made a number of detailed recommendations, but left the main practices of the reform intact. Its most radical but still extremely mild provision was a concession to objections to automatic payment; in the case of individual suppliers who were 'not conscientious' Gosbank could rule their invoices would not be paid until accepted by the purchaser.[447] Such complacency was wholly inadequate, and a few days later the deputy chairman of the bank complained that the 'higher controlling agencies' – this must have referred to the Politburo or Sovnarkom – while criticising credit policy as too liberal, had 'failed to afford the bank the necessary help in its struggle with those agencies which are trying to turn this liberalism into a rule'.[448] This remarkably frank public criticism reflected the extreme exasperation of a party member made responsible for carrying through the reform and now unable to extricate the bank from the resulting disorder without firm intervention from above.

[447] SZ, 1930, art. 504.
[448] I, August 16, 1930 (Kaktyn').

CHAPTER EIGHT

THE XVI PARTY CONGRESS, JUNE 26–JULY 13, 1930[1]

The draft resolution for the party congress, 'On the Fulfilment of the Five-Year Plan of Industry', published in *Pravda* on May 21, 1930, celebrated the triumphant advance of industrialisation in enthusiastic terms. It declared that 'the USSR is being transformed with unprecedented speed from a backward agrarian country into an advanced country', and condemned the Right for their 'attack on the line of the party on the main decisive question – the question of the rapid rate of industrialisation'. It claimed that the optimum variant of the five-year plan adopted in May 1929 would be achieved in three years in several major industries, including coal, oil and agricultural and general engineering.

Articles and speeches in advance of the congress also saluted the ambitious plans now in force as entirely realistic, and stressed their urgent necessity in view of the increased military danger to the USSR presented by the growing crisis in the capitalist world. Kaganovich, at the Moscow regional party conference, praised the 'Bolshevik tempos' prevailing in industry, and noted the 'exceptional role' of Rabkrin in the adoption of higher plans in face of ignorance and wrecking. Boldly asserting that 'History gave us no other way out but tense plans', he warned the delegates that 'we must live through the next 1–1 $^1/_2$ years – they are the most difficult years'. But the rewards for this effort would be immense: while the *New York Times*' correspondent had admitted that the USSR might be the second great world power in 1940, this was an underestimation:

---

[1] Agricultural aspects of the congress are discussed in vol. 1, pp. 330–6.

We are convinced that 1940 will see only one great world power – the USSR![2]

The continuing danger of Rightist influence in the party was a prominent theme of pre-congress speeches. At the XI Ukrainian party congress Rudzutak condemned the 'cowardly' attempts of the Right to prove that 'we have run too far ahead':

They say that we have begun to build 5 houses this year when there are bricks only for 4; and ask whether it wouldn't be better to give up building the 5th house and complete the building of 4. But we say – let's press ahead with all our might and we will also build the 5th house.[3]

Both Rykov and Tomsky condemned their own past errors and supported the central committee in pre-congress speeches (see vol. 1, p. 327). Bukharin, however, was conspicuously silent. A *Pravda* editorial strongly criticised him for failing to renounce his own views on 'organised capitalism'[4], and he was also vigorously condemned by the bureau of the party cell of the scientific research sector of Vesenkha, which he headed.[5] At party meetings held before the congress, open criticisms of the central committee were mainly concerned with collectivisation (see vol. 1, pp. 322–7). A few voices were also raised against excessive rates of industrialisation: according to one report, at party meetings Rightists opposed the slogan 'the five-year plan in four years' as a 'second dizziness with success', and called for 'a return to the five-year plan'.[6]

Trotsky, in exile in Turkey, was also strongly convinced that

[2] P, June 8, 1930; the *New York Times'* correspondent was Duranty. For Molotov's similar speech to the Leningrad regional conference, see P, June 11, 1930.

[3] P, June 14, 1930.

[4] P, June 7, 1930.

[5] ZI, July 2, 1930; the bureau resolution, dated June 30, argued rather unconvincingly that he had failed to place sufficient stress on socio-economic relations and the class struggle in an article on socialist reconstruction and the natural sciences; the offending article appeared in a brochure issued by the sector in preparation for the congress, and was reprinted in Bukharin, *Etyudy* (1932), 211–35. For similar criticisms of Bukharin, see P, July 2, 1930, disk. listok 26 (Vasil'kovskii and Treivas) and P, July 9, 1930 (Pozern).

[6] P, June 23, 1930, disk. listok 18 (Kruglikov).

industrialisation was being forced ahead at an unrealistic pace.[7] In an 'Open Letter to the CPSU', dated March 23, 1930, he condemned as *'adventurism'* both the excesses of collectivisation and the unrestrained tempos of industrialisation, reflected in the slogan 'the five-year plan in four': the excessive rate of growth had led to 'the symptoms of a threatening economic crisis'. He called for 'an end to the "racetrack-gallop" pace of industrialisation', which had reduced the living standards of the population, and for an end to inflation.[8] He reverted to this theme frequently in the weeks before the congress, writing in June 1930 of 'the necessity for a decisive revision of all the supplementary industrial plans of the last eighteen months or two years'.[9] Members of the Left opposition in exile within the USSR differed on how to react to the 'ultra-leftism' of the party leadership. Rakovsky, V. Kosior, N. Muralov and Kasparova, in their statement of April 1930, while strongly critical of the collectivisation drive and the increasing oppression within the party, argued that the retreat from collectivisation 'might turn into disorderly flight, a *catastrophe*'. For this reason the renunciation of comprehensive collectivisation must be combined with 'increased construction of sovkhozy' and with 'the retention of the tempo of industry (so sokhraneniem tempa promyshlennosti)'.[10] Rakovsky's support for the tempo of

---

[7] For a further discussion of the views of Trotsky and the Left opposition at this time, see vol. 1, pp. 327–8.

[8] *Writings of Leon Trotsky (1930)* (1975), 135–50, first published in BO (Paris), x (April 1930), 2–7.

[9] *Writings of Leon Trotsky (1930)* (1975), 263; BO (Paris), xii–xiii (June–July 1930), 28–9; this is the text of a letter dated June 1930. See also *ibid.* 168–85 (article of April 13, first published in *The Militant*, June 21, 28, 1930), and BO (Paris), xi (May 1930), 11–19).

[10] The full text first appeared in BO (Paris), xvii–xviii (November–December 1930), 11–19 (see also vol. 1, p. 328). Extracts were published at the time of the party congress (BO (Paris), xiv (August 1930), 23–4 – Trotsky wrote 'we are publishing this issue while having in our hands only the reports of the first sittings of the congress' – *ibid.* p. 2). These extracts reached Trotsky in a letter sent from the USSR to the French Trotskyist Pierre Naville in Paris; this letter, written in French, is in the Trotsky archives (T 17307), and gives the phrase about the tempo of industrialisation as *'tout en maintenant le rhythme du développement industriel'* (*'while maintaining the rate of industrial development'*); this is mistranslated in the extract in Trotsky's bulletin by the much stronger expression 'vsemernaya podderzhka tempa promyshlennogo razvitiya' ('complete support for the rate of industrial development'), but appears in the correct Russian in the full version published in the bulletin at the end of the year.

industrialisation divided the exiles. A letter sent to Rakovsky from a colony of exiles in Kazakhstan reported these divisions of opinion. One group supported his view that the urgent task was to prevent the retreat from going too far: 'we call upon the workers and the working peasants to support with their shoulders the cart which the bureaucrats almost allowed to fall, in order to save its socialist load'. Another group argued that the 'adventurist period of ultra-leftism' in industrialisation was continuing, and claimed that to support it would deepen the economic crisis and impoverish the working class: 'we are for achievable industrialisation'. Trotsky rather lamely declared himself unable to adjudicate without full information, adding that disagreement about whether growth would be 25 or 30 per cent this year 'cannot be a subject for a dispute *of principle*'.[11]

While Soviet official hostility was primarily directed towards the Right, Trotsky also came in for abuse. An article in *Pravda* indignantly repudiated his criticism of the slogan 'the five-year plan in four', insisted that 'the past seven months have shown that the rates adopted are entirely realistic' and even claimed that plans were likely to be still further increased.[12] Yaroslavsky, addressing the Moscow regional party conference, cited a letter allegedly written by a Trotskyist which declared that Trotskyists were willing to place themselves at the head of peasant uprisings(!). Yaroslavsky, setting out on the path which led a few years later to the arraigning of oppositionists as spies of the Gestapo, claimed that this demonstrated 'the *fascisation* of the Trotskyists'.[13] Oppositionists in exile suffered worsening living conditions on the eve of the congress, and many of them were subjected to rigorous and humiliating searches.[14]

---

[11] BO (Paris), xiv (August 1930), 23–4; the letter from the exiles appears in the Trotsky archives as T 17307 (in French); it was addressed from 'Khodzhent', presumably Khodzhikent, South Kazakhstan, 75km. from the nearest railway station. When he received the full text of the Rakovsky statement, Trotsky supported it in his journal as good tactics which had played a part in 'the revival of the Left opposition during the pre-congress discussion', but in the same issue he again declared that 'the revision of the five-year plan to four years was a mistaken step' (BO (Paris), xvii–xviii (November–December 1930), 10–11).

[12] P, May 7, 1930 (Berezin).

[13] P, June 9, 1930.

[14] BO (Paris), xvii–xviii (November–December 1930), 39–41; T 14564 (letter

The congress opened on June 26, 1930. In his lengthy report on the following day, Stalin put his full weight behind the revised plans for industry, asserting that the experience of the first two years demonstrated that 'we can fulfil the five-year plan in four years'.[15] In a whole number of industries, including oil and engineering, the plan could be fulfilled 'in three or even in two-and-a-half years'. But this should provide no grounds for complacency. While the rate of growth was high, in the absolute level of industrial production 'we are devilishly *backward*'; '*a further acceleration*' of the rate of industrial growth was essential. Stalin declared uncompromisingly:

> People who chatter about the necessity of *reducing* the rate of development of industry are enemies of socialism, agents of our class enemies. (*Applause.*)

Later passages in the report stressed that Soviet difficulties, unlike those facing the capitalist countries, were 'not difficulties of decline or *stagnation*, but difficulties of *growth*, of *development*, of the *forward movement*'. Behind the difficulties lurked the 'frantic opposition of dying classes' supported from abroad, which could be overcome only by 'organising an offensive against the capitalist elements *along the whole front* and isolating opportunist elements in our own ranks which hinder the offensive, toss about in panic from side to side and induce in the party lack of confidence in victory'. In a passage which was frequently cited throughout his lifetime and after, Stalin particularly emphasised the importance for the victory of the offensive of socialist emulation and the 'huge break-through in the psychology of the masses', transforming their attitude to labour (see p. 257 above).

Turning to the specific tasks facing the party, Stalin specifically endorsed several of the revised five-year targets. He supported the increase of the five-year plan for the production

---

from Kansk in Siberia). They were able, however, to correspond irregularly with each other, sometimes even by telegram (see BO (Paris), xiv (August 1930), 23–4), and even to communicate with Trotsky by writing to intermediaries living outside the USSR (the Trotsky archives contain a number of letters written in 1930 from his supporters in exile in the USSR – T 15741 provides an incomplete list).

[15] For the report, see Stalin, *Soch.*, xii (1949), 235–373.

of pig-iron in the last year of the plan from 10 to 17 million tons,[16] and the increased plans for tractors (raised from 55,000 to 170,000), vehicles (from 100,000 to 200,000), non-ferrous metals and agricultural engineering. The target for combine-harvesters, which did not appear at all in the five-year plan, was set at 40,000. In another much-cited passage, Stalin stressed the flexibility of the plans, but solely in terms of the desirability of increasing the original targets:

> For us the five-year plan, like any other plan, is a plan adopted merely as a first approximation, which must be corrected, changed and improved on the basis of local experience, on the basis of experience of carrying out the plan ... Only bureaucrats could think that the work of planning is *completed* by compiling the plan. Compiling the plan is only the *beginning of planning*.

Stalin contrasted the '*attenuating* Trotskyist curve' of the Osvok plan of 1925–6 with the '*rising* Bolshevik curve' of industrial production and investment which had actually been attained in 1925/26–1929/30, and drew the lesson that the Trotskyists lacked confidence in socialist construction and hence now regarded the Bolshevik rates of growth as extreme: '*one cannot now distinguish the Trotskyists from our Right deviationists*'.[17]

Although Stalin's report referred briefly to weaknesses in rationalisation, cost reduction and the quality of output which 'press upon our whole economy and prevent it from advancing', the overwhelming stress throughout was on maintaining and extending the rate of growth. Displaying an extravagant confidence in future expansion, he asserted that light industry as well as heavy industry could now develop rapidly:

> We have already restored heavy industry. It is merely necessary to develop it further. Now we can turn towards light industry and move it forward at an accelerated rate.

[16] In *Soch.*, xii, 331, published in 1949, '17 million tons' is replaced by '15–17 million tons'.

[17] For the Osvok plan, compiled under Pyatakov's leadership, see Carr and Davies (1969), 844–51. Stalin failed to mention that Pyatakov urged higher rates of growth upon Osvok and that Trotsky condemned all its estimates as hopelessly inadequate.

On July 2, in reply to the debate, Stalin strongly emphasised the charge that 'the former leaders of the Right opposition do not comprehend our Bolshevik tempos of development, do not believe in these tempos and in general do not accept anything which goes outside the framework of gradual development and the spontaneous flow of events'.[18] In a well-judged peroration much relished by his supporters, Stalin mocked the leaders of the Right, comparing them with Chekhov's 'Man in a Case', who wore galoshes and a padded jacket in July, and always carried an umbrella for fear of bad weather. They were frightened of the smallest cloud on the horizon and were terrified when they saw even a single cockroach, believing that it meant catastrophe. Bukharin wrote to the central committee saying that it was not a cockroach but a thousand raging animals, and predicting that Soviet power would be destroyed within a month, while Rykov declared that disaster would arrive in a month plus two days, and Tomsky nervously warned them not to write documents at all. (The minutes recorded at this point 'Homeric shouts of laughter from the entire hall'.) Then a year later they realised their error and boldly declared that they were not afraid of cockroaches, and that it was a tiny cockroach anyway.[19]

This was the first party congress at which Stalin was fully in command. His fiftieth birthday celebrations had elevated him to a position in which public criticism of any aspect of his policy seemed almost sacrilegious. In his report to the congress he presented himself to the delegates as a tough, shrewd politician, not lacking in humour, combining an impressive grasp of political reality and a clear vision of the socialist future of the Soviet Union – their own image of a heroic version of themselves.

Stalin's report and reply to the discussion dominated and set the tone for the rest of the congress. Ordzhonikidze's report on the work of CCC/Rabkrin discussed at length the efforts of Rabkrin to increase the five-year plans for industry, and amounted to a thorough-going condemnation of the inefficiency of Vesenkha. According to Kuibyshev's biography, after the first half of Ordzhonikidze's report had been delivered on the

---

[18] *Soch.*, xiii (1951), 12.
[19] *Soch.*, xiii (1951), 12–16.

evening of July 2, Kuibyshev was deeply upset, paced about his study most of the night, and then wrote a letter to his young colleagues in Vesenkha in which he declared that the criticisms were 'absolutely true'. In a striking phrase, he compared Vesenkha with a 'ploughman who must plough up his land before sunset because the weather will be bad tomorrow':

(1) the party and its general line speak through Sergo;

(2) the party as always is right;

(3) economic administrators (khozyaistvenniki) must not turn into a kind of caste, they must go with the party, help it disclose faults without fear and fling themselves into the work;

(4) economic administrators must purge themselves and fill their ranks more boldly with fresh proletarian forces.

Consequently 'it is not necessary to permit economic administrators to come forward with criticism of Ordzhonikidze's report'.[20] An editorial published in the industrial newspaper on Kuibyshev's advice praised the work of Rabkrin in industry, especially in bringing about an increase in the targets for the iron and steel industry, and called upon economic administrators to learn to use the methods of work of Rabkrin.[21]

In the course of the debate on Ordzhonikidze's report, Zatonsky from Rabkrin claimed that the initiative in the reorganisation of industry as well as the revision of the five-year plan had been taken by Rabkrin.[22] Mezhlauk, deputy chairman

---

[20] Kuibysheva *et al.* (1966), 300–1, quoting from the archives. Z. Fazin, *Tovarishch Sergo* (1970), 100–3, reports that Ordzhonikidze's wife had 'never seen Sergo so agitated as on that evening' and that he decided not to ring Kuibyshev after delivering the report because he knew 'this would bring no comfort' to him. After Kuibyshev's death his brother showed Kuibyshev's letter to his Vesenkha colleagues to Ordzhonikidze, who commented 'I know how hard it was for the economic administrators, and especially for Valerian, and what a superhuman burden they bore on their shoulders' (Kuibysheva *et al.* (1966), 302). The incident is further discussed in SS, xxxvii (1985), 160–2 (Fitzpatrick).

[21] ZI, July 4, 1930; Ordzhonikidze's report was published in ZI, July 6, 1930, with a large photograph of Ordzhonikidze and a small one of a worried-looking Kuibyshev; in a photograph in ZI, July 13, 1930, Kuibyshev is next to Stalin, and Ordzhonikidze has a friendly hand on Kuibyshev's shoulder.

[22] *XVI s"ezd* (1931), 327.

of Vesenkha, following the line recommended by Kuibyshev, praised Rabkrin for helping the central committee to push through higher plans in the iron and steel industry in spite of strong resistance from industrial officials, and also praised the OGPU for eliminating wreckers. He anticipated that the target of 17 million tons would be reached as early as 1931/32, the fourth year of the plan.[23] This extreme position was not taken up by others in the debate, who were content to suppose that the slogan 'The five-year plan in four' meant that the optimum variant of the plan approved in the spring of 1929 would be reached in four years, so that the new plans were as it were an alternative rather than an addition to the slogan. Lobov, chairman of Vesenkha of the RSFSR, also declared that Ordzhonikidze was 'completely right' to put his criticisms so sharply.[24]

Kuibyshev's report on the five-year plan in industry, delivered on July 7, concentrated on industrial achievements but also praised the work of Rabkrin.[25] The Rabkrin onslaught on Vesenkha continued in this debate. M. Kaganovich, a senior official of Rabkrin, criticised Kuibyshev in hostile terms for his formal attitude to rationalisation.[26] Only Krzhizhanovsky attempted to say a kind word for Vesenkha. While praising Ordzhonikidze for his 'exhaustive picture of negative elements' he also pointed out that the achievements recounted by Kuibyshev in his report far outweighed any defects of industry.[27] In his summing-up Kuibyshev again insisted that the rates of development must be 'maintained and forced up', and singled out the plan to produce '17 million tons of metal' as 'a red thread which runs through the whole period until the end of the five-year plan':

To the question: what is the plan for the remaining three years? the direct short answer can be given – 17 million tons of pig-iron, because 17 millions tons of pig-iron determines all the rest. 17 million tons of pig-iron means a certain amount of machine-building; 17 million tons of pig-iron

[23] *Ibid.* 329–31.
[24] *Ibid.* 361.
[25] *Ibid.* 476–504.
[26] *Ibid.* 521–2.
[27] *Ibid.* 557.

means a certain amount of chemical production; 17 million tons of pig-iron means a certain amount of coal and coke; 17 million tons of pig-iron means that the question of developing transport is solved, and so on. 17 million tons of pig-iron is the most important task.[28]

The debates at the congress reflected the tension within industry resulting from the pressures of industrialisation and from the imposition upon Vesenkha by the central party authorities of unrealistically high targets. Ordzhonikidze, supported by the machinery of Rabkrin, correctly diagnosed that Vesenkha under its present leadership would be unable to cope with the revised five-year plan, and was passionately if erroneously convinced that the revised plans could be achieved. The efforts of Rabkrin were welcomed and encouraged by Stalin and his immediate entourage in the Politburo, as Ordzhonikidze was able to report to the congress. The policies of the Politburo and Rabkrin were eagerly supported by an enthusiastic minority of lower party officials and ordinary members; many of these were primarily younger party members who had reached maturity since the middle of the 1920s. For this minority the high targets and the struggle against wreckers and fainthearts were the banner behind which they rallied for the cause of socialism.[29] Many Vesenkha officials and factory managers, however, were privately sceptical about the viability of the new plans. It is impossible to guess how many silent sceptics there were, as any sign of hostility even to individual features of the new plans, let alone the plans a whole, risked the charge of Right deviation or worse. Even the confidential reports of Gosplan to Sovnarkom, while frank in describing failures to achieve the plans, carefully avoided any hint that the plans themselves were unrealistic.[30] Ordzhonikidze aptly remarked to the congress:

[28] *Ibid.* 563–4.

[29] For reminiscences by young Communists who welcomed the industrialisation drive and found it accorded with their experiences and desires, including Zverev (later Minister of Finance), Patolichev (later a secretary of the party central committee), and two dissidents of the 1960s, Lev Kopelev and General Grigorenko, see Kuromiya (forthcoming), ch. 5.

[30] See for example the Gosplan survey of industrial conjuncture in 1929/30, reproduced from the archives in *Industrializatsiya, 1929–1932* (1970), 224–31.

I think that the CC of our party in reporting its work to you has not and will not be reproved or condemned by the congress for these changes in the five-year plan.[31]

In spite of the prevailing political atmosphere, the revisions of the plans of individual factories and even of whole industries continued to be strongly resisted, albeit in guarded terms. An unsigned article in *Izvestiya* claimed that 'it is not a secret for anyone that some leaders of industrial enterprises, a certain part of the engineering-technical personnel and in some places even the voluntary [i.e. party and trade-union] organisations of industry consider that the high rates of development of the economy, and particularly of industry, are a temporary transitory phenomenon'.[32] At the party congress Ordzhonikidze described the disputes about the iron and steel five-year plan as 'heated',[33] and also referred to 'a certain light-hearted and somewhat contemptuous attitude towards Rabkrin officials on the part of some economic agencies and particular officials'. Faced with this scepticism in industry, his own report, written from the viewpoint of Rabkrin, was couched in such critical terms that some delegates accused him privately, to his shocked astonishment, of presenting 'the secretary of the party cell as the only bright spot in our whole economy and all business managers as worth nothing'.[34] Mezhlauk also acknowledged that the general line of the party had 'often met frantic resistance' from the industrial administration, sometimes supported by party members: the proposal to launch the UKK and the pig-iron target of 17 million tons had been adopted 'by direct decisions of the CC against the soviet apparatus'.[35] The energy and the length of time which Stalin and the other leaders devoted to defending the revised plans at the congress reflected their knowledge of the extent of this scepticism.

Industrial managers, and economic administrators in general, found it equally difficult to accept that the non-party economists and engineers who resisted the higher plans were deliberate

[31] *XVI s"ezd* (1931), 301.
[32] *I*, May 20, 1930.
[33] *XVI s"ezd* (1931), 304.
[34] *Ibid.* 404.
[35] *Ibid.* 300–1; for Mezhlauk's own earlier objections to irresponsible higher targets see p. 213 above.

wreckers set upon undermining the Soviet system. In September 1929, Ordzhonikidze himself, while strongly criticising Groman for his *'dangerous and harmful'* ideology, had nevertheless admitted that he was 'incorruptible'.[36] At the XVI congress, however, he praised the 'tremendous work' of the OGPU in exposing wreckers, explaining that earlier 'a tremendous number of our officials' did not believe that there were many wreckers; 'they thought the OGPU had overstepped the mark, and a great deal of effort was needed to persuade them that wrecking was taking place'.[37] At the congress a pamphlet compiled by the OGPU was distributed to the delegates as information supplementary to Ordzhonikidze's report, with the intention of convincing doubters. It consisted of extracts from the depositions of industrial and Gosplan specialists who were under arrest, and purported to show that 'certain communist economic administrators', lacking adequate technical knowledge, 'were not in a position to rebuff the counter-revolutionary wreckers'; I. Kosior and Lomov were singled out for criticism. It lacked hard evidence of wrecking; and much of the testimony simply bore witness to muddle. But Larichev, former head of the fuel section of Gosplan, confessed to preparing five-year plans that were deliberately set too low; a senior engineer admitted corrupt links with the Swedish communications' equipment firm of Ericsson; and a railway specialist admitted economic espionage for Germany. The leading engineers were portrayed in some detail as a hostile group, influential on economic policy, with strong connections with capitalist firms, elevated in their social origins and linked closely and protectively with one another.[38] None of this amounted to a serious and consistent story of counter-revolutionary activity; but it had an air of verisimilitude for delegates who had no reason to doubt the genuineness of statements made to the OGPU.

At the congress, following Ordzhonikidze's report and the distribution of the pamphlet, Mezhlauk confirmed that in industry 'many officials over a long period were not convinced

---

[36] Ordzhonikidze, ii (1957), 176–7.

[37] *XVI s''ezd* (1931), 319.

[38] *Material k otchetu TsKK* (1930), a 59-page pamphlet; see especially pp. 39 (Larichev), 54–5 (Khibarov on Ericsson), 47 (Gaiduk on German espionage), 5–15 (social origins and behaviour of engineers). It is carefully discussed by S. Fitzpatrick, who first drew attention to it, in SS, xxxvii (1985), 160–2, 169.

that wrecking was taking place right under their noses'.[39] A few months later Krzhizhanovsky admitted at a meeting of the Communist Academy that he and 'probably the majority of economic administrators' had not expected to find that so many leading planning officials were wreckers.[40] But the systematic publicity for forced confessions from those under arrest, the unrelenting pressure for higher targets, the atmosphere in which to resist was dangerous, while to support official policy was to be identified with a great cause: all these factors persuaded doubters to accept both the circumstantial tales of wrecking and the higher targets. Mezhlauk assured the congress that comrades who earlier had been 'quite unable to get used to the rates of growth set by the central committee' were now 'most active organisers' and could be 'fully relied upon'.[41] But this was conviction based on loyalty and false evidence rather than on rational persuasion.

The central committee plenum following the party congress removed Tomsky from the Politburo, so that Rykov was the only remaining former Right-wing leader. Kirov, Kaganovich and S. Kosior, all powerful opponents of the Right, were promoted from candidate to full membership; and Syrtsov was appointed a candidate member.[42] The Orgburo underwent even more drastic changes. Only five of the thirteen members continued in office; and one of these was removed in the following November.[43] Kaganovich now joined Stalin and Molotov as the only Orgburo members who were also members of the Politburo.

The great anomaly in these decisions was the retention of Rykov as a full member of the Politburo and as chairman of Sovnarkom. This decision, or lack of decision, is in striking contrast to the prevailing atmosphere at the congress. In his

[39] *XVI s"ezd* (1931), 330.
[40] PKh, 10–11, 1930, 6–7 (report to technology section, November 4, 1930).
[41] *XVI s"ezd* (1931), 330.
[42] SPR, vii, ii (1930), 174.
[43] Bauman, Molotov and Stalin continued as secretaries and members of the Orgburo, and Bubnov and Moskvin as members. New members elected were Kaganovich and Postyshev, who were also appointed secretaries, and Akulov, Gamarnik, Lobov and Shvernik (SPR, vii, ii (1930), 174). In November Moskvin, who was deputy head of the cadres' allocation department (raspredot-del), was transferred to Vesenkha; his post, and presumably his membership of the Orgburo, were taken over by Ezhov (P, November 19, 1930).

speech at the congress Rykov claimed that he had not displayed 'a shadow of fractionalism or disagreement in principle' since the November plenum; but he was frequently interrupted, strongly criticised in the speeches of other delegates, and mocked by Stalin.[44] In the congress resolution the Right were now formally condemned as 'objectively an agency of the kulak class', pursuing a line which would lead to 'the restoration of capitalism in our country'.[45] The retention of Rykov in office does not seem explicable solely in terms of Stalin's characteristic caution about removing his opponents. While Stalin possessed great authority at the congress and among party activists, his authority in the smaller world of the Politburo had been severely damaged during the crisis over collectivisation.[46] Knowledge of this may have stayed his hand. But it seems more likely that Syrtsov, chairman of Sovnarkom of the RSFSR since May 1929, was being groomed to replace Rykov as chairman of Sovnarkom of the USSR;[47] Syrtsov, appointed a candidate member of the Politburo only at the time of the XVI congress, was hardly yet senior enough to take on an office held only by Lenin and Rykov.

In the weeks following the XVI party congress, the most important change in Sovnarkom was the replacement of the Rightist Uglanov as People's Commissar for Labour by Tsikhon, in whose charge Narkomtrud became much more malleable.[48] Perhaps even more important than the appointment of Tsikhon was the transfer of Kraval', a notoriously tough supporter of Stalin, from Vesenkha to Narkomtrud to act as Tsikhon's

[44] *XVI s"ezd* (1931), 148–54; for criticism of Rykov, see for example the speech of Kabakov (pp. 160–2); for Stalin, see p. 335 above.

[45] *KPSS v rez.*, iii (1954), 21.

[46] According to the Italian ambassador, at the end of February 1930, Stalin secured only the vote of Molotov in a Politburo discussion on collectivisation; seven votes were recorded against him (see Haslam (1983), 122, citing the Italian archives). This report fits well with the account of these events in vol. 1, pp. 261–8, 311–12.

[47] On this see Avtorkhanov (Munich, 1959), 189 (sometimes an unreliable source).

[48] SZ, 1930, ii, art. 268 (dated August 3). Tsikhon, a former metal-worker who joined the party in 1906, was employed as a Rabkrin official for a short period in 1923–4; in 1924–8 he was secretary of the Bauman district party committee in Moscow; in May 1928 he was transferred to the building workers' trade union (ZI, August 6, 1930).

deputy;[49] moreover, Gindin, the most prominent adviser to Narkomtrud, was removed from its presidium.[50] Other substantial changes were delayed. In spite of the ferocious criticism of Vesenkha at the congress by Ordzhonikidze and other Rabkrin officials, for the moment Kuibyshev remained at the head of Vesenkha; and Krzhizhanovsky continued at Gosplan in spite of its weakness under his leadership. The transformation of Sovnarkom awaited the political crisis at the end of the year.

Shortly after the party congress, between July 27 and August 7, 1930, Rakovsky prepared in exile his 14,000-word article 'At the Congress and in the Country', which was the first programmatic criticism of Soviet economic policy prepared within the USSR since Bukharin's 'Notes of an Economist' of September 1928.[51] According to Rakovsky, the result of the XVI congress was to provide even greater freedom of action for the authorities; it constituted a major step towards 'Bonapartisation' of the party. But it evaded the real situation. A crisis was approaching, in which history would exact its payment for seven years of opportunist policy. While industrial production had risen by 27·4 per cent in October 1929–June 1930, this increase was almost entirely due to the more intensive use of existing capital through the *nepreryvka*, the increase in the labour force, and more intensive use of labour. Owing to the fall in quality, moreover, the official figures were a *'statistical fiction'* – a limit was being approached at which to increase the quantity of output would merely reduce its quality. The centrists (i.e. Stalin and his supporters) had hoped to 'jump across in a single leap, by-passing all the stages, to super-American tempos on the basis of pressure on the working class', and had accordingly increased all disproportions to a point at which no

---

[49] SZ, 1930, ii, art. 268 (dated August 3). For Kraval', see SR, lxii (1984), 215–16, n. 72 (Davies).

[50] SZ, 1930, ii, 307 (dated September 14). Earlier, Rudzutak was replaced by Rukhimovich as People's Commissar for Transport, but remained deputy chairman of Sovnarkom (SZ, 1930, ii, arts. 194–5 (dated June 11)); this appointment, which does not seem to be politically significant, occurred immediately before the transport crisis of the summer of 1930 (see pp. 348–9 below).

[51] The article was published in BO (Paris), xxv–xxvi (November–December 1931), 9–32; for agricultural aspects, see vol. 1, pp. 335–6. A translation into English appears in *Critique*, no. 13 (1981), 13–53.

real reserves existed. The capital investment programme was being considerably underfulfilled, and new factories would therefore not become available as soon as planned: the breach through which the crisis would break, and was already breaking, would be '*the gap between old fixed capital going out of service and the impossibility of new fixed capital being introduced to replace it in time*'. The real resources did not exist which would enable industrialisation to be carried out fast enough to extricate the Soviet economy from the crisis. Rakovsky accordingly predicted that quantitative indicators would fall sharply (he did not make it clear whether he expected output or only the rate of growth to fall), and that a crisis of fixed capital would occur simultaneously or subsequently. At the same time transport was in a 'catastrophic position'. Finance was in disarray. A united front of the countryside would develop against the state, while the delay in the development of industry would result in a further fall in the productive forces of agriculture. The centrists were now 'dogs chasing their own tails', 'rotating in the closed circle of their fictitious paper resources', and any movement forward would create new disproportions.

In view of this alarming prospect, Rakovsky concluded that the only possible solution was a retreat in which the party secured the support of the working class by fundamentally improving their material position, while simultaneously developing the class struggle in the countryside. The number of factories under construction in industry must be reduced, concentrating resources on key objects, and freeing them for lagging branches of the economy such as transport and electrification. Budgetary expenditure and currency issue must also be reduced. To achieve this required the replacement of the political leadership and the 'radical reconstruction of the whole political system'. But even with the removal of the present leadership this programme would take years, and a decline in productive forces in the first period was inevitable.

In some major respects this diagnosis was obviously too pessimistic. Capital investment in industry was far in excess of capital repair; in 1929/30 it was almost treble the 1913 level. The danger of a general decline in industrial production was far less than Rakovsky supposed. But Rakovsky was correct, at least for certain major industries, in estimating that existing capital was almost fully utilised, in concluding that the period before new factories would be completed was far longer than the leadership supposed, and in accordingly anticipating an immediate crisis.

CHAPTER NINE

THE INDUSTRIAL ECONOMY IN DISORDER, JUNE–SEPTEMBER 1930

(A) FIVE SECTORS IN CRISIS

(i) Industry

At the time of the XVI party congress, which celebrated industrial progress in a mood of complacent enthusiasm, industry was already entering a serious crisis. The preliminary Vesenkha report for June 1930, published shortly after the end of the congress, revealed a significant decline in industrial production and labour productivity.[1]

The decline of industrial production continued during July–September 1930, the final quarter of the economic year. This was in sharp contrast to the previous year, when the normal summer decline was replaced by a substantial increase in production (see pp. 80–1 above). In July–September 1930, production was 4 per cent lower than in the previous quarter, and only 12·3 per cent higher than in July–September 1929.[2] The output of consumer goods declined, and the output of producer goods grew much more slowly than in the earlier part of the year.[3] The crisis was at its most acute in July and August: production in both months was lower than in the previous January, and in August it was only 8·7 per cent higher than in the same month of 1929. In September 1930, following

---

[1] ZI, July 22, 1930 (Vesenkha-planned industry in 1926/27 prices), which reported that production had declined by 4·5 and productivity by 0·7 per cent. For the final production figures, which show almost the same rate of decline, see Table 7(c); the final report revised the decline in productivity (output per worker per day) to 2·6 per cent (*Ezhemesyachnyi statisticheskii byulleten'*, 9(84), June 1930, 27).

[2] *Industrializatsiya, 1929–1932* (1970), 230.

[3] Group B production was 11·6 per cent lower than in the previous quarter, Group A 4·7 per cent higher (see Table 7(b)).

a vigorous campaign by the party, a rapid recovery took place, but production was still lower than in the previous April.[4] Labour productivity also declined in July, and did not exceed the April–May 1930 level until September. The more rapid increase in the labour force than in production which characterised the summer of 1930 reversed previous trends, and was described by Gosplan as 'a special kind of scissors'.[5] While the decline in labour productivity was primarily due to the crisis in the consumer goods industries in September 1930, productivity also remained below the April 1930 level in several major producer goods industries, including coal and coke, iron and steel, and non-ferrous metals.[6] Labour discipline also deteriorated in July–September 1930: absenteeism without due cause amounted to 1·66 days as compared with 1·14 days in the previous quarter, and labour turnover increased from 13·7 to 14·3 per cent per month.[7] These were industry's worst results for many years. The deterioration of industrial performance was so marked that even the published annual survey by Gosplan admitted 'fairly important departures from the plan, which have created a number of difficulties and breakdowns'.[8]

The most alarming decline occurred in the metal-producing and coal industries, previously distinguished for their steady progress. The production of pig-iron, which had fallen only slightly in July–September 1929, fell much more rapidly in July–September 1930, with a consequent decline in the production of crude and rolled steel; the production of copper ore declined sharply from April 1930 onwards.[9] Metal, already in short supply, became the bottleneck of bottlenecks for all the capital goods industries. So alarming was the shortage that a report submitted to the presidium of Vesenkha at the end of July proposed that only first-priority consumers should receive

[4] See Table 7(c); the campaign of September 1930 forms part of the policies for dealing with the crisis fully implemented in October–December 1930, and is discussed in ch. 11 below.

[5] *Kon"yunktura . . . za sentyabr' i 12 mesyatsev 1929/30* (n.d. [1930]), Trud, pp. 2–4.

[6] *Ezhemesyachnyi statisticheskii byulleten'*, 1–2 (86), August–September 1930, 25–7.

[7] *Itogi VSNKh* (1932), 84–7, 80–3.

[8] PKh, 7–8, 1930, 26 (Guberman).

[9] See Table 9(e)–(f), and (for copper ore) *Ezhemesyachnyi statisticheskii byulleten'*, 10(85), July 1930, 18.

steel in July–September 1930: Narkomtorg, Narkomfin, and all hospitals and schools should receive no allocation whatsoever.[10] But the most severe decline was in coal production, which was more than 30 per cent lower in both August and September 1930 than in the previous April (see Table 9(a)). The consequent inadequate supply of coke, and its deteriorating quality, in turn hindered attempts to expand the production of pig-iron.[11] Other Group A industries fared better, but their expansion was on the whole much slower than in the summer of 1929: the engineering industries were hindered by the growing scarcity of coal and metal.[12]

(ii) Railway transport

In the first six months of 1929/30 persistent complaints were voiced about the inadequate performance of the railways. In November 1929 the plenum of the party central committee warned that the '*transport and roads problem*' was increasingly becoming a bottleneck in the economy.[13] In March 1930, a sharply-worded report from Rabkrin declared that 'bureaucratism, inertness and direct wrecking continue to reign in the *apparat* of Narkomput''.[14] In the same month a report to the central planning department of Narkomput' castigated the results for the first five months of the year as 'shameful': the amount of freight remaining unloaded on March 15 was more than three times as great as on October 1, 1929. The report warned that the failure to improve the utilisation of rolling stock to the planned extent was 'catastrophic'. If the plan were not carried out in the second half of the economic year transport would '*enter a period of prolonged crisis*'.[15] Following these strictures,

[10] EZh, July 27, 1930 (report by Lauer); the presidium of Vesenkha approved this proposal, but it was slightly modified by Gosplan, which cut the planned production of rails so that construction steel could be provided to major sites and to Narkomtorg (EZh, July 31, 1930).

[11] *Industrializatsiya, 1929–1932* (1970), 233–4.

[12] In July–September 1930 production of 27 out of 66 products of engineering and electrical engineering for which quarterly figures are available declined; this included important items such as tractors, railway wagons, internal combustion engines and ball-bearings (*Itogi VSNKh* (1932), 23–32).

[13] *KPSS v rez.*, ii (1954), 625.

[14] P, March 15, 1930.

[15] EZh, March 20, 1930.

performance improved. Between February and June 1930 the number of goods wagons loaded per day rose from 42,298 to 51,039.[16] A Gosplan survey reported in May that transport was 'coping with the plan' and provided 'no grounds for alarm'.[17] The number of wagons loaded on June 12, 1930 – 54,100 – proved, however, to be a peak figure: average daily loadings fell to 47,466 in July, 45,013 in August, and 46,746 in September, and the figure for June 1930 was not regained until May or June 1931.[18]

A Gosplan report attributed the decline primarily to the failure of industry and other sectors to achieve their production plans, which reduced the demand for transport facilities; it pointed out that unloaded stocks on October 1, 1930, were substantially lower than on October 1, 1929.[19] But more alarming symptoms of approaching disorder could also be observed. According to Gosplan, the continuous increase in passenger traffic resulted in a great increase in the proportion of passenger locomotives needing repair, so that during the summer freight locomotives had to be diverted to passenger trains. Simultaneously, the stock of available wagons declined 'to the point of complete exhaustion'. By the beginning of October 1930, rolling stock was 'at the limit of its carrying capacity'. The strain on the railways was reflected in an increase in the number of accidents and a decline in the average speed of trains.[20] Transport was on the eve of crisis.

(iii) Construction

On June 1, 1930, almost twice as many construction workers were employed in the Soviet economy as on June 1, 1929 (see

[16] SO, 3–4, 1930, 108; EZh, October 26, 1930. The figure for June was later revised to 54,000 (*Zheleznodorozhnyi transport* (1970), 117).

[17] EZh, May 13, 1930.

[18] *Zheleznodorozhnyi transport* (1970), 90, 130–1; for June 12, 1930, see EZh, October 26, 1930.

[19] *Kon''yunktura . . . za sentyabr' i 12 mesyatsev 1929–30* (n.d. [1930]), Transport, pp. 2–3; the decline was from 24,000 to 15,000 wagon-loads.

[20] *Ibid*. Transport, pp. 4–8. Accidents increased from 5·67 per 100,000 km. in 1928/29 to 6·87 in October 1929–June 1930, and the number was expected to be higher in the rest of the year; the average commercial speed for goods trains declined from 13·7 to 12·7 km. per hour. Accidents in river transport increased even more dramatically (*ibid*. Transport, p. 10).

Table 17), and expenditure on capital investment in industry in October 1929 – May 1930 was twice as high as in the first eight months of the previous year (see p. 249 above). But this substantial increase was far less than planned. A report to the Vesenkha presidium noted that only 36 per cent of the annual expenditure plan had been fulfilled by June 1, 1930, and that the required priorities had not yet been established: contrary to the intentions of the plan, producer goods industries lagged behind consumer goods industries, and investment in new factories behind investment in existing factories.[21] Gosplan reported in the same month that 'capital construction in industry has developed in unfavourable conditions, as a result of which there has been a considerable lag in rates of growth, which is creating an extremely tense position for the remainder of the building season'.[22]

The fulfilment of the capital investment plan for the year as a whole therefore required a further enormous increase in expenditure in July–September 1930. In the last quarter of 1928/29, the average number employed in capital construction increased by as much as 58 per cent, and as a result the annual investment plan was almost achieved. In July–September 1930, however, the average number employed increased by only 27 per cent, far less than the normal seasonal increase.[23] Moreover, the number employed on both August 1 and September 1, 1930, was less than on July 1 (see Table 17). This was an unprecedented reversal of the normal seasonal trend. As a consequence, investment fell even further behind the plan. Even in Vesenkha, the number of construction workers employed at the height of the building season was far below requirements, amounting to only 750,000 instead of one million.[24] At the end of the economic year, Zolotarev, who was in charge of capital construction in Vesenkha, reported to a Conference of Giant Projects a '*most enormous breakdown*' in capital construction, worse than in industrial production, as a result of which 'we have not reached the summit which we must attain in our steep ascent'.[25]

[21] ZI, July 26, 1930 (report by Ratner to session of July 25).
[22] *Industrializatsiya, 1929–1932* (1970), 141.
[23] See Table 17; the quarterly percentage increases are calculated by comparing the average of July 1–October 1 with the average for April 1–July 1.
[24] *Materialy VSNKh* (1931), 15.   [25] ZI, September 30, 1930.

(iv) Finance

During July–September 1930, the financial situation continued to deteriorate: with each successive month, the reduction in costs lagged further behind the plan, and over the whole year it amounted to only 6·9 per cent as compared with the plan of 11 per cent.[26] In the economy as a whole, expected savings from improvements in costs amounted to only 1,500 instead of 3,000 million rubles, most of this gap being due to the underfulfilment of the cost reduction plan in industry.[27] In consequence, expenditure of the state budget under the heading 'national economy' in the period June–September increased to a monthly average of 427 million rubles as compared with 337 millions in the first eight months of the year: most of the increase was allocated to industry.[28] Additional financial resources were also provided by the issue of substantial short-term credits in excess of the plan. These credits, primarily made available to industry, resulted in a very substantial unplanned issue of currency (see Table 23). Currency issue in July–September 1930 was larger as a proportion of the total currency in circulation than in any previous quarter since the currency reform of 1924, and in absolute terms currency issues in this single quarter were larger

---

[26] The following table shows cost reduction in large-scale industry, excluding the food industry, in 1929/30 as a percentage of the equivalent period of 1928/29:

October 1929 –March 1930 average	April	May	June	July	August	Average (11 months of 1929/30)
6·4	8·9	8·6	8·3	7·1	6·7	7·3

(*Industrializatsiya, 1929–1932* (1970), 238).

The percentage decline for the whole year (6·9) appears in a Vesenkha report (ZI, November 23, 1930); if these figures were comparable, costs in September 1930 would have been about 5 per cent lower than in September 1929, but an alternative figure of 7·3 per cent for Vesenkha-planned industry appears in PI, 2, 1931, 14–15.

[27] P, September 9, November 20, 1930.

[28] Calculated from data in *Industrializatsiya, 1929–1932* (1970), 30–2, and SO, 6, 1930, 153; the monthly expenditure on industry amounted to 217 against 167 million rubles.

than the total issue in any previous economic year since 1924. Even so, they were not always adequate to cover authorised expenditure. The Turksib railway reported at the end of 1929/30 a substantial accumulation of reserves in its current account because the lack of bank notes prevented it from meeting its obligations.[29]

The rapid expansion of the currency in the summer of 1920 was accompanied and reinforced by a characteristic manifestation of repressed inflation: the disappearance of silver and even copper coin. This began in May or June 1930, and became exceptionally severe in the following month: a ten-kopek coin was treated as equivalent to a ruble note.[30] Telephone booths stood idle; municipal authorities issued 'scrip' in small denominations; shops gave credit slips instead of change.[31] Bryukhanov, while admitting the existence of a tense market situation, blamed kulaks and priests for urging the hoarding of silver, and condemned 'counter-revolutionary rumours' that silver was to be removed from circulation, and that money was to be entirely replaced by rationed supplies. Acknowledging that this agitation had influenced 'elements with a low degree of consciousness in town and country', Bryukhanov repudiated the rumours, and announced that silver coin was to be issued in larger quantities, 'as planned', during August and September.[32] According to western reports, the hoarding of coins was made a capital offence.[33] *Pravda* reported in August 1930 that a 'considerable group of speculators' had been arrested in Moscow region on the dubious charge that they pursued deliberate counter-revolutionary objectives in persuading cashiers and tramway officials to hide silver in their apartments; arrests also took place in other towns.[34] An American journalist resident in Moscow reported that within 'a week or two' of these severe measures, coins were back in circulation.[35]

---

[29] TsGANKh, 1884/80/452, 4, 6.
[30] VT, 7–8, 1930, 75; Maynard (1942), 261.
[31] Lyons (1938), 364.
[32] P, July 26, 1930.
[33] Lyons (1938), 365; Friedman (1933), 338.
[34] P, August 2, 1930.
[35] Lyons (1938), 364–5; Lyons wrongly dates the small change crisis as 'late in 1930'. According to an unpublished Gosplan report, 'the crisis of small change was eliminated almost everywhere by August–September' (*Kon"yunktura . . . za sentyabr' i 12 mesyatsev 1929/30* (n.d. [1930]), Finansy, p. 7).

(v) *Internal trade*

The high currency issues of the special quarter facilitated the rapid expansion of the money incomes of the employed population. In industry, as compared with the previous quarter, the average wage increased by 4 per cent in July–September 1930, and the number of workers and apprentices by 5·9 per cent (see Tables 15(b) and 20); the total wage bill in industry probably increased by about 8 per cent.[36] In construction, the number of workers increased by 27 per cent and the average wage by as much as 14 per cent, so the wage bill increased by over 40 per cent.[37] But the supply of consumer goods declined. In July Mikoyan warned the second congress of consumer cooperatives that in the final quarter of the economic year the supply of industrial goods to the market was likely to be no higher than in the same period of 1928/29.[38] This apparently pessimistic forecast proved far too optimistic; the production of Group B industries in July–September 1930 was 5·5 per cent lower than in July–September 1929.[39] In spite of the widening gap between demand and supply, retail prices in socialised trade were not increased.[40] A large additional demand remained unsatisfied, and a Gosplan survey reported 'a big jump in the growth of the goods famine'.[41]

Following the removal of the restrictions on peasant markets in March 1930, some small traders sought to resume their

---

[36] *Nar. kh.* (1932), 458–9; *Trud* (1932), 61. In the above estimate of the wage bill I have tried to allow for the fact that the figure for workers includes lower-paid apprentices, the number of which increased sharply in this quarter, while they are not included in the figure for the average wage.

[37] For the number of workers see p. 350 above; for the average wage see *Nar. kh.* (1932), 468; the average wage always increased in July–September, but this was a larger increase than in 1929 (9 per cent) or 1928 (11 per cent).

[38] P, July 30, 1930.

[39] *Industrializatsiya, 1929–32* (1970), 230. For individual products see *Ezhemesyachnyi statisticheskii byulleten'*, 1–2 (86), August–September, 1930, 18–21.

[40] The index for urban cooperative retail trade was 99·0 on both July 1 and October 1, 1930 (average annual prices in 1928 = 100) (*Tovarooborot* (1932), 132–5); it is not known whether retail sales at higher commercial prices increased in this period.

[41] PKh, 7–8, 1930, 43 (Guberman).

activities. According to a Narkomfin survey, former traders who were no longer registered would re-appear at market places in the guise of peasants, 'most often trading from stalls, little tables, from their hands, the ground, or from baskets and other devices which can be moved by one person with all the goods': they sought to buy up supplies from peasants and, legally or illegally, from the consumer cooperatives.[42] In the countryside, traders bought authorisations to trade from peasants who had been issued them by the local soviets.[43] But 'speculators' – traders reselling goods originally purchased by others – continued to be harried and persecuted. In the summer of 1930, as in the previous autumn and winter, many 'speculators' were arrested in raids on market-places carried out without warning by the GPU.[44] Almost all this trade was on a very small scale. An American journalist visiting Moscow in the autumn of 1930 reported that 'the Okhotny Ryad, the sidewalk market in the centre of the town, where one could buy anything from suckling pigs, game and caviare to fancy fruit and vegetables has been wiped off the map', and replaced by a 'huge, long, empty cooperative store'. The Sukharevka, the famous flea market, was 'as crowded and agitated as ever', but was a 'bull market pre-eminent'. Typical items for sale included patched pants, second-hand slippers and empty watch-cases; new footwear made by peasants was sold at enormous prices.[45]

The excess of demand over supply resulted in an increase in bazaar and private market prices which was frankly described by *Pravda* as 'exceptionally large in magnitude'.[46] In the single month of June 1930, private industrial prices rose by 15·7 per cent, and private agricultural prices by 20·3 per cent.[47] Henceforth monthly price figures were no longer published. But according to an unpublished index for peasant sales of food at urban bazaars, after an increase of 22·2 per cent in June, bazaar prices increased by a further 53·4 per cent between July 1 and

[42] FP, 7–8, 1930, 93, 98.
[43] FSKh, 6, 1931, 7.
[44] See, for example, P, July 27, 1930: *Pravda* reported that some of those arrested were sent to camps for various periods, others were exiled to Siberia and the Far North.
[45] Knickerbocker (1931), 22–6.
[46] P, October 2, 1930.
[47] VT, 7–8, 1930, 75.

October 1 (see Table 24(c)).[48] Such a rapid increase during the months of the harvest has neither precedent nor successor in the USSR in years of peace. Even in the famine year 1932 urban bazaar prices for food increased by only 13·3 per cent between May and October.[49] This indicates the extraordinary pressure of demand in the summer months of 1930. In consequence of the rapid increase in prices, sales of food and consumer goods on the free market increased greatly in value terms. The proportion of workers' expenditure on goods purchased on the free market increased from 21 per cent in May to 30 per cent in August 1930; the equivalent percentages for white-collar employees were 39 and 49 per cent.[50] But this represents a substantial decline in free-market sales in real terms.

Total supplies of both industrial consumer goods and foods to the non-agricultural population greatly deteriorated in the summer of 1930. In July and August 1930 the amount spent by workers on industrial consumer goods was lower than in the same months of 1929; expenditure on clothing and footwear was only two-thirds of the 1929 level.[51] The decline in the amount of rationed food available was also very substantial. According to an unpublished Gosplan report, the food situation was most tense in the second half of 1929/30; high food issues

---

[48] This is the index for five food products; the index for nine products increased by 16·7 in June and 56·4 per cent from July 1 to October 1 (*Tovarooborot* (1932), 143).

[49] *Itogi . . . po torgovle*, November 1932, 81 (this is the index for nine food products); prices began to increase much more rapidly from November 1932.

[50] *Kon''yunktura . . . za sentyabr' i 12 mesyatsev 1929/30* (n.d. [1930]), Tablitsy.

[51] The following table, measured in current prices, shows the change in workers' budgets (including expenditure on the free market) (same period of previous year = 100):

	October 1929 –August 1930	Jan.– March 1930	April– June	July	August
Income spent on goods:	112·2	117·1	108·7	111·7	111·7
agricultural	113·6	112·4	112·4	112·9	126·0
industrial goods	103·8	119·1	101·1	91·6	84·3
of which clothing and footwear	96·7	122·7	91·1	67·1	68·9

(*Kon''yunktura . . . za sentyabr' i 12 mesyatsev 1929/30* (n.d. [1930]), Obmen i raspedelenie, p. 5).

in the first half of the year and poor collections during 1930 led to a decline in stocks. Meat issues declined from 178 thousand tons in October–December 1929 to 38 thousand tons in April–June, increasing to 55 thousand tons in July–September 1930; supplies of vegetable oil 'declined from month to month'; butter supplies were even worse. Vegetable supplies, which were expected to have a major effect on food consumption with the new season, no doubt increased, but were lower than planned, and by October 1930 many towns reported that potatoes were in very short supply and the position with other vegetables was even worse. For most of the year the availability of flour and bread had been 'even and continuous', but by September there were 'interruptions in supply even in respect of the capitals'.[52] Even according to the official Soviet estimates, in August calories consumed by workers were 4·5 per cent less than in August 1929; there was a slight decline even in the favoured areas, Moscow, Leningrad and the Donbass; and in the Urals the decline amounted to as much as 16·7 per cent.[53]

If the decline in real wages could perhaps have been a matter of genuine controversy on the eve of the XVI party congress (see pp. 307–9 above), it should have been indisputable by the summer of 1930. While the average wage for workers in industry increased by no more than 13 per cent between September 1929 and September 1930,[54] the index for the cost of the standard food basket used for estimating workers' budgets, which in April–June 1930 was 17·8 – 21·3 per cent higher than in the same period of the previous year, had increased by October 1, 1930, to 44·8 – 63·4 per cent above the index for October 1, 1929; even if the retail prices of non-food products remained stable, this would imply a rise in the cost of living as a whole by at least 20–30 per cent.[55] In spite of these unambiguous figures,

---

[52] *Kon"yunktura . . . za sentyabr' i 12 mesyatsev 1929/30* (n.d. [1930]), Obmen i raspedelenie, pp. 5–7.

[53] *Ibid.* Tablitsy.

[54] The average monthly wage in September 1929 was 76r 31k (Mendel'son, ed. (1930), 43, 152); and for the two quarters July–September and October–December 1930 it averaged 86r 17k (see Table 20).

[55] PKh, 5–6, 1931, 68–9 (Pollyak); the lower index uses end-period weights, the higher initial-period weights – this difference is plausibly explained by Pollyak as due to the higher proportion of meat and dairy products in 1929, the prices of which grew particularly rapidly. It is thus a kind of 'Gerschenkron effect' – it should be called a 'Pollyak effect' – in relation to food (see Zaleski

by the end of 1929/30 the dogma that the standard of living was continuously increasing was almost unchallengeable.

The more efficient administration of rationing was an urgent necessity. According to Soviet accounts, the issue of ration books earlier in 1930 was undertaken hastily and apparently without proper supervision: it was alleged that no proper record was kept by housing administrations, and that they did not recover the books of those leaving Moscow: 300,000 books had been issued to 'dead souls' in Moscow alone, and were thus available for speculative purposes, while genuine ration books often failed to be honoured.[56] According to an American visitor to Moscow, in the autumn of 1930 there was 'no certainty about any food except bread', and the rest-day in the five-day week was largely spent hunting for goods.[57]

The alarming food situation, in which even the basic rationed supplies were uncertain, was reflected in the decision of a Moscow district in August 1930 to establish an experimental system of 'closed distribution' for workers in fifty factories; they were specifically registered with 24 retail cooperative shops to which only they had access. The initiative was supported by *Pravda*, and by the beginning of September both Narkomtorg of the RSFSR and Tsentrosoyuz agreed that this should be the basic form of rationing for factory workers and staff, with the rest of the urban population attached to open shops.[58] Within a few weeks, the new system had already been introduced for the food rations of 500,000 workers, employees and their families, and was being introduced in other major towns.[59] Another form of 'closed distribution' established in Moscow at this time was Torgsin (an abbreviation for 'torgovlya s inostrantsami', trade with foreigners); this predecessor of the present *Berezka* shops was an agency of Narkomtorg of the USSR attached to Mosgortorg, the Moscow town trade department, and sold

---

(Chapel Hill, 1971), 143, n. 199). The index refers to food consumption at home only, *not* to all consumption, the prices for which rose less rapidly (*pace* Zaleski, *loc. cit.*, and Schwarz (New York, 1952), 137–8).

[56] P, August 16 (Volgina), September 1 (Moscow Rabkrin resolution), 1930; EZh, October 18, 1930.

[57] Knickerbocker (1931), 10, 14–15.

[58] VT, 11–12, 1930, 117–18.

[59] VT, 11–12, 1930, 119, 125; a figure of 587,780 for Moscow is given in EZh, October 18, 1930.

goods to foreigners in exchange for foreign currency.[60] Thus the 'closed distribution' system ensured more reliable supplies for crucial groups of the population at a time of worsening food shortage.

(B) DEFICITS AND BOTTLENECKS

After the recovery of large-scale industry to the pre-war level its further rapid development in the second half of the 1920s, and the vast expansion of capital investment, involved the rapid transformation of the Soviet economy, from the summer of 1927 onwards, into an economy of shortages, repressed inflation and physical allocation, an economy in disequilibrium. Until the summer of 1930 this was an economy in dynamic disequilibrium in which production and investment were expanding at an increasing rate. The 'Bolshevik ascending curve' had apparently triumphed. But in the summer of 1930 shortages were much more severe, and played a large part in the temporary interruption and even reversal of the progress of industrialisation.

The impact of the shortages varied between industries and sectors. The labour shortage had become endemic; but its most serious impact was in the coal industry and capital construction, where the number of workers declined in July and August 1930. The shortage of capacity, in circumstances of declining technical efficiency, primarily affected the iron and steel industry and the railways. The shortage of agricultural raw materials was the crucial bottleneck in the consumer goods industries; the shortage of industrial materials, notably iron and steel, was a bottleneck factor everywhere, and particularly in those engineering industries which were not treated as of high priority.

(i) The labour shortage

Before 1929/30, in spite of the rapid expansion of urban employment, only certain types of skilled labour were in short supply. Even in 1929 new jobs created were barely sufficient to absorb the continuous net flow into the towns of labour from the countryside. On October 1, 1929, the number of unemployed

[60] EZh, August 26, 1930.

registered at labour exchanges still amounted to 1,242,000 (see Table 18). Even the most optimistic prognoses supposed that unemployment would continue at a high level throughout the five-year plan.[61] But during 1930 the average number employed in the non-agricultural sectors increased by over two millions, more than three times as many as in the previous year (see p. 126 above and Table 14(a)).

The winter of 1929/30 was the first occasion on which unemployment was reduced between October 1, always a moment of peak employment, and April 1, a moment of minimum employment. By the spring of 1930, in many skilled trades hardly any workers remained registered at labour exchanges.[62] A skilled worker could get a new job in a couple of days.[63] Faced with the increase in job vacancies, Narkomtrud proposed that labour exchanges should enlarge the categories entitled to register for work, including artisans and their children, widows and divorced wives of workers, employees and invalids, women who had ceased work for family reasons, and other categories which had previously been excluded.[64] In the discussion supplement issued by *Pravda* before the XVI party congress, the wisdom of recruiting former 'bourgeois and petty-bourgeois elements' into industry was hotly debated. But no one doubted that such ideologically dubious recruitment was frequently practised by industrial managers in face of the labour shortage.[65]

The total number of unemployed continued to decline throughout the summer of 1930, and by October 1, 1930, amounted to about 570,000 in terms of the definition current in 1929, and to a mere 335,000 in terms of the new definition adopted in September 1930.[66] The number of semi-skilled and

[61] See Carr and Davies (1969), 467.

[62] VTr, 7–8, 1930, 52.

[63] ZI, June 19, 1930; according to this article, 'bezrabotitsa' (lack of work) had now been replaced by 'bezrabochitsa' (lack of workers). Another report, however, described long queues for work, which allegedly consisted of 'rural people' who were lazy and 'alien to large-scale construction', and registered merely to get unemployment benefit (ZI, June 12, 1930 – Mokhov).

[64] P, May 11, 1930.

[65] P, May 27, disk. listok 3 (Markus), June 14, disk. listok 12 (Bobkov), June 20, disk. listok 15 (Rusatskii), 1930.

[66] See Table 18; for an earlier narrowing in the definition of unemployment, see Carr and Davies (1969), 456–7.

skilled industrial workers registered as unemployed declined to a mere 47,100.[67] By the summer of 1930, the shortage of skilled workers had given way to a general shortage of labour. In a desperate effort to fulfil their plans, the producer goods and construction industries eagerly sought additional workers. But relatively few were forthcoming. In industry, the number employed increased by 118,000 between May and September 1930,[68] but this was far less than the demand: on September 1, 1930, the labour exchanges recorded an unsatisfied demand for 1,067,000 workers.[69] In the coal industry, the number of workers fell drastically, from 249,000 in May to 197,000 in September; this reduction by 21 per cent was far greater than the normal seasonal decline, and a dramatic reversal of the achievement in the summer of 1929, when the number of workers slightly increased. In all three months July, August and September 1930 the number of workers in the coal industry was lower than in any month in 1928/29.[70] In capital construction, the decline in the number employed from July 1, 1930 onwards (see Table 17) took place in spite of growing demand. In May 1930, labour exchanges met 79 per cent of all requests for building workers; in August, they were able to meet only 29·5 per cent.[71] The shortage of building workers was so great that a 10-hour day was introduced on many sites during the summer, particularly on high-priority sites.[72]

The shortage of labour was particularly acute wherever a high proportion of workers retained their links with the countryside. In 1930 as a whole the influx of labour from the countryside greatly increased: according to Soviet data, the net number of new settlers in the towns increased from 1·06 million in 1928 to 1·39 million in 1929 and 2·63 million in 1930.[73] But for the first time since the early 1920s this increase was insufficient to satisfy the hunger for labour of the industrial

[67] See Lane, ed. (1985), 45 (Davies and Wheatcroft).

[68] *Ezhemesyachnyi statisticheskii byulleten'*, 1–2 (86), August–September 1930, 2–5.

[69] Rogachevskaya (1973), 281.

[70] *Ezhemesyachnyi statisticheskii byulleten'*, 1–2 (86), August–September 1930, 2–5.

[71] *Industrializatsiya, 1929–1932* (1970), 389; the number of requests rose from 283,000 in May to 314,000 in August.

[72] *Kon"yunktura ... za sentyabr' i 12 mesyatsev 1929/30* (n.d. [1930]), Stroitel'stvo, p. 9.

[73] *Trud* (1936), 7.

economy; and in the coal industry, and in certain sections of the construction industry, the inflow gave way to an outflow. This did not of course reflect an absolute shortage of potential rural recruits: in 1931–5, a further 12·7 million persons settled in the towns, in spite of the restrictions introduced on rural–urban migration at the end of 1932.[74] But in the delicate balance between agriculture and the industrial economy the advantage from the point of view of the potential peasant migrant had temporarily swung to the countryside. The good harvest encouraged potential migrants to remain in the countryside and some ex-peasants to return there. In the uncertain year of collectivisation, another impulse which affected the peasant-workers was no doubt their desire to be on the spot in their own village so as to ensure a fair share of the harvest for themselves and their families. But the main factor discouraging peasants from settling or remaining in the towns was the absolute deterioration of living and working conditions. This was most clearly illustrated in the case of the coal industry. In the spring of 1930, the industrial newspaper already warned that deteriorating housing conditions were leading to a drift of labour from the Donbass.[75] In August, a report to the presidium of Vesenkha admitted a 'catastrophic shortage of labour' in the industry and blamed it on 'unsatisfactory distribution of food and bad physical and welfare conditions'.[76]

Similar conditions prevailed in the construction industry. In April and May, when building workers were still available at the labour exchanges in the big towns, some major sites in less attractive areas were already short of labour.[77] In May, a survey of the industry noted that workers left the sites if housing and canteens were lacking.[78] In the summer, these problems were a major factor in the net decline in the number of construction workers: a Gosplan report attributed the unavailability of labour to 'the sceptical attitude of seasonal workers to the verbal offers of good conditions' and the 'lack of

[74] *Trud* (1936), 7.
[75] ZI, March 14, 1930 (Limarev).
[76] ZI, August 13, 1930; for another report on poor food supplies in the Donbass, see P, August 11, 1930 (editorial).
[77] *Kon"yunktura . . . za sentyabr' i 12 mesyatsev 1929/30* (n.d. [1930]), Stroitel'stvo, p. 7.
[78] I, May 13, 1930, referring to the site of the Bobriki chemical works.

food supply and the bad housing conditions, resulting in a number of cases in mass refusal to travel to distant places'; attempts authorised by Sovnarkom to transfer workers to priority sites were 'counter-productive in many places'.[79] According to Gosplan, the attempt to overcome the labour shortage by increasing the working day to ten hours was 'resisted by part of the workers and some lower trade-union organisations in spite of pay increases of 25 to 50 per cent'. Here too 'the refusal was in most cases explained by the lack of food'.[80] Poor food and housing were also described as major causes of labour shortages in numerous reports in the Soviet press. Thus in Magnitogorsk workers would arrive barefoot and inadequately clothed, after being promised 'paradise' by the recruiting agents; in view of the poor conditions, they immediately left again after collecting their allocation of industrial clothing.[81] According to its deputy manager, at Magnitogorsk 'medicine, sanitation, hygiene, canteens, water and cultural diversions are all on such a low level that they couldn't be worse', and 'even the most primitive barracks are lacking'; in consequence, at the beginning of September, 'when it suddenly became cold, workers eagerly climbed aboard the trains leaving Magnitogorsk'.[82] But even such better-placed sites as Dneprostroi failed to recruit and retain sufficient workers as a result of poor housing and food.[83] While many of those departing from construction sites sought better conditions elsewhere in industry or construction, others went back to the countryside, and potential recruits, lacking adequate assurances about wages and living conditions, refused to leave their villages.[84] Mezhlauk, summing up the evidence presented by delegates to the conference of giant building sites in October 1930, concluded that housing must be constructed for building workers before work began on the main buildings on a site. The final resolution of the conference pointed out that adequate

---

[79] *Kon''yunktura . . . za sentyabr' i 12 mesyatsev 1929/30* (n.d. [1930]), Stroitel'stvo, pp. 8–9; the report also noted the unwillingness of district soviets to allow peasants to take up building work.

[80] *Ibid.* Stroitel'stvo, p. 8.

[81] ZI, September 27, 1930.

[82] ZI, October 1, 1930 (Valerius).

[83] Yantarov, 2nd edn ([Kharkov], 1935), 53.

[84] ZI, October 4, 1930 (Sviderskii, referring to Chelyabinsk site).

centralised food supply was essential if workers were to be recruited.[85]

Labour shortages would have been mitigated if the planned increases in labour productivity had been achieved. But throughout June–August 1930 productivity in Vesenkha-planned industry was lower than in April and May (see p. 347 above). The simplest economies had already been made in previous years; and resources now tended to be channelled away from improvements in existing plant towards new investment. At the XVI party congress, M. Kaganovich complained that while 'cde. Kuibyshev usually presents us with rationalisation on formal occasions . . . like a fine meal offered for us to taste', industry failed to take it seriously in practice.[86] The intermittent and worsening shortages of materials, and their deteriorating quality, also hindered improvements in productivity. These deficiencies were countered by the enthusiasm of a substantial minority of dedicated workers. But the deteriorating physical conditions at home and at work discouraged such enthusiasm. Above all the unavailability of additional skilled labour and the influx of raw as yet untrained labour from the countryside had lowered the average level of skill and made increases in productivity more difficult. The annual report of Narkomtrud drew attention to the 'huge number' of 'poorly-trained and second-class' workers recruited into industry as a result of the shortage of skilled workers, particularly into producer goods industries. It also pointed out that the high rate of turnover and scarcity of labour led management to take on a reserve of more workers than they really needed, which further reduced the rise in labour productivity.[87] In the summer of 1930 the Soviet Union had become the first country to experience 'full employment' in the towns in peace-time, and confronted unprecedented problems of recruitment and discipline.

The labour shortages of the summer of 1930 thus resulted from what amounted to a new kind of scissors' crisis between town and country. The blades of the new scissors represented not agricultural and industrial prices but rural and urban living

[85] ZI, October 5, 11, 1930.
[86] *XVI s"ezd* (1931), 521–2.
[87] *Industrializatsiya, 1929–1932* (1970), 377–8.

conditions; the dependent variable was not marketed agricultural food supplies but the supply of rural labour, particularly seasonal labour, to the towns. Even if living conditions were everywhere deteriorating, when the blades opened in favour of the countryside, the supply of rural labour would fall or even be replaced by a reverse movement of labour into the countryside in those sectors of the industrial economy in which workers retained close ties with the countryside, such as the coal industry and construction. This dilemma was first posed in an acute form in the summer of 1930. The Soviet authorities made half-hearted efforts to improve workers' conditions; but food supplies and other resources were lacking. Behind the scenes desperate measures were suggested, including a fanciful proposal to recruit large numbers of Chinese labourers.[88] The dilemma of the agriculture–industry price scissors had been solved by using compulsion to transfer agricultural products from the countryside. Following this precedent, Narkomtrud and Vesenkha made strenuous efforts in the summer of 1930, not yet to compel potential workers to leave the countryside, but to direct recruits they had enticed into the construction industry to unattractive priority sites. But for the moment these efforts were largely unsuccessful.

(ii) The problem of full capacity

The shortage of capacity had been anticipated and feared ever since the mid-1920s, but in practice substantial increases of production had unexpectedly been obtained from existing capacity in 1926–30 (see pp. 82–3 above). In the summer of 1930 unutilised capacity still remained in the consumer goods industries and in several branches of engineering. In the crucial iron and steel industry, however, many smaller or older furnaces, and whole factories which had previously been shut down on grounds of economy, were now again in use. But new capacity due to be introduced in 1929/30 was greatly delayed. Thus Blast-Furnace No. 5 at the Rykov works, Yenakievo, due to begin production on May 1, 1930, did not start up until after

---

[88] At the conference of giant sites, a speaker attacked 'Yaglomist proposals on 200,000 Chinamen' as 'pure opportunist nonsense' (ZI, October 2, 1930); Ya. Yaglom was a former editor of the newspaper *Trud*, closely associated with Tomsky (see Carr and Davies (1969), 553).

the end of the economic year.[89] At the Kerch works difficulties in bringing new plant into production were particularly acute. The plant was originally intended to use local ore, but this proved unsuitable, so ore had to be transported from Krivoi Rog. Transport difficulties with the ore and non-arrival of electrical equipment resulted in great delays in starting Blast-Furnace No. 2, and the change in the supply of ore made it impossible to use steel processing plant already installed.[90]

But even if all the new capacity planned for 1929/30 had been successfully installed in the iron and steel industry, this would have supplied only a small proportion of the planned increase in production. Until the large new furnaces and factories under construction were completed, further expansion of production depended on the more efficient use of existing capacity.[91] But priority in men, materials and equipment was afforded to the new factories, and no serious preparation was made for improving the utilisation of existing furnaces. In this world of shortages and pressures for higher production, the quality of fuel and raw materials supplied to the industry began to fall, and this was a crucial factor in furnace productivity. Thus the quality of coke sharply deteriorated between February and September 1930, and as a result of the labour crisis in the coal industry the quantity supplied fell during the July–September quarter. The quality of the ore, and the arrangements for sorting it, failed to improve.[92] The turning point came in the last quarter of 1929/30. The 'coefficient of utilisation' of blast-furnaces, which measures the yield per unit of furnace, improved both in January–March and April–June 1930, but sharply deteriorated in July–September.[93] The industry had entered a period of declining technical efficiency.

The railways provide a second conspicuous example of a bottleneck resulting from the insufficient availability of capacity. In the previous five years, the low level of capital investment in the railways was a recurrent theme for vociferous complaints

[89] *Metall*, 10–12, 1930, 13.
[90] ZI, June 4, 1930 (Birman); Gershberg (1971), 3–15, 93–4; on Kerch ores see Clark (1956), 155–8.
[91] PKh, 1, 1931, 26 (Mednikov).
[92] PKh, 1, 1931, 26; *Industrializatsiya, 1929–1932* (1970), 233–4; B, 18, September 30, 1930, 16 (Mezhlauk).
[93] *Industrializatsiya, 1929–1932* (1970), 234.

from Narkomput'. A leading railway expert, contributing to the discussion before the XVI party congress, pointed out that between 1924/25 and 1928/29 fixed capital on the railways had increased by only 4·5 per cent, as compared with 17·3 per cent for the economy as a whole.[94] By 1929/30 the railways were being worked far more intensively than before the war. Between 1913 and 1929/30 goods traffic increased by 67 per cent.[95] But the carrying capacity of locomotives and goods wagons had increased by a little over one-third in the same period.[96]

In the course of 1930 the extent to which existing capacity could be used even more intensively was hotly disputed among rival railway economists. Bessonov condemned von Mekk and other 'wreckers' for their plans to spend large sums immediately on basic reconstruction of the railways rather than on improving the efficiency of their operation; according to Bessonov, young railway engineers had demonstrated that rolling stock could carry more freight for longer periods than the old engineers had believed possible. Improvements in the efficiency with which existing capacity was utilised could therefore provide a breathing space before major new capital construction need be undertaken.[97] His opponents, notably the young Red Professor Tverskoi, naturally acknowledged the need to condemn the 'wreckers', but argued that large-scale reconstruction (i.e. investment in new capacity) must accompany the improved use of existing facilities.[98] At the XVI party congress, Stalin stressed the importance of transport for the economy and for defence,

---

[94] P, May 31, 1930, disk. listok 5 (Tverskoi).

[95] It amounted to 27,400 wagons per day in 1913 (P, August 12, 1930 – D. Sulimov), and 45,774 in 1929/30 (EZh, October 26, 1930).

[96] In P, May 31, 1930, disk. listok 5, Tverskoi gave the increase in the *number* of locomotives as 4·4 per cent and in the carrying capacity of goods wagons as 20·7 per cent; in P, June 6, 1930, Bessonov pointed out that the *capacity* of locomotives was 35 per cent above the 1913 level, and gave figures purporting to show that the number of wagons in operation had increased by 16 per cent and the capacity per wagon by 10 per cent. The higher figure of 34 per cent for total capacity of wagons was given by Sulimov, deputy People's Commissar for Transport, in P, August 12, 1930.

[97] P, February 1, 1930 (discussion article); June 6, 1930, disk. listok 8; EZh, March 1, 1930; on this controversy see Hunter (1957), 45–6.

[98] P. March 1, 1930, May 31, 1930, disk. listok 5; for Tverskoi, see Hunter (1957), 296, n. 7.

warned that there was a risk that transport, especially river transport (*sic*) would become a bottleneck, and added:

> In spite of the tremendous importance of transport and the transport economy, the reconstruction of this economy still lags behind the general rate of development.[99]

This delphic utterance was promptly cited by both Bessonov and Tverskoi in justification of their own approach.[100]

It soon became apparent that, as in industry, the authorities supported Tverskoi's view that preparation for basic reconstruction and improved efficiency must take place simultaneously. This view was strongly supported both by an American delegation inspecting the Soviet railways and by a Soviet delegation which had inspected railways in the United States.[101] An editorial in the contrary sense, which had been written by Bessonov, was withdrawn by the economic newspaper after *Pravda* intervened.[102] Narkomput' had already prepared a bold plan of reconstruction, involving the use by the railways of 2·4 million tons of iron and steel in 1930/31, including 800,000 tons of rails, more than twice as much as in 1929/30.[103] These proposals indicated the urgency with which Narkomput' regarded the fundamental reconstruction of the railways. Their spokesman argued that 'transport is not in a position to cope with the tasks which will be posed in 1931/32 unless decisive measures are taken to change its structure'.[104]

While these arguments were proceeding, the daily number of

---

[99] *Soch.*, xii, 337.

[100] P, July 8, 1930, disk. listok 29; Tverskoi also pointed out that the congress resolution called for 'development and reconstruction' of transport.

[101] Mr. Budd, president of the Great Northern railway, recommended the use of more powerful locos, improved track, automatic coupling and automatic braking in two articles in EZh, July 25, 30, 1930; V. Dokunin, a member of the Soviet delegation, described United States railways in enthusiastic terms in B, 14, July 31, 1930, 54–63.

[102] EZh, August 20, 1930 (editorial); P, August 30 (Dokunin), September 9, 1930; in an avowal of error three months later, Bessonov apologised for not correcting his line after Stalin had called for 'decisive and rapid [*sic*] reconstruction of transport' (P, December 11, 1930).

[103] EZh, August 5, 1930; a new five-year plan for the railways along similar lines was summarised in EZh, September 2, 1930.

[104] B, 14, July 31, 1930, 50 (Dokunin).

goods wagons loaded declined by 11·6 per cent between June and August 1930, and failed to recover to the June level in September (see p. 349 above). It was obvious to both sides in the controversy that the looming crisis of the next few months could be solved only by patching up the existing capital stock. In the capital investment plan for 1930/31 submitted by Narkomput' in August 1930, only one-sixth of the allocation was for 'reconstruction', i.e. new construction; the rest was to be used for replacing rails, providing new goods wagons and so on.[105] Meanwhile, the annual report of Narkomput' firmly concluded that it was the shortage of capacity which was the main cause of the halt in the expansion of goods traffic:

> In some months of 1929/30, especially during the autumn traffic and in June, when the load reached its maximum level, railway transport was working almost at the limit. The colossal pressure from traffic in certain periods of the year often exhausted the carrying capacity of certain sections and junctions, so that diversions and stipulated prohibitions had to be introduced for longer periods than in previous years.

In spite of the reduced pressure on the railways resulting from the failure of production plans, in July–September 1930 the railways continued to work under strain, and sought to spread their load by increasing their operations on Sundays and religious holidays.[106]

(iii) Raw materials in deficit

In 1929/30 most industrial inputs were in short supply as a result of inflationary pressures, and the system of physical allocation of materials was firmly established. The inadequate supply of certain materials, notably iron and steel, was a particular cause for anxiety. After the demands of priority industries had been dealt with, supplies to other industries and sub-industries declined absolutely. In July–September 1930,

---

[105] EZh, August 5, 1930; the sum for reconstruction was later increased (EZh, September 5, 7, 1930).
[106] Reprinted from the archives in *Zheleznodorozhnyi transport* (1970), 88; the main material of the report was published in EZh, October 26, 1930.

the total production of iron and steel declined by 4·3 per cent,[107] and supply to non-industrial users was severely cut (see pp. 347–8 above). In August, the industrial newspaper reported that 'the country is going through a most severe metal famine', as a result of which iron beams and girders were not available for capital construction, and some agricultural repair shops had ceased work.[108]

The shortage of materials was even more serious in the cotton textile industry. The cotton harvest in 1929 was somewhat higher than in 1928, although lower than planned, and the control figures for 1929/30 anticipated that owing to 'a certain increase in imports' the rate of growth of the industry would be greater in 1929/30 than in 1928/29.[109] But the unfavourable balance of payments (see pp. 394, 397–8 below) compelled the Politburo to reduce cotton fibre imports drastically; they amounted to only 68,000 tons as compared with 123,000 tons in 1928/29. In April–September, normally a peak period for cotton imports, only 34,000 tons were imported as compared with 88,000 tons in April–September 1929 (see Table 13(d)). This represented a cut of about 15 per cent in the total of home-produced plus imported cotton supplied to the textile industry, mainly occurring in the second half of the economic year. Many factories had to close down for some weeks. In July 1930, 64 of the 191 cotton textile factories in Vesenkha-planned industry were closed for the whole month, and employment was reduced to 265,000 as compared with 457,000 in October 1929.[110] These cut-backs in the summer of 1930 must have demoralised and infuriated many textile workers, particularly as they followed a two-year campaign to introduce a three-shift system and impose night work on female workers. In July–September 1930 the production of cotton textiles amounted to only 296,000 linear metres as compared with 612,000 in the previous quarter, when

---

[107] *Itogi VSNKh* (1932), 38, measured in value terms in 1926/27 prices; for output in physical terms, see Table 9(a)–(c).

[108] ZI, August 3, 1930.

[109] *KTs . . . na 1929/30* (1930), 91; cotton fibre consumption was expected to increase by 11·8 per cent in 1929/30 as compared with 9·9 per cent in 1928/29 (p. 93). The control figures anticipated that the 1929 harvest would be 977 thousand tons (p. 118), but in fact it was only 860 thousand tons. This corresponds to cotton fibre weighing about 250,000 tons.

[110] *Ezhemesyachnyi statisticheskii byulleten'*, 1(76), October 1929, 65–7, and 10(85), July 1930, 71–3; see also B, 6, March 1931, 38 (Rapoport).

production was already much less than normal, and 697,000 in July–September 1929 (see Table 9(f)). This decline in cotton textile production, together with a smaller decline in the production of linens, was entirely responsible for the decline in the production of consumer goods as a whole.[111]

(c) CAUSES OF ECONOMIC DISORDER

These acute shortages of labour, capital and materials in crucial industries in the final quarter of 1929/30 were primarily due to the enormous increase in capital investment in the producer goods industries which had been imposed by the annual control figures and the revised five-year plans. The investment plans made necessary a massive expansion of Group A industries: the increased plans for the production of cement, brick, timber, iron beams and girders, and capital equipment, were directly derived from the capital investment plan. Simultaneously, Group A production normally allocated to other sectors of the economy was diverted to investment. The most obvious example of the process was the high requirement imposed on the metal-producing industries by the capital equipment plans, which restricted the use of metal for other purposes: the proportion of rolled metal consumed by the metal-working and iron and steel industries increased from 51·7 per cent in 1926/27 to 60·4 per cent in 1928/29 and 67·8 per cent in 1929/30.[112] Building materials were similarly diverted to industrial construction from housing and other kinds of lower-priority construction (see Table 10). Moreover, when capital equipment was not produced in the USSR, imports were increased; and this in turn led to the reduction of imports for other purposes and

---

[111] Gross production was as follows in 1930 (million rubles at 1926/27 prices):

	Jan.–Mar.	Apr.–June	Jul.–Sept.
Cotton textiles	760	581	327
Linen textiles	76	72	50
All other Group B	961	982	1090
Total Group B	1797	1635	1467

(*Itogi VSNKh* (1932), 43–4). These figures exclude the food industries.

[112] Gorelik (1937), 44 (for 1928/29); SMe, 5–6, 1932, 313 (for 1926/27 and 1929/30).

necessitated the increased export of both food products and industrial goods (see pp. 392–4 below).

The restrictions on the lower-priority sectors of the economy were so severe that investment in urban housing and in the education and health services declined (see p. 378 below). The production of consumer goods also declined (see p. 346 above); the deficit in the supply of cotton, the main cause of this decline, was in turn due primarily to the reduction of imports to make way for the increased import of capital equipment, though the deteriorating terms of trade for agricultural products on the world market worsened the foreign trade difficulties. The limited supplies of consumer goods had to be made available to a larger non-agricultural labour force, because the expansion of investment brought about a substantial increase in employment. In consequence, real wages declined. The high labour turnover of 1929/30, which reached a peak in the second half of the year, partly took place because workers changed their jobs in search of better food or wages. The labour shortage of the summer of 1930 was a consequence both of the absorption of the unemployed by industry and construction, and of the reluctance of peasants to seek work in towns and industrial settlements in view of the deterioration in real wages and working conditions in non-agricultural employment. All these inter-related factors which helped to bring about the crisis of the summer of 1930 thus stemmed from the expansion of capital investment in 1929/30.

The huge increase in industrial investment, and the associated pressure throughout industry and all other sectors of the economy, was thus a major contributory cause of the crisis. But this is not the whole story. The capital investment plan for 1929/30, the associated plans for industrial production, and the revised five-year plans, were not merely high; they were unrealistically high. This circumstance exacerbated all difficulties. The attempt to achieve an unrealistically high level of investment evoked feverish efforts to acquire additional labour and materials in order to make up lost ground, and placed an additional strain on resources. Moreover, the adoption of the vastly increased five-year plans led to an increase in the number of new projects started, and a rise in the proportion of capital investment allocated both to major new long-term projects and to expanded versions of existing projects. Investment was not diverted to major projects to the extent planned (see pp. 381–2 below). But the proportion of investment allocated to projects which were not completed in the course of the year was much higher than in any previous year (see p. 380 below), and the proportion of investment which became immediately available to facilitate current production consequently fell.

The difficulties created by the over-ambitious plans were dramatically illustrated by the travails of the outstanding construction of 1929/30, the Stalingrad tractor factory, following its official completion in June 1930. The factory planned to produce 2,000 tractors in July–September 1930.[113] In fact it produced eight in June, none in July, ten in the last five days of August and 25 in September, a total of 43 in all.[114] Moreover, according to an American technician:

> *None of the few tractors produced by the factory has stood the test run. It is a fact that after 70 hours of work they begin to go to pieces.*[115]

The source of all the difficulties was that the factory started production prematurely.[116] Machinery continued to arrive throughout the summer, so that much work had to be done by hand in the tool-room; only 75 per cent had arrived even by the end of September.[117] Moreover, plans to supply from Soviet factories most of the metal required for tractor production had to be temporarily abandoned. Tests of steel from the main supplier, the Stalingrad 'Krasnyi Oktyabr'' works, showed it was of hopelessly poor quality. Copper ribbon to make radiators arrived from the Leningrad 'Krasnyi Vyborzhets' works with 'no protective packing, torn and scratched', and was unusable. Nuts of inadequate quality were supplied by workshops which

[113] ZI, June 19, 1930 (Ivanov); the original plan was 3,500 tractors (I, September 11, 1930).

[114] Il'in, ed. (1931), 17. Knickerbocker (1931), 93, reported that 20 tractors were made in August and 60 in September; Dodge (1960), 278, cites slightly different figures, totalling 35, for the first four months.

[115] ZI, October 8, 1930.

[116] A fictionalised history of the factory later commented that 'social opinion drove them, the wish to offer the first tractor to the XVI party congress as the Promise (slovo) for 1930, the year of the developed offensive on all fronts of construction' (Il'in (1934), 108).

[117] P, July 30, 1930 (Osinskii), ZI, October 8, 1930.

had previously made nails for peasant huts.[118] While building was in progress little attention was paid to preparation for production: a leading construction worker later admitted that 'we all thought that as soon as we finished building the factory everything would be complete at once and tractors would start to come off the conveyor-belt'.[119] According to a report from the factory:

No-one paid any attention to the plan for developing production, no-one thought about it in the days when the construction was being completed. Everything was directed to getting the first tractor off the production line. But they forgot about how the second, third, fifth, one-hundredth and one-thousandth tractor would be produced, how the flow of production would be organised . . . No-one thought about producing tooling, or about training people properly to work on the first-class American automatic machine tools. No-one thought about producing experimental tractors, and carefully checking their work.[120]

The workers were almost completely untrained. They included 7,000 young workers, many of whom had never held a nut, and other unskilled workers who damaged the machines. The courses provided while the factory was being completed were badly organised, endeavouring to teach trigonometry to people who did not even know their multiplication table.[121] Margaret Bourke-White, the American industrial photographer, vividly described the situation in the autumn of 1930:

Our familiar American scene of the production line with rows of men on each side popping nuts and bolts and sprocket-wheels and camshafts into their respective places along a steadily moving conveyor belt is something that the Russians as a body have never experienced or imagined. Instead the production line usually stands perfectly still. Half-way down the factory is a partly completed tractor. One Russian is screwing in a tiny little bolt and twenty other

[118] P, July 30, 31, 1930 (Osinskii); Il'in, ed. (1933), 407 (Tsmyg, editor of the factory newspaper *Daesh' traktor!*); Dodge (1960), 293.
[119] Il'in, ed. (1933), 188 (Lipkin).
[120] I, September 11, 1930 (Vishnyakov).
[121] Il'in, ed. (1933), 56, 131–4, 138, 140, 155; Dodge (1960), 190.

Russians are standing around him watching, talking it over, smoking cigarettes, arguing.

In this perfectly designed factory, 'peasants, theorists, young political enthusiasts' were 'like children marvelling over new toys . . . religious fanatics worshipping before a new shrine':

> they do not even know how to take directions to use it. Instead they make long speeches about the power of the machine and write eloquent articles about the glory of industry. In all this there is a flaming religious fervour. For the new ikon is a drill press.

When the radiator shell is lowered:

> A veritable army guides it into the assembly. A boy with a striped shirt wearing a sailor hat, a worker with a cigarette, a comrade in an embroidered blouse, an old man with side-whiskers, a serious-faced girl, all hurry forward, anxious to give a helping hand.[122]

At the centre of the difficulties, the factory director, Ivanov, found that the curses and exhortations which had proved effective in getting the factory built were not effective in mastering production. At the end of August, 'the whole factory collective, from manual workers to engineers', was buzzing with the story that he had sworn at the head of the power station and pushed him out of the building in the presence of indignant workers. In the course of the next few weeks, he struck a workman, and accused a foreman of being a counter-revolutionary when he was caught smoking after the conveyor belt had stopped.[123] The fictionalised history of the factory described his increasing loss of confidence which eventually made him frightened of being alone.[124]

In the middle of September 1930, the Politburo, indignant at failure, heard a report on the work of the factory; such detailed attention to the major new projects and factories by the highest

[122] Bourke-White (1931), 118–19, 125.
[123] I, September 11, 1930; Il'in, ed. (1933), 78 (Lapidus, party secretary); Knickerbocker (1931), 90.
[124] Il'in (1934), 118.

party authority was by now becoming normal practice.[125] But the extraordinary degree of haste and muddle had been generated by the over-ambitious plans forced upon the management and the workers by the Politburo itself, and it was unable to offer a viable immediate solution to the problems of the factory.

The enthusiasm of the minority of politically active workers helped to mitigate such problems. In the summer of 1930, the socialist emulation movement, including the production collectives and communes, was at its height, and many of the large number of new recruits to the party eagerly sought to win their spurs. But 1930 was also a year of social and administrative upheaval. From the end of 1929, every major government department, and most factories and other economic units, were successively subject to the purge of specialists and officials directed against the conservative and the faint-hearted, and sometimes accompanied or followed by charges of wrecking (see pp. 111–12 above). Simultaneously, the party purge was directed against those actually or purportedly influenced by Rightist views (see pp. 61–2, 117–18 above).

The disruptive effect of the purges on normal administration was greatly enhanced in industry and internal trade by the thoroughgoing organisational reform, which continued at least until the summer of 1930 (see pp. 241–3 above). In industry the reform brought about more administrative restructuring than any of the reforms of the 1920s; it was possibly more disruptive of normal administrative activity than any other reform except the Khrushchev regionalisation of 1957. Most industrial administrators spent a substantial part of their time changing jobs or shifting offices, or at least changing the labels on their doors and the arrangement of their files. But the major defect of the reorganisation was not its protracted complexity but its inappropriateness for the new central planning system which was emerging. The formal and informal connections established in the 1920s between the factories and their administrative superiors were breaking down, and a satisfactory new system of connections failed to emerge. At best, something like the old arrangements continued by inertia and necessity.

---

[125] Il'in, ed. (1933), 75–6; Stalin, Molotov and Postyshev took part in the discussion.

The credit reforms had a similar effect on financial arrangements (see pp. 320–8 above). All these changes had a cumulative effect on the daily operation of industry, and undoubtedly contributed to the economic crisis of the summer of 1930.

The administrative upheaval was accompanied by a social upheaval, as new workers moved in to industry, and many of the most experienced workers departed for new factories. This was in large part an inevitable cost of industrial expansion, inevitably putting a brake on labour productivity. But the unexpected complexity and chaos resulting from the collectivisation of agriculture made unexpectedly large claims for the transfer of politically active workers and officials from the towns, temporarily or permanently. The troubled relations with agriculture also contributed directly to the exacerbation of the crisis in the industrial economy in the summer of 1930. If the forced collectivisation drive itself was a response of the leadership to the disruption of the food market by the pressures of industrialisation, socialised agriculture in turn placed unexpected demands on industry which greatly complicated all the plans for industrial development. Socialised agriculture imperatively demanded mechanisation, and this requirement led to further substantial increases in the plans for the major producer goods industries. When the pig-iron plan for 1932/33 was increased from 10 to 17·6 million tons, 3·3 million tons of the increase were intended for the industries producing agricultural implements, tractors, combine-harvesters and vehicles.[126] When the five-year plan for the output of crude oil in 1932/33 was increased from 22 to 40 million tons, the major factor was the need for fuel for tractors and vehicles. It was estimated that they would consume some 14 or 15 million tons of the 18 million tons of petrol and kerosene which would be obtained from 40 million tons of crude oil.[127]

In 1929/30 these longer-term needs of socialised agriculture already imposed themselves on the established priorities of current plans. The major capital projects which were hurriedly completed in time for the XVI party congress – Turksib, Rostsel'mash and the Stalingrad tractor factory – were all

[126] EZh, January 12, 1930 (Tseitlin); a substantial proportion of the vehicles was intended for use in the countryside.

[127] ZI, February 14, 1930 (prof. A. Sakharov); P, May 14, 1930 (Kviring).

closely associated with the improvement of agriculture and were presented to the congress as practical evidence that the agricultural problem could be solved in the very near future. The priority afforded to these projects in turn hindered the completion of plans for the introduction of new capacity in the iron and steel and coal industries.

When the Soviet leaders imposed high grain collections and collectivisation on the peasantry, they failed to anticipate that this would bring about a substantial deterioration in agriculture, and an immediate livestock crisis. These unexpected developments in turn seriously undermined the plans for industrialisation. The precipitate decline in livestock greatly reduced the food available to the non-agricultural population and was a major factor in the decline of real wages in the summer of 1930.[128] The decline in the number of horses available for agricultural work made agricultural mechanisation much more urgent. The expansion of the money incomes earned by collective farmers and individual peasants on the free market disrupted all the plans of the authorities for the control of trade and consumption, and contributed to the labour shortages and increased labour turnover which were a major feature of the crisis of July–September 1930.

---

[128] The consumption of livestock products per head of the non-agricultural population, measured in 1928 prices, declined from 63r 99k in 1929, 41 per cent of all their food consumption, to 50r 45k in 1930, 33 per cent of all their food consumption (*Materials* (1985), 204).

CHAPTER TEN

THE ECONOMIC YEAR 1929/30 IN RETROSPECT

(A) CAPITAL INVESTMENT

The outstanding feature of the second 'spinal' year of the five-year plan was the vast expansion of capital investment and its concentration on the producer goods industries. Total gross investment for the whole economy, including capital repair, increased by over 30 per cent.[1] The increase in net investment was even more rapid: according to Soviet estimates, in the calendar year 1930 net investment or 'real accumulation' increased by 69 per cent when measured in current prices and by 92 per cent in 1928 prices (see Table 1). As much as two-thirds of the total increase in gross investment was attributable to the producer goods industries; investment in Group A industries (including electric power) amounted to 1,453 million rubles in 1928/29 and 3,240 millions in 1929/30, an increase of 123 per cent. Within this total, investment in the construction of new factories expanded most rapidly of all.[2] Investment in agriculture and transport increased much more slowly, while in urban and rural housing, education and health, and in the consumer goods industries, it declined absolutely, reversing the trend of previous years.[3] Within the service sectors, the needs of

---

[1] Detailed figures were not published. Our incomplete estimates in current prices in Table 7 show an increase of 35 per cent. Shortly after the end of the economic year, *Pravda* reported that investment in fixed prices (evidently 1926/27 prices) increased from 8,800 million rubles in 1928/29 to 11,500 millions in 1929/30, or by 30·7 per cent (P, October 28, 1930 – Maimin).

[2] *Materialy VSNKh* (1931), 12; nearly all the investment in new factories was located in Group A industries.

[3] See Tables 2, 3 and 4; the data for several sectors are available only for the calendar years 1929 and 1930. The figure for consumer goods excludes the food industries. According to *Pishchevaya industriya* (1937), 19, investment in

industry were treated as paramount: thus investment in urban housing controlled by industry rose by 173 per cent, while investment in housing controlled by the local soviets and the cooperatives, and in private housing, declined (see Table 3).

The major achievements in the producer goods industries were nevertheless failures if judged by the criterion of plan fulfilment. In industry and electric power capital investment in 1929/30 amounted to only 81 per cent of the revised plan, and some 90 per cent of the original plan.[4] Moreover, these figures in current prices underestimate the failure to fulfil the plan in real terms, as the cost of capital construction fell less rapidly than planned.[5] According to Vesenkha, industrial investment in real terms amounted to only about 77 per cent of the revised plan.[6]

The fulfilment of the investment plan was at least as unfavourable in most other sectors of the economy. Only 84 per cent of the capital investment programme for the railways (1,200 million rubles) was fulfilled in terms of current prices,[7] some 77 per cent in real terms. Rails supplied amount to 79 per cent and goods wagons to only 73 per cent of the plan.[8] Moreover, capital investment in the construction of new railways reached only 65 per cent of the plan in current prices, about 60 per cent in real terms.[9]

The failure to reach planned levels of investment in crucial

---

the food industries increased from 155 million rubles in 1929 to 256 millions in 1930, but what is included under this heading is not stated.

[4] See Table 4, and *Materialy VSNKh* (1931), 19.

[5] Building costs for industry were planned to decline by 14 per cent (*KTs . . . na 1929/30* (1930), 578) but in fact declined, according to one report, by 5·9 per cent in 1929/30 (P, October 6, 1930), according to another, by 7·7 per cent; investment costs, including the cost of capital equipment, declined by 8·5 per cent (see Table 24(d)). These figures may exaggerate the extent of cost reduction.

[6] ZI, November 23, 1930.

[7] P, October 8, 9, 1930 (report by Mironov of Narkomput' to the eighth congress of the building workers' union).

[8] EZh, October 26, 1930; *Zheleznodorozhnyi transport* (1970), 102; 307,000 tons of rails were supplied against 250,000 tons in 1928/29 (ZI, June 21, 1930).

[9] *Zheleznodorozhnyi transport* (1970), 99–100. The annual report on the state budget, which shows moneys passed to the railways rather than actually absorbed in construction, recorded a somewhat better performance (million rubles at current prices):

producer goods industries called the future of the revised five-year plan into question.[10] The achievement of the revised five-year plans approved at the XVI party congress required a substantial improvement in the output from existing capacity and a huge increase in new capacity. The halt in the growth of production in the summer of 1930 demonstrated that it would be difficult to obtain substantial production increases from existing capacity. But as a result of the lag in capital investment a much smaller amount of new capacity became available in industry than planned. The control figures planned an increase of fixed capital in use of 37·2 per cent;[11] the actual increase recorded was only 21 per cent.[12] New factories starting work during the year were valued at only 600 million rubles as compared with the plan of 940 millions.[13] In spite of the huge increases in industrial investment in 1929/30, the total amount put into operation, including both new and existing factories, was only slightly higher than in 1928/29.[14] This lag resulted from a large unintended increase in unfinished construction. In view of the high planned increases of investment it seemed feasible to

	Plan	1929/30 Actual	Percentage
Capital investment: existing railways	625·7	527·8	84·4
new railways	265·4	223·0	84·0
	891·1	750·8	84·3

(*Otchet . . . 1929–1930* (1931), ob. zapiska, 64–6). These figures exclude capital repair.

[10] The following percentages of fulfilment in real terms were reported from Vesenkha, as compared with 77 per cent for Vesenkha-planned industry as a whole: machine tools 45, coking and chemicals 59, building materials 65, vehicles and tractors 64, oil 82, coal 85 (ZI, November 23, 1930); for revised figures in current prices see Table 4. Investment in power stations lagged particularly badly.

[11] *KTs . . . na 1929/30* (1930), 447.

[12] P, October 2, 1930 (Guberman), presumably referring to large-scale industry; *Materials* (1985), 168, gives an increase of 28 per cent in the calendar year 1930 for all industry.

[13] *Industrializatsiya, 1929–1932* (1970), 133; P, November 3, 1930; the figure of 940 million rubles is explicitly stated to exclude industries working for defence, and presumably the figure of 600 millions also excludes these industries.

[14] *Materialy VSNKh* (1931), 16 (1,446 against 1,424 million rubles; these figures are for Vesenkha-planned industry, excluding the food industry and non-industrial power-stations).

start a larger number of projects, and the number of new starts greatly increased in the course of 1929/30. But the underfulfilment of the plan resulted in what *Pravda* described as 'the overextension of the front'.[15] The increase in unfinished construction in 1929/30 amounted to 55 per cent of the total investment in industry during the year.[16]

Even the major new producer goods factories, the backbone of the revised five-year plan, did not receive sufficient priority. Some prestige projects undoubtedly enjoyed considerable advantages in the supplies of men, money and materials. A large accumulation of metal was reported at Dneprostroi,[17] and of cement and timber at the Tomsky (Makeevka) iron and steel works.[18] Such major projects were supported by the intervention of the presidium of Vesenkha, which issued *ad hoc* orders allocating specific materials to specific sites,[19] and reducing allocations to sites which were working badly.[20] But no special mechanism yet existed for the control of priority sites, and Vesenkha switched its attention from site to site, neglecting those to which it paid attention earlier. Thus the number of construction workers at the Stalingrad tractor factory was cut by 7,000 immediately after the factory was started, although much remained to be built.[21] In the course of an extensive survey of the capital investment programme for 1929/30, a Vesenkha spokesman let fall this revealing comment:

It is difficult to say which of the construction jobs of heavy industry are 'shock' jobs. In essence they are all 'shock' jobs.[22]

During the summer of 1930, even such important sites as

[15] P, November 3, 1930.
[16] According to *Materialy VSNKh* (1931), 16, unfinished construction increased in value by 1,765 million rubles in 1929/30 against only 235 million rubles in 1928/29; for coverage see note 14 above.
[17] *Metall*, 10–12, 1930, 124–131 (Tovbin).
[18] P, May 31, 1930.
[19] See for example P, August 25, 1930 (cable for Berezniki chemical plant).
[20] ZI, October 4, 1930 (Zolotarev on Voskresenskii chemical plant).
[21] I, September 11, 1930 (report from Stalingrad), ZI, October 1, 1930 (Myshkov).
[22] I, February 5, 1930 (Mednikov).

Magnitogorsk,[23] the Kramatorsk engineering works[24] and the
Kharkov tractor factory[25] complained of serious shortages of
workers, money and materials. Even in these crucial industries
the five-year plan was already in jeopardy.

(B) INDUSTRIAL PRODUCTION

The massive increase in investment and the labour force in the
producer goods industries resulted in an increase in their
production by as much as 39 per cent in 1929/30 (see Table
7(a)). The increase in the production of the engineering
industries was particularly impressive (see Table 8(a)).
Significant developments took place in branches of engineering
previously little developed in the USSR. With the development
of the Moscow vehicle factory and the tractor shop at the
Putilov factory, the production of lorries and tractors greatly
increased. The production of machine tools rose by over 60 per
cent. The electrical engineering corporation VEO increased
production by as much as 81 per cent, and overfulfilled its
annual plan; new items of production included a 24,000kW
steam turbogenerator and a 115,000V transformer.[26]

These achievements in the producer goods industries in
1929/30 contrasted with the pervasive difficulties in the
consumer goods industries. Production of Vesenkha-planned
Group B industries, including the food industry, increased by
only 12 per cent (see Table 7(a)). As a result of the reduction in
supplies (see p. 369 above), the production of several major
consumer goods manufactured from agricultural raw materials,
notably cotton textiles, drastically declined.[27] The food industry
was also in difficulties. Production of sugar fell drastically,

[23] ZI, October 4, 1930; expenditure was reported to have been much less
than planned throughout 1929/30, except in the very last month of the economic
year.
[24] ZI, October 1, 1930 (Kuz'min, head of construction).
[25] P, May 28, July 31 (Osinskii), October 25, 1930; ZI, October 1, 1930.
[26] TsGANKh, 3429/1/5242, 18–20. The turbogenerator was manufactured
in Leningrad under licence from Metropolitan Vickers and to their design
(*Machinery*, vol. 94, January 21, 1959, pp. 165–6).
[27] See Table 8(b). The production of woollens and footwear increased owing
to the availability of wool and leather in large quantities due to the slaughter
of animals.

owing to the bad harvest of 1929, and was supplemented by imports (see p. 392 n. 57 below); production of animal products, such as butter, also declined. This bleak picture was modified, or concealed, by the continued expansion of the production of alcoholic drink and tobacco, and by substantial increases in the factory manufacture of clothing and preserved foods, previously made almost entirely domestically or by artisans (see Tables 7(a)–(b) and 8(b)). But this shift to large-scale production did not indicate a corresponding increase in real consumption.

Supplementing large-scale industry, artisan and other small-scale industry, responsible for over one-third of the production of consumer goods, displayed a remarkable capacity for survival in face of the powerful forces acting against them. A survey of fourteen artisan metalworking artels in Melitopol' and district reported that in spite of the metal shortage they were producing oil and diesel motors, pumps and children's bicycles; they were able to use any grade of metal 'to the last gram', but also obtained metal on loan from factories in order to carry out orders.[28] A report on the footwear industry in October 1930 declared that 'the private trader has begun to busy himself more intensively; work with the customer's raw material is vast in scale; coopers are busy in almost every village, and even in kolkhoz and sovkhoz systems the working of leather is being carried out on a considerable scale under the guise of various kinds of artisan cooperation'.[29] The net effect of the countervailing pressures on small-scale industry is difficult to assess. Statistics are not available for the economic year 1929/30, and are unreliable for 1930.[30] The official statistics for 1930 purport to show that while the total production of small-scale industry slightly declined, its production of consumer goods slightly increased.[31] These figures are doubtless exaggerated. But even

[28] *Metall*, 10–12, 1930, 140–2 (Tovbin).

[29] ZI, October 11, 1930, reporting conference of October 7.

[30] Estimates were made by the expert evaluators of district and regional planning commissions on the basis of a questionnaire to the private sector and a comprehensive census of the socialised sector, and then corrected with the aid of other material (*Materials* (1985), 292).

[31] According to an estimate made in 1931, the number of persons engaged in small-scale industry increased from 4,500,000 in 1928/29 (average) to 4,636,000 in October 1929–December 1930 (average), while production in 1930 grew by 7·5 per cent in current prices and declined by 2·3 per cent in 1926/27 prices (see Table 16 and PI, 5–6, 1931, 74, 77 – Sen'ko). According to the estimate

taking them at their face value, their inclusion with the figures for census industry greatly reduces the total rate of increase of the production of consumer goods.[32]

The statistics for both Vesenkha-planned and small-scale industry exaggerate the increase in production in a further important respect, particularly in the case of consumer goods. They take no account of the further decline in quality in 1929/30, which affected the whole of industry, but particularly consumer goods. In the spring of 1930, the Vesenkha presidium, following a report from Kraval', noted the 'threatening position' in regard to quality, and the 'further deterioration' in quality which had occurred in several industries.[33] A survey of the quality of textiles in April–June 1930 revealed that defective production had more than doubled in a number of areas as compared with the previous year.[34] A Gosplan survey of the results of 1929/30 noted that the woollen industry had gone over to 'cruder forms of raw material', while the footwear industry had gone over to substitutes.[35] In October 1930, at a USSR conference on the quality of consumer goods, Kuibyshev castigated the *'conveyor belt of irresponsibility and spoiled production'* which stretched from the coal industry via the iron and steel industry, the engineering industry and light industry to the

---

in *Materials* (1985), 155, 179, production of small-scale industry was as follows (million rubles at 1928 prices):

	1928	1929	1930
Net output	1812	1662	1620
Gross turnover			
Producer goods	1116	1045	971
Consumer goods	4753	4661	4878
Total	5869	5706	5849

[32] According to *Materials* (1985), 179, gross turnover of consumer goods produced by census industry increased by 20·7 per cent in 1930 (in 1928 prices) but gross turnover of all consumer goods, including the production of small-scale industry, increased by only 14·8 per cent.

[33] TsGANKh, 3429/1/5193, 92 (the session appears to be dated May 20); this was followed by a lengthy Vesenkha order of June 20, signed by Kuibyshev (SP VSNKh, 1929/30, art. 1553).

[34] It had increased from 6·8 to 14 per cent in Ivanovo region, 9 to 22 per cent in Leningrad and 4 to 14 per cent in Moscow region (*Za rabotoi*, 11–12, 1930).

[35] *Industrializatsiya, 1929–1932* (1970), 237–8 (Gosplan survey).

consumer, as a result of which the quality of cotton and woollen textiles had deteriorated from quarter to quarter. Kuibyshev pointed out that while the failure of managers to achieve the quantitative production plan resulted in dismissal, no manager was ever called to account for deteriorating quality of output, and announced that '*quality is now being placed on the same level as the fulfilment of the production programme*'. The conference resolved that all industrial plans should henceforth contain indicators 'guaranteeing a minimum level of quality'.[36] But for some time to come these firm resolutions would remain no more than pious hopes.

(c) FINANCE AND INTERNAL TRADE

In 1929/30 the expenditure on the unified state budget exceeded the estimates approved in December 1929 by over 6 per cent, and increased by as much as 60 per cent as compared with 1928/29. This was more than double the rate of growth in each of the previous two years, and far outstripped the growth of the national income, which increased by no more than 16 per cent in 1929/30.[37]

The rapid growth of budgetary expenditure was mainly a direct consequence of the growth of capital investment. Allocations to industry and agriculture doubled in 1929/30; these two items alone accounted for more than 50 per cent of the net increase in expenditure. In spite of the considerable underfulfilment of the capital investment plan, budget expenditure on industry exceeded the estimates by 17·8 per cent. This was a consequence of the underfulfilment of the profit plan of industry, which was in turn due to its failure to reduce costs as much as planned. The control figures for 1929/30, following the principles set out in the five-year plan, anticipated that a high proportion of the financial plan would consist of the internal resources of the major branches of the

[36] ZI, October 12, 15, 1930.
[37] Data on the state budget in this section are derived from Table 22(a)–(b) unless otherwise stated. According to Maimin, the national income amounted to 32·7 milliard rubles in 1929/30, an increase of 15·7 per cent (P, October 28, 1930 – estimated in 'fixed prices' – evidently 1926/27 prices). For the national income in the calendar years 1928–30 see Table 1.

economy, and that the role of the budget in providing finance
for industry would decline.[38] These hopes proved entirely
unwarranted. The proportion of investment in Group A
industries financed by the state budget increased from 64 per
cent in 1928/29 to 78 per cent in 1929/30.[39] Moreover, the
resources contributed by Group A industries to capital
investment consisted almost entirely of depreciation allowances;
these were calculated as an automatic percentage of costs, and
in no sense reflected financial efficiency. The paramountcy of
state budget allocations in financing investment was implicitly
recognised by a decree of May 23, 1930, which ruled that all
allocations from the budget to state industry, trade and
transport and to state agricultural enterprises should be in the
form of non-returnable grants with effect from October 1, 1929;
this brought an end to the long controversy about whether
loans or grants were the best means of financing investment.[40]

The financial authorities were apparently brilliantly successful
in finding revenue to cover these huge increases in expenditure.
Budgetary revenue increased even more rapidly than expenditure, by as much as 65·7 per cent, and exceeded the estimates
by over 1,100 million rubles. The budget surplus, planned at a
mere 30 million rubles, amounted to as much as 648 million
rubles, a much larger surplus than in any previous year.

Four major sources of revenue contributed to this success.
First, the excise from vodka and other alcoholic drink almost
doubled: the rate of tax was sharply increased in the autumn of
1929, and production increased by over 10 per cent.[41] The
decision in 1929 to reduce the sales of vodka in the course of the
five-year plan was silently reversed.[42]

[38] *KTs . . . na 1929/30* (1930), 275.

[39] PKh, 5, 1932, 115 (Putilov).

[40] SZ, 1930, art. 316; the controversy temporarily re-emerged in 1932 (see
SR, lxii, 209 (Davies)), but was not seriously resumed until the 1960s.

[41] According to *Ezhemesyachnyi statisticheskii byulleten'*, 1–2 (86), August–
September 1930, production of grain alcohol and table wine increased from
527 to 582 million litres; according to Nutter (1962), 454, 489, citing *Pishchevaya
promyshlennost'*, 1–2, 1932, 13, the production of 40° vodka rose from 527 to 613
million litres. For the increases in the rate of tax, see SZ, 1929, arts. 591–2 (dated
September 27) and 630 (dated October 21).

[42] Grain allocation for the production of all types of alcohol, including
industrial alcohol, increased from 124,000 tons from the 1928 harvest to 509,000
tons from the 1929 harvest (see vol. 1, Table 9(c)).

The second major source of additional revenue was the state loan system, consisting primarily of mass loans to the population and sums loaned by the savings banks from the net increase in their deposits. For wage-earners, these loans were more or less compulsory in character, and amounted to about 5 per cent of the total wage bill, a slightly higher proportion than in 1928/29. In the countryside, much pressure was exerted to secure subscriptions to loans by peasants, particularly during the collectivisation drive of the winter of 1929–30: their contributions quadrupled as compared with the previous year, but remained a small proportion of the total.[43] Until 1930 the sale back to the state of loan obligations was a widespread practice. But in 1929 a Narkomfin pamphlet insisted that 'the sale-back of obligations while capital construction is developing is equivalent to pulling the bricks out of a building under construction', and in February 1930 the Elektrozavod factory, Moscow, which was the official 'patron' of Narkomfin (see p. 117 above), launched a campaign to prevent this practice. Henceforth sale-back awaited the permission of the local loan commission, and occurred much less frequently.[44]

A third source of additional revenue was provided by the railways. The transport system as a whole earned a surplus of 47 million rubles in 1929/30 as compared with a planned deficit of 312 million rubles; the deficit in 1928/29 amounted to 86

---

[43] Sources of the main mass loans of 1928/29 and 1929/30 were as follows (million rubles, with percentage of total in brackets):

	Second industrialisation (launched in 1928)	Third industrialisation (launched in 1929)
Workers and white-collar employees	412 (82)	671 (72)
Peasants	45 (9)	199 (21)
Other	47 (9)	64 (7)
Total	504 (100)	935 (100)

(Martynov (1973), 108); these are subscriptions, not actual amounts paid in.

[44] P, February 21, 1930, Kul'chitskii (Kiev, 1979), 205. It was simultaneously announced that all loans to the population would be absorbed in the new mass loan 'The Five-Year Plan in Four' (SZ, 1930, art. 137, dated February 21, and art. 379, dated July 3); this effectively reduced the interest due on loans issued before 1929.

million rubles. This unexpected achievement was partly a result
of the failure of capital investment on the railways to increase
as much as planned.[45] But it was mainly due to the increased
profit on current operations. Owing to the vast expansion of
traffic in 1929/30, more goods and more passengers were carried
per unit of rolling stock than in 1928/29. The huge increase of 48
per cent in the number of passengers carried by the railways,
which exceeded the plan by as much as 26 per cent, reflected
the enormous upheaval of 1929/30, when millions of citizens, in
response to the expansion of employment and the deteriorating
conditions, travelled in search of better jobs.[46] Freight carried
also increased substantially. The total traffic on the increasingly
overcrowded trains rose by 31 per cent. Passenger fares were
increased from August 1, 1930, and freight charges also rose
slightly, providing additional income. The surplus on current
account increased from 653 million rubles in 1928/29 to 1,184
million rubles in 1929/30.[47] This was the only sector of the
economy in which operating costs per unit were lower than

---

[45] See p. 379 above, and *Otchet . . . 1929–1930* (1931), ob. zapiska, 55–66; the
rest of the information in this paragraph is also derived from the latter source.

[46] The average length of passenger journey increased from 87 to 93km., so
passenger traffic increased more rapidly than the number of passengers carried.
These figures are for 'paying passengers', and may therefore exclude the
passenger traffic resulting from the exiling of kulaks and others (*Otchet . . .
1929–1930* (1931), ob. zapiska, 58).

[47] The summary results are as follows (income and expenditure are in million
rubles):

		1928/29	*1929/30*	*Percentage increase*
1	Paying passengers (milliard passenger-km.)	29·7	47·5	59·9
2	Income from passengers and luggage	412·5	695·0	68·3
3	Freight (milliard ton-km.)	106·7	131·5	23·5
4	Income from freight	1731·4	2189·7	26·5
5	Total traffic in milliard standard ton-km.[a]	136·3	179·3	31·5
6	Other income	105·3	101·0	−4·1
7	Total income (1 + 4 + 6)	2249·2	2985·7	32·7
8	Operating expenditure	1596·0	1801·8	28·9

(*Otchet . . . 1929–1930* (1931), ob. zapiska, 58–62).
[a] 1 passenger-km. is taken as equivalent to 1 ton-km. of freight.

planned, declining by as much as 14·1 per cent instead of the planned 9·1 per cent. But the penalties were severe. The average speed of freight trains, 13·8 km. per hour in 1928/29, declined to 12·3 km. in 1929/30. Locomotives and rolling stock were exploited to the point of breakdown. The annual budget report slightingly described the financial success as 'a positive result according to the numerical data', but brusquely commented that 'this was not a consequence of initiatives by Narkomput' itself . . . but due to causes independent of it'.

The fourth source of additional budgetary revenue was provided by state and cooperative enterprises. This was by far the most important single item: revenue from industrial tax, income tax and deductions from profits paid by the socialised sector increased by 1,729 million rubles, 121 per cent. Part of the increase was due to the transfer of excises on textiles and other commodities into industrial tax, and should properly appear under excises.[48] But most of it was obtained by intensive efforts to mop up income available in enterprise accounts, particularly those of trading enterprises and republican and local industry. Thus in 1929/30 deductions from profits, previously collected from profits of the previous year, were collected from previous-year and current-year profits simultaneously; 408 million rubles were raised from current-year profits, including 306 million rubles from local industry. The rates of income tax on socialised enterprises were also increased. The largest single increase was in the industrial tax, but the devices by which the increase was obtained were not clearly explained in the report on the fulfilment of the state budget.[49]

This squeeze on the accounts of enterprises in the socialised sector deprived them of the working capital needed for their

[48] The excise on textiles amounted to 134 million rubles in 1928/29 (*Otchet . . . 1928/1929* (1930), 35); no equivalent figure for 1929/30 has been available.

[49] The main sources of revenue from socialised enterprises were as follows (million rubles):

	1928/29	*1929/30*
Industrial tax	885	1841
Income tax	119	321
Deductions from profits of state industry	254	791
Other	166	200
Total	1424	3153

current operations, and a large part of the resources transferred to the budget was promptly replaced by the vast and largely uncontrolled short-term loans made by Gosbank after the credit reform (see pp. 326–7 above). Precise figures have not been available: according to one source, the bank issued unplanned credits amounting to 1,100 million rubles in 1929/30, most of them in the second half of the year. The short-term credits issued by the bank not merely cancelled out the budget surplus, but were also responsible for net currency issues amounting to 1,621 million rubles as compared with the plan of 600 million rubles.[50] Deficit finance was concealed behind the facade of a state budget in surplus.

The currency issue of 1929/30, which amounted to 61 per cent of the total currency in circulation on October 1, 1929 (see Table 23), fuelled an increase of money incomes which far outstripped the increase in the supply of goods in real terms. The incomes of the non-agricultural population in 1929/30 were estimated as 20 per cent and of the agricultural population as 22 per cent greater than in 1928/29, as compared with the planned 11 per cent in each case.[51] But the supply of goods at the relatively low fixed prices of state and cooperative trade increased at a lower rate. Even according to the official statistics, retail trade in the socialised sector increased by only 18·3 per cent in 1929/30 (see Table 12). And a Gosplan report published

[50] FP, 1–2, 1931, 73 (Saigushkin), and Table 23 below.
[51] The following figures (million rubles) were reported in *Kon''yunktura . . . za sentyabr' i 12 mesyatsev 1929/30* (n.d. [1930]), Obmen i raspredelenie, p. 1:

	1928/9	1929/30	Planned increase (control figures) (per cent)	Actual increase (per cent)
All income of non-agricultural population	12363	14806	10·8	19·7
of which, proletariat [i.e. wage-earners]	8942	11387	16·3	27·3
Income of agricultural population	10267	12515	10·9	21·8
of which, from sale of agricultural production	6600	7590	5·5	15·0

See also P, October 2, 1930; PKh, 7–8, 1930, 39–40 (Guberman).

at the time recorded a growth in the supply of goods at current prices (including higher commercial prices) of only 9 per cent,[52] and in the case of twelve key industrial commodities supplies to the retail market declined by 3 per cent in real terms in 1929/30.[53]

The gap between supply and demand was even larger than is indicated by these figures, because organised private retail trade, in spite of a substantial increase in prices, declined by 50 per cent in 1929/30 (see Table 12, note h). It was partly replaced by peasant bazaar trade, which declined in real terms, but increased considerably in terms of current prices. But in 1929/30 a substantial part of bazaar trade merely transferred surplus purchasing power from the urban to the rural population. The growth of private trade in agricultural goods at high prices, together with the unavailability of many industrial goods, resulted in huge increases in the cash holdings of the population. According to rough calculations by Narkomfin and Gosplan, cash held in the countryside increased between October 1, 1929, and October 1, 1930, from 1,500 to 2,690 million rubles, and urban personal cash holdings increased from 250 to 500 million rubles, a total increase of 1,440 millions.[54]

(D) FOREIGN TRADE

The enormous growth of capital investment in industry in 1929/30 resulted in very substantial increases in the import of capital equipment. Machinery employed in modern enterprises such as the Stalingrad tractor factory was either not manufactured at all in the USSR, or was manufactured in insufficient quantities. The reconstructed vehicle assembly

---

[52] PKh, 7–8, 1930, 43 (Guberman); the increase was 4–5 per cent if commercial prices were not taken into account.

[53] *Tovarooborot* (1932), 9 (measured in 1926/27 prices).

[54] FP, 1–2, 1931, 76 (Saigushkin); cash held by the peasants on December 1, 1927, was estimated at only 450 million rubles (see Carr and Davies (1969), 45). A lower estimate gave the increase in cash as 840 million rubles for the agricultural and 360 million rubles for the non-agricultural population (*Kon"yunktura . . . za sentyabr' i 12 mesyatsev 1929/30* (n.d. [1930]), Obmen i raspredelenie, p. 2).

works in Moscow was equipped with machine tools from Ford and in the first stages merely assembled components purchased from Ford.[55] Even in the case of the long-established agricultural engineering industry, 45 per cent of the capital equipment installed in Rostsel'mash was imported from abroad.[56] Several other long-established industries such as iron and steel continued to depend on foreign suppliers for their major items of equipment. The total import of machinery and apparatus (including machine parts) more than doubled in the single year 1929/30, and absorbed 22 per cent of all imports, as compared with 13 per cent in 1928/29. Imports of metals and metal components, also primarily required for capital investment, increased by 63 per cent, and electrical engineering imports by 31 per cent (see Table 13(c)).

The decision to accelerate the mechanisation of agriculture also made substantial claims on imports as well as on domestic production: the import of agricultural machinery and implements increased by as much as 163 per cent in 1929/30, and was responsible for 11 per cent of all imports as compared with 5 per cent in 1928/29. The increased import of industrial and agricultural machinery, together with the associated expansion of metal imports, was entirely responsible for the total increase in imports by 28 per cent in 1929/30.[57] Imports of cotton, wool and other agriculture raw materials were drastically reduced: while the import of metals, metal products and machinery, and electrical goods increased by 304 million rubles, the total import of all other items declined by 17 million rubles. (See Table 13(c).)

The increase in imports in 1929/30 imperatively required an expansion of exports. In the 1920s considerable efforts were made to increase the export of industrial products, including timber and oil. By 1928/29 the export of timber in physical terms already equalled 64 per cent of the 1913 level, and nearly four times as much oil was exported as in 1913. Soviet exports of asbestos, chemicals, cement and various food products also

---

[55] TsGANKh, 3429/1/5196, 119 (this is the *Metallicheskii byulleten'* dated November 5, 1930).

[56] P, June 15, 1930; the total cost of the equipment was 39 million rubles (Yakovlev (1932), 9).

[57] The only other substantial increase was in the import of sugar, following the bad harvest of 1929.

exceeded the 1913 level.[58] In 1929/30 the export of timber increased by 54 per cent and for the first time almost equalled export in 1913, and the export of oil increased by 25 per cent (see Table 13(b)). But in spite of strenuous efforts the export of manufactured goods increased by only 11 per cent.[59] The more difficult market conditions resulting from the world economic crisis, and the increasing hostility of foreign powers to the Soviet Union (see pp. 394–6 below), were both a major hindrance to the expansion of Soviet exports. The unsatisfactory export performance of manufactured goods was also attributed in the Soviet press to their poor quality. Soviet industry had great difficulty in reaching international quality standards even in the case of timber and oil. The quality of manufactured goods intended for export was often very low, and it deteriorated in a number of industries in 1929/30. The industrial newspaper reported that as a result of poor packaging 50 per cent of the window glass sent to Persia was broken, and complained that production was not adjusted to the demand of the foreign market, so that Soviet potash was supplied in lump rather than powdered form and Soviet kaoline was manufactured in an unacceptable colour.[60] A letter sent to Soviet factories from Arcos, the Soviet cooperative trading agency in London, pointed out that while the London poor purchased Soviet matches because they were cheaper than British or Swedish matches, they complained that the striking surface of the box was poor, the match-head too small, and the match-stick inadequately paraffined. Three or four matches were often needed to light a pipe, and matches tended to go out in 'damp and windy' English conditions, or when trying to light a gas mantle.[61]

The substantial increase in the export of timber and oil in physical terms did not earn as much foreign currency as expected owing to the decline in the price of these products on international markets in the first stage of the world economic

[58] *Memorandum* (Birmingham), No. 2, July 1931, 14–15.
[59] This refers to 'other industrial products' in Table 13(a). Of the total increase in this item by 15 million rubles, 4 millions were obtained from the growth in sales of 'antiques and art products' from 3·3 to 7·3 million rubles (*Vneshnyaya torgovlya*, 1929/30, 6(65), July–September 1930, 21).
[60] ZI, January 25, 1930.
[61] ZI, February 18, 1930; Soviet matches still suffer from these defects in the 1980s.

crisis. The Soviet authorities were impelled to place greater reliance on traditional agricultural exports. Exports of animal and poultry products declined as a result of the Soviet livestock crisis, but exports of grain and most other agricultural products increased. Export of grain increased from 99,000 to 2,269,000 tons. Of this total, 1,229,000 tons was exported in July–September 1930 from the harvest of 1930, which in the agricultural year July 1930–June 1931 as a whole provided 5,502,000 tons, 59 per cent of the amount exported in 1913 and 2$'/_2$ times the highest export figure of the 1920s. But the misfortunes of the world agricultural crisis shattered Soviet hopes of achieving a positive balance of trade as a result of grain exports: the average amount earned for a ton of grain was a mere 54 rubles in 1929/30 as compared with 161 rubles in the previous year. Exports failed to keep up with imports, and the trade returns recorded an unfavourable balance of trade amounting to 66 million rubles (see Table 13). This reversed the favourable foreign trade balance achieved in 1928/29.[62]

Soviet efforts to increase exports in conditions of world economic crisis were hindered in several major western countries by a vociferous campaign against Soviet dumping. The United States' market confronted Soviet foreign trade with the greatest problems. The United States, with its advanced technology and its mass production, had long been presented to the Soviet public as the example to emulate and the best source of imports for the capital investment programme. Articles in the Soviet press at the beginning of 1930 described growing collaboration. American technology was popularised by lectures in Soviet towns, and by July 1930 over 100 Soviet commissions had visited the United States, signing contracts with 1,700 firms.[63] The United States was the major supplier of industrial equipment to the Soviet Union, followed by Germany, France and Britain. But Soviet exports to the United States were small: according to a Soviet estimate, the United States supplied 26·5 per cent of Soviet imports in 1929/30 but purchased only 5·5

---

[62] According to a western study carried out at the time, the value of exports was over-estimated by the Soviet authorities, and the foreign trade deficit in 1929/30 actually amounted to 103 million rubles (see *Memorandum* (Birmingham), No. 4, February 1932, 13, and accompanying text).

[63] ZI, January 30 (Shukhgal'ter), July 6 (Tsukerman), 1930.

per cent of Soviet exports.[64] Moreover, economic relations with the United States deteriorated in the spring of 1930, when a vigorous campaign was launched in the American press against political and religious persecution in the USSR and alleged Soviet dumping of timber and other products. As a result of the exertions of the Special Committee to Investigate Communist Activities in the United States chaired by Congressman Hamilton Fish, on May 23 an anti-dumping tariff was introduced for Soviet safety matches, together with special formalities for other Soviet exports, and on July 26 the US Treasury imposed an embargo on Soviet timber exports on the grounds that convict labour was employed in the industry.[65] The Soviet Union reacted by reducing the placing of orders in the United States[66] and by a vigorous campaign drawing attention to the advantages of European technology. An editorial in the economic newspaper called for a '*re-examination of our Americanomania*' and urged Soviet managers to remove the 'American spectacles which block out their view of Europe'.[67] An authoritative industrial economist persuasively argued that United States' technology was best for cheap mass production of tractors and other standard equipment but Germany was superior in research-based technologies in the chemical and electrical engineering industries.[68]

Trade relations with Europe were also far from smooth. In France, mounting anxiety in business circles about Soviet dumping led to the introduction of a crippling licence system for Soviet goods on October 3, 1930.[69] British economic relations with the Soviet Union greatly improved under the Labour Government in 1929–30, but the British balance of trade with the Soviet Union was unfavourable, and Britain urgently sought

---

[64] *Dokumenty vneshnei politiki*, xiv (1968), 402–5 (dated July 1, 1931).

[65] *Dokumenty vneshnei politiki*, xiii (1967), 457–8, 776–7, 830–1; EZh, July 31, 1930; see also Libbey (1975), 217–19, and Haslam (1983), 38–9; the government over-ruled the Treasury decision, but the Treasury retained the right to challenge imports, the burden of proof that convict labour was not used resting with the supplier.

[66] EZh, July 6, 1930.

[67] EZh, August 12, 1930.

[68] ZI, August 6, 1930 (Perel'man).

[69] *Dokumenty vneshnei politiki*, xiii (1967), 568–9; see also Haslam (1983), 41–5.

to persuade the Soviet Union to take more British exports.[70] Trade relations with Germany were temporarily soured by a raid by the Munich police on the Soviet trade agency.[71] But it was above all the world economic crisis which dominated and fostered all the obstacles which stood in the way of Soviet exports.

In these bleak circumstances the Soviet authorities intensified their efforts to increase the range and quantity of machinery produced in the USSR. In March 1930, Kuibyshev published an appeal to Soviet industry to economise on the import of machinery;[72] a vigorous campaign purported to show that machinery manufactured in the USSR could meet many of the needs which had so far been satisfied by imports of equipment.[73] In its written report to the XVI party congress, Vesenkha emphatically returned to this theme:

> The general tension resulting from the success of socialism in the USSR has found expression in a series of hostile acts against our republic (such as the unsuccessful attempt to 'test' us with bayonets, the financial and economic blockade, and the 'crusade'). This has posed much more sharply the question of liberating the USSR as quickly as possible from economic dependence on the capitalist states, and of the *maximum reduction of imports*.[74]

After the congress STO established a Commission on Imports, headed by Ordzhonikidze, and supported by a commission of Vesenkha.[75] Every construction project, however important, was constrained to reduce the import content of its estimates. From June 1930 the construction department of the Tractor and Vehicle Corporation VATO battled for many months with

[70] *Dokumenty vneshnei politiki*, xiii (1967), 771–2. The Board of Trade claimed that British exports to the USSR in 1930, including re-exports, amounted to £9·35 million, but the Soviet authorities argued that Soviet purchases in the colonies and dominions amounting to £6·71 million and invisible exports to the USSR amounting to £8·07 million should also be taken into account.
[71] VI, 5, 1977, 67.
[72] EZh, March 25, 1930 (letter dated March 24).
[73] See, for example, the extensive coverage of this theme in ZI, April 9, 1930.
[74] *Vypolnenie* (1931), 15.
[75] SP VSNKh, 1929/30, art. 1826 (dated August 14); the Vesenkha commission was headed by Sushkov, a senior official of its foreign department.

Lovin, manager of the Chelyabinsk project, in an endeavour to replace imported iron girders by home-produced iron or reinforced concrete for the frame of the building.[76]

In practice, the major projects of the five-year plan continued to rely heavily on imported capital equipment; and the Soviet authorities continued to encourage the systematic application in the USSR of foreign technical experience. The number of technical assistance agreements increased from 75 to 134 in the course of 1929/30: during the economic year nearly twice as many agreements were signed as in 1928/29. The agreements were primarily concerned with the producer goods' industries: there were 26 agreements for machine building, 25 for chemicals, 15 for metals, but only three for textiles and six for the whole of agriculture. The vast majority of the agreements were with United States and German firms.[77] The agreements ranged from large schemes, such as the assistance of the Freyn Engineering Co. in the design, construction and equipment of iron and steel plants, to contracts with individuals such as Rukeyser and Karner (see pp. 217, 125 n. 39 and 189–90 above).[78]

The cost of foreign technical assistance formed a relatively small part of the balance of payments: according to a Western estimate, it amounted to only 15 million rubles in 1928/29 and 18 millions in 1929/30.[79] But the cost of all invisible imports, including Soviet activities abroad and interest on foreign credits, is estimated to have exceeded the value of invisible exports by about 127 million rubles in 1929/30. The net increase in all Soviet debts to foreign firms and banks amounted to 210 million rubles in 1929/30; this included 72 million rubles net credit from Britain following the extension of the Export Credit Scheme to the USSR in August 1929. The new credits had the effect of providing the Soviet government with sufficient foreign

---

[76] TsGANKh, 7620/1/601, 72; 7620/1/603, 23, 25–6; Lovin was supported in his opposition to reinforced concrete by the American engineer John Calder.

[77] *Economic Conditions* (Moscow, 1931), 162–3; 55 agreements were with the United States, 53 with Germany, 9 with France, 8 with Sweden, 3 with Britain, 3 with Italy, and one each with Switzerland, Spain and Norway; 85 of the firms and individuals involved are listed on pp. 225–30.

[78] Technical assistance agreements with individuals were unusual; individuals generally signed an 'agreement with foreign specialists' (see *ibid.* 139–43).

[79] *Memorandum* (Birmingham), No. 4, February 1932, 13; these figures, which purport to include payments to foreign labour in foreign currency, seem to be underestimates.

currency to cover the deficit on invisibles and the foreign trade deficit of 66 million rubles.[80] But the foreign debt was held entirely in the form of short-term bills and credits. Ways of repaying it would soon have to be found.

---

[80] *Memorandum* (Birmingham), No. 4, February 1932, 10, 13–14, 20; the figures for invisibles were approximate estimates based on incomplete information.

CHAPTER ELEVEN

THE SPECIAL QUARTER: OCTOBER–DECEMBER 1930

(A) TWO ROADS TO SOCIALISM

The economic difficulties of the summer of 1930 led to a re-emergence of policy conflicts in the party. Our limited knowledge of the disputes reflects the increasing secrecy in Soviet political life. In 1924–7, documents from the various Left oppositions were partly published in the official press, and widely circulated in leading party circles. The views of the Right opposition in 1928–9 are also known in some detail, in spite of the fact that the political battles were largely fought behind closed doors. But criticisms of party policy in the summer and autumn of 1930 are known only from the veiled statements of the dissident leaders, the polemics of their official opponents, the brief later reminiscences of some of the participants, and equally brief and tantalising references to the archives by Soviet historians.

Significant critical murmurs came from Kuibyshev. From early in 1927, as head of Vesenkha, he had been one of the most persistent and active Politburo members pressing for an increased pace of industrialisation. And in the winter of 1929–30 he does not appear to have resisted the efforts of Ordzhonikidze and Rabkrin to increase the five-year plan. In the early months of 1930 he headed Vesenkha commissions which visited the provinces in search of increased productivity and resources, and strongly advocated increases in the official five-year plan for pig-iron (see pp. 200–1 above). At the XVI party congress in June 1930 Vesenkha was strongly criticised by Rabkrin for its failure to cope with the increased plans; Kuibyshev still strongly supported the plan to produce 17 million tons of pig-iron in the final year of the five-year plan, and stressed its crucial importance (see pp. 337–8 above). But an account by Khavin, who worked on the Vesenkha newspaper at

the time, claims that while Kuibyshev at first fully supported
the target of 17 million tons, he came to realise 'within two or
three months' that it was not feasible. Khavin claims that in
August 1930, at a joint session of the presidiums of Gosplan
and Vesenkha, Kuibyshev demonstrated that in order to achieve
this target capital investment in the iron and steel industry
must rise to 2,500 million rubles in 1931. As it was not feasible
to obtain this large sum from the budget, the presidium of
Vesenkha asked for and was granted only 1,000 million rubles.[1]
This session was not reported in the press; and, despite
Kuibyshev's doubts, on September 7 Vesenkha established a
commission under his chairmanship 'to work out the necessary
measures for obtaining the production of 17 million tons of pig-
iron in 1932/33'.[2] Kuibyshev's scepticism about the revised
plan for pig-iron would logically have led him to a general
rejection of the revisions of the five-year plan approved by the
XVI party congress, but it is not known whether he permitted
himself to draw these more general conclusions, either privately
or in a narrow circle.

Bolder and more far-reaching criticism came from Syrtsov,
chairman of Sovnarkom of the RSFSR.[3] Syrtsov, a prominent
enthusiast for rapid industrialisation and collectivisation in the
autumn of 1929, came forward in February 1930 as one of the
earliest and most vigorous advocates of a more moderate policy
towards the peasantry; at that time he also made some far-
reaching criticisms of the centralised administrative machinery
(see vol. 1, p. 213). At the XVI party congress, he attacked the
Right wing and defended both the rate of industrialisation and
the existence of disproportions in the economy, but also stressed
the need to set 'a necessary limit' to disproportions, so that they
should not reach a level at which 'certain crisis phenomena for
the whole national economy were imminent'.[4] So far all these
statements appeared to be within the boundaries of authorised

[1] Khavin (1968), 78. While inaccurate in detail (in August 1930, plans were
still being prepared in terms not of the calendar year 1931, but of the economic
year 1930/31), this account, by a knowledgeable contemporary, is likely to
reflect the disputes behind the scenes.

[2] SP VSNKh, 1929/30, art. 1908; this order was also reported in ZI, September
9, 1930.

[3] For Syrtsov, see vol. 1, p. 375, and SS, xxiii (1981), 30–1 (Davies).

[4] XVI s"ezd (1931), 221–7.

criticism, and Syrtsov remained in favour: he was promoted to candidate membership of the Politburo after the congress (see p. 341 above).

On August 30, 1930, Syrtsov delivered a two-hour speech on the control figures for 1930/31 at a joint session of the Sovnarkom and Ekoso (Economic Council) of the RSFSR. This major speech still remained formally within the framework of official policy, insisting that the planned rate of growth must be achieved, particularly in heavy industry. But in substance it was a far-reaching condemnation of major trends in policy. He claimed that plans prepared by the People's Commissariats of the USSR had deteriorated in quality: there was 'a certain decline in energy, almost a prostration, an absence of creative initiative'. 'Failures in the third and fourth quarter [of 1929/30] have cast a definite shadow over our economic development.' Hasty planning decisions had resulted in 'a feverish and senseless excitement which is sometimes assumed to be real work'. Factory directors and other leading officials lacked the considerable civil courage required to oppose high plan proposals which they believed to be unrealistic, while 'energetic, shouting groups of unprincipled careerists, who have no real interest in the plan, try to draw the attention of the management to themselves by their zeal':

> It seems to me a somewhat incomprehensible and alarming circumstance that our Gosplan has not warned us about the disruptions in our planning. The question must be raised of the lack of planning (besplanovost') and arbitrariness in a number of important areas and the lack of coordination between certain very important decisions.

In explanation of these deficiences, Syrtsov summoned the campaign against the bourgeois specialists to his aid. Hitherto the specialists had been accused of imposing 'minimalist' plans on the economy. But Syrtsov, while admitting there were some open wreckers of this kind, also claimed that other 'alien elements' caused harm by their 'deference to their communist bosses, their flattery and their readiness to agree with and support everything which comes into the head of the bosses, without responsibility for its correctness and expediency'.

In a passage of his speech which was particularly strongly

attacked subsequently, Syrtsov castigated the Stalingrad factory for rushing to produce its first tractor to display at the XVI party congress. This was a 'deception'. The tractor was not a real product of the factory, and could have been assembled in any workshop: 'This tractor mock-up was worthy of any Potemkin village'.[5]

Syrtsov ranged over many other deficiencies in the course of his speech. He acknowledged that the real wages of the working class were in important respects deteriorating; workers had to resort to the private market to an increasing extent, and food was insufficient. Simultaneously many managers were trying to make up for their own failures by putting pressure on the workers and depriving them of days off. In the sphere of goods' circulation 'alarming symptoms' were 'the subject of alarmed discussion by the whole country' and were 'particularly intensively, if incorrectly, discussed in queues'. The prevailing attitude to money and costs was one of contempt. As a result of the huge gap between official prices and prices on the private market, speculation was growing, involving a 'considerable part of the working population and the working class'. Syrtsov concluded that it was essential to increase revenue so as to bring currency in circulation into line with the goods available. The forthcoming year must become 'a year of decisive correction of mistakes':

> The useful energy of the working masses must be emancipated from its serfdom, our faults must be subjected to greater criticism, and deception and falsification must be eliminated from this criticism.

Syrtsov, having praised Gosplan of the RSFSR for its relative restraint, concluded by calling on the Sovnarkom and Ekoso of the RSFSR to approve 'a resolution which will draw the attention of the government of the USSR to the need to secure a balance in the main elements of the plan (metal, fuel, the food balance of the population, etc.)'.[6] This was in effect a demand

---

[5] For 'Potemkin villages', see vol. 1, p. 213; in February 1930 Syrtsov had already criticised 'Potemkin kolkhozy' (*loc. cit.*).

[6] S. I. Syrtsov, *K novomu khozyaistvennomu godu* (1930): this 32-page pamphlet published in 10,000 copies by the department of press and information of Sovnarkom of the USSR and STO was described as the 'reworked stenogram'

from the Russian Republic that the government of the USSR should plan more realistically.

In the Transcaucasus, a declaration by the regional party committee, drafted by its secretary Lominadze, closely accorded with the tenor of Syrtsov's speech, condemning 'the lordly feudal attitude to the needs and interests of the workers and peasants' prevalent in the Transcaucasian soviets, and describing district and village soviets as generally being mere 'policing and taxation points'. Lominadze's resolution called for the 'narrowing of the front of capital construction'.[7] Like Syrtsov's speech, the Transcaucasus declaration, while implicitly criticising official party policies, formally endorsed and supported them.[8]

Sweeping aside the pretensions of Syrtsov and Lominadze, the majority of the Politburo held fast to the prescription that the difficulties of the summer of 1930 were entirely due to the activities of enemies, and the insufficient vigilance and determination of the administration; and pressed on with the revised five-year plan. On September 3, faced by the unsatisfactory performance of July and August, the central committee issued an Appeal to all party, economic, trade-union and Komsomol organisations to complete in full the economic programme for September, the last month of the economic year 1929/30. The Appeal frankly admitted a 'shameful reduction in rates of growth', and called for the mobilisation of all organisations to fulfil the plan, improve labour discipline and reduce labour turnover. The Appeal also stressed that the forthcoming economic year 1930/31, the third year of the five-year plan, was of 'decisive importance for the fulfilment of the five-year plan in four years'.[9] Two days later, a central committee resolution arranged to send out 20–25 brigades, headed by

---

of the speech of August 30; I am indebted to Professor N. Shiokawa for providing me with a copy. Summaries and extracts, sometimes presented tendentiously, appeared in articles by his critics published in October–December 1930: see my accounts in *Soviet Studies*, xxxiii (1981), 40–1, and in vol. 1, 375–6 of the present work, written before I had seen the pamphlet. The speech is wrongly dated October 1930 in my vol. 1, p. 375.

[7] P, December 2, 1930; B, 21, November 15, 1930, 40–1: NAF, 11–12, 1930, pp. vii, xiv–xv; see also vol. 1, p. 376, and SS, xxiii (1981), 33–5, 41–2 (Davies).
[8] This was acknowledged by official spokesmen: see B, 21, November 15, 1930, 39 (Tal').
[9] P, September 3, 1930.

central committee plenipotentiaries, to lagging industrial districts; the brigades were to include economists, journalists and shock workers.[10] This call for plan fulfilment by means of better organisation, exhortation and greater exertion closely followed the similar and largely successful Appeal issued on January 25, 1930, after the lag of October–December 1929 (see p. 246 above). Its immediate outcome was also positive: the performance of industry in September 1930 was substantially better than in previous months (see pp. 346–7 above). But industry still lagged far behind the plan. Further emergency measures were evidently required.

The Appeal of September 3 took it for granted that the economic year would continue to run from October 1 to September 30, as it had ever since 1922; at this time the preparation of the control figures for 1930/31 was in full spate.[11] The protracted earlier discussion of the merits of transferring all planning from the economic year to the calendar year had recently lapsed.[12] The publication on September 20, 1930, of a decree of TsIK and Sovnarkom 'On the Transfer of the Beginning of the Economic Year from October 1 to January 1'[13] was entirely unexpected. The decree interposed the October–December 1930 quarter between 1929/30 and the year 1931, and required the economic plan and state budget for the quarter to be approved by Sovnarkom not later than October 5. On the same day as the decree, September 20, an order by the presidium of Vesenkha declared that plans for the special quarter must be submitted to its planning sector by 3 p.m. on

---

[10] P, September 5, 1930.

[11] On September 10, a Vesenkha order instructed industrial corporations which had not done so to submit detailed figures for 1930/31 to its presidium within three days (SP VSNKh, 1929/30, art. 1931).

[12] For references to the earlier discussion see Davies (1958), 59, n. 4; Lenin's original advocacy of the October 1–September 30 economic year inhibited its replacement.

[13] SZ, 1930, art. 510. The decree ingenuously explained that the economic year no longer neeeded to begin after the results of the harvest were already known because the socialisation and planning of agriculture now 'to a considerable extent make it possible to determine the results of the following agricultural year'; somewhat more plausibly, it also argued that the whole building season, 'which finishes in November–December', should be included in the planning year. Capital construction was planned on a calendar-year basis in 1929 and 1930.

September 22![14] At this session of the Vesenkha presidium, Kuibyshev called upon industry to 'reject all tendencies to use the October–December quarter as a period for "correcting" the result of the present economic year', and Vesenkha specifically ruled that shortfalls in 1929/30 must be covered as an 'extra target' in the special quarter.[15] Unkind foreign critics, however, suggested that the special quarter provided a convenient means of pretending to make up lost ground.[16] Plans for the special quarter were eventually approved by Vesenkha on October 25 and, with minor modifications, by Sovnarkom on October 30.[17] The foreign critics proved to be at least partly right: the planned increase in industrial production by 38·5 per cent above the average quarterly production in 1930, far from covering the underfulfilment in 1929/30, was substantially lower than the increase of 45–50 per cent provisionally planned for 1930/31.[18] Although the plans for the special quarter thus concealed the extent of past failure, they did not imply any relaxation of tension: industrial production was planned at 46·9 per cent above the unsuccessful July–September quarter.[19] Pig-iron production was to increase, fairly modestly by the standards of that time, by 26·2 per cent, coal production by as much as 130·7 per cent.[20] Capital investment in Vesenkha-planned industry was planned at 965 million rubles in current prices, some 20 per cent above the actual quarterly expenditure in 1929/30. As usual, the plan provided for very substantial productivity increases, cost reductions and other economies in

---

[14] SP VSNKh, 1929/30, art 1983a; the term 'special quarter' appears in the Vesenkha order but not in the decree of TsIK and Sovnarkom; it was soon in general use.

[15] P, September 21, 1930; see also SP VSNKh, 1929/30, art. 1983a.

[16] See BP (Prague), lxxxi, August–September 1930, 24–5.

[17] SP VSNKh, 1929/30, art. 2209; SZ, 1930, art. 575

[18] EZh, March 9, 1930, reported that the preliminary outline figures (tochki) of Vesenkha for 1930/31 assumed an increase of 49·3 per cent; Grin'ko later referred to an expected increase of 45–50 per cent (PKh, 5, 1930, 6); an editorial in ZI, September 17, 1930, anticipated an increase of 50 per cent above the underfulfilled *plan* for 1929/30.

[19] *Cit.* Zaleski (Chapel Hill, 1971), 148.

[20] The results for July–September are from *Ezhemesyachnyi statisticheskii byulleten'*, August–September 1930, 18–21; the plan for October–December appears in PKh, 10–11, 1930, 341–5.

industry.[21] The optimistic endeavour to sustain extremely rapid growth by means of substantial improvements in financial indicators continued long-established planning devices in increasingly adverse circumstances.

(B) WRECKERS ON TRIAL

In the context of the bitter struggle to achieve the plan, the Soviet Union was presented to its population as a fortress besieged by enemies without and within. The further deterioration in Soviet international relations provided some objective evidence for this campaign. In spite of the appointment of the flexible and realistic Litvinov as People's Commissar for Foreign Affairs in place of the ailing Chicherin,[22] a definite improvement in relations occurred only in the relatively minor case of Mussolini's Italy.[23] Some friction occurred even with the British Labour Government.[24] In the United States, a fierce campaign against Soviet forced labour and the Soviet dumping of cheap exports had been cut short during the summer, but resumed even more vigorously in the autumn.[25] Further sorties were undertaken, apparently by Russian émigrés, against the Chinese Eastern Railway.[26] But the relations with France and her Polish and Romanian allies gave rise to the greatest anxiety. At the beginning of 1930, the seizure of the White-Russian General Kutepov by Soviet agents in Paris, together with Comintern involvement in an uprising in Indo-China, aroused great French hostility.[27] In September, the tactless Czechoslovak

[21] Capital investment costs were to be 8 per cent, and industrial production costs 7 per cent, lower than in 1929/30, while the productivity of labour was to rise by 12·6 per cent (*Industrializatsiya, 1929–1932* (1970), 250; SP VSNKh, 1929/30, art. 2209 (order of October 25)).

[22] SZ, 1930, ii, arts. 252–3 (dated July 21).

[23] See Haslam (1983), 48–51.

[24] On December 3, Foreign Secretary Henderson commented 'I am bitterly disappointed at the results of one year's experience of renewed relations with the Soviet government' (Woodward and Butler, eds., vii (1958), 190).

[25] *Dokumenty vneshnei politiki*, xiii (1967), 555.

[26] *Ibid.* 594–5, 819.

[27] See Haslam (1983), 23–4, 34–7. For Soviet confirmation that the OGPU was responsible for the abduction of Kutepov, see *ibid.* 129, note 12. Kutepov ran a para-military organisation which sought to overthrow the Soviet regime (see Pipes (1980), 379–87).

Prime Minister Beneš confirmed the worst Soviet fears when he told the Soviet representative in Prague 'confidentially that not so long ago in Geneva the French strongly insisted on action of Poland against the USSR with the active support of all members of the Little Entente'.[28] On October 3, the French imposed strict sanctions on Soviet exports which, when followed by Soviet counter-measures, effectively brought Franco–Soviet trade to an end.[29]

Within the Soviet Union, the lull which followed the arrests and denunciations of bourgeois specialists in the winter of 1929–30 proved to be merely temporary. The campaign against the bourgeois specialists reached its climax in the course of the last few months of 1930. On September 3, 1930, an inconspicuous notice in the daily newspapers reported that nine prominent specialists had been arrested, 'together with others'. They were accused of being 'participants and leaders in counter-revolutionary organisations', with the aim of overthrowing Soviet power and restoring the power of the landlords and the capitalists.[30] The nine included leading figures from several major groups of specialists of the NEP years: Groman and Bazarov, ex-Menshevik economists from Gosplan; Ramzin, an influential engineer from Vesenkha; and Kondratiev, Chayanov, Makarov and Yurovskii, economists from Narkomzem and Narkomfin, formerly of an SR or liberal persuasion.[31]

In the course of September 1930, a number of summary executions by the OGPU were briefly announced. Six 'wreckers' from Moscow consumer cooperatives were shot, and others sent to concentration camps, for diverting 'hundreds of tons' of foodstuffs to speculators who sold them at 'pillaging prices'.[32] Three fire-brigade officials were shot and five sent to

[28] *Dokumenty vneshnei politiki*, xiii (1967), 485–6 (despatch dated September 4); Beneš did not improve matters with his explanation that Czechoslovakia had undermined the scheme by agreeing to join in only if it had the support of Britain and Italy as well as France. The Little Entente included Czechoslovakia, Romania and Yugoslavia.

[29] See Haslam (1983), 43–5; normal trade relations were not restored until July 1931 (*Dokumenty vneshnei politiki*, xiv (1968), 427, 432).

[30] P, September 3, 1930.

[31] The other two named were Dadyrin, prominent in the agricultural cooperatives, and Sukhanov. According to Medvedev (London, 1971), 122, Groman was arrested on July 13 and Sukhanov on July 20.

[32] ZI and EZh, September 9, 1930.

concentration camps for allegedly creating conditions leading to the outbreak of fire and hindering the putting out of fires.[33] This was followed by the summary execution after a secret trial of 48 Narkomtorg officials for sabotage of food supplies (see vol. 1, p. 374).

The Narkomtorg food-sabotage case was the prelude to the Industrial Party trial. A lengthy indictment was published in the daily newspapers on November 11, and the trial lasted from November 25 to December 6. The eight accused were headed by Ramzin and included Kalinnikov, former chairman of the industrial section of Gosplan, Larichev, former chairman of its fuel section, Charnovsky, head of the scientific and technical council of the metal industry of Vesenkha, and the prominent textile engineer Fedotov.[34] The indictment also announced that Khrennikov, formerly a prominent planner in Vesenkha, 'died under questioning'; other sources claim that he was arrested as early as the summer of 1929 in the hope of forcing him to become a defendant in a major trial.[35]

The trial and its mechanism have been fully discussed by many authors.[36] It was an important moment in the history of Soviet economic policy. The trial, and the further arrests in these months preparatory for later trials, involved the majority of the senior non-party officials in Gosplan, Vesenkha, Narkomzem and Narkomfin, and finally destroyed the constellations of non-Bolshevik economic administrators which had taken shape in the 1920s. The charges and the confessions linked all opposition to official economic policy with deliberate sabotage and treason, and attributed current economic difficulties to this sabotage. Ramzin, whose evidence most

[33] EZh, September 16, 1930.

[34] The other accused were Kupriyanov and Sitnin, textile engineers in Vesenkha, and Ochkin, who had worked for some years as secretary of Ramzin's Thermo-technical institute. For Ramzin, see p. 197 above, and Carr and Davies (1969), 803; for Kalinnikov, Charnovsky and Fedotov, see references in Carr and Davies (1969).

[35] Solzhenitsyn (London, 1974), 375, 396.

[36] For eye-witness accounts see Rothstein, ed., *Wreckers on Trial* (1931); Goode, *Is Intervention in Russia a Myth?* (1931); Lyons (1938), 370–80. For accounts of the trial and the surrounding circumstances see Solzhenitsyn (London, 1974), 376–99; Medvedev (London, 1971), 114–21. The verbatim report of the trial is available in French as *Le procès des Industriels de Moscou* (Paris, 1931); the following account is based on this source.

closely followed the wishes of the managers of the trial, claimed that the plotters had tried to underestimate production possibilities until 1929, and then had exaggerated them in the second half of 1929 and in 1930, in each case with the aim of damaging the economy; but according to Ramzin and his prosecutors the economy had worked so well that the exaggerated targets had often after all proved realistic! The prosecution treated a variety of discredited policies as conscious attempts to harm the economy, including the wasteful construction of textile factories with high ceilings and the use of machinery manufactured in England, as well as such acts of passive sabotage as the failure to develop power stations in the Donbass on the grounds that it would eventually obtain power from Dneprostroi. According to the prosecution, such waste and chaos was designed to produce a situation in which the intervention planned by France, under Poincaré, could succeed in establishing a counter-revolutionary government. In view of such charges and admissions, non-communist specialists and officials who remained at liberty were even less willing than before to criticise official policies. At the same time the elaborate account of the conspiracy provided the general public with a persuasive explanation of goods shortages, repressed inflation and other difficulties.

The publicity for the trial was vast. For three weeks it was the major feature of all the daily newspapers, including even the agricultural newspaper *Sotsialisticheskoe zemledelie*, occupying several full pages every day. It thus received as much publicity as the XVI party congress and more publicity than the adoption of the first five-year plan in the spring of 1929. The need for discipline in face of internal and external enemies, and their responsibility for the economic crisis, was rammed home.

The substance of the charges was very widely accepted. A clandestine correspondent of the émigré Menshevik journal reported that the masses passionately demanded the shooting of the accused, exchanging such remarks about the specialists as 'They sold themselves to the capitalists'; 'However much you feed a wolf, he always looks back to the forest'; 'They got 3,000 [rubles a month] and travelled in cars, while we live on bread and potatoes'.[37] A young Soviet journalist, who acted as *Izvestiya*

----

[37] SV (Paris), 24 (238), December 20, 1930, 14.

correspondent at the complementary Menshevik trial of March 1931, assumed that the accused were guilty, even though one of his own friends had been arrested.[38] A hostile witness acknowledged that when the death sentences were commuted to ten years' imprisonment 'this unexpected act of mercy shocked Russia more deeply than the verdict'.[39] The expressions of shock, and apologies for lack of vigilance, from Krzhizhanovsky, Strumilin and even Bukharin seem to the present author to convey a certain air of sincerity.[40] Trotsky, in emigration, and Rakovsky, in exile in the USSR, fully accepted the evidence at the trials as genuine, and held that the accused were 'a gang of agents of international imperialism'.[41] Thus the official ethos on

[38] Gnedin (Amsterdam, 1977), 276; he later became a prominent official of Narkomindel, and was himself arrested after the dismissal of Litvinov in the spring of 1939.

[39] Lyons (1938), 379.

[40] See for example Krzhizhanovsky in PKh, 10–11, 1930, 5–26 and in EZh, November 14, 1930; Strumilin, EZh, November 4, 1930; and N.B. [Bukharin], ZI, December 17, 1930. On Krzhizhanovsky's role, see also p. 416 below. It is significant that in 1958, at a relaxed time in matters of publication, Strumilin added the following remarks to a reprinted article on Kondratiev, indicating his continued conviction that deliberate damage was done, at least by this group of specialists (*Na planovom fronte* (1958), 366) (see also p. 416, note 65 below):

In 1927 when we wrote these lines, the Kondratiev school still benefited from considerable weight and authority in Soviet circles. Our slogan at that time – 'it must be exposed and rendered harmless' and our forecast that 'it will finish badly' seemed to many to be a very understandable polemical exaggeration. But it finished even worse than one could expect.

The complete moral degeneration of the Kondratievshchina was manifested in the fact that it *itself* in the words of its leaders, who abandoned all their ideological assumptions, recognised its whole past as a single unbroken mistake.

[41] BO (Paris), xvii–xviii (November–December 1930), 17–18, 20–1; BO (Berlin), xxiv (September 1931), 19. According to a fellow-exile, Rakovsky even claimed that his period of work in Paris had provided him with valuable material on the link of the wreckers with the 'White emigration and the French bourgeoisie'. A letter in the Trotsky archives from one of his supporters living in internal exile, dated January 1, 1931, also assumed that the accused in the Industrial Party trial were guilty (T 5732, L. Vol'fson). Trotsky withdrew this interpretation in 1936 (see Deutscher (1963), 163). Medvedev (London, 1971), 115, concludes that 'public confidence in Soviet courts was only slightly shaken in 1930'.

the political environment of economic policy-making to a substantial extent became a mass ethos.

But there can be no doubt that the accused were not guilty of the serious charges preferred against them. Reports in the émigré Menshevik journal published at the time demonstrated the internal inconsistencies of the Industrial Party and Menshevik trials, and described the methods by which the OGPU obtained confessions.[42] In 1967, Yakubovich, a defendant in the Menshevik trial, stated that Krylenko, the state prosecutor, frankly admitted to him during questioning: 'I have no doubt you personally are not guilty of anything. We are both performing our duty to the Party'.[43]

In the course of the autumn, the number of engineers and other specialists involved in charges of wrecking rapidly increased. In September, Milyutin claimed that wrecking was confined to 'an insignificant group of specialists'.[44] But by the end of 1930 a high proportion of non-party specialists who had held leading positions in Vesenkha and Gosplan were in prison, and the alleged wrecking activities were publicly acknowledged to have been widespread:

> It was difficult to imagine in advance the scale of the wrecking organisations, the scale of the activity, the scale of their organisational interconnections, the scale of their crimes.[45]

(C) THE SYRTSOV–LOMINADZE AFFAIR

The extent to which Syrtsov and Lominadze attempted to form an organised opposition, jointly or severally, is not known with certainty.[46] Frank discussions occurred among groups of old

---

[42] SV (Paris), 5 (243), March 14, 1931, 9–12; 10 (248), May 23, 1931, 15–16. Medvedev (London, 1971), 117–22, also discusses the internal inconsistencies.

[43] Medvedev (London, 1971), 130.

[44] NAF, 9, 1930, 11.

[45] N.B. [Bukharin], in ZI, December 17, 1930. On July 16, 1987, a decision of the Supreme Court of the USSR recognised the innocence of Chayanov, Kondratiev, Makarov, Yurovskii and ten other economists (*Literaturnaya gazeta*, August 5, 1987).

[46] The evidence is examined by the present author in SS, xxxiii (1981), 42–5.

associates in which party policy and Stalin were criticised and
alternative policies were advocated. The people concerned no
doubt tried to use their official positions to modify policy. But
on balance the evidence for organised groups or fractions or for a
'bloc' around Syrtsov and Lominadze is not convincing. The
discussions appear to have involved only a small number of
people: Yaroslavsky's reference to their 'powerlessness' and
'insignificant numbers' seems to be accurate.[47]

For over two months after his speech of August 30 no explicit
criticism of Syrtsov appeared in the press. At the beginning of
October, Ryutin, a former supporter of Uglanov who now
worked in Vesenkha as head of the film industry, was expelled
from the party by the presidium of the central control
commission for 'treacherous double-dealing conduct in relation
to the party and for attempting clandestine propaganda of
Right-opportunist views'.[48] Two weeks later, on October 22,
Nusinov and Kavraisky, two associates of Syrtsov from his
Siberian days, were expelled from the party for 'anti-party
double-dealing fractional work'.[49] Veiled attacks on Syrtsov
now began to appear in the press: at the end of October, the
economic newspaper attacked an anonymous orator's 'recent'
two-hour speech, citing many of the phrases in Syrtsov's speech
of August 30.[50]

After this cautious start, characteristic of Stalin's dealings
with his opponents, on November 3 Syrtsov was replaced by
Sulimov as chairman of the Sovnarkom of the RSFSR,[51] and on
the same day an enlarged meeting of the bureau of the Moscow
party committee condemned Syrtsov for organising an
'underground fractional centre' and Lominadze for organising a
'conspiratorial group'.[52] Later in the month, Lominadze and a
number of his associates were deprived of their positions in the

[47] P, November 7, 1930.
[48] P, October 6, 1930.
[49] P, October 23, 1930; Nusinov and 'those who stand behind him' were
attacked for '"Leftist" Ryutinshchina' (P, October 30, 1930).
[50] EZh, October 31, 1930.
[51] P, November 4, 1930; D. E. Sulimov, born in the Urals 1890, son of an iron
worker, worked in a Ural iron works as apprentice, clerk, and underground
Bolshevik organiser; from 1917–27 he worked in the Urals as an administrator,
primarily in industry; from 1927–30 he was first deputy People's Commissar
for Transport (P, November 5, 1930).
[52] P, November 12, 1930.

Transcaucasian party.[53] On December 1, both Syrtsov and Lominadze were expelled from the party central committee by a joint resolution of the Politburo and the presidium of the central control commission.[54] The resolutions accused them of forming a '"Left"–Right bloc' on a 'common political platform, coinciding in all fundamental respects with the platform of the Right opportunists'.[55]

While the resistance by Syrtsov and Lominadze to Stalin's policies was weak and easily overcome, the Syrtsov–Lominadze affair was a significant incident. Syrtsov and Lominadze had both been active supporters of Stalin during the 'great break-through'; this was the first example of a publicly-announced major disagreement within the Stalin camp. These two important figures from different wings of opinion had found common ground on four major related issues. First, both Syrtsov and Lominadze held that the planned pace of industrialisation could not be supported by existing physical resources: the number of capital projects must be reduced, and production plans must not be inflated by the operation of the mechanism of counter-planning (they also clearly believed – though they did not say this in public – that existing plans could not be achieved). Secondly, pressure on the peasantry must be relaxed: Syrtsov wanted a halt to collectivisation, Lominadze criticised high-handed attitudes to the peasants. Thirdly, the excessive centralisation and lack of initiative of the system must be curbed. This in turn required, according to Syrtsov, a revamping of the system to provide greater flexibility; to encourage the sale of agricultural products, market incentives must be partly resuscitated. Fourthly, the situation in the country must be faced, and must be reported more honestly.

This was not the Bukharin programme of 1928–9. Bukharin's criticism of 'super-industrialist' plans was based both on the unavailability of physical resources (you cannot build with

[53] P, November 26, December 2, 1930; one of the new members of the bureau of the Georgian party was Beriya.

[54] P, December 2, 1930. In expelling members of the central committee, the Politburo assumed powers rightly belonging only to the central committee in plenary session. The resolution, like other Politburo decisions, was reported as coming from the central committee (and central control commission), but the plenum of the central committee did not meet till later in the month.

[55] For a further account of this resolution see SS, xxxiii (1981), 43; among those associated with Lominadze was Shatskin (see vol. 1, p. 43).

future bricks) and on the necessity of maintaining market equilibrium with the peasants. There was no hint that either Syrtsov or Lominadze believed that it was possible to cut back industrialisation so as to restore the market to the point at which the state could offer prices at which the peasant would be willing to part voluntarily with his major foodstuffs. Nor was this the Rakovsky programme of July 1930. There was no hint that either Syrtsov or Lominadze believed that to resolve the crisis industrialisation must be brought to a halt. But all these critics agreed that there was a substantial element of adventurism and bureaucratic excess in Stalin's policies. This assessment was undoubtedly partly or wholly accepted by a wide stratum of party members in the administration and in industrial management, as well as by most non-party specialists. It would provide the common ground of the Ryutin platform and the affairs of A. P. Smirnov and of Eismont and Tolmachev in the autumn of 1932.

Measures against Syrtsov and Lominadze and their associates were accompanied by continued pressure against the former Right-wing party leaders. After his silence at the party congress, Bukharin stated on September 16 'I agree in essence with the decisions of the XVI congress'. This declaration was condemned as ambiguous.[56] Numerous appeals were issued to Bukharin, Rykov and Tomsky to speak out on current political issues.[57] The party district committee in which the scientific research sector of Vesenkha was situated condemned Bukharin for his 'Right-wing opportunist attitude' to the work of the sector, and called for 'more decisive organisational measures' against him.[58] On November 19, evidently in response to this pressure, and following the publication of the indictment of the Industrial party, Bukharin sent a declaration to the party central committee condemning both the Syrtsov–Lominadze group and Ryutin, and stressing the growing tension of the class struggle within and outside the USSR. He went so far as to affirm that wrecking and counter-revolutionary gangs must be dealt with 'by the sword' and that all party members must display maximum discipline.[59] This declaration was accepted as

[56] P, November 4, 1930.
[57] See, for example, P, October 28, 29, 1930.
[58] SZe, November 5, 1930.
[59] P, November 20, 1930.

'satisfactory in the main' by the party central committee.[60] But
the treatment of Bukharin was quite exceptional. In the summer
and autumn of 1930, Tomsky and Uglanov were dismissed
from their government offices, and Rykov followed before the
end of the year.[61] Bukharin, head of the research sector of
Vesenkha since 1929, was the only former leader of the Right to
remain in post after 1930.

(D) THE UPHEAVAL IN ECONOMIC ADMINISTRATION

This extensive campaign against the 'Right-"Left" bloc', the
'Right opportunists' and the wreckers was accompanied by
major changes in Sovnarkom. With this exception of Mikoyan,
People's Commissar for Trade, and of Yakovlev, already
appointed from Rabkrin as People's Commissar for Agriculture
when Narkomzem of the USSR was formed in November 1929
(see vol. 1, p. 169), all the People's Commissars concerned with
economic affairs were replaced. Before the autumn upheaval,
Rudzutak was replaced by Rukhimovich as People's Commissar
for Transport on June 11 (see p. 343 n. 50 above), and on August
3 the former Rightist Uglanov was replaced in Narkomtrud by
Tsikhon, supported by Kraval' as his deputy (see p. 342 above).
The revamping of Narkomtrud heralded a more vigorous and
uncompromising policy of strengthening labour discipline. Then
on October 18, Bryukhanov was freed 'at his own request' from
Narkomfin, and replaced by Grin'ko, until then deputy People's
Commissar for Agriculture. Pyatakov was simultaneously
replaced as chairman of Gosbank by Kalmanovich.[62] Grin'ko

---

[60] P, November 22, 1930; the central committee reproved the newspapers *Za
industrializatsiyu* and *Trud* for attacking the declaration in their issues of
November 21.

[61] On September 13, 1930, Tomsky was removed 'at his own request owing
to illness' from the chairmanship of Vsekhimprom, the chemical combine,
after a vigorous press campaign against the management of the chemical
industry (SP VSNKh, 1929/30, art. 1948): for examples of the press campaign,
see P, August 25, 1930, in which a full page on the industry was headed 'The
Opportunism of Vsekhimprom'. For the dismissal of Uglanov and Rykov, see
pp. 342 above and 439 below.

[62] SZ, 1930, ii, arts. 326–9; Grin'ko, a Right-wing Socialist Revolutionary in
October 1917 (see *Writings of Leon Trotsky, 1934–1935* (1971), 176), was an
active supporter of industrialisation and planning who worked in the Ukrainian

and Kalmanovich were both identified with tough policies of industrialisation.[63]

The most dramatic changes took place in Gosplan and Vesenkha. According to his biographer, following the arrest of the leading non-party specialists in Gosplan Krzhizhanovsky wrote to Menzhinsky in alarm, and was told that all government departments were in the same situation; he should 'clench his teeth, select honest cadres and keep working'. Nevertheless he sent his resignation to Stalin.[64] On November 11, the day on which the indictment of the Industrial party conspirators was published, Krzhizhanovsky was freed from the chairmanship of Gosplan 'at his personal request', and replaced by Kuibyshev. On the same day Ordzhonikidze replaced Kuibyshev as chairman of Vesenkha.[65] The transfer of Kuibyshev to Gosplan, and his simultaneous appointment as deputy chairman of Sovnarkom, was hardly a demotion. In view of the widespread arrests of ex-Mensheviks and other specialists in Gosplan, whose 'treachery' had not been noticed by Krzhizhanovsky (see p. 410 above), and the resulting confusion in its administration, a senior political figure was certainly needed to put things in order. But in view of the critical attitude which Kuibyshev had apparently expressed about the revised five-year plan for the iron and steel industry (see pp. 399–400 above), and the ruthless criticism of Vesenkha by Ordzhonikidze and Rabkrin (see

Gosplan until 1928, and was then transferred to the USSR Gosplan (see references indexed in Carr and Davies (1969)), until his further transfer to Narkomzem in December 1929 (see vol. 1, p. 169). Kalmanovich, born 1888 in Siberia, joined Bolsheviks 1917, worked in food industry and food supplies 1918–1926, chairman Prombank 1926, chairman Zernotrest 1928, deputy People's Commissar for Agriculture responsible for sovkhozy December 1929. Pyatakov was appointed chairman of the chemical combine Vsekhimprom on October 18 (SP VSNKh, 1929/30, art. 2168), and a member of the presidium of Vesenkha on October 21 (SZ, 1930, ii, art. 340).

[63] For the circumstances of these appointments, see p. 431 below.

[64] Kartashev, *cit*. Kuromiya (forthcoming), ch. 6; Stalin characteristically remarked 'In my opinion, you need not leave. But if you have decided to, don't leave altogether – at least keep your hat on the hanger in Gosplan'.

[65] I, November 11, 1930; SZ, 1930, ii, arts. 354–8 (dated November 10); Krzhizhanovsky remained a deputy chairman of Gosplan until February 11, 1931, when he was transferred to the presidium of Vesenkha (SZ, 1931, ii, arts. 14, 45). Strumilin was removed from his deputy chairmanship of Gosplan on December 8, but remained a member of its presidium (SZ, 1930, ii, art. 427).

pp. 335–9 above), the change undoubtedly represented a defeat for Kuibyshev and a triumph for Ordzhonikidze and Rabkrin. Ordzhonikidze proceeded immediately to instal Rabkrin men in Vesenkha, while most of the leading officials who had been appointed by Dzerzhinsky or Kuibyshev were transferred. First Unshlikht and Lobov,[66] and then Osinsky, Dogadov and Tomsky,[67] were removed from deputy chairman-ships of Vesenkha, and a number of other officials, including Ronin, K. Rozental' and Lomov, were removed from its presidium;[68] Unshlikht, Ronin and Rozental' joined Kuibyshev in Gosplan. Within five days of Ordzhonikidze's appointment, Pavlunovskii, a former Rabkrin official, was appointed deputy chairman of Vesenkha, and twelve new members, mainly former Rabkrin officials, were appointed to its presidium.[69] A. Gurevich was placed in charge of planning, Zangvil' of finance and M. Kaganovich of the engineering industry; these were all prominent former members of the Rabkrin staff.[70] G. Prokof'ev, a member of the OGPU collegium soon to be in charge of the economic administration of the NKVD, was appointed a member of the presidium of Vesenkha and head of a 'temporary group' for the elimination of the consequences of wrecking.[71] Several former opposition leaders, including Bukharin, Pyatakov and Smilga, retained their Vesenkha posts when Ordzhonikidze assumed office.[72] Other leading officials who had served under Kuibyshev continued to remain in charge of Vesenkha corporations, while V. Mezhlauk and I. Kosior were transferred back to Moscow

---

[66] SZ, 1930, ii, arts. 426, 409 (decrees of December 8 and 12).

[67] SZ, 1930, ii, art. 430 (decree of December 20).

[68] SZ, 1930, ii, arts. 380 (decree of November 17), 404–5 (decree of November 28); SZ, 1931, ii, art. 13 (decree of January 18).

[69] SZ, 1930, ii, arts. 374–5, 397–400 (decrees of November 13).

[70] SP VSNKh, 1929/30, arts. 2356, 2358 (orders of November 29); I. Moskvin, formerly deputy head of the personnel department of the party central committee, was placed in charge of cadres in Vesenkha – P, November 19, 1930, reported that he was replaced in the central committee by Yezhov, who had been in charge of personnel in Narkomzem since the end of 1929 (see vol. 1, p. 169).

[71] SZ, 1930, ii, arts. 397–400; SP VSNKh, 1929/30, art. 2358; for Prokof'ev see Orlov (New York, 1953), 86–7, 225, 256; for his membership of the OGPU collegium see SZ, 1929, ii, art. 238 (dated October 26, 1929).

[72] Smilga had been appointed head of the mobilisation-planning department on July 17, 1930 (SP VSNKh, 1929/30, art. 1673).

from the iron and steel combines in order to undertake permanent work in the presidium of Vesenkha as deputy chairmen, restoring them to the position they had held before 1930.[73] While some continuity with the former administration of Vesenkha was thus maintained at the top level, this was nevertheless a most considerable upheaval, and placed former Rabkrin staff in a dominant position in the administration of industry. Even more sweeping changes took place in the staff of many of the sectors and corporations: thus only six of the 72 staff in the planning and economic administration of Vesenkha continued in office in 1931.[74]

The last major change in the economic commissarists affected Narkomtorg, the People's Commissariat for Internal and Foreign Trade. On November 22, it was split into Narkomsnab (the People's Commissariat for Supply) and Narkomvneshtorg (the People's Commissariat for Foreign Trade).[75] Narkomsnab had acquired a name corresponding more closely to its function: in addition to its responsibility for internal trade and agricultural collections, in June 1930 it had taken over the food industry from Vesenkha.[76] But the new name also reflected the conviction which prevailed throughout 1930 that trade was a survival of NEP which would soon be superseded (see pp. 167–71 above). Mikoyan, appointed People's Commissar for Trade in place of Kamenev in January 1926, remained People's Commissar for Supply. The establishment of Narkomvneshtorg involved another promotion for a Rabkrin official, Rozengol'ts, who was appointed People's Commissar.[77]

The upheaval in Sovnarkom was completed in December with the appointment of Andreev, transferred from his post as secretary to the North Caucasus region of the party, as chairman

[73] SP VSNKh, 1929/30, art. 2371 (dated December 3), art. 2428 (dated December 21).

[74] See SS, xxxvii (1982), 170, n. 81 (Fitzpatrick); this valuable article provides further details on the changes in Vesenkha.

[75] SZ, 1930, art. 592.

[76] SP VSNKh, 1929/30, art. 1589 (order of June 26, based on Sovnarkom decree of June 17); republican Narkomtorgs and local trade departments simultaneously took over the republican and local food industry.

[77] SZ, 1930, ii, arts. 359–360 (decrees of November 22); Rozengol'ts, former deputy People's Commissar for Workers' and Peasants' Inspection, was transferred from Rabkrin to Narkomtorg on October 1 (SZ, 1930, ii, art. 312).

of CCC/Rabkrin,[78] and the new edifice was crowned by appointing Molotov in place of Rykov as chairman of Sovnarkom (see p. 439 below).

(E) WORKERS UNDER PRESSURE

Still convinced that their ambitious plans could be achieved by stubborn effort and improved organisation, during the special quarter the Soviet authorities introduced far-reaching measures to tighten control over the industrial workers. During the 1920s, the urban working class was in a relatively favoured position. By the summer of 1930, in spite of the encroachment on their standard of living and privileges since 1928, the position of the workers still remained anomalously favourable in important respects. They retained the right to change their job at will, and in many cases exercised this right; and unemployed workers could refuse to accept work inappropriate to their qualifications without losing benefit. Efforts by the central authorities to regulate seasonal labour from the countryside in the spring of 1930 had been ineffective, and were temporarily abandoned (see vol. 2, pp. 163–5). Urban labour thus appeared to be an unplanned element in an economy which was increasingly planned from the centre. The central committee Appeal of September 3 drew attention to the 'great change in the environment' due to the absorption of all former skilled workers and the influx of new workers from the countryside, and complained that the economic commissariats and the trade unions had not taken this new situation into account. The Appeal criticised in particular Narkomtrud and some of the trade unions, which had taken a 'bureaucratic attitude' to economic issues:

> Until recently Narkomtrud has confined itself to publishing bureaucratic data about hundreds of thousands of unemployed and paying out of tens of millions of rubles of 'unemployment' benefit; instead it should struggle against selfish elements, flitters and those refusing to work.

[78] SZ, 1930, ii, arts. 431–2 (dated December 22); following normal practice, he was also appointed vice-chairman of Sovnarkom, joining Rudzutak and Kuibyshev.

The party should ensure that 'social pressure', including boycott, was exercised to reduce labour turnover, and that bonuses and extra rations were awarded to workers remaining at their job for a long period; labour legislation and the Statute about labour exchanges should be re-examined; women and young people without jobs should be encouraged to work.[79]

Even before the publication of this Appeal, Narkomtrud under its new leadership had drafted decrees designed to strengthen labour discipline.[80] Until the autumn of 1930, the only provision for personal records had been that workers could be given a reference at their own request. The 1922 Labour Code of the RSFSR and a subsequent circular of the Narkomtrud of the RSFSR explicitly provided that no 'hostile statements' should be included, and that personal qualities and the reason for leaving the job could be mentioned only at the request of the worker.[81] On September 6, 1930, however, a decree of Sovnarkom of the RSFSR proposed major changes in the rights of workers; and a further decree of September 23 provided that reasons for a worker's discharge should be entered in the wage books (raschetnye knizhki) which recorded their earnings at the factory concerned, or in a special certificate which must be made available to the labour exchange.[82]

The decrees of September 6 and 23 were systematised and applied to the whole USSR in three major all-Union decisions in October and December 1930. The first, dated October 9, was an order of Narkomtrud which instructed insurance offices 'in view of the huge shortage of labour in all branches of the economy' to cease paying all unemployment benefits immediately. Those who were still unemployed were to be allocated to vacant jobs forthwith, including unskilled work not

[79] P, September 3, 1930; see also pp. 342–3 above. A Politburo resolution in August 1930 had already impatiently impugned the majority of unemployed as 'connected with agriculture and handicrafts and interested only in getting a little extra' (Suvorov (1968), 218).

[80] ZI, August 12, 1930; for further details, see Filtzer (1986), 109.

[81] Labour Code, art. 42; and circular of April 10, 1923 (Tsaregorodtsev, in VTr, 1, 1931, 81–2).

[82] For the decree of September 6 (I, September 8, 1930) see Filtzer (1986), 109–10. The decree of September 23, approved jointly by Narkomtrud, Vesenkha and VTsSPS of the RSFSR, is reprinted in Mordukhovich (1931), 157–9; standard reasons for discharge to be recorded in the wage books included 'own wish, expiry of work, unsuitability, absenteeism'.

related to their own training; work could be refused only with an authorised medical certificate, in which case sickness benefits would be paid on the unemployment benefit scale. Those refusing jobs offered by the labour exchange must be removed from the unemployment register.[83]

The second major decision, approved on October 20, was a lengthy resolution by the party central committee 'On Measures for the Planned Supply of the National Economy with Labour, and Against Labour Turnover'.[84] Its most important provision was that skilled workers and specialists could be transferred, if the trade unions agreed, from less important to more important branches of the economy (coal, iron and steel, transport and large-scale construction were specifically mentioned as priority branches), and from one part of the country to another. At the same time, promotion of workers from the bench to any administrative position, except those directly concerned with production or forming part of the staff of the trade unions, was suspended for two years.[85] In order to strengthen labour discipline 'socially alien' elements were to be removed from industry, the rules of internal order and tables of fines and penalties were to be revised, and 'deserters' and 'flitters' were to be deprived of the right to work in industrial enterprises for six months. These stringent provisions were accompanied by positive incentives: long-established and shock workers were to receive priority in flats, higher education, holidays and the allocation of scarce goods, and in key industries those in post for more than two years after November 1, 1930, were to receive three days' additional holiday, or pay in lieu. The resolution strongly endorsed the movement to obtain voluntary agreement to remain at one's job for a definite period (samozakreplenie). It also urged that the training of skilled workers should be speeded up and expanded. To bring more

[83] P, October 11, 1930. A later order of Narkomtrud stated that unemployed must be offered work within three days; if they refused it, they should be removed from the register for six months. Work elsewhere could be refused if housing were not offered at the new place of work, or if it would involve a wife moving away from her husband (ZI, December 26, P, December 27, 1930).

[84] P, October 22, 1930.

[85] On March 25, 1931, a decree of the central committee and Sovnarkom restricted the ban to promotion 'from production to soviet work' (SZ, 1931, art. 172).

labour into the industrial economy, additional categories were henceforth entitled to register at labour exchanges, including children and relatives of urban manual and white-collar workers, artisans, poor peasants, batraks and collective farmers.

On December 15, a third decree, approved by TsIK and Sovnarkom, called for 'fuller and planned utilisation of the existing labour force' and 'a decisive and consistent struggle with all disorganisers of production', and repeated the main provisions of the October decisions of Narkomtrud and the party central committee. It also ruled that all hiring of labour must in future be carried out via Narkomtrud agencies, except in the case of administrators, specialists and certain minor groups. The decree also provided for the introduction of labour contracts between management and worker for periods of up to three years. Chemicals, engineering and electric power were added to the list of priority industries to which skilled workers and specialists could be compulsorily directed from less important branches of the economy. Workers thus compulsorily directed to other parts of the USSR would retain the right to their original accommodation.[86]

The implementation of these decrees involved major changes in the operation of Narkomtrud. The labour exchanges of Narkomtrud were replaced by cadres' departments (otdely kadrov), with much wider functions in training and supplying labour for the industrial economy.[87] The new approach to labour was much in evidence at the all-Union conference of labour agencies held in November 1930, the first under the auspices of the new leadership of Narkomtrud. Welcoming the decision to replace labour exchanges by cadres' departments, Kraval' told the conference:

> The words 'labour exchange' and 'labour market' should be finally driven out of our vocabulary, as it is completely inappropriate for the proletarian state that the labour force should be quoted on some 'market'.[88]

A corollary of the view that workers in a socialist economy must not be commodities subject to market forces was that they

[86] SZ, 1930, art. 641.
[87] P, November 10, 1930 (decision of Narkomtrud collegium).
[88] ZI, November 17, 1930.

should be subject to greater planned control. In this spirit, speakers at the labour conference urged that all workers should be issued with individual 'labour books' recording their career in production. This proposal went much further than the decision to include the reason for leaving in the wage book: the wage books were temporary documents issued at each place of employment, the labour books would be permanent documents which accompanied the workers for the rest of their lives. To help the struggle against 'alien elements and flitters', the labour book for workers and ITR should record both achievements and deficiencies; the latter could include drunkenness, absenteeism and violations of labour discipline.[89] The proposal to introduce labour books was subsequently endorsed at numerous factory meetings. No action along these lines was taken by the authorities until 1938. But the cadres' departments were asked not to register potential workers unless a note in their wage book, or a special certificate, disclosed their reason for leaving the last place of work; and all organisations were instructed not to take on workers who had left their previous job without permission or had been dismissed for indiscipline.[90] An article published in the party journal summarised the current vision of the planning of labour in the socialist economy:

A situation must be reached in which Narkomtrud of the USSR and its local agencies have become militant staffs for the planned training of the cadres required by the economy and the planned and organised allocation of these cadres. Narkomtrud must turn from a bureaucratic *apparat*, dragging at the tail of events, at the tail of the stormy rates of growth of socialist construction, into a real agency of the proletarian dictatorship, concerned with the truly socialist organisation of labour.[91]

The far-reaching legislation of the autumn of 1930 did not, however, bring into being the disciplined, stable and planned labour force of which the central authorities dreamed.

---

[89] P, November 24, 1930. During the Civil War, labour books had been introduced in Moscow in 1919–20 for men aged 16 to 50 and women aged 16 to 40 (Sakwa (London, 1988), 89–90).

[90] Mordukhovich (1931), 119.

[91] B, 2, January 31, 1931, 35.

Most of these measures foundered as a result of the shortage of labour, which soon drove managers to violate the regulations, and the authorities to overlook these violations: 'it is better to appear in court for taking on flitters', admitted the assistant director of a Leningrad factory, 'than for failing to fulfil the promfinplan'.[92] With the growing scarcity of labour, an increasing proportion of all workers were hired directly by their employers, by-passing the labour exchanges; and the proportion greatly increased of workers offered permanent rather than temporary work, and therefore gaining the rights which went with permanent work.[93] Thus the instruments for control and discipline continued to diminish in importance at the very time when the authorities were seeking to greatly increase control over labour.

For the next eighteen months, the massive and chaotic influx of new labour into industry continued, labour productivity declined instead of rising, and nominal wages rose rapidly; labour turnover fell slightly, but it remained much higher than in 1929. Many of the compulsory powers worked badly in practice, and the attempt to maintain a single central agency responsible for the administration and planning of labour was eventually abandoned. The authorities made very extensive use of monetary incentives to persuade workers to change their jobs and to encourage skill and effort. A 'labour market', though an imperfect one, continued to exist.[94] The legislation of the autumn of 1930 was nevertheless of very great significance in the development of the Soviet system. It greatly increased the legal powers of the economic authorities in relation to the industrial workers. It drastically changed the tone in which their rights and grievances were discussed. It marked a decisive move towards the compulsory transfer of large numbers of workers as a standard procedure in carrying out the plan. Henceforth more severe penalties and strong moral pressure were brought to bear on a rapidly expanding labour force in order to discipline it.

[92] Mordukhovich (1931), 129.
[93] The proportion of workers hired at the labour exchanges fell from 84 per cent in July–September 1929 to 61 per cent in July–September 1930; the proportion of temporary workers fell from 70 per cent of all hirings at the end of 1929 to 40 per cent at the end of 1930 (Mordukhovich (1931), 90, 86–7).
[94] These developments will be discussed in vol. 4.

The crisis in the coal industry (see pp. 348, 361 above) provides a striking illustration of the attempt to facilitate the achievement of the plan by the better organisation of labour and its direct allocation. The authorities recognised that poor food and housing, and deteriorating working conditions, were a major cause of the departure of workers from the mines.[95] But their main emphasis was on poor leadership and organisation, and particularly on bad handling of the labour force. *Pravda* blamed the party and the trade unions, and the 'criminal ineptness of economic and administrative-technical personnel'.[96] The central committee of the Ukrainian party reprimanded Soyuzugol' and the Ukrainian committee itself, presumably with the encouragement of Molotov, who was present as a special plenipotentiary of the USSR central committee.[97] Molotov, at meetings of party activists in the Donbass mining towns, attacked those who criticised the excessive rate of growth of the industry as Right wingers, Trotskyists and 'singing to the tune of the class enemy'. He argued that the main trouble was insufficient use of machinery, and emphasised the desirability of employing a permanent mechanised labour force. But he also stressed at length the role of the shock-workers' movement as a means of mass participation in socialist construction and of overcoming the coal crisis.[98] The main emphasis in the practical solution of the crisis was placed on the control and recruitment of mining labour. The Ukrainian central committee called for the 'cleansing' of ex-kulaks from the labour force, and for the abolition of traditional labour organisation in the industry. The artels, groups of workers usually recruited from the same village, paid collectively, and headed by an elder, were castigated for their 'petty-bourgeois pragmatism'; and 'artificial production communes' supported by 'leftist phrasemongers' were equally condemned. The committee insisted that such 'spontaneous' artels and 'artificial' communes should be replaced by production brigades.[99]

Fresh labour was recruited to the coal industry by means of a

[95] ZI, August 13, 1930 (Kuibyshev); P, October 5, 1930 (Ukrainian central committee).

[96] P, September 25, 1930 (editorial).

[97] P, October 5, 1930.

[98] P, October 1, 2, 1930 (speeches of September 27, 29).

[99] P, October 5, 1930.

highly organised campaign. Early in the crisis, *Pravda* called upon the Komsomol to 'throw thousands into the breech'.[100] Kolkhoztsentr issued a directive calling for the recruitment of 20,000 collective-farmers for the mines,[101] and the central authorities also instructed the coal corporation Ugol' to recruit 30,000 Komsomol members and 28,000 batraks, making 78,000 altogether, as compared with a total labour force in September 1930 of 187,000. By October 20, 71,000 had already been recruited.[102] It is not known how many of these were retained. Complaints soon appeared that batraks were promised industrial goods and free food which they did not receive, so that more than half the first batch of recruits soon left, taking with them the special clothing with which they were issued.[103] Later reports claimed that many collective farmers had remained in the mines.[104] Organised and semi-compulsory recruitment evidently played an important part in the immediate resolution of the crisis. The crucial factor, however, was probably the end of the agricultural season, and the consequent greater readiness of workers to leave the countryside for the mines.[105] Nevertheless, this experience in the coal crisis encouraged the authorities in their belief that direct controls over labour were effective.

Measures to tighten central control over the labour force were accompanied by renewed efforts to draw upon the enthusiasm of the committed rank-and-file worker. October 1 was declared a national shock-workers' day, and simultaneously

---

[100] P, August 11, 1930.

[101] P, August 22, 1930. The recruits from kolkhozy were to retain all their rights as kolkhoz members, including the right to purchase part of the harvest at state collection prices, and only the minimum deduction was to be made to kolkhoz funds from their wages.

[102] *Industrializatsiya, 1929–1932* (1970), 376; those actually recruited included 24,700 Komsomol members, 15,000 collective farmers and 30,400 batraks.

[103] P, September 3, 1930. Kraval' later complained that most peasants in one district were wearing special miners' clothing; this abuse was curbed by the simple expedient of marking the clothes (ZI, November 12, 1930).

[104] VTr, 12, 1930, 77 (Fominikh). Unemployed miners were also recruited from the Ruhr; an American correspondent reported that more than a thousand started work, but many of them returned home, declaring that unemployment in Germany was preferable to coal-mining in the USSR (Knickerbocker (1931), 167–74).

[105] On this, and on the coal crisis generally, see *Annals* (Tokyo), 24 (1982–3), 133–8 (Shiokawa).

a competition was launched for the best industrial enterprise.[106] Short courses were established for shock-brigade organisers, and engineers and technicians were urged to work with the shock brigades; the AUCCTU called upon the voluntary society of inventors to set up a group in every enterprise, so as to coordinate the various efforts to rationalise production.[107]

The most dramatic and ironic of these endeavours in the autumn of 1930 was the 'counter-planning' movement. Earlier in 1930 preliminary attempts had been made to break down factory plans to the workers at the bench and to involve them directly in planning. Elektrozavod, the Moscow electrical factory, endeavoured to work out a five-year plan for each shop and machine tool.[108] On March 11, 1930, a joint letter of Vesenkha and the AUCCTU stressed that plans should be provided for every shop and even for every group of machines (agregat).[109] On April 28, the presidium of the AUCCTU called upon trade unions to participate in compiling the control figures for 1930/31, claiming that the plan would be fulfilled if every enterprise and every worker properly comprehended their own plan.[110] By May 1, the Karl Marx textile engineering factory in Leningrad disaggregated the promfinplan to every bench: their well-developed shock-workers' movement is said to have played a crucial part in the overfulfilment of the plan by 10·4 per cent in October 1929–June 1930. When the factory turned its attention to the control figures for 1930/31, it established brigades of shock workers, each including an engineer, which drew up a 'counter-promfinplan' based on the production possibilities of every machine tool. The counter-plan ambitiously envisaged that production could be expanded to 220 per cent of the 1929/30 level, far beyond the initial intentions of the factory administration; it was forwarded to the trust so that it could be tied in with the availability of raw materials.[111] On July 25–26, 1930, the 6,000 workers approved an Appeal to the Soviet

[106] P, October 1, 2, 1930.
[107] VTr, 10–11, 1930, 46.
[108] See VI, 8, 1973, 205.
[109] SP VSNKh, 1929/30, art. 997.
[110] See VI, 8, 1973, 205.
[111] P, July 30, 1930; B, 15–16, August 1930, 20–1; VI, 8, 1973, 206. The counter-plan was eventually increased to 240 per cent of 1929/30 (P, September 1, 1930).

public at large, and especially to the iron and steel workers, responsible for the supply of the main raw materials to the factory, to extend counter-planning to the whole of industry.[112]

Such developments were greeted by the economic administration with considerable scepticism. On June 26, 1930, Vesenkha of the RSFSR issued a circular suggesting that preliminary drafts of the 1930/31 control figures should not be discussed in shops and enterprises, as later changes due to government directives would result in 'confusion' in the planning process. On July 2 the Moscow regional sovnarkhoz tried to restrict such discussions to factory directors and the regional departments of trade unions.[113] Numerous reports in the press claimed that factory directors and industrial officials were hostile to counter-planning. An article in the party journal admitted 'stubborn opposition to the counter-promfinplan',[114] while the industrial newspaper complained that 'as a rule it is not greeted with joy by economic officials, and it is sometimes even held off at bayonet point'.[115] But the party authorities responded with great enthusiasm to a movement which seemed to provide both an objective basis and mass support for high rates of growth. On August 3, an editorial in *Pravda*, defining the counter-plan as '*a plan constructed on the maximum production possibilities of the enterprise and freed from the burdens of planning defects*', warned that attempts at factories to reduce the plan were '*a Right-wing deviation in practice*'. During August, a series of articles in the industrial newspaper from different industries and areas, under the general heading 'From the Factory Bench to Gosplan', favourably reported the activities of shop-floor workers in raising the plan targets. An editorial in *Pravda* praised the counter-planning movement as 'new and gigantic in its significance' and condemned communist officials who resisted increased plans under the influence of conservative specialists as 'haemorrhoidal petty bureaucrats'.[116] On August 30, the industrial newspaper, claiming that the 'unique production élan of the working masses is of course one of the major arguments for increasing the plan', delphically remarked that 'if someone

[112] P, July 30, 1930.
[113] P, July 30, 1930.
[114] B, 15–16, August 31, 1930, 24.
[115] ZI, October 21, 1930.
[116] P, August 26, 1930.

or other has already spoken of the declining curve of workers' enthusiasm, we can say confidently and without ambiguity: *these are Right-wing opportunist voices*'.[117]

These criticisms of Right-wing opportunism reflected a serious division of opinion behind the scenes. On August 30, Syrtsov, in his speech to Sovnarkom and Ekoso of the RSFSR, complained that 'discussion of the counter-promfinplan is often replaced by wordy declarations and the imposition of figures plucked out of the air in an atmosphere of auction and speculation'. According to Syrtsov, those who defended realistic planning were frequently accused of deviation and wrecking; managers who 'lack adequate civil courage (which is required in substantial quantities)' accept high targets in which they do not believe, and genuine initiative was stifled by 'shouting groups of unprincipled careerists'.[118] Lominadze, in the declaration of the Transcaucasian party central committee, while describing the counter-plan as 'a new form of activity of the masses', demanded that it must be 'protected in every way from vulgarisation, rubber-stamping, and irresponsible playing about with figures'.[119]

The counter-plan campaign was a step towards the transformation of the annual plan from a plan for the factory as a whole into a detailed operational document on the factory floor. It thus marked a significant stage in the history of Soviet industrial planning. But the failure of the authorities, obvious in retrospect, to endeavour to tie in the new plans with raw material possibilities produced a situation in which the plan of every enterprise could assume that 100 per cent of the capacity of every machine would be utilised irrespective of the availability of materials. This was bound to cause a rapid increase of plan targets – a further departure from realism. It was particularly ironic that the movement should have started in the Karl Marx textile engineering factory. Iron and steel, on which the factory depended for its main materials, was the scarcest of all commodities, and allocations were particularly restricted for

[117] ZI, August 30, 1930; a similar line was taken by Kapustin in B, 15–16, August 31, 1930, 23–4.

[118] Syrtsov, *K novomu khozyaistvaistvennomu godu* (1930), 8–9; for other aspects of this speech see pp. 400–3 above.

[119] *Cit.* B, 21, November 15, 1930, 40 (Tal').

factories connected with the consumer industries.[120] Moreover, in view of the drastic cuts in cotton imports (see p. 369 above), which continued in the special quarter, much of the textile machinery produced by the Karl Marx factory was not required.

Certain warning notes were sounded in the course of the autumn of 1930. An article in *Pravda* criticised the error of seeing plans from above and plans from below as two separate flows and argued that plans from above must be an '*obligatory prerequisite*' of plans from below:

> The attempt of certain overheated comrades to construct plans *only from the benches*, only from abstract production possibilities, is baseless and useless building of castles in the air (prozhekterstvo).[121]

A prominent industrial economist similarly argued that the counter-plan at the bench level should be constructed within the framework of the control figures, jointly with the foreman and with help from the engineers, so that a single plan emerged at shop and factory conferences.[122] But these were isolated voices in an atmosphere in which managers and engineers feared charges of Right-wing opportunism, and shock-workers and party enthusiasts had received no clear directives restricting their proposals to the framework of available resources.[123] In the vast majority of factories, the control figures and the counter-plans were not properly coordinated.[124]

(F) TIGHTENING THE FINANCIAL SCREW

During 1929/30, although the state budget was nominally in surplus, huge currency issues through short-term credit provided by Gosbank had resulted in large accumulations of cash by

[120] The factory complained of inadequate supplies of metal in P, September 1, 1930.

[121] P, September 25, 1930 (Dol'nikov and others); the word 'prozhekterstvo' was again used 34 years later in attacks on Khrushchev's plans after his fall.

[122] ZI, December 8, 1930 (Kvasha).

[123] In the Dnepropetrovsk iron and steel works, when 'former Trotskyists' wanted to reduce the counter-plans, the workers formed in response a shock brigade named after the OGPU (ZI, November 20, 1930).

[124] ZI, December 8, 1930 (Kvasha).

individual citizens (see p. 391 above). On September 16, 1930, the Politburo, after hearing a report from a 'commission on improving the financial position', recommended to Sovnarkom that strong action should be taken in relation to economic organisations which violated financial discipline.[125] This decision reflected a major shift in financial policy, and was followed a month later, on October 18, by the replacement of Bryukhanov and Pyatakov by Grin'ko and Kalmanovich. A contemporary Western observer commented on the dismissal of Bryukhanov and Pyatakov that 'Moscow believes it was because they refused to sponsor a deliberate inflation'.[126] But, according to Vareikis, the leadership of Narkomfin and the board of Gosbank were removed for the opposite reason: the credit reform had not been adequately prepared and supervised, so that excess spending had occurred; this resulted in 'some currency tension' throughout the country. Vareikis added that the party central committee was now insisting on the mobilisation of money from the population, and on strict economy.[127] This account seems far more plausible. Immediately after the Politburo decision of September 16, the financial screw was tightened. The huge net increase in currency of July and August 1930, amounting to 175 per cent of the issue originally planned for the whole of 1929/30, was followed by a much more modest increase in September and a minute increase in October. This was quite contrary to the normal seasonal pattern.[128] The squeeze caused extreme financial tension throughout the economy. Gosplan noted in an unpublished report that currency restrictions had led to delays in the payment of wages for periods varying from 4–6 days to

---

[125] *Industrializatsiya, 1929–1932* (1970), 594.

[126] Knickerbocker (1931), 226; similar reports appeared elsewhere.

[127] Vareikis (Voronezh, 1931), 233–4 (speech to Central Black-Earth regional party committee, December 5, 1930); for Pyatakov's role in the credit reform, see pp. 320–3 above.

[128] Monthly net currency issues were as follows (million rubles):

	1929	1930
July	75·7	405·6
August	171·8	312·6
September	181·8	85·8

In October 1930 the issue amounted to 25·6 million rubles in the first 27 days. (*Kon"yunktura . . . za sentyabr' i 12 mesyatsev 1929/30* (n.d. [1930]), Finansy, p. 7.)

two weeks, and even in some cases to delays of $1^1/_2$–2 months. In some areas, these delays, which affected workers in production more than those in trade, had forced workers to sell clothing, domestic goods and even part of their rations. Lack of currency had also hindered agricultural collections and the floating of timber.[129]

These troubles did not deflect the authorities from their new policy of strict control over currency. The decree on the national economic plan for the special quarter, approved on October 30, while not giving a figure for currency issue, called for strict financial and credit discipline.[130] A few days later, on November 3, Grin'ko told a joint session of the collegium of Narkomfin and the board of Gosbank that in October–December no currency at all was to be issued; instead a 'free reserve' was to be accumulated of 600 million rubles. According to Grin'ko this severe financial programme was not proposed by the financial agencies but 'dictated to them by the party and the government'. It would involve '*putting the screws on the financial economy*': the psychology of treating the financial plan as secondary must not be tolerated, and investment must be made dependent on successful accumulation.[131] A subsequent *Pravda* editorial condemned '"leftists" who assist Right-wing opportunism, disorganising our monetary economy', and urged financial agencies to supervise economic construction 'via the ruble' on a daily basis.[132] A fortnight later, on November 17, a conference of financial officials was summoned to discuss the prospects for currency circulation. Addressing the conference, Maimin, while still condemning Yurovsky's 'kulak–capitalist support for market equilibrium and currency circulation based on gold', also vigorously criticised Kozlov's view that money was turning into labour coupons as 'a contemptuous "leftist attitude"', which was 'complete rubbish'. While the nature of money would change, it would remain 'in full force'. Grin'ko pragmatically called upon the assembled officials to cease the 'endless discussions' about the nature of the Soviet ruble and to turn instead to 'burning questions', such as the amount of working capital needed for the grain collections and the organisation of

---

[129] *Ibid.* Obmen i raspredelenie, pp. 2–3, Finansy, p. 8.
[130] SZ, 1930, art. 575.
[131] FP, 9, 1930, 3–4.
[132] P, November 5, 1930.

inter-enterprise cashless accounts.[133] The financial situation was now being treated as a matter of great urgency by the Politburo, which discussed it on two occasions in November. On November 15 it approved the draft of a Sovnarkom decision on the progress of the fulfilment of the financial plan of the special quarter, and on November 30 it adopted a resolution of its own on the same subject.[134] Subsequently, CCC/Rabkrin instructed local control commissions to keep a continuous watch on the fulfilment of the financial plan.[135] Ordzhonikidze, recently transferred to Vesenkha, sent a strongly worded letter to the industrial corporations stressing the need to improve financial and credit discipline (see p. 436 below). Financial stringency was now the order of the day.

In the midst of all these tribulations, a major reform was introduced in the system of budgetary revenue with effect from October 1, 1930.[136] All existing indirect taxes, including the industrial tax and the various excises, were unified into a 'turnover tax'.[137] This was imposed on each industrial corporation as a percentage of its turnover. The rates varied between the corporations in rough conformity with the taxes which had been replaced, from 8 per cent on Soyuzkhleb to as much as 87·2 per cent on Tsentrospirt, which held the state monopoly of vodka and other spirits (the tax of 87·2 per cent was included in the turnover, and was thus the equivalent of a mark-up of 681 per cent (87·2:12·8) on the production price). The corporation had the right to vary the individual rates it charged on particular goods, provided the total sum was collected as planned. Simultaneously the income tax and profits tax on enterprises were combined into a single 'deduction from

[133] P, November 20, 1930. In I, November 13, 1930, Miroshnikov, however, continued to insist that increased financial programmes had to be accepted in order not to harm economic growth; during the special quarter, which was not a 'rest period' but a period of further advance, the 'main part' of the working capital required for the whole year would be issued in order to cover debts.

[134] *Industrializatsiya, 1929–1932* (1970), 595–6; the content of the Politburo decisions is not known.

[135] ZI, December 11, 1930 (resolution dated December 10).

[136] SZ, 1930, art. 476 (decree of September 2 'On the Tax Reform').

[137] SZ, 1930, art. 483 (dated September 3).

profits': 81 per cent of planned profits were transferred to the budget, and 19 per cent remained with the trust, 10 per cent for capital expenditure, and 9 per cent for the Fund for Improving Workers' Welfare (FUBR).[138]

These new taxes ultimately provided flexible instruments for reducing inflationary pressure and providing some financial incentive to enterprises. But in their initial form they were crude, over-centralised and over-simplified, and within a year or two were substantially modified.[139]

(G) RESULTS

Following the improvement in industrial performance in September 1930 (see pp. 346–7 above), production increased substantially during the special quarter, and was 17·4 per cent higher than in the previous quarter, increasing by 11·9 per cent for producer goods, and as much as 26·7 per cent for consumer goods.[140] A temporary victory was achieved in the battle for coal: production increased by 43 per cent. Substantial increases were also recorded in the production of oil and electricity while the engineering industries continued to expand rapidly. With the arrival of the new cotton harvest, the summer crisis was overcome; production of cotton textiles more than doubled in the special quarter. (See Table 9(f).)

In spite of these achievements, production fell far short of the plan, which had proposed an increase by over 40 per cent (see p. 405 above): the report of Gosplan on the special quarter frankly stated that production had been 'insufficient to compensate for the "trough" (progib)' of July–September.[141] The most serious failure was in the iron and steel industry. The output of crude steel continued to rise because of the greater availability of scrap.[142] But the production of iron ore and pig-iron failed to increase: pig-iron production was only 3·8 per cent higher than in October–December 1929. And coal

[138] SZ, 1930, art. 478 (decree of September 2).
[139] For further discussion see Davies (1958), 211–22.
[140] See Table 7(b) (Series 3). The provisional figures in the quarterly Vesenkha report were slightly lower (see ZI, January 24, 1931).
[141] *Industrializatsiya, 1929–1932* (1970), 241.
[142] ZI, January 24, 1931.

production, in spite of the dramatic recovery, remained lower than in January–March 1930. The increase in the production of producer goods by 40 per cent between October–December 1929 and October–December 1930[143] was primarily due to the expansion of the engineering industries, and rested on the shaky foundation of an inadequate increase in coal and metal production. The report by Vesenkha on the special quarter frankly admitted that the failure to achieve the plan in the coal, iron ore and iron and steel industries 'must give rise to the most serious alarm', as 'the work of all other industries depends on these industries'.[144] In the iron and steel industry, as a result of the shortfall in the delivery of coal and other fuel, barely two days' coal stocks remained at the beginning of December, resulting in partial stoppages at four major works.[145]

Labour productivity recovered in October–December 1930 from the alarming decline which had occurred in the previous quarter. The increase in output per worker by 17·3 per cent was, however, almost entirely due to the recovery of cotton textiles and associated consumer goods; the increase amounted to 36·6 per cent for consumer goods as against only 1·8 per cent for producer goods. Moreover, as compared with October–December 1929 output per worker for industry as a whole had increased by a mere 1·3 per cent.[146] The same pattern was followed by other indicators of industrial performance. Labour turnover and absenteeism without due cause declined in the special quarter, in consequence of the stricter labour legislation, but remained higher than at the beginning of 1930.[147] In conditions of acute fuel shortage, the product-mix and quality of fuel continued to decline. Gosplan reported that in consequence 'in a number of industries fuel consumed per unit of output during the special quarter, instead of declining, exceeded the level of 1929/30'.[148]

---

[143] See Table 5(b) (Series 2).

[144] ZI, January 24, 1931.

[145] TsGANKh, 4086/1/2941, 42–3 (session of Stal' board, December 12, 1930); this refers to coal used for fuel, not coking coal.

[146] PI, 5–6, 1931, 85; these figures have the same coverage as Series 2 in Table 8(b) and (c) below.

[147] See note to Table 19, and *Itogi VSNKh* (1932), 80–7; *Industrializatsiya, 1929–1932* (1970), 252.

[148] *Industrializatsiya, 1929–1932* (1970), 250–1.

In these unpropitious circumstances, the plan to reduce industrial costs completely failed. While the planned reduction for the special quarter was an ambitious 6·8 per cent, in October 1930 costs were only 1·7 per cent below the average level for 1929/30; and in November they actually increased slightly.[149] In December, Ordzhonikidze, now chairman of Vesenkha, addressed a letter to all industrial corporations declaring that the failure to fulfil the costs plan was 'particularly seriously alarming': profits deductions to the state budget were much lower than planned, and industry had failed to accumulate its own resources to finance capital construction to the planned extent. Failure to observe financial and credit discipline was 'disrupting the promfinplan and increasing financial tension'.[150] But his appeal was unsuccessful. In its report on the special quarter, submitted before cost data for December 1930 was available, Gosplan optimistically estimated that costs had declined by 2·5 per cent in the quarter as a whole.[151] But the Narkomfin journal later reported, without giving a precise figure, that in industry as a whole costs had increased in the special quarter, the increase reaching 8·7 per cent in the coal industry, and 7·2 per cent in iron and steel.[152]

The special quarter saw the achievement of a substantial positive balance of foreign trade. The imports of various agricultural materials and consumer goods were still further reduced; and the previously high imports of agricultural machinery were cut drastically. Only the import of industrial machinery and parts was retained at the level of 1929/30. (See Table 13.) But the positive trade balance was primarily a statistical improvement due to the seasonal concentration of grain exports into this quarter. The conflict between the impossibility of achieving adequate exports and the necessity of importing more industrial equipment and materials was not resolved.

The substantial imports of industrial machinery, together with the continued expansion of the Soviet engineering industries, provided the basis for maintaining a high level of

---

[149] *Industrializatsiya, 1929–1932* (1970), 250.

[150] ZI, December 12, 1930; these arguments were reiterated at greater length in ZI, December 25, 1930.

[151] *Industrializatsiya, 1929–1932* (1970), 251.

[152] FP, 1–2, 1931, 14 (Maimin).

capital investment in industry, amounting during October–December 1930 to 1,242 million rubles in Vesenkha-planned industry as compared with 1,248 million rubles in the previous quarter.[153] The normal seasonal decline in construction was far less marked in 1930 than in previous years: between October 1, 1930 and January 1, 1931, the number of persons employed in capital construction declined by only 28·7 per cent as compared with 41·0 per cent in 1929, and for the quarter as a whole was 92 per cent higher than in October–December 1929 (see Table 17). With the available data it is impossible to compare these results with the capital investment plan for the special quarter. According to Gosplan reports, only 80–85 per cent of the quarterly expenditure plan was achieved.[154]

In view of the failure of the plan for industrial costs, it is not surprising that the plan to reduce currency in circulation was not achieved. But the net increase in currency issued amounted to only 38 million rubles, less than in the October–December quarter in any of the previous three years.[155] This was a significant move towards a stable currency. But it involved the imposition of severe financial restrictions throughout the economy. In industry, delays in paying wages occurred at a number of enterprises.[156]

The extraordinary efforts of the special quarter thus brought about a further expansion of industrial production, and maintained capital investment at an unprecedented level. These results refuted Rakovsky's pessimistic conclusion that no further increase in production was possible before major new investments had been brought into operation. On the other hand they also demonstrated that plans exceeded all realistic possibilities, in spite of the concealed reduction in plans in the special quarter. But, with Syrtsov dismissed and Kuibyshev silenced, this conclusion continued to be rejected by Stalin and his supporters.

---

[153] *Itogi VSNKh* (1932), 116–20; these figures, which include investment in electric power, are for 'the value of work actually carried out'.
[154] PKh, 12, 1930, 22; *Industrializatsiya, 1929–1932* (1970), 143–5; *Materialy VSNKh* (1931), 17; at 34 priority sites plan fulfilment amounted to only 73·1 per cent.
[155] See Table 23 below, and Carr and Davies (1969), 976.
[156] FSKh, 6, 1931, 2 (Grin'ko); in the iron-ore corporation Yurt, wage debts to workers for November 1930 had to be met by a special allocation (TsGANKh, 4086/1/2941, 44, report at Stal' board, December 14, 1930).

(H) THE DECEMBER PLENUM

The joint plenum of the party central committee and central control commission, held from December 17 to 21, 1930, was the first since November 1929, apart from a formal session at the time of the XVI party congress. The first item was a report by Kuibyshev, in his new capacity as chairman of Gosplan, on 'The National Economic Plan for 1931 (Control Figures)'. The annual planning document had previously been known only as the 'control figures', and its new title emphasised the importance and the success of planning in the eyes of the authorities. In his report Kuibyshev elaborated the familiar theme of the contrast between economic expansion in the Soviet Union and economic decline and increasing unemployment in the capitalist countries. Taking as his standard the original five-year plan of April 1929, rather than the revised targets of 1930, he argued that the plan had been substantially overfulfilled in 1928/29, and 1929/30; in the special quarter, in spite of defects due to 'the subjective factor', there had been a 'positive break-through' in rates of growth after the disruptions of the previous quarter. A very rapid advance in 1931 was therefore proposed, including an expansion of national income by 38·9 per cent and of the gross production of Vesenkha and Narkomsnab industry by 43·6 per cent. Kuibyshev described the plan to produce 17 million tons of pig iron in 1933 as 'the characteristic feature which runs through the planning of Vesenkha and Gosplan'.[157] Kuibyshev's pessimism about the iron and steel plans (see pp. 399–400 above) had now been dissipated, or was carefully concealed from the public. The year 1931 was characterised in Kuibyshev's report, and by other speakers at the plenum, as the year in which 'the construction of the foundations (fundament) of the socialist economy must be completed'.[158]

The struggle against the Right wing was strongly emphasised at the plenum. In a further speech, Kuibyshev castigated Rykov

[157] The only specific target included in preliminary instructions of the presidium of Vesenkha on the compilation of the plan issued on November 16 was 'the unconditional fulfilment of the programme to produce 17 million tons of pig iron in 1933 and 82 millions in 1937' (TsGANKh, 3429/1/5195, 189–91).

[158] Kuibyshev's report, 'revised for the press', appeared verbatim in PKh, 12, 1930, and in Kuibyshev, V (1937), 9–43.

as an opponent of rapid industrialisation, and declared that as Rykov had not become an active advocate of the general line after the XVI congress, a 'crack' of a disruptive kind had appeared between the leadership of the government and the party, which was impermissible in view of the 'tremendous cohesion' required for achieving the 1931 plan.[159] The plenum resolved to dismiss Rykov from the Politburo, and he was simultaneously replaced as chairman of Sovnarkom by Molotov.[160] Molotov made it abundantly clear in his own speech to the plenum that Sovnarkom would henceforth be unambiguously subordinate to the party. He reminded the plenum that he had worked in the central committee under 'the direct leadership of Lenin's best pupil Stalin', and avowed that in Sovnarkom he was also going to work 'as a party worker, an executant of the will of the party and its central committee'. He reported to the session the good news that the Council of Labour and Defence, STO, which he described as 'a kind of economic general staff', was to be strengthened by appointing Stalin as one of its members. Parallel to STO, and also under Molotov's chairmanship, a new 'Commission for Fulfilment' was established under Sovnarkom; this commission would have a common staff with Rabkrin, and would check the fulfilment of party and Sovnarkom directives and decisions.[161] The new commission does not appear to have played an important role in practice. Its establishment was significant as one of the endless series of administrative devices, reminiscent of the days of War Communism, designed to bring some order into the chaos of overlapping plans and instructions from different central agencies, and to put the distribution of scarce supplies on a sound and regular basis. But Molotov's appointment to the chairmanship of Sovnarkom, a post which he held for over

[159] Speech of December 19, first published in Kuibyshev, V (1937), 51–62.

[160] *KPSS v rez*, iii (1954), 74; I, December 20, 1930 (decree dated December 19); in view of his new duties, Molotov ceased to be a secretary of the party central committee and a member of the Orgburo. Following the usual practice, Andreev, who had been appointed head of CCC/Rabkrin in place of Ordzhonikidze (see pp. 418–19 above), ceased to be a candidate member of the Politburo.

[161] Molotov's report to the plenum on re-electing the soviets was published in abbreviated form in B, February 15, 1931, 16–25. For the government decree establishing the Commission for Fulfilment, see SZ, 1931, art. 18 (dated December 24, 1930).

ten years, was a major step towards ensuring the subordination of the whole governmental machine to the Politburo and to Stalin.

CHAPTER TWELVE

THE ARMAMENTS INDUSTRIES, 1929–30

The claims of defence reinforced the claims of industrialisation. Tsarist Russia had developed a strong artillery, naval shipbuilding and military chemical industry, and good aircraft design and production facilities. The rapid expansion of armaments production in 1909–14 was made possible by the advance of heavy industry in the 1890s, and in turn played a major role in the industrial boom on the eve of the first world war. But in the mid-1920s the armed forces were only half their pre-war size, while armaments production was probably lower than in 1913.[1] The technical level of Soviet armaments generally lagged far behind those of the major capitalist powers. Artillery was entirely based on pre-war designs and war-time modifications. The Soviet Union had as yet no tank industry, though it had benefited from German technical assistance in establishing design facilities. Even at the end of 1928 the Red Army possessed only 350 lorries and 700 motor cars.[2] The aircraft industry alone challenged the advanced countries with Tupolev's designs of metal aircraft; but its batch production consisted almost entirely of simple aircraft of foreign design, and aero-engines were largely imported.[3]

In the spring of 1927 the defeat of the Chinese communists and the rupture of diplomatic relations by Britain dramatically demonstrated that the Soviet Union was a weak and isolated

---

[1] The armed services numbered 630,000 in December 1926 as compared with 1,200,000 in the Army alone in April 1914 (Wheatcroft (1982), 7; *Californian Slavic Studies*, vol. 7 (1973), 133 (Kenez)); for armaments production in 1913, 1925/26 and 1927/28 see p. 20 n. 83 above.

[2] VIZh, 12, 1964, 9.

[3] See Davies, ed. (1988) (Lewis and Cooper). For Voroshilov's assessment of the backwardness of the Soviet defence industry in 1927, see *Pyatnadtsatyi s"ezd* (1962), ii, 988.

power in a hostile world. The subsequent war scare in the summer of 1927 was promoted by the party leaders to strengthen their hand against the Left Opposition.[4] But the international events of 1927 undoubtedly strengthened the resolve of the leadership to accelerate the development of the capital goods industries as a basis for a modern defence industry. In December 1927, the XV party congress explicitly resolved:

> Bearing in mind the possibility of a military attack . . . it is essential in elaborating the five-year plan to devote maximum attention to a most rapid development of those branches of the economy in general and industry in particular on which the main role will fall in securing the defence and economic stability of the country in war-time.[5]

In 1927–9 the plans to develop a large-scale vehicle and tractor industry, and to establish major iron and steel and chemical facilities in the Urals and beyond, were strongly influenced by the need to establish an industrial capacity which would sustain a large modern armaments industry.[6]

But the production of modern armaments could not await these long-term industrial developments. Even before the international events of 1927, the Soviet authorities had already sought to revive and strengthen armaments production, following the deterioration of Soviet relations with Britain, France and Poland in 1926. Henceforth the short-term needs of defence competed with as well as reinforcing the claims of industrialisation. Simultaneously greater attention was devoted to the integration of military and civil production by using armaments factories to produce civilian goods, and by adapting civilian factories so that they were ready for war-time conversion to military needs.[7]

In the course of 1928 and 1929, as the rising ambitions of every sector of the economy were recorded in successive drafts

---

[4] See *Soviet Union/Union Soviètique*, vol. 5, i (1978), 1–25 (Meyer); the author underplays the leaders' sense of danger by underestimating the significance of the party central committee resolution of June 1, 1927.

[5] *KPSS v rez.*, ii (1954), 452.

[6] See Carr and Davies (1969), 426–31, 439 and SS, xxvi (1974), 272–4 (Davies).

[7] See Carr and Davies (1969), 426–31.

of the five-year plan, influential military leaders stressed the immediate claims of the armaments industries.[8] Early in 1928, a report by Tukhachevsky, chief of staff since November 1925, pointed out that the Soviet armed forces lagged technically behind the rest of Europe, and called for immediate and comprehensive technical rearmament, including the establishment of a powerful air force, and of tank units with fast-moving tanks armed with guns.[9] According to a Soviet historian, Tukhachevsky's proposed figures were 'really grandiose for that time', and were condemned by Voroshilov and Stalin as unrealistic.[10] In May 1928, following this incident, Tukhachevsky resigned from the post of chief of staff and was relegated to the command of the Leningrad military region.[11] Tukhachevsky, who had commanded the Warsaw offensive in 1920, combined his call for increased armaments with strongly advocating the use of the Red Army as a spearhead of world revolution. He was replaced by the cautious non-party professional soldier, Shaposhnikov, and this temporarily restrained plans for massive rearmament.[12] The plan approved by the government on July 30, 1928, envisaged that the stock of tanks would reach a mere 1,075 by the end of 1932.[13]

In the debate on the five-year plan at the XVI party

[8] In his careful study of Soviet military literature, Boetticher (1979) argues that the military stressed the importance for defence both of heavy industry and of the supply of food, fodder and horses from a stable agriculture. He claims that there was no 'rational justification, from the point of view of security', for the rapid industrialisation policies of the party leadership at the end of the 1930s (Boetticher (1981), 17). But this does not refute the view that increasing pressure from the military for the expansion of heavy industry was one of the factors influencing the party leadership in 1927–30; moreover, Boetticher underestimates the significance of the campaign by Tukhachevsky and his colleagues.

[9] A further unpublished report, 'Future War', prepared in the IV Administration of the Red Army in 1928 by Tukhachevsky, Ya. K. Berzin and others, called for the establishment of (1) motorised rifle and machine-gun units (chasti), supported by fast-moving tanks, (2) large cavalry units supported by armoured cars and fast-moving tanks, and (3) large air-attack units (VIZh, 5, 1983, 79, 82–3 – Savushkin).

[10] VIZh, 4, 1963, 66 (Isserson); Tukhachevsky's figures have not been published.

[11] *Ibid.* 66; Tukhachevskii, i (1964), 11.

[12] On the replacement of Tukhachevsky, see Carr (1971), 319–20.

[13] VIZh, 8, 1968, 105; the production of tanks and other armaments will be recorded in the Tables to vol. 4 of the present work.

conference in April 1929, Krzhizhanovsky, speaking on behalf of Gosplan, acknowledged, in response to complaints from the military, that military needs were insufficiently elaborated and 'possibly underestimated' in the plan, while Unshlikht, deputy People's Commissar for War, was extremely critical of the military aspects of the plan.[14] This marked the beginning of a major shift in armaments policy. Shortly after the conference, even though the first Soviet tanks were only just being completed, the five-year plan for tank production was greatly expanded: 5,000 tanks were to be manufactured in the course of the plan.[15] Two months later, on July 10, Chinese troops acting on instructions from Chiang Kai-Shek seized the Chinese Eastern Railway in Manchuria, which was jointly owned and managed by the Soviet and Chinese governments, and expelled its Soviet employees.[16] This was certainly the most serious direct challenge of a foreign power to the authority of the Soviet government since the years of civil war. Five days later, on July 15, 1929, the Politburo adopted an important resolution 'On the Conditions of the Defence of the USSR'. While the resolution must have been in preparation for some time, it was presumably hurried through as a result of the Chinese attack. The resolution noted with satisfaction that the past five years had seen 'the creation of a strong army prepared for battle, fully reliable *in a political respect*, and corresponding *in a technical respect* to the level of development of the productive forces of the country'. According to the resolution, the adoption of the five-year plan created 'favourable conditions for the considerable qualitative and quantitative improvement of the defence of the USSR'; the next stage must be that in the course of the plan 'a modern military–technical basis for defence must be established'. As well as the modernisation of existing armaments, this would involve 'in the course of the next two years the acquisition of prototypes of modern artillery and of all modern types of tanks, armoured cars, etc., followed by the introduction of them into the army'. In the case of the air force, which was more advanced, the resolution called for 'the rapid development of its quality to the level of advanced bourgeois countries' and the 'inculcation, cultivation and development of Soviet research

---

[14] See Carr and Davies (1969), 431.

[15] VIZh, 8, 1968, 106; the plan was approved on May 6.

[16] See Carr, iii (1978), 898–900.

and design capacity, especially for aircraft engines'.[17] A few days later, the Revolutionary Military Council (RVS) of the USSR undertook the revision of its five-year plan in the light of the Politburo resolution.[18] The increased importance attached to the rapid development of the defence industries was marked by the establishment of the very senior post of Chief of Armaments to which Uborevich was appointed, and by the creation of a new Administration for Motorising and Mechanising the Red Army under Khalepskii.[19]

In response to the seizure of the Chinese Eastern Railway, the Soviet authorities established a Far Eastern Army under Blyukher and broke off relations with the Chiang Kai-Shek government.[20] In the next two months strenuous but unsuccessful efforts were made by the Soviet side to reach agreement with Chiang Kai-Shek; until November the Far Eastern Army undertook only minor military operations.[21] Behind the scenes the appropriate response to Chinese aggression was hotly debated. At the Moscow party conference in September 1929 Korostelev, from the Moscow party control commission, criticised 'a certain – I would call it – delicacy' on the part of the Soviet authorities in dealing with the Chinese attack:

> It seems to me that we have not displayed enough force or sufficiently rebuffed these rash adventurers. The more law-abiding restraint there is on our part, it seems to me, the more insolence and attacks on our territory there would be; and it is probable that the more rebuff we give to these attacks the less inclination there will be to seize our territory.[22]

Another delegate even more bluntly declared that 'the central committee is following an insufficiently harsh line'.[23] In a confused reply, Molotov argued that the object of the Chinese

---

[17] *KPSS o vooruzhennykh silakh* (1969), 264–6; the resolution is published with some omissions.

[18] *50 let* (1968), 569 (dated July 17); the previous five-year plan, of which details have not been available, was approved in 1928.

[19] *Ibid.* 569 (decisions of July 18; on the same day RVS approved decrees on the tank-tractor-armoured car and artillery equipment of the army).

[20] See Degras, ed., ii (1952), 391–2.

[21] *Ibid.* ii (1952), 393–7; Carr, iii (1978), 908–9.

[22] *Pervaya Moskovskaya*, i (1929), 110.

[23] *Ibid.* 143; the delegate, Fomin, was described as an ordinary worker.

attack was to '*unwind the offensive against the USSR* by the imperialists', with the implication that the Soviet Union should avoid becoming the victim of provocation through hasty response; but he also admitted that the aim of the attack was 'to discredit the Soviet Union as a powerless country eaten up by economic difficulties and internal political complications'.[24] In November the Red Army acted more forcefully, and successfully routed the Chinese forces, using some of its new aeroplanes as well as troops; and Soviet rights on the railway were fully restored.[25]

This alarming incident strengthened the argument for an immediate effort to increase military strength, reinforcing the claim for expanding the military five-year plan at a time when all sectors of the economy were pressing for higher targets. On January 11, 1930, Tukhachevsky sent a report from Leningrad to Voroshilov arguing that 'the successes of our socialist construction . . . pose the urgent task of reconstructing the armed forces taking into account all the latest technical factors, the possibilities of military-technical production and the developments in the countryside'; he called for an increase in the number of divisions and an expansion of artillery, aviation and tank armies.[26] This report was not published; but in a public lecture to the newly-established military section of the Communist Academy, later printed in the Academy journal, Tukhachevsky took the same line. He urged that the new mass production facilities in Soviet industry should be utilised, and criticised conservative fears that the mass use of motor vehicles was ruled out in the USSR by the state of the roads. Military thought, according to Tukhachevsky, also lagged behind the advance of industrialisation, and in contrast to other military experts he strongly advocated the use of large-scale offensive operations, condemned the strategy of defence in depth modelled on the Napoleonic war of 1812, and rejected the view that the proletarian state did not have the right to overthrow the bourgeoisie of another country by force.[27] Elsewhere he repudiated the claim of another expert that it was 'better to

[24] *Ibid.* 150–1.
[25] See Carr, iii (1978), 909; the protocol signed between the Chinese and Soviet sides was published in P, December 23, 1929.
[26] Tukhachevskii, i (1964), 12.
[27] VKA, xxxix (1930), 202–10.

give up Minsk and Kiev than take Belostok and Brest', rejecting such views as 'the influence of bourgeois ideology on the theory of the art of war'.[28]

Tukhachevsky's report of January 1930 remained unanswered for several months; he wrote to Stalin in April requesting a reply, but Stalin bluntly responded that the adoption of this programme would lead to the elimination of socialist construction and its replacement by some kind of system of 'Red militarism'.[29] According to a Soviet account, Stalin also observed that 'it was incomprehensible that a marxist could have such unrealistic ideas – to adopt such a project would mean to militarise the whole country and this was worse than any wrecking'.[30] To Tukhachevsky's humiliation, Stalin's reply was read out by Voroshilov to the RVS. Nevertheless, Tukhachevsky returned unsuccessfully to the argument on several occasions in the course of 1930.[31] Tukhachevsky was not alone in pressing for a rapid improvement in Soviet military strength, though others did not associate themselves with Tukhachevsky's offensive strategy. Military and planning officials concerned with the defence industries insistently urged both the immediate expansion of armaments production and the reorientation of the whole of industry to defence needs (see pp. 448–50 below). How far this new campaign had the active support rather than the mere acquiescence of Stalin and his supporters in the Politburo is not known. It was soon followed by a further substantial shift in defence policy. According to the official Soviet history of the second world war:

[28] Tukhachevskii, ii (1964), 144–6; this attack on Verkhovskii, the expert concerned, and on Svechin and Melikov was originally published in 1930 as a preface to a translation of the German military historian Delbrück's history of the art of war.

[29] Tukhachevskii, i (1964), 12.

[30] VIZh, 4, 1963, 67 (Isserson); only brief extracts have been made available both of Tukhachevsky's report and of Stalin's reply. In his commentary Marshal S. Biryuzov approves the spirit of Tukhachevsky's report, but remarks that 'the specific figures need further refinement', frustratingly failing to cite any figures (Tukhachevskii, i (1964), 12).

[31] *Ibid.* i (1964), 12; in a letter to Stalin dated December 30, 1930, Tukhachevsky complained that the terms of Stalin's reply had made it impossible for him to raise for discussion various matters concerned with the development of defensive capacity; he had been removed from his responsibilities for the teaching of military strategy in the Military Academy.

In the period of preparation for the XVI congress of the party the CC CPSU (b) and the Soviet government required the RVS USSR to examine again the plan of military construction on the following principles:

(a) numerically – not to lag behind our probable adversaries in the most important theatre of war;

(b) in technology – to be stronger than our adversary in the three decisive types of armament, i.e. air force, artillery and tanks.[32]

This campaign for strengthening the defence industries reached its climax at the time of the XVI party congress, though without any public reference to the new guide-lines. On June 2, Unshlikht was transferred from his post as deputy People's Commissar for War to a deputy chairmanship of Vesenkha.[33] Unshlikht was a vigorous protagonist of the development of modern armaments,[34] and his appointment was evidently intended to augment the priority afforded to military orders within industry. Two weeks later, a striking article by Mekhonoshin, the head of the defence section of Gosplan, called for the forced development of the production of high-quality alloys, non-ferrous metals and machine building, including precision engineering, so that industry was ready for war-time military needs: tanks and tractors, civilian and military aircraft, armoured cars and automobiles, field and civil communications and electricals, and merchant and military shipping, must all be adapted so as to enable a rapid shift from civilian to defence production in time of war. Mekhonoshin insisted that developments so far were too slow; 'the whole attention of industrial and planning agencies, party and trade-union agencies' must be concentrated on this issue.[35] On the day on

---

[32] *Istoriya vtoroi mirovoi voiny*, i (1973), 258; no date is given for these guide-lines. On June 13, 1930, RVS USSR approved a 'corrected plan for the construction of the Red Army' (*50 let* (1968), 569); *Istoriya vtoroi mirovoi voiny*, i (1973), 258, implies that this plan was based on the new guide-lines, but according to Kardashov (1976), 242, it was based on the more circumspect guide-lines of July 15, 1929 (see pp. 444–5 above).

[33] SP VSNKh, 1929/30, art. 1478 (dated June 6), reporting TsIK decree of June 2.

[34] See Carr and Davies (1969), 431, and p. 444 above.

[35] I, June 16, 1930.

which the congress opened, *Izvestiya* published a full-page article on 'Military Development for the XVI Congress', in which Ventsov, the head of the Mobilisation Section of the Staff of the Red Army, insisted, implicitly contradicting the Politburo resolution of July 1929, that 'until recently the utilisation of technology for defence purposes and saturation of the army with technology have lagged behind the general technical development of industry'.[36]

At the congress itself Voroshilov, after discussing in some detail the substantial rearmament recently undertaken by the Western powers, including Poland and Romania, also claimed that industrial officials 'do not yet take the question seriously enough':

> Our war industry, and industry as a whole, both in the quantity and in the quality of its supplies of everything required for defence, is still hobbling quite badly.[37]

He added that he would return to this question in the debate on Kuibyshev's report, and would 'have to say something not entirely pleasant for our industry', but in the event he did not speak again at the congress. Instead Muklevich, from the Political Administration of the Red Army, resumed the attack on industry, complaining that 'often under the cover of secrecy nothing at all is done'. Civilian and military output were not yet interchangeable, the plans of armaments factories were vague and general and 'with many military orders there are delays, high costs and poor quality'. Shipbuilding was a case in point; with the development of a merchant fleet, the officials of the industry had neglected military orders, and endeavoured to push military shipbuilding out of their factories altogether.[38] Unshlikht, from his new vantage point within industry, also complained that orders from the Commissariat for War were frequently 'considered to be second-priority orders of secondary importance, with which there is no need to hurry', and insisted that an immediate improvement was essential:

[36] I, June 26, 1930 (Ventsov and Petukhov).
[37] *XVI s"ezd* (1931), 285.
[38] *Ibid.* 506–7; Muklevich was former head of the navy (see Carr, ii (1976), 630–1).

In the year 1930/31 the break-through must certainly take place. *It is absolutely essential to obtain a sharp reduction in prices, a considerable improvement in the quality of production; orders must not be left incomplete, and the period in which they are carried out must be shortened,* both for prototypes and for batch production.[39]

The major reports at the congress by Stalin and Kuibyshev had little to say about the defence industries, and the congress resolutions merely insisted on their importance in general terms. But soon after the congress Smilga, a prominent old Bolshevik and former oppositionist with considerable experience both in the Red Army and in planning, was appointed head of the Mobilisation-Planning Administration of Vesenkha, and both he and Budnyak, a prominent official concerned with the armaments industries, were appointed to the presidium of Vesenkha: Unshlikht, Smilga and Budnyak now constituted a formidable pressure group within the industrial administration.[40] The needs of the defence industries gradually received greater emphasis. In an article in the economic newspaper on August 13, 1930, Zarzar, in charge of 'aerofication and automobilisation' in Gosplan, called for major improvements in the aircraft industry. He pointed out that the design and production of engines was lagging behind airframes; and complained that Soviet civil aviation received less of its income in subsidies than its European equivalents and must be developed rapidly.[41] In a further article he proposed more attention to airships, and more generally complained that the 1928 and 1930 variants of the five-year plan for 'aerofication' were inadequate; Dirazhblestroi, responsible for constructing airship factories, and Aviastroi, responsible for constructing aircraft factories, must be developed on a par with Dneprostroi.[42] The issues continued to be hotly disputed behind the scenes, and the higher party authorities intervened on several occasions in favour of the needs of defence. On August 16, 1930, three days after the publication of Zarzar's first article, Stalin and

[39] *XVI s"ezd* (1931), 538.
[40] SP VSNKh, 1929/30, arts. 1673 (dated 17 July), 1734a and 1735 (both dated July 28); SZ, 1930, ii, arts. 160 (dated July 16), 212 (dated July 21).
[41] EZh, August 13, 1930; Zarzar was apparently transferred from the air force to the presidium of Gosplan in 1930 (ZI, September 6, 1933).
[42] P, September 10, 1930.

Voroshilov, on holiday in Sochi, wrote to the Politburo objecting to the dilatoriness of the commission on civil aviation headed by Rudzutak:

> The military air force of the largest imperialist countries is mainly based on the might of the civil air force . . . In view of our almost complete lack of a civil air force and the related absolute weakness of the military air force, we consider it necessary to make up for lost time . . . In connection with this it is necessary to construct a number of factories (East of the Volga) for engines, aircraft and airships, so as to raise the Civil Air Force to 10–15 thousand tons within a short period of time. Of course this will involve setting up a special agency.

Such developments would cost 'hundreds of millions' of rubles.[43]

The party leaders also intervened in support of aero-engine development at this time. While Stalin and Voroshilov were still in Sochi, Baranov, head of the Air Force, and Uborevich sent them a telegram complaining that aircraft engine design was hampered by lack of facilities. After talking to the designer Charomskii, Voroshilov sent a telegram of support to the party central committee headquarters, and a subsequent meeting attended by Politburo members agreed to the formation of an Aero-Engine Institute.[44]

As in other industries these efforts to strengthen the defence industries were undermined by the large number of arrests of specialists in the course of 1929 and 1930. In October 1929, for example, five former generals working in war industry were found guilty of spying and sentenced to death; their associates were imprisoned in concentration camps.[45] In the aircraft

---

[43] Cited from the archives in Kardashov (1976), 250–1. The five-year plan adopted in the spring of 1929 allocated 100 million rubles to civil aviation, presumably for aerodromes and other infrastructure (*Pyatiletnii plan*, i (1930), 68).

[44] *Byli industrial'nye* (1970), 109–15 (Charomskii). The Aero-Engine Institute was established by a decision of RVS on December 3, 1930; it was later renamed Central Institute for Aviation Engine Construction (TsIAM) (Yakovlev (1982), 315).

[45] *Pravda*, October 20, 1929; Krzhizhanovsky later reported that ten former generals and 19 former colonels had been found guilty of wrecking in war industry (P, February 12, 1930).

industry, the leading designers Polikarpov and Grigorovich were arrested in September 1929, but from 1930 were employed in a Central Design Bureau (TsKB) established at the 'Aviarabotnik' factory No. 39 in Moscow, under the supervision of the Technical Section of the OGPU. The TsKB, formed in the spring of 1930, combined a number of separate design bureaux, and employed both imprisoned and free staff.[46]

The TsKB had a staff of 300 by the end of 1930, and 500 by the autumn of 1931.[47] According to the aircraft designer Yakovlev, who worked there with other free engineers, 'the organisation was overstaffed and senseless, the expenditure great and the results small; only Polikarpov worked brilliantly'.[48] Polikarpov and Grigorovich were eventually released in 1933.[49]

Firm evidence is lacking on the extent to which the mounting attention devoted to the defence industries in 1929 and 1930 resulted in practice in an increase in their share of industrial resources: only scrappy statistics are available on investment and production in 1928–30. In 1929, after long delays, Tupolev's first military aircraft, the all-metal reconnaissance bi-plane ANT-3, went into production.[50] In the summer and autumn of that year Soviet aviation undertook a series of remarkable and well-publicised flights, including a flight from Moscow–London and back by the nine-seater three-engined passenger aircraft ANT-9 and from Moscow–New York via Siberia by the ANT-4; this was the heavy two-engined bomber monoplane TB-1 with its armour removed. Both of these aircraft went into batch production at this time.[51] In 1930 aircraft production was substantially higher than in 1928 and 1929; and, under the peculiar conditions of GPU control, research and design facilities expanded.[52] Investment in civil aviation, presumably in the infrastructure, expanded from the minute figure of 5 million rubles in 1929 to 30 million rubles in 1930.[53] In 1930, with the

[46] Yakovlev (1967), 96; Gunston (1983), 89, 238. The Aviarabotnik factory was renamed the 'Menzhinsky' factory after the head of the OGPU.

[47] Lewis (1979), 135; Shavrov (2nd edn, 1978), 408.

[48] Yakovlev (1967), 96.

[49] Gunston (1983), 89, 238.

[50] Yakovlev (1967), 58; it passed its state tests in 1926.

[51] Yakovlev (1982), 20–1, 265, 359–60.

[52] See Lewis (1979), 135.

[53] P, February 9, 1933 (A. Gol'tsman).

batch production of the MS-1 based on the Renault light tank, tanks were manufactured in substantial numbers for the first time.[54]

After the XVI Party Congress, production in the defence industries evidently accelerated. In October–December 1930, the production of 'other machine building', the main item in which was the defence industries, was 25·6 per cent higher than in the previous quarter, while the production of machine building and metalworking as a whole increased by only 18·1 per cent. But the increase of capital investment in 'other machine building' was slightly less rapid than in the sector as a whole.[55]

In spite of this progress, the defence industries were often less successful in fulfilling their plans than the other sectors of heavy industry. The production of tanks amounted to only 20 per cent of the plan in 1929, 65 per cent in January–March 1930, and 20 per cent in April–June and July–September 1930.[56] In 1930, passengers and freight carried by civil aviation also lagged far behind the five-year plan approved in the spring of 1929;[57] and in October–December 1930, in spite of Politburo support, investment in civil aviation amounted to only 50 per cent of the quarterly plan.[58] While defence factories and military orders were supposed to be afforded top priority, the urgent claims of the key civilian projects, such as the Ural–Kuznetsk combine and the tractor and lorry factories – which themselves had considerable military potential – frequently overrode the

[54] See VIZh, 8, 1968, 106.
[55] Estimated from data in *Itogi VSNKh* (1932), 117–19; further data will be provided in the Tables to vol. 4.
[56] *Istoriya vtoroi mirovoi voiny*, i (1973), 260.
[57]

	1927 (Actual)	1928 (Actual)	1928/29 (Plan)	1929 (Actual)	1929/30 (Plan)	1930 (Actual)	1930/31 (Plan)	1931 (Actual)
Passengers (thousands)	7·9	9·5	12·8	12·0	30·0	14·9	51·7	22·6
Freight & posts (thousand tons)	190·0	248·0	340·7	287·6	827·9	339·5	1560·0	669·1
Distance flown (th.km.)	2044·9	2497·8	4399·9	3561·9	9252·6	4879·4	12766·5	6144·3

(Plan figures from Kokorin (1930), 28; actual figures from *SSSR za 15 let* (1932), 187; the actual figures are higher than those in *Sots. str.* (1935), 455, which excludes airlines of local significance and flights by the Derulyuft company.)

[58] ZI, February 21, 1931 (Kuibyshev).

claims of the directly military projects.[59] High priority civilian research sometimes drove out military research. In 1930, when the automobile-engine research institute NAMI was transferred to the administrative control of the vehicle and tractor corporation, its aviation department, with its equipment, was ejected from NAMI premises and transferred physically as well as administratively to the aviation research institute TsAGI, even though the latter was so short of space that it was partly accommodated in an old church.[60] And urgent civilian production sometimes drove out military production. In October 1930 Vesenkha ruled that the maximum use should be made of defence industry factories for civilian production for the heavy machine-building industry, as part of the drive to reduce imports.[61] In December, Voroshilov complained to Ordzhonikidze that a mere 29·6 per cent of the quarterly allocation of 24,000 tons of pig-iron to artillery factories had been received by December 14;[62] in contrast total production of pig-iron in October–December 1930 amounted to as much as 79·8 per cent of the quarterly plan of 1,546,000 tons.[63]

The problems of affording priority to the defence industries partly reflected the inherent difficulties of the task of assimilating what in many respects required a more complex technology, and was more demanding in terms of materials, workmanship and quality standards than anything previously produced in Russia. But at the end of 1930 the defence industries were evidently still of lower priority in practice than the tractor or iron and steel industries. The authorities proceeded on the assumption that there was no immediate threat of a major war,

---

[59] See TsGANKh, 3429/1/5197, 20 (materials attached to Vesenkha presidium decree of October 30, 1930, on the geological survey of the raw material basis for industry).

[60] *Byli industrial'nye* (1970), 111; for the Politburo intervention in this matter see p. 451 above.

[61] TsGANKh, 3429/1/5195, 146 (decree of Vesenkha presidium dated October 29, no. 1537). The importance of this was stressed by Ordzhonikidze at the XVI party congress in June 1930 (*XVI s"ezd* (1931), 309–10).

[62] Akshinskii (1974), 156–7; 2,900 tons were received in October, 2,900 in November, and 1,300 from December 1–14.

[63] For the plan, see SZ, 1930, art. 575; for actual production, see *Chernaya metallurgiya* (1935), 62. Artillery works also received iron and steel from their own metallurgical facilities.

and the delicate balance between longer-term and immediate military strength was still tilted towards the construction of a powerful heavy industry as a basis for future defence.

CHAPTER THIRTEEN

CONCLUSIONS

It is not the clear-sighted who lead the world. Great achievements are accomplished in a blessed, warm mental fog.

Joseph Conrad

(A) EFFECTS OF THE REVOLUTION

The consequences of the social and economic transformation wrought by revolution and civil war were complex and paradoxical. The implementation of an anti-capitalist urban-based revolution in a country in which capitalism was relatively weak removed or restricted private capital, but did not fully replace it by public enterprise. In the countryside, the social revolution eliminated the landowners' estates and greatly weakened the better-off peasants, diminishing the commercial sector of agriculture. In internal trade, partly as a result of the limitations on the private sector, both the total number of retail trading outlets and the number of persons engaged in retail trade were considerably smaller than before the revolution (see pp. 31–2 above).

In agriculture, the commercial sector was further weakened as a result of state policy. The balance was tilted, even after the introduction of the New Economic Policy in 1921, towards industry and the urban worker. Throughout most of the 1920s the terms of trade between industrial and agricultural products were more unfavourable to agriculture than in 1913. These unfavourable terms of trade, together with the decline of commercial agriculture, brought about a substantial reduction in agricultural marketings (see vol. 1, pp. 14–18). This in turn inhibited the development of the industrial economy. The shortage of agricultural raw materials hindered the recovery of the consumer goods industries; the lack of agricultural products for export was the main cause of the drastic decline in foreign trade (see pp. 20–1, 33 above).

Other consequences of the social revolution also caused difficulties for the industrial economy. The introduction of the eight-hour day was a popular measure, which encouraged the urban population to believe that the new regime identified itself with their interests. But it meant that throughout the industrial sector working hours per person were reduced by 15–20 per cent. On the railways pre-war levels of operation were attained only by a substantial increase in the number employed, while in industry the recovery to pre-war levels of production involved a combination of higher employment and higher labour productivity. (See pp. 28–9 above.)

Post-revolutionary limitations on private capitalism removed the major pre-revolutionary internal sources of investment. All large-scale industry was nationalised; private industry consisted only of small factories and artisan workshops with relatively trivial profits. Private trade was also small in scale and restricted in scope. But the almost complete absence of loans from abroad after the revolution meant that all the resources for investment had to be obtained from within the Soviet Union. The great decline in all forms of private wealth therefore meant that the state itself enthusiastically but painfully shouldered the burden of obtaining resources for investment. If the Bolsheviks had not been committed to state planning, they would have had to invent it.

Other consequences of the social revolution were more favourable to economic development. The humbling of the wealthy resulted in a drastic decline in both home production and imports of luxury goods, and in the number of domestic servants, freeing labour and industrial capacity for less sybaritic purposes. The abrogation of the external and internal national debt removed an incubus from the state budget and the balance of payments. The reduction in state military expenditure as compared with the eve of the first world war substantially reduced a major item of the pre-revolutionary budget, released industrial capacity, and facilitated the direction of state resources towards civilian investment.

But the crucial role was played by the policy of the state, which strongly favoured industrial expansion. A combination of financial and price controls, together with some physical controls, enabled a substantial shift of resources towards industrialisation (see pp. 42–5, 50–1 above). Imports were directed towards the needs of industry, and particularly the needs of industrial investment, to a much greater extent than in 1913 (see pp. 34–5 above). Although construction (building work) and total capital investment had not recovered to the 1913 level, investment in industry had substantially increased, at the expense of investment in housing and in transport. Investment in agriculture was also higher than in 1913; this was primarily due to increased investment in livestock (see pp. 50–1 above).

The pattern of industrial recovery was strongly influenced by these developments. The production of producer goods (capital goods) was greater than in 1913, though it still lagged behind the 1916 level. Factory production of some consumer goods previously manufactured by artisans substantially increased, continuing the war-time trend. But many consumer goods industries were hampered by the chronic shortage of agricultural raw materials.

In spite of the rapid recovery of Soviet industry, in 1926/27 the gap in production between the USSR and the advanced capitalist nations was as wide as in 1913. Soviet industry relied on pre-revolutionary capital stock, which had suffered a decade of neglect, and was often urgently in need of replacement rather than overhaul. The technological gap was therefore wider than the production gap. The recovery of industry also restored its geographical distribution; as before the revolution, it was concentrated into a few areas embracing a minority of the population (see pp. 23–7 above). Moreover, the growth of industry had failed to curb the scourge of mass urban unemployment, a far more prevalent evil under NEP than before the revolution (see pp. 11–13, 27 above).

(B) THE INDUSTRIALISATION DRIVE, 1927–9

This was the ambiguous context in which the Soviet Communist party was committed to overtaking the industrial level of the advanced capitalist countries 'in a relatively minimum historical period' (resolution of XV party conference, November 1926). At the end of the economic year 1926/27, the Soviet authorities had neither defined this 'relatively minimum historical period' nor determined the methods by which their goal would be reached. Before the end of the calendar year 1927, however, the grain crisis urgently confronted the party with the major dilemmas posed by the policy of rapid industrialisation.

Hic Rhodus, hic salta!

Like other moments of decisive change in history, the grain crisis does not lend itself to straightforward explanations. The substantial increase in capital investment during the summer of 1927, and the consequent rise in purchasing power in both town and country, was certainly an important cause of the crisis. The relatively low grain prices introduced from the summer of 1926 onwards were also a major reason for peasant reluctance to sell grain to the state after the harvest of 1927. Moreover, the reduction of the prices of industrial consumer goods in the spring of 1927, carried out in spite of rapidly rising demand, exacerbated the goods shortages, particularly in the countryside.

While more sophisticated price policies in 1926–7 would have mitigated the grain crisis of 1927, and might have avoided it altogether, the large further rise in industrial investment during 1928 and 1929 was not compatible with the market relation with the peasants which was the cornerstone of NEP. Some western economists have argued that the Soviet state could have successfully turned the terms of trade against the peasant by increasing the prices of essential industrial consumer goods and holding down the prices of agricultural products.[1] But it is by no means certain that this proposition is correct even in principle.[2] And in practice such a switch of terms of trade against the peasants could have been effective only if the state had been able to hold down the prices not only of grain and industrial crops, but also of meat and dairy products, and vegetables, most of which in 1927/28 were sold in the private sector.[3] The state would also have needed to establish control

---

[1] *Problems of Communism*, July–August 1976, 59 (J. Millar).

[2] See Harrison (1977), 18, and Davies, ed. (1988) (Harrison).

[3] According to a TsSU questionnaire to 10,000 families in the 117 largest towns, the private sector (including peasant bazaar trade) was responsible in the agricultural year 1927/28 for the sale of 26·1 per cent of grain products, 48·3 per cent of meat, 53·4 per cent of dairy products and eggs, and 77·3 per cent of vegetables (SO, 7, 1929, 67 – D. Lyubimov).

over the prices of rural as well as urban handicrafts. Without these measures peasant activity would have shifted to the uncontrolled sector, and the required increase in extra-rural food supplies would not have been obtained. But such extensive price controls would require a very substantial administrative mechanism for their enforcement, and, like the course actually followed by the Soviet authorities, would have brought the non-coercive economic relation with the peasants to an end.

For nearly all Soviet politicians and economists, whatever their school of thought, the pace of industrialisation was the central issue. The debate began two or three years before the grain crisis. Opinion in the party, with very few exceptions, assumed as early as the end of 1925 that industrialisation was an urgent necessity. Dzerzhinsky, head of Vesenkha until his death in July 1926, combined strong support for the market relation with the peasants with an equally strong conviction that *'our industry must be constructed on a new technological basis, by utilising all the achievements of technology which are available in the bourgeois world'*.[4] Rykov, Bukharin and their colleagues took the same view. Lenin's injunction to 'catch up and overtake' the capitalist west was central to party policy.

But how rapid a pace of industrialisation was feasible? Rykov and Bukharin took it for granted that the market relation with the peasants must be maintained. But ever since 1923 Trotsky and his supporters, while not abandoning their support in principle for NEP, had insisted that the pace of industrial development was dangerously slow: the platform of the United Opposition in September 1927, supported by three of the six party leaders who had been full members of the Politburo at the time of Lenin's death, declared that 'the present tempo of industrialization and the tempo indicated for the coming years are obviously inadequate'.[5]

Following the grain crisis, in 1928 and 1929 nearly all the critics of official policy argued that the pace of industrialisation must be reduced.[6] Bukharin and his colleagues on the Right

[4] Dzerzhinskii, ii (1977), 311 (speech of December 11, 1925); see also SS, xi (1959–60), 382–4 (Davies).

[5] *Platform* (1973), 36.

[6] Bukharin, in 'Notes of an Economist' (P, September 30, 1928), in order to keep within the bounds of official policy, merely called for no increase in the existing tempo of industrialisation, but his arguments were clearly designed to demonstrate that the existing tempo was too high.

saw 'over-strain in capital expenditure' as the cause of all the difficulties,[7] and the non-party specialists in Narkomfin and Narkomzem advocated the reduction of industrial plans as the only practical means of avoiding inflation and shortages.[8] Trotsky at first assumed in discussions with his supporters in exile after the grain crisis that a high rate of industrialisation could be obtained by squeezing the Nepman and the kulak but, following the further acceleration by the end of 1929, even Trotsky concluded that the pace of industrialisation was too high. In contrast, Stalin, strongly encouraged by Kuibyshev in Vesenkha and by leading personalities in Gosplan and elsewhere, from 1927 onwards increasingly insisted that the pace of industrialisation must be accelerated even if this caused difficulties on the market. In February 1928, in the midst of the grain crisis, Mikoyan explained to Narkomtorg that the choice was between slower development, or more rapid development at the risk of difficulties: *'we chose the second road'*.[9]

There were weighty reasons for this choice. The major technological advances in the United States and Germany in the 1920s meant that the goal of overtaking the capitalist world was receding further into the distance: 'in the capitalist countries', Stalin pointed out in November 1928, 'technology is not only advancing, but simply rushing ahead'.[10] Soviet agricultural difficulties also seemed to the Soviet leaders to be rooted in backward technology, and soluble only with comprehensive mechanisation. Even Bukharin declared with pride that 'the blades of tractor-drawn ploughs are turning over the virgin land of the steppes . . . the free feathergrass is singing its last song before its death'.[11] According to Stalin and his supporters serious dangers menaced the Soviet Union if it failed to industrialise rapidly. The growth of employment lagged behind the spontaneous movement of potential workers into the towns: without industrialisation, Ordzhonikidze asked rhetorically in July 1927, 'what will you do with the unemployed who come from the villages, and with the workers' children who have grown up and cannot work?' (see p. 53 above). But

[7] See Carr and Davies (1969), 319.
[8] See, for example, Yurovskii (1928), 371.
[9] TPG, February 18, 1928.
[10] Stalin, *Soch.*, xi (1949), 247.
[11] P, September 30, 1928.

the major new factor in 1927 was the recognition by the Soviet leaders of the dangerous international isolation of the Soviet Union. The immediate danger of war was exaggerated for reasons of political tactics both by the United Opposition and by the party leadership. But Soviet fears were grounded in a series of alarming events: the defeat of the Chinese revolution in April 1927, the abrogation of diplomatic relations by the British Conservative government in May, the assassination of the Soviet representative in Poland and the simultaneous bomb-explosion in the Leningrad party club in June. Henceforth the party leaders were determined to establish an industrial economy strong enough to provide modern armaments capable of repulsing hostile capitalist powers. Kuibyshev, his tongue loosened by alcohol, is said to have told a Soviet official in May 1928 that 'Stalin recently summed it all up brilliantly in a single phrase: we need real industrialisation, not industrialisation *at shabby little tempos* (plyugavenkie tempy)'.[12]

But the headlong Soviet rush along the road to industrialisation cannot be explained merely as a response to these threatening circumstances. The approach of the Bolshevik leaders to the great economic issues of the end of the 1920s was shaped by their life-experiences and their revolutionary ideology, as well as the international and internal environment in which they operated. They had grown up as dissidents within the Russian Empire, with its long-established centralised autocratic state. In tsarist Russia independent legal institutions, liberty of expression, and democracy all had a brief and somewhat exiguous history. The leaders and members of the Bolshevik party had been hardened by the political persecution and economic exploitation which they suffered before the revolution. They had witnessed and endured mass slaughter and chaos in Russia during the first world war. All this helps to explain the strength and the triumph of the Leninist wing of Russian marxism; and the decision of the Bolsheviks, supported by many industrial workers, to seize and hold on to political power.

The maintenance and consolidation of Bolshevik power against tremendous obstacles during the Civil War and after

[12] Valentinov (Stanford, 1971), 250; the record of the conversation was prepared by the émigré deputy editor of the industrial newspaper in 1956, 28 years after it occurred, and so cannot be presumed to be accurate.

strengthened the authoritarian trends in state and party. The Bolsheviks only partly destroyed the old state machine. Even during the Civil War, and to an even greater extent in the 1920s, they found themselves relying on the administrative procedures and practices of the tsarist regime in order to govern this vast territory of heterogeneous peoples, drawing upon former tsarist officials and still more on the filing systems of tsarist institutions. At the summit of state power, the tsar, his court and his ministers were replaced by the Politburo of the Bolshevik party and by the leading party members who headed the People's Commissariats which succeeded the tsarist Ministries. Even before the death of Lenin, the Soviet Union had become a one-party state, and several fateful strands had already become prominent in Bolshevik thought and practice. The so-called 'Stalinist' notion that opponents of party policy were objectively – and sometimes subjectively – agents of the class enemy has a long history. As early as the spring of 1918 Lenin denounced the Menshevik Groman and his associates as supporters of counter-revolution because they advocated greater economic incentives to the peasants.[13] In March 1921, simultaneously with the introduction of NEP, Lenin condemned the Workers' Opposition in the party for its 'anarchist spirit, the response to which should be a rifle'.[14]

The bitter struggles of the Civil War also strengthened the Cheka. The treatment of opponents as agents of the class enemy by Soviet political thought and by the political police found dramatic practical expression in the first major public trial of political opponents, the trial of the Socialist-Revolutionary leaders in March 1922. Several ingredients of the trials of 1928–31 were already present in the 1922 trial. The party central committee took the decision to organise the trial; major defendants, one of whom denounced his own sister, avowed their guilt; the defendants were condemned by the press before they were found guilty (Bukharin and Lunacharsky called them 'vermin' and 'microbes').[15] Political justice was already subordinated to the will of the party leaders.

---

[13] Lenin, *Soch.*, xxvii, 397: 'Go to Skoropadskij', he jeered, 'go to the bourgeoisie'. Skoropadskij was the Ukrainian nationalist leader.
[14] *Desyatyi s"ezd* (1963), 123; he used a similar phrase a year later (see Lenin in *Odinnadtsatyi s"ezd* (1961), 24, and Shlyapnikov's reply, *ibid*. 102).
[15] See Jansen (London, 1982), 23, 81, 152.

Such developments were not the sole trend in Bolshevik thought and practice. Traditions of stormy debate and democracy, and even of recognising the right to differ, remained strong. But Stalin, in his lectures on Leninism shortly after Lenin's death, could lean on one major aspect of Lenin's thought and practice in presenting the party as the 'leading and organising detachment of the working class', 'the embodiment of unity of will, incompatible with the existence of fractions' – a party which 'becomes strong by cleansing itself of opportunist elements'.[16]

Historians have not yet satisfactorily assessed the relative importance of these various influences in determining the complex of decisions which led to the transformation of the Soviet system at the end of the 1920s. Bolshevik ideology and political practice, the Russian heritage, and the imperatives of industrialisation all played a significant part; no one factor provides a sufficient explanation. Leninist ideology was not the decisive factor: it proved by and large compatible not only with the Stalin regime, but also with the more flexible political and economic orders of the 1920s and of the decades since Stalin's death in 1953. Nor does the heritage from the Russian past provide a sufficient explanation. Other countries with quite different histories – including Cuba and China – have developed political and economic regimes similar in important respects to the Soviet system of the 1930s and 1940s.

Some historians have attempted to cut through these difficulties by arguing that Stalin's personality was a decisive if accidental factor in determining the outcome. But despotic individuals have played a major role in the history of many industrialising countries in the twentieth century, both communist and non-communist, as well as in some advanced industrial countries, notably Nazi Germany. Historians of the 'Stalin' period, the 'Mao' period, the 'Hitler' period and the 'Nkrumah' period are each tempted to explain their period in terms of the accident that a particular tyrant managed to grasp the levers of power, but the common institution of despotism calls for an analysis which does not depend on individual personalities.

The account in the present book of the development of

[16] Stalin, *Soch.*, vi (1947), 169–86.

industrial policy and the Soviet economic system at the end of the 1920s confirms that both the ideology and the experience of the Bolsheviks influenced their decisions about economic dilemmas. A foreshortened vision of what is possible and a conviction that public ownership would easily solve all problems was a central feature of Marx's as well as Lenin's thought. Bolshevik confidence in the economic power of the centralised state was perhaps derived more from the Russian past than from Lenin or Marx. But their willingness to abandon the market in favour of planning through administrative orders found support both in Marxism generally and in its Leninist variant, which placed social and economic relations rather than the market mechanism at the centre of economic analysis. Even more important perhaps was the influence of the economic experience of the Soviet leaders: both the war-time Russian and post-revolutionary Soviet economies were shortage economies in which the state frequently intervened to control or defeat market forces. The view that it was possible and essential for the proletarian state to overcome the laws of the market in the course of planned socialist industrialisation was widely held in the party. In 1924 and 1925 Preobrazhensky, Krzhizhanovsky and Strumilin all insisted with varying degrees of emphasis and with various qualifications that the market must be subordinate to the plan, while in 1927 first Mikoyan and then Kuibyshev defended price controls, which imposed the will of the state at the expense of shortages, as a victory for planning (see vol. 1, pp. 34–6). In any case, rapid industrialisation necessarily tended to upset market equilibrium; a high level of industrial investment could not have been enforced without state intervention; the shortage economy was primarily a consequence of the economic goals of the authorities. But the domination of a certain cast of mind in the Bolshevik party of the mid-1920s meant that market levers were abandoned precipitately and with little consideration of the consequences.

The shift from NEP to the centrally-planned economy did not take place without a serious struggle within the party. The battle between what we might call the 'War Communism' and the 'NEP' traditions took place not only between groups and individual leaders in the party, but also within the mind and conscience of every party member. Stalin's inner thoughts cannot be known. But as late as November 1926 Stalin as party general secretary strongly defended the compatibility of industrialisation with the economic alliance with the peasantry. 'The socialist method of industrialisation', he declared, 'leads not to the sharpening of internal contradictions but to smoothing them out and overcoming them'.[17]

Even after the grain crisis Stalin and his colleagues had no clear conception of the extent to which the industrialisation drive would lead to the breakdown of the market and the collapse of NEP. In the course of 1928 they embarked upon a series of emergency measures in the hope of partially or fully overcoming the crisis. They switched resources to the production of consumer goods for the peasant market. They imposed currency and credit restrictions in order to halt the growth of inflation. They embarked upon a crash programme to construct sovkhoz 'grain factories' which would increase bread supplies to the towns. They revived the policy of offering investment concessions to foreign capitalists. They combined a vigorous productivity drive with restrictions on wages and overheads, in order to reduce costs so as to obtain profits for industrial investment. (See pp. 63–5 above.)

Only the last of these policies was at all successful; the drive to reduce costs by increasing productivity more than wages eventually became a firm feature of the economic system of the Stalin period. But this success did not provide sufficient resources. In 1928 and 1929 inflationary pressures mounted. Rapid industrial growth and increased industrial investment were accompanied by a halt in the growth of agriculture and its partial decline. The outcome was paradoxical. Inflation was incompletely repressed. With the expansion of purchasing power fuelled by the acceleration of industrialisation, prices on the free market rose rapidly, particularly food prices. In spite of the low prices paid by the state for grain and industrial crops, the scissors between the retail prices of industrial consumer goods and the average price received by the peasants for agricultural products as a whole returned to the 1913 level in 1928, and then opened in favour of agriculture in 1929 (see pp. 60–1 above). Simultaneously the inability of the state to obtain agricultural goods for export forced it to reduce the import of capital equipment (see pp. 74–5 above). Contrary to the

[17] Stalin, *Soch.*, viii (1948), 286–8.

assumption of many western historians, it was not the collectivisation of agriculture in 1929–30 which caused the crisis which turned the terms of trade in favour of agriculture; it was the shift in the terms of trade in favour of agriculture in 1928 and 1929 which led a desperate but self-confident Politburo to embark on collectivisation in 1929–30.

Within the party the agricultural crisis was at the centre of the clash with the Right wing. Bukharin condemned the imposition of what Stalin called a 'tribute' on the peasants as their 'military-feudal exploitation'.[18] The Politburo seized the opportunity of the clash with the Right to impose greater conformity within the party, condemning the resistance of Bukharin and his supporters to the new policies as an attempt to establish 'party feudalism' – a 'formless conglomerate consisting of feudal princedoms including the *Pravda* princedom, the AUCCTU princedom, the princedom of the Comintern secretariat, the Narkomput' princedom, the Vesenkha princedom, etc. etc.'.[19] By this time Stalin had already enunciated his new doctrine that the class struggle would not diminish but intensify in the course of the transition to socialism (see vol. 1, p. 467). Resistance to the acceleration of industrialisation by non-party specialists, and their non-compliance, were countered by arrests, imprisonment and executions (see pp. 61–2, 91 above).

(C) ACCELERATED INDUSTRIALISATION, 1929–30

Following these drastic measures in 1928 and the early months of 1929, the further acceleration of industrialisation in the autumn of 1929 was accompanied by a determined drive to impose the will of the party on the economy and on society. Stalinism has often been assailed by western critics for 'economic reductionism'. This is an odd criticism, for a major distinguishing feature of Stalin's doctrines was his insistence on the crucial role of the political system in the transition to socialism in the USSR. Following Lenin, he argued that the Soviet political

[18] Cited in *KPSS v rez.*, ii (1954), 558.
[19] *KPSS v rez.*, ii (1954) 562 (resolution of joint session of Politburo and presidium of party central control commission, February 9, 1929).

order was already more advanced than the political order of the advanced capitalist countries: the power of the proletarian state must be used to create the advanced economic basis required by socialism (see pp. 139–40 above). The charge of 'economic reductionism' has some validity insofar as higher production was treated as the paramount objective in the 1930s and 1940s. But even in this respect the critics have missed their mark. Stalin and his colleagues treated not production as such but production in the interests of the socialist state as the over-riding goal. 'We do not need *just any* growth of the labour productivity of the people', Stalin pointed out to the party central committee in April 1929, 'we need a growth which will ensure a systematic preponderance of the socialist sector of the economy over the capitalist sector'.[20] The trouble was rather that the kind of political order and society which was created did not accord with the socialist system envisaged either by Stalin's critics or by classical marxism (see pp. 162–3 above).

Soviet doctrine strongly emphasised that in order to construct the economic base of socialism the proletarian state would have to mobilise the mass of the population and its creative initiative. Great stress was placed on the importance of 'socialist emulation' and 'shock work' in the factories; these movements purported to include most workers (see pp. 256–61 above). In 1929–30 more direct participation of politically-active workers in the control of the factory was also encouraged: bureaucracy would be overcome by creative initiative exercised by elected voluntary personnel. In 1930, workers' collectives and communes were at their most popular; in their various forms they involved some ten per cent of all industrial workers. (See pp. 272–8, 261–7 above.) At the same time industrial workers, as the most reliable support for the regime, were encouraged to spread socialist understanding and practice in other sectors of the economy. Workers' brigades in the countryside played a significant role in the collectivisation of agriculture (see vol. 1, pp. 204–9); workers' brigades were also prominent in the Bolshevisation of the state apparatus (see pp. 117–18 above). Skilled and politically conscious workers were sent in substantial numbers to lagging factories and to crucial construction sites, while simultaneously rank-and-file workers were recruited to

[20] Stalin, *Soch.*, xii (1949), 80–1.

the party in large numbers to assist it in coping with its greatly expanded tasks (see pp. 135–7 above).

Soviet leaders claimed that as a result of these endeavours the Soviet working class was being transformed: 'a new human being', Kuibyshev announced, 'is being created in production' (see p. 131 above). These claims were greatly exaggerated. But there is no doubt that the enthusiastic support of a significant minority of the urban population, embodied in hard work and often in self-sacrifice, helped the regime to overcome many obstacles. The cause of socialist construction was also actively supported by a minority of convinced marxists in every profession from economics to education, from physics to history (see pp. 143–53, 155–62 above). The efforts to create a new world were encapsulated in the continuous working week, the *nepreryvka*, which destroyed the fixed boundaries between work and leisure by making Sunday a normal working day and attempting to abolish fixed working days and working hours (see pp. 252–5 above). In the winter of 1929–30 a government commission sought to mark the new era by introducing a revolutionary calendar (see pp. 143–4 above).

The socialist transformation was not a spontaneous process, either in intention or in practice; Stalin admitted or boasted in retrospect that during the first five-year plan 'the party as it were whipped on the country, accelerating its forward movement'.[21] In the same spirit, Krzhizhanovsky told TsIK (the Soviet Central Executive Committee) that to achieve the 1929/30 control figures 'a war is taking place . . . a war with the highest goals' (see pp. 183–4 above). What was universally known as the 'socialist offensive' was not intended merely to overcome the forces of nature and the inertia of loyal citizens. It was primarily directed against all the 'remnants of capitalism' in the USSR. Nepmen, kulaks and disloyal and even neutral specialists were treated as enemies and arrested, exiled and even executed. A parallel battle was waged against hostile ideology and its advocates, including not only religion and the church, and the wide variety of non-marxist intellectual activities which had been tolerated in the 1920s, but also such heretical varieties of marxism as Deborin's 'menshevising idealism' in

---

[21] *Soch.*, xiii (1951), 183 (report to central committee plenum, January 7, 1933).

philosophy and Rubin's political economy (see pp. 149–52, 155–60 above).

Social terror and ideological control, together with the greater centralisation of the economy, involved the tightening up and consolidation of the machinery of political power. In the course of 1929–30 Stalin and his supporters established their undivided power in the Politburo and Orgburo, in each of which the Right wing of the party had been a strong minority in 1928–9; these changes at the top were accompanied by a purge at all levels in the party, directed partly against those suspected of Rightist views (see pp. 134, 234–6, 241 above). Following a parallel purge of the state administration, a similar consolidation took place in Sovnarkom, culminating in the replacement of Rykov by Molotov in December 1930. During 1929–30 the full-time staff and the committee membership of the trade unions were radically changed at every level (see p. 278, n. 225 above).

In 1929–30 the authority of CCC/Rabkrin (the party central control commission and the jointly-staffed Workers' and Peasants' Inspectorate) was at its height. As the principal advisory agency to the Politburo, CCC/Rabkrin advocated and to a considerable extent itself designed the policies of accelerated industrialisation and socialisation which dominated this period. It effectively took over control of the new Narkomzem of the USSR in December 1929 and of Vesenkha in November 1930; its agents managed the economy together with Pyatakov, Grin'ko and other enthusiasts for socialist transformation. As the organiser of the purges in the party and the state administration, CCC/Rabkrin headed the campaign against class enemies and Right-wing deviationists. Here it was supported, encouraged and driven on by the OGPU.

In 1929–30 the power of the OGPU and the range of its activities also greatly increased. The OGPU was responsible for the arrest and questioning of unreliable specialists and the exiling of kulaks, and for summary executions. It organised the many secret political trials of 1929–30, and set up the major trial of the 'Industrial Party' in November 1930 (see pp. 115–17, 407–10 above).

On December 21, 1929, the Soviet Union celebrated Stalin's fiftieth birthday (see vol. 1, pp. 174–5). A Russian fiftieth birthday is a great event in the life of every citizen; Lenin objected to the celebration of his anniversary on April 23, 1920, but could not prevent the Moscow party committee from organising a special meeting or from publishing a pamphlet about the aniversary.[22] Stalin was not so reticent; a vast display of public enthusiasm for him coincided with the launching of an all-out 'socialist offensive' in the towns as well as the countryside. Stalin was presented as a wise as well as a determined leader, far-sighted and sensible, harsh but flexible. The Stalin presented to the public in 1929–30 personally launched the elimination of the kulaks as a class in December 1929, but also personally halted the collectivisation campaign in March 1930 when it had gone too far. But both the official and the private Stalin of 1930 was primarily the man of the socialist offensive, determined to destroy the remnants of capitalism and to transform NEP Russia into socialist Russia at breakneck speed. 'We are advancing at an accelerated tempo', he told the XVI party congress in June 1930, but 'we are devilishly *backward* in the level of development of our industry, . . . only *further acceleration* of the rate of development of our industry will enable us to catch up and overtake the advanced capitalist countries in a technical and an economic respect'; 'those who chatter about the necessity of *reducing* the rate of development of our industry are enemies of socialism and agents of our class enemies'.[23] This was the image of the Bolshevik leader with which party members loyal to Stalin identified themselves: progressive and constructive, unyielding to the enemy.

Bolshevik doctrine under the influence of Stalin and his supporters did not obviously conflict with Lenin's; it was rather an hypertrophied form of one aspect of Leninism. The official ideology of the Stalin period was not fully established until 1938, when the *History of the Communist Party of the Soviet Union (Bolsheviks): Short Course* was published. But significant features were already in place. Stalin's stress on leadership by a monolithic party in 1924 and on the intensification of the class struggle in 1928 was followed in 1930 by his insistence that in Soviet conditions the state must not wither away but grow stronger during the transition to socialism (see pp. 139–40 above).

Three further features of the doctrine were particularly

[22] Lenin, *Soch.*, xxx, 491–3.
[23] Stalin, *Soch.*, xii (1949), 271, 273–4.

prominent from 1929 onwards, and served to curb creative marxist thought. First, opponents on all matters, large and small, whether bourgeois intellectuals or party stalwarts, were crudely dismissed either as enemy agents, or at best as behaving like enemy agents. The identification of disagreement with treachery was far more blatant than in Lenin's post-revolutionary writings, and was extended to debates among intellectuals where tolerance had previously been the norm. Thus, as we have seen, Stalin dismissed those who suggested lower rates of growth as 'agents of our class enemies', while Yaroslavsky castigated the *'fascisation* of the Trotskyists' (see pp. 332–3 above). In political economy Rubin and his associates, previously permitted to propound and defend their theories, were denounced for 'Menshevik and Trotskyist conceptions' (see p. 157 above).

Secondly, misrepresentation and falsehood on a much wider scale were used to conceal unpleasant realities. When party economists claimed that their ambitious industrialisation plans were compatible with a balanced budget and a stable currency, this was perhaps merely an extreme form of self-deception: it was justified by optimistic extrapolations from the best Soviet experience and foreign practice (see pp. 180–1, 189–90 above). But when Stalin denounced the Osvok draft of the five-year plan for its *'attenuating* Trotskyist curve', he must have known that the principal Trotskyist involved in the plan had fought for higher growth rates within Osvok (see p. 334 above); and Stalin's insistence in face of the evidence that real wages were continuing to increase imposed a simple falsehood in the name of a higher truth (see p. 308 above).

Thirdly, active support for the whole policy of the regime was regarded as an essential manifestation of loyalty. Krzhizhanovsky bluntly told the specialists that *'who is not with us is against us'* (see p. 114 above); both wings of the party, Bukharin and his former followers on the Right, and the former oppositionists of the Left, were badgered to display full and active support for the party leadership.

In this atmosphere of enthusiasm, orthodoxy and fear, remaining traditions of frank discussion within the economic administration were further restricted, together with the independence of the statistical services; the range of economic information which could be published was greatly reduced.

Confidential reports to Sovnarkom as well as published statements had to work within the official policy that plans were in no way exaggerated and the official falsehood that real wages were not declining. But in spite of these severe constraints such reports often sought to convey as much reliable information as possible.[24] And it is clear that while non-party specialists remained silent, party members in industry and elsewhere continued to speak up for more realistic policies when they were strongly convinced that official policies would fail.

While debate about economic policy, though muted, did not cease, the party endorsed the over-ambitious revisions of the five-year plan supported by Rabkrin; their principal targets were enshrined in Stalin's report to the XVI party congress in June–July 1930 and the associated resolution (see pp. 333–4, 329 above). The plans were based on three inter-related assumptions. First, the new factories under construction would be built within the time period achieved by the best United States or German practice: the disadvantage of Soviet inexperience would be compensated by foreign advice and by the advantage of socialist central planning. Secondly, the efficiency of existing capital equipment would be greatly increased. Thirdly, in the remaining years of the five-year plan additional costs savings in industry would exceed those achieved in 1928/29, and large cost reductions would also take place in capital construction. Everywhere unit costs of overheads, fuel and raw materials would decline systematically. Above all, labour productivity would continue to increase more rapidly than wages. The revised plans would enable Soviet industry to rapidly overtake that of the United States. The production of pig-iron, for example, merely one-tenth of the United States' level in 1928/29, would reach nearly 40 per cent of that level at the end of the first five-year plan in 1932/33; and for the last year of the second five-year plan, 1937/38, even the most modest plan for pig-iron production amounted to nearly 90 per cent of the United States' 1929 level (see p. 226 above).[25] The plans of

---

[24] See for example the mimeographed report on 1929/30 by the Conjuncture Group of the Sector of Reproduction of Gosplan, *Kon"yunktura . . . za sentyabr' i 12 mesyatsev 1929/30* (n.d. [1930]), part of which is reprinted in *Industrializatsiya, 1929–1932* (1970), 224–40.

[25] These estimates have taken United States' pig-iron production in 1929 at 43·3 million tons, the highest level achieved before 1941 (see Nutter (1962),

1930 therefore provided statistical support for Kaganovich's bold claim that the USSR would be the greatest single world power by 1940.

Between the summer of 1929 and the XVI party congress in June 1930, simultaneously with the upward revision of the plans, heroic efforts to set the Soviet economy firmly on course for overtaking the United States resulted in an enormous expansion of industrial production. In May 1930 production of large-scale industry was 35·5 per cent higher than in May 1929.[26] Even more remarkable was the increase in capital investment, reflected in the number of persons engaged in building work, which more than doubled between May 1929 and May 1930 (see Table 17).

These successes seemed to the party leaders to justify the methods of mobilisation by which the all-out drive was put in motion. The leap in industrial production was achieved by two major campaigns, the first in the summer of 1929 (see pp. 80–1 above), the second in the first few months of 1930 (see pp. 246–7 above). But the precipitate advance concealed underlying weaknesses. The increase in industrial production in the summer of 1929 and the first eight months of 1929/30 was accompanied by a substantial decline in quality, which was not reflected in the production statistics. Many of the new building workers were untrained and inexperienced, and their productivity was low. Most new capital projects were incomplete when handed over to production, and suffered many months of disorganisation and low production. Existing factories were deprived of resources for extensions and repairs in favour of the new projects. Balance of payments difficulties, together with the disorganisation in agriculture, led to a reduction in the supply of important raw materials. Inflationary pressures mounted, reflected in the rise of urban food prices on the peasant market by 76·5 per cent between October 1, 1929, and June 1, 1930 (see Table 24(c)).

In consequence of these strains, the rapid advance until May

5–83). These figures underestimate the relative size of the US iron and steel industry. The greater availability of scrap in the United States enabled the production of crude steel to exceed the production of pig-iron by 30–50 per cent, whereas in the USSR the production of crude steel and pig-iron were approximately equal.

[26] *Ezhemesyachnyi statisticheskii byulleten'*, 1–2 (86), August–September 1930, 17.

1930 was followed in the summer of 1930 by a serious crisis in the industrial economy. Both the gross production of large-scale industry and output per worker systematically declined in June, July and August 1930; recovery began only in September. The number employed in the construction industry, instead of increasing, slightly declined at the height of the building season. In spite of the good harvest, food shortages grew worse; this was reflected in a further rise in urban food prices on the peasant market by nearly 80 per cent between June 1 and October 1 (see Table 24(c)).

The pattern of crisis differed between industries. First, a crisis of capacity hit the iron and steel industry and the railways: existing capacity in these industries was more or less fully utilised, and in this economy of pressures and shortages it proved impossible to use existing capacity more efficiently. Secondly, a severe labour crisis led to a substantial decline in coal production and prevented the planned increase in capital construction generally. In coal-mining and building, many workers retained close ties with their villages, or worked seasonally. The deteriorating food and accommodation in the mining areas and on the building sites meant that workers remained in or returned to the countryside. This was a 'scissors' crisis' in labour supply, the blades of the scissors measuring living and working conditions in industry and in the villages: in the summer of 1930 the blades opened in favour of the villages. Thirdly, a crisis of raw materials affected several industries, above all cotton textiles: the authorities drastically reduced the import of cotton in order to ameliorate the balance of payments crisis resulting from inadequate agricultural exports and the deteriorating terms of trade for agricultural goods on the world market.

While the economic disorders of the summer of 1930 took different forms in different industries, they were due to common underlying causes. In ch. 9(C) above four inter-related factors are shown to be of major importance. First, the increase of investment in the producer goods industries, the pivot of the industrialisation drive, drew resources from the whole of industry: in the course of 1929/30, an 'economy of shortages' was firmly established (see pp. 358–70 above). Secondly, the upheaval in agriculture caused far greater damage to the urban standard of living than the political leaders had anticipated, and led to the diversion of an unexpectedly high proportion of industrial resources to investment and production in the agricultural engineering industries (see pp. 376–7 above). Thirdly, purges and reorganisation temporarily disrupted the industrial economy; the disorder was exacerbated by the inappropriateness of major features of the reorganisation, though mitigated by the enthusiasm of politically committed workers and officials (see pp. 375–6 above). Finally, the five-year, annual and operational plans adopted in the course of 1929/30, at every level from the Politburo to the work-bench, were not merely ambitious or taut, but wildly unrealistic (see pp. 371–5 above). This imposed an additional strain throughout industry, and led to the misallocation of resources to unfeasible objectives.

Many factory managers and economic officials believed that the plan – either for their own unit, or for industry as a whole – was over-ambitious. The censorship of the press, and the self-censorship imposed by officials anxious not to be impugned as Rightists, make it impossible to determine how widespread such criticisms were. In the party leadership Kuibyshev apparently shared such doubts in August 1930; and in the same month Syrtsov publicly criticised unrealistic plans and called for balanced planning (see pp. 399–403 above). Syrtsov also pleaded for restraint in collectivisation, and for the provision of greater incentives in agriculture (see vol. 1, pp. 375–6). He also strongly attacked excessive centralisation and the insufficient scope for initiative, and called for greater honesty in statistical and other information. It would be an error to suppose that his views were close to those advanced by Bukharin and his associates in 1928–9. Bukharin wanted to restrict industrial development to a level compatible with a market relation with the peasants. There is no evidence that Syrtsov or his associates believed that industrialisation should be cut back to the point at which peasants would be willing to part voluntarily with their major foodstuffs; their criticisms were rather directed at what they regarded as a substantial element of adventurism and bureaucratic excess in Stalin's policies.

The party leadership, headed by Stalin, swept aside these criticisms, and pressed ahead with their endeavour to achieve the revised five-year plans approved by the XVI party congress. The mobilisation of every organisation at every level, and of the mass of the population, would overcome all difficulties; an emergency 'special quarter' was introduced in October–December 1930 in which this would be achieved. One significant modification in existing policies was the determined effort to achieve financial stability through ceasing currency issues. Mobilisation in the special quarter combined further appeals to the population to exert every effort to achieve the plan with much stronger legislation to control the movement of labour and impose labour discipline, and with a further harsh drive against wreckers and traitors, culminating in the 'Industrial party' trial. (See ch. 11 above.)

These measures succeeded in overcoming the crisis. During the special quarter the production of Vesenkha-planned industry increased by 17 per cent, and was therefore over 10 per cent higher than in the April–June quarter before the crisis. In spite of the onset of winter, capital construction was maintained at a high level. But these achievements lagged far behind the plans. This did not deter the authorities from their determination to press ahead with the revised five-year plan, with its central aim of producing 17 million tons of pig-iron in 1933. The annual national-economic plan for 1931, approved by the party central committee in December 1930, proposed that gross production of large-scale industry should increase by the unprecedentedly high figure of nearly 45 per cent in a single year, and ambitious targets were also set for agriculture. Such extremely over-ambitious planning was not abandoned until the beginning of 1933, when the Soviet Union was in the grip of a severe economic crisis, and about to suffer a disastrous famine.

(D) INDUSTRIALISATION AND THE ECONOMIC SYSTEM, 1929–30

During the course of the turmoil of 1929–30, major features of the Soviet economic system emerged. In 1930 the Soviet concept of socialism included both Marx's familiar principles: public ownership of the means of production, and remuneration according to work done. Soviet politicians and economists, following Marx, also assumed that a socialist economy would be a moneyless economy. Payment for work might take the form of some kind of labour token, but this would not be money, because it would not circulate. Trade in commodities would be replaced by product-exchange. Soviet economists therefore regarded the rationing of food and consumer goods, together with the physical allocation of producer goods, as major steps towards socialist distribution. In February 1930 a Gosplan report explained that '*market relations controlled by the state*' were being replaced by '*planned and organised product-exchange between town and country and planned and organised distribution of products between classes within the town and the country*': the laws of the market were giving way to 'organised human will'.[27] At the XVI party congress Stalin defended the shortage economy of the Soviet Union by contrasting it with under-consumption in the capitalist economies:

> Here in the USSR the growth of consumption (purchasing power) always goes ahead of the growth of production, driving it forward, but over there, with the capitalists, the growth of consumption of the masses (purchasing power) never catches up the growth of production and always lags behind it, thus condemning production to crises.
>
> They consider it entirely normal ... to burn 'surplus' agricultural products ... while in the USSR those guilty of such crimes would be sent to a madhouse.[28]

In the winter of 1929–30 many prominent officials and economists assumed that the gradual elimination of trade, together with the large currency issues characteristic of this period, meant that money was already losing its significance. Throughout 1930 monetary incentives – whether economic accounting (khozraschet) in industry or wage incentives to the worker – were treated as of secondary importance. The financial control system and the arbitration system were in large part

[27] EZh, February 9, 1930 (V. A. Levin, addressing All-Union Conference of Planning and Statistical Agencies).
[28] Stalin, *Soch.*, xii (1949), 322–3. Excess purchasing power had already been treated as a stimulus to industry by Mikoyan in December 1926 and Rykov in January 1927 (see Carr and Davies (1969), 631). For the triumph in Comintern of the 'underconsumptionist' analysis of the world capitalist economic crisis, see Day (1981), chs. 5–8. This view continued to dominate marxist thinking until the advent of the second world capitalist economic crisis in the mid-1970s, which displayed markedly different characteristics.

abolished; the budget was downgraded in favour of the broad 'unified financial plan'; the credit reform in practice gave free rein to the issue of credits (see pp. 310–28). Piecework partly gave way to time work.[29]

In 1929–30 central planning in physical terms, which dominated the Soviet economic system in the Stalin period, was firmly established, and remained largely unreformed until 1987. For Soviet communists – as for most socialists throughout the world – planning offered the alternative to the anarchy of the capitalist market, which in 1929–30 was resulting in economic crisis and mass unemployment on an unprecedented scale. Grin'ko put this in an extreme form:

> In the process of carrying out the five-year plan we physically experience and feel with every fibre of our being that we need to organise a social and political mechanism with which 150 million people will act, guided by a single plan, a single concept, a single will, a single effort to accomplish what is laid down by the plan.[30]

These hopes and assumptions had formed part of the Bolshevik concept of the future throughout the slow years of NEP, with Krzhizhanovsky as their standard-bearer and Dneprostroi as the model and augury of future development. Every aspect of the economy would be brought into the plan. Thus the physicist Academician Ioffe proclaimed in 1930 that golden prospects for science were already on offer:

> Our research institutes already exceed the European and almost equal the American in their size. Their structure possesses all the advantages of the socialist system: planning instead of a collection of accidental and competing work; unification into large collectives instead of handicraft cells; direct connection with all sides of life and production; a healthy social base and revolutionary enthusiasm.[31]

---

[29] In Leningrad, for example, the percentage of working hours in industry remunerated by piece payments declined from 63·7 in October 1929 to 57·3 in October 1930 (NFI, 2, 1931, 10 – A. Rotshtein).

[30] EZh, December 26, 1929 (speech of December 24 to Gosplan specialists).

[31] *Sotsialisticheskaya rekonstruktsiya* (1930), 24–5. A major conference on the planning of science in April 1931 was addressed by Bukharin, Krzhizhanovsky,

In the conception of 1930, labour as well as materials would be centrally planned and allocated. By the autumn of 1930 the planning and control of labour was an urgent task. Mass unemployment had been eliminated, and workers were no longer available to fill vacancies for skilled and semi-skilled jobs; the ready availability of work strengthened the position of the individual worker.[32] In the autumn of 1930, when compulsory powers over labour were greatly strengthened, an all-Union conference even decided that labour agencies throughout the USSR must prepare 'monthly operational reports on the recruitment and planned distribution of the labour force'.[33]

The major principles by which the central planning system should be guided had already been established, pragmatically or in the course of fierce debate, in the second half of the 1920s, and were consolidated in 1929–30. The battles of 1927–9 had already seen the victory of the view that the rapid industrialisation of a developing country must necessarily involve the disruption of economic equilibrium.[34] Accordingly Vesenkha, in its report to the XVI party congress, insisted that 'we cannot have a plan variant "balanced in advance" in our system of planning':

> The rushing ahead of some branches and the lagging of others is naturally accompanied by a number of disproportionalities, by the violation and breaking-up (lomka) of balances. And this breaking-up is inevitable, insofar as the establishment of new proportions is inevitable. Through disproportionality, the continuous violation of balances, the new proportionality is formed.[35]

In 1927–9 Soviet planning doctrine already maintained that these inevitable disproportions must be overcome by widening the bottlenecks rather than by cutting the plans.[36] This doctrine

---

Molotov and Kuibyshev (see Lewis (1979), 828, and P, April 8, 9, 10, 11, 12, 13, 14, 15, 1931).

[32] See, for example, VTr, 1, 1930, 34 (Mokhov), 6, 1930, 27–8 (Mokhov), and p. 279 above.

[33] VTr, 10–11, 1930, 138 (conference of labour agencies, November 1930).

[34] See Carr and Davies (1969), 794–9.

[35] *Vypolnenie* (1931), 30.

[36] See Carr and Davies (1969), 794–9.

found dramatic expression in a remarkable article by Kaktyn',
'Overcome the Bottlenecks':[37]

> A situation in which almost all the main branches of the
> economy have to be treated as bottlenecks is a reductio ad
> *absurdum* if the problem is approached from the point of view
> of a 'realistic' justification of the plans. Insofar as all these
> branch limits mutually affect each other, insofar as in this
> situation we would have to base ourselves on the 'narrowest'
> 'realistically' secured branch, this would mean the reduction
> of the surplus possibilities of the others in conformity with
> the narrowest. But in future development the most restricted
> of the most restricted branches could involve pressure on
> other branches . . . and the development of the economy as a
> whole could follow a contracting spiral of negative
> reproduction. From our point of view, from the point of view
> of an active Bolshevik struggle against obstacles, a situation
> in which all the main branches are included among the
> bottleneck branches merely reflects the general tension of the
> national-economic plan.

This view was deeply entrenched in the new generation of
planners. Thus in the Lower Volga a planning official insisted
that '*planning indicators showing low rates of growth should be adapted
to indicators with higher rates of growth, and planning indicators for
secondary branches to indicators for leading branches;* . . . the opposite
methodology would be the antipodes to the methodology of
socialist planning'.[38] Readers wishing to understand the
mentality with which the Bolshevik planners of 1930 'stormed
heaven' should seek for a moment to empathise with this crucial
doctrine. Its application in the preparation of the plans has
been amply illustrated in ch. 6 above.

In the concept of the authorities the heart of central planning
was the centrally-administered capital investment programme
which would introduce the most advanced world technology
into every industry. To this end the network of nation-
wide capital project institutes for particular industries was
considerably enlarged. Thus in the metal group of industries

[37] P, November 3, 1929.
[38] NP, 8–9, 1930, 91.

the iron and steel projects institute Gipromez was joined by the engineering institute Gipromash: in the spring of 1930 3,000 persons were employed in engineering project-making, including those working in the trusts and on the building sites.[39] Throughout industry foreign firms or individual engineers were involved in the preparation of all major and many minor projects (see pp. 123–5, 216–8 above). Simultaneously strenuous efforts were made to centralise, rationalise and specialise the building industry.[40] In October 1930, a Vesenkha conference resolved that the construction corporation Soyuzstroi, which included building materials factories as well as building trusts, should become the 'general staff' for the construction industry in Vesenkha; a strong project bureau within Soyuzstroi would control all project-making.[41]

The dynamic approach to the development of industry was enforced in existing factories by the drive to fulfil the production plan, which increasingly dominated the working life of every administrator, from the central offices of Vesenkha in the 'Business House' on Nogin Square to the factory foreman. With the elimination of the operation of market forces within large-scale industry – never very powerful even in the mid-1920s – and the drive to transfer resources to the capital investment programme, it became essential in every industry to centralise both the planning of production, and its distribution between rival claimants. This was accomplished by 'material balances' (budgets in physical terms), and by the subordination of financial to material balances. Material balances were prepared in Vesenkha and Gosplan, and subjected to intensive scrutiny by both organisations, and in crucial matters by Sovnarkom and even by the Politburo. At the end of 1930, a senior planning

[39] ZI, March 16, 1930; *Metall*, 3–4, 1930, 25–9 (Dobrovol'skii); Gipromash was based on Mosgipromez, which had primarily worked for the industry of the Moscow region.

[40] For the crucial Sovnarkom decree on the industry, dated December 26, 1929, see *Nashe stroitel'stvo*, 3–4, 1930, 95–107; it is summarised in *Industrializatsiya, 1929–1932* (1970), 564–5.

[41] ZI, October 11, 1930 (conference of giant construction projects); Soyuzstroi, first known as Stroiob"edinenie, established in January 1930 with the aim of 'the industrialisation of construction', incorporated a large number of existing building trusts, offices and bureaux from a wide range of industries (SP VSNKh, 1929/30, art. 595, dated January 12); its first head was N. P. Komarov (*ibid*. art. 674, dated January 24).

official, V. A. Levin, while admitting that material balances had been crude approximations 'until recently' ('they simply put down a figure and challenged others to refute it'), claimed that they were now more elaborate and precise.[42] The balances were not in themselves operational instruments of planning; they allocated products in fairly broad categories between fairly broad sectors and sub-sectors of the economy, and needed to be disaggregated into specific plans for specific operational units. According to Levin, the watchwords for supply planning were, or should be, *operativnost'* and *ocherednost'*, which may roughly be translated as 'specific operationality' and 'a priority system'.[43] These terms – together with *adresnost'* (meaning 'every operational plan must refer to a specific economic unit') – soon became everyday planning jargon.[44]

Before the end of 1930 the most extreme plans propounded during the socialist offensive of 1929–30 had already been abandoned. Wildly optimistic assumptions about the likely efficiency which could be achieved by socialist enterprises, coupled with the doctrine of planning to 'widen the bottleneck', had resulted in Sabsovich's fantastic plans in which United States' production would be exceeded several-fold within a few years. Before the XVI party congress in June 1930, the Politburo had rejected these plans, and the associated schemes to build luxurious towns, including agro-towns for the whole agricultural population (see vol. 2, pp. 41–7, 51–4, and pp. 152–3, 225–8 above).

This move towards somewhat greater realism was accompanied by significant modifications in prevailing notions about the social and economic organisation appropriate to the transition

[42] ZI, November 17, 1930.
[43] ZI, November 17, 1930.
[44] The role of mathematical methods in planning also received attention at this time. In a major article, Kol'man, the senior official of the party central committee responsible for science (see p. 142 above) abused the western mathematical school in political economy, including Pareto, Clark and Fisher, as 'a "scientific" cover for fascism', and condemned heretical Soviet proponents of mathematical methods, notably Kondratiev and Bazarov in economics, but insisted that mathematical methods should be used by marxist economists, as they were at an elementary level by Marx himself, and should be compulsory subjects in advanced economics courses (P, October 31, 1930). But Kol'man acknowledged that many people opposed mathematical methods in principle; and their view, by default or design, eventually prevailed.

to socialism. While the experiments in workers' participation in planning and administration continued, the more egalitarian variants of workers' communes in factories were condemned, and stronger measures were introduced to control and discipline workers. In the countryside, attempts to strengthen the kolkhoz by transferring to it the functions of the village soviet, and by entrusting it with agricultural machinery, were rejected in favour of the maintenance of village soviets and the establishment of a network of state-owned Machine-Tractor Stations (see vol. 1, pp. 225–6, and vol. 2, pp. 25–8). While sound practical arguments can be advanced in support of each of these measures, they formed part of a long-term tendency to strengthen central state control at the expense of the 'free and equal association of the producers' regarded by Marx and Engels as a cardinal feature of socialism.

From March 1930, the party officially rejected the notion that the time had already come when money could be eliminated from the socialist economy. Just as the eventual elimination of the state was to be achieved by temporarily strengthening it, so the eventual elimination of money would be achieved by strengthening the ruble. The closing months of 1930 also saw a re-emphasis on the importance of economic accounting (khozraschet) in the relation between enterprises and the central authorities.

These modifications in policy and system eventually had far-reaching repercussions. But for the moment they were extremely limited in their scope. The plans approved by the XVI party congress, though less fantastic than those proposed by Sabsovich and others, still envisaged overtaking the United States by the end of the second five-year plan. An unmodified doctrine of 'widening the bottleneck' guided the counter-planning movement, a debased form of workers' participation, in the autumn of 1930. Soviet marxists at the end of 1930 still envisaged the socialist economy as a moneyless economy, in which no private or individual sector would exist either in the towns or in the countryside; the market economy would be replaced by product-exchange. And the optimistic assumptions about the speed of industrial transformation meant that socialism as thus defined would soon be achieved. As will be shown in succeeding volumes of this history, in the course of 1931–3 sights were lowered; over-ambitious plans gave way to realism, and the definition of socialism was drastically modified.

In 1930 the planning system was still struggling into life. The inherent difficulties in creating a complex system of centralised controls were aggravated by the huge gap between plans and their fulfilment, which caused great confusion throughout the industrial sector. An effective system of priorities, essential in Soviet-type planning, had not yet been established. A conference on capital construction in May 1930 revealed that no proper system of priorities between sites yet existed;[45] Vesenkha did not approve a list of high priority building sites for supply purposes until October 1930, and it did not immediately become fully effective.[46] Throughout 1930 the supply system, and planning as a whole, were in disorder.

The emerging system of central planning also carried with it more fundamental disadvantages characteristic of shortage economies. In conditions of supply uncertainty, factories presented exaggerated claims for materials, and where they could hoarded stocks; but the relentless pressure for greater production resulted in a dangerous decline of stocks of materials which were particularly scarce.[47] Official and unofficial agents or 'fixers (tolkachi)' in increasing numbers sought to secure scarce materials for their factory or construction site. 'I have twelve agents who go round factories and find out what can be exchanged where', admitted the head of supply at Elektrozavod, 'if *we did not have stocks for commodity exchange with other factories* we would have a permanent standstill'.[48] The production drive led enterprises to neglect quality, while the sellers' market enabled them to produce so as to fulfil the plan with minimum trouble, rather than in accordance with customers' needs.[49] The establishment of strong central controls over industry fettered initiative and discouraged risk. Complaints were already voiced about a feature of Soviet planning which is perhaps the major

[45] ZI, May 30, 1930.

[46] ZI, October 23, 1930.

[47] For evidence of the existence of these conditions even before 1929, see Carr and Davies (1969), 833–4.

[48] *Komissiya po mobilizatsii*, svodka No. 7, August 1930, 42; SGRP, 10, 1930, 140, reported that there were nearly 2,500 'representatives' of the regions in Moscow, excluding people on temporary business trips.

[49] See, for example, M. Kaganovich's report to the first conference on planning production in the metal and electrical industry, January 1931 (*Metall*, 1, 1931, 4).

problem of the 1980s and 1990s: 'it is no secret for anyone that in the drive to fulfil quantitative indicators we frequently push to the rear the establishment of new production and the organisation of new technology'.[50]

These defects in the system were contested by the elaboration of countervailing devices. 'Norms' or standard quantities of permitted consumption of materials and fuel per unit of output sought to check extravagant claims.[51] Fierce legislation sought to ban fixers from Moscow and close down their offices.[52] Numerous commissions were established and penalties introduced to overcome the decline in quality (see pp. 384–5 above). While such arrangements mitigated these inherent regularities of the planning system, they could not eliminate them.

In spite of its major imperfections and defects, Soviet planning achieved notable successes. The outstanding achievement was the astonishing expansion in industrial investment, which was in 1929/30 more than 90 per cent above the level of the previous year, and several times as large as in 1913. With the aid of the increased investment, the building season of 1930 saw the completion of the first three major projects – the Turksib railway, the agricultural machinery factory at Rostov-on-Don, and the Stalingrad tractor factory. Construction of the Dneprostroi hydro-electric plant was reaching its peak. At the Uralmashzavod heavy engineering factory in Sverdlovsk, the main production shops of the greatly-expanded project began to be constructed. After many vicissitudes, construction was started at both ends of the grandiose Ural–Kuznetsk combine. The vast construction programme which began the transformation of the USSR into a great industrial power was under way.

---

[50] *Pervaya vsesoyuznaya konferentsiya* (1931), 38, referring to the electric cable factory Sevkabel'.

[51] For the introduction of norms in capital construction, see Venediktov, ii (Leningrad, 1961), 765–7. Stock norms were as yet rudimentary or non-existent (see ZI, March 12, 1930 – Ratskin).

[52] See EZh, October 14, 1930 (decree of CCC/Rabkrin).

TABLES

Note: in all Tables, — = not applicable.

         n.a. = not available in sources used.

         ( ) = calculated as residual by present author.

         [ ] = estimated by present author.

Metric tons (tonnes) are used throughout this volume.

Tables for industrial production and for the defence industries will be included in vol. 4.

Table 1.   National income by sector of origin, 1928–1930 (million rubles)

	Current prices			1928 prices		
	1928	*1929*	*1930*	*1928*	*1929*	*1930*
Census industry	5829	7832	10801	5829	7835	10977
Small-scale industry	1812	1849	1849	1812	1662	1620
Building	1870	2266	3000	1870	2346	3303
Agriculture	10410	10694	13630	10154	9986	10267
Forestry	1404	1734	1813	1404	1696	1815
Other (fishing, hunting, etc.)	752	748	918	752	720	885
Transport (freight)	1135	1489	2002	1135	1261	1497
Trade	2961	3271	3916	2961	3289	3904
Customs duties	272	254	404	272	250	370
Total national income	26442	30136	38333	26187	29045	34637
Of total, real accumulation[1a]	4489	4838	8193	3697	4801	9230
Of total, socialist sector[2b]	11022	15513	23926	11070	15910	24397
private sector[2b]	15420	14623	14408	15117	13105	10240

Sources: Except where otherwise stated, *Materials* (1985), 155.
    [1]*Materials* (1985), 127.
    [2]*Materials* (1985), 156.

Notes: For coverage and methods of estimation, see *Materials* (1985).
    [a] (National income minus non-productive consumption) = (Accumulation Fund).
       (Accumulation Fund − Losses ± Deficit/Surplus on Balance of Trade) = (Real Accumulation).
    [b] Production on the individual holdings of collective farmers, individual handicraft enterprises, etc. are assigned to the private sector.

Table 2. Gross capital investment by sector of the economy, 1926/27–1930 (million rubles at current prices)

	1926/27[1]	1927/28[1]	1928/29	1929/30	1928[7]	1929[7]	1930[7]
Vesenkha-planned industry	1098	1325	1644[2e]	3268[5]	1511[i]	2103[i]	3921[i]
Electrification	247[a]	269[a]	207[2]	303[5]	218	308	457
Other socialised industry	172	290			192	266	358
Private and small-scale industry	63	64	} (449)	n.a.	53	70	48
Total industry and electrification	1580	1948	2300[3f]	n.a.	1975	2747	4784
Socialised agriculture	164	243	900[3]	n.a.	392	844	2622
Individual agriculture	3147	3055	2699[ig]	n.a.	2901	2402	1454[l]
Total agriculture[b]	3311	3298	(3599)	n.a.	3261	3140	3667
Timber	8	13	21[ig]	n.a.	n.a.	n.a.	n.a.
Transport	695	943	1100[3]	n.a.	919[j]	1161[j]	1682[j]
Communications	34	38	56[ig]	90	54	70	100
Trade, etc.	148[c]	176[c]	n.a.	n.a.	68	154	341
Education	66	114	215[4]	202[4]	130	221	237
Health	60	89	114[4]	102[4]	99	116	130
Municipal	121	170	242[4h]	271[4h]	194	253	268
Administration	53	61	58[4]	112[4]	61	71	96
Socialised urban housing[d]	247	312	289[4]	248	280	294	253
Private urban housing	191	202	243[4]	110[4]	236	223	125
Total investment	6534	7363	8531[1]	11500[6]	7276[k]	8451[k]	11680[k]
Of which, socialised	3133	4042	5400[3]	n.a.	4117	5862	10455
private/individual	3401	3321	(3100)	n.a.	3116	2647	1598

Sources: [1] *KTs . . . na 1929/30* (1930), 454.
[2] *Materialy VSNKh* (1931), 19; *Ezhemesyachnyi statisticheskii byulleten'*, 3 (78), December 1929, 116–17.
[3] *Itogi* (1933), 42.
[4] *Materials* (1985), 276.
[5] *Otchet . . . 1929–1930* (1931), ob. zapiska, 39–40.
[6] P, October 28, 1930; this figure was compared with 8,800 million rubles in 1928/29.
[7] *Materials* (1985), 426–30.

Notes: n.a. = not available in sources consulted.
 [a] Includes all power-stations except factory stations, which appear under industry.
 [b] Includes all housing in the agricultural sector (see Table 3).
 [c] Includes investment for primary reworking and collection of agricultural products, as well as in trade as such.
 [d] Does not include industrial housing (see Table 3).
 [e] Vesenkha-planned industry as in 1931, plus part of food industry.
 [f] Socialised sector only.
 [g] Provisional figure.
 [h] Figure in source less estimate for municipal electrification based on data for calendar years in *Materials* (1985), 426–30, by taking 25 per cent of first year and 75 per cent of second year.
 [i] Includes Narkomsnab-planned industry; food industry was transferred to Narkomsnab in 1930, but this item may also include some investment which appeared under 'Trade' in data for 1926/27 and 1927/28.
 [j] Includes civil aviation.
 [k] Discrepancy between total and sum of individual items is explained in *Materials* (1985), 430.
 [l] This is a very rough figure: according to Gosplan, 'owing to the absence of any statistical or departmental data for the second half of 1930', investment in that period was estimated simply by assuming 'simple reproduction' of capital stock (i.e. no net investment) (see *Materials* (1985), 273).

Table 3.   Gross investment in housing, 1926/27–1930 (million rubles at current prices)

	1926/27[1]	1927/28[1]	1928[2]	1929[2]	1930[2]
Factory housing, etc.	173	205	173[b]	224[b]	612[b]
Other urban socialised housing	247	312[a]	280	294	253
Urban private housing	191	202[a]	236	223	125
Housing in agricultural sector	1015	989	931[c]	867[c]	611[c]
Total housing	1626	1707	1620	1588	1601

Sources: [1] *KTs . . . 1929/30* (1930), 454–61.
      [2] *Materials* (1985), 426–30.

Notes: The data for factory housing are included with Industry and the data for all housing in the agricultural sector are included with Agriculture in Table 2 above.
 [a] The following revised figures appear in *Materials* (1985), 276: industry 168; other urban socialised 278; private 238.
 [b] Excludes housing built for transport and electrification: it may be calculated from *KTs . . . na 1929/30* (1930), 454–61, that this amounted to 46 million rubles (1926/27), 67 millions (1927/28) and 67 millions (1928/29 preliminary).
 [c] Mainly peasant *izby* (cottages); investment in housing in socialised sector of agriculture amounted to only 20 million rubles (1928), 32 millions (1929) and 159 millions (1930). For the unreliability of the figure for 1930, see Table 2, note[l].

Table 4. Gross capital investment in Vesenkha-planned industry, by type of industry, 1926/27–1930 (million rubles at current prices)

	1926/27[1] Fulfilment	1927/28[3] Fulfilment	1928/29 Final Plan[4]
1. Electric power: regional	199[2]	215[2]	311
Coal	139	134	168
Oil	180	208	232
Peat, etc.	n.a.	n.a.	3
2. Total fuel	(319)[b]	(342)[b]	(403)
3. Ore	15	17	18
Iron and steel	117[7]	186	261
Non-ferrous metals	27[7]	31	47
Machine building and metal working	(141)[c]	137	184
Electrical	17	20	32
4. Total metal group	(302)[c]	(373)[e]	(530)[e]
Chemicals Group A	n.a.	66	114
Chemicals Group B	n.a.	20	30
5. Total chemicals	60	(85)	(144)
6. Timber and woodworking	30	39	68
7. Paper	38	45	34
8. Building materials	43	40	96
9. Glass		17	15[i]
10. Pottery		4	4[i]
Textiles Group A	171	16[f]	13[f]
Textiles Group B		201	216
Tailoring	3	6	13[j]
11. Total textile group	(174)	(222)	(242)
12. Leather and footwear	17	29	38
13. Printing	3	4	3
14. Food, drink and tobacco	65	94	87
15. Other	(2)	(13)	(25)
Total Vesenkha-planned industry	(1267)[d]	(1539)[d]	(2018)[d]

1928/29[4g] Fulfilment	1929/30 Final Plan[5]	1929/30[5g] Fulfilment	October–December 1930[6] Fulfilment
207[5]	451	313	156
161	362	273	93
226	346	289	90
3	90	56	14
(391)	(798)	(618)	198
16	26	24	21
255	526	413	128
39	119	90	26
187	594	574	284
33	62	62	22
(514)[e]	(1301)[e]	(1139)[e]	(460)
91[h]	389	262	125
26	49	27	6
(118)	(438)	(289)	131
57	184	234	64
37	60	47	11
78	275	200	49
16[i]	27	28	8
5[i]	6	6	3
13[f]	40[f]	40[f]	7[f]
217	185	157	32
16[j]	5	11	11
(246)	(230)	(208)	(50)
41	30	47	11
4	8	10	3
86	9[k]	8[k]	2[k]
(29)	(427)[l]	(353)[l]	(75)[l]
(1845)[d]	(4270)[d]	(3524)[d]	1242

Sources: [1] *Industrializatsiya, 1926–1928* (1969), 119, except where otherwise stated.

    [2] *KTs . . . na 1929/30* (1930), 454.

    [3] *Industrializatsiya, 1926–1928* (1969), 247, except where otherwise stated.

    [4] *Ezhemesyachnyi statisticheskii byulleten'*, 3 (78), December 1929, 116-17, supplemented by *Industrializatsiya, 1929–1932*, 121, and *Materialy VSNKh* (1931), 19; in each case the figure has been taken which appears to be the latest compatible with data for other years.

    [5] *Materialy VSNKh* (1931), 19.

    [6] *Itogi VSNKh* (1932), 110–20.

    [7] *Promyshlennost' . . . 1926/27* (1928), 210–11.

Notes: Changes in classification were frequent in these years: various minor changes have not been noted.

    [a] Factory stations are included with the industry concerned.

    [b] Peat and minor fuels not included.

    [c] Total for metal group, less electrical industry, is given in *Promyshlennost' 1926/27* 1928), 210–11, as 282 million rubles, including ore (11 millions); this total is equivalent to 288 million rubles in our Table (282 − 11 + 17), and implies that machine building and metalworking amounts to 127 million rubles.

    [d] Vesenkha-planned industry plus investment in regional power stations, which was planned by Vesenkha, and was included in the total from 1930 onwards. These totals were obtained as follows:

	1926/27	1927/28	1928/29 Plan	1928/29 Fulfilment	1929/30 Plan	1929/30 Fulfilment
Vesenkha-planned	1068	1324	1707	1638*	3819†	3211
Electric power	199	215	311	207	451	313
Total	1267	1539	2018	1845	4270	3524

    * *Materialy VSNKh* (1931), 19, gives investment excluding food and drink as 1552 (Glavkhlopkom has been deducted), and *Ezhemesyachnyi statisticheskii byulleten'*, 3 (78), December 1929, 116–17, gives food and drink as 86.

    † Total as in source *less* Glavkhlopkom, food and drink omitted (see note [k] below).

    Note that 1928/29 and 1929/30, and possibly other years, omit the gold and platinum industries (*Materialy VSNKh* (1931), 19).

    [e] Metal group as in original source plus electrical industry.

    [f] In 1927/28 includes Glavkhlopkom (8 million rubles); in later years Glavkhlopkom has been omitted.

    [g] Stated to be preliminary figures, but later revisions have not been available.

    [h] Excludes 'special works'.

    [i] Glass is given as 7 million (both plan and fulfilment) in *Ezhemesyachnyi statisticheskii byulleten'*, 3 (78), December 1929, 116–17.

    [j] Includes toilet requisites industry.

    [k] Salt industry only; rest transferred to Narkomsnab. In 1930 Narkomsnab investment in sugar, fish and meat industries amounted to 123 million rubles; and its remaining investment, which included some investment in this group of industries, amounted to 147 millions (*Sots. str.* (1935), 468–9).

[1] This total includes investment in research, geological survey and the cinema and building industries, but about one-third of the total is not explicitly accounted for in 1929/30 (see data for 1930 in *Itogi VSNKh* (1932), 110–20). Most if not all expenditure in the defence industries, however, appears under 'machine building' and 'chemicals Group A'.

Table 5.   Planned capital investment in industry, 1929/30 (million rubles at current prices)

	Proposed for Vesenkha-planned industry during negotiations	Equivalent figure: five-year plan classification
Actual expenditure in 1928/29		1629[a]
Five-year plan (April 1929) for 1929/30, optimum variant		2331[b]
Central directive, August (?) 1929	3000[c]	3200–3300[d]
Claims to Vesenkha, August 1929	3700[c]	
Vesenkha proposal, August 25, 1929	3070[f]	3300–3400[d]
Gosplan proposal, September 1929	2922[g]	3100–3200[h]
Approved by Sovnarkom, October 1929		3331[i]
Control figures volume, October 1929		3267[j]
Revised plan, 1929/30		3606[k]
Actual investment, 1929/30		[2990][l]

Sources and notes: The rival investment proposals and plans for industry advocated in the course of the discussion were rarely comparable with the classification used in the five-year plan. This Table struggles to present them systematically.

[a] *Ezhemesyachnyi statisticheskii byulleten'*, December 1929, 116–17.

[b] *Pyatiletnii plan* (1930), i, 162–3.

[c] See text and note 3, p. 180 above.

[d] The Vesenkha figure of 3,070 million rubles which followed this directive excluded investments amounting to 229 million rubles, including allocations to reserve (100 million rubles), shipbuilding (64 million rubles) and building offices (55 million rubles); all of these were apparently included in the five-year plan figure. It is unclear whether the five-year plan figure also included 'special needs' (presumably defence industries) which were planned by Vesenkha at 115 million rubles. (For these details, see *Kontrol'nye tsifry promyshlennosti 1929/30* (n.d. [1929]), 88–90.)

[e] TPG, October 11, 1929 (Kuibyshev).

[f] See p. 180 above.

[g] TPG, September 25, 1929.

[h] According to TPG, October 5, 1929 (Gordon), the Gosplan proposal for total capital investment in Vesenkha-planned industry amounted to 3,374 million rubles as compared with the Vesenkha proposal of 3,584 millions; these figures evidently need to be reduced by 200–300 million rubles to enable comparability with the five-year plan.

[i] Krzhizhanovskii *et al.* (1930), 5, states that 'the figure of 3,331 million rubles corresponds for the control figures of 1929/30 to the investment figure in the five-year plan of 2,331'.

[j] *KTs . . . na 1929/30* (1930), 462, which treats this figure as comparable to 1,679 million rubles investment in 1928/29, the figure in the five-year plan; on pp. 506–8, the control figures claim that the equivalent to the five-year plan of 2,331 million rubles in 1929/30 is 3,435 millions, but this mistakenly includes electric power, loans to housing cooperatives and investment in industrial higher education establishments, which in all other sources are treated as not included in the five-year plan figure.

[k] Supplementary investments in iron and steel, coal, oil, coke and other industries to the value of 339 million rubles were authorised by SZ, 1930, art. 239 (dated April 2, 1930).

[l] So many changes in classification were made in the course of the year that I have been unable to estimate a comparable figure. According to *Otchet . . . 1929–1930* (1931), ob. zapiska, 40, 'expenditure reached about 83 per cent of the plan' (preliminary figure); this has been used to estimate the above figure. For a wider coverage, *Otchet . . . 1929–1930* (1931), *loc. cit.*, gives a fulfilment figure including the food and drink industries of 3,268 millions as compared with the plan of 3,960 millions. None of these estimates take into account the failure to reduce building costs as planned.

Table 6.   Plans in 1929 and 1930 for production of pig iron by new works, 1932/33 (million tons)

	April 1929: Five-year plan[1]		December 1929: VMS[2]	June 1930[3]	June 1930: XVI Congress[4]	August 1930: Stal'[5]	New capacity actually in operation: end 1936[6h]
	Initial variant[1]	Optimum variant[1]					
Southern region:							
Krivoi Rog	0·35	0·20	1·10	1·05[a]	1·0	1·05	0·71
Zaporozh'e	0·05	0·15	1·10[a]				0·82
Old Mariupol'			1·00[b]				[h]
New Mariupol'						0·70+	0·40[d]
Kerch	0·35	0·73	0·75	0·42[d]	0·6	0·50[d]	
Other		0·05					
Total Southern	0·75	1·13	3·95	1·47		2·3	1·93
Urals and Siberia:							
Magnitogorsk	0·35	0·60	1·10	2·50[a]	2·6	2·60	2·15
Kuznetsk	0·16	0·33	0·55	1·00[a]	1·0	1·01	1·74
Nizhnii Tagil'			0·50	[e]	0·3	0·90	—
Bakal				[e]	?[f]	(1·10[8])	—
Other	0·04	0·10		0·04		0·04	
Total Urals and Siberia	0·55	1·03	2·15[c]	3·54		(4·65)	3·89
Lipetsk		0·47				0·15[g]	[h]
Total USSR	1·30	2·63	6·10	5·01		(7·10)	5·82

Sources: [1] *Pyatiletnii plan,* i (1930), 42–4.

[2] TPG, December 17, 1929 (VMS report to Glavchermet).

[3] P, June 8, 1930 (Birman); similar figures are reported in I, June 16, 1930.

[4] *XVI s"ezd* (1931), 483 (Kuibyshev).

[5] ZI, August 10, 1930.

[6] Gorelik (1937), 64.

Notes: [a] Already envisaged as the *ultimate* capacity of these works when five-year plan was compiled (I, June 16, 1930).

[b] 0·95 proposed in I, January 19, 1930.

[c] 1·1 proposed in I, January 19, 1930.

[d] This capacity was installed in 1926–9.

[e] According to I, June 16, 1930, capacity would be 1 million tons but would not be available until early years of second five-year plan.

[f] According to Kuibyshev, it was 'very probable' that 'a certain quantity of metal' would be obtained from this works during the first five-year plan.

[g] Listed in source but not included in total.

[h] According to Clark (1956), 320–1, in addition to the totals listed here two large blast-furnaces had been installed at Mariupol', two at Lipetsk and two at Tula – each would produce some 0·35 million tons a year.

Table 7 Industrial production in value terms

(a) Gross production of large-scale industry, by industry, 1913–30 (million rubles at 1926/27 prices)

	1913	*1927*	*1928*	*1929*	*1930*
Fuel and power[a]	796	808	1313	1593	2092
Iron and steel[b]	807	673	787	951	1147
Other metals[c]	147[2]	156[i]	216[i]	295[i]	382[i]
Building materials and glass	299[e]	288[i]	374[i]	479[i]	633[i]
Rubber and asbestos	120	159	184	247	339
Metalworking, etc.	434[f]	305[i]	504	707	1197
Machine building	697[f]	1348[ij]	1735	2347	3772
Chemicals	255	(364)[ik]	412	487	774
Woodworking	393	479	555	777	1078
Food, drink and tobacco	2722[g]	2865[g]	3655[l]	4070[l]	4810[l]
Textiles: cotton	2124[h]	2528[h]	3002[h]	3378[h]	2943[h]
woollen	316	425	535	631	703
linen	168	196	192	281	324
silk	163	57[2]	75	103	171
other	129	96	130	193	272
Clothing and knitwear	31	328	621	1080	2023
Leather, fur and footwear	199	530	680	1102	1606
Paper and printing[d]	324	269	314	433	500
China and earthenware	35	38[i]	52[i]	60[i]	71[i]
Other	(92)	(767)	(1524)	(1990)	(2862)
Total census industry[m]	—	n.a.	16860	21204	27699
Group A	—	n.a.	7727	10098	14293
Group B	—	n.a.	9133	11106	13406
Total census industry on 1913 definition[n]	10251	12679	15818	19923	25837
Group A	4290	5735	6807	8966	12664
Group B	5961	6944	9011	10957	13173

Sources: except where otherwise stated, *Promyshlennost'* (1936), 3–22.
[1] *Sots. str.* (1934), 30.
[2] *Sots. str.* (1935), 14–15.

Notes: This series includes state, cooperative and private census industry.
[a] Power, coal, peat, oil and oil-refining.
[b] Including ore.
[c] Includes ores, which according to the source 'were not separated in the records in the old years'.
[d] Paper includes wood pulp, cellulose, paper, carton and fibres; and except for 1930 also includes cardboard. Printing includes all enterprises with 16 workers or more, even without an engine.
[e] Cement, brick including fire-resistant brick (from *Sots. str.* (1934), 30) and glass.
[f] Excludes rail workshops.
[g] Excludes fish industry.
[h] Includes cotton-cleansing.
[i] All building materials and glass.
[j] Includes cables and light-bulbs.
[k] Given together with rubber and soap industries; this figure was obtained by deducting these from the total.
[l] Includes fish industry, amounting to 122 million rubles (1928), 149 (1929), 233 (1930) (derived from *Sots. str.* (1935), 14–15, figure for food, drink and tobacco excluding fish industry).

ᵐ Includes timber and fish industry, and services (including electric power and repair work) supplied outside the factory (*Sots. str.* (1934), 25).

ⁿ Excludes timber and fish industry (*Sots. str.* (1934), 25).

(b) Gross production of large-scale state industry by quarters,
1927/28–1930
(million rubles at 1926/27 prices)

| | | Group A | | |
		Series 1[1a]	Series 2[2b]	Series 3[3c]
1927/28:	October–December	998		
	January–March	1090		
	April–June	1081		
	July–September	1156		
1927/28:	Total for year	4324		
1928/29:	October–December	1235	1297	
	January–March	1309		
	April–June	1381		
	July–September	1536		
1928/29:	Total for year	5461		
1929/30:	October–December	1627	1713	
	January–March	1893		2318
	April–June	1989		2413
	July–September	2084	(2177)	2503
1929/30:	Total for year	7595		
1930:	October–December		2405	2802
1930:	Total for year			10035

Group B			Total		
Series 1[1a]	Series 2[2b]	Series 3[3c]	Series 1[1a]	Series 2[2b]	Series 3[3c]
1407			2404		
1556			2645		
1438			2518		
1386			2542		
5786			10110		
1695	2002		2929	3300	
1783			3092		
1785			3166		
1814			3350		
7076			12537		
2083	2277		3712	3990	
2205		1797	4098		4115
1929		1635	3918		4048
1706	(1644)	1467	3791	(3820)	3969
7929			15520		
	2546	1858		4951	4660
		6757			16792

(c)   Gross production of large-scale state industry by months,
1928/29–1930
(million rubles at 1926/27 prices)

	Group A			
	Series 1[1a]		Series 3[3c]	
	1928/29	*1929/30*	*1929/30*	*Oct.–Dec. 1930*
October	413	528	—	891
November	395	515	—	891
December	426	584	—	1019
January	434	593	737	—
February	412	598	736	—
March	462	702	845	—
April	475	662	810	—
May	435	658	800	—
June	470	669	803	—
July	470	642	782	—
August	507	667	814	—
September	559	775	907	—

	Group B				Total		
Series 1[1a]		*Series 3*[3c]		*Series 1*[1a]		*Series 3*[3c]	
1928/29	*1929/30*	*1929/30*	*Oct.–Dec. 1930*	*1928/29*	*1929/30*	*1929/30*	*Oct.–Dec. 1930*
575	701	—	614	989	1229	—	1505
548	648	—	574	943	1164	—	1465
572	734	—	670	998	1319	—	1690
589	720	576	—	1023	1313	1313	—
584	710	580	—	997	1308	1316	—
610	775	640	—	1072	1477	1486	—
682	754	640	—	1158	1416	1450	—
542	619	518	—	977	1277	1318	—
561	556	477	—	1031	1225	1280	—
537	498	427	—	1007	1140	1209	—
611	549	472	—	1119	1216	1286	—
665	659	567	—	1224	1435	1474	—

Sources and Notes to Table 7(b) and (c)

Sources: [1] 1927/28 and 1928/29: EO, 3, 1930, 178–9.

1929/30: *Ezhemesyachnyi statisticheskii byulleten'*, 1–2 (86), August–September 1930, 17.

[2] PI, 5–6, 1931, 85.

[3] *Itogi VSNKh* (1932), 46–7.

Notes: The coverage of these three series varies considerably, and no series provides data for the whole period. The available data do not make it possible to chain the series together satisfactorily. All series exclude cooperative and private industry.

[a] This series includes the food industry, and industries with seasonal interruptions (vegetable-oil, starch and molasses and sugar-refining); it excludes seasonal industries (sugar-beet, wine-making, timber, brick and peat) and regional power stations.

[b] This series includes industry planned by Vesenkha and Narkomsnab (i.e. it includes the food industry), and, unlike series 1, it also includes sugar-beet and wine-making; it also excludes the timber industry (coverage is otherwise not explained).

[c] This series includes industry subordinate to Vesenkha in 1931 (i.e. it excludes the food industry); it excludes the seasonal timber, brick and peat industries. It includes defence industries as part of machine building and metal working; these may have been excluded from series 1 and series 2, though series 1 includes 42 factories employing 141,000 workers (including MOP) whose functions are merely described as 'general engineering' (*Ezhemesyachnyi-statisticheskii byulleten'*, 10 (85), July 1930, 58–9, line 50).

(d)   *Indexes of industrial production*

(i)   *1913 = 100*

	1913	*1927/28*	*1928/29*	*1929/30*
Nutter (in 1927/28 prices)[1]	100	103[a]	116[b]	134[b]

	1927	*1928*	*1929*	*1930*
Official: all industry[2]	100	111	132	158	193
large-scale industry[2]	100	122	152	190	249

(ii)   *Previous year = 100*

	1928/29	*1929/30*
Nutter (in 1927/28 prices):		
all industry[1]	114[c]	115[c]
Hodgman: large-scale industry[3]	120	116

	1928	*1929*	*1930*
Official: all industry[2]	119	120	122
large-scale industry[2]	125	125	131

Sources: [1] Nutter (1962), 525–6.
[2] *Promyshlennost'* (1957), 31; this index for large-scale industry is a little lower than is implied by the data in Table 7 (a) above, where 1930 = 252 (1913 = 100).
[3] Hodgman (1954), 73.

Notes: [a] Includes miscellaneous machinery but not armaments; with 1955 weights, amounts to 107 (1913 = 100) (p. 527).
[b] Excludes miscellaneous machinery and armaments; with 1955 weights, amounts to 125 in 1928/29 and 141 in 1929/30 (p. 527).
[c] Excludes miscellaneous machinery and armaments; with 1955 weights, amounts to 117 in 1928/29 and 113 in 1929/30 (p. 527).

General note to Table 7:   Large-scale or 'census' industry included (with some exceptions) enterprises with engines which employed at least 16 workers and enterprises without engines which employed at least 30 workers. The increase in production in this period was exaggerated in the official statistics by several factors: (1) some production was transferred to large-scale from small-scale industry or from domestic peasant production, and therefore did not reflect an equivalent increase in total industrial production (e.g. footwear, clothing); (2) quality declined, especially in 1929–30, and this was not reflected in the statistics; (3), further upward distortions occurred in the frequent reclassification of industries, and in the transfer from current to fixed 1926/27 prices.

But Nutter's estimates in Table 7(d) above underestimate the increase (see Davies (1978)).

Table 8. Industrial production in physical terms, 1928/29 and 1929/30

(a) Engineering industries

	1928/29	1929/30
Diesel engines (th. h.p.)	68·8	99·4
Other engines (th. h.p.)	77·9	152·0
Steam turbines (th. h.p.)	140·6	284·5
Steam boilers (th. h.p.)	4017	6274
Metalworking machine tools (units)	8287	13447
Equipment for spinning factories (units)	740	1112
Equipment for weaving factories (units)	4990	5349
Equipment for dyeing and finishing (units)	151	147
Tobacco and paper machines (units)	393	299
Sewing machines (thousands)	425·1	538·1
Calculating machines (arithmometers) (units)	8257	14850
Electrical machines (th. kW)	463·6	767·0
Locomotives (units)	713[1]	828[1]
Goods wagons (number in 2-axle units)	15940[1]	20965[1]
Lorries (units)	858	4630
Other vehicles (units)	292	515
Bicycles (th.)	20·5	29·0
Shipbuilding (mill. r., 1926/27 prices)	85·0	149·8
Machine components (mill. r., 1926/27 prices)	51·5	72·4
Tractors (units)	3267	9364
Ploughs with iron and wooden beams (th.)	1709	2083

Source: Except where otherwise stated: *Ezhemesyachnyi statisticheskii byulleten'*, 1–2 (86), August–September 1930, 18–21, 136.

[1] *Industrializatsiya, 1929–1932* (1970), 344.

(b) Consumer goods

	1928/29	1929/30
Finished cotton textiles (m.m.)[1]	2826	2410
Finished woollen textiles (m.m.)[2]	100·6	114·5[a]
Linen textiles (m.m²)[2]	179·6	185·9[a]
Leather footwear: census industry[3]	48·8[b]	75·4[a]
non-census industry[3]	48·3[b]	37·2[a]
Total footwear (in m. pairs)[3]	97·1[b]	112·6[a]
Household soap (th.t.)[2]	221·3[b]	207[a]
Matches (th. boxes)[2]	6845[b]	9419[a]
Butter (th.t.)[2]	78[b]	41[a]
Vegetable oil (th.t.): large-scale industry[2]	363	318[a]
Sugar (granulated) (th.t.)[2]	1282	823
Confectionery (th.t.)[2]	118	241[a]
Vodka and table wine (th. hectolitres)[1]	5271	5815
Beer (th. hectolitres)[2]	2723	3383
Preserves (m. jars)[4]	(94)[c]	160
Tobacco (th.t.)[2]	27·3[b]	33·1[a]
Cigarettes (milliards)[2]	57·7[b]	61·7[a]

Sources: [1] *Ezhemesyachnyi statisticheskii byulleten'*, 1–2(86), August–September 1930, 18–21.
[2] *Industrializatsiya, 1929–1932* (1970), 345–6.
[3] *Materials* (1985), 362.
[4] EZh, October 8, 1930.

Notes: These figures do not allow for reduction in quality.
[a] 1930.
[b] 1929.
[c] 160 is stated to be 70·2 per cent above 1928/29.

Table 9. Monthly industrial production in physical terms, 1928–1930

(a) Coal (thousand tons)[1a]

	1928	1929	1930
January	3233	3491	4361
February	3118	3342	4258
March	3267	3612	4787
April	2526	3479	4411
May	2736	2811	3991
June	2680	3164	3936
July	2707	3274	3414
August	2737	3233	3019
September	2737	3232	2910
October	3304	3850	4085
November	3197	3756	4404
December	3557	4240	4789
Total for year	35799	41483	48392
	1927/28	*1928/29*	*1929/30*
Total for economic year	34935[b]	39696	46932
Revised total for economic year (1936)[3c]	35510	40067	47780

(b) Crude oil (thousand tons)[1d]

	1928	*1929*	*1930*
January	854	1085	1256
February	808	898	1137
March	922	992	1358
April	934	992	1460
May	1036	1206	1545
June	1002	1166	1494
July	1025	1273	1596
August	1013	1286	1629
September	1047	1233	1646
October	1099	1273	1722
November	1072	1256	1728
December	1099	1324	1785
Total for year	11910	13926	18356
	1927/28	*1928/29*	*1929/30*
Total for economic year	11419[f]	13401	16974
Revised total for economic year (1936):			
excluding gas[4]	8882	11034	16172[e]
including gas[3]	11749	13810	18923[e]

Tables

(c) Pig-iron (thousand tons)[1]

	1928	*1929*	*1930*
January	278	341	414
February	264	302	386
March	291	352	440
April	279	344	430
May	299	367	446
June	272[g]	364	440
July	268	353	428
August	267	347	403
September	274	366	396
October	290	395	407
November	277	358	410
December	315	393	416
Total for year	3374	4320	5017
	1927/28	*1928/29*	*1929/30*
Total for economic year	3282[h]	4018	4969
Revised total for economic year (1936)[3c]	3282	4021	4964

(d) Crude steel (thousand tons)

	1928^2	1929^2	1930^2	1930^1
January	357	401	487	500
February	348	354	445	458
March	383	419	497	510
April	341	417	478	492
May	351	397	500	514
June	337	396	474	488
July	314	380	450	463
August	339	402	439	453
September	365	408	458	473
October	387	431	478	492
November	372	433	503	518
December	387	468	489	503
Total for year	4281	4906	5698	5864
	1927/28	*1928/29*	*1929/30*	*1929/30*
Total for economic year	4159[h]	4720[h]	5560[h]	5683[h]
Revised total for economic year (1936)	4251	4854	5761	5761

(e) Rolled steel (thousand tons)

	1928[2]	*1929*[2]	*1930*[2i]	*1930*[1i]
January	292	309	381	393
February	279	276	362	374
March	316	339	395	407
April	277	366	375	384
May	297	299	379	388
June	273	328	373	384
July	234	323	359	370
August	275	325	343	356
September	296	342	394	407
October	327	346	387	402
November	308	342	386	398
December	319	376	392	416
Total for year	3494	3971	4526	4678
	1927/28	*1928/29*	*1929/30*	*1929/30*
Total for economic year	3371[h]	3861	4425	4628
Revised total for economic year (1936)[3]	3408	3898	4503	4503

(f) Cotton textiles (million linear metres)[1]

	1928	*1929*	*1930*
January	226	228	259
February	217	229	262
March	230	238	276
April	194	277	282
May	221	201	165
June	195	261	165
July	173	193	83
August	215	231	68
September	231	273	145
October	249	281	206
November	221	241	194
December	227	264	229
Total for year	2599	2917	2334
	1927/28	*1928/29*	*1929/30*
Total for economic year	2539[h]	2828	2491
Revised total for economic year (1936)[5]	2678[c]	2996[c]	2351[e]

Sources for Table 9(a)–(f):
  [1] *Osnovnye pokazateli*, 1933, 36–9.
  [2] *Ibid.* August 1932, 54–7.
  [3] *Promyshlennost'* (1936), 25.
  [4] *Ibid.* 196–7.
  [5] *Ibid.* 29.

Notes: [a] These figures are in physical terms, including brown coal and anthracite. The equivalent figure in hard-coal fuel equivalent is 34,067 in 1927/28, 34,439 in 1928/29 and 45,485 in 1929/30 (*Promyshlennost'* (1964), 192; and see note [c] below).
  [b] Output in January–September 1928 as above, plus output in October–December 1927 from Mendel'son, ed. (1930), 23; the latter figures are from a series which reports somewhat lower output than in the Table above (e.g. 9,309 thousand tons in January–March 1928 as against 9,618 thousands).
  [c] In *Promyshlennost'* (1957) and *Promyshlennost'* (1964) these totals are reported as for the calendar year concerned.
  [d] Stated to exclude gas; but revised total excluding gas is substantially lower (see below).
  [e] For calendar year 1930.
  [f] Output in January–September 1928 as above, plus output in October–December 1927 from Mendel'son, ed. (1930), 24; the latter figures are from a series which reports somewhat higher output than in the Table above (e.g. 2,615 thousand tons in January–March 1928 as against 2,584 thousands).
  [g] Misprinted as 572 in original.
  [h] Includes October–December 1927 from Mendel'son, ed. (1930), 26–8, 32.
  [i] Later (higher) series in source [1] does not give data for 1928–9.

Table 10.   Allocation of building materials, 1928–1930

	1928	1929		1930	
	Amount	Amount	% Increase (+) or Decrease (−)	Amount	% Increase (+) or Decrease (−)
Roofing iron (th.t.)					
Total production	390	391	+0·3	321	−17·1
For industrial building	59	71	+20·3	103	+45·0
For agricultural building	91	87	−4·4	35	−59·8
For other building, etc.[a]	218	247	+13·3	208	−15·8
Change in stocks	+22	−13		−24	
Cement (th.t.)					
Total production	1907	2368	+24·2	3170	+33·9
For industrial building	880	1164	+32·3	1644	+41·2
For agricultural building	91	82	−9·9	69	−15·9
For other building, etc.	843	977	+60·0	1239	+26·8
Net exports	69	79	+14·5	70	−9·1
Increase (+) or decrease (−) in stocks	+24	+68		+149	
Building brick (m.)					
Total	3419	4370	+28·2	5649	+29·3
For industrial building	676	926	+47·9	1648	+78·0
For agricultural building	460	463	+0·7	330	−28·3
For other building, etc.[a]	2269	2868	+26·4	3421	+19·3
Change in stocks	+14	+112		+250	

	1928	*1929*		*1930*	
		Amount	*% Increase (+) or Decrease (−)*	Amount	*% Increase (+) or Decrease (−)*
Window glass (th. m³)					
Total	34242	40320	+17·8	43094	+6·9
For industrial building	4748	6866	+44·6	11225	+63·5
For agricultural building	11960	14136	+18·2	9383	−33·6
For other building, etc.[a]	13560	14723	+8·6	15632	+6·2
Net exports	33	−24		943	
Losses	1712	2303	+34·5	2638	+14·5
Change in stocks	+2229	+2316		+3275	
Sawn timber	26032	28837	+10·8	32872	+14·0
Total					
For industrial building	4177	5287	+26·6	9737	+84·2
For agricultural building	5532	5099	−7·8	3429	−32·8
For other building, etc.[a]	12591	13852	+10·0	14036	+1·3
Net exports	3261	4009	+22·9	4098	+2·2
Change in stocks	+471	+590		+1572	

Source: Materials (1985), 338–46.

Note: [a] Includes housing, and production 'consumed in production'; the latter item is substantial only in the case of roofing iron.

Table 11.   Number of retail trade enterprises, 1925/26–January 1, 1931

Series (a)	1925/26	1926/27	1927/28	1928/29
Towns: socialised	50036	54893	66574	90799
private	269065	256172	202633	124283
Total towns	319101	311065	269207	215082
Countryside: socialised	80137	85989	92037	99779
private	155822	154557	120191	62444
Total countryside	235959	240546	212228	162228
Total: socialised	130173	140882	158611	190578
: private	424887	410729	322824	186727
: both sectors	555060	551611	481435	377305

Series (b)	Apr. 1, 1928	Jan. 1, 1929	Jan. 1, 1930	Jan. 1, 1931
Towns: socialised	47705	68000	71088	64402
: private	144406	104000	34765	9500
Total towns	192111	171500	105853	73902
Countryside: socialised	75500	87500	91933	107748
: private	70500	49500	12385	8100
Total countryside	146000	137000	104318	115948
Total: socialised	123000	155000	163021	172150
: private	214500	153000	47150	17700
: both sectors	338000	308500	210171	189850

General note: The data for the number of retail trade enterprises appear in two separate series, which are only roughly comparable. Series (a) shows the total number of enterprises registering in the course of a year, and therefore exaggerates the number by including those which ceased to be registered in the course of the year. Series (b) shows the number of enterprises registered on a specific date, but unfortunately does not begin until April 1, 1928.

Sources:
   Series (a): Tovarooborot (1932), 50.
   Series (b): January 1, 1930 and 1931: *ibid.* 50.
         April 1, 1928: towns: *ibid.* 55.
         April 1, 1928: countryside and total, and January 1, 1929: estimated (to nearest 500) from percentages *ibid.* 52 and the absolute data for January 1, 1930 *ibid.* 55.

Table 12. Retail trade turnover by social sector, 1926/27–1930 (million rubles at current prices)[a]

	1926/27			1927/28			1928/29			1929/30			October–December 1929/30		
	Urban	Rural	Total	Urban	Rural	Total	Urban	Rural	Total	Urban	Rural	Total	Urban	Rural	Total
State	1525	292	1817	1867	340	2207	2363	531	2894	3045	1065[g]	4110	810	390	1200
Cooperative	4075	2762	6838	5487	3398	8885	6981	4081	11061	7635	4765	12400	2320	1680	4000
Total socialised retail trade	5600	3054	8654	7354	3738	11092	9343	4612	13955	10680	5830	16510	3130	2070	5200
Private[b]	4015	1048	5064	2888	760	3649	2141	539	2680	n.a.	n.a.	1240[h]	n.a.	n.a.	n.a.
Total organised retail trade	9615	4103	13718	10242	4499	14741	11484	5151[f]	16635	n.a.	n.a.	(17750)	n.a.	n.a.	n.a.
Urban peasant trade[c]	n.a.[d]	n.a.	n.a.	n.a.[d]	—	n.a.	2000[2][e]	—	2000[2][e]	2800[2][e]	—	2800[2][e]	n.a.	n.a.	n.a.
Total retail trade	n.a.	n.a.	n.a.	(12242)	—	(16741)	(13484)	—	(18635)	n.a.	—	(20550)	n.a.	n.a.	n.a.

Sources: Except where otherwise stated, *Tovarooborot* (1932), 18.

[1] *Sovetskaya torgovlya*, 4 (9), 1931, 1.

[2] Malafeev (1964), 131, citing the archives.

Notes: [a] Excludes public catering, reported as follows for calendar years (million rubles at current prices) (*Sovetskaya torgovlya* (1935[?1936]), 59):

1928:	300 (urban)	50 (rural)	350 (total)
1929:	471	79	550
1930:	1140	150	1290

[b] 'Stationary intermediary trade only.'

[c] Free-market trade by peasants and others.

[d] According to SO, 7, 1929, in 117 towns in 1927/28 bazaar trade in agricultural products amounted to 338 million rubles, as compared with socialised trade in these products amounting to 1,100 millions and private trade amounting to 591 million rubles.

[e] The source reports that agricultural products acquired on the 'private market' by the urban population amounted to 2,900 million rubles in 1929 and 4,000 millions in 1930; according to the source, some 65–70 per cent of these sales were by peasants (and the rest presumably partly by private traders and partly by individual urban citizens).

[f] Misprinted as 5551.

[g] Misprinted as 106.

[h] This source reports private trade as 3,906 million rubles in 1927/28 and 2,379 millions in 1928/29.

Table 13. Foreign trade, 1928/29–1930

(a) Exports in value terms (million rubles at current prices)

	1928/29	1929/30	October–December 1930
Grain	15·9	121·6	100·0
Other products of agriculture[a]	67·2	73·5	12·9
Livestock and poultry products	138·4	98·1	13·6
Fur	109·1	83·1	8·7
Other products of farming[b]	15·7	17·4	5·6
Total products of farming[b]	346·3	393·7	141·8
Timber and products	138·6	180·2	41·9
Food, drink and tobacco	79·9	71·8	36·1
Oil	132·6	157·3	35·3
Other mining	44·3	48·9	9·0
Other industries	135·9	150·4	32·6
Total industrial	531·3	608·6	154·9
Total exports	877·6	1002·3	296·7

(b) Exports in physical terms (thousand tons)

	1928/29	1929/30	October– December 1930
Grain	99	2269	2784
Other products of agriculture[a]	214	205	34
Livestock and poultry products	198	131	23
Fur	3·55	3·48	0·55
Other products of farming[b]	34	42	21
Total products of farming[b]	549	2651	2863
Timber and products	4778	7368	1965
Food, drink and tobacco	457	541	121
Oil	3642	4555	1169
Other mining	2810	3336	785
Other industries	382	419	103
Total industrial	12069	16219	4143
Total exports	12618	18870	7005

(c) Imports in value terms (million rubles at current prices)

	1928/29	1929/30	October–December 1930
Tea	29·5	23·4	3·4
Sugar	3·8	29·8	3·7
Other food products	38·8	39·8	11·5
Total food, drink and tobacco	72·1	93·0	17·6
Total animal products	70·0	54·4	21·9
Agricultural machines	43·1	113·2	6·8
Other machines and apparatus	78·6	161·7	38·5
Machine parts	26·6	69·8	24·5
Vehicles, etc.	13·8	26·5	5·8
Ocean-going ships	9·4	12·0	4·3
Other metals and metal goods	123·0	200·6	55·7
Total metals and metal goods	294·5	583·8	135·6
Total electrical goods, etc.	49·9	65·3	14·4
Cotton	131·1	64·7	10·2
Wool	71·0	47·9	11·4
Other spinning materials and products	54·8	49·3	5·6
Total spinning materials and products	256·9	161·9	27·2
Other	92·9	110·3	21·0
Total imports	836·3	1068·7	237·7

(d) Quarterly imports of cotton and other spinning materials

	Cotton		Other spinning materials and products		Total spinning materials and products	
	thousand tons	*million rubles*	*thousand tons*	*million rubles*	*thousand tons*	*million rubles*
October–December 1928	27·9	32·8	21·7	31·8	49·6	64·6
January–March 1929	6·6	12·7	28·1	30·3	34·7	43·0
April–June 1929	40·9	37·0	19·4	31·5	60·3	68·5
July–September 1929	47·6	48·6	22·2	32·2	69·8	80·8
Total for economic year 1928/29	123·0	131·1	91·4	125·8	214·4	256·9
October–December 1929	19·9	18·9	35·9	34·4	55·8	53·3
January–March 1930	14·0	13·7	26·5	27·2	40·5	40·9
April–June 1930	13·1	12·6	17·1	19·1	30·2	32·3
July–September 1930	20·8	19·3	20·6	16·1	41·4	35·4
Total for economic year 1929/30	67·8	64·5	100·1	97·4	167·9	161·9
October–December 1930	9·9	10·2	26·1	17·0	36·0	27·2

Sources to
Table 13(a)–(d): Derived from monthly data in *Vneshnyaya torgovlya Soyuza SSSR (statisticheskii obzor)*, 3 (62), December 1929; 4 (63), January–March 1929/30; 5 (64), April–June 1929/30; 6 (65), July–September 1929/30; 7 (66), October, November, December 1930.

Notes to
Table 13(a)–(d): [a] *Zemledelie.*
                      [b] *Sel'skoe khozyaistvo.*

Table 14.   Number of persons in non-agricultural employment, 1926/27–1930 (annual average, thousands)[a]

(a) By economic sector

	1926/27	1927/28	1928/29	1929	1930
Large-scale industry[b]	2839	3033	3270	3366	4264
Small-scale industry	423	408	408[c]	279[c]	290
Building	547	684	822	918	1623
Railways	961[b]	957[b]	933[b]	984[d]	1084[d]
Water transport	111	110	113	111	132
Other transport[e]	185	188	215	207	283
Posts and telegraphs	95	95	94	120[f]	153[f]
Trade	515	515	589	627	815
Public catering, etc.	68[g]	73[g]	80[g]	79	181
Banking, etc. (kredit)	86	91	100	108	101
Education	715	777	825	819	921
Health	365	406	429	438	477
Administration, economic and other establishments[h]	1120 }	1244	1257	1255	1470
Municipal enterprises	105 }			123	131
Domestic work	317	368	399 }	706	399
Day work	388[j]	432[k]	475[l] }		
Total	8866	(9381)	(10009)	10140	12323

Source: Except where otherwise stated: 1926/27, 1927/28 and 1928/29: *Trud* (1930), 3. 1929 and 1930: *Trud* (1936), 10–11.

Notes: [a] This Table does not include self-employed, particularly numerous in small-scale industry, building and trade (see pp. 528–9 below). It excludes forestry and fishing as well as agriculture, and also excludes the armed services. Only one job is included for persons engaged in more than one job, in sectors where this practice is 'widespread' (especially education and health). (*Trud* (1936), 359.) For details of the coverage, and comparisons with other sources, see Redding (1958), a valuable and neglected Ph.D. thesis, and Wheatcroft (1981).
  [b] Excludes staff of railway boards (see *Trud* (1930), 97).
  [c] The discrepancy between the 1928/29 and 1929 figures for small-scale industry is not explained.
  [d] Apparently includes staff of railway boards.
  [e] Includes local transport and (presumably) civil aviation.
  [f] Includes rural letter-carriers.
  [g] Includes staff of hostels and 'hygiene establishments'; public catering alone amounted to 49,000 in 1926/27 and 53,000 in 1927/28 (*Trud* (1936), 10–11, 24).
  [h] Includes administration of the economy, administrative and legal agencies, staff of voluntary organisations (e.g. the party, trade unions), entertainment, capital project organisations, geological survey, publishing, etc.
  [j] Obtained by deducting domestic labour in *Trud* (1930), 3, from total for domestic and day-labour in *Trud* (1936), 10–11.
  [k] 1928: *Trud* (1932), 60.
  [l] 1929: *loc. cit.*

(b) By social sector[a]

	1926/27				1927/28				1928/29				1930			
	State	Coop	Private	Total	State	Coop	Private	Total	State	Coop	Private	Total	State	Coop	Private	Total
Large-scale industry	2708	81	50	2839	2906	89	39	3033	3152	95	23	3270	4064	179	21	4264
Small-scale industry	108	89	227	423	128	102	179	408	118	185	106	408	179	134	12	325
Building	496	35	16	547	624	47	13	684	755	54	12	822	1490	108	8	1666
Local and other transport	150	18	18	185	159	16	13	188	182	22	11	215	259	29	1	289
Trade and public catering	162	336	85	583	146	381	61	588	178	467	23	660	250	726	2	978
Other	3220	339	23	3584	3274	384	20	3680	3302	435	15	3751	3901	530	7	4438
Day work	n.a.	n.a.	n.a.	388[1]	362[2c]	48[c]	22[c]	432[2c]	398[2d]	67[2d]	10[2d]	475[2d]	125	20	1	146
Domestic	0	0	317	317	0	0	368	368	0	0	399	399	0	0	253	253
Total	6844[b]	898[b]	736[b]	8866	(7599)	(1067)	(715)	(9381)	(8085)	(1325)	(599)	(10009)	10268	1726	305	12299

Sources: Except where otherwise stated: 1926/27, 1927/28, 1928/29: *Trud* (1930), 3.
1930: *Trud* (1932), 60.

[1] See Table 14(a), note [i].
[2] *Trud* (1932), 60.

Notes: [a] For coverage, see Table 14(a), note [a].
[b] Excludes day work.
[c] 1928.
[d] 1929.

Table 15. Number of employed persons in large-scale industry, 1928–30 (thousands)

(a) All employed persons (January 1 of each year)

	1928	*1929*	*1930*	*1931*
Manual workers[a]	2399	2656	2981	3894[d]
Apprentices	133	133	136	353[d]
Ancillaries (MOP)[b]	127	132	147	194
White-collar[c]	266	287	343	521
Total	2925	3208	3606	4962

Source: Trud (1932), 17.

Notes: [a] *Rabochie.*

[b] Junior ancillary personnel (includes janitors, messengers, cleaners, etc.).

[c] *Sluzhashchie*, including all office-workers, and engineering and technical staff.

[d] Workers and apprentices, totalling 4,246,000 on this date, were employed as follows: Vesenkha 3,473 thousands; Narkomsnab 286; other commissariats 207; other state establishments 78; cooperatives 188; concessions 14 (*ibid.* 63).

(b) Manual workers and apprentices (quarterly average)[a]

	1928	1929	1930
January–March	2538	2786	3230
April–June	2655	2857	3579
July–September	2778	2990	3789
October–December	2791	3052	4085[b]
Annual average	2691	2921	3675

Source: Trud (1932), 61.
Notes: [a] These data, collected by Gosplan section of labour statistics, refer to the 'main branches of industry'.
　[b] The number of apprentices increased substantially during this quarter.

Table 16. Number of persons engaged in small-scale industry by social
sector, 1926/27, 1928/29 and 1930 (annual average; thousands)[a]

	1926/27[1b]	*1928/29*[2c]	*1930*[4]
State sector	39	203	} 1832
Cooperative sector[h]	178	922	
Capitalist sector [d]	227[3e]	47[g]	25[i]
Individual sector[d]	3348[f]	3327[g]	2804
Total	3791	4500	4636

Sources: ¹ *St. spr. 1928* (1929), 500–2, except where otherwise stated.
² *Melkaya promyshlennost'*, i (1933), 22–45, 189.
³ *Trud* (1930), 3.
⁴ NPF, 23–4, 1930, 47–8; PI, 5–6, 1931, 74, 77 (Sen'ko).

Notes: ᵃ These figures cover industry in the normal Soviet sense. They include all
mining and manufacturing industry, including flour-milling, and exclude
timber cutting and hauling, fishing and building. Both the 1926/27 and 1928/29
censuses included all enterprises operative during the economic year concerned
(the 1928/29 census specified that the enterprises must have been working for at
least one week uninterruptedly or at least two weeks discontinuously – *Melkaya
promyshlennost'*, i (1933), p. x). In 1928/29 the average person worked in small-
scale industry for only 16 weeks a year; assuming a 45-week year, the full-time
equivalent of 4,500,000 persons is 1,650,000.
ᵇ 'Industrial fishing' has been deducted from the original total.
ᶜ Data for flour milling and for the production of groats and vegetable oil
(p. 189 of the source) have been added to the data in the basic table (pp. 22–
45 of source).
ᵈ What are termed above 'capitalist sector' and 'individual sector' are not
separated in the souce for 1926/27, but are all included in the 'private sector'.
The source for 1928/29 describes these two sectors as 'capitalist' and 'small-
scale commodity production'.
ᵉ This figure is annual average for hired labour in the private sector of small-
scale and artisan industry, and may not be strictly comparable with the figure
for 1928/29; source ³ gives the number in this sector in 1928/29 as 106,000.
ᶠ Obtained by deducting the figure for the capitalist sector from 3,575,000, given
in the original source for both sectors combined.
ᵍ According to the source, in the flour, groats and vegetable-oil industries,
10,000 persons were employed in the 'private capitalist sector' and a further
316,000 were 'participants' in the production of the 'private capitalist sector'.
The latter category is evidently the equivalent of 'small-scale commodity
production' in the rest of small-scale industry, but classified pejoratively
because individual millers were perceived as a threat to the grain collections.
In the above Table 10,000 have been included with 'capitalist' and 316,000 with
'individual'.
ʰ Includes consumer and agricultural cooperatives as well as artisan cooperatives.
ⁱ Employing 3 or more hired workers.

Table 17. Monthly number of persons employed in building, January 1, 1928–January 1, 1931 (thousands; 1st of each month)

	1928	*1929*	*1930*
January	437	514	789
February	409	476	819
March	390	460	871
April	438	515	1115
May	531	597	1394
June	819	942	1836
July	911	1161	2008
August	960	1205	1954
September	1043	1337	1983
October	1067	1377	2113
November	935	1257	2116
December	699	1037	1949[a]
Annual average	723	918	1623

Source: Trud (1936), 244; for alternative lower monthly figures see *Industrializatsiya, 1929–1932* (1970), 387, 440.

Notes: These figures exclude the large number of self-employed persons in the building industry. According to the December 1926 census, 325,000 persons were employed in building as their main and 105,000 as their first secondary occupation, but a further 216,000 persons reported building as their main occupation under various categories of self-employed and 377,000 as their first secondary occupation. The census figures include unskilled workers with specific tasks but exclude general labourers (chernorabochie), who were not divided by occupation (*Vsesoyuznaya perepis'*, xxxiv (1930), 120–73). The average annual number of persons employed in building in 1926/27 was 548,000 (SO, 12, 1928, 60).

[a] The number employed on January 1, 1931, was 1,854,000.

Table 18. Number of unemployed registered at labour exchanges, October 1, 1928–October 1, 1930 (thousands)

	Total	Total excluding juveniles[a]
October 1, 1928	1365	1125
April 1, 1929	1741	1483
October 1, 1929	1242	959[b]
April 1, 1930	1081	850[b]
July 1, 1930	778	579[b]
October 1, 1930	335	220[b]

Sources: See Lane, ed. (1986), 44 (Davies and Wheatcroft).

Notes: The decline between October 1, 1929, and October 1, 1930, was partly a genuine decline in unemployment and partly due to the removal from the register of what a Narkomtrud report described as 'the alien element and "dead souls"', amounting to 230,000 persons; according to the report, 'until September 1930 the records included a considerable number of persons not interested in receiving work, and also people registered for trades for which there was no demand' (*sic*) (*Industrializatsiya, 1929–1932* (1970), 385–6).

[a] *Podrostki.*

[b] An alternative source reports a decline from 932,000 on October 1, 1929, to 140,000 on October 1, 1930.

Table 19. Quarterly labour turnover in census industry, 1928/29–1929/30 (as percentage of labour force)[a]

	Oct.–Dec.	Jan.–Mar.	Apr.–June	Jul.–Sept.	Total for year
1928/29					
At personal request	6·1	5·4	8·9	14·6	35·0
For indiscipline[b]	3·3	3·7	4·7	6·1	17·8
Other causes[c]	13·8	10·9	13·6	12·1	50·4
Total	23·2	20·0	27·2	32·8	103·2
1929/30					
At personal request	13·9	14·6	20·7	19·0	68·2
For indiscipline[b]	5·7	6·0	9·7	13·1	34·5
Other causes[c]	13·9	12·4	11·5	9·6	47·4
Total	33·5	33·0	41·9	41·7	150·1

Source: Estimated from data in Mordukhovich (1931), 34, 39.

Notes: Turnover in Vesenkha-planned industry in October–December 1930 was reported at 36 per cent as compared with 42·9 per cent in the previous quarter (*Itogi VSNKh* (1932), 80–3).

[a] Estimated by the 'method of the lowest indicator'; for problems of measurement of turnover, see p. 279, notes 230–1 above.

[b] 'Violation of rules of internal order'.

[c] The largest item in this group is 'reduction in the labour force', which declined from 27·6 per cent in October 1928–June 1929 to 13·0 per cent in October 1929–June 1930 (*Kon''yunktura . . . za sentyabr' i 12 mesyatsev 1929/30* (n.d. [1930]), Trud, p. 7.

Table 20.   Average monthly earnings, 1927–1930 (by quarters, in rubles and kopeks)

	1927	*1928/29*		
	Oct.–Dec.	*Oct.–Dec.*	*Jan.–Mar.*	*Apr.–June*
All insured persons[1a]	63·38	67·98	68·10	69·80
Large-scale industry:				
Manual workers[b] and apprentices[2]	64·03[c]	67·86	67·87	71·95
Manual workers[3b]	64·64[e]	70·94[f]	—	—
White-collar[4h]: all	118·21	125·72	126·45	131·22
: administrative and technical	—	—	—	—
Ancillary (MOP)[4]	43·45	47·81	48·31	51·54
Railway workers: permanent[5]	70·52[i]	76·06[i]	76·47[i]	78·89[i]
	—	—	74·99[j]	77·07[j]

Sources: [1] *Nar. kh.* (1932), 419.

[2] *Kon"yuktura . . . za sentyabr' i 12 mesyatsev 1929/30* (n.d. [1930]), Tablitsa 7.

[3] *Nar. kh.* (1932), 458–9.

[4] *Trud* (1932), 133.

[5] *Ibid.* 144.

Notes: [a] Includes both fully and partially insured.

[b] *Rabochie.*

[c] Jan.–Mar. 1928.

[d] Rough figure, estimated from data for Jan.–Mar., Apr.–June, and Jan.–Sept. (latter is 74r 50k).

[e] 1927 average.

[f] 1928 average.

[g] 1929 average.

[h] *Sluzhashchie.*

[i] Includes railway repair works.

[j] Excludes railway repair works.

	Average	1929/30				Average	Oct.–Dec.
July–Sep.	*1928/29*	*Oct.–Dec.*	*Jan.–Mar.*	*Apr.–June*	*July–Sept.*	*1929/30*	*1930*
72·53	(69·60)	75·70	76·71	79·85	82·76	78·76	86·54
75·80	(70·87)	75·00	72·89	75·21	(75·40)[d]	(74·63)	n.a.
—	77·65[g]	—	79·40	81·44	84·69	—	87·65
138·08	130·37	139·62	142·52	150·19	153·99	146·58	159·42
—	—	—	206·14	216·11	216·68		219·71
52·09	49·94	52·73	51·80	57·75	57·49	54·94	58·71
80·98[i]	(80·60)	81·12[i]	—	—	—	—	—
78·95[j]	—	79·09[j]	83·34[j]	87·80[j]	93·06[j]	(85·82)[j]	93·44[j]

Table 21.   Party membership, January 1, 1924–January 1, 1931

	Number of members and candidates (thousands)	Workers by social situation (%)	Workers by occupation (%)
January 1, 1924[1]	446000[1]	43·9[1]	18·8[7]
January 10, 1927	1144000[2]	55·7[2]	30·0[3]
January 1, 1929	1535000[4]	62·1[9]	41·3[6]
January 1, 1930	1678000[4]	65·8[9]	43·3[6]
April 1, 1930	1852000[5]	68·2[9]	45·5[6]
January 1, 1931	2212000[4]	n.a.	40·9[8]

Sources: [1] *Sotsial'nyi i natsional'nyi sostav VKP(b)* (1928), 22, 31.

[2] *Ibid.* 51.

[3] Estimated from *ibid.* 51–2.

[4] Andrukhov (1977), 123.

[5] *XVI s"ezd* (1931), 83.

[6] Estimated from data in *Sostav VKP(b)* (1930), 35, applied to figure for total number of members and candidates in Table.

[7] B, 21–2, November 30, 1926, 42.

[8] Workers by occupation amounted to 44·0 per cent of 2,057,000 members and candidates excluding Red Army and members serving abroad (Gooderham (1983), Table I; Zolotarev (1979), 107), i.e. to 905,000; the percentage above was obtained by applying this figure to the total.

[9] *Sostav VKP(b)* (1930), 34; these percentages are for membership excluding those serving in the Red Army or working abroad.

Table 22. State budget in comparable classification, 1913, 1926/27, 1928/29 and 1929/30 (million rubles at current prices)

(a) Net revenue

	1913	1926/27	1928/29	1929/30 Plan	1929/30 Fulfilment
Tax on alcoholic drinks	718	585	980[1]	1529[1]	1854[1]
Other excises	301	625	822	688	789
Profit from special commodity fund	—	—	—	181[2]	299[2]
Customs dues	353	190	258	372	304
Total indirect taxes	1372	1400	2060	2770	3246
Personal income tax	—	114	187[3a]	213[4a]	213[4a]
Industrial tax: private sector	150	109	170[5]	176[6]	144[6]
Agricultural tax	—	358	449	415	406
Other direct taxes (mainly on private property)	122	—	—	—	—
Taxes and deductions from profits, etc.: socialised sector	75	626	1424	—[b]	3153
Timber revenue	92	287	308	450	477
Dues (poshliny), etc.	231	176	128	162	109
Other revenue	221	134	237	—[b]	386
Net revenue from transport and posts	25	0	0	0	47
State loans: net receipts	—	218	407	985	873
Carried forward from previous year	—	—	205	0	186
Total net revenue	2288	3422	5575	8111	9240

Sources: 1913 and 1926/27: derived from Davies (1958), 4–5, 83–4, and Carr and Davies (1969), 975–6.
1928/29 and 1929/30: except where otherwise indicated, derived from *Otchet . . . 1929–1930* (1931), ob. zapiska, 6–17.
[1] *Otchet . . . 1929–1930* (1931), ob. zapiska, 23, 31.
[2] *Otchet . . . 1929–1930* (1931), 56.
[3] *Ob"yasnitel'naya zapiska . . . 1928/29* (1930), 28–32.
[4] *Otchet . . . 1929–1930* (1931), ob. zapiska, 21–3.
[5] *Ob"yasnitel'naya zapiska . . . 1928/29* (1930), 26.
[6] *Otchet . . . 1929–1930* (1931), ob. zapiska, 20.

Notes:
General note: 'Self-balancing' revenue from transport and posts, and that part of the revenue from state loans which was expended on repayments and interest, have been omitted. Administrative costs for the vodka monopoly have been omitted for 1913 and 1926/27; they do not appear in the 1928/29 and 1929/30 budgets.
[a] Includes tax on superprofits, and inheritance and gifts tax.
[b] Not available as separate item.

(b) Net expenditure

	1913	1926/27	1928/29	1929/30 Plan	1929/30 Fulfilment
Industry	65[a]	448	996	1781	2099
Electrification	n.a.	103	180	310	229
Agriculture	139[b]	204	497	773	986
Net expenditure on transport and posts	0	177[f]	86	312	0
Trade	—	91[f]	262	407	612
Municipal economy and housing	—	43	68	120	76
Other	—	134	139	250	248
Total on national economy	204	1199	2228	3953	4250
Social and cultural	143[c]	356	521	889	916
Defence	953[d]	634[g]	912	1114	1113
OGPU	—	n.a.[h]	54	59	60
Administration	495[e]	369	265	249	275
Transferred to low budgets	n.a.	582	1265	1561	1701
Other, including reserves	74	226	141	256	277
Payments on state loans	424	0	0	0	0
Total net expenditure	2293	3366	5386	8081	8592
State budget surplus or deficit (−)	−5	56	189	30	648

Sources: 1913 and 1926/27: form data in Davies (1958), 4–5, 65, 83–4.

1928/29 and 1929/30: derived from *Otchet . . . 1929–1930* (1931), ob. zapiska, 6–17.

Notes: [a] Ministry of Trade and Industry.

[b] Department of agriculture and land settlement, and state horse-breeding.

[c] Ministry of Education.

[d] Includes expenditure by military department for economic and strategic purposes.

[e] Includes 247 million rubles of Ministry of Finance, which includes various expenditures on the economy.

[f] Includes food industry.

[g] For comparability with 1913, should include budget allocations to defence industries, and probably shipbuilding. Allocations to 'other' industries, presumably defence industries, amounted to 51 million rubles in 1926/27 (*Promyshlennost, . . . 1926/27* (1928), 72), 76 millions in 1928/29 (*Otchet . . . 1928–1929* (1930), 86), 124 millions in 1929/30 (Plan), and 130 millions in 1929/30 (Fulfilment) (*Otchet . . . 1929–1930* (1931), 84). The allocation to shipbuilding in 1926/27 was 18 million rubles (*Promyshlennost' . . . 1926/27* (1928), 72); it is not available for 1928/29 and 1929/30.

[h] Presumably included in Administration.

Table 23.   Currency in circulation, October 1, 1926–January 1, 1931 (million rubles)

October 1, 1926	1291[1]	April 1, 1929	1998[1]	April 1, 1930	2876[2]
October 1, 1927	1628[1]	July 1, 1929	2213[1]	July 1, 1930	3455[2]
October 1, 1928	1971[1]	October 1, 1929	2642[2]	October 1, 1930	4264[3]
January 1, 1929	2028[1]	January 1, 1930	2773[2]	January 1, 1931	4302[3]

Sources: [1] Mendel'son, ed. (1930), 126.
[2] *Kon"yuktura . . . za sentyabr' i 12 mesyatsev 1929/30* (n.d. [1930]), Finansy, p. 7.
[3] See Arnold (New York, 1937), 412–13.

Table 24. Price indexes, 1926/27–1930
(a) Average annual retail prices (1913 = 100)

	1926/27[1]			1927/28[2]		
	Agricultural goods	Industrial goods	All goods	Agricultural goods	Industrial goods	All goods
Socialised	176	199	191	177	188	184
Private	207	242	226	278	242	244
All trade	186	210	201	194	198	197

	1928/29[1]			1930[2]		
	Agricultural goods	Industrial goods	All goods	Agricultural goods	Industrial goods	All goods
Socialised	192	191	192	196	203	200
Private	367	269	308	826	433	564
All trade	222	203	210	291	219	260

Sources: [1] Mendel'son, ed. (1930), 98–106; these figures will also be found in Malafeev (1964), 401, with slight errors. [2] Malafeev (1964), 401, citing archives.

Notes: This series apparently does not include peasant bazaar trade, and increases less rapidly than series (b) below (1930 prices for All trade, All goods, are 23·8 per cent above 1928/29, whereas in series (b) in 1930 they are 26·1 per cent above 1929).

(b) Average annual retail prices (1928 = 100)

	1929	*1930*
Agricultural goods	116·1	177·3
Industrial goods	103·3	101·2
All goods	109·7	138·3

Source: Tovarooborot (1932), 123.

Notes: This series is based on retail prices collected at 60 geographical points for same type and grade of good; labour statistics, showing prices paid by workers rather than the population as a whole, give an index for 1930 of only 128·0 (1928 = 100) for all goods (see *ibid.* 125–6). The price index in *Materials* (1985), 147, for all products consumed by the population in 1930 is 130·4 (1928 = 100).

(c) Monthly urban bazaar prices for agricultural goods (July 1, 1926 = 100)[a]

	1926	*1927*	*1928*	*1929*	*1930*[c]
January 1	n.a.	93·4	104·8	125·9	209·3
February 1	n.a.	97·2	104·2	131·9	217·2
March 1	n.a.	97·9	104·0	141·5	241·9
April 1	n.a.	95·1	103·6	149·7	264·8
May 1	n.a.	97·0	110·8	171·0	294·3
June 1	n.a.	97·3	115·7	172·0	317·4
July 1	100·0	101·2	130·4	176·8	388·0
August 1	103·0	101·3	136·7	181·3	505·8
September 1	93·9	97·5	117·4	174·0	562·0
October 1	91·9	96·0	117·8	179·8	595·2
November 1	90·6	99·8	120·5	195·1	616·6
December 1	91·9	102·8	126·3	204·2	609·9
Average annual prices (previous year = 100)[b]	n.a.	103·7	118·3	145·7	245·9

Source: Tovarooborot (1932), 143.

Notes: [a] This table covers five products: rye flour, potatoes, beef, butter and eggs.

[b] Average of seven months in 1926 (July 1, 1926–January 1, 1927), and thirteen months in other years.

[c] 618·1 on January 1, 1931.

(d) Indexes of cost of investment inputs, 1926/27–1931 (annual averages, 1927/28 = 100)

	1928/29	1929/30	1931
1. Building costs			
Industry	92·0	84·9	97·9
Railways	94·7	98·3	111·0
Housing: socialist sector	92·9	83·0	95·8
Housing: private sector	97·0	103·7	124·4
2. Equipment costs			
Imported	99·5	89·6	79·6
Home-produced	97·8	97·8	92·8
Weighted costs	101·8	94·6	88·6
3. All investment costs			
Industry	95·7	87·6	94·0
Railways	100·6	101·4	106·3

Source: Materials (1985), 148–9.

Note: For methods by which these cost indexes were estimated, see *ibid.* 278–84.

GLOSSARY OF RUSSIAN TERMS AND ABBREVIATIONS USED IN TEXT

aktiv	activists (politically-active members of a community)
AMO	avtomobil'nyi zavod (automobile factory, Moscow)
art.	article (stat'ya)
AUCCTU	All-Union Central Committee of Trade Unions (VTsSPS – Vsesoyuznyi tsentral'nyi sovet professional'nykh soyuzov)
batrak	rural labourer
CC	Central Committee [of Communist Party] (Tsentral'nyi Komitet)
CCC	Central Control Commission [of Communist Party] (Tsentral'naya Kontrol'naya Komissiya – TsKK) (joint staff with Rabkrin)
Cheka	Chrezvychainaya Komissiya (Extraordinary Commission) [political police], *later* GPU or OGPU
CPSU(b)	Communist Party of the Soviet Union (Bolsheviks)
disk. listok	diskussionyi listok (discussion sheet)
Dneproges	Dneprovskaya gidroelektricheskaya stantsiya (Dnepr Hydro-electric Power Station)
Dneprostroi	Upravlenie gosudarstvennogo Dneprovskogo stroitel'stva (Administration for State Dnepr Construction)
Donbass	Donetskii ugol'nyi bassein (Donets coal basin)
Donugol'	Donetskii gosudarstvennyi kamennougol'nyi trest po proizvodstvu i prodazhe kamennogo uglya i antratsita VSNKh

SSR (Donets state coal trust of Vesenkha USSR for production and sale of coal and anthracite)

Ekoso
Ekonomicheskii sovet RSFSR (Economic Council of RSFSR [equivalent to STO of USSR])

Energotsentr
Gosudarstvennoe vsesoyuznoe ob"edinenie energeticheskogo khozyaistva VSNKh SSSR (State All-Union Corporation of Vesenkha USSR for the Energy Sector)

FUBR
Fond uluchsheniya byta rabochikh (Fund to.Improve Workers' Welfare)

FZU
fabrichno-zavodskoe uchenichestvo (factory apprenticeship [schools])

genplan
general'nyi plan (general [10–15 year] plan)

Gipromash
Gosudarstvennyi institut po proektirovaniyu mashinostroitel'nykh zavodov (State Institute for Projects of Engineering Factories)

Gipromez
Gosudarstvennyi institut po proektirovaniyu metallicheskikh zavodov (State Institute for Projects of Metal Works)

Glavchermet
Glavnoe upravlenie po chernoi metallurgii VSNKh SSSR (Chief Administration of Vesenkha USSR for the Iron and Steel Industry)

glavk (pl., *glavki*)
glavnoe upravlenie (Chief Administration)

Glavkhim
Glavnoe upravlenie khimicheskoi promyshlennosti VSNKh SSSR (Chief Administration of Vesenkha USSR for the Chemical Industry)

Glavkhlopkom
Glavnyi khlopkovyi komitet VSNKh SSSR (Chief Cotton Committee of Vesenkha USSR)

Glavnauka
Glavnoe upravlenie nauchnymi, nauchno-khudozhestvennymi, muzeinymi i po okhrane prirody uchrezhdeniyami (Chief Administration [of Narkompros] for Scientific, Fine Art, Museum and Nature Protection Establishments)

Goelro
Gosudarstvennaya komissiya po elektrifi-

	katsii Rossii (State Commission for the Electrification of Russia)
Gosbank	Gosudarstvennyi bank (State Bank)
Gosfinkontrol'	Glavnoe upravlenie gosudarstvennogo finansovogo kontrolya NKF SSSR (Chief Administration of State Financial Control of Narkomfin USSR)
Gosplan	Gosudarstvennaya planovaya komissiya (State Planning Commission)
Group A	producer goods or capital goods industries
Group B	consumer goods industries
GPU (OGPU)	*see* OGPU
IKKI	Ispolnitel'nyi Komitet Kommunisticheskogo Internatsionala (Executive Committee of Communist International)
khozraschet	khozyaistvennyi raschet (economic [profit-and-loss] accounting)
kolkhoz	kollektivnoe khozyaistvo (collective farm)
kolkhozsoyuz	soyuz sel'skokhozyaistvennykh kollektivov (union of agricultural collectives)
Kolkhoztsentr	Vserossiskii (*from November 1929* Vsesoyuznyi) Soyuz Sel'skokhozyaistvennykh Kollektivov (all-Russian (*from November 1929* All-Union) Union of Agricultural Collectives)
Komsomol	Kommunisticheskii soyuz molodezhi (Communist League of Youth)
kopek	1/100 ruble
Kuznetskstroi	Kuznetskoe stroitel'stvo (Kuznetsk Construction)
Magnitostroi	Magnitogorskoe stroitel'stvo (Magnitogorsk construction)
Lenmashtrest	Leningradskii gosudarstvennyi mashinostroitel'nyi trest VSNKh SSSR (Leningrad State Engineering Trust of Vesenkha of USSR)
MOP	mladshii obsluzhivayushchii personal (junior ancillary staff)
NAMI	Nauchnyi avtomotornyi institut (Vehicle and Engine Research Institute [Moscow])

Narkomfin	Narodnyi komissariat finansov (People's Commissariat of Finance)
Narkomindel	Narodnyi komissariat inostrannykh del (People's Commissariat of Foreign Affairs)
Narkompros	Narodnyi komissariat prosveshcheniya (People's Commissariat for Education [of RSFSR])
Narkomput'	Narodnyi komissariat putei soobshcheniya (People's Commissariat of Ways of Communication [i.e. of Transport])
Narkomsnab	Narodnyi komissariat snabzheniya (People's Commissariat for Supply – formed November 1930)
Narkomtorg	Narodnyi komissariat vneshnei i vnutrennei torgovli (People's Commissariat of External and Internal Trade [until November 1930])
Narkomtrud	Narodnyi komissariat truda (People's Commissariat of Labour)
Narkomvneshtorg	Narodnyi komissariat vneshnei torgovli (People's Commissariat for Foreign Trade – formed November 1930)
Narkomzem	Narodnyi komissariat zemledeliya (People's Commissariat of Agriculture [of RSFSR up to December 1929, then of USSR])
NEP	Novaya ekonomicheskaya politika (New Economic Policy)
nepreryvka	*nepreryvnaya rabochaya nedelya* (continuous working week)
NKVD	Narodnyi komissariat vnutrennikh del (People's Commissariat of Internal Affairs)
Novostal'	Vsesoyuznoe ob"edinenie po stroitel'stvu novykh predpriyatii chernoi metallurgii VSNKh SSSR (All-Union Corporation of Vesenkha USSR for Construction of New Enterprises of Iron and Steel Industry)
ob"edinenie (pl. ob"edineniya)	corporation(s) [in industry replaced *glavk* and syndicate at beginning of 1930]

OGPU (GPU)	Ob"edinennoe Gosudarstvennoe Politicheskoe Upravlenie (Unified State Political Administration [Political Police])
okrug	administrative unit between a region (oblast') and a district (raion) (see vol. 1, p. xx)
Orgburo	Organizatsionnoe byuro (Organisation committee [of party central committee])
Osvok	Osoboe soveshchanie po vosstanovleniyu osnovnogo kapitala (Special Conference [of Vesenkha] for the Restoration of Fixed Capital)
Pereval	'Mountain-pass' [group of writers]
Prombank	Bank dolgosrochnogo kreditovaniya promyshlennosti i elektrokhozyaistva (Bank for Long-Term Credit to Industry and Electrification)
promfinplan	proizvodstvenno-finansovyi plan ([industrial] production and financial plan)
PTEU	Planovo-tekhniko-ekonomicheskoe upravlenie VSNKh SSSR (Planning-Technical-Economic Administration of Vesenkha USSR)
pud	0·01638 tons
rabfak	rabochii fakul'tet (Workers' Faculty)
Rabkrin	Narodnyi komissariat raboche-krest'yanskoi inspektsii (People's Commissariat of Workers' and Peasants' Inspection)
rabochie	[manual] workers
RAPP	Russkaya assosiatsiya proletarskikh pisatelei (Russian Association of Proletarian Writers)
Rostsel'mash	Rostovskii zavod sel'skokhozyaistvennogo mashinostroeniya (Rostov agricultural engineering factory)
RSFSR	Rossiiskaya Sovetskaya Federativnaya Sotsialisticheskaya Respublika (Russian Soviet Federative Socialist Republic)
RSK	raion sploshnoi kollektivizatsii (district of comprehensive collectivisation)

ruble (rubl')	unit of currency, at par = £0·106 or $0·515
RVS	Revolyutsionnyi voennyi sovet SSSR (Revolutionary Military Council of the USSR)
Sel'mashstroi	Stroitel'stvo Rostovskogo-na-Donu zavoda sel'skokhozyaistvennogo mashinostroeniya (Rostov-on-Don Agricultural Machinery Factory Construction)
sluzhashchie	white-collar workers (often includes engineering and technical workers, sometimes only lower-grade white-collar)
SNK	*see* Sovnarkom
sovkhoz	sovetskoe khozyaistvo (Soviet [i.e. state] farm)
Sovnarkom	Sovet Narodnykh Komissarov (Council of People's Commissars)
Soyuzkhleb	'Union Grain' (All-Union Grain Corporation of Narkomtorg)
Soyuzneft'	Gosudarstvennoe vsesoyuznoe ob''edinenie neftyanoi i gazovoi promyshlennosti VSNKh SSSR (State All-Union Corporation of Vesenkha USSR for Oil and Gas Industry)
Soyuzugol'	Vsesoyuznoe ob''edinenie ugol'noi promyshlennosti VSNKh SSSR (All-Union Corporation of Vesenkha USSR for the Coal Industry)
SR	sotsialist-revolyutsioner (Socialist Revolutionary)
Stal'	Vsesoyuznoe ob''edinenie metallurgicheskoi, zheleznorudnoi i margantsevoi promyshlennosti VSNKh SSSR (All-Union Corporation of Vesenkha USSR for the Iron and Steel, Iron-ore and Manganese Industry)
STO	Sovet Truda i Oborony (Council of Labour and Defence [Economic sub-committee of Sovnarkom])
TsAGI	Tsentral'nyi aerogidrodinamicheskii institut (Central Aero-Hydronamic Institute)
tsentner	0·1 tons

Tsentrospirt	Tsentral'noe upravlenie gosudarstvennoi spirtovoi monopolii (Central Administration of State Alcohol Monopoly)
TsGANKh	Tsentral'nyi gosudarstvennyi arkhiv narodnogo khozyaistva SSSR (Central State Archive of the National Economy of the USSR) – *see* Section I of Bibliography, p. 551
TsIAM	Tsentral'nyi institut aviatsionnogo motorostroeniya (Central Aero-engine Institute)
TsIK	Tsentral'nyi Ispolnitel'nyi Komitet (Central Executive Committee [of Soviets of USSR])
TsKB	Tsentral'noe konstruktorskoe byuro (Central Design Bureau)
TsPA	Tsentral'nyi partiinyi arkhiv Instituta marksizma-leninizma pri TsK KPSS (Central Party Archives of Institute of Marxism–Leninism attached to CC CPSU)
TsSU	Tsentral'noe statisticheskoe upravlenie (Central Statistical Administration)
TsUNKhU	Tsentral'noe upravlenie narodnokhozyaistvennogo ucheta (Central Administration of National Economic Records) (statistical agency, formed in December 1931 attached to Gosplan)
Turksib	Turkestano–Sibirskaya Zheleznaya Doroga (Turkestan–Siberian Railway)
Ugol'	Vsesoyuznoe ob''edinenie kamennougol'noi promyshlennosti zapadnoi chasti SSSR VSNKh SSSR (All-Union Corporation of Vesenkha USSR for Coal Industry of Western USSR [formed August 1930]
UKK	Uralo–Kuznetskii kombinat (Ural–Kuznetsk Combine)
Uralmash *or* Uralmashzavod	Ural'skii zavod tyazhelogo mashinostroeniya (Urals Heavy Engineering Works)
VEO	Vsesoyuznoe elektrotekhnicheskoe ob''edinenie VSNKh SSSR (All-Union

	Electrical Engineering Combine of Vesen-kha USSR)
Vesenkha	Vysshii Sovet Narodnogo Khozyaistva (Supreme Council of National Economy [in charge of industry])
VMS	Vsesoyuznyi metallurgicheskii sindikat (All-Union Metal Syndicate)
Vsekhimprom	Vsesoyuznoe ob"edinenie khimicheskoi promyshlennosti VSNKh SSSR (All-Union Corporation of Vesenkha USSR for the Chemical Industry)
Vsekopromsovet	Vsesoyuznyi sovet respublikanskikh tsentrov promyslovoi kooperatsii (All-Union Council of Republican Centres of Industrial Cooperatives)
Vsekopromsoyuz	Vserossiskii soyuz promyslovykh kooperativov (All-Russian Union of Industrial Cooperatives)
VSNKh	*see* Vesenkha
Yugostal'	Gosudarstvennyi yuzhnyi metallurgicheskii trest VSNKh SSSR (State Southern Metallurgical Trust of Vesenkha USSR)
Yurt	Yuzhno-rudnyi trest VSNKh SSSR (Southern Ore Trust of VSNKh USSR)
Yuzhmashtrest	Yuzhnyi mashinostroitel'nyi trest (Southern Engineering Trust)
Zernotrest	Grain Trust ([for new grain sovkhozy])

ABBREVIATIONS OF TITLES OF BOOKS AND PERIODICAL PUBLICATIONS, ETC., USED IN FOOTNOTES

(For full titles, see appropriate section of Bibliography; items listed below are periodical publications unless otherwise stated.)

AER	American Engineers in Russia (*see* Section I of Bibliography, pp. 551–2)
B	*Bol'shevik*
BFKhZ	*Byulleten' finansovogo i khozyaistvennogo zakonodat-el'stva*
BP	*Byulleten' ekonomicheskaya kabineta prof. S. N. Prokopovicha*
BSE	*Bol'shaya sovetskaya entsiklopedia* (series of books)
EHR	*Economic History Review*
EO	*Ekonomicheskoe obozrenie*
EZh	*Ekonomicheskaya zhizn'*
FP	*Finansovye problemy sotsialisticheskogo khozyaistva*
FSKh	*Finansy i sotsialisticheskoe khozyaistvo*
I	*Izvestiya*
IA	*Istoricheskii arkhiv*
IS	*Istoriya SSSR*
KPSS v rez.	*Kommunisticheskaya partiya Sovetskogo Soyuza v rezolyutsiakh* (books)
KTs ... na ...	*Kontrol'nye tsifry narodnogo khozyaistva SSSR ... for* (followed by year) (books)
NAF	*Na agrarnom fronte*
NFI	*Na fronte industrializatsii*
NPF	*Na planovom fronte*
P	*Pravda*
PE	*Problemy ekonomiki*
PI	*Puti industrializatsii*
PKh	*Planovoe khozyaistvo*

PS	*Partiinoe stroitel'stvo*
PZM	*Pod znamenem marksizma*
SGRP	*Sovetskoe gosudarstvo i revolyutsiya prava*
SKhG	*Sel'skokhozyaistvennaya gazeta*
SO	*Statisticheskoe obozrenie*
SPR	*Spravochnik partiinogo rabotnika* (series of books)
SP VSNKh	*Sbornik postanovlenii i prikazov* (VSNKh)
SR	*Slavic Review*
SS	*Soviet Studies*
SU	*Sobranie uzakonenii*
SV	*Sotsialisticheskii vestnik*
SZ	*Sobranie zakonov*
SZe	*Sotsialisticheskoe zemledelie*
TPG	*Torgovo-promyshlennaya gazeta*
TsIK 2/V	*2 [Vtoraya] sessiya TsIKa . . . 5 sozyva* (book)
TsIK 3/V	*3 [Tret'ya] sessiya TsIKa . . . 5 sozyva* (book)
TsIK 3/IV	*3 [Tret'ya] sessiya TsIKa . . . 4 sozyva* (book)
VF	*Vestnik finansov*
VIZh	*Voenno-istoricheskii zhurnal*
VKA	*Vestnik Kommunisticheskoi Akademii*
VT	*Voprosy torgovli*
VTr	*Voprosy truda*
ZI	*Za industrializatsiyu*
ZART	*Zakonodatel'stvo i administrativnye . . .*
ZRT	*Zakonodatel'stvo i rasporyazheniya . . .*

BIBLIOGRAPHY

Letters used as abbreviations for items in the bibliography are listed on pp. 549–50. All other books are referred to in the text footnotes either by their author or editor, or by an abbreviated title (always including the first word or syllable) when there is no author or editor, and by date of publication. Place of publication is Moscow or Moscow–Leningrad, unless otherwise stated. Only items referred to in the text are included in the bibliography.

SECTION I ARCHIVES, THESES AND OTHER UNPUBLISHED MATERIALS

Soviet archives
Tsentral'nyi gosudarstvennyi arkhiv narodnogo khozyaistva SSSR:
fond 1884 (Narodnyi komissariat putei soobshcheniya SSSR)
fond 3429 (Vysshii sovet narodnogo khozyaistva SSSR)
fond 4086 (Uchrezhdeniya metallurgicheskoi promyshlennosti VSNKh SSSR i NKTP SSSR)
fond 5240 (Narodnyi komissariat vnutrennei i vneshnei torgovli SSSR)
fond 7620 (Vsesoyuznoe avtotraktornoe ob''edinenie VSNKh SSSR)
(referred to as TsGANKh, followed by fond/opis'/delo, list)
US government archives
State Department files: referred to by Decimal classification, followed by document number.
Trotsky archives (Houghton Library, University of Harvard):
referred to by document number
Hoover Institution: American Engineers in Russia (referred to as Hoover, AER):

Box 2: L. M. Banks, J. S. Ferguson, J. H. Gillis, R. W. Stuck mss.

Box 3: F. R. Harris, W. S. Orr mss.

Box 4: R. W. Stuck (second ms.)

Personal interviews of Soviet émigrés in Israel by K. Miroshnik and R. W. Davies, April 1982: referred to by interview number (tapes and transcripts are in possession of present author)

Unpublished theses and papers

Barber, J. D. 'The Composition of the Working Class in the USSR, 1928–1941', unpublished Discussion Papers SIPS (Soviet Industrialisation Project Series) 16 (CREES (Centre for Russian and East European Studies), University of Birmingham, 1978)

Boetticher, M. V., 'Soviet Defence Policy and the First Five-Year Plan', unpublished working paper, West European Conference on Soviet Industry and the Working Class in the Inter-War Years; University of Birmingham, June 3–6, 1981 (CREES, University of Birmingham, 1981)

Cooper, J. M., 'Defence Production and the Soviet Economy, 1929–1941', unpublished Discussion Papers SIPS 3 (CREES, University of Birmingham, 1976)

Cooper, J. M., 'The Development of the Soviet Machine-Tool Industry, 1917–41,' unpublished Ph.D. thesis (University of Birmingham, 1975)

Davies, R. W., 'Soviet Industrial Production, 1928–1937: the Rival Estimates', unpublished Discussion Papers SIPS 18 (CREES, University of Birmingham, 1978)

Dodge, N. T., 'Trends in Labour Productivity in the Soviet Tractor Industry: a Case Study in Industrial Development', unpublished Ph.D. dissertation (Harvard University, 1960)

Gooderham, P. O., 'The Regional Party Apparatus in the First Five-Year Plan: The Case of Leningrad', unpublished Discussion Papers, SIPS 24, i, ii (CREES, University of Birmingham, 1983)

Harrison, R. M. 'Soviet Peasants and Soviet Price Policy in the 1920s', unpublished Discussion Papers SIPS 10 (CREES, University of Birmingham, 1977)

Libbey, J. K., 'Alexander Gumberg and Soviet-American Relations, 1917–1933', unpublished Ph.D. dissertation (University of Kentucky, 1975)

Martynov, V.I., 'Rabochii klass v bor'be za razvitie tyazheloi promyshlennosti v gody pervoi pyatiletki, 1928–1932 gg.', unpublished kandidatskaya dissertatsiya (Moscow, 1973)

Merridale, C. A., *The Communist Party in Moscow, 1925–1932*, unpublished Ph.D. thesis (University of Birmingham, 1987)

Redding, A. D., 'Nonagricultural Employment in the USSR, 1928–55', unpublished Ph.D. thesis (University of Columbia, 1958)

Rees, E. A., 'Rabkrin and the Soviet System of State Control, 1920–1930', unpublished Ph.D. thesis (CREES, University of Birmingham, 1982)

Sadler, A., 'The Party Organisation in the Soviet Enterprise, 1928–34', unpublished M.Soc.Sc. thesis (CREES, University of Birmingham, 1979)

Shiokawa, N., 'A "Socialist State" and the Working Class: Labour Management in the Soviet Factory, 1929–1933', unpublished working paper to Soviet Industrialisation Project Seminar (CREES, University of Birmingham, May 1986)

Wheatcroft, S. G., 'Changes in the Pattern of Employment in the USSR, 1926–1939', unpublished paper presented to Social Science Research Council Conference on Soviet Economic Development in the 1930s (CREES, University of Birmingham, 1982)

Wheatcroft, S. G., 'Towards an Analysis of the Class Divisions in the USSR in the 1920s and 1930s, with Special Reference to the Non-Agricultural Non-Labouring Classes', unpublished working paper (University of Birmingham, 1984)

SECTION II   NEWSPAPERS, JOURNALS AND
OTHER PERIODICAL PUBLICATIONS

Annals of the Institute of Social Science (University of Tokyo)
Bol'shevik
British–Russian Gazette (London)
Bulletin of the Society for the Social History of Medicine
Byulleten' ekonomicheskogo kabineta prof. S. N. Prokopovicha (Prague)
Byulleten' finansovogo i khozyaistvennogo zakonodatel'stva
Byulleten' Gipromeza (Leningrad) (*Gipromez* from No. 4, 1930)
Byulleten' Gosplana
Byulleten' Kon"yunkturnogo Instituta

Byulleten' Oppozitsii (bol'shevikov-lenintsev) (Paris/Berlin)
Californian Slavic Studies
Canadian Slavonic Papers
Critique (Glasgow)
Dneprostroi
Economica (London)
The Economic History Review
EKO (Novosibirsk)
Ekonomicheskaya zhizn'
Ekonomicheskoe obozrenie
Ekonomika i matematicheskie metody
Ezhemesyachnyi statisticheskii byulleten' (VSNKh SSSR)
Finansovye problemy planovogo khozyaistva (*Vestnik finansov* until No. 2, 1930)
Finansy i sotsialisticheskoe khozyaistvo
Gipromez (Leningrad) (*Byulleten' Gipromeza* until No. 3, 1930)
Informatsionnyi byulleten' Gosplana SSSR
Istoricheskii arkhiv
Istoriya SSSR
Itogi vypolneniya narodno-khozyaistvennego plana po torgovle i snabzheniyu (TsUNKhU)
Izvestiya
Komissiya po mobilizatsii vnutrennikh resursov pri Prezidiume VSNKh SSSR, svodka No. . . .
Literaturnaya gazeta
Machinery (London)
Memorandum (Birmingham Bureau of Research on Russian Economic Conditions, University of Birmingham)
Metall
Na agrarnom fronte
Na fronte industrializatsii (Leningrad)
Na planovom fronte
Nashe stroitel'stvo
Nizhnee Povolzh'e (Saratov)
Novyi mir
Osnovnye pokazateli vypolneniya narodno-khozyaistvennogo plana (TsUNKhU)
Partiinoe stroitel'stvo
Planovoe khozyaistvo
Pod znamenem marksizma
Pravda

Predpriyatie: proizvodstvenno – ekonomicheskii i tekhnicheskii zhurnal
Problems of Communism (Washington, D.C.)
Problemy ekonomiki
Protokol zasedaniya Prezidiuma Vysshego Soveta Narodnogo Khozyaistva
  SSSR
Puti industrializatsii
Review of Socialist Law
Sbornik postanovlenii i prikazov po promyshlennosti (VSNKh SSSR)
Sel'skokhozyaistvennaya gazeta (*Sotsialisticheskoe zemledelie* from
  January 29, 1930)
Severnyi rabochii (Yaroslavl')
Slavic Review (Urbana–Champaign)
Sobranie uzakonenii i rasporyazhenii RSFSR
Sobranie zakonov i rasporyazhenii SSSR
Sotsialisticheskii vestnik (Paris)
Sotsialisticheskoe zemledelie (*Sel'skokhozyaistvennaya gazeta* until
  January 28, 1930)
Sovetskaya metallurgiya: tekhniko-ekonomicheskii zhurnal
Sovetskaya torgovlya
Sovetskoe gosudarstvo i revolyutsiya prava: zhurnal instituta sovetskogo
  stroitel'stva i prava
Soviet Studies (Oxford to xix, 1967–8, then Glasgow)
Soviet Union/Union soviètique
Statisticheskoe obozrenie
Statistika truda
Torgovo-promyshlennaya gazeta (*Za industrializatsiyu* from beginning
  of 1930)
VARNITSO
Vestnik finansov (*Finansovye problemy planovogo khozyaistva* from
  No. 3, 1930)
Vestnik Kommunisticheskoi Akademii
Vneshnyaya torgovlya Soyuza SSR: statisticheskii obzor
Voenno-istoricheskii zhurnal
Voprosy istorii
Voprosy literatury
Voprosy torgovli
Voprosy truda
Vypolnenie narodno-khozyaistvennogo plana (Gosplan SSSR)
Za industrializatsiyu (*Torgovo-promyshlennaya gazeta* until end of
  1929)
Zakonodatel'stvo i administrativnye rasporyazheniya po vneshnei i

vnutrennei torgovle, renamed *Zakonodatel'stvo i rasporyazheniya po torgovle* in 1930
Za rabotoi
Za tempy, kachestvo i proverku

SECTION III   BOOKS, ETC. IN RUSSIAN

Abramov, A., *U Kremlevskoi steny* (2nd edn, 1978)
Akshinskii, V., *Kliment Efremovich Voroshilov: biograficheskii ocherk* (1974)
Andrukhov, N. R., *Partiinoe stroitel'stvo v period bor'by za pobedu sotsializma v SSSR, 1917–1937* (1977)
Arkheograficheskii ezhegodnik: 1968 (1970)
Atlas, Z. V., *Den'gi i kredit (pri kapitalizme i v SSSR)* (1930)
Atlas, Z. V., *Sotsialisticheskaya denezhnaya sistema: problemy sotsialisticheskogo preobrazovaniya i razvitiya denezhnoi sistemy SSSR* (1969)
Bardin, I. P., *Rozhdenie zavoda: vospominaniya inzhenera* (Novosibirsk, 1936)
Barun, M. A., *Osnovnoi kapital promyshlennosti SSSR* (1930)
Bessonov, S. A., and Kon, A. F., *Rubinshchina ili marksizm?* (1930)
Bol'shaya sovetskaya entsiklopediya, vols. V (1930), LXI (1934)
Borilin, B., and Leont'ev, A., eds., *Protiv mekhanisticheskikh tendentsii v politekonomii* (1929)
Bukharin, N., *Etyudy* (1932)
Burdyanskii, I. M., *Osnovy ratsionalizatsii proizvodstva* (1930)
Buzlaeva, A. I., *Leninskii plan kooperirovaniya melkoi promyshlennosti SSSR* (1969)
Byli industrial'nye: ocherki i vospominaniya (1970)
Chernaya metallurgiya, zhelezorudnaya, marganetsevaya i koksovaya promyshlennost' SSSR: statisticheskii sbornik (1935)
Chistka sovetskogo apparata k XVI s"ezdu VKP (b) (1930)
Den, V. E., ed., *Tyazhelaya industriya v SSSR: ugol', neft', zhelezo i med'* (1926)
Desyatyi s"ezd RKP (b), mart 1921 goda: stenograficheskii otchet (1963)
Dikhtyar, G. A., *Sovetskaya torgovlya v period postroeniya sotsializma* (1961)
Dinamika rossiiskoi i sovetskoi promyshlennosti v svyazi s razvitiem

narodnogo khozyaistva za sorok let (1887–1926gg.), vol. I, iii (1930)

Direktivy KPSS i sovetskogo provitel'stva po khozyaistvennym voprosam: sbornik dokumentov, vol. II, *1929–1945 gody* (1957)

Direktor I. A. Likhachev: *v vospominaniyakh sovremennikov; o zavode i o sebe* (1971)

Dokumenty vneshnei politiki SSSR, vols. XIII, *1 yanvarya – 31 dekabrya 1930* (1967), XIV, *1 yanvarya – 31 dekabrya 1931* (1968)

Dzerzhinskii, F. E., *Izbrannye proizvedeniya,* 3rd edn, vol. II, *1924–1926* (1977)

Elektrifikatsiya SSSR: sbornik dokumentov i materialov, 1926–1932gg. (1966)

Fabrichno-zavodskaya promyshlennost' Soyuza SSR: osnovnye pokazateli ee dinamiki za 1924/25, 1925/26 i 1926/27gg. (1929); *ibid. Tablitsy* (1929)

Fabrichno-zavodskaya promyshlennost' SSSR i ego ekonomicheskikh raionov, vol. I (1928)

Fazin, Z., *Tovarishch Sergo* (1970)

Formirovanie i razvitie sovetskogo rabochego klassa (1917–1961gg.): sbornik statei (1964)

Frankfurt, S. M., *Rozhdenie stali i cheloveka* (1935)

Galiguzov, I. F., and Churilin, M. E., *Flagman otechestvennoi industrii: istoriya Magnitogorskogo metallurgicheskogo kombinata imeni V. I. Lenina* (1978)

Gan, L., *Arsenal sotsialisticheskoi rekonstruktsii: metallo- i elektrozavody Leningrada* (Leningrad, 1931)

Gershberg, S., *Rabota u nas takaya: zapiski zhurnalista-pravdista tridtsatykh godov* (1971)

Glebov-Avilov, N., *Sel'mashstroi: Rostovskii na Donu zavod sel'sko-khozyaistvennogo mashinostroeniya* (Rostov, 1930)

Gnedin, E., *Katastrofa i vtoroe rozhdenie: memuarnye zapiski* (Amsterdam, 1977)

God devyatnadtsatyi. Almanakh devyatyi (1936)

God raboty pravitel'stva: materialy k otchetu za 1928/29g. – pervyi god pyatiletki (1930)

Gorelik, I. G., *Metodika planirovaniya chernoi metallurgii* (1937)

Guznyaev, A. G., *Problemy predmeta politicheskoi ekonomii sotsializma (teoriya, istoriya, metodologiya)* (Kazan', 1976)

Illarionov, S. I., *Problema tovarnogo proizvodstva: perekhodnyi period* (1984)

Il'in, Ya., *Bol'shoi konveier* (1934)
Il'in, Ya., ed., *Bol'sheviki dolzhny ovladet' tekhnikoi (chemu uchit' opyt Stalingradskogo traktornogo)* (1931)
Il'in, Ya., ed. (sostavitel'), *Lyudi stalingradskogo traktornogo* (1933) *Industrializatsiya Severo – Zapadnogo Raiona v gody pervoi pyatiletki (1929–1932gg.)* (Leningrad, 1967)
Industrializatsiya SSSR, 1929–1932 gg.: dokumenty i materialy (1970)
Industrializatsiya SSSR, 1926–1928 gg.: dokumenty i materialy (1969)
Istoriya industrializatsii Nizhegorodskogo–Gor'kovskogo kraya (1926–1941gg.) (Gor'kii, 1968)
Istoriya industrializatsii Srednego Povolzh'ya, 1926/1941 gg. (Kuibyshev, 1974)
Istoriya industrializatsii Urala (1926–1932 gg.) (Sverdlovsk, 1967)
Istoriya Kommunisticheskoi partii Sovetskogo Soyuza, vol. IV, ii (1971)
Istoriya Moskovskogo avtozavoda imeni I. A. Likhacheva (1966)
Istoriya Moskovskogo Instrumental'nogo Zavoda (1934)
Istoriya vtoroi mirovoi voiny, vol. I (1973)
Itogi desyatiletiya Sovetskoi vlasti v tsifrakh, 1917–1927 (n.d. [? 1928])
Itogi i perspektivy khozyaistvennogo stroitel'stva (Kon''yunktura za period oktyabr'–iyun' 1926–27 goda i osnovnye direktivy po sostavleniyu kontrol'nykh tsifr narodnogo khozyaistva na 1927–28 god), ([i]), Stenogramma ob''edinennogo zasedaniya SNK SSSR i STO 5 iyulya 1927g., (ii), Stenogramma ob''edinennogo zasedaniya SNK SSSR i STO 12 iyulya 1927g. (1927)
Itogi raboty promyshlennosti VSNKh za 1931g. i perspektivy tyazheloi promyshlennosti na 1932g.: materialy k dokladu tov. Ordzhonikidze XVII vsesoyuznoi konferentsii VKP (b) (1932)
Itogi vypolneniya pervogo pyatiletnego plana razvitiya narodnogo khozyaistva Soyuza SSR (1933)
Iz istorii Magnitogorskogo metallurgicheskogo kombinata i goroda Magnitogorska (1929–1941 gg.) (Chelyabinsk, 1965)
Izmeneniya sotsial'noi struktury sovetskogo obshchestva, 1921 – seredina 30-kh godov (1979)
Izmeneniya v chislennosti i sostave sovetskogo rabochego klassa (1961)
Kardashov, V., *Voroshilov* (1976)
Kas'yanenko, V. I., *Zavoevanie ekonomicheskoi nezavisimosti SSSR, 1917–1940 gg.* (1972)
Khavin, A., *U rulya industrii (dokumental'nye ocherki)* (1968)
Khmel'nitskaya, E. L., ed., *Ekonomika sotsialisticheskoi promyshlennosti: uchebnik dlya vuzov,* vol. I (1931)

Kholmyanskii, I., *Spetsializatsiya i kooperirovanie mashinostroeniya v pervoi pyatiletke* (1933)

Khromov, S. S., F. E. *Dzerzhinskii na khozyaistvennom fronte, 1921–1926* (1977)

Kirov, S., *Leningradskaya organizatsiya nakanune XVI s"ezda VKP (b): doklad o rabote obkoma VKP (b) na III oblastnoi partkonferentsii* (Leningrad, 1930)

Kokorin, M., *Oborona SSSR i pyatiletka* (1930)

Kol'man, A., *My ne dolzhny byli tak zhit'* (NY, 1982)

Kolomenskii, A., *Kak my ispol'zuem zagranichnuyu tekhniku* (1930)

Kommunisticheskaya partiya Sovetskogo Soyuza v rezolyutsiyakh i resheniyakh s"ezdov, konferentsii i plenumov TsK, 2nd edn, vol. II, *1924–1930*, vol. III, *1930–1954* (1954)

Kommunisticheskii Internatsional v dokumentakh (1919–1932) (1933)

Kontrol'nye tsifry narodnogo khozyaistva SSSR na 1928/1929 god (1929)

Kontrol'nye tsifry narodnogo khozyaistva SSSR na 1929/30 god, odobrennye Sovetom Narodnykh Komissarov SSSR (1930)

Kontrol'nye tsifry promyshlennosti na 1929/1930 g.: materialy k dokladu VSNKh SSSR Gosplanu SSSR (n.d. [1929])

Kontrol'nye tsifry pyatiletnego plana promyshlennosti (1927/28–1931/32 gg.) (1927)

Kon"yunktura narodnogo khozyaistva SSSR za sentyabr' i 12 mesyatsev 1929/30g. (n.d. [1930])

Kostyuchenko, S., Khrenov, I., Fedorov, Yu., *Istoriya Kirovskogo zavoda, 1917–1945* (1966)

KPSS o vooruzhennykh silakh Sovetskogo Soyuza: dokumenty 1917–1968 (1969)

Krzhizhanovskii, G. M., *Izbrannoe* (1957)

Krzhizhanovskii, G. M., Kviring, E. I., and Kovalevskii, N. A., *Problemy postroeniya general'nogo plana* (1930)

Krzhizhanovskii, G. M., Strumilin, S. G., Kviring, E. I., Kovalevskii, N. A., Bogolepov, M.I., *Osnovnye problemy kontrol'nykh tsifr narodnogo khozyaistva SSSR na 1929/30 god* (1930)

Kuibyshev, V. V., *Brigady sotsializma: doklad na I Vsesoyuznom s"ezde udarnykh brigad* (1930)

Kuibyshev, V. V., *Stat'i i rechi*, vol. V, *1930–1935* (1937)

Kuibysheva, G. V., Lezhava, O. A., Nelidov, N. V., Khavin, A. F., *Valerian Vladimirovich Kuibyshev: biografiya* (1966)

Kul'chitskii, S. V., *Vnutrennie resursy sotsialisticheskoi industrializatsii (1926–1937)* (Kiev, 1979)

Kuz'min, V. I., *Istoricheskii opyt sovetskoi industrializatsii* (1969)

Kuz'min, V. I., *V bor'be za sotsialisticheskuyu rekonstruktsiyu, 1926–1937: ekonomicheskaya politika Sovetskogo gosudarstva* (1976)

Lakin, G. V., *Reforma upravleniya promyshlennost'yu v 1929/30g.* (1930)

Lapidus, I., and Ostrovityanov, K., *Politicheskaya ekonomiya v svyazi s teoriei sovetskogo khozyaistva* (1930)

Leikina-Svirskaya, V. R., *Russkaya intelligentsiya v 1900–1917 godakh* (1981)

Lauer, G., *My sozdali chernuyu metallurgiyu* (1933)

Lel'chuk, V. S., *Sozdanie khimicheskoi promyshlennosti SSSR* (1964)

Lenin, V. I., *Sochineniya*, 4th edn, vols. XXI (1948), XXVII (1950), XXX (1950), XXXII (1950), XXXIII (1950)

Leninskii plan sotsialisticheskoi industrializatsii i ego osushchestvlenie (1969)

Leninskii sbornik, vol. XL (1929)

Literaturnoe nasledstvo, vol LXV (1958)

Lyando, A., *Voprosy finansovogo balansa (ocherki narodnogo khozyaistva istorii i metodologii sostavleniya)* (1963)

Malafeev, A. N., *Istoriya tsenoobrazovaniya v SSSR (1917–1963 gg.)* (1964)

Material k otchetu TsKK VKP(b) XVI s"ezdu VKP(b) sostavlennyi OGPU (k dokladu tov. Ordzhonikidze) (1930)

Materialy k pyatiletnemu planu razvitiya promyshlennosti SSSR (1927/28–1931/32 gg.) (1927)

Materialy k pyatiletnemu planu promyshlennosti VSNKh SSSR na 1928/29–1932/33 gg. (1929), vols. I–III

Materialy k VI s"ezdu sovetov SSSR – kratkie itogi raboty promyshlennosti VSNKh SSSR za period mezhdu V i VI s"ezdami sovetov SSSR (1931)

Materialy po balansu narodnogo khozyaistva za 1928, 1929 i 1930 gg. (1930) – See Materials

Materialy po istorii SSSR, vol. VII (1959)

Matushkin, P. G., *Bor'ba kommunisticheskoi partii za sozdanie vtoroi ugol'no-metallurgicheskoi bazy SSSR* (Chelyabinsk, 1966)

Mednikov, N., *Promyshlennost' na vtorom godu pyatiletki* (1930)

Melkaya promyshlennost' SSSR po dannym Vsesoyuznoi perepisi 1929g., vol. I (1932)

Mendel'son, A. S. ed., *Pokazateli kon''yunktury narodnogo khozyaistva SSSR za 1923/24–1928/29 gg.* (1930)
Minaev, S. V., ed., *Osnovnye momenty rekonstruktsii promyshlennosti SSSR (ocherki)* (1930)
Mordukhovich (Mokhov), E., *Na bor'bu s tekuchest'yu rabochei sily* (1931)
Moshkov, Yu. A., *Zernovaya problema v gody sploshnoi kollektivizatsii sel'skogo khozyaistva SSSR (1929–1932 gg.)* (1966)
Na novom etape sotsialisticheskogo stroitel'stva: sbornik statei (1930), vols. I, II
Na putyakh k obobshchestvleniyu melkoi promyshlennosti SSSR (1927)
Narodnoe khozyaistvo SSSR: statisticheskii spravochnik 1932 (1932)
Narodno-khozyaistvennyi plan SSSR na 1931 (kontrol'nye tsifry): doklad Gosplana SSSR Sovetu Narodnykh Komissarov SSSR (1931)
Narodnoe obrazovanie, nauka i kul'tura v SSSR: statisticheskii spravochnik (1971)
Neiman, G. Ya., *Vnutrennyaya torgovlya SSSR* (1935)
Obshchii svod po Imperii rezul'tatov razrabotki dannykh pervoi vseobshchei perepisi naseleniya, proizvedennoi 28 yanvarya 1897 goda, vols. I and II (St. Petersburg, 1905)
Ob''yasnitel'naya zapiska k otchetu Narodnogo Komissariata Finansov Soyuza SSR ob ispolnenii edinogo gosudarstvennogo byudzheta Soyuza Sovetskikh Sotsialisticheskikh Respublik za 1928–1929 g. (1930)
Ocherki Gor'kovskoi organizatsii KPSS, vol. II (Gor'kii, 1966)
Ocherki po istorii statistiki SSSR (1957)
Odinnadtsatyi s''ezd RKP (b), mart-aprel' 1922 goda: stenograficheskii otchet (1961)
Ordzhonikidze, G. K., *Stat'i i rechi*, vol. II, *1926–1937 gg.* (1957)
Ostavnov, A. V., *Avtomobili Forda: modeli A i AA* (1931)
Otchet Narodnogo Komissariata Finansov Soyuza SSR ob ispolnenii edinogo gosudarstvennogo byudzheta Soyuza Sovetskikh Sotsialisticheskikh Respublik za 1928–1929g. (1930)
Otchet Narodnogo Komissariata Finansov Soyuza SSR ob ispolnenii edinogo gosudarstvennogo byudzheta Soyuza Sovetskikh Sotsialisticheskikh Respublik za 1929–1930g. (Leningrad, 1931)
Paramonov, I. V., *Puti proidennye* (2nd edn, 1970)
Pashkov, A. E., *Ekonomicheskie problemy sotsializma* (1970)
Pervaya Moskovskaya oblastnaya konferentsiya Vsesoyuznoi kommunisti-cheskoi partii (bol'shevikov): stenograficheskii otchet [September 14–18, 1929], vols. I, II (1929)

Pervaya vsesoyuznaya konferentsiya rabotnikov sotsialisticheskoi promyshlennosti [January 31–February 4, 1931] (1931)
Pervye shagi industrializatsii SSSR 1926/27gg. (1959)
Pervyi Vsesoyuznyi s"ezd udarnykh brigad (k tridtsatiletiyu s"ezda): sbornik dokumentov i materialov [December 5–10, 1929] (1959)
Pishchevaya industriya SSSR k 20-letiyu sovetskoi vlasti (1937)
Politicheskii dnevnik, 1963–1970 (Amsterdam, 1972)
Polyakov, Yu. A., Dmitrenko, V. P., Shcherban', N. V., *Novaya ekonomicheskaya politika: razrabotka i osushchestvlenie* (1982)
Problemy rekonstruktsii narodnogo khozyaistva SSSR na pyatiletie: pyatiletnii perspektivnyi plan na V s"ezde Gosplanov [March 7–14, 1929] (1929)
Profsoyuznaya perepis', 1932–1933g., vol. I (1934)
Promyshlennost': sbornik statei pod redaktsiei A. P. Rozengol'tsa po materialam TsKK VKP (b) – NK RKI (1930)
Promyshlennost' SSSR (1936)
Promyshlennost' SSSR: statisticheskii sbornik (1957)
Promyshlennost' SSSR: statisticheskii sbornik (1964)
Promyshlennost' SSSR v 1926/27 godu: ezhegodnik VSNKh SSSR (1928)
Promyshlennost' SSSR v 1927/28 godu: ezhegodnik VSNKh SSSR, ([i]) (n.d. [1930]), ii (1930)
Promyslovaya kooperatsiya SSSR (1934)
50 [Pyat'desyat] let vooruzhennykh sil SSSR (1968)
Pyatiletnii plan narodno-khozyaistvennogo stroitel'stva SSSR, 3rd edn (1930), vols. I, II (i), II (ii), III
Pyatnadtsatyi s"ezd VKP (b): dekabr' 1927 goda: stenograficheskii otchet (1962), vols. I, II
Rabochii klass – vedushchaya sila v stroitel'stve sotsialisticheskogo obshchestva, 1921–1937 gg. (1984) (*Istoriya sovetskogo rabochego klassa*, vol. II)
Rashin, A. G., *Naselenie Rossii za 100 let (1811–1913 gg.): statisticheskie ocherki* (1956)
Rashin, A. G., *Formirovanie rabochego klassa v Rossii* (1958)
Resheniya partii i pravitel'stva po khozyaistvennym voprosam, vol. II, *1929–1940 gody* (1967)
Rogachevskaya, L. S., *Likvidatsiya bezrabotitsy v SSSR, 1917–30 gg.* (1973)
Rogachevskaya, L. S., *Sotsialisticheskoe sorevnovanie v SSSR: istoricheskie ocherki, 1917–1970 gg.* (1977)

Rozengol'ts, A. P., See *Promyshlennost': sbornik statei* . . .

Sabsovich, L. M., *Gorod budushchego i organizatsiya sotsialisticheskogo byta* (1929)

Sabsovich, L., *SSSR cherez 15 let: gipoteza general'nogo plana* (1929)

Sed'moi s"ezd professional'nykh soyuzov SSSR (1927)

Serebrovskii, A. P., *Ratsionalizatsiya proizvodstva i novoe promyshlennoe stroitel'stvo SSSR v suyazi s pyatiletnim planom razvitiya godsudarstvennoi promyshlennosti* (1927)

Serebrovskii, A. P., *Na zolotom fronte* (1936)

Shavrov, V., *Istoriya konstruktsii samoletov v SSSR do 1938g.* (2nd edn, 1978)

XVI [Shestnadtsatyi] s"ezd Vsesoyuznoi Kommunisticheskoi partii (b): stenograficheskii otchet (2nd edn, 1931)

Shirokorad, L. D., *Metodologicheskie problemy politicheskoi ekonomii sotsializma v sovetskoi ekonomicheskoi literature perekhodnogo perioda* (Leningrad, 1974)

Shtikh, M., *Zavod gryadushchikh urozhaev: rostovskii krasnoznamenskii sel'mash* (1931)

Slovo o Magnitke (1979)

Sostav VKP (b) k XVI s"ezdu: dinamika osnovnykh pokazatelei rosta partii mezhdu XV i XVI s"ezdami (1930)

Sotsialisticheskaya rekonstruktsiya i nauchno-issledovatel'skaya rabota: sbornik Nauchno-Issledovatel'skogo Sektora PTEU VSNKh SSSR k XVI s"ezdu VKP (b) (1930)

Sotsialisticheskoe sorevnovanie v promyshlennosti SSSR (1930)

Sotsialisticheskoe sorevnovanie v SSSR, 1918–1964: dokumenty i materialy profsoyuzov (1965)

Sotsialisticheskoe stroitel'stvo SSSR: statisticheskii ezhegodnik (1934)

Sotsialisticheskoe stroitel'stvo SSSR: statisticheskii ezhegodnik (1935)

Sotsial'nyi i natsional'nyi sostav VKP (b): itogi Vsesoyuznoi partiinoi perepisi 1927 goda (1928)

Sovetskaya torgovlya (1935 [? 1936])

Spravochnik partiinogo rabotnika, vols. VII, i–ii (1930), VIII (1934)

SSSR: 4 s"ezd sovetov: stenograficheskii otchet (1927)

SSSR: 5 s"ezd sovetov: stenograficheskii otchet [May 20–28, 1929] (1929)

SSSR za 15 let: statisticheskie materialy po narodnomu khozyaistvu (1932)

Stalin, I. V., *Sochineniya*, vols. VII (1947), VIII (1948), XI (1949), XII (1949), XIII (1951)

Statisticheskii spravochnik SSSR za 1928 (1929)

Strumilin, S. G., *Na planovom fronte, 1920–1930 gg.* (1958) (referred to in present volume as Strumilin (1958 (1)))

Strumilin, S. G., *Statistiko – ekonomicheskie ocherki* (1958) (referred to in present volume as Strumilin (1958 (2)))

Suvorov, K. I., *Istoricheskii opyt KPSS po likvidatsii bezrabotitsy (1917–1930)* (1968)

Syrtsov, S. I., *K novomu khozyaistvennomu godu: pererabotannaya stenogramma rechi S. I. Syrtsova na ob"edinennom zasedanii SNK i EKOSO RSFSR, 30 avgusta 1930g. po dokladu Gosplana [RSFSR] o kontrol'nykh tsifrakh na 1930/31g.* (1930)

Syrtsov, S., *Nakanune partiinogo s"ezda* (1930)

Tekhnicheskie kul'tury (statisticheskii spravochnik po posevnym ploshchadyam, urozhainosti, valovym sboram i zagotovkam k 1936g.): kartofel', ovoshchi (1936)

Tovarooborot za gody rekonstruktivnogo perioda (1932)

3 [Tret'ya] sessiya Tsentral'nogo Ispolnitel'nogo Komiteta Soyuza SSR 4 sozyva (1928)

3 [Tret'ya] sessiya Tsentral'nogo Ispolnitel'nogo Komiteta Soyuza SSR 5 sozyva: stenograficheskii otchet i postanovleniya [January 4–12, 1931] (1931)

Trifonov, I., *Ocherki istorii klassovoi bor'by v period NEPa (1921–1937)* (1960)

Trud v pervoi pyatiletke (1934)

Trud v SSSR: ekonomiko-statisticheskii spravochnik (1932)

Trud v SSSR: spravochnik 1926–1930 (1930)

Trud v SSSR: statisticheskii spravochnik (1936)

Trudy Komissii po metallu, xvi (1927)

Trudy pervoi konferentsii proektiruyushchikh i ekspertiruyuschchikh organizatsii VSNKh SSSR [June 19–20, 1930] (1931)

Trudy Tsentral'nogo Statisticheskogo Upravleniya, vols. XXIX, ii (1926) (Popov, P. I., ed. *Balans narodnogo khozyaistva Soyuza S.S.R. 1923–24 goda*, and *ibid. Tablitsy*), XXXVI, i (1926) (*Vserossiiskaya promyshlennaya i professional'naya perepis' 1918g. Fabrichno-zavodskaya promyshlennost' v period 1913–1918 gg. Promyshlennaya perepis'*)

Tukhachevskii, M. N., *Izbrannye proizvedeniya*, vol. I, 1917–1927gg., II, 1928–1937gg. (1964)

Tyazhest' oblozheniya v SSSR (sotsial'nyi sostav, dokhody i nalogovye platezhi naseleniya Soyuza SSR v 1924/25, 1925/26 i 1926/27 godakh): doklad komissii Soveta Narodnykh Komissarov SSSR po izucheniyu tyazhesti oblozheniya Soyuza (1929)

Uglanov, N. A., ed., *Trud v SSSR: sbornik statei* (1930)

Umanskii, S. A., ed., *Mirovoe khozyaistvo: sbornik statisticheskikh materialov za 1913–1927 gg.* (1928)

Unpelev, G. A., *Rozhdenie Uralmasha (1928–1932 gg)* (1960)

Uproshchenie finansovoi sistemy (1930)

Ural'skii zavod tyazhelogo mashinostroeniya, 1928–1933 (Sverdlovsk, 1933)

Vaganov, F. M., *Pravyi uklon v VKP(b) i ego razgrom (1928–1930)* (1970)

Vainshtein, A. L., *Narodnoe bogatstvo i narodnokhozyaistvennoe nakoplenie predrevolyutsionnoi Rossii* (1960)

Vainshtein, A. L., *Tseny i tsenoobrazovanie v SSSR v vosstanovitel'nyi period, 1921–1928 gg.* (1972)

Valentinov, N. (Vol'skii), *Novaya ekonomicheskaya politika i krizis partii posle smerti Lenina: gody raboty v VSNKh vo vremya NEP: vospominaniya* (Stanford, 1971)

Valovoi, D., and Lapshina, G. E., *Sotsializm i tovarnye otnosheniya: problemno-istoricheskie ocherki politicheskoi ekonomii sotsializma* (1972)

Vareikis, I., *V bor'be za general'nuyu liniyu na praktike* (Voronezh, 1931)

Vdovin, A. I., Drobizhev, V. Z., *Rost rabochego klassa SSSR, 1917–1940 gg.* (1976)

Venediktov, A. V., *Organizatsiya gosudarstvennoi promyshlennosti v SSSR*, vol. II, *1921–1934* (Leningrad, 1961)

Vneshnyaya torgovlya SSSR za 1918–1940 gg.: statisticheskii obzor (1960)

Vsesoyuznaya perepis' naseleniya 1926 goda, vol. XXXIV (1930)

2 [Vtoraya] sessiya Tsentral'nogo Ispolnitel'nogo Komiteta Soyuza SSR 5 Sozyva: stenograficheskii otchet [November 29 – December 8, 1929] (1929)

Vypolnenie plana pervogo goda pyatiletki (1930)

Vypolnenie pyatiletnego plana promyshlennosti: materialy k dokladu V. V. Kuibysheva na XVI s"ezde VKP(b) (1931)

Yakhot, I., *Podavlenie filosofii v SSSR (20–30 gody)* (New York, 1981)

Yakovlev, A. S., *Tsel' zhizni* (1967)

Yakovlev, A. S., *Sovetskie samolety: kratkii ocherk*, 4th edn (1982)

Yakovlev, Ya., *Rostovskii kombinat Sel'mashstroi: ob"yasnit. broshyura k serii kinoplenochnykh diapozitivov* (1932)
Yantarov, S., *Velikoe istoricheskoe stroitel'stvo*, 2nd edn ([Kharkov], 1935)
Yurovskii, L., *Denezhnaya politika sovetskoi vlasti (1917–1927)* (1928)
Zheleznodorozhnyi transport v gody industrializatsii SSSR (1926–1941) (1970)
Zolotarev, N. A., *Vazhnyi etap organizatsionnogo ukrepleniya Kommunisticheskoi partii (1928–1937 gg.)* (1979)
Zuikov, B. N., *Sozdanie tyazheloi industrii na Urale (1928–1932 gg)* (1971)

SECTION IV   BOOKS, ETC. IN OTHER
LANGUAGES

Arnold, A. Z., *Banks, Credit and Money in Soviet Russia* (New York, 1937)
Avtorkhanov, A., *Stalin and the Soviet Communist Party: a Study in the Technology of Power* (Munich, 1959)
Bailes, K. E., *Technology and Society under Lenin and Stalin: Origins of the Soviet Technical Intelligentsia, 1917–1941* (Princeton, N.J., 1978)
Barber, J. *Soviet Historians in Crisis, 1928–1932* (London, 1981)
Bergson, A., *The Structure of Soviet Wages: A Study in Socialist Economics* (Cambridge, Mass., 1944)
Boetticher, M. V., *Industrielisierungspolitik und Verteidigungkonzeption der UdSSR, 1926–1930: Herausbildung des Stalinismus und aussere Bedrohung* (Dusseldorf, 1979)
Borodin, N. M., *One Man in his Time* (London, [1955])
Bourke-White, M., *Eyes on Russia* (New York, 1931)
Brown, E. J., *Russian Literature since the Revolution* (New York, 1969)
Brutzkus, B., *Economic Planning in Soviet Russia* (London, 1935)
Carr, E. H., *The Bolshevik Revolution, 1917–1923*, vol. II (London, 1952)
Carr, E. H., *Foundations of a Planned Economy, 1926–1929*, vol. II (London, 1971), vol. III, i–iii (London, 1976–8)
Carr, E. H., *The Interregnum, 1923–1924* (London, 1954)
Carr, E. H., *Socialism in One Country, 1924–1926*, vol. I (London, 1958), vol. II (London, 1959)

Carr, E. H. and Davies, R. W., *Foundations of a Planned Economy, 1926–1929*, vol. I (London, 1969)

Chamberlin, W. H., *Russia's Iron Age* (Boston, 1934)

Clark, M. G., *The Economics of Soviet Steel* (Cambridge, Mass., 1956)

Cohen, S. F., *Bukharin and the Bolshevik Revolution: a Political Biography, 1888–1938* (London, 1974)

Collette, J.-M., *Politique des investissements et calcul économique: l'expérience soviètique* (Paris [1964])

Crisp, O., *Studies in the Russian Economy before 1914* (London, 1976)

Davies, R. W., *The Development of the Soviet Budgetary System* (Cambridge, 1958)

Davies, R. W., ed., *From Tsarism to the New Economic Policy: Continuity and Change in the Economy of the USSR* (London, 1988)

Davies, R. W., ed., *Soviet Investment for Planned Industrialisation, 1929–1937: Policy and Practice: Selected Papers from the Second World Congress for Soviet and East European Studies* (Berkeley, 1984)

Day, R. B., *The 'Crisis' and the 'Crash': Soviet Studies of the West (1917–1939)* (London, 1981)

Degras, J., ed., *Soviet Documents on Foreign Policy*, vol. II, *1925–1932* (London, 1952)

Deutscher, I., *The Prophet Outcast, Trotsky: 1929–1940* (London, 1963)

Economic Conditions in the USSR: Handbook for Foreign Economists, Specialists and Workers (Moscow, 1931)

Engels, F. *Herr Eugen Dühring's Revolution in Science (Anti-Dühring)* (London, n.d. [?1939])

Engels, F. *The Origin of the Family, Private Property and the State* (London, 1940)

Feinstein, C. H., ed., *Socialism, Capitalism and Economic Growth: Essays Presented to Maurice Dobb* (Cambridge, 1967)

Filtzer, D., *Soviet Workers and Stalinist Industrialization: the Formation of Modern Soviet Production Relations, 1928–1941* (London, 1986)

Fischer, M., *My Lives in Russia* (New York and London, 1944)

Fitzpatrick, S., *Education and Social Mobility in the Soviet Union, 1921–1934* (Cambridge, 1979)

Fitzpatrick, S., ed., *Cultural Revolution in Russia, 1928–1931* (Bloomington, Indiana, 1978)

Friedman, E. M., *Russia in Transition: a Business Man's Appraisal* (London, 1933)

Goode, W. T., *Is Intervention in Russia a Myth?* (London, 1931)

Graham, L. R., *The Soviet Academy of Sciences and the Communist Party, 1927–1932* (Princeton, NJ, 1967)

Gregory, P. R., *Russian National Income, 1885–1913* (Cambridge, 1982)

Grossman, G., *Soviet Statistics of Physical Output of Industrial Commodities: their Compilation and Quality* (Princeton, N.J., 1967)

Gunston, B., *Aircraft of the Soviet Union: the Encyclopedia of Soviet Aircraft since 1917* (London, 1983)

Haslam, J., *Soviet Foreign Policy, 1930–33: the Impact of the Depression* (London, 1983)

Hodgman, D. R., *Soviet Industrial Production, 1928–1951* (Cambridge, Mass., 1954)

Hubbard, L. E., *Soviet Trade and Distribution* (London, 1938)

Hunter, H., *Soviet Transportation Policy* (Cambridge, Mass., 1957)

Ilf, I., and Petrov, E., *The Little Golden Calf* (London, 1932)

Jansen, M., *A Show Trial under Lenin: the Trial of the Socialist-Revolutionaries, Moscow 1922* (The Hague, 1982)

Joravsky, D., *Soviet Marxism and Natural Science, 1917–1932* (New York, 1961)

Kaufman, A., *Small-scale Industry in the Soviet Union* (Washington, D.C., 1962)

Kirstein, T., *Die Bedeutung von Durchführungsentscheidungen in dem zentralistisch verfassten Entscheidungssystem der Sowjetunion: eine Analyse des stalinistischen Entscheidungssystems am Beispiel des Aufbaus von Magnitogorsk (1928–1932)* (Berlin, 1984)

Kirstein, T., *Sowjetische Industrialisierung – geplanter oder spontaner Prozess?: eine Strukturanalyse des wirtschaftpolitischen Entscheidungsprozesses beim Aufbau des Ural–Kuzneck–Kombinats 1918–1930* (Baden-Baden, 1979)

Knickerbocker, H. R., *The Soviet Five-Year Plan and its Effect on World Trade* (London, 1931)

Kravchenko, V., *I Chose Freedom: the Personal and Political Life of a Soviet Official* (London, 1947)

Kuromiya, H., *Hope and Despair: Stalin's Revolution in Industry, 1928–1931* (Cambridge, forthcoming)

Lampert, N., *The Technical Intelligentsia and the Soviet State: a Study of Soviet Managers and Technicians, 1928–1935* (1979)

Lane, D., ed., *Labour and Employment in the USSR* (Brighton, 1986)

Leggett, G., *The Cheka: Lenin's Political Police: the All-Russian Extraordinary Commission for Combating Counter-Revolution and Sabotage (December 1917 to February 1922)* (Oxford, 1981)

Lewin, M., *The Making of the Soviet System: Essays in the Social History of Interwar Russia* (London, 1985)

Lewis, R. A., *Science and Industrialisation in the USSR: Industrial Research and Development, 1917–1940* (London, 1979)

Littlepage, J. D., and Bess, D., *In Search of Soviet Gold* (London, 1939)

Lorimer, F., *The Population of the Soviet Union: History and Prospects* (Geneva, 1946)

Lyons, E., *Assignment in Utopia* (London, 1938)

Malle, S., *The Economic Organization of War Communism, 1918–1921* (Cambridge, 1985)

Materials for a Balance of the Soviet National Economy, 1928–1930, ed. S. G. Wheatcroft and R. W. Davies (Cambridge, 1985)

Maynard, J., *The Russian Peasant: and Other Studies* (London, 1942)

Medvedev, R. A., *Let History Judge: the Origins and Consequences of Stalinism* (London, 1971)

Nutter, G. W., *Growth of Industrial Production in the Soviet Union* (Princeton, NJ, 1962)

Orlov, A., *The Secret History of Stalin's Crimes* (New York, 1953)

Pipes, R., *Struve, Liberal on the Right, 1905–1944* (Cambridge, Mass., 1980)

The Platform of the Joint Opposition (1927) (London, 1973)

Preobrazhensky, E., *The New Economics* (Oxford, 1965)

Le procès des Industriels de Moscou (25 novembre–8 decembre 1930): stenographie integrale des débats du procès des industriels de Moscou publiée par le Gosisdat (édition d'état de l'U.R.S.S.) (Paris, 1931)

Rees, E. A., *State Control in Soviet Russia: the Rise and Fall of the Workers' and Peasants' Inspectorate, 1920–34* (London, 1987)

Reiman, M., *The Birth of Stalinism: the USSR on the Eve of the 'Second Revolution'* (Bloomington, Indiana, 1987)

Rothstein, A., *Man and Plan in the Soviet Economy* (London, 1948)

Rothstein, A., ed., *Wreckers on Trial: a Record of the Trial of the Industrial Party held in Moscow November–December, 1930* (London, 1931)

Rubin, I. I., *Essays on Marx's Theory of Value* (Detroit, 1972)

Rukeyser, W. A., *Working for the Soviets: an American Engineer in Russia* (London, 1932)

Sakwa, R., *Soviet Communists in Power: a Study of Moscow during the Civil War, 1918–21* (London, 1987)

Schlesinger, R., *History of the Communist Party of USSR* (Bombay, 1977)

Schwarz, S. M., *Labor in the Soviet Union* (New York, 1952)

Solzhenitsyn, A., *The Gulag Archipelago, 1918–1956*, vol. [I] (London, 1974), II (London, 1976)

Susiluoto, I., *The Origins and Development of Systems Thinking in the Soviet Union: Political and Philosophical Controversies from Bogdanov and Bukharin to Present-day Re-evaluations* (Helsinki, 1982)

Sutton, A. C., *Western Technology and Soviet Economic Development, 1930 to 1945* (Stanford, 1971)

Tucker, R. C., *Stalin as Revolutionary, 1879–1929: a Study in History and Personality* (New York, 1973)

Valentinov, N., *Encounters with Lenin* (Oxford, 1968)

Wheatcroft, S. G., and Davies, R. W., eds., See *Materials*

Woodward, E. L. and Butler, R., eds., *Documents on British Foreign Policy 1919–1939*, 2nd series, vol. VII, *1929–34* (London, 1958)

Rigby, T. H., *Communist Party Membership in the USSR, 1917–1967* (London, 1967)

Writings of Leon Trotsky (1930) (New York, 1975), *(1934–35)* (New York, 1971)

Zaleski, E., *Planning for Economic Growth in the Soviet Union, 1918–1932* (Chapel Hill, 1971)

NAME INDEX

SUBJECT INDEX